MEMOIRS: 1921-1941

ILYA EHRENBURG

Memoirs: 1921–1941

*

Translated by
TATANIA SHEBUNINA

in collaboration with
YVONNE KAPP

THE WORLD PUBLISHING COMPANY

CLEVELAND AND NEW YORK

L. G.

Published by The World Publishing Company
2231 West 110th Street, Cleveland 2, Ohio

Library of Congress Catalog Card Number: 64-12061
FIRST EDITION

Grateful acknowledgment is made to S. G. Phillips, Inc.
for permission to reprint from Walter Morison's translation of
the *Collected Stories of Isaac Babel*, copyright 1955 by S. G. Phillips, Inc.

WP764
English translation copyright© by Macgibbon & Kee Ltd. 1963.
Biographical sketches copyright© by The World Publishing Company 1964.

TRANSLATORS' NOTE

We wish to acknowledge the following sources for quotations in the text: the extract from Pascal's *Pensées* (p. 86) is Martin Turnell's translation of the Lafuma Edition (Harville Press, 1962); some short passages (pp. 109, 113 and 117) are from Walter Morison's translation of *The Collected Stories of Isaac Babel* (Criterion Books, Inc., 1955). Desnos' last poem (p. 140) and sonnet (p. 143) have appeared in *L'Evolution poétique de Robert Desnos* by Rosa Buchole (Palais des Académies, Brussels, 1956). The *Couplets de la rue Saint-Martin* (p. 141) were very kindly photocopied in Paris at our request from *Etat de Veille* (Robert-J. Godet, Paris, 1943). The verse from Toller's *Swallow-Book* (p. 200) is Ashley Dukes' translation (Oxford University Press, 1924). The passage from *A Soviet Writer Looks at Vienna* (p. 258) is Ivor Montagu's translation (Martin Lawrence, 1934); the passages from *The Journals of André Gide* (Vol. IV) (pp. 298–99, 301) are Justin O'Brien's translation (Alfred A. Knopf); the passages from E. M. Forster's speech (p. 307) are taken, with the author's kind permission, from *Abinger Harvest* (Harcourt, Brace & World, Inc.); the quotations from Hemingway are from *A Farewell to Arms* (p. 385) and *For Whom the Bell Tolls* (pp. 389, 391) (Charles Scribner's Sons); the extract from *Don Quixote* (p. 400) is from Samuel Putnam's translation (The Viking Press, 1949); the Apollinaire verse (p. 481) is from the collected *Oeuvres Poétiques* (Gallimard, 1956).

The translation of all other quotations, from the Russian or other original languages, and the footnotes are ours.

TRUCE: 1921-1933

1

IN THE late autumn of 1921, coming from Brussels, well-nourished and serene, I saw Berlin. The Germans were living as though they were at a railway station, no one knowing what would happen the next day. Newspaper men were shouting: '*Bay Tset!*[1] Latest edition! Communist demonstration in Saxony! Preparations for a putsch in Munich!' People read the paper silently and went on their way to work. Shopkeepers changed their price-tickets every day: the mark was falling. Herds of foreigners wandered along the Kurfürstendamm: they were buying up the remnants of former luxury for a song. In the poorer quarters several bakeries were looted. It seemed as though everything was bound to collapse, but factory-chimneys went on smoking, bank-clerks neatly wrote out astronomical figures, prostitutes painstakingly made up their faces, journalists wrote about the famine in Russia or the noble heart of Ludendorff, schoolchildren learnt by heart the chronicle of Germany's past victories. At every turn there were small *Diele*, dance-halls where lean couples conscientiously jigged up and down. Jazz blared. I remember two popular songs: 'Yes, we have no bananas' and 'Tomorrow's the end of the world'. However, the end of the world was postponed from one day to the next.

Bernhard Kellermann published a novel on the revolution in Germany under the title *The Ninth of November*. I do not know whether this date means anything to young readers. On 9th November 1918 the Kaiser hastily left for Holland, and the Social Democrats declared the Republic. But in the Ministries the same high officials and civil servants remained, and the doorman said respectfully: 'Good day, *Herr Geheimrat*'.

I took a room in a boarding-house in the Pragerplatz; round the corner was the broad avenue of the Kaiserallee; I went out for a stroll and found myself in a huge square – it was called the Hohenzollern-platz. Portraits of Kaiser Wilhelm hung in the rooms of my boarding-house.

[1] *Berliner Zeitung*.

I struck up a friendship with the poet Karl Einstein, a jovial romantic man, who had a huge bald head adorned with a wen. He told me that he had fought as a soldier on the Western front and had had a nervous breakdown. He reminded me of my friends of former days – Rotonde habitués – with his admiration for Negro sculpture, his blasphemous poems and that combination of despair and hope which now seemed like the breath of a bygone era. He wrote a play about Christ. He was prosecuted for blasphemy. I attended the trial. The proceedings took place in a gloomy, ill-lit hall. The idea of religious fanaticism is usually associated with Roman Catholicism, with papal Bulls, with the Inquisition. Yet Doctor Servetus was burnt at the stake not by Catholics but by Calvinists whom the Catholics regarded as free-thinkers, and he was burnt for refusing to attribute the functions of the body to Providence. Experts at Einstein's trial quoted from the works of enlightened twentieth-century theologians.

(In 1945 I saw war-shattered Berlin. There remained one wall of the building where Einstein's trial had taken place, and on it a Russian sapper had written: 'This area has been cleared of mines.')

In the Berlin of 1921 everything seemed unreal. Big-bosomed Valkyries stonily supported the façades of houses as before. The lifts worked, but there was hunger and cold in the flats. The conductor courteously helped the *Geheimrat's* wife out of the tramcar. The tram-routes remained unchanged but no one knew the route of history. Catastrophe assumed the guise of prosperity. I was struck by the sight in shop windows of pink and blue dickeys as substitutes for shirts that had become too expensive; the dickeys were a sign, a proof, if not of prosperity at least of respectability. In the Josti café where I sometimes went, the wishy-washy so-called 'Mocha' was served in metal coffeepots with a little glove on the handle to prevent the customer burning his fingers. Sweet cakes were made of frostbitten potatoes. As before, the Berliners smoked cigars labelled Havana or Brazilian though in fact they were made of cabbage leaves steeped in nicotine. All was orderly, pleasant, almost as it had been under the Kaiser.

One night we were out walking with V. G. Lidin who had just arrived in Berlin. The cafés closed early: the *Polizeistunde* was a remnant of the war years. A man approached us and offered to take us to a night spot, a *Nachtlokal*. We travelled by underground, then walked a long way through sparingly lit streets and finally found ourselves in a respectable flat. On the walls hung portraits of members of the family in officer's uniform and a painting of a sunset. We were given champagne – lemonade laced with spirits. Then the host's two daughters appeared – naked – and began to dance. One of them talked to Lidin and it turned out that she admired Dostoyevsky's novels. The mother hopefully eyed the foreign guests: perhaps they would be tempted by her daughters and would pay; in dollars of course, marks were no use, their value would fall during the night. 'Is this life?' sighed the respectable mamma. 'It's the end of the world . . .'

A short time before my arrival in Berlin the rabid nationalists had killed Erzberger, one of the leaders of the Centre Party. Members of the monarchist Bismarck League quite openly applauded the murder. Lawyers pretended to be studying the articles of the code, the Social Democrats sighed shamefacedly, while the future SS men were learning to shoot at live targets.

None of this prevented catastrophe from being presented as a well-ordered existence. The artificial limbs of war-cripples did not creak, empty sleeves were pinned up with safety-pins. Men whose faces had been scorched by flame-throwers wore large black spectacles. The lost war took care to camouflage itself as it roamed the streets.

The newspapers reported that out of every hundred newborn babies admitted into foundling hospitals thirty died within the first few days. (Those who survived were called up in 1941 and became Hitler's cannon-fodder.)

UFA was busy making films which were about anything except the last war. The audiences, however, were hungry for the semblance of suffering, brutal cruelty, tragic endings. I once happened to be present at the shooting of a film of this kind. The heroine's father tried to wall her up, her lover lashed her with a whip, she threw herself out of a seventh-floor window while the hero hanged himself. The producer told me that the film would have a different, a happy ending – for export. I observed more than once with what rapture pale, skinny adolescents watched the screen when rats gnawed a man to death or a venomous snake bit a lovely girl.

I went to the *Sturm* exhibitions; what I saw was not painting, not art, but the hysterical outbursts of people armed with brushes and tubes of paint in place of revolvers and bombs. In my notes I have recorded the titles of some of the pictures: 'Symphony in Blood', 'Radiochaos', 'The Colour-Scale of the End of the World'. Spiritual discord demanded an outlet, and what the critics called 'Neo-Expressionism' or

'Dadaism' had more to do with the battle of the Somme, with uprisings and putsches, with dickeys worn next the skin than with what we usually consider art. Walden, the moving spirit of *Der Sturm*, had the face of an emaciated bird and long untidy hair. He liked talking about *Doppelgänger*, intuition, the end of civilization. In the picture gallery where the walls were in a state of frenzy, he felt perfectly at home and treated me to coffee and whipped-cream cake brought from a neighbouring café.

I went to Magdeburg: the façades of the houses, the trams, the newspaper kiosks were richly ornamented with the same hysterical painting. The head of the building authority of the city was a gifted architect, Bruno Taut. Le Corbusier found inspiration in geometry, but then he lived in France, while Bruno Taut lived in a country where everything was confused: hunger and speculation, yesterday's dreams about Baghdad and tomorrow's expedition to India, beerhall putsches and workers' risings. (When Hitler came to power Bruno Taut went to Japan where he was delighted to find modern architecture – the traditional Japanese houses, light and bare.)

Although I remembered the Suprematists' canvases in the Moscow streets, Magdeburg dismayed me. No matter how unusual, even sometimes arid, was the language of Tatlin, Malevich, Popova, Rodchenko, it was still the language of art. What made me uneasy about German painting was its literariness as well as the total absence of any sense of proportion: the pictures shrieked.

I remember the cover of Hasenclever's book of verse: a desperate screaming man's face. An exuberance of prophecies ran riot in poetry; both Werfel and Unruh predicted annihilation. Meanwhile the man in the street, indifferent to poetry, remained mistrustfully silent.

I used to meet Leonhard Frank. He was already forty and a well-known author, but he was still a visionary youth: it would be enough for men to look into one another's eyes and smile – and the evil spell would be broken immediately. Even later he did not change much, nothing could toughen him. I met him after the war, during the fascist years in Paris; he was then living in West Germany and had come to Berlin where he had friendly talks with writers from East Germany. One of his books is called *Man is Good*; this is a very subjective appraisal – Frank had learnt what SS men were like, but he himself was indeed a good man.

Arthur Holitscher shook his grey curls. 'You'll see – before the year is out working Berlin will hold out its hand to Moscow.'

In the district much frequented by foreign profiteers and the new rich, known as *Schieber*, there was the Romanisches Café, the haunt of writers, artists, small speculators and prostitutes. There one met Italians who had fled from Mussolini's castor oil, Hungarians who had evaded Horthy's prisons. There the Hungarian painter Moholy-Nagy argued with Lissitzky about Constructivism. There Mayakovsky told Piscator about Meyerhold. There Italian visionaries dreamt about an international march of workers on Rome, while crafty dealers bought and sold American banknotes of small denomination. Stolid citizens on their way to Sunday service at the Gedächtniskirche glanced apprehensively at the Romanisches Café: it seemed to them that the headquarters of the world revolution had been established opposite the church.

Even in those days west Berlin was 'Western'; this fact is connected not only with the winds of history but with ordinary winds as well: in Berlin, in London, in Paris the western districts are favoured by the rich – ordinary winds blow from the ocean and factories are built in the eastern districts.

In west Berlin people pinned their hopes on the West and at the same time hated it: dreams of protection against Communism mingled with dreams of revenge. In the shop windows there were notices such as: 'No French goods sold here'; this was seldom true, and a *Schieber*'s wife did not have to rack her brains about where to buy Guerlain scent: patriotism retreated before greed. Nevertheless when the Moscow Kamerny theatre came for a season to Berlin it had to change the title of the French operetta *Giroflé-Girofla* to *The Twins*, and that of *Adrienne Lecouvreur* to *Maurice of Saxony*.

In east and north Berlin one could occasionally hear the *Internationale*. There people did not trade in dollars or mourn the Kaiser. There people went hungry, worked, and waited for the revolution to break out. They waited patiently, perhaps too patiently. I saw several demonstrations. Rows of grim men passed with clenched fists raised. But every demonstration ended exactly at two o'clock, at dinnertime. I recall a conversation I had with one worker. He tried to prove to me that the fact that the membership of his union was growing meant victory for the proletariat. A passion for organization is an estimable thing; but in Germany it seemed to me exaggerated. (In 1940 I saw a

13

Berlin without cars – Berlin cars were dashing about the highways of Europe: the Third Reich was conquering the world. But the pedestrians stopped short at the sight of a red light, none dared to cross the street.) The worker I talked to in 1922 lived in terms of elementary arithmetic, but this was the era of Lenin and Einstein.

It was in a beerhall in the Alexanderplatz that I first heard the name of Hitler. One of the customers was voicing his admiration for the Bavarians: those were the fellows! They would soon get going. They were no strangers, they were workers and true Germans. They would make short shrift of all those Frenchmen, Jews, *Schiebers* and Russians. His listeners protested, but this supporter of a certain Hitler repeated obstinately: 'I'm telling you, he's a German and a worker'.

The mark continued to fall; when I arrived a newspaper cost one mark; soon I had to pay thirty marks for it. A new underground line was opened. In the *Diele* couples danced till they were exhausted, danced conscientiously as if doing a hard job. Lloyd George declared that the Germans would be made to pay reparations down to the last *Pfennig*. Mortality from chronic undernourishment was rising. Everybody talked about Stinnes and Spengler. Stinnes was well known: he was the new Kaiser, Lord of the Ruhr, the Hephaestus of the new Olympus. Few read Spengler's books but all knew the title of one of his works – *The Decline of the West* (in Russian this was translated as *The Decline of Europe*)in which he lamented the passing of a culture he cherished. Unscrupulous speculators, murderers, glib journalists invoked Spengler too, for, if the time had come to die, there was no need to stand on ceremony; even a scent called 'Decline of the West' appeared on the market.

Strikes broke out time and again. In the Café Josti a decently-dressed customer fell to the floor. A doctor who was sitting at the next table examined him and said in a loud voice: 'Give him some real coffee. This is simply inanition'. All the time life was becoming more difficult but the people went on working methodically and perseveringly.

In a crowded tramcar I was once called 'Polish dog'. On the wall of a good bourgeois house, with a notice by the front door saying '*Nur für Herren*', I saw the chalked slogan 'Death to the Jews'.

Everything was colossal: prices, abuse, despair.

Poets writing in the journal *Die Aktion* said that since NEP they no longer believed in Russia: the Germans would show the world what a true revolution is. One poet declared: 'One must begin by simultaneously killing ten million people in different countries.' (Herzen wrote about the 'Sobakevich[1] of the German revolution', Heinzen, whose idea was that: 'it would be sufficient to kill off two million people in the world for the revolution to run smoothly.') A man on the staff of the *Rote Fahne* said to me: 'Your *Jurenito* is a revolting book. I can't understand how it could be published in Moscow. When we come to power, we'll have none of that kind of thing.'

The Chancellor Josef Wirth was the man in power. He did what he could to save the Republic and signed the Rapallo treaty with Soviet Russia. The English and the French were disgusted. As for the Germans, they continued to wait, some for the revolution, others for the fascist putsch. I met Chancellor Wirth in Vienna in 1952, at the World Peace Congress. He was then seventy-five. Once, after a protracted meeting, we happened to fall into conversation. Wirth said: 'When an author finishes a novel he must feel satisfied – at least a few pages have come out well. The evening of a politician's life is a very different thing; what matters there is not occasional successes but the conclusion. I could say that my life has been cancelled out. First there was Hitler. I knew there would be war. I had to go abroad. When the war ended there was Adenauer. We belonged to the same party, he's three years older than I am. I told him that he was repeating the mistakes of his predecessors. He's an intelligent man, but he couldn't understand what I meant. I don't wish to live to see another war. But what can I do? Perhaps speak at your Congresses, but that, if you will forgive me, is childishness.' He closed his tired, lack-lustre eyes.

On a summer's day in Grünewaldstrasse fascists of the *Organisation Konsul* shot the Minister of Foreign Affairs, Walther von Rathenau. When the police tracked down the gang, the men committed suicide. The fascists were buried with military honours.

The shopkeepers did not have time to change their prices. They found a way out: prices were supposed to remain unchanged but they had to be multiplied by a 'key-number', a coefficient. Yesterday this was four hundred, today it became six hundred. On the screens of suburban cinemas Dr. Caligari pursued his insane antics. In one day nine suicides were registered in Berlin. A magazine was brought out called *Friendship*, devoted to the theory and practice of homosexuality.

[1] Character in Gogol's *Dead Souls*.

The Germany of those days found her portraitist – Georg Grosz. He depicted *Schiebers* whose fingers were like short sausages. He depicted the heroes of past and future wars as man-haters hung with iron crosses. The critics classified him as an Expressionist, and his drawings as a combination of ruthless realism and of that foresight which some people for some reason call fantasy. Yes, he dared to show Privy Councillors sitting naked at their desks, plump, over-dressed ladies disembowelling corpses, murderers carefully washing their bloody hands in a washbasin. In 1922 this might have seemed sheer fantasy; in 1942 it became a commonplace. Grosz's drawings are poetical in their cruelty; they evoke the carved Ledas of Hildesheim, the goblins of Gothic lettering, the taverns under guildhalls, the smell of grief and malt which fills the narrow medieval streets.

Grosz had the light eyes of a baby and a shy smile. He was a mild and kindly man who hated cruelty and dreamt of human happiness. It was precisely this, perhaps, that helped him to depict ruthlessly those well-manured hotbeds in which were taking root the future *Obersturmführers*, the ladies who had a taste for war trophies, the stokers of Auschwitz.

In those days the entire world was watching Berlin. Some with dread, some with hope: in that city the fate of Europe for the next decades was being decided. Everything was alien to me there: the houses, the customs, the well-ordered vice, the faith in numbers, screws and diagrams. And yet I wrote at the time: 'I accompanied my loving words about Berlin with such unattractive descriptions that you will probably be glad that you are not in Berlin. I beg you, take my word for it, and think of Berlin with affection – that city of hideous monuments and anxious eyes'. I spent two years there in anxiety and hope: I felt as if I were at the front and that the brief hour when guns fall silent was dragging on. But I often asked myself: what am I waiting for? I wanted to believe and I could not.

Mayakovsky, when he came to Berlin in the autumn of 1922, protested his love: 'Today I tread your earth, Germany, and my love for you blossoms forth romancier and romancier.' 'Romancier' sounds odd to us. The word was evidently coined from 'romance', not in a literary but in the colloquial sense of the word. A poet sometimes sees what critics do not see, and then the poet is accused of making mistakes. Sometimes the poet makes the same mistakes as others and then the critics, like benevolent examiners, nod approvingly. Writing of

Germany, Mayakovsky said what many millions of men thought in 1922. True, there had already been the crushing of the Soviet republic in Bavaria, the murders of Karl Liebknecht and Rosa Luxemburg, but ahead were the shining lights of the Hamburg rising. For those then living nothing had yet been decided, and in the autumn of 1922 I waited for the revolution like the rest.

It is a mistake to ascribe moderation, love of the golden mean, to the Germans: not only the art of the Expressionists but also too many pages of German history are marked by excesses.

Mayakovsky wrote that 'through Wilhelm's arch of the Brandenburg gate' would pass the workers of Berlin, victors in the struggle. History decided otherwise: eleven years later through those gates passed fanatical Hitlerites; and in May 1945 – Soviet soldiers.

2

I DO not know how many Russians there were in Berlin in those years; certainly a great many – at every step you could hear Russian spoken. Dozens of Russian restaurants were opened – with balalaikas, and zurnas, with gypsies, pancakes, shashlyks and, naturally, the inevitable heartbreak. There was a little theatre that put on sketches. Three daily newspapers and five weeklies appeared in Russian. In one year seventeen Russian publishing firms were started. They published Fonvizin and Pilnyak, cookery books, works by Fathers of the Church, technical reference books, memoirs, lampoons.

Somewhere in Siberia Wrangel's generals were still signing military orders. The newspaper *The Two-Headed Eagle* printed edicts of 'His Imperial Majesty'. In *Novoye Vremya* (New Time) Suvorin junior compiled lists for the future cabinet, Foreign Affairs going to Markov the Second, Home Affairs to Burtsev. Shady characters recruited hungry men into imaginary 'death battalions'. However, yesterday's lieutenants and cavalry officers no longer dreamt of storming Russian towns, but rather of obtaining a French or German visa. Ataman Krasnov, laying aside his baton, wrote at one go the huge novel *From Two-Headed Eagle to Red Flag*.

It was difficult for some of the cut-throats to become taxi-drivers or factory workers all of a sudden; they tried to prolong their past. As the Bolsheviks were far away they fell back on settling accounts with their companions in exile. At a lecture by Milyukov, monarchists shot Nabokov, a Kadet leader. Members of the 'Black Hundred' vented their wrath on Kerensky, declaring that he was the son of the well-known revolutionary Gesya Helfman. The 'Black Hussar' Posazhnoy wrote: 'Milyukov babbles nonsense with a loose tongue, forgetting that patience is wearing thin. Fires of revenge are blazing up. He will perish at my hands, O Black Hussars!' I remember how diverted we were by the book of one Bostunich, *Freemasonry and the Russian Revolution*, in which it was claimed that the Socialist Revolutionary Chernov was in reality Lieberman and that the Octobrist Guchkov was a Freemason and Jew called Vaquier: Russia had been destroyed by Waterman fountain pens and Kuppenberg's champagne, stamped with diabolical pentagrams.

Vasilevsky-Ne-Bukva, a journalist well-known in pre-revolution days, wrote that 'the Bolsheviks had debauched Sologub', referring to his novel *The Snake-Charmer* written before the revolution. Burtsev called Yesenin 'the Soviet Rasputin'; K. Chukovsky, for his article *Akhmatova and Mayakovsky*, was declared 'a Soviet hanger-on'; and the same Koyransky who had made up some anti-semitic verses about me exercised his wit by saying that 'Mayakovsky's Flute is a sewer-pipe'. Some writers of repute behaved no better than the journalists. Zinaida Hippius constantly attacked Andrey Bely. The novelist E. Chirikov, who owed so much to Gorky, produced a scurrilous satire *The Smerdyakov[1] of the Russian Revolution*. Bunin threw mud at everybody. 'White' newspapers declared almost every day that the end of the Bolsheviks was at hand.

All this was merely a storm in a teacup, the hysterical outbursts of discarded dignitaries, the work of a dozen foreign intelligence services, or the delirium of isolated fanatics. There were many among the *émigrés* who did not understand why they found themselves in exile. Some had fled in panic, some had fled from hunger, and some because their neighbours were leaving. Some people had remained, others had left; one man went out on a *Subbotnik* in Kostroma, his brother washed plates in the Berlin restaurant Medved; they shared the same opinions, and were also akin by nature. The fate of millions of people had been decided by pure chance.

It might have been supposed that everything had settled down, that the dry land had been separated from the waters, but in fact the confusion of a time of transition still prevailed. The publisher Ladyzhnikov published books by Gorky and Merezhkovsky. Another publisher, L. I. Grzhebin, put the imprint: 'Moscow – Petersburg – Berlin' on his editions and brought out works by the most diverse authors: Bryusov and Pilnyak, Gorky and Victor Chernov.

The firm which published *Julio Jurenito* bore the poetical name 'Helikon'. The mountain once inhabited by the Muses proved to be non-existent; it was just a small office in the Jakobstrasse, and there sat a young man of poetical appearance – A. G. Veshnyak. I was immediately won over by his love of art. He published works by

[1] Character in *The Brothers Karamazov*.

Soviet authors and quarrelled with the *émigrés*. I grew fond of him and his wife, Vera Lazarevna; they were my close friends, kind, good people, and they perished in Auschwitz.

There was a place in Berlin that reminded one of Noah's Ark, where the clean and unclean met peaceably; it was called the House of Arts and was just a common German café where Russian writers gathered on Fridays. Stories were read by Tolstoy, Remizov, Lidin, Pilnyak, Sokolov-Mikitov. Mayakovsky declaimed. Yesenin, Marina Tsvetayeva, Andrey Bely, Pasternak, Khodasevich recited poetry. Once I met Igor Severyanin who had come from Estonia; as before, he was full of self-admiration and read the same 'poesies'. A storm broke out at a lecture by the painter Pougny; Arkhipenko, Altman, Shklovsky, Mayakovsky, Gabo, Lissitzky and I argued furiously. On the other hand, the evening devoted to the thirtieth anniversary of Gorky's literary activity passed off peacefully. The Imaginists organized their own evening and behaved uproariously, as they had always done in the Moscow 'Pegasus' Stable'. On one occasion E. Chirikov came in, sat down next to Mayakovsky and listened quietly.

Today this strikes me as almost incredible. Two or three years later the poet Khodasevich (to say nothing of Chirikov) would not have dreamt of entering a place where Mayakovsky was present. Apparently not all the dice had been cast yet. There were people who called Gorky a 'semi-*émigré*'. Khodasevich, who later worked on the monarchist newspaper *Vozrozhdeniye* (Regeneration), edited a literary journal together with Gorky and talked of going back to Russia. Alexey Tolstoy, surrounded by *Smena Vekh* ('Change of Landmark') people, alternately praised the Bolsheviks as 'unifiers of the Russian land' and indulged in angry abuse. The fog was still swirling.

The success of the House of Arts was greatly helped by its first president, the Symbolist poet Nikolay Maximovich Minsky. He was then sixty years old; he was short and rotund, and smiled and purred like an affectionate cat. Now everyone has forgotten his name, but when I was a youth he was much talked about. Vyacheslav Ivanov argued with him, Blok wrote about him, young ladies adored his verses which happened to appear in a volume of *The Reader and Reciter:* 'Fleeting dreams, carefree dreams, are dreamt only once ...'

In 1905 Minsky, like many Symbolist poets, went through a phase of enthusiasm for the revolution. He had a permit to publish a newspaper, and by some irony of fate this advocate of the cult of 'absolute individuality' became the official editor of the first legal Bolshevik newspaper *Novaya Zhizn* (New Life). He did not interfere with the editorial work but contributed to the paper the poem: 'Proletarians of all countries unite! Ours the strength, ours the will, ours the might. Gather for the last struggle as for a festival. He who's not with us is our foe and shall fall'. He was in general a rather indifferent poet, but his role in the development of aesthetic culture at the end of the last century is beyond dispute.

The newspaper *Novaya Zhizn* was soon banned by the Tsarist authorities, and Minsky was prosecuted. He went abroad and stayed there till the end of his days (he died at the age of eighty-three).

Perhaps precisely because he had witnessed neither the Revolution nor the Civil War, he conversed happily both with Soviet writers and with the most irreconcilable *émigrés*. I think he did not clearly realize what it was exactly that divided them, and often put his foot in it: he tried to prove to L. Shestov that the collective also has its rights, he demanded that Mayakovsky should give recognition to freedom of speech, calling to witness the traditions of Korolenko, and when speaking to Alexey Tolstoy he never failed to praise Futurism, Imaginism and other new-fangled notions. But it was all very well meant, and no one took offence. He had a smile for everybody, and a particularly tender one for young women.

Talking to me he constantly insisted that 'the victory of the manual workers is not enough, it's necessary to unite intellectual workers. Children should be educated – the future depends on them. Setting up educational centres, that's a task for the young.' He was quite out of touch with reality, especially Russian reality. I could barely suppress my laughter when he called the children's homes that he was planning 'almas'; in Latin *alma* is a foster-mother, but in Russian it sounds funny, and it happened that some friends of mine had a German sheepdog called Alma. But Minsky went on purring and smiling. On the occasion of a New Year's celebration at the House of Arts he recited a rhymed toast: 'Let us, like children gay and free, see in the year nineteen hundred and twenty-three. Let all the silly quarrels end, Andrey Bely'll be Sasha Chyorny's friend. Shklovsky will Shakespeare's plots admire, and Pasternak inherit Lermontov's lyre. And president Minsky's efforts for the good cause will be rewarded by stormy applause.'

There was yet another 'no man's land' in Berlin where Soviet writers met *émigré* writers – the pages of the magazine *Novaya*

Russkaya Kniga (The New Russian Book). This was edited by professor Alexander Semyonovich Yashchenko, a lawyer and an amateur of letters; he had left Russia with a Soviet passport and, like Minsky, did his best to bring everybody together. There was hardly anyone who did not contribute to his journal. I extolled the works of Tatlin and joined issue with those who ran down Soviet poetry. Alexander Semyonovich sighed: 'It's harsh, too harsh', but none the less printed my articles. In the same issue he published the exhortations of a former Tolstoyan, the monarchist I. Nazhivin: 'Old Russia fast became the kingdom of Cham . . . But the young men were perishing, the generals were drinking, stealing, breaking the law, while those at the rear speculated in blood and wallowed in debauchery. In exile I energetically carried on national and monarchist work, but every day menacing doubts grew in my mind. Everybody has become vile, everybody is exhausted. Our future is heartbreaking and sombre'. And in the next issue Mayakovsky wrote: 'I have started writing for *Izvestia*. I am organizing the publishing house MAF. I am mustering the Futurists of Communism'.

All around was Berlin with its long, depressing streets, with hideous art and handsome cars, with hopes of revolution and the first shots of the fascists. The poet Khodasevich described the Berlin night as seen through Russian eyes: 'Clinging couples like statues. A heavy sigh. The heavy sigh of a cigar. Wait – a sharp wind will whistle down the alleyways of Berlin's clumsy mass, and a harsh day will rise behind the houses over the "stepmother of Russian cities"'.

It was not easy to understand the 'stepmother of Russian cities'. In her schools there were well-behaved boys destined twenty years later to scar the mother of Russian cities[1]. It must be admitted that, like the majority of Russian writers, Khodasevich remained aloof from German life.

Alexey Remizov sat hunched up at home and wrote in elaborate old Russian lettering *Russia in Script*. Andrey Bely said he was writing about Blok. Alexey Tolstoy worked with the painter Pougny on a book about Russian art. In Berlin Marina Tsvetayeva wrote one of her best books: *Craftsmanship*.

I worked hard; in two years I wrote *The Life and Death of Nikolay Kurbov, Trust D. E., Thirteen Pipes, Six Stories about Easy Endings,*

[1] The traditional epithet for Kiev.

and *The Love of Jeanne Ney*. After *Julio Jurenito* it seemed to me that I had found my path, my themes, my language; actually I was drifting, and one book cancelled out the last. I shall revert to this later on. At the moment I want to talk about something else: the journal *Veshch* (Object) which I brought out together with the Constructivist Lissitzky.

Lissitzky firmly believed in Constructivism. In ordinary life he was mild, exceedingly kind, at times naïve; he was often ill; he fell in love in the way that people used to fall in love in the past century – blindly, self-sacrificingly. But in art he was like a fanatical mathematician, finding his inspiration in precision and working himself up over austerity. He was marvellously inventive, could get up a stand at an exhibition so that the paucity of the exhibits looked like superabundance and knew how to present a book in a new way. His works show feeling for colour and masterly composition.

Veshch was published by the 'Scythians'. It is not difficult to realize how alien the ideas which we preached were to the revolutionary Slavophils and incorrigible Narodniki. After the first issue they could not stand it and dissociated themselves from us publicly. For my part, in each of my books I 'dissociated' myself from myself. It was precisely at that time that Viktor Shklovsky nicknamed me 'Paul, son of Saul'. On his lips this did not sound unkind. In life he did what nearly all his contemporaries did; that is, he more than once switched his judgments and estimations, though without bitterness and even with a certain bravado; only his eyes were sad – as they had probably been from birth. It seems to me that such a passionate man must often feel cold. In Berlin, too, he felt cold. There he wrote what I consider to be his best book, *A Sentimental Journey*. Its style – suddenly darting from one subject to another ('there's an elderberry tree in the garden and an uncle in Kiev' as the Russian saying goes), associations by juxtaposition, a swift succession of settings and an emphatically personal idiom – all this was dictated by the content. Shklovsky was describing the terrible years in Russia and his own inner confusion.

In Berlin Shklovsky's sad eyes were doubly sad: he was quite unable to adjust himself to life abroad; he was then writing *Zoo*.

This book had an unforeseen extension in life: it contributed to the birth of an authoress whom some younger readers think of as a French-woman. Elsa Triolet was living at the time in Berlin and we often met She is a Muscovite, and a sister of Lily Brik. In the early days of the

Revolution she married a Frenchman, André Triolet – Andrey Petrovich – whom, taking our cue from Elsa, we called simply Petrovich – and she went with him to Tahiti. (Petrovich is a character; his passion is horses. One day in Paris he told me he was going to Denmark for his holidays: there were wonderful pastures there and his horses could be put out to grass.) After their return from Tahiti André Triolet remained in Paris, while Elsa went on to Berlin. She was very young, attractive, with the pink colouring of a Renoir picture, and sad. Viktor Shklovsky included four or five of Elsa's letters in his book *Zoo*. When the book came out Gorky told Shklovsky that he liked the letters written by a woman. Two years later the Moscow publishing house *Krug* (The Circle) published Elsa Triolet's first book *In Tahiti*. Later Elsa lived in Paris where I saw her almost every day in Montparnasse. There she met Aragon in 1928, and shortly began to write in French.

In *Zoo* Shklovsky reproved his heroine for being too fond of 'pan-European culture' and for thus being able to live outside Russia. His feelings were understandable: having got stranded by chance in Berlin he was homesick and longed to go back.

Boris Pilnyak, when he came to Berlin, observed the alien life with curiosity. He was a gifted and muddle-headed man. He knew what he was writing about, and impressed both Russian and foreign readers not only by the cruel details of the life he described but also by the unusual form of his narrative. Pilnyak's books of the nineteen-twenties, like those of many of his contemporaries, bear the stamp of the epoch: a combination of crudeness and mannerism, of hunger and the cult of art, enthusiasm for Leskov and for squabbles overheard in the market-place. He perished in the thirties, and it is difficult to tell what direction his path as a writer might have taken. In Berlin in 1922 he said that the Revolution was a 'muzhik', a 'national' revolution, he accused Peter the Great of 'wrenching Russia away from Russia'. His simplicity had an admixture of cunning: that traditional Russian psychological mechanism known as *yurodstvo* (which he adored).

Yesenin spent several months in Berlin; he languished and, of course, behaved rowdily. He was always accompanied by the Imaginist Kusikov, who played the guitar and declaimed: 'They say of me that I'm a scoundrel, I am a wicked and cunning Circassian'. They drank and they sang. In vain did Isadora Duncan try to restrain Yesenin; one scene followed another. When in drink Pilnyak tried to work out a philosophy based on the havoc in Russia, and Yesenin in despair smashed crockery.

The newspaper *Nakanune* (On the Eve) began to appear. I had occasion to talk to its ideologists two or three times. The *Smena Vekh* people openly admitted that they had no love for Communism, but they liked the fact that the Bolsheviks had created an army, ousted the interventionists and rebuffed Poland. 'We stand for a strong power,' they said, 'the rest will fall into place.' I wrote to the poetess M. M. Shkapskaya: 'The *Nakanune* people cannot forgive me for refusing to write for them, but what can I do? I am too much to the left for them'. The journalist Vasilevsky-Ne-Bukva published in *Nakanune* a racy article about me saying that I ought to be beaten about the head with a hefty hambone.

Alexey Tolstoy sat in silent gloom puffing at his pipe, then, suddenly appeased, he would break into a smile. He once said to me: 'You'll see, no literature will come out of the emigration. Emigration can kill any author within two or three years'. He knew that he would soon be going home.

The 'Scythians' were all for Razin, for Pugachev, they quoted *The Twelve*, then Yesenin's verses about the 'iron guest'. The *Smena Vekh* people said that the Bolsheviks were the heirs of Ivan the Terrible and Peter the Great. They all swore by Russia, and all kept talking about 'roots', 'traditions', 'the national spirit', while the rank-and-file *émigrés*, after drinking a few glasses at the Troika restaurant and hearing the song about Stenka Razin, wept and cursed as they had wept and cursed in the last Russian heated goods-wagon when they bolted across the frontier.

Tolstoy was right: for the majority of Russian writers emigration was death. Why was this? Is it true that any kind of emigration destroys a writer? I do not think so. Voltaire spent forty-two years in exile, Heine twenty-five, Hugo nineteen, Mickiewicz twenty-six. *Candide, Germany, Wintermärchen, My Past and Thoughts, Les Misérables, Pan Tadeusz* were all written in emigration. The root of the matter does not lie in the separation from one's country, however painful. Writers of different types may become exiles – those in the vanguard and those who bring up the rear. I think it was Danton who said that you could not carry away your country on the soles of your shoes; this is true, but one can carry it away in one's consciousness, in one's heart. One can go to the ends of the earth without petty hatred and with generous ideas. This is what distinguishes the fate of Herzen from that of Bunin.

The 'Scythians', the Eurasians, the *Smena Vekh* group had one thing in common: they contrasted Russia with the decaying West. These indictments of Europe were a curious echo of the bygone judgments of the Slavophils.

(A quarter of a century after these years about which I am writing, some thoughts, and even some words come to life again. Servility is certainly an unedifying spectacle, it degrades both the flatterer and the flattered. Already in the eighteenth century satirists ridiculed Russian noblemen who tried to Gallicize themselves. I detest the Soviet petty bourgeois who, after seeing a vulgar American film, says to his spouse—with that kind of fellow it is always a spouse, not a wife: 'How far ahead of us they are!' I am prepared, however, to render homage not only to Shakespeare and Cervantes, but to Picasso, Chaplin, Hemingway, and I do not feel that this degrades me. Unending talk about one's superiority is linked with grovelling before things foreign – they are but different aspects of an inferiority complex; and I detest no less the other kind of petty bourgeois who is ready to decry, sincerely or hypocritically, everything and anything if it is foreign.)

In E. G. Lundberg's *Memoirs of a Writer* there is a note made at the beginning of the year 1922: 'A group of Russian writers were gathered to drink tea and liqueurs in the smart café over the Willi restaurant. Toasts began. Some drank to literature, some to wisdom, some to freedom. "Against violence!" an expatriate philosopher raised his glass, biting his lips with inner pain. All fell silent. It was clear at whom this toast was aimed. After a short silence people embraced and drank. Only Ehrenburg and I took no part. What Ehrenburg was thinking I do not know. But I was thinking of the slavery of the semi-destitute human beings in this graveyard of Europe so dear to the hearts of cultured men.' I do not, of course, recall the gathering itself. But I know all right what I was thinking about during those years.

The 'Scythians' were the outcome of Blok's famous poem. No matter how powerful Blok's word-magic, I could not and do not share some of its sentiments: 'We shall disperse into the thickets and forests leaving the wide plains to fair Europe. We shall turn to you our sinister Asiatic faces. Come, come all to the Ural! We are clearing the field for battle, for the steel machines with their precision heartbeats to meet the wild Mongolian horde!'

26

No, I did not want to accept the 'sinister Asiatic face'. These words sound historically unjust, for in India there are undoubtedly no fewer philosophers and poets than there are in England. At the time, Europe seemed to Lundberg a well-loved graveyard. But I did not sing requiems for Europe. My novel *Trust D.E.*, written in those years, is the history of the destruction of Europe as a result of an American trust's activities. It is a satire; I could write the same thing today under the title: *Episodes of the Third World War*. For me Europe was not a graveyard but a battlefield, at times beloved, at others not at all: such I had seen it as a youth in Paris, such I found it in the uneasy Berlin of 1922. (Such I see it also today. One can, of course, have different attitudes towards Europe – 'open a window', or stop all the cracks in the doors; and one can also remember that the whole of our culture, from Kiev Rus to Lenin, is indissolubly bound up with the culture of Europe.)

What else did I think about in those days? About how to reconcile the 'precision heartbeats' with humanity, justice, art. I knew that one could be proud of the heroic achievement of a people which was the first to set foot upon an unexplored path, but this path seemed to me much broader than the traditions of one country or the soul of one nation.

I do not remember exactly who drank the liqueurs in the Café Willi. Perhaps one of those present went on later to the Troika and there, over a glass of vodka, declaimed about Russia's mission. Chekhov once took down this remark: 'A Patriot: "Did you know that our macaroni is better than the Italian kind? I'll prove it to you! Once in Nice I was served sturgeon – I almost burst out crying".'

Since the time of the toasts in the Café Willi nearly forty years have passed. The old emigration has disappeared; people have aged, died; their children have become good Frenchmen, Germans, Englishmen. The son of the Kadet leader Nabokov (shot by an ultra-monarchist) is now one of the most popular writers in America; at first he wrote in Russian, then in French, now he writes in English.

The newspapers have more than once pointed out the shortcomings of our fishing industry. But that sturgeon of which Chekhov wrote is with us still.

3

IN 1922 there came to the bourgeois boarding-house in Trauten-strasse where I lived a man whom I did not know and who said with unassuming pride: 'I am Tuwim'. I did not know his poetry at the time but was immediately flustered: before me stood a poet. Everybody knows that there are many versifiers in the world, but few poets, and to meet them is overwhelming. Pushkin has said that outside the hours of inspiration a poet's soul is 'wrapped in cold slumber'. Could it not be this seeming cold that scorches those who approach them? Tuwim's 'cold slumber' was passionate, bitter, frenzied.

He questioned me about the Russian poets, about Moscow. He lived by two passions: his love for human beings and the difficult intimacy with art. We immediately found a common language.

Almost the whole of our lives we existed in different worlds, meeting seldom and by chance (formerly one used to say 'like ships that pass in the night', I would say now 'like passengers at a noisy airport when loud-speakers yell: "Flight number . . .'"). And yet there are few people whom I have loved so tenderly, so solicitously, so unaccountably as I loved Julian Tuwim.

At our first meeting I was struck by his beauty. He was then twenty-eight. As a matter of fact, he retained his good looks till the end of his life. A large birthmark on his cheek lent something tragic to his clear-cut features, and he had a sad, almost apologetic smile; his abrupt movements were part and parcel of a profound shyness.

Poets are not destined to linger long on this earth, and young men of letters called Tuwim 'an old man', yet he died before the age of sixty.

The line of life is tortuous not only in the palm of the hand. Some pundits rebuked Tuwim: this he had failed to understand, there he had withdrawn, missed his footing, advanced too far, turned away. During the years of the Second World War Tuwim wrote: 'Politics is not my profession. It is a function of my conscience and temperament'. Of course his way was not a straight highway, but where and when have poets marched along a macadamized road? Tuwim suffered from a fear of space – agoraphobia: he found it difficult to cross a large square. Yet he was compelled to cross wastes and deserts, to step out of one epoch and into another.

Mayakovsky wrote about him that he was 'unquiet, excited', and, noting contradictions, ascribed them to the conditions of life in Poland in 1927. 'Evidently he would have liked to write things like *A Cloud in Trousers*, but in Poland one could not make a living even with official poetry – what "clouds" could there be?' Yet Mayakovsky had written *A Cloud in Trousers* in Tsarist Russia and Tuwim translated it in reactionary Poland. If he did not write *A Cloud in Trousers* it was only because the two poets were dissimilar.

In 1939 a critic of the left asserted that 'an absence of ideology, a fleeing from life' were characteristic of Tuwim. Some months before Tuwim's death I listened to a broadcast of the Congress of Freedom and Culture (an organization sponsored by the Americans); the commentator said that Tuwim had betrayed Poland, proved false to poetry, had lost his conscience.

One cannot understand a man's course by watching this or that step; the path of life can be seen from a hilltop, not from under a gateway. Years alter both the form of a State and the thoughts of people, but a poet carries throughout the whole of his creative activity something which is more important than anything else. Mayakovsky was right in calling Tuwim 'unquiet, excited'. And so he remained all his life: when he frequented the Mala Zemianska café with his friends the *Skamandrites* – Slonimski, Iwaszkiewicz, Leczon (a group of poets who, trying to give a new trend to Polish poetry, called themselves *Skamandr*); and when he broke with many old friends, having decided to return to the new Poland; and when in his early youth he cursed the classical canons, indulged in impudence and all sorts of foolery; and also when, shortly before his death, he exclaimed: 'I am full of such commonplace feelings as faith, hope, love for noble people, hatred for scoundrels'.

In November 1950 a World Peace Congress was held in Warsaw. A very well-informed and influential person said to me, pointing to Tuwim who was modestly sitting at the back of the hall: 'You see what re-moulding means? The poet of the fleeting moods takes part in the struggle for peace'. I smiled in reply; I remembered an old poem by Tuwim for which he had been abused left, right and centre: he wrote about oil, about blood and called on the soldiers to lay down their rifles. This was a quarter of a century before the first World Peace Congress. But some people who drive about in cars and preserve a memory of horse-drawn transport only in the form of the everlasting horseshoe, have long arms and short memories.

Marina Tsvetayeva wrote that every poet 'lives in a ghetto'. Tuwim liked these lines and repeated them to me more than once. And at a time when he had not yet reached thirty he wrote about those who put poets into a ghetto and those who, in the ghetto, do not surrender: 'No, you will not either by service or by flattery attain to my free calling of poet. The Lord God will not fasten those constellations on your epaulets and uniforms'.

Poland has not always been kind to Tuwim, but he always loved Poland. The character of Polish patriotism is bound up with the history of the three partitions; I never forgot this when I listened to Tuwim's outpourings. (They were, so to speak, spiced with that tincture of irony that is dictated by reserve.) He was passionately attached to his native Lodz, a town distinctly not made for admiration. In 1928 I was in Warsaw, and later in Lodz where I gave readings from my books. Tuwim implored me not to fail to see Petrovska street, the market, the Savoy Hotel, the factories, the slums of Baluti. I stayed in the Savoy in Lodz, I saw the factories, Baluti, the large prison; I saw men of letters, workers, gendarmes, secondary school boys, the industrialist Poznanski, members of the underground. I noted at the time: 'Lodz is a short name. There are short phrases such as: "five cases", "three goods-wagons", "a portion of goose", "call the doctor", "call the police", "the undertaker". Thoughts are even shorter: "eight zlotys to the dollar", "I'll die!", "I'll get out of it!", "the devil!", "arrest him!" A good town, an outspoken town. In all Europe you will not find such anger, such a will to live, nor yet such despondency.' When I next saw Tuwim I said to him: 'A wonderful town!' He smiled. I am sure he saw a different Lodz. I was there for a week, he had grown up in it, and the power of love is that it transfigures so many things. Not long ago I read Tuwim's poem: 'Let those extol Sorrento and the Crimea who have a taste for their beauty. But I am from Lodz. And black smoke was to me pleasant and sweet'.

Probably Tuwim was more complex than he seemed, not only to the dogmatists from various monastic orders but also to his friends. But I shall have more to say about this. I am concerned now with his attachment to Poland.

In 1940 Tuwim reached Paris. That winter was a strange one; as the French said, *une drôle de guerre*. At night the city was blacked out but in the restaurants and cafés, behind the screened windows, there was light and noise – the military were enjoying themselves. At the front the soldiers were bored, while in Paris the police were working hard: no one knew for certain whom France was fighting – the Germans or the Communists. Windowpanes were criss-crossed with strips of paper: the Parisians were protecting the glass against expected bombings; but all was quiet, unbearably quiet, and hardly anyone guessed that within a few months what would be shattered to smithereens was not the window of the cautious concierge, but the whole of France. During that winter I was ill and saw few people; many friends did not wish to see me: some were afraid, others angry – friendship was one thing, politics another. But Tuwim sought me out. He thought of one thing only – Poland, and that winter Paris was meaningless to him. Our friendship had survived a severe test: we embraced and understood one another.

We parted for six years. No need to say what these years were. In the autumn of 1941, when the communiqués of the *Sovinformbureau* announced every day: 'Our troops have withdrawn from . . .', and elderly Home Guards straggled along the Moscow sidestreets, when in the West they were singing our funeral dirge, I received a cable from New York. Tuwim spoke of friendship, of love, of faith. (All that I have left is my notebooks and I do not remember the exact wording.) Later Tuwim wrote: 'At the time of Hitler's greatest triumphs on the eastern front, I sent a cable to Ehrenburg – a cable full of faith in the coming victory of the Red Army'.

In the spring of 1946 I sat in Tuwim's flat in New York among trunks and suitcases: the following week he was due to leave for France and from there for Warsaw. He was exceptionally gay and in high spirits. Many Poles who were at that time living in New York tried to talk him out of it: they called a return to Warsaw a 'betrayal'. It was naturally not easy for Tuwim to break with some of his old friends but he was possessed by a single idea – the coming meeting with Poland; he was happy and excited, like a boy going to his first lovers' meeting.

In the autumn of 1947 I was in Poland. By day, by evening and by night Tuwim took me over the ruins of Warsaw. 'Just look – how beautiful it is!' The city was terrifying. Ruins of ancient cities are beautiful: time is an architect of genius, it knows how to lend harmony even to desolation; but cities that have just been destroyed by war torment the eyes and the heart: mounds of rubble, gutted houses with shreds of wallpaper, a spiral staircase hanging in the sky, people huddling in cellars, mud-huts, dugouts. But Tuwim saw the beauty of burnt and ravaged Warsaw because he was a Pole and because he was a poet.

I should like to speak of Tuwim's love for the Russian people and for Russian poetry. The past might have been expected to loom large for him: he well remembered the Tsarist order and the policemen in the streets of Lodz. For twenty years the ruling circles of Poland fomented hostility: everything Russian was maligned. This did not affect Tuwim. He devoted many years to translating Russian poets. When he read to me his translation of the *Bronze Horseman* I could detect Pushkin's complex rhythm. At one of our last meetings he said to me: 'The Russian language seems to have been expressly created for poetry'.

As early as the nineteen-twenties his dream was to visit the Soviet Union. He came to Moscow in the spring of 1948. On the day of his arrival we went to a restaurant. He explained exactly what he wished to see, which was, in fact, everything. That same evening he fell ill; he was taken to the Botkinsky hospital. The doctors suspected cancer, and he got wind of this (he had an ulcer of the stomach, but five years later he died of a heart attack). And so he never saw anything of Moscow but a hospital ward and a room at the Hotel National, about which he said that it strongly reminded him of the rooms in the Lodz Savoy.

I have close friends amongst foreigners; when talking to them I suddenly feel: here is the frontier. For we have lived, and are living now, too differently. I never had that feeling with Tuwim; not only was there no 'iron curtain' dividing us, but not so much as a flimsy veil.

Heine wrote: 'When I die they will cut my tongue out of my dead body'. The books of the poet who brought fame to Germany, who enriched her lyrical poetry, were burnt a hundred years later on bonfires in his native Düsseldorf: the racialists could not forgive the author of the *Wintermärchen* for being a Jew. When I was in Poland in 1928 anti-semites persecuted Tuwim: he showed me a newspaper where it was said that his poetry 'smelt of garlic'.

Tuwim has a poem about a Jewish beggar-boy who sings a sad little song in the street hoping that some gentleman will throw him a copper. Tuwim wants to throw his heart to him, go with him and sing with him the song of sorrow under other people's windows. 'But there is no refuge in the world of men for Jewish wanderers with a wild song.'

In 1944 Tuwim issued a declaration entitled: *We – the Polish Jews.* Here are some passages from it: 'And at once I hear the question: "Where does this 'we' come from?" A question to some extent well-founded. It is put to me by Jews to whom I have always said I was a Pole. Now it will be put to me by Poles for whom I remain more or less a Jew. Here is the answer to both . . . I am a Pole because I like being a Pole. This is my own business, and I am not obliged to account to anyone. I do not divide the Poles into those with a pedigree and those without; I leave that to the racialists, foreign and home-grown. I divide Poles, as I do Jews, and men of any nationality, into intelligent and stupid ones, honest and dishonest, interesting and dull, oppressors and oppressed, worthy and unworthy. I divide Poles into fascists and anti-fascists . . . I could add that, on the political plane, I divide Poles into anti-semites and anti-fascists, for anti-semitism is the inter-national language of fascists . . . I am a Pole, because I was born, grew up and studied in Poland, because in Poland I came to know happiness and grief, because I want, at all costs, to return to Poland from exile, even if in some other place an earthly paradise is promised me. I am a Pole because it was in Polish that I voiced the troubles of first love, and in Polish, too, that I babbled of happiness and the storms it creates. I am a Pole, also, because the birch and the willow are nearer to me than the palm and the cypress, and Mickiewicz and Chopin are dearer to my heart than Shakespeare and Beethoven, dearer for reasons which, again, I cannot explain by any rational arguments . . . I hear voices: "Very well. But if you are a Pole, why do you write 'We – Jews'?" I reply: "Because of my blood." "Then it is racialism?" Nothing of the kind. On the contrary. There are two kinds of blood: the blood that flows in the veins and the blood that flows out of them. The first is the sap of the body, to study it is the business of the physiologist. Those who ascribe to this blood any kind of properties other than physiological ones are those who, as we have seen, reduce towns to ruins, kill millions of human beings and, in the end, as we shall see, doom their own people to destruction. The other kind of blood is that which the leader of international fascism pumps out of

33

humanity in order to prove the superiority of his blood over mine, over the blood of millions of people tortured to death . . . The blood of Jews (not "Jewish blood") flows in deep, broad streams; the dark streams flow together in a turbulent, foaming river, and in this new Jordan I accept holy baptism — the bloody, burning brotherhood in martyrdom of the Jews . . . We, Shloims, Sruls, Moishkes, dirty, garlicky, we with our endless insulting nicknames, we have proved ourselves the peers of Achilles, of Richard Coeur de Lion and other heroes. In the catacombs and bunkers of Warsaw, in the stinking sewers we amazed our neighbours, the rats. We, with rifles on the barricades, we, below planes that bombed our wretched dwellings, we arose as soldiers of freedom and honour. "Aronchik, why are you not at the front?" He was at the front, honoured sirs, and he died for Poland . . .'

These words, written in blood — 'that flows out of the veins' — were copied by thousands of people. I read them in 1944 and for a long time could not speak to anyone: Tuwim's words were the vow and the curse that lived in the hearts of many. He had found the means to express them.

Years passed. Hitler poisoned himself. The leaders of the Polish anti-semites emigrated to England, to America. But the wound in Tuwim's heart did not heal. I remember my last meeting with him; it was at a difficult time, in 1952. We conjured up many memories, we spoke about many things. Yulek (that is how I should like to refer to him) rose suddenly, came up to me, embraced me and immediately said to cover his emotion: 'And now let's go to the Cinderella, they make coffee there in the Italian way'.

I have mentioned Heine: Tuwim had something in common with him (besides what interests the race experts), and that was an irony born of heightened sensibility. At times Tuwim seemed almost arrogant; many of his poems annoyed people who respect hierarchies; he could come out with caustic sayings. 'You know, the hedgehog must have a very tender heart,' he once said. When moved, he tried to hide the fact with a joke. In 1950, at the Peace Congress, a young girl approached him and described rapturously how she loved his book, *The Seventh Autumn*. Filled with embarrassment Tuwim suddenly turned to me: 'And do you remember how a *shpik* (police spy) turned out to be an admirer of mine?' This had happened in 1928, in Warsaw, where I was under the surveillance of two *shpiks*: one tall, with the face

34

and gait of a boxer, the other puny, dark and so myopic that he often lost sight of me in the street. I had got used to him, sometimes asked him to buy me a newspaper or a packet of tobacco; in short I tamed him. One day, when we were going along a street with Tuwim and talking about poetry, I suddenly noticed that the dark one, instead of trotting behind, was walking at Tuwim's side. This annoyed me, and I reminded the *shpik* of the rules of good manners, but he replied: 'I'm not doing this in the line of duty. How could I not listen when Tuwim is talking?' This was so unexpected that it made us laugh.

Tuwim has many wicked poems about the bourgeoisie. I recall the Café Mala Zemianska in the winter of 1928. It was frequented not only by the Skamandrite poets, by Pilsudski's dashing A.D.C. Duglawa-Wieniawski, who was fascinated by the art world, but also by those Warsaw characters who wanted to be thought refined and came there to drink coffee and gobble cream cakes an hour before dinner. Tuwim ridiculed them: 'At one o'clock a gentleman of leisure entered the café religiously, he sat down, self-important and vigorous, almost a foreigner; the poor fellow nearly burst out of his skin trying to look like a boxer or a Varangian, or perhaps even a lord. No one noticed him, and with a wry smile he decided to be the Spaniard Mendoza y Oliva, a businessman from Pamplona, a singer from Alicante, a Spanish monarchist, a Spanish *émigré*. But all in vain, even were he from Toledo; so he went off to Water y Closedo. And there, having poured out his troubles to a silly old woman, he returned to No. 17 Mala Koszikova Street.'

Many people thought that Tuwim was on the point of angrily echoing Pushkin's words: 'Away with you! What has a peaceful poet to do with you?' As a matter of fact, Tuwim loved those whom he called 'the ordinary people' before these words had become a newspaper catch-phrase. It is not an accident that he dedicated one of his best poems, *The Barbers*, to Charlie Chaplin, that touching jester who in our terrible age has championed the little man: 'Along the wall of the empty barber's shop the barbers doze for hours; they wait, they look – no customers appear, they are bored, they wander about with nothing to do, they shave themselves, they cut each other's hair, they exchange a few words, doze, snore and wake up again . . . A thunderstorm is gathering, everything grows dark blue, cocks crow, the barbers are frightened, they scuttle about – d'you hear the thunder? The barbers weep, sing, the barbers go crazy, they stand stock-still, then bustle about almost at the double.' It is doubtful whether in 1926 the politicians of Poland, sitting in barbers' shops or even in the chamber of the Sejm, heard the first peals of thunder. But the poet heard them.

In 1928 I wrote about Tuwim: 'One cannot argue with him. He thinks in associations, he argues in assonances'. Yes, Tuwim was first and foremost a lyrical poet, which did not prevent him from understanding the epoch better than it was understood by solemn souls who think in diagrams and argue in quotations. Tuwim was expressing himself in his poems, perhaps that is why they were accepted by people as the expression of their own thoughts and emotions, as something common to everyone. A Pole once told me that when he was a partisan during the war years he used to recite, like an incantation, Tuwim's verses: 'I may have lived there but one day, or perhaps it was a century . . . All I remember is a morning and white, white snow.'

In his youth Tuwim had been a passionate admirer of Rimbaud, the scapegrace and the seer, the rebel and the youth with the face of a despairing angel. During our last meeting Tuwim suddenly said to me: 'But you know, I believe that no one has written better about the most difficult things than Blok'. His love for other poets was disinterested, and he translated with the same eagerness *A Cloud in Trousers* and *The Lay of Igor's Host*, though he never tried to borrow from anyone. Yet Blok was certainly akin to him. I am very fond of Tuwim's poem *At the Round Table* with its epigraph taken from Schubert's song: 'Oh lofty art, how often in the hours of sorrow . . .': 'But perhaps again, my dear, we might go for a day to Tomaszow. There the same golden blizzard swoops and the September quiet dwells. In that white house, in that same room where someone's furniture is stacked, our old unfinished quarrel we must end, my dear'. Perhaps this is precisely that 'most difficult thing' – poetry is stripped here, it seems to be made out of nothing, as in Blok's *Hours of the Night*, as in Verlaine's lyrics.

When I said that even his friends did not always understand Tuwim this is what I was thinking of: of the extreme complexity that becomes simplicity, of the man who knew a great deal, who was wise and at the same time childlike, of the author of humorous sketches and subtle lyric poems. He wrote poetry for children, and in one poem told the story of the odd character Janek who does everything the wrong way round. Children laughed when they listened to the verses, while

Tuwim smiled deprecatingly; he himself was like the Janek whom he ridiculed.

When I visited him for the last time in his home, he was joking with eight-year-old Eva. For some reason we both felt sad, but I never could have imagined that I should not see him again.

He loved trees. I remember a poem of his: in the forest he tries to identify the tree from which they will make his coffin; the limpid melancholy of this poem is not unlike Lermontov's 'Whether I wander through noisy streets . . .'

In the parks of Warsaw, outside the town, in the garden of the poet Iwaszkiewicz, when I looked at the trees I thought about Julian Tuwim's tree. He was ten years younger than I, and now seven years have passed already since he died.

I am accustomed to losses and yet I do not feel reconciled: it hurts. But how good to have known him!

4

RUSSIAN writers sometimes went to the café Prager Diele. Their conversations were noisy and confused; the waiters could not get used to these strange customers. On one occasion Andrey Bely got into an argument with Shestov; they were talking about the disintegration of personality and used the kind of language that only professional philosophers can understand. Then the curfew hour struck, the lights in the café went out, but the philosophical dispute was still not finished.

Never shall I forget the scene that ensued. In two of the segments of the revolving door Andrey Bely and Shestov were shouting. Each, without noticing it, was pushing at his part of the door, and they could not get out into the street. Shestov, with his hat, his beard, his large walking-stick, looked like the Wandering Jew, while Bely fulminated, wildly gesticulating, his fluffy hair on end. An old waiter, who had seen much in his day, said to me: 'That Russian must be a famous man'.

In 1902 Andrey Bely, or more correctly, Boris Nikolayevich Bugayev, studying physics and mathematics at Moscow University, was twenty-two. At the time he was writing feeble Symbolist verse, and introduced himself to Valery Bryusov who was regarded as the master of the new poetry. Here is the entry Bryusov made in his diary: 'Bugayev came to see me, he read some poems of his, talked about chemistry. He is probably the most interesting man in Russia. Maturity and senility of mind coupled with a strange youthfulness'. An old friendship bound Alexander Blok and Andrey Bely. Their relationship was compounded of intimacy, painful quarrels, reconciliations. One might have thought that Blok would get used to Bely, but no, it was impossible to get used to him. In 1920 after a meeting with Bely, Blok notes: 'He is the same as ever: full of genius, strange'.

A genius? An eccentric? A prophet? A jester? Andrey Bely made a tremendous impression on all who met him. In January 1934, when he heard of Bely's death, Mandelstam wrote a poem-cycle. He realized Bely's greatness: 'The Caucasian mountains shouted to him as did the jostling crowd of the tender Alps, on the sheer masses of vastnesses of sound his seeing footfall trod'; and yet, he also wrote, expressing the confusion felt by others: 'Tell me, they say that some Gogol or other has died? It's not Gogol, but a mediocre writer, a *gogolek*[1]. The chap who organized some nonsense that time, who showed off, rather a lightweight, forgot something, didn't grasp something else, started a shindy, whipped up the snow'.

In 1919 this is how I described Andrey Bely: 'Huge, wide-open eyes – blazing fires in a pale, emaciated face, a too-high forehead with an islet of hair standing on end. He recites poetry as a Sybil prophesies, and as he reads he waves his hands about: he stresses the rhythm, not of the verse, but of his secret thought. This is almost funny, and at times Bely seems a magnificent clown. But when he is close to you, anxiety and yearning, the feeling of some immense unhappiness, takes hold of everyone. Bely is greater and more important than his books. He is a wandering spirit that has not found a body, an unbounded torrent. Why does the fiery word "genius" sound like a title when applied to Bely? Bely could have been a prophet, his innocent madness is lit by divine wisdom. But the "six-winged seraph", having flown down to him, did not finish the job: he opened the eyes of the prophet, allowed him to hear unearthly rhythms, gave him "the tongue of the wise serpent" but did not touch his heart'.

When I wrote these lines I knew Andrey Bely only from his books and from fleeting encounters. In Berlin and at the seaside resort of Swinemünde I often met Bely and came to realize that in speaking about the seraph and the heart I had been mistaken: what I had taken for coldness was unhappiness, broken wings, a shattered personal life and an exuberantly brilliant vocabulary.

Now, reflecting upon the fate of this truly extraordinary man, I can find no solution. Probably the ways of the great (and not only of the great) artists are unfathomable. Raphael died young but had time to say all he had in him. Whereas Leonardo da Vinci lived a long life, discovered, invented (his scientific works were published when all his discoveries and inventions had only an historical value), painted with colours prepared by himself, which quickly dried, dulled and scaled off, and what millions of people know is not Leonardo's artistic genius but the spurious legend of La Gioconda's 'mysterious smile'. There are authors smaller than the books they have written: one calls the

---

[1] *Gogol* is the Goldeneye, a duck, *gogolek* – the diminutive.

man to mind and marvels that he could have written such things. But there are others. Even now, as forty years ago, I believe that Andrey Bely was greater than anything he wrote.

I do not mean to say that his works are insignificant or of little interest. I consider some of the poems in his book called *Ashes* perfect; his novel *Petersburg*, no matter how one regards its approach, is a great event in the history of Russian prose; Andrey Bely's memoirs are fascinating. But these books have not been republished, they are not translated, and they are unknown both at home and abroad.

The Great Soviet Encyclopedia found a kind word for Bely's father, the mathematician N. V. Bugayev, but the son, Boris Nikolaye-vich, was unlucky, being described, in the manner of 1950, as a 'calumniator'. (Again I think of the advantages of the exact sciences: one cannot stick the label 'calumniator' on the work of a mathe-matician.)

For the modern reader a book by Andrey Bely is heavy going: he is baulked by word-derivations invented by Bely, by an arbitrary transposition of words, by the deliberately stressed rhythm of the prose. Even in his remarkable memoirs written shortly before his death, Andrey Bely constantly tries to 'whip up the snow': 'Baltru-shaitis, grim as the rocks, whom they called Yurgis, was a friend of Polyakov . . . And without taking off his overcoat would sit down, fold both his hands on his stick and wreath himself with the smoke of a cigarette, like a crag in the clouds, shake off the ash with a most terrible grimace, his elbow at an angle and blinking from under a transverse wrinkle at his own nose laced with conspicuous red veins'. This seems to be written in an ancient language, it must be deciphered like *The Lay of Igor's Host*. Not all young Soviet prose writers are acquainted with Andrey Bely's books. However, without him (as without Remizov) it is difficult to imagine the history of Russian prose. Andrey Bely's contribution to it can be felt in the works of some modern authors who quite possibly have never read *Petersburg* or *Kotik Letayev*.

The ways of the development of literature are even more mysterious than those of individual authors. Essential oils extracted from the orris-root or from the flowers of the ylang-ylang are never used in their pure form, but they are distilled by all the perfumers of the world. The essence is always diluted with water. Very few people are capable of reading from end to end the complete works of Velemir Khlebnikov.

Yet this considerable poet still exercises an influence on modern poetry in hidden, roundabout ways – through those whom Khlebnikov has influenced. The same can be said of Andrey Bely's prose.

His road was tortuous and as hard to understand as his syntax. In 1932, not far from Kuznetsk, in a hamlet where the Siberian Shortsi lived, I saw the last of the shamans. He realized that his days were numbered and would begin his ritual with reluctance, perhaps driven by hunger, or perhaps simply by habit; but some minutes later he would fall into ecstasy and shout inspired words that no one could understand. When I recall some of Andrey Bely's readings I think of this shaman. It seems to me that Bely often both spoke and wrote in a state of frenzy, performing a shaman's ritual – he hurried, he was always seeing and foreseeing something but could not find intelligible words to express it.

He was inspired by Steiner, by anthroposophy, he helped to build the temple in Dornach, not like Voloshin, but quite seriously and with zest. In 1922 there were numerous small dance-halls in Berlin; bewildered, half-starved Germans, men and women, danced the popular foxtrot for hours on end. What dream possessed Andrey Bely when he first heard jazz? Why did he furiously take up dancing, frightening young shop-girls with his prophet's eyes? His hair had gone white at an early age; his skin was deeply tanned, and his eyes detached themselves more and more from his face, living their own life.

Whatever he touched turned to misfortune: tragedies in his love life, his friendship with Blok, continuous disillusionments, literary loneliness. As early as 1917 he wrote his own epitaph: 'He believed in the golden glitter, but died from the arrows of the sun; he measured centuries with his thought, but did not know how to live his own life'. He died at the age of fifty-four, not from the arrows of the sun, but from exhaustion; he wanted to march with the age, but either outstripped it or lagged behind: 'did not know how to live his own life'. He seems to have tried everything: mysticism and chemistry, Kant and Solovyev and Marx; after Dornach he was director of the Proletkult literary workshop, wrote essays on the growth of Socialist economy for Soviet newspapers, produced the abstruse *Glossalalia*, more than once gave up writing, then again 'started a shindy'.

Hardbitten *émigrés* hated him; they saw him as a turncoat: had he not spent his evenings conversing with Shestov, Berdyayev, been friendly with Merezhkovsky? And then suddenly, in 1922 in Berlin, he asserted that true culture was in Soviet Russia and that those who had fled from the Revolution were dead and stinking.

The Scythians regarded him as one of themselves – on what grounds it is hard to say, probably because he admired Blok's moral courage. There was nothing 'Scythian' about Andrey Bely, and he feared the 'pan-Mongolism' about which Solovyev had written and which had inspired Blok. He condemned the automatism of the West European bourgeoisie not as a Scythian, dreaming of ancient nomad camping grounds, but as a humanist of the Renaissance.

I remember two pronouncements of his. Talking to Mayakovsky in Berlin (I have mentioned how highly Bely admired the poem *Man*), Bely said: 'I accept everything in you – Futurism, the revolutionary spirit, but there is one thing that divides us: your love for the machine as such. The danger of utilitarianism is not that the young people will be drawn to the applied sciences, that I should welcome. The danger lies elsewhere – in the apologia for America. The America of Whitman no longer exists, the leaves of grass are withered. Now there is the America that has taken up arms against man'. On another occasion Bely got into an argument with a writer close to the *Smena Vekh* group. He shouted: 'You don't really like the Revolution, you believe in NEP, you admire order, the strong hand. But I stand for October! Do you see? Whatever it is that I don't like, it's just the thing you like.'

I have already said that in 1919 he had predicted the atom bomb. When he talked to me he often said that mathematicians, engineers and chemists were traitors to their duty of serving mankind and worked at perfecting destruction, catastrophe, death. (He wrote about this in his diary for the years 1915–16 *On the Mountain Pass*.)

Undoubtedly he was a genius. An impotent genius. A short time before his death he tried to unravel this contradiction. 'For thirty years I have been dogged by the refrain: "He has betrayed his convictions. He is neglecting literature ... He has burnt the artist within him, having, like Gogol, gone mad. He is a frivolous creature, a lyricist ... A deadly rationalist ... A mystic ... He has become a materialist". I have given plenty of cause for such opinions: by trying to be too clever (as a result of a premature complication of themes), by the contrapuntal technique of the orchestration of my world outlook, which I see as a symphony of many voices; thus a composer bereft of his instruments cannot reproduce with his pitiful hoarse throat the parts of the horns, the flutes, the violins, the cymbals in their interlacing of sounds. The most correct explanation is, possibly, an extremely complex score and a feeble human voice.'

Hence the loneliness. At the seaside, seemingly in good spirits, he said to me: 'The most difficult of all is to find a bond with men, with the people'. When he gave me his *Petersburg* he inscribed it: '... with the feeling of a permanent bond'. What I am talking about is not the chance coincidence of words, but an obsession. He wanted so badly to forge a living bond with people. And fate frustrated him. His personal grief seemed cold, 'gold in the azure'. In a poem dedicated to Bely, Mandelstam wrote: 'Between you and the country an icy link is forming'. These lines were written on the day following Andrey Bely's death.

5

I HAVE said that the development of our prose was influenced by Andrey Bely and Alexey Remizov, although their books have been forgotten now by nearly everyone. These two writers were not at all alike. Andrey Bely soared in the clouds, could not live a single day without philosophical generalizations, travelled a great deal, went into ecstasies, worked himself up, argued. Remizov was a stay-at-home, he lived on the earth, even underground, like a sorcerer or a mole, found inspiration in the roots of words and indulged in oddities rather than in involved abstractions.

In the years 1921–2 young Soviet prose writers – Boris Pilnyak, Vsevolod Ivanov, Zoshchenko and many others – made their appearance in literature; nearly all of them had passed through a phase of admiring Andrey Bely and Remizov. I once took a look at the books I wrote in those days (*Incredible Stories*, *Life and Death of Nikolay Kurbov*, *Six Stories about Easy Endings*) and was surprised: involved and broken sentences, words in the wrong order or simply coined; yet when I wrote in that way this kind of language seemed to me natural. Pilnyak's *The Bare Year* and many other works by the young Serapions were written like that too. If this is to be regarded as a malady, one might call it growing pains.

The influence of Bely and Remizov on young authors was so marked that Gorky wrote to Konstantin Fedin: 'But do not take this to mean that I recommend Bely and Remizov as teachers – nothing of the kind. Yes, they have a marvellously rich vocabulary and of course this deserves attention, as it is deserved by the third repository of the treasures of pure Russian, Nikolay Leskov. But – try and find yourself. That, too, is interesting, important and maybe very significant.'

I have spoken about Andrey Bely. Now I should like to recall Alexey Remizov whom I got to know in Berlin in 1922. In a lower-middle-class German flat cluttered with other people's belongings, sat a small hunched-up man with a long inquisitive nose and lively, twinkling eyes. His wife, Serafima Pavlovna, was busy offering tea to the guests. On the desk I noticed manuscripts written, or rather traced, by a master calligrapher. On strings stretched across the room swayed all kinds of devils cut out of paper: domesticated and wicked, cunning and good-natured as newborn kids. Remizov smiled quietly: on that day, in addition to his usual toys, he had a new one – Pilnyak, who told fantastic stories about life in Kolomna.

In Berlin Remizov was exactly the same as he had been in Moscow or in Petrograd, writing the same kind of stories, playing the same kind of games, cutting out the same kind of devils: I say this now as I read notes made by those who had met him before he went abroad. Vladimir Lidin's entry made in 1921 says: 'Such men – Russian, earthy, mouselike – have not yet all gone: he lives and enjoys good health, and may God give him many years of life, this Russian man, who at night scratches and scratches with his pen – in hunger and cold – the king of monkeys, Alexey Mikhailovich Remizov'. In 1944, in his book *Gorky Among Us*, Fedin recalled the first years of the Revolution: 'Stooping, in some way reminding one of the Little Hump-backed Horse, knees slightly bent, a man is scurrying along the Nevsky, looking sharply from behind his spectacles, in a little overcoat and a little fur cap. He hides the big-brained back of his head in his turned-up coat collar, and sticks out his chin and lips, while his sizeable hooked nose with its sensitive tip quivers, probably savouring the words that fly from his puffed-out lips.' (Lidin wrote these lines in the years when everybody was imitating Remizov, and Fedin's were written twenty years later, but he, too, when speaking about Alexey Remizov unconsciously fell into the long-discarded Remizov idiom.)

Remizov played, among other games, at a certain mysterious society he had created, the *Obezyanya velikaya i volnaya palata* ('The Great and Free Chamber of Monkeys'), or *Obezvolpal*. He raised his writer friends Yevgeny Zamyatin, Pavel Shchegolev, the Serapions to the dignity of knights, princes and bishops. I figured on his list as the 'knight with the caraboid proboscis'.

In 1946, when I came to Paris, I visited Remizov. I had not seen him then for some twenty years. There is no need to recall what those years had been like. Remizov, too, had suffered many misfortunes. During the German occupation he had endured hunger, privation and cold. In 1943 his wife had died. I saw an old man bent almost double. He lived alone, forgotten, abandoned, and in great poverty. But the same mischievous twinkle gleamed in his eye, the same devils swung in the room, and he wrote in the ancient script, as he always had, setting down

45

his dreams, writing letters to his dead wife and working on books which nobody wanted to publish.

N. Kondryanskaya recently sent me a book devoted to Alexey Remizov's last years. I look at the photographs. He was losing his sight, wrote with difficulty, called himself 'the blind scribe', but his eyes astonishingly retained their former expressiveness, and he worked to the last day; he wrote the same things in the same way: *The Mouse's Pipe, The Peacock's Feather, The Tale of Two Beasts.* He died in 1957 at the age of eighty. A short time before his death he recorded in his diary: 'A pressing swarm of fancies, but no means of realizing them – it's my eyes. Today I wrote all day in my mind but could not put it down on paper'. He played his games to the end: on his books published in the last years stands the legend: 'Censored by the Supreme Council of the *Obezvolpal*'.

One might envy such tenacity, such truth to one's own self, such strength of mind. Yet there is nothing to envy: Remizov knew the full measure of human misery. He was often accused of piling it on in his books, but his own fate was far more absurd than anything he could have invented.

An author always tries to show a reason for the actions of his characters, even if they are in complete contradiction to commonly accepted logic. Poets logically justify their illogicality. We understand why Raskolnikov kills the old woman and why Julien Sorel kills Madame de Rênal. But life is not an author; life can, without any explanation at all, tangle things up or, in Remizov's words, turn everything upside down. Remizov was the most Russian of all Russian writers, yet he spent thirty-six years abroad and said: 'I don't know how this came about'.

In his early youth, when he was a student, Remizov was attracted to politics, became a Social Democrat, was jailed, spent six years in administrative exile together with Lunacharsky, Savinkov and the future expert on Pushkin, Pavel Shchegolev. In exile he met his future wife, Serafima Pavlovna, a naïve Socialist Revolutionary. When he talked, Remizov always stressed that he had abandoned revolutionary activities because he considered himself a poor organizer, and also because he had become engrossed in his writing. Not long before his death he recorded in his diary how he had been drawn into revolutionary activity: 'How revolution was made in Russia. Rearrangement of life – of the order of life. My feeling begins – beggars in the church porch, and factory slums'. Three months later he continued: 'History seems to me bloodthirsty, war and oppression, somebody has to be tortured and tortured to death. A man wants to eat his fill, to sleep in peace, to think freely. It is not everyone who can do so on an empty stomach. If you have not eaten your fill, you will not sleep soundly. Worry stuns and kills thought. Revolution starts with bread'.

In one of his last books, writing about Turgenev, Remizov returns to the same problem: 'During the Revolution everybody rushed to Dostoyevsky's *The Devils*[1] trying to find out about the revolution. And no one thought about the unappeased, blazing Marianne of *Virgin Soil* who, I know, will never be appeased, or about her sister Elena in *On the Eve,* nor to seek the "devils" in quite a different place – man's life is difficult and it is his dream to ease this life, no time for "devils" – no, not there, and if we have to talk about devils, here is the world as pictured by Turgenev, Tolstoy, Pisemsky and Leskov – here are legions of devils, and their name is sloth, deliberate sloth'.

In his books *The Pond* and *Sisters of the Cross* Remizov showed the real devils of pre-revolutionary Russia. In his preface to the French translation of *Sisters of the Cross* Romain Rolland says that the book shows up the injustice of the old society and explains and justifies the storm.

Bunin knew why he lived and died in exile, whereas Remizov, when speaking about the White *émigrés,* always used the unfriendly 'they', and often said: 'No matter what they say, the true life is in Russia'. N. Kondryanskaya quotes the following words of Remizov: 'Out of the year 1947 I have retained three strong epithets they used about me: "reactionary", "rascal", "Soviet scoundrel".' When I visited him in the summer of 1946 he said: 'My passport is a Soviet one', finding some consolation in the fact, and he smiled ruefully.

Abroad he was driven from pillar to post, he was evicted from his home, he was deported. In Berlin, Thomas Mann intervened on his behalf. In Paris he was accused of breeding mice. He was always in debt and worried over the rent of his small flat.

Konstantin Fedin wrote: 'Remizov could be and usually was a very peculiar "Right Front" in literature'. The word 'Right' concerns, of course, not politics but aesthetics: Fedin opposes Remizov to LEF (Left Front). But to me it seems that the passion for old demotic turns

[1] Generally known in English as 'The Possessed'.

47

of speech, for the roots of words, which distinguishes Remizov, was also characteristic of Khlebnikov without whom one cannot imagine LEF.

Remizov said that of all his contemporaries the closest to him were Andrey Bely, Khlebnikov, Mayakovsky and Pasternak. His tastes were not so very 'Right' after all. In painting he liked Picasso and Matisse. His archaisms were dictated not by conservative leanings but by the search for a new idiom.

Remizov often recalled Mikhail Prishvin with affection. In a letter written just before his death he expressed his joy that Prishvin's memory had been solemnly honoured in Moscow. In his autobiography Prishvin, trying to explain the nature of art, wrote: 'In his day the writer Remizov was friendly with Kalyayev and a revolutionary graft "took" on him. Remizov was no lightminded deserter to literature. Kalyayev lost none of his respect for him when he started on his elegant, exquisite writings. Once, in the last days of his life, Kalyayev ran into Remizov at a railway station, gave him a friendly smile and, in passing, asked him with simple good-nature: "Are you still writing about your little bugs?" '

Of course Remarque is more read than Hoffmann, and Apukhtin was more popular than Tyutchev. But it is not statistics that decide the case: there are wings of different sizes for different flights.

Remizov was a poet and a spinner of fairy-tales. In one of the books he gave me he wrote: 'Everything here is for the Christmas tree'. At one time Christmas trees were out of favour with us; later they were reinstated. Remizov was the same in his books as in his life: he played, he invented, sometimes he amused, at other times he made one sad. Children are not alone in loving Christmas trees, and it is rare to meet someone who has not at some time desperately longed for a Christmas tree. And in this lies the justification for the 'little bugs', the long labours of the writer Alexey Mikhailovich Remizov.

6

WHEN bestowing upon me the accolade of *Obezvolpal* Remizov dubbed me 'caraboid'; this was no accident, for the carabus beetle when attacked ejects a stinging liquid. The critics called me a sceptic, a malicious cynic.

I said at the beginning of these memoirs that I wanted to write a confession: I probably promised more than I can fulfil. In Catholic churches the confessionals have curtains so that the priest shall not see who is confiding secrets to him. They say that a writer's biography is in his books; this is true. However, when he endows his fictional characters with his own traits, the author masks himself, covers up his traces; he has, besides his books, a personal life, love, joys, losses. When I was writing about my childhood and my early youth I more than once pulled aside the curtain of the confessional. Having come to my adult life, I pass a great deal over in silence, and the more I advance the more often I have to omit events in my life about which it would be difficult for me to speak even to an intimate friend.

Yet, in spite of this, my book is still a confession. I have mentioned that I have often been called a sceptic. A book by I. Tereshchenko entitled *A Modern Nihilist – I. Ehrenburg*, came out in Leningrad in 1925. (Turgenev who had launched the word 'nihilist' wrote: 'I have used this word not as a reproach, not with any desire to insult, but as an exact and fitting expression for an emerging historical fact; it has been transformed into a weapon of indictment, of irrevocable condemnation, almost a brand of dishonour'.) I should like to make clear how much truth there is in the label which has so often been attached to me.

In my childhood I lived in doubt of the absolute value of the truths I heard from my parents, my teachers and other adults. It was the same later on; blind faith seemed to me at times admirable, at times repulsive, but always alien. Occasionally in my youth I tried to force myself to believe but, having reached the age which Dante calls 'the middle of life's road', I realized that one can alter one's judgments but not one's nature. Three years ago I expressed in verse my attitude towards blind faith, to which I opposed critical thinking and loyalty to an ideal, to men and to oneself: 'I was not a model pupil and with years have not grown irreproachable; of all the apostles, Doubting Thomas seems to me the most human. When he heard, he did not simply believe – many were the fables that were told. And very probably more than one apostle said that he was very dangerous. Perhaps Thomas was a slow thinker, but when he had thought he got down to work, he said only what he thought and did not go back on his word. He measured with his own yardstick, he had his own Tables of the Law. Is it not because he was "doubting" that he remained silent when he was tortured?'

I have referred more than once in these memoirs to the nature of my doubts. Had I been a sociologist or a physicist, an astronomer or a professional politician I should certainly have found it easier to cross the field of life[1]. I do not mean to say that the paths of politicians or scholars are strewn with roses; but when they experience temporary setbacks or defeats they see that in the end reason prevails. But I became a writer, that is, a man the nature of whose work compels him to be interested not only in the organization of society but also in the inner world of the individual, not only in the destiny of mankind, but also in the destiny of individual human beings.

Today we often talk about the decline of literature and art and say that the 'physicists' have outstripped the 'lyricists'. In 1892 Chekhov wrote: 'Are not Korolenko, Nadson and all the dramatists of today just lemonade? Have the pictures by Repin or Shishkin really enraptured you? They are nice, they show talent. You admire, and at the same time you cannot manage to forget that you want to smoke. Science and technology are passing through a wonderful period, but for us this is a flabby, sour, dull time, and we ourselves are sour and dull, all we can bring into the world are guttapercha boys[2], and the only man who does not see this is Stasov whom Nature has endowed with the rare faculty of getting drunk on slops'. Occasionally, peering into the past, one is comforted: when Chekhov wrote the letter I have quoted, he did not know that his path was on the ascent, that Maxim Gorky's first story had been published in a Tiflis newspaper, that the twelve-year-old boy Sasha Blok would become a great poet and that Russian poetry was on the eve of an upsurge. Flow and ebb always follow one another. Sometimes the flow becomes prolonged. The

---

[1] Russian saying: 'To live through life is not as easy as to cross a field.'
[2] Allusion to a story by Dmitry Vasilyevich Grigorovich (1822–1900).

French Impressionists made their début in the seventies of last century. Many of them were still at the height of their powers when they were succeeded by Cézanne, Gauguin, Van Gogh, Toulouse-Lautrec; in the early days of our generation pictures by Bonnard, Matisse, Marquet, Picasso, Braque, Léger were exhibited for the first time, and only a quarter of a century later did the ebb set in. Modern American literature has been created by writers born in and about the year 1900: Hemingway, Faulkner, Steinbeck, Caldwell; they were called 'the lost generation', but it was not they, it was the next generation that lost its way, got stuck in a morass. Between the death of Nekrasov and the first collection of poems by Alexander Blok almost thirty years passed.

I witnessed the emergence of important writers and painters and cannot complain of having lived at a time of decadence in art. No, what has been depressing is something different: I have lived through an epoch of discrepancy between, on the one hand, the swift progress of the natural sciences, of the development of technology, of the triumph of Socialist ideas and, on the other, of the spiritual impoverishment of millions of human beings. I have too often come across extraordinarily complicated machines and incredibly primitive men with the prejudices and the crude reactions of cavemen.

I have described the Moscow of my childhood: dark, with its *Moskovsky Listok*, its snobs with their eyes fixed on Paris, its illiterate working class, its foreign wares; in the West people seldom spoke about Russia: the land of the knout, of brave Cossacks, of wheat and furs, the land of bombs and gallows. Today it is enough to glance at any paper in any continent to see what a lot they have to say about us; everybody looks to Moscow, some with hope, others with apprehension; the green, sleepy town of my childhood has become a true world capital. A new China has been born, India has its independence, a storm has broken out and, one after another, the countries of Asia and Africa are throwing off the domination of the white man. Yes, everything has changed. Could I, as a boy, have imagined that I should be able to cross the ocean in a few hours, that there would be radio and television, that man would travel into space? Miracles, seven-league boots!

But could I either, in those years of my adolescence, imagine that Auschwitz and Hiroshima lay ahead? We were brought up on the books of the last century, and I knew wo poles: progress and barbarism, enlightenment and ignorance. The twentieth century has brought confusion into many things. I recall a German officer's diary brought to me at the front in 1943. The owner of the diary was a student who quoted Hegel and Nietzsche, Goethe and Stefan Georg, who was keenly interested in the prospects for modern physics, and yet he recorded: 'Today in Kielce we liquidated four Jewish brats, they were hiding under the floor, and afterwards we laughed at the way we had starved out the rats'. More recently we have seen how Patrice Lumumba was subjected to brutality. Reporters photographed the torturing, and they had excellent cameras.

Savagery can be explained when it is linked with ignorance; it is more difficult to understand in educated and even sometimes talented people. The future SS men went to school in the Germany I knew; from their childhood they had been told that Kant had written the *Critique of Pure Reason*, and that Goethe's dying words had been: 'More light!' All this did not prevent them ten years later from throwing Russian babies down wells. I shall be told: 'The insane ideas of a maniac.' Of course. But what astounded me was not the appearance of Hitler on the world stage, but the rapidity with which the face of German society changed: men of excellent education were transformed into cannibals; the brakes of civilization proved too weak and failed at the first test.

But why speak of the fascists? I have seen how, in an advanced society, some men, who were thought to have been inculcated with noble ideas, committed base actions, betrayed their comrades, their friends, for the sake of personal security; how a wife repudiated her husband, a clever son defamed his father who had got into trouble.

I do not know whether it was because a struggle was going on for the building of a new society, a struggle that was at times a bloody one, in which the opponents stopped at nothing, or because in the space of a few years it was necessary to make up for the leeway of centuries, but many people developed one-sidedly. The author of the book *A Contemporary Nihilist*, which I have referred to, accused me of the 'cult of love', which he regarded as petty bourgeois. 'In individual cases, sexual love may, for weak or underdeveloped persons, play the part of a progressive motive force, but on condition that it is assigned its proper place.' I called to mind Petrarch, Lermontov, Heine, and it seemed to me that my accuser was a 'weak or underdeveloped man', and that, although he considered himself a Communist, his conception of love 'assigned to its proper place' was an apology for petty bourgeois vulgarity.

Am I really a sceptic, a cynic, a nihilist? I look back on my past. I myself wanted to understand, to verify a great deal, and was more than once mistaken. But I was firm in the knowledge that, no matter how much I was saddened or revolted by this or that thing, I would never dissociate myself from a people that was the first to have had the courage to put an end to the world of greed, of hypocrisy, of racial and national arrogance which I hated. I believe that a sceptic would have spent his whole life smiling bitterly in some intellectual retreat, while a cynic would have written exactly the sort of thing that pleases the most rigorous critics.

Sartre told me once that Determinism was an error, that we always have freedom of choice. He is a man of great intellect, of sensitive conscience and of rather childlike naïvety. As I think now of the road he has taken, I realize once again how much our choice is shackled by historical circumstances, by our environment, by the feeling of responsibility for others, by that social climate which cannot help but make a man's voice louder or, on the contrary, mute it and alter all proportions.

There are epochs when, having chosen a place 'above the battle', it is possible to retain a love of man and humaneness; and there are others when spiritually independent Cynics become cynics, and Diogenes' barrel turns into the 'house that is always on the outskirts'[1]. But at all events, man cannot choose his epoch.

In which way, then, were the critics right? They were right in so far as, owing to my nature, I see not only what is good but also what is bad. They are right also because I tend to be ironical; the more deeply I am disturbed and moved, the sharper do the thorns bristle; this is quite a common phenomenon; there even used to be a term for it: 'romantic irony'.

In my earlier books satire predominated; grabbers, spiteful vulgarians, hypocrites often suddenly took the centre of the stage. Later I saw that, more often than not, good and evil co-exist in the same person. I wrote *The Second Day*. But the label still stuck. Alexander Afinogenov, whom I got to know in the thirties, recorded this in his diary: 'Ehrenburg's attitude to all that is going on is sceptical'. This

[1] Russian saying: 'My house is on the outskirts, I know nothing'.

was written by a friendly hand but the remark shows the momentum of a reputation once acquired. And it is not necessary to talk of a quarter of a century ago. In 1953 I wrote *The Thaw*; the very title of the book would seem to demonstrate the author's faith in the epoch and the people; yet the critics were indignant because I depicted a factory director as a bad and unfeeling man.

There are writers who apparently see only goodness and kindness everywhere. This has nothing to do with the author's own kindness. Chekhov seems to me to have been gentler, kinder, more tolerant than Tolstoy. But Chekhov wrote with justice: 'Every night I wake up and read *War and Peace*. One reads it with as much curiosity and naïve surprise as though one had never read it before. It is wonderfully good. The only parts I don't like are those where Napoleon appears. As soon as Napoleon comes on the scene there is strain and every kind of trick is used to prove that he was more stupid than he really was. Everything Pierre, Prince Andrey or that utter nonentity Nikolay Rostov does or says is good, intelligent, natural and moving . . .' Tolstoy made Nikolay Rostov seem a charming person, but he was unable to describe Napoleon. As for Chekhov, he was able to depict with great skill people who harm others, and in his stories those who are harmed are far from angelic.

Which of the two is more necessary: to show up vice, moral defects, social pestilence, or to affirm nobility, beauty, harmony? I think it is a pointless question: men need everything. Derzhavin and Fonvizin lived at the same time; 'The voice of time! The ringing of metal!' has remained, and so has *Nedorosl* ('The Minor'). There has never been, there is not, and there is hardly ever likely to be a society without vices; a writer's duty, if he hears the call, is to speak out about them, undaunted by the possibility that someone will have the happy thought of classifying him among the sceptics or the cynics.

I like Belinsky for his social passion, his love of art, and his deep honesty. I have often recalled his words: '. . . when we find in a novel that only scoundrelly types of people are well drawn while decent ones are badly drawn, it is a clear sign either that the author has undertaken a task which is foreign to him, is beyond his capacity, the limits of his talent, and he has therefore sinned against the fundamental laws of art, that he has been inventing, straining and writing rhetorically instead of creating; or else that he has superfluously, in contradiction to the inner meaning of his work, and solely at the behests of morality, introduced these characters into his novel, and has thus also sinned against the fundamental laws of art'.

At times I have sinned against the laws of art, at times I have been mistaken in my appraisal of events, of people. Of one thing I am innocent: of indifference.

My ratiocinations may seem to be literary polemics. After all, I was talking about confession, and here I am constantly quoting Belinsky, Tolstoy, Turgenev, Chekhov. But I had to talk about the eyes and the heart, about loyalty to one's epoch, which is paid for by sleepless nights and unsuccessful books. Without this chapter I should have found it difficult to continue my tale.

7

I HAVE said that my generation can count on its fingers the relatively peaceful years; amongst these should be counted the time of which I now relate.

In the autumn of 1923 everybody thought that Germany was on the eve of a civil war. There was shooting in Hamburg, in Berlin, in Dresden, in Erfurt. There was talk about Communist 'proletarian hundreds', about the 'black Reichswehr' of the fascists. The Chancellor, Stresemann, made an appeal to patriotism. General Seeckt made sure that the artillery had enough shells. Foreign correspondents hung on the telephones. The storm seemed inevitable. Faint peals of thunder rumbled. But nothing happened. The workers were discouraged, worn out. The small bourgeois was completely bewildered; he no longer believed anyone; he hated Stinnes and the French and, though slightly nervous of the guardians of the law, he longed at the same time for a stable and firm regime. The Social Democrats boasted of their exemplary organization. The Trade Unions methodically collected membership dues. But determination was weak. The Chancellor gave orders to dissolve the Workers' Governments of Saxony and Thuringia. I saw leaflets with a call to revolution; people read these and trudged silently to work.

Munich was regarded as the headquarters of the fascists. The well-known General Ludendorff and the so far little-known Hitler made an attempt to seize power. This preliminary rehearsal of a tragedy was recorded in history as 'the beerhall putsch', a title better suited to a farce. The Berliners skimmed through the reports from Munich with indifference: one more putsch – Captain Roehm – someone called Hitler . . . The days of the 'Dawes Plan' were approaching, the days of Stresemann's shrewd diplomacy, of sudden plenty after years of unremitting want. The papers gave their attention to sensational murders or the love affairs of film stars.

The factories could not cope with the flood of orders. The previously empty shops began to fill with customers. The 'heroes' of the

56

painter Grosz drank French champagne to 'the new era' in the Kurfürstendamm restaurants.

There is a vast literature on the transition from war to peace economy. It is just as difficult for an ordinary man to pass from a life overflowing with historic events to a humdrum existence. I had spent two years in Berlin with the constant feeling of a gathering storm, and suddenly I realized that the wind had died down. To tell the truth I was dismayed: I was not prepared for a peaceful life.

The House of Arts had long since closed. The ephemeral publishing firms had gone bankrupt. The Russian writers had dispersed: Gorky to Sorrento, Alexey Tolstoy and Andrey Bely to Soviet Russia, Tsvetayeva to Prague, Remizov and Khodasevich to Paris.

The foreign speculators had also left Berlin: the mark was back on its feet. The newspapers declared that the new American President would oblige the French to evacuate the Ruhr, that the rehabilitation of Germany had begun. Some Germans wholeheartedly enjoyed the tranquillity, others said it was necessary to prepare for revenge – the occupied could not relinquish the dream of being the occupiers again. The needle of the barometer was rising, however; people thought less about a future war than of the coming holidays.

I wrote a great deal, and perhaps during those months (as more than once later in my life) my profession came to my rescue. I do not know whether it is a 'sacred' profession or merely a very difficult one; I am not referring now to plans, to imagination, but simply to sweat. I recorded the number of books written (then followed a list of titles). What this represented in the first place was labour, and torn up pages, a line ten times rewritten, sleepless nights – the things that every writer knows. There were days when I was so angry with myself that I was ready to forswear writing; and then once more I would be sitting over a sheet of paper: I had become engrossed in this work and it was too late now to speculate whether I had talent or not.

I finished and sent off to Petrograd my sentimental novel *The Love of Jeanne Ney*, a tribute to the romanticism of the revolutionary years, to Dickens, to enthusiasm for the plots of novels, and to my (this time non-literary) desire to write not only about a Trust concerned with the destruction of Europe, but also about love.

Tramping the long streets of Berlin, all so much alike, I sometimes composed verse which I did not publish. Here is one of the poems written at the time: 'To die so that lights should shudder, that cheeks should smell of smoke, that the fast train's "sh, you, shut up, shut up!" should be nurse's hush to the abandoned heart, that this should be without you, to be clinging to the window-strap instead of to your hands; that there should be no "oh stay!" dying to cast your future by the rash of stars and by the fever of stations; so to die, to understand that the noise, the tea, the station-buffet waiter, the eternal rose in the lapel, that this is death and that to your "farewell" I am not fated to reply'. The form looks borrowed, borrowed from Pasternak, but the content was mine. I continued to work, to storm, to indulge in irony, of course, and all the while I was sick at heart.

(In one of his novels Mauriac says: 'Even suffering is a luxury. Yes, too many years fell to our lot when people could not permit themselves the luxury of feeling sad, of suffering from a bruised soul, from un-shared love, or from loneliness'.)

Coming towards me in the opposite direction were respectable citizens, smartly dressed women, civil servants, schoolboys. Dachs-hunds, tied up at the doors of sausage shops, waited for their mistresses with unhappy yawns.

I parted from Berlin without regret. But to part from certain illusions that lived on in the 'nihilist's' heart was much harder.

We ridiculed romanticism but in reality we were romantics. We complained that events were developing too swiftly, that we could not meditate, concentrate, realize what was going on; but no sooner had history put on the brakes than we fell into despondency – we could not adapt ourselves to the new rhythm. I wrote satirical novels, had the reputation of being a pessimist, but privately nursed the hope that, before ten years had passed, the whole face of Europe would have changed. In my thoughts I had already buried the old world, yet suddenly it had sprung to life again, had even put on weight and was grinning.

The period which historians call 'the temporary stabilization of capitalism' was setting in. As they read this part of my memoirs readers may think: the first parts were far more interesting, there's a definite falling off . . . Ah well, the interval is not the play, and the year 1924 is neither 1914 nor 1919.

During the years of respite writers realized that they could write; it is precisely in those years that Hemingway's splendid novels, Babel's *Red Cavalry*, Mayakovsky's *About This*, Roger Martin du Gard's *Les Thibault*, Tsvetayeva's best poems, Thomas Mann's *Magic Mountain*,

Aragon's *Le Paysan de Paris,* Fadeyev's *The Nineteen,* and other remarkable works were written. But to write about the years when there were no mobilizations, no battles, no concentration camps, when people died in their beds, and to write about them interestingly, is very difficult. Flaubert dreamed of writing a novel in which nothing happened, but somehow he never wrote it; plainly, even for a quiet narrative, events of some sort are necessary. However, the reader may take comfort: the respite was a short one.

8

I THINK it was in September 1923 that a friend of Mayakovsky and of Elsa Triolet arrived in Berlin from Prague. This was red-haired Romka – the linguist Roman Osipovich Yakobson, who worked at the Soviet Representation. In a poem that has been included in anthologies Mayakovsky recalled how the diplomatic courier Nette 'squinting at the wax of the seal, babbled endlessly about Romka Yakobson and sweated oddly, memorizing poetry'. Roman was pink-faced and blue-eyed, with a squint in one eye; he drank a great deal but his head remained clear, and only after the tenth glass would he button his coat the wrong way. What struck me about him was that he knew everything: the structure of Khlebnikov's verse, old Czech literature, Rimbaud, the machinations of Curzon and Ramsay MacDonald. Occasionally he made things up, but when anyone tried to catch him out in an inaccuracy he replied with a grin: 'That was just a working hypothesis of mine'. Roman Yakobson tried to persuade me to go to Prague, tempting me with baroque houses, young poets and even Moravian sausages. (Roman liked his food and was beginning to put on flesh, though he was still very young.)

Towards the end of the year I went to Prague. The young poets gave me a friendly welcome and questioned me about Mayakovsky, Meyerhold, Pasternak, Tatlin: I was the first Soviet writer they had met. (This is mentioned in Nezval's memoirs published posthumously.)

František Kubka, referring to his meetings with Soviet writers, says that he often saw me in Prague but cannot remember to which occasion this or that conversation belongs. I also cannot recall when I first met many of my Prague friends – in 1923 or later – but I well remember one of my first evenings there when Roman Yakobson took me to the café Narodna Kavarna, a favourite resort of the members of *Devetsila*, as the Czech champions of left-wing art called themselves. The poets Vítězslav Nezval, Jaroslav Seifert, the prose-writer Vladislav Vančura and the theoretician of *Devetsila*, the critic Karel Teige, sat on a divan by a long table. There were also some young artists but I do not remember exactly who they were. Nezval drank *slivovice* and emitted joyful cries. Then Vančura went home while we set off on a round of wineshops, finishing up at dawn in an empty cold snack-bar where local custom demanded that one should eat giblet soup.

When Nezval was present it was difficult to notice anyone else; he filled not only the room but, so it seemed, the whole of Prague. He shouted ecstatically, jumped on to the table and recited poetry, embraced every one of us, all the while waving his short broad arms that reminded one of flippers. He was altogether like a sea-lion. His appearance was so unusual that the artist Adolf Hoffmeister drew portraits of him as children draw a tree or a house – in a few lines – drew them without looking, in a flash, and all these portraits were wonderful likenesses. One night, in a quiet street, Nezval was loudly declaiming poetry. A policeman asked him not to wake people, but Nezval went on shouting. He had no identity papers, but after rummaging in his pockets he produced a crumpled scrap of newspaper with Hoffmeister's caricature and condescendingly showed it to the policeman: 'Nezval. Poet'.

The power of Nezval's poetry lies first of all in its spontaneity, its simplicity. People usually say 'simple as a child'. I have said that François Villon, who was regarded as an artless composer of ballads and rondos, was in fact a skilled master. Nezval had a wide knowledge of poetry, he loved the Czech romantics, and also Novalis, Baudelaire, Rimbaud, Guillaume Apollinaire, Mayakovsky, Pasternak, Eluard, Tuwim. There was not a single form of poetry to which he did not set his hand, from the sonnet to verse held together only by internal rhythm, from Classicism to Surrealism; the struggle to overcome the problems of his material always attracted him, and he always emerged victorious. He was simple, not like a child, but like a nightingale, like an anemone, like summer rain. Hourly he discovered the world; he approached the world and human emotions, and even pots and pans, as if the thousands of years of civilization before him had never existed. He was new not because he wished to be an innovator, but because he saw and felt everything in a new way: 'Rose-coloured paintings are exhibited under an open sky in the middle of a plain. The terra-cotta roofs are there, that's the view of Milan from a height. Daybreak has suddenly fallen apart. Sun, sun, eat up the little pies'.

Poetry was his element, like water for a fish; deprived of it even for a single day he felt unable to breathe. He loved the poets, he felt a kinship with them, a community – from his early friendship with André Breton and Eluard to his late meetings with Nazim Hikmet; he went into ecstasies when he discovered other poets. One day he asked me to read aloud to him poems by Leonid Martynov, was delighted and beat the air with his flippers. He had a kindly face, and it did not belie him. During the last years of his life he was writing a book of reminiscences; he told me he did not find it easy: he knew that a great deal had changed in the world, but he did not want to be disloyal to the friends of his youth; he betrayed no one, and wrote courageously and with feeling. I think that he was able to do so precisely because he was a poet. (I recall Pasternak's simple and wise words that 'a bad man cannot be a good poet.')

In his poems Nezval often wrote about poetry: 'Be severe and beautiful! Good luck! Starfalls of tears, and the pledges of women's eyes, and love in the mountains where hundreds of stars fall out of their nests straight into one's hands. Till we meet! Till we meet! So be it. Once again I shall wind up the alarm-clock. How many people live around us here. That's what poetry is, my friend'.

When I first got to know Nezval he was twenty-three. Years passed. The critics, as is their way, admonished him: he was moving away from the Revolution, he was becoming a formalist – worse still, he had fallen in love with Surrealism, he was moving away from poetry, he was immersed in politics, he was too complicated, he was too simple, he had not mastered his art, he was spent. But Nezval remained what he always had been. I have never met anyone who resisted so stubbornly the whittling, the levelling, the proof-correcting of the years.

When he was a young man he wrote that he was dedicating himself to the Revolution; he looked upon justice and beauty as sisters. Often neither pundits nor poets care to recognize this. But Nezval stood firm. His naïvety was apt to cause some amazement: in 1934 he approached the Central Committee of the Communist Party in an attempt to prove that Surrealism, which greatly attracted him at the time, was quite consistent with historical materialism. And even very much later, towards the end of his life, he did not sneer at the past, did not renounce his former friends even if their ways had parted. In 1929, when it was suggested to him that he should leave the Communist Party, he refused; twenty years later he would not repudiate what he regarded as art.

Revolution was for him no abstract political idea, but the essence of life. In art, too, he passionately loved all that broke away from the canons of the past. I knew his friends: the daring producer Emil

Burian, who in those days found his inspiration in Meyerhold, and the artists Šima, Filla, the young Slaviček, Štirski, Tojaen. When in the late forties they were classed with the 'formalists', Nezval could not stomach it. He once said to me: 'Why is it that one man has no head, another no heart, and the third has a head and a heart but no eyes: he does not see the painting but never fails to judge the artist'. The epoch more than once presented him with the alternative: 'Choose – one thing or the other ...' He did not agree, he was too big for any kind of frame. His poetry, like a river in flood, recognized no banks, and his kindness disarmed everyone.

In the late forties he was working in the Film Department, but even in this service he found poetry: the films of Trnka. We saw *The Nightingale*, from Andersen's tale, with him. The mechanical toy could not replace the live bird. Nezval was delighted: 'Things are bad for painting ... But here's Trnka. Chase art out of the door, and it will come back through the window'.

He loved the trees of Moravia and the new architecture of Prague. He loved the landscapes of the impressionist Slaviček, and wrote a book about him; he loved Chaplin's films, the roofs of Paris, heart-to-heart talks. When he wrote the *Song of Peace*, the sternest critics were moved. And yet Nezval had always written about peace.

A long time ago, in the twenties, as we strolled about Prague, I told him that I had learnt much in the courtyards of the old town, those courtyards that stretch far back between the houses, where children play and old women gossip, and where there are ill-lit taverns of the sort where Schweik told his involved stories. In 1951 Nezval recalled our conversation and wrote that I knew Prague not only from Hradčany or the Vaclavske Namesti, that I loved her courtyards. He, of course, was familiar with every courtyard, every blind-alley in Prague. We met both in Prague and in Moscow, but when I think of him I always see him on the embankment of the Vltava or in a narrow, stuffy street near the Staro Mesto. He devoted many wonderful poems to his beloved city, and one of his books is called *Prague with Fingers of Rain*.

He once saw a woman who had been drowned in the Vltava, then remembered the mask seen in Paris, and wrote the poem *The Unknown Woman from the Seine*. He had been struck by the drowned woman's smile in death. 'Oh dead unknown! We are stepchildren of Fate. Will death open to us star-filled gardens?'

Throughout the whole of Nezval's life there persisted a vague, yet at the same time solid, realistic dream. I have read somewhere that he was the last of the romantics; no, the word 'last' does not apply to him: in everything and at all times he was a pioneer.

At this moment there comes to my mind his old poem from the volume *Woman in the Plural*. The poet is walking in a strange town past an enormous house in which, he is sure, there is a museum of stuffed birds. The streets are deserted; at the corner he sees a woman: she is too warmly dressed for a summer day, her hat hides half her face; the woman thinks she knows Nezval, and he, too, thinks that he knows her, but the town is strange, familiar but unloved. They reach the house, go up to the third floor and she sits down without taking off her hat. Nezval says to her: 'You do not exist. You are here. All my life I have been writing for you'. But the woman is again not there. Again he paces the streets, seeking. 'I think it is she . . . I feel that she is near, as we feel the nearness of death.'

This book is not about poetry but a story of my life, and that is why I have to talk of Nezval's poems – they entered into my days.

Not so long ago we were sitting with Hoffmayer recalling the past; very few of our common friends, patrons of the Metro, the Slavia and other cafés were still living. Vančura, mild but unyielding, was shot by the Germans. The first of the poets to go was Galas who died in 1949. The lives of Bibl and Teige were tragically cut short. The architect Feuerstein, who produced the scenery for Nezval's plays, had already shot himself in the nineteen-thirties. The artist Filla was also dead.

Nezval had often thought about death over the years. In a poem written in 1915 he said that people who tried to fence off the idea of death 'had purple faces, and their nails bit into the palms of their hands'. But Nezval was not reconciled to death. 'Better be bowed down in life than straightened out in death. Better the whole burden of life than an easy death.' All his life he cast horoscopes; it was a game. But about death he thought in earnest. In 1955, in a poem written in the South of France he repeated: 'Sea, the water grows, sea, the years do not count, what is grief to you? The grass grows, the water flows, man wants to live, man dies. What is he to you? You are the sea'.

He was like the sea: there was so much inexhaustible and turbulent vitality in him. Soon after the end of the war he took Galas and me to a wineshop: he had dug up some bottles of old wine that had been hidden away from the Germans. Behind us were years, each the equivalent of ten. Galas was depressed. But Nezval was happy and boisterous; I found myself thinking: here is someone for whom years don't count.

On one of my visits to Prague I found Nezval much subdued. Friends said that he had heart trouble, the doctors had forbidden him to drink or smoke. But two or three days later there was the turbulent Nezval waving his flippers, looking admiringly at women, drinking wine, declaiming poetry and, of course, casting horoscopes. One day he told me that his horoscope foretold evil: he preferred to die not according to the timetable of an electrocardiogram but to that of the magic map of constellations.

The last time we met was in the spring of 1958, at the airport in Prague. I was sitting in the refreshment room waiting to catch the plane to Delhi. Suddenly I caught sight of Nezval – he had just flown in from Italy. He said to me with his usual enthusiasm: 'Italy's wonderful!' Then he embraced me and added in a low voice: 'But things are bad with me', and pointed to his heart.

He died soon after.

In one of his best poems, *Edison*, written in 1911, there are lines about passion, death, immortality: 'But, above all, that the buried treasure should not be lost without trace. Death fights us dishonestly, we shall be put to bed by force to drink oceans of medicine. You who were hastening into the future will be betrayed by all the centuries. How can I be calm when at every step there is a gathering of marvels? Before me is a ferry, the slime of wet mill-wheels. You, posterity, forgive me. We were turned by the cogs of the age, the fever of war gripped us, separation waved handkerchiefs to us. It may be that in my delirium I bridled souls with the harness of art, may it not be that I, fleeing heartbreak, saved you from the madhouse? People, people! What suffering and passion have said cannot be lost'.

I do not believe that a future historian will be able to understand our times by reading exclusively newspapers, minutes of meetings, or the archives of academies and law courts; he will be compelled to have recourse to poetry, and the first book for which his hand will reach will be the poems of the unquenchable Nezval.

9

I WAS astonished when I saw Moscow again. I had gone abroad in the
last weeks of War Communism. Everything looked different now.
Ration cards had disappeared, people were no longer 'registered'.
Administrative personnel was greatly reduced and no one was working
out grandiose projects. *Proletkult* poets had ceased writing on cosmic
subjects. The poet Mikhail Gerasimov said to me: 'It's right, but it
makes me sick'.

The former TEO typist, a red-haired girl whom for some reason
we used to call Cleopatra, had long forgotten 'October in the Theatre'
and Meyerhold's screams. She stood in the Petrovka near the arcades
and sold brassières.

Old workers and engineers were painfully getting production on its
feet. Consumption goods had made their appearance. The peasants had
begun to bring poultry to the markets. The Muscovites had grown
fatter and were more cheerful. I was both pleased and saddened. The
newspapers wrote about the 'grimaces of NEP'. From the point of
view of the politician or the production expert the new line was correct;
we know now that it produced what it was intended to produce. But
the heart has its reasons: NEP often seemed to me to have a sinister
grimace.

I remember how, on arriving in Moscow, I stood stock-still before
a delicatessen shop. What things it had! Most significant of all was the
shop sign: *Estomak*. The belly had not only been rehabilitated but
exalted. A notice in a café at the corner of Petrovka and Stoleshnikov
Lane made me laugh: 'Children come here to eat cream'. I did not
detect any children, but there were many customers, and they seemed
to put on weight as I watched.

A number of restaurants had been opened: here The Prague, there
The Hermitage, farther on The Lisbon, The Bar. The waiters wore
dress clothes (I never could find out whether these tail-coats had been
made for them or had been preserved in trunks from pre-revolutionary
days). At every corner there was a noisy beerhouse with foxtrotting,
with Russian choirs, with gypsies, with balalaikas, or simply with

brawling. Customers drank beer and port to get drunk quickly, ate peas or smoked fish, bellowed and used their fists.

Near the restaurants smart drozhkys waited for the customers, and, as in the ancient days of my childhood, called out: 'Your Highness, can I take you anywhere?'

Here, too, one could see beggarwomen, homeless children; they whined: 'Give us a kopek'. There were no kopeks: there were millions ('lemons') and new 10-rouble notes. At the casinos millions were gambled away in a night: the profits of brokers, speculators or common thieves.

In the Sukharevka I heard ditties being sung; they describe better than anything else the 'grimaces of NEP'. There was a philosophical one: 'Chicken roasted, chicken steamed, chickens also want to live. I'm not Soviet, I'm no Kadet, I'm just a chicken commissar. I cheated no one, and I shot no one, I only pecked the grain'. There was the song of the woman selling bread-rolls: 'My father's a drunkard, he craves for his vodka, he lies and he blusters, and my brother's a thief; my sister's a trollop, she's gone to the devil, my mother's a smoker, oh what a disgrace!' There was also a bandit song apparently from Odessa: 'Comrade, comrade, my wounds are aching, comrade, comrade, what did we fight for, what did we bleed for – the bourgeois are feasting, the bourgeois are gloating . . .'

I met a gypsy who, before the Revolution, had sung in a restaurant. In 1920 she came to see Meyerhold every day demanding that he should get her a ration card. He sent her to MUZO (the Music department). She told me with a smile: 'I've been a nomad for four years, now I've settled down, I sing at the Lisbon.'

An actress I knew invited me to her house. I have no idea how she had managed to keep a flat in a private house near the Kropotkinskaya entirely to herself. There were a lot of guests; they danced the foxtrot solemnly, as though performing a rite. At midnight a young man arrived, dressed in a tight-fitting bright ginger suit, and explained patronizingly that in Moscow people were unable to distinguish between the foxtrot and the onestep. He had lately returned from a mission and had seen how they danced in Leipzig. Everybody listened attentively. Then the gramophone was put on: the same tunes as in the *dancings* of Paris and Berlin: 'Yes, we have no bananas', 'I'm looking for Titine'. The actress told me that the young man who had been to Leipzig had studied with her at the drama school and was now working in the Commissariat for Foreign Trade. 'He'll get locked up soon, he's got sticky fingers.'

The middle class had known what it was to live well since childhood, spending money was their regular occupation. The old bourgeoisie had dispersed all over the world; for many of them life abroad was hard; the change from opulence and idleness to destitution, to rough work, drove people to despair, to suicide, to crime. The social origin of the NEPmen was exceedingly mixed. A former junior barrister, after working for two years in the Commissariat of Justice, suddenly started to trade in sleeping-car reservations. I knew a poet who in 1921 read semi-Futuristic verse at the Domino. Now he was peddling French scent and cosmetics and Estonian brandy. A former worker at Goujon's factory, a veteran of the Civil War, was prosecuted: he had stolen a vanload of textiles and was caught by accident – he got drunk and smashed a mirror, and they found eight million roubles on him. Of course he was as unlike an hereditary bourgeois as some lieutenant – the son of a rich landlord, driven by necessity into a Paris factory – is unlike a proletarian. The millions of roubles went to the NEPmen's heads; they behaved wildly, created scandals, and soon perished. There were few who saved something for a rainy day: people did not believe in NEP's survival, nor in the banknotes. There was a very fine dividing line between permissible profit and illegal speculation. From time to time the GPU arrested a dozen or a hundred enterprising traders; this was called 'skimming the NEP'. The cook knows when to skim the fish-soup, but I doubt whether all the NEPmen understood which they were: the scum or the fish. Uncertainty about the morrow gave a special character to the amusements of the new bourgeoisie. The Moscow that Yesenin called 'Tavern Moscow' lived in a state of morbid tempestuousness; it was like a mixture of the nineteenth-century gold-fever in California and an exaggerated Dostoyevskian moral climate.

Side by side was the other Moscow. The former Metropole was still the Second House of the Soviets; here lived party executives who ate humble rissoles in the canteen. They still worked fourteen hours a day. Engineers and doctors, teachers and agronomists continued, if not with the former romantic inspiration, yet with the same determination, to rebuild a country ruined by civil war, blockade and years of drought. It was still difficult to push one's way into the lecture-rooms of the Polytechnic Institute, books were snapped up as soon as they appeared in the shops: the storming of knowledge continued.

This is what I wrote in 1924: 'I do not know what these young people will become – builders of Communism or Americanized technicians – but I love this new generation: heroic and spirited, capable of sober study and cheerfully going hungry, not like in Leonid Andreyev's plays about students, but in earnest; of passing from machine-guns to "teach-yourself" manuals and back; a generation that roars with laughter at the circus and is terrible in sorrow; a generation without tears, callous, a stranger to tender passion and to art, devoted to the exact sciences, to sport, to the cinema. Its romanticism does not lie in producing myths about a world beyond, but in the bold attempt to mass-produce tangible myths, in series, in the factories; such romanticism is justified by October, and is sealed by the blood of seven revolutionary years'. (Of course in this formulation there was some of my former enthusiasm for Constructivism, but I think I had correctly observed the typical characteristics of the young people of those days.) I added: 'It is good that they can approach facts critically. When someone starts to echo a popular speaker, he is held up to ridicule, called a "yes-man".'

The Rabfak[1] men, about whom I was writing, had been born early in the century. I was only some ten or twelve years older than they, but the change from one generation to the next had been abrupt. My contemporaries were Mayakovsky, Pasternak, Tsvetayeva, Fedin, Mandelstam, Paustovsky, Babel, Tinyanov. Our youth had belonged to the pre-revolutionary years, we remembered a great deal which sometimes helped and sometimes hindered us. But the students of 1924 had seen the Revolution with the eyes of adolescents, they were formed in the years of Civil War and NEP. This was the generation of Fadeyev and Svetlov, of Kaverin and Zabolotsky, of Yevgeny Petrov and Lugovskoy. Their ranks were soon to thin. Now those who have survived are retiring on a pension; they have the time to study the subject that Hugo called *l'art d'être grandpère*, and I have noticed that the young find a common language with them more easily than with their own fathers.

The snow covers everything with a compassionate blanket. When the first thaw sets in the earth is bared. In the years of NEP we were staggered, and at times driven to despair, by the tenacity of petty

[1] *Rabochiy Fakultet* – Pre-University training course attended part-time by workers.

bourgeois mentality, for we were naïve in those days and did not know that it is far more difficult to change man than to change the system of a country's government.

I did not have a room in Moscow and was given hospitality in the *Tsekubu* (Central Committee for Welfare of Scientists and Scholars) in Kropotkinskaya. Old scholars used to come there to chat or sigh quietly; it was difficult for them to understand what it was all about.

Many poets, too, sighed in those days; but as they did it not in the *Tsekubu* canteen but in the pages of journals, they were taken to task for their sighs, because a smile was considered a certificate of political soundness. The journal *Na Postu* (At Your Post) came out; the title sounded heroic, but in fact the 'post' was of the militia type rather than a fighting one. The *Na Postu* group abused everybody – Alexey Tolstoy and Mayakovsky, Vsevolod Ivanov and Yesenin, Akhmatova and Veresayev. Nevertheless the poets went on sighing. Aseyev wrote a melancholy poem about love call *Lyrical Digression*, and in high glee *Na Postu* quoted lines from it torn out of their context: 'How can I become your poet, Communist tribe, if time is painted ginger, not red?'

I went to see Mayakovsky. The Briks had heaps of guests as usual; they were drinking tea and eating cold meatballs. Mayakovsky was there too, morose, putting the last touches to a poster. A few days later I met him at the club; he maintained that one ought to help the government in its struggle against private trading; he wrote advertising slogans: 'Clothe the body, feed the stomach, fill the mind – everything man needs at the GUM he will find', or: 'The problems of the world are solved – "Embassy" cigarettes are the best thing in life'. In the middle of the night he suddenly began to recite beautiful passages from the poem *About This*; in his verses he tried to persuade himself that he would never voluntarily part with life.

The time for prose had come: people could reflect on all they had lived through. Fadeyev wrote *The Nineteen*, Babel *Red Cavalry*, Tynyanov *Kukhlya*, Zoshchenko *Tales*, Fedin *Cities and Years*, Leonid Leonov *The Badgers*.

I wanted to travel about the country; I had no money and was tempted by an offer from someone who organized Literary Evenings, of which there were very many at the time. He suggested that I should go to Petrograd, Kharkov, Kiev and Odessa to read lectures on Life in Western Europe. The promoter wanted to keep in step with the times, which meant making a good profit out of the venture; he was no longer young and was consistently unlucky. He had everything perfectly mapped out: the lectures were organized by the Red Cross Society which was to receive part of the proceeds; scouts were sent ahead to various towns; one of these was the promoter's son Lenya, a young student, a shy and at the same time rather impudent lad. He decided to write a book about me without delay and bewildered me with his questions: 'Tell me how you happened to fall in love for the first time.' 'Whom do you put higher – Voltaire or Anatole France?' 'What's your view, is Eros winged or wingless?' Another organizer was completely businesslike; he ate goose with relish, at the stations he found young ladies whom he enticed into the sleeping-car, he haggled with the institutions that let the halls, and told me: 'Today I've got to earn 200 roubles and I shall, you'll see'.

We had to find a title for the lectures. Mayakovsky had accustomed the public to posters which any American would have envied: 'Poetry is a Manufacturing Industry', 'An Analysis of the Infinitely Small', 'Conductor of Three Americas', 'The White Sausages of Lysistrata', 'And Yet Ehrenburg Moves', 'The Smoking Veresayev', 'Ball in Honour of a Young Queen', 'Bryusov and the Bandage'. The promoter beseeched: 'Something unintelligible . . .' I chose the first thing that came into my mind: 'The Drunken Operator'.

In Kharkov the promoter hired the Missouri Circus. There were no microphones in those days. I shouted, straining my voice, something about Chaplin's films, while the audience roared: 'We can't hear!' I wanted to leave but the promoter stopped me: 'They'll want their money back. I've got a large family. I beg you, go on trying. My wife's already beating up an egg-nog for you'.

I saw Odessa for the first time now; I knew it from funny stories and 'Mamma Odessa' astonished me, it looked depressing. The port was empty of shipping. Here and there black ruins showed. The former lightheartedness of the inhabitants had obviously disappeared; life was still disorganized. In one of the squares I saw the head of a bearded feudal prince with the inscription underneath: Karl Marx. The young cashier at the theatre where I was giving my lecture struck Lenya dumb by suddenly saying to him: 'Why d'you keep making sheep's eyes at me? We've passed that stage long ago. Take me out to supper at the Londonskaya, and then we can talk, because I'm no longer on government pay now'.

The Londonskaya hotel was a picturesque place. Some of the rooms were still occupied by party executives; their wives cooked the dinner on primuses and nursed their children; in the evening the conversations were about the current leader in *Pravda*, the agenda for the Thirteenth Party Congress. The occupants of the other rooms were speculators, journalists, music-hall artists, NEP merchants; drinking went on and occasional brawling. In the market I heard the song: 'It's awfully noisy in Schneerson's house . . .' But at Schneerson's it was very quiet; it was quiet in the streets which bore new names: International, Proletarian, Lassalle, The Commune. In Pechesky's Café speculators, having ordered a glass of tea, tried to sell tattered orange or green dollar bills to each other. Jobbers kept on yawning nervously: from time to time there were police raids and everyone was rounded up.

At the *Odessa News* the editor's secretary showed me a poem by a young Odessan; he wrote about the sea, the birds, birdcages. I liked it and asked the poet's name. 'Eduard Bagritsky', the secretary said.

I broke the glass of my wristwatch and went to a watchmaker's. He took a long time to fit in a new glass. I waited in silence while he talked ceaselessly: 'Today they're attacking Curzon in the paper. But I can tell you that Curzon isn't afraid of them. It's me that's afraid of them. First of all I'm afraid of the tax inspector, secondly I'm afraid of the GPU, thirdly I'm afraid of you – how can I tell what sort of man you are and why you want me to tell you everything?'

Beggarwomen said: 'Comrade, give me something', 'In God's name, dear Citizen . . .' 'A kopek, Sir'. Modes of address were jumbled up and so were the epochs.

In Kiev I was driving along the Kreshchatik when the sledge suddenly disintegrated, the horse trotting away with the driver, while I landed with the seat in a snowdrift. The sledge had not managed to hold out, but in the market they were selling well-made pre-revolutionary things: samovars, Singer sewing-machines, Moser's watches, pot-bellied merchants' teacups.

Where the grip of the past was strongest was in man's consciousness. At one of the stations a peasant woman carrying a sack got into the 'soft coach' by mistake. The conductor yelled: 'Where d'you think you're going? Get out! This isn't nineteen-seventeen!'

In Gomel, in the refreshment room at the station hung a notice: 'He that does not work neither shall he eat'. Passengers from the sleeping-car were dining at the small tables. Here, too, wandered homeless children in the hope of scraps. A passenger handed one girl his plate with some bits of meat and gravy: 'Here, gobble it up!' A waiter (or as they used to say then a 'serving citizen') ran up, tore the plate out of the child's hands and threw the pieces of meat and potatoes all over the rags she was wearing. I was revolted, but nobody backed me up. The little girl cried and ate hastily. In Gomel I saw a match factory; the director, a former factory-hand, wounded in the battles against Denikin and in poor health, worked from morning till night; there was no gum for sticking the boxes; he kept saying: 'The country needs matches'. Young men in that town talked about the fighting in Hamburg, about Mayakovsky's poems, about the future. And before my eyes were the obtuse, indifferent faces in the station buffet and the humiliated child.

The promoter's agent was satisfied – he had over-fulfilled the plan. Lenya did not write a book about me and told everybody: 'And why write about him? I know him like a book'. Lenya's father lost on the business, for although the proceeds were very good, snowdrifts on the line between Odessa and Leningrad held us up for two days at a wayside halt, and my promoter had to pay a forfeit for the hall. There was nothing to be done – he was doomed to failure. For my part, I was satisfied, for I had seen a lot.

After every lecture I was bombarded with questions, some of which I wrote down: 'Why did the Revolution misfire in Germany?' – 'What are the fashions today in Paris?' – 'What were you trying to say in your *Jurenito*?' – 'Who are worse: the Social-traitors or the Fascists?' – 'Explain briefly the theory of relativity.' – 'Why has schooling got to be paid for again?' – 'Why do you writers put ideas into girls' heads about declarations of love?' – 'Do they accept foreign volunteers in India for the struggle for independence?' – 'They say in the papers that you are a product of corruption, in that case tell us how much you get paid for your lecture.' – 'Mayakovsky says that poetry is production, but Pushkin says differently. Which of them is right in your view?' – 'Will Communism discover how to conquer death?' – 'Are you in favour of Association football or do you also recognize Rugby?' – 'Tell us something about Rutherford's work in the field of atomic transformation.' – 'In what way is the onestep different from the two-step and which is more popular in Berlin?' – 'Why do we have translations of *Tarzan* while Marcel Proust's novel is not translated?' – 'Do you think that the monetary reform will reduce the "scissors"?'[1]—'Do you know Picasso and what is he up to now?' – 'Sexual love is a bourgeois relic, why don't they say so frankly?' – 'A short time ago a lecturer spoke here and said that art survived during the period of transition, but that under Communism it will disappear. I don't agree, can you help me to get this clear?'

I have quoted these questions in the same order, or rather disorder, in which I took them down. I think that they may help towards an understanding of those already distant years.

I often talked to young people; they were of all kinds: intelligent and stupid ones, honest ones and careerists. NEP helped to restore the economy, but it was not exactly a good school for the young. They all still remembered the years of civil war: the great deeds, the glory, the atrocities, the heroism, the plundering. These young men and women who had come to the universities from the front, from the villages, were passionate and vigorous. The students worked well, and they also behaved well, oscillating between naïve utilitarianism and the romanticism characteristic of their age. But there were also quite a few who lost their heads: the ambitious ones, the imaginative ones without the rudiments of morality, the weak-willed ones who, when they found themselves in the wrong company, were ready for anything. Side by side with earnest student life there was debauchery. 'Tavern Moscow', where Yesenin was agonizing, breathed its wine-laden breath into the young people's faces and led many astray.

One young man told me a long, involved, though not very complicated story: not so long ago he had been an honest member of the Komsomol, a promising student. A friend drew him into some shady business; it seemed quite high-minded on the surface: he was entrusted with collecting money for the Air Force, but it turned out that the collection was organized by a gang of swindlers. The student was very angry, he wanted to go to the GPU, but after having been given a wad of notes, he was tempted by the fleshpots. He fell in love with a girl who kept asking for presents, and began to speculate; he was expelled from the Komsomol and was awaiting arrest. He had very expressive hands: they flew up, they threatened, they implored.

I wanted to write about him, about others like him. I began to attend

[1] Discrepancy between the price of bread and manufactured consumer goods.

74

law court sessions; I got permission to talk to the prisoners in the *isolators* (this was what the prisons were called in those days). What attracted me, of course, was not the fascination of the environment, not the criminal activities, but the history of the rise and fall of those steep, slippery years.

A new word, *rvach* ('grabber'), was coming into use, and I called my hero, the son of a Kiev waiter, a *rvach*. I described his childhood, his thirst for glory, his egocentricity, his uplift during the years of the Revolution, his studies, his fall. Mikhail Lykov (this was the name of my hero) had a brother, Artem, honest, not very good at understanding romantic feelings, but kind, who tried to save Mikhail from final ruin. My hero was no Rastignac; there were various, sometimes conflicting emotions within him. Having fallen in love with a greedy frivolous woman, he behaved like a silly boy. At the same time he thought him-self exceptional and superior to his comrades. You might say there was something of Julien Sorel in him, born a hundred years later in the country of the Socialist Revolution. Convicted, he committed suicide in his prison cell.

I wrote in a letter: 'I am finishing *Rvach*. I have even become fond of my hero, although he is a rascal, a scoundrel, with a tendency to romanticism, a pathetic speculator'. Even today it seems to me that a writer, when shedding light on the interior world of those characters whom the critics call 'negative', becomes attached to them; for he sees the elements of good which are inherent in the heart of a man who has sunk to the bottom. It was never my intention to justify grabbers. As the epigraph of my book I took the words of an ancient prayer which condemns individualism: 'Thy will be done, so that this year be dewy and rainy, and so that Thou shalt not hearken to the prayers of travellers on the roads whom rain may hinder, though all the world be in need of rain'.

I knew that once again I should be criticized: why write about some wretched grabber when all around there are plenty of noble and inspired characters? It seems to me that it is a doctor's duty to make a diagnosis, and only a lunatic could suppose that a doctor who estab-lishes a case of infectious disease thereby spreads the infection. In my novel *Rvach* the attempt to disclose the spiritual world of the misguided Mikhail Lykov was accompanied by a satirical description of the mode of life in those years. Even the *Na Postu* people recognized in theory the necessity for satire, yet they immediately called it calumny if anyone tried to show up this or that seamy side of our life. ('We need our own Shchedrins and Gogols' – so I heard it said much later. In theory, satire was regarded as necessary, but in practice almost as an act of sabotage; a poet even wrote a doggerel verse: 'We need Shchedrins who are more humane, and such Gogols as will not cause us pain'.)

I wrote in 1924: 'If in my books the so-called negative types stand out as more expressive, this is not indicative of some cunning intrigue on my part but of a certain inadequacy, a limitation of human nature. How I should like to read, instead of the indictments of my books, some splendid epic about a new, healthy, active man! Alas, the well-meaning critics are in no hurry to write it; they prefer to condemn me. For my part I prefer to go on with the work for which I feel a natural inclination and not wait for the time when an inspired book will be written by Artem. I want to tell my contemporaries the story of his brother'.

On 26th January 1925 I recorded: 'Popov has refused *Rvach*, so it is not very likely to be published'. (I do not remember who this Popov was.)

One of the most prominent *Na Postu* spokesman, calling me an 'open enemy of the Revolution', wrote: 'The emotional appeal of *Rvach* consists in admiration for the predatory atmosphere of the NEP, in approving of the seizure of our entire economic apparatus by bourgeois beasts of prey. This is the final collapse of yesterday's candidate for the title of the Russian Spengler'.

In a melancholy sonnet Bagritsky wrote: 'Let a breath of wind blow, let the North be felt a little – and we come fluttering down. Whose path do we now strew with our bodies? Whose feet will pass over our rust? Shall we be trampled by young trumpeters? Will alien constellations rise above us? We are the shed comfort of rusty oaks!'

In the window of a bookshop in the Kuznetsky I noticed 'The tree of Soviet literature'. The branches bore explanatory labels: 'Proletarian Writers', 'LEF', 'Peasant Poets', 'Left-wing Fellow-travellers', 'Centrist Fellow-travellers', 'Right-wing Fellow-travellers', 'Neo-bourgeois Literature', and so on. Under the tree lay fallen leaves, and one of them was called 'Ehrenburg'.

There was a great deal of wind later on, of wind and of the North. By some miracle I did not flutter to the ground.

10

NOT so long ago I dug up in a library a half-disintegrated copy of the one-day literary newspaper *Lenin* which was issued on the day of Vladimir Ilyich's funeral. It contains among others an article of mine written hastily, in that state of mind when one does not think about style. I want to quote some passages from this clumsy article; they may explain the later chapters of these reminiscences.

Thinking back about pre-war Paris I wrote: 'In those years that were on the eve, what did we know? Disquiet and wanderings, bombs and poetry. . . . Were not his those penetrating and dignified words: "We have made mistakes, we have made many, many mistakes"? Yes, here there could be frustration and mistakes, because here there was life. But over there, among the sad grey houses, in a country where the glib speaker never tires of talking about freedom, about the dignity of the individual, no hero has emerged, no builder, no leader. There could not be any mistakes: there was no life there.

'. . . Europe was given Versailles for the four years of terrible war, but Russia by her sufferings won October.

'. . . To understand Lenin's creative power it is enough to glance over there where, every Sunday, Poincaré shouts passionately above the ruins and the graves: "As for us, no! We have never made any mistakes!"

'He knew, we did not know. We did not know that the national revolution of half-savage peasant Russia would grow into an era of peace. We did not know that the "Give us land!" of February would become in October "Give us the Earth!" He knew this. He knew it when he lived in Geneva. He knew it when he worked at night by the light of an oil-lamp in a small room.

'And only a few months ago, at St Pauli in Hamburg, after the rising was crushed, I heard the following conversation. Two brothers were arguing, both workers. Brothers. Workers. Enemies. The one had taken part in the rising, the other had helped to crush it. But the one who had risen had been wounded and had been smuggled home. The one who had helped to put down the rising said: "What need was there to rise? After all, the Socialists in the Senate had promised the issue of half a pound of margarine. You hear that? We shall be getting margarine". His brother retorted: "And *we* shall be getting *him*!" And as he said it he pointed at the portrait hanging in his room, as it hangs in hundreds of thousands of workers' rooms in all the cities of every land.

'. . . We have often been dismayed. We had our own new art, our disquiet, our wanderings over the world. And it seemed to us that all this was alien to him. We did not know that without his work there was neither growth nor life for us. No matter that the building of the house is not finished. No matter that inside it is very hard and cold. Its walls are rising. While there, where all the houses are intact, where ten years ago writers rebelled and languished in the city of grey houses, what is there? There is no room for us there. The storm in a teacup is over. What remain are odes in honour of the academician Foch in return for a decent three-course dinner. The despair of the vast European night – he knew that too. He was a man of one idea, he thought about one thing only so that other, happy, people might be able to think about many things.'

When a great man dies people involuntarily look back at what we call history and sometimes at their own small lives as well. So it was with me when I wrote about the death of Lenin: I recalled the feeling of being on the eve, the Rotonde, the revolt of the writers and critics and, in my anger, probably unjustly, called it all 'a storm in a teacup'. Self-denigration was dictated by the bitterness of the loss, an understanding of those decisive and truly universal things realized by the man whose death had bereaved humanity.

Those words of mine, written so long ago about the meaning of October, the contrasting of Russia's difficult road with the spiritual impoverishment of the West seem true to me today.

'What if the building of the house is not finished?' Yes, in 1924 we did not know the cost in sweat, in tears, in blood, of that house whose walls were already rising in Lenin's time. We did not know that in the thirties, in the forties, we should not be told our mistakes in a friendly way, in a comradely way. But the house has been built, and the spiritual strength of our people has manifested itself in the fact that it was built in spite of everything.

Those were days when the frosts were severe even for a Moscow winter. It was useless to try and persuade the children to stay at home. Adults carried small children on their shoulders. Red Army men wept.

At night in Okhotny Ryad, in the Dmitrovka, in the Petrovka, everywhere bonfires were lit, and round the bonfires sombre men in sheepskin coats gathered in silence. There were many bearded delegates, for in those days peasant Russia was still bearded.

I could not stay at home. I watched the funeral procession in Balchug. I was in the Hall of Columns where sobbing drowned the strains of the funeral march. Moscow which, according to the saying, does not believe in tears, wept aloud. I went to my comrade of the old clandestine school organization, he lived in the Second House of the Soviets. Usually cheerful, he was silent now, and I suddenly noticed tears in his eyes. The old woman porter of the *Tsekubu* was crying. The people's grief was immense and genuine.

In those cruel January nights I saw, as though from afar, in the perspective of centuries, what our people had achieved; and no matter what doubts I may have had in the succeeding, far more oppressive decades, Lenin's concept was always before me, sustaining me, preventing me from going astray.

I was a young non-party writer; to some a 'fellow-traveller', to others an 'enemy', but in reality an ordinary member of the Soviet intelligentsia, formed in pre-revolutionary times. No matter how we were abused, no matter what suspicious looks were thrown at our prematurely greying heads, we knew that the way of the Soviet people was our way too.

In Paris on several occasions I had the opportunity of talking to Lenin; I knew he loved Pushkin, loved classical music and was a complex man with a generous soul. But all his passion, all the power of his creative genius was dedicated to a single purpose – the struggle to free the workers from exploitation, to build a new Socialist society.

That is why I wrote in 1924: 'He thought about one thing only, so that other, happy, people might be able to think about many things.'

The word 'happy' may grate upon the ear. The small children who were carried on their fathers' shoulders into the Hall of Columns are the orphans of the thirties, the soldiers of the Patriotic War, men whose heads are touched with grey, who read the reports of the Twentieth Congress. And yet the words about happiness are true; when I go to meetings of our young people now, I see that the boys and girls of 1961 think about many things, are enthusiastic about many things and know many things.

I should like to conjure up some more memories of Vladimir Ilyich, say something ordinary, simple. When I was talking to him in Paris, he suddenly interrupted me: 'Have you got a room? The hotels here are expensive,' and turning to Krupskaya: 'Who can help him? Ludmila? Ah yes, she knows . . .' When A. I. Altman was modelling Lenin's head in his study, the sculptor had to stop and leave because some comrades had come to see Lenin. Vladimir Ilyich did not forget to moisten the clay. Lunacharsky told me that when he asked Lenin whether the 'left' artists could be allowed to decorate Red Square for May Day, Vladimir Ilyich replied: 'I'm no expert in this; I don't want to impose my taste on others'.

There is an article by Stalin on Lenin's political style. It was written long ago in the twenties and everything it says is absolutely right. But Lenin's personal, human style – the boldness of creative thought and the exceptional modesty, the strength, the resolution, that excluded neither gentleness nor deep respect for spiritual values, for reason, for art, humaneness, genuine humaneness – proved to be unique.

11

In May 1924 I went with Lyuba to Italy. There were many tourists there, speaking many languages; among them were Germans who had come with firm currency in marks and the no less firm conviction that they had safely escaped an earthquake and could enjoy the land where the lemon-trees bloom.

(The French say that a scalded cat fears cold water. Men are more thoughtless than cats. The ten thousand inhabitants of the new Pompeii look upon Vesuvius as a father-provider, for they make their living on the curiosity of tourists. In 1944 Vesuvius, waking up for a moment, destroyed the little town of San Sebastiano. The inhabitants of the neighbouring towns, however, stayed where they were.)

There was an international exhibition in Venice where Soviet artists were represented for the first time. We were sitting at Florian's in St Mark's Square; I remember the woman artist Alexandra Ekster and Boris Ternovets. Florian's café was then 163 years old; now it has reached the age of 200, it ought to celebrate its jubilee. There Longhi, Canaletto, Goldoni, Gozzi must have sat over cups of chocolate. I cannot remember what we talked about, perhaps Meyerhold's latest production or Saryan's pictures that were exhibited in Venice, or maybe about the *maschera*.

Lean Englishwomen fed the clumsy pigeons. Shoeblacks and coral sellers contorted themselves like classical harlequins. The tourists expressed their admiration vocally and in writing, industriously signing stacks of brightly-coloured postcards. The whole thing was reminiscent of a stage setting in the Kamerny Theatre.

About us lay the city with its hundreds of mysterious, evil-smelling canals, with phalanxes of mewing cats, with seventeenth-century houses in which people, just as they do in ordinary houses, dream, suffer from jealousy, quarrel, flick through the evening paper, go down with 'flu or appendicitis. Everyday life was framed in enchanting vistas, a pistachio-coloured sky, rose-tinted water, small bridges, columns, fountains. This is where a man needs eyes. But I watched the Black-shirts who strolled about the Piazza or sat eating ices.

We went to Murano and saw the most skilled glassblowers. On the walls of the factory a slogan in black stood out: 'Long live Lenin!' *Fascisti* in small black caps scowled and shifted from one pocket to another their new toys – revolvers.

I have said that for men of my generation the respite was a short one and, what is more, we seldom managed to forget what the papers call 'historical events'. Why could I not enjoy the beauty of Tintoretto's pictures and of the waters of the canals in quiet? Something disturbed me, perhaps the novelty: this was the first time in my life that I was seeing real, live Fascists.

As a young man I had greatly admired the Campo Santo frescoes and told Lyuba that we must visit Pisa. Lyuba looked at the luminous paintings of Benozzo Gozzoli who had covered the walls of the cemetery with the sweetness of earthly life; but I looked at the Black-shirts. During the war a German bomb destroyed part of the Pisan frescoes. Not long ago I found myself again in Pisa and saw the wreck of the former visions. It pained me to think that at the time I had not looked my fill at the frescoes; but what can you do? You live not as you would like, but as life comes along.

It could hardly have been foreseen in 1924 that fascism, having made its way from semi-patriarchal Italy into well-organized Germany, would destroy fifty million lives and cripple the existence of several generations. But I was sorry for Italy, sorry and anxious. Who were these people, yelling, marching, raising their outstretched arms? Surely they must be misfits, sons of bankrupt shopkeepers, provincial notaries or lawyers, ambitious men seduced by high-sounding phrases. They could have been taken for masqueraders at some idiotic carnival, but I realized then already that men do not live according to Descartes.

Something took us to a small town in central Italy, Bibiena. It has no sights and tourists seldom stop there. But it is a lovely little town. In the evening I dropped into the ill-lit *bottiglieria* where there were huge round demijohns of red wine. An old man was telling the proprietor and two customers a long story about the stonecutter Giulio who had returned from America. He had saved a little money and was planning to get married. Then one night the secretary of the local Fascists arrived in a car from Arezzo. They were drinking wine at different tables when suddenly this man began to bait Giulio, ordering him to shout: '*Evviva* Mussolini!' Guilio replied: 'Let the asses bray it!' Then and there the Fascist shot him dead. The murderer was arrested as a matter of form, and a week later was released. That was the whole story. The old man drank his wine and crumbled bread between his gnarled fingers. I went out. The small hill looked like a starry sky with myriads of fireflies flitting about. Frogs croaked gently. Lovers were exchanging kisses and vows in the darkness. But I thought about the fate of the unknown Giulio.

When we reached Rome all seemed quiet. We went to the embassy. The ambassador said that trade relations with Italy were beginning to take shape; he also told me that the poet Vyacheslav Ivanov had arrived in Rome and visited the embassy. Tourists were scurrying to the Vatican or the Colosseum. In the Corso, in the café Aragno politicians were discussing what the Corfu expedition had cost Italy. I haunted the museums, admired the Byzantine mosaics and for several days forgot politics. Suddenly, in the Piazza Montecitorio, we saw excited crowds of people shouting and burning newspapers. The same thing was happening in other public squares; I heard shouts of 'Down with the Fascists! Down with the murderers!' Indignant people were burning batches of Fascist newspapers: *Corriere Italiano*, *Popolo d'Italia*, *Impero*. A few minutes later I learnt that the Fascists had kidnapped the young Socialist deputy Giacomo Matteotti.

It is difficult to foretell how people will react to events; sometimes the annihilation of a thousand victims passes practically unnoticed and sometimes the killing of one man shakes the world. The murder of Matteotti had the simplicity of an object lesson, like an ancient parable. Wherever I went I heard the victim's name.

(In my book *10 H.P.* I wrote about the end of Matteotti, though it had no direct relation to the Citroën factories or to the struggle for oil. I could not keep silent about it, for what happened on 10th June 1924 in Rome had become part of my life too.)

There was still a parliament in Italy at the time; in the spring elections had been held. The Fascists, with the help of wine and castor oil, cudgels and promises, insured a majority for themselves; nevertheless the opposition parties won some forty per cent of the votes. On 30th May the young deputy Matteotti had made a courageous speech in parliament exposing the violence and the killings. The Fascists interrupted him with howls; one shouted: 'Go to Russia!' When Matteotti left the tribune the deputies of the Left congratulated him; he said to one of them laughingly: 'You'd better get my obituary ready'. Eleven days later he stepped out of his house to buy some cigarettes and never came back.

By this time Mussolini was no longer admitting criticism, yet he still hesitated to arrest a deputy; he had given his friend Cesare Rossi the job of getting rid of Matteotti. Rossi was head of the Press Department of the Ministry of the Interior; this was only a cover, the Press Department's real work was the assassination of political opponents. Rossi summoned the editor of the *Corriere Italiano*, Filippelli. The editor in his turn called upon the services of a certain Dumini.

On the Lungotevere, not far from his home, Matteotti was surrounded by a number of unknown men who hustled him into a car. The car sped out of the city. The kidnappers gagged Matteotti. Dumini knew his job (he later confessed to the murder of twelve anti-fascists). Matteotti suffered from T.B., the struggle was short; when he tried to open the door of the car, Dumini stuck a knife into him.

In a deserted spot near Quartarella the Fascists hastily buried Matteotti's body. Mussolini learnt with satisfaction that it had been a clean job; he did not expect publicity: the man had disappeared and that was that. It so happened, however, that some women had seen a man being forced into a red car. Opposition newspapers were still coming out at the time. Investigations were started. Filippelli's car was discovered and there were bloodstains on the seat. They were forced to arrest Dumini. Even Rossi was questioned but his case was soon quietly dropped. Shortly after, Rossi quarrelled with Mussolini, escaped to Paris and there began to denounce his former friend.

Rome seethed; it was as if at any moment a revolution would break out. Opposition deputies swore that they would resist the gang of assassins. In every country people were revolted by the cynicism of the Fascists. The Duce was frightened. He declared that he was shocked by the murder of a deputy, that the culprits would be severely punished; he even went so far as to accept the resignation of the general secretary of the Fascist Party. Apparently he, too, thought that the smouldering fires would burst into flame.

The national character of the Italians is quite different from that of the Germans, but the upshot was the same. Deputies made angry speeches. The Romans burnt sheaves of Fascist newspapers and then dispersed to their homes. Mussolini swiftly recovered his self-assurance. I was still in Italy when I was given a copy of the *Impero* in which the

Fascists ridiculed those who were protesting: 'Let lunatics bluster. He laughs best that laughs last ... No one will prevent Fascists from shooting criminals in all the public squares of Italy'. Later I read a speech by Mussolini on the murder of Matteotti: 'It is useless and stupid to look for the culprits. We have a language of our own: the language of the revolution'.

Yes, the Italians are unlike the Germans. They have an innate love of freedom, a spirit of rebellion, of insubordination, they have imagination. Yet Mussolini ruled Italy for twenty-three years, and the partisans executed him only a few days before Hitler's suicide. I happened to read the arguments of a French writer who claimed that a people will tolerate any crimes committed by a dictator so long as he leads it where it wants to go. I do not believe that the average Italian was eager to conquer Ethiopia, repress the Spaniards, see the Don. And how can anyone believe that the people who gave the world Don Quixote is created for fascism, that the people of Quevedo and Goya is fore-doomed to obscurantism, to stupid, ignorant despotism? Yet it will soon be a quarter of a century that a general of small stature and even less calibre has ruled Spain. No, nothing can be explained by national character, and all one can say about the Italians is that they performed the role of 'Roman legionaries' badly – the more honour to them.

At the start, the Fascists tried to prove with a wealth of argument that the Duce was leading Italy to greatness, to social justice, to libera-tion from foreign capital. Later they became more sparing of words and launched the slogan: 'The Duce does not make mistakes'; later still they simply shouted 'Long live the Duce!' In 1934 I saw the im-mense arcades in Milan entirely plastered with posters bearing the single word 'Duce!'

Professor S. S. Chekhotin was a pupil of Pavlov; basing himself on the theory of conditioned reflexes, he tried to analyse certain pheno-mena of social life, in particular the effects of propaganda. Pavlov conducted a great number of experiments with dogs. Chekhotin studied fascist literature. He told me that among the dogs that undergo experiments there are always some that do not react, or rather, react only feebly to the stimuli. Professor Chekhotin thinks that a certain, very small, proportion of humans is capable of resisting methods of primitive propaganda (emblems, special gestures of greeting, laconic slogans, uniforms, etc.). I am no physiologist and do not take upon myself to judge how far S. S. Chekhotin is right. But in my life I have only too often seen the triumph of mindless stupidity, of sheer bombast.

I had another spell of admiring the Roman pines, the marble nymphs shedding tears, the gentle smiles of the destitute inhabitants of the Trastevere, and then we pushed on to Paris.

I continued to write books, frequented cafés, worked up enthusiasms, had a little fun, was sometimes gay and sometimes wretched – life went on, reasonably calm, reasonably pleasant but, on the whole, it was the sad life of the nineteen-twenties. There often rose before me the dim shadows of the Blackshirts, Matteotti's murder, the first trying-out of those decades that I was destined to live through.

Suddenly I picked up again Pascal's small volume and found solace in it: for the first time I dwelt on the words: 'Man is only a reed, the feeblest thing in nature, but he is a thinking reed. It is not necessary for the entire Universe to take up arms in order to crush him: a vapour, a drop of water is sufficient to kill him. But if the Universe crushed him, man would still be nobler than the thing which destroys him, because he knows that he is dying; and the Universe which has him at its mercy is unaware of it. All our dignity therefore lies in thought.' Events might have persuaded me to doubt the truth of Pascal's words, for I saw how quickly people gave up thinking. But the first years of the Revolution had not gone by without leaving their trace; I was immunized against blind faith and against blind despair.

Pascal could hardly have believed that every man is capable of thinking, whatever the circumstances may be. Mussolini turned many Italians into robots; when they met each other they raised their arms and imagined that this lent them dignity. But side by side with them were others who thought, ridiculed, told sardonic stories, read prohibited books – the reed did not break. Antonio Gramsci spent ten years' solitary confinement in the prison at Turi di Bari. There he wrote articles on Benedetto Croce's philosophy, on Pirandello's works, on Dante, Machiavelli and much else; he wrote to his Russian wife Giulia, to her sister Tatyana, letters that are heartfelt, passionate, wise and very human. I often re-read them and each time I feel proud – yes, there it is, the thinking reed!

Time does not hurry, it is death that hurries. Gramsci died in 1937. Time does not hurry, but sooner or later it puts everything in its place. Not so long ago I was walking along a street in Florence. It

86

was a blue April morning. Children were playing about. An old man was taking his dog for a walk. Lovers were whispering things to each other. Without thinking I glanced at the name of the street: Via Matteotti.

12

IN the spring of 1924 the 'left bloc' triumphed at the French elections.
The head of the new government was the Radical, Edouard Herriot, a
highly cultivated man, a patriot devoid of chauvinism, benevolent and
broadminded; he liked the way they cooked in Lyons (where he had
been mayor), had written a book on the private life of Madame Récamier, and at the same time was alive to the traditions of the Jacobins;
in short, he was a typical representative of the nineteenth-century
French intelligentsia. In 1924 the British and the Americans wanted
France to come to terms with the Germans as quickly as possible.
Herriot condemned the occupation of the Ruhr and Poincaré's
stubbornness but, being a Frenchman, he wanted to have safeguards,
for this was a matter that touched the security of France: 'We must
avert the dagger which constantly threatens us while you talk about
peace.' Dear God, how easily politicians change not only their words
but their principles! In 1924 the British replied: 'First disarmament,
and after that guarantees of safety'.

Briand was referred to as the nightingale of Europe; when he spoke
old cynics, deeply moved, blew their noses. Briand naturally spoke
about peace, about European solidarity, about magnanimity. Herriot
tried to make the British and the Americans see reason: 'Careful! The
Reichswehr is reviving. The German army has modern weapons. I want
peace, like everyone else, but how can peace be maintained if the
security of France is ignored?' Herriot was overthrown and replaced
by Briand. At the Swiss resort of Locarno the famous Treaties were
signed. That evening fireworks rocketed into the sky. Stresemann
wrote to the Crown Prince: '. . . Secondly, my aim is to protect Germans
living abroad, I mean those ten or twelve million of our countrymen
who are at present living in foreign countries, under a foreign yoke.
The third big task is the rectification of our eastern frontier, the return
to Germany of Danzig and of the Polish Corridor, and the rectification
of the Upper Silesian frontier. And there is the prospect of an *Anschluss*
with German Austria'.

(It is unfortunate that in a book about my life I should be obliged to

88

recall not only poets and artists, not only people whom I like, but also Stresemann. It cannot be helped, for we lived in an epoch when history unceremoniously broke into our lives by day and by night, like a Poltava policeman.)

I was reminded of the fireworks in Locarno fifteen years later when the Paris sky burst into flames and we heard the crash of the first incendiary bomb. As for Herriot, the Germans carted him off to a concentration camp.

The victory of the 'left bloc' had produced some changes, but for me Paris remained forbidden. In Rome I asked Lyuba to go to the French consulate: my appearance always frightened the clerks and Lyuba could placate them more easily. I was right: the consul, not knowing that we had been expelled from France, stamped our passports with perfectly good visas. This was enough to get us to Paris, but we could not stay there: the deportation order was still in force.

Friends directed me to the secretary of the Masonic Lodge 'The Great East'. I found myself in that very den that had frightened the monarchist Bostunich. The den was an ordinary study, and the secretary of the Lodge an elderly Radical who was very well up in the gastronomic niceties of all the small Parisian restaurants. There were very many Freemasons in France but, contrary to Bostunich's fantasies, they did not worship the devil Bafamet or the Jewish god Jahveh, or Karl Marx; the Lodges were simply mutual assistance societies of a special kind. The secretary told me that he had dealt with far more difficult cases: the Prefect of Police was a Freemason and his friend.

I was obliged to go to the Prefect. He was not at all like the good-natured Radical and his manner towards me was overbearing. 'What do you intend to do in Paris?' I said that I intended to write books. The Prefect smiled: 'Books, Monsieur, are of different kinds. Bear in mind that the French police, too, are not idle.' (He was speaking the exact truth. The Minister de Monzie, who in 1940 became interested in my police 'case', told me: 'You have probably written twenty books, but I can assure you that the police have written far more than that about you'.)

I took up quarters in an hotel in the avenue du Maine, with a dark winding staircase, stinking passages and dirty rooms. Under its windows stood the usual round *pissoir*, and the usual scarred bench where lovers sat and kissed in the evening.

In the autumn the French government decided to recognize the

Soviet Union. Once more I stepped over the threshold of the mansion in the rue de Grenelle, my first visit since the February Revolution. Posses of uniformed and plain-clothes police were gathered outside the embassy. They were visibly excited: it was no joke that in broad daylight demented Russians should be raising the red flag and singing the *Internationale* in this aristocratic quarter of Paris. L. B. Krassin was smiling quietly. Mayakovsky was pacing the courtyard saying that he was fed up with Paris and the Americans were holding up his visa.

Mayakovsky came every day to the Rotonde. He wrote that he was conversing with the shades of Verlaine and Cézanne. The Rotonde was living like a *rentier*, on its invested past. Those with whom I had once spent restless nights of talk were no longer there: Modigliani and Apollinaire were dead, Picasso had moved to the Right Bank and had grown cool to Montparnasse. Rivera had gone to Mexico. The few old regulars were surrounded by cosmopolitan tourists. No one argued any more about how to blow up society or reconcile justice and beauty.

It is hard to say why I went every day to Montparnasse, to the Rotonde or the Dôme; it must have been sheer force of habit. Sometimes I met old friends: Léger, Chantal, Zadkine, Cendrars, Lipschitz, Per Krohg, Feyder, Fotinsky. Of course we talked about art, about the Russian revolution, about Picasso, about the international exhibition, about Chaplin, but none of it was like the pre-war Rotonde. It was not that we were old (Léger, the oldest among us, was then forty-four) but our former turbulence had vanished. We were like soldiers retired from active service and wearing out their faded tunics.

In a letter to the poetess Shkapskaya I wrote: 'I am sitting in the Rotonde, smoking a new pipe of cubist design. The sun is wonderful today. There goes a tom-cat and even the angle of his upright tail bears witness to the unusualness of the day. But Ehrenburg, as befits a devastated individual, goes on smoking his pipe. I am in the doldrums. At one moment I am amazed that art is everywhere and long for ordinary conversation or for fat *escargots* which give me indigestion; at another, behaving like Turgenev's "fathers" and looking at the new generation with contemptuous pity, I demand the inspiration that has been abolished. Everybody decries *Jeanne Ney*, and they have christened me "Verbitskaya"[1]. What am I to do? Order a skirt? Commit

---

[1] Authoress of the popular novel *The Keys of Happiness*.

suicide on Heine's tomb? The French write good prose and bad verse. But who wants it? Brother writers, why are we trying so hard?'

The Montparnasse cafés were crowded: the lights of the pre-war Rotonde attracted dreamers, adventurers, men of ambition. Young Swedes, Greeks, Poles, Brazilians, rushed to Paris; they wanted to turn the world upside down, but the world stood as firmly on its feet as ever.

Cubism had rather surprisingly caught the fancy of the great *couturiers* and luxury shops; for a paltry sum young artists painted shawls or made eccentric gewgaws for visiting American ladies. A number of art dealers had set up in business hoping to discover another Modigliani. They made contracts with promising artists and bought up all their paintings cheap, believing, I suppose, that hunger stimulates inspiration. Pictures became stock-exchange shares, a market for speculation; prices were artificially boosted or reduced.

Argentine artists and Serbian poets wrote to their parents that Surrealism was soon going to conquer the world, that they would become famous, but in the meantime would the old people make an effort and send them a couple of hundred francs?

Caravans of tourists transformed Montparnasse into a centre of night life. At the Cigale, at the Jockey, they danced till the small hours, and the lovely Kiki, with eyes like an owl, sang bawdy songs in a mournful voice.

In the summer of 1925 the International Exhibition of Decorative Art opened in Paris. The Italian fascists exhibited their arrogance and stupidity (they called it Neo-Classicism). Among the French pavilions, which were exceptionally grey and drab, the one built by Le Corbusier for the journal *Esprit Nouveau* stood out. The chief attraction of the exhibition was the Soviet pavilion built by the young Constructivist architect K. S. Melnikov. Like many things produced by our Constructivists and LEF people, the pavilion could not claim to be an assertion of Utilitarianism: the staircase was difficult to climb, slanting rain penetrated the building. It was an expression of the romanticism of the first revolutionary years. Most of the exhibits were by 'left' artists: scale-models of Meyerhold's and Tairov's productions, Rodchenko's constructions, L. Popova's textiles, Lissitzky's posters.

Many Muscovites gathered in Paris: Mayakovsky, Yakulov, Melnikov, Sterenberg, Rodchenko, Rabinovich, Ternovets. Talking to them I felt at home, as though I was back in the Moscow of 1921.

The Parisians regarded Soviet art as the most advanced: in addition to the exhibition they saw *Battleship Potemkin*, Tairov's production of *Phèdre*, Vakhtangov's *Princess Tourandot*. But the pavilion at the exhibition, as so much else, was more in the nature of an epilogue; the counter-offensive of Naturalism was beginning, that of Bytovism[1], academic forms, decorum, simplification, and the photographic conventionality which, claiming to precision of detail, tried to pass itself off as a true reflection of life.

This is what I wrote in 1925: 'The simple-minded think that the faithful depiction of great deeds is great art. They do not realize that on a sensitized plate one cannot distinguish the sun from a brass button. There is heroic nature, but there can be no heroic Naturalism. A photographer taking a picture of a provincial wedding in the October days is still a photographer. At the moment vulgar Naturalism has triumphed. It is kept alive by human weakness; for if it is the faculty of legs to leap or at least to step out, there is another part of the body that invariably tends towards a soft seat. People are trying to organize a cosy tea-party on a tightrope'.

I had already said farewell to Constructivism: 'The triumph of industrial beauty means death to "industrial" art. To copy a machine is more vulgar than to copy a rose, for in the latter case one is at least robbing an anonymous author. "Left" art, which created true masterpieces, has quickly disintegrated. It set out to persuade people that nothing in the world remained but grain elevators, geometrical figures and naked ideas. The battle-cry "Art into life!" has hardly died down before this art itself is going . . . into museums'.

I no longer had an aesthetic programme. I rushed from one thing to another. Mayakovsky, on his return from America, said that it was good for machines there but not for men. When I asked him whether he had any doubts about LEF's programme, he said: 'No, but much ought to be revised. In particular the approach to technique'.

I wanted to know what it was that inspired French writers and artists. I got to know MacOrlan, Duhamel, Jules Romains; with the architect Le Corbusier I went to see Barbusse at the office of *Clarté*. I developed an enthusiasm for the cinema and talked to the directors René Clair, Abel Gance, Jean Renoir, Feyder, Epstein.

It would be a sin to describe these years as fruitless: since I have

[1] From *byt* – material, practical part of life.

mentioned the cinema, it is enough to say that in 1925 I saw Chaplin's *The Gold Rush* and *The Pilgrim*. Nor was there any lack of noise; now and again various new schools came into being; the Surrealists made the most noise. But there was something lacking – perhaps hope, perhaps uneasiness. (The fate of many of those whom I used to meet in Montparnasse has recurred to me just now. René Crevel and Pascin committed suicide, Feyder was killed by the Hitlerites. Soutine perished during the years of occupation, the hunted Desnos died after suffering in a concentration camp. Those years, too, were 'eves'; but people thought that it was just a grey, weekday morning.)

I was no longer a Rotonde recluse, nor an art fanatic. From morning till night I wandered about Paris, went into cafés, where I found and talked to brokers, barristers, cattle-dealers, salesmen, workers. What struck me was the mechanization of life, the speed of movement, the advertisements in lights, the stream of cars. Of course there were a hundred times fewer cars then than now, there were no television sets, radios were only just coming into use and in the evening no discordant voices on different wavelengths poured out of open windows into the street. But I felt that the rhythm of life and its pitch were changing. At night the name of the 'automobile king' Citroën glittered on the Eiffel tower. Electric goblins climbed up the façades of the ashen houses in an endeavour to tempt the very moon with the apéritif Dubonnet or the face cream 'Secret of Eternal Youth'.

The outskirts of Paris were changing; the fortifications had disappeared as well as the waste ground and the shacks. The first houses in the new industrial style were being built. Here was Constructivism, not on Rodchenko's drawing-board but in reality. The artist Ozenfant invited me to his house. It had been built by Le Corbusier: light, austerity, the whiteness of a hospital ward or of a laboratory. I thought of Tatlin's constructions, of the enthusiastic *Vkhutemas*[1] crowd. It was the same, and yet different. We had been discovering America – of course an imaginary one. But in the meantime the real America had come to Europe, not with the romantic pronouncements of the LEFs but with dollars, with hard calculation, with vacuum cleaners and the mechanization of human emotions.

Politics interested very few people; the Parisians read neither the speeches of Briand nor accounts of the rebirth of the German army.

[1] *Vkhutemas* – Institute of Higher Education in the Applied Arts.

People thought that whoever did not succumb to chauvinist propaganda must be a firm believer in peace, and this suited everybody: people wanted to enjoy life peacefully. When they unfolded a newspaper some looked for the Stock Exchange prices, some for the football results, others for the weather forecast. The pale horse and other apocalyptic beasts had made room for Renaults and Citroëns. The trenches of Chemin-des-Dames, the soldiers' mutinies, the demonstrations had receded into the distant past. Jazz bellowed late into the night, and snobs admired the syncopated rhythm. Women wore very short skirts and said that they adored sport. *Dancings*, boxing matches, coachloads of tourists, vacuum cleaners, crosswords and a number of other innovations made their appearance.

Life, newly re-hashed, needed exotic spicing. Shop-girls from the department stores and notaries' wives revelled in Pierre Benoit's *Atlantide*. For the more sophisticated there were the books by Paul Morand, the diplomat-writer. Each year he published collections of stories: *Fermé la Nuit*, *Ouvert la Nuit*, *L'Europe Galante*, in which he related how he had slept or not slept with women of different nationalities. For the Paris ladies who did not wish to lag behind the age, love had become a provincial anachronism, and now Paul Morand's lovers modernized it; even in bed they talked like businessmen: 'You're like a dud cheque', 'Don't live on the capital of your nerves'.

It was harder and harder to come across the traditional bourgeois who continued to survive in the pages of *Poivre Rouge*, the stout, carefree lazy paterfamilias who clips coupons, or the hedonist sauntering along the boulevards. He had been superseded by the businessman, full of energy, who preferred motor racing to girls and violets, had a taste for risky enterprises, for any kind of shady deal, an economist or engineer by education, well up in the new production methods and world-prices, the struggle of trusts, the venality of Ministers, all that went on behind the scenes in politics. His sons despised the romantic notions dear to a former generation – the tears of the drunken Verlaine, Anatole France's scepticism, the anarchists' ranting. They went in for physical training, respected the strong and, nine years later, on the night of the fascist putsch, slashed the police horses' legs with razors.

Although the American soldiers had long since gone home, everything that came from the New World was held in high esteem. Jazz had replaced the consumptive fiddlers and jaunty accordion players. In the dance-halls they now had 'hostesses' who danced with the customers for a fixed sum. Snobs, who not so long ago had taken part in scrimmages at the First Nights of Diaghilev's ballets or at the Private View of the Salon des Indépendants, now frenziedly yelled 'Bravo, Joe!' at boxing matches. Writers had begun to write novels about sport in which the heroes were boxers, footballers, cyclists.

In summer Paris was overrun by tourists; the list of sight-seeing 'musts' included the Champs Elysées, the Venus of Milo, the Eiffel tower, Napoleon's tomb, Montmartre, the Rotonde, the brothel in the rue Chabanais called *Société des Nations*, which had rooms in the Spanish, Japanese and Russian style; the tourists were taken round by a prim manageress who explained the various details.

Before the war the French seldom crossed their frontiers; now many of them spent their holidays in Switzerland, Italy, Austria, England. Dekobra's *La Madonne des Sleepings* (the French *wagon-lits* sounded too provincial) was tremendously popular with the ordinary reader.

Every last vestige of the past century had disappeared; the street carnivals, the confetti, bowler hats, plush-covered seats in dark cafés; the men had shaved off their beards, the women had cut their hair short.

All this applies to the year 1925 rather than to Paris. Now when I look back on that time, Paris appears to me idyllic, provincial, something like Utrillo's pictures. The times were changing, and Paris resisted longer perhaps than did Berlin, Brussels or Milan. But I was then living in Paris, and it was there that I witnessed the first results of the American rejuvenation of old Europe.

Everybody realized that law and order had prevailed; some with bitterness, others with joy. Politics were conducted behind the scenes and had little interest for the spectators. Not so long ago the Bolsheviks had been depicted as men with knives between their teeth. Now there were Bolsheviks settled in the rue de Grenelle where big industrialists called in the hope of getting orders. On 7th November our embassy entertained various deputies, prominent journalists, businessmen, society ladies. They all looked askance at Marcel Cachin but were reassured by the sight of caviare on the tables.

In some society drawing-rooms it was fashionable to admire 'Slav mysticism', 'the Russian temperament'. Those snobs who praised everything Soviet were dubbed *bolchévisants*. One tennis champion, a half-wit, said to me: 'I hear money's been abolished in your country. That's splendid! I hate having to reckon my expenses'. Somebody else asked Lyuba: 'Is it true that Potemkin is a better actor than Mosjoukhine?' He had heard something or other about the success of Eisenstein's film and thought Potemkin was the name of an actor.

From time to time tragic events broke into the illusory calm of the city. One of these was the news of the shooting of women workers in the Douarnenez canning factories in Brittany. A big meeting was held in Paris; the speakers called for action; the workers applauded and whistled. Then everything was quiet again. The wars in Morocco and Syria somehow started unobtrusively. The shooting was far away, and life in Paris went on as before.

In the Soviet Union in those days great popularity was enjoyed by the works of Pierre Hamp. He described production, his novels were like feature-articles, which many found thrilling. In his early youth Pierre Hamp had been a worker. What I saw, however, was a respectable man of letters aged about fifty. He knew nothing about LEF, but after rapturously describing some new machine-tool exclaimed: 'How much more beautiful are the movements of a machine than those of a human being!'

I sometimes met MacOrlan. He had the face of a melancholy bulldog and was good at telling stories about the war years. I liked his book *L'Hôpital de la Madeleine*, a fantastic tale about a man who suddenly sweats blood; the medical staff is shaken; all the newspapers are full of this unprecedented case; they decide to exhibit the patient for money; the amount of blood increases – barrels, tons of it; a company is formed to exploit it, the government intervenes; meanwhile the half-dead patient lies and listens to the trickling of the hot stream. It is customary to think that the *roman noir* came into being after the Second World War, but this book was written in the early twenties. MacOrlan lived in an enchanting cottage near the Marne; he sometimes played the accordion and was as bitter as wormwood. He said to me one day: 'You know what? If the human race goes on for a few thousand years more, rabbits will bite and carrots will jump out of the earth and nip people's calves'.

I realized that the October Revolution had brought many changes. Writing about my feelings for the new times I said: 'We love it with a no less "strange love" than our predecessors loved the "fatherland". This feeling also demands both blood and certain silences'. What was I chiefly thinking of? I believe it was of man's destiny, of the fact that writers cannot be satisfied with describing events, they must disclose the spiritual world of the man of today.

In 1925 they produced Čapek's play *R.U.R.* in Paris; a new word appeared: *robot*. We often spoke at the time about 'thinking' machines, and it seemed to me that for Pascal's 'reed' inner degeneration was more terrifying than all the storms. What I was afraid of was not that the 'thinking' machines would be exceedingly complicated, but that the machines would gradually eliminate the habit of thinking, supplant the web of emotions.

The Summer of 1925 is perhaps the saddest of all my books, not the most bitter nor the most hopeless one, but simply the saddest. Its story is not complicated. It is told in the first person. The hero of the novel comes to Paris, goes downhill, tramps about the brightly-lit street, picks up butt-ends, then finds a job at the slaughterhouses driving sheep. A certain Italian adventurer tries to get the weak-willed confused man to kill the capitalist Piquet. Nothing comes of this but the hero grows very fond of a small abandoned girl and nurses her. The child dies. The plot did not interest me much; what I wanted to describe was the loneliness of a man in a large city, the despair of many people I had met, the fate of the generation that had fought at Verdun. 'We believed in many things, we believed firmly and for a long time, if only in the God of shepherds and inquisitors, who made wine out of water and water out of blood; we believed in progress, in art, in every pair of spectacles, in every test-tube, in every pebble in a museum. We believed in social justice and in the symbols of flowers. Now we were excited by the aesthetics of skyscrapers, now by the discovery of a new serum. We believed that everything was advancing towards something better. We argued until we were hoarse, adopted resolutions, read poetry and compared different Constitutions. In those days we had stiff collars and firm souls. And then? Then we lay in the mud of the trenches, put on gas-masks instead of carnival masks. We stabbed with our bayonets, scrounged food, shivered with typhus or 'flu. We learnt that war smells of excrement and blood, and peace of carbolic acid and prison.'

Quite a few sad books were written in those years: it seems clear that actors suffer greater torment during the intervals than when they are on the stage.

A newspaper article entitled *On the Roads of Life* was sent to me from Moscow. The critic wrote: 'I. Ehrenburg relates here how "unable to bear hunger and freedom any longer" he "settled down", got himself a job: "my job was to drive sheep from the cattleyards of la Villette to the neighbouring slaughterhouses". The means chosen by I. Ehrenburg for temporarily supplementing his earnings deserves serious attention, it seems to us . . . I. Ehrenburg's example merits closer social examination. Ehrenburg himself sees in his temporary job at the slaughter-houses something heroic, something of the martyr's halo on the writer's brow furrowed with deep thought: "I accurately counted the rumps of the sheep. At times they baulked and bleated piteously. I then shouted 'Hi! Hi!', and my voice, which could be gentle enough when I tried to get round young women or read certain chapters from *Jeanne Ney* in public, was now able to frighten these agonized creatures." A writer must be tragically cut off from real life if such a simple thing as finding a temporary job seems to him a supreme, almost a world tragedy. . . . After all this a perfectly proper and healthy road.'

It must have been the only time in those days that something praiseworthy was found in my writings, but it was undeserved praise: I had never worked in slaughterhouses and had never driven sheep. But I did see the trenches on the Somme, the heavy stupor of the respite, the misery of Belleville, Italian Blackshirts and much else.

13

As I was walking past the Rotonde I caught sight of a familiar face on the terrace: it was the poet Peretz Markisch whom I knew from Kiev days. It would have been difficult not to notice him, his handsome, inspired face stood out in any company. Boris Lavrenev always said that Markisch looked like portraits of Byron. Possibly. Or perhaps he was like that image of the romantic poet which hundreds of paintings and drawings, lines of poetry, the atmosphere of a different epoch had imprinted on our imagination. Markisch was a Romantic in more than poetry; the curl of his hair was romantic and the way his head was set on his slender neck (he disliked ties and always went about with an open shirt-collar); and the youthful appearance he retained thoughout life was also romantic.

Warszawski, a Jewish writer from Poland, was also sitting at his table, and an artist whose name I have forgotten. I knew Warszawski from his novel *The Smugglers* which had been translated into various languages; he was shy and said little. The artist, on the contrary, talked without stopping about exhibitions, critics, the difficulty of making a living in Paris: he was a Bessarabian and had only recently come to France where he worked as a house-decorator, painting landscapes in his spare time.

Was it Warszawski, or was it the painter, who told the story about the little whistle? This was a Chassidic legend (the Chassids are a mystic and rebel sect of Jews who rose against the rabbis and the rich bigots in the eighteenth century). I remembered the legend and later used it in my book *The Stormy Life of Laẓik Roitschwanẓ*; the book is little known, and I shall repeat the story here.

In a small Volhynian town there lived a famous *Zaddik* – as the Chassids called the true good men. In this little town, as everywhere else, there were rich men, who lent money at high interest, landlords, merchants; there were men who were eager to enrich themselves by fair means or foul; in short, there were plenty of unjust people. The Day of Atonement came, when according to the belief of pious Jews, God judges men and determines their future destiny. On the Day of

Atonement they neither drink nor eat until the evening star appears and the rabbi allows them to go home. On that particular day a brooding silence had reigned in the synagogue. By the Zaddik's face the people saw that God was angry with the evil deeds of the inhabitants of that little town; the star took a long time to come out; everyone expected a severe verdict. The Zaddik prayed to God to forgive the sins of the people, but God pretended to be deaf. Suddenly the silence was broken by whistling. Among the poorer men who were standing at the back was a tailor with his five-year-old son. The prayers had bored the little boy, and he suddenly remembered that in his pocket was a penny whistle his father had bought him the day before. Everybody turned on the tailor: for such unheard-of behaviour God would chastise the town! But the Zaddik saw that the stern God had relented and was smiling. That is all there is to the legend. It greatly moved Markisch, and he cried: 'Ah, that's a story about art!' Then we got up and started to go home. Markisch accompanied me to the corner of the street and suddenly (we had been talking about other things) he said: 'But today a whistle's not enough, what we need is Mayakovsky's trumpet'.

This phrase seems to me to explain the many difficult years of his life. He was not made either for loud appeals or for heroic poems, he was a poet with a little pipe that produced clear, piercing notes. But there was no imaginary deity about who could smile, the age was a noisy one; and men's ears were not able to discern music.

Versifiers have always existed and have grown particularly numerous since the production of verse has become a profession. Markisch was a poet. It is, of course, difficult to judge poetry in translation (I do not know Hebrew) but every time I talked to Markisch his attitude of mind struck me: he perceived as a poet both the great events and the petty details of everyday life. This impression was shared by many others. Such different people as Alexey Tolstoy, Tuwim, Jean-Richard Bloch, Zabolotski and Nezval remarked on it.

He was not afraid of well-worn themes and often wrote what all the poets of the world have written about. The forest in the autumn: 'The leaves there do not rustle in secret alarm, they lie crumpled and drowsing in the wind; but now one, awakened, has set off sleepily along the road like a golden mouse seeking its nest'. The tear of a beloved woman: 'It does not fall from your lashes but rests quivering between your eyelids. In it the world leaves its frontiers and in its depths the glistening pupil grows larger'.

He was a master and worked tirelessly; one could say the same thing about him that he said of an old tailor: 'What else could he bring to the dark hamlets? Back-stitched years and a spiky needle'.

Markisch did not turn away from life; not only did he accept the times, but he loved them ardently; he wrote epic poems about construction, about the war. Himself a man of exceptional integrity, he jealously guarded what he loved from the shadows of doubt; he was a Soviet man from top to toe; and although we are of the same generation (he was four years younger than I), I admired his singleness of heart.

He witnessed the pogroms, he lived in Poland when anti-semitism was rife, but there was not a scrap of nationalism in him, not even the nationalism of a mouse under the floorboards who knows that cats are stretching themselves overhead. If I were asked to cite an exemplary internationalist I should boldly name Markisch.

Critics have commented that in his poems they sometimes sense sadness, bitterness, disquiet. What else could they expect? One of his first poems, *The Heap*, is dedicated to the pogrom in Gorodishche; recently I read a translation of his unpublished novel, finished not long before he perished: it is a chronicle of suffering, of struggles, of the destruction of the Warsaw ghetto.

However, I do not want to talk only of the times he lived in; I want also to say something about what made the poet. Let me recall a very old dialogue between two Spanish poets: the Marquis of Santillana and the Rabbi Shem Tov. It took place in the first half of the fifteenth century when Spain was ruled by Pedro the Cruel. The Jews and the Arabs introduced gnomic verse, i.e. short philosophical maxims, into Spanish poetry. One such gnomic poet was Rabbi Shem Tov. Pedro the Cruel, who suffered from insomnia, ordered Rabbi Shem Tov to write some poetry for him. The poet called the book *Advice*, and it began with the following consolation: 'There is nothing in the world that grows eternally. When the moon is full, it begins to wane'. The court poet, the Marquis of Santillana, replied with an epigram: 'As good wine that is sometimes kept in a rotten barrel, so truth occasionally issues from the lips of a Jew'. Rabbi Shem Tov had the last word: 'When the world was created, it was so divided that some had the good wine, others the thirst'. (I came upon these polemics by accident when, half a century ago, I was studying old Spanish poetry. Rabbi Shem Tov's aphorism struck me then as a happy one, and still does.)

Markisch was one of the poets not of good wine but of dry lips, hence the faint tinge of bitterness that occasionally makes itself felt in poetry that is full of the joy of living.

We seldom met each other for we lived in different worlds, but at every encounter I felt that Markisch was a wonderful man, a poet and a revolutionary who would never hurt anyone without good cause, never betray his friends or turn away from those in trouble.

I remember a big meeting in Moscow in 1941; it was transmitted by radio to America. Peretz Markisch, Sergei Eisenstein, S. M. Mikhoels, P. L. Kapitsa and I were among the speakers. Markisch appealed fervently to American Jews to call upon their country to join in the struggle against fascism (America at that time being neutral).

The last time I saw Markisch was on 23rd January 1949 in the Writers' Union at the funeral of Mike Gold. Markisch pressed my hand sorrowfully; we exchanged a long look, wondering who would be the next to draw the lot.

Boris Lavrenev has written: 'Markisch's considerable talent was at its height and he would certainly have produced even greater works had his life not been cut short in its prime. He fell, falsely accused, the victim of enemies. Those enemies of our country destroyed a remarkable singer physically, but they could not destroy his song'. Markisch was arrested on 27th January 1949, the date of his death was 12th August 1952.

Like all those who knew Markisch, I think of him with almost anxious tenderness. I recall his lines: 'Two dead birds fell to the ground. It was a lucky blow . . . What is better than the earth? Here, in this sunny blessed land if one has to fall, so be it. So I see it dimly . . . I have taken a step, come on let's go, d'you hear, let's go! If you've fallen, so be it. Don't regret anything. If you must fly, then fly. How blinding is the light! The prospects are vast and have no bounds'. It is hard to reconcile oneself to the idea that of the singer only the songs have survived.

But in those days long ago, when I met the youthful inspired Markisch in Montparnasse, when he spoke about the child's whistle and Mayakovsky's thundering voice, he was trying out destiny. For me he was the pledge that poetry and the age we lived in could not be divorced: 'I have shouldered you, O age! I have girt myself with you, as with a broad stone belt. The road rises in sheer steepness, and I must climb it. Through the howling of the wind, through deep snowdrifts I climb. Many will perish amid the drifts . . .' No, this was no dreamy simpleton, no blind fanatic; the pipe was held to the dry lips of a ripe intrepid man.

14

When I arrived in Moscow in the spring of 1926, I took up quarters in an hotel in Balchug; the room was expensive, and I was short of funds. Soon I was offered hospitality by Katya and Tikhon Sorokin; they were living in Protochny Lane, between the Smolensky market and the Moskva, in an old dilipadated house. (At the beginning of the war this house got a direct hit from a German incendiary bomb and was burnt down.)

For some reason Protochny Lane was at that time the favourite haunt of thieves, petty speculators, market stall-holders. Riff-raff thronged to the Ivanovka dosshouse. In the little seedy houses, painted pink, apricot or chocolate-brown – with their signboards of private trades-men, their wrenched-out bells, their rubber plants and throat-cutting – the stifling, brutal life of NEP's last years was being played out. Everybody traded in everything, wrangled, prayed, swilled vodka and, dead drunk, fell like corpses in the gateways. The yards were filthy. Vagrant children huddled in the cellars. Militiamen and agents of the Criminal Investigation Department peered warily into the lane.

I was seeing one of the backdoors of the epoch, and I decided to describe it. I knew, of course, that to write about heroic characters is more pleasant and less trouble, but an author is not always free to choose his characters; it is not he who seeks them, but they who seek him. Artists have an expression 'to paint from nature'; this does not by any means imply Naturalism: the Impressionists, for instance, painted only from nature, while the Naturalists, who usually call themselves realists, paint portraits quite happily from photographs. I found my inspiration in Protochny Lane, with its callousness and its heartbreak, its shallow understanding of great events, its cruelty and its remorse, its darkness and its deep despondency; for the first time I made an attempt to write 'from nature'.

The plot turned on something that really happened: the owner of one of the little houses, an apricot or chocolate-coloured one, a greedy and heartless huckster, incensed by the homeless children who had stolen a ham from him, blocked up the entrance to the cellar where they had sought refuge from the terrible night frosts.

A landscape changes not only according to the light but also according to the artist's frame of mind. I could no longer exist on mere negation, my satirical sneering chilled me. In my novel *Rvach* I had tried to make a social analysis of events; there are many general descriptions in it. In *Protochny Lane* there is little irony: I was bent on finding in my characters that spark of goodness which beckoned them out of the dirt, the meanness, the moral desolation. I did not write any poetry in those years and the novel was something of a lyrical outpouring.

I not only became fond of my characters, I projected myself into them. The landlord, who had tried to destroy the homeless children, as well as his lodger, a puny wastrel who had married a baron's daughter before the Revolution and lived on her money, remained in the background. All the other characters flounder in confusion, searching and suffering. My thoughts and emotions of those years can be traced in the ordinary Soviet girl Tanya, with her casual affairs, her yearning for a great love, her books and her work; and in the unsuccessful poet Prakhov, who has become a hack journalist, ambitious but without will power, ready to commit a meanness and even a baseness, but who is beginning to recognize the vanity and the shallowness of his dreams; and in the hunchback musician Yuzik who plays the fiddle in the Electra cinema, a homespun philosopher with a hopeless love of life; and in the old Czech, a former Latin teacher, who has become a beggar but has raised himself spiritually, seen the light, and whom the homeless children have come to love.

The hunchback Yuzik asks the old beggar:

'Then why have you, a teacher of Latin, been thrown out into the street? It's one thing or the other: either you're right, or they are.'

'I was right – that's the past tense. They are right – that's the present tense. And the babies playing with their rattles today will be right – *futurum*. I've been watching with keen pleasure their flags, their processions, their enthusiasm. Young man, the blood that flushes their cheeks and the fire of self-abnegation in their eyes are beautiful.'

I do not think any book of mine has been so reviled as the novel *In Protochny Lane*. I do not remember all the reviews but one of them I have before me now; it is entitled *Soviet Russia without Communists*, and it was published in the Leningrad *Krasnaya Gazeta* (Red

Journal): 'The Soviet Russia seen and shown through the muck that oozes out of Protochny Lane is not our real country, but the cherished ideal of Milyukov: Soviet Russia without Communists. Ehrenburg is carrying out the social commission of the *émigré* intelligentsia by giving a picture of a corner of Soviet Moscow without Socialist construction, without the inspiration of building a new life ... Ehrenburg has behaved like a bristly rootler among rubbish heaps who, having accidentally wandered into a rose-garden, does not see the rich and fragrant blooms but only the prickly thorns, and finds pleasure in the muck that manures the flower-beds'.

There is a passage in Stendhal's *Le Rouge et le Noir*: 'A novel is a mirror on the highway. It reflects now the azure sky, now the dirt, the puddles and the ruts. Yet the man who holds the mirror is accused of immorality. The mirror reflects dirt, and you accuse the mirror. You would do better to accuse the uneven road or the inspector of highways.'

In 1926, when I was writing *In Protochny Lane*, Konstantin Fedin was working on *Transvaal*, Leonid Leonov on *The Thief*, Valentin Katayev on *The Embezzlers*, Vsevolod Ivanov on *The Mystery of Mysteries*. The old Literary Encyclopedia calls all these books 'a distortion of Soviet reality', 'an apology of the petty bourgeoisie', 'a slander'.

This goes to show that Milyukov's political dreams had nothing to do with it. During the first years of the Revolution, writers of my generation tried to get an over-all picture, to realize the significance of what was going on; later on, quieter and, if you like, greyer times set in; writers began to take a closer look at individual human destinies. In olden days a beggar boy was whipped for the pranks of a prince; writers were and still are the critics' whipping-boys for the ruts in the road.

Protochny Lane was not in the least like a rose-garden. And I, being a bristly fellow, though in all honesty not a pig, was distressed by the dirt. I have very often felt cold in the world and have sought kindness, warmth. On the banks of the Moskva, in the summer, buttercups and dandelions grew, the sorry flowers of the waste land, trampled and smothered in filth. It was such flowers that I wanted to describe.

It is idle to argue with the past, but it is worth reflecting on it, trying to find out why the written pages so often turned out paler, shallower than those the author saw in his imagination during his sleepless nights.

All my life I have devotedly admired Gogol. I am writing these lines in the dimly-lit room of an hotel in Rome. (A few days between two Congress sessions happened to be free, and I decided to get back to my unfinished chapter.) Yesterday I revisited the Café Greco which Gogol frequented once upon a time; I sat down under his portrait and fell into thought: what light this moody, sickly, deeply unhappy man threw both on Russia and on the world!

In the novel about Protochny Lane the hunchback Yuzik reads and re-reads the same book; its first pages are missing, he knows neither the title, nor the author's name. He says to Tanya: 'Ah, just listen to what I read yesterday: "A great depth of soul is needed to light up a picture taken from contemptible life and to turn it into a pearl of creation". ' Tanya laughs: 'You read silly books, Yuzik. Who talks about "pearls" nowadays? The author's a writer, not a jeweller. You should study methodology!'

The quotation comes from Gogol. Depth of soul enabled him to impress his contemporaries deeply, and it impresses us deeply too. Sitting at his table I reflected that neither I nor many of my contemporaries possessed sufficient depth of soul, and that too often we find ourselves defeated, not by the critics, but by the times, precisely because we have proved incapable of throwing light on the everyday, the unimportant, the 'contemptible', with the true depth, the boldness of concept, the courage of the author of *Dead Souls* and of *The Overcoat*.

I do not speak of others, but I have the right to judge myself. The weakness of my novel lay not in the subject, nor in the fact that I fixed my gaze on the unsavoury inhabitants of Protochny Lane without contrasting them to the builders of the future, but in that I shed the light of art too timidly, too meanly, too intermittently on this world that I was depicting. The crux of the matter lies not in the quality of such gifts as I have, but in spiritual hastiness, in the fact that we were living blinded by tremendous events, deafened by cannonades, by roaring, by intensely loud music, so that at times we ceased to detect the nuances, hear the heartbeats, and so lost the habit of discovering that spiritual detail which is the living tissue of art.

All this I realized not in the year 1926, but much later: a man goes on learning till his last day.

15

I<small>T</small> was hot in Moscow that summer; many of my friends were living at their *dachas* or elsewhere in the country. I wandered aimlessly about the scorching city. One of those sultry days that precede a thunderstorm brought me an unexpected joy: I met the man who became my most intimate and true friend, the author to whom I looked up as an apprentice to a master – Isaak Babel.

He came to me unheralded, and I still remember his first words: 'So that's what you're like'. I on my side stared at him with even greater curiosity: so here was the man who had written *Red Cavalry, Odessa Tales, The Story of My Dovecote*. Several times in my life I have been introduced to authors whose books I revered: Maxim Gorky, Thomas Mann, Bunin, Andrey Bely, Heinrich Mann, Machado, Joyce; they were much older than I; they were universally recognized, and I looked at them as at distant mountain peaks. But twice I was as excited as a lover who meets the object of his secret love for the first time: it was like that in the case of Babel and, ten years later, in that of Hemingway.

Babel immediately carried me off to a beerhouse. When we entered the dark, crowded room, I was astounded. Here shabby speculators, habitual thieves, cabbies, suburban market-gardeners, down-at-heel representatives of the old intelligentsia forgathered. Someone was shouting that 'the elixir of life has been invented, it's disgusting because it's fabulously expensive, so the scoundrels will outlive everybody else'. At first no one paid any attention to the shouter, then his neighbour knocked him over the head with a bottle. In another corner a scuffle broke out over a girl. Blood streamed down the face of a curly-haired young fellow. The girl yelled: 'You needn't try so hard. Harry Piel – he's the one I like!' Two men who had drunk themselves unconscious were dragged out by their feet. A little old man, very polite, seated himself at our table. He started telling Babel how his son-in-law had tried to cut his wife's throat 'and Verochka, you know, didn't turn a hair, she just said: "Clear out, if you don't mind" – this girl of mine, you know, she's very refined.' I could not stand it any longer: 'Shall we go?' Babel was taken aback: 'But it's so interesting here'.

He looked less like a writer than anyone I have ever seen. In his sketch *The Beginning* he relates how when he first came to Petersburg (he was then twenty) he rented a room in an engineer's flat. After taking a good look at his new lodger the engineer gave orders that the door leading out of Babel's room into the dining-room should be locked and that all the overcoats and galoshes should be taken out of the hall. Twenty years later Babel lodged with an old French lady in the Paris suburb of Neuilly; his landlady locked him in at night for fear he should cut her throat. And yet there was nothing terrifying about Babel's appearance; it was just that he puzzled people: heaven knew what kind of man he was and what his occupation might be.

Mike Gold, who met Babel in Paris in 1935, wrote: 'He is not at all like a man of letters or a former cavalryman but reminds one rather of a village schoolmaster'. This impression was largely due to his spectacles whose role in *Red Cavalry* had assumed alarming proportions ('They send up chaps like you without asking us, and here anyone wearing glasses can get his throat cut', 'You bespectacled fellows have about as much pity for us as a cat has for a mouse', 'You've ruined that mount, four-eyes'.) He was short, stocky. In one of the stories in *Red Cavalry* he speaks of Galician Jews, contrasting them with 'the stout and jovial Jews of the South, bubbling like cheap wine': the stevedores, carters, cabbies, bandits like the notorious Mishka Yaponchik, the prototype of Benya Krik. (The epithet 'jovial' is a Gallicism; in Russian we say 'jolly', 'cheerful'.) In spite of his glasses Babel was far more like a jovial Odessan – though one who had known his share of grief – than a village schoolmaster. His spectacles could hide the unusually expressive eyes, now mischievous, now sad. His nose, tirelessly inquisitive, also played an important part. Babel wanted to know everything: what his brother-soldier, a Kuban Cossack, felt when, after a two days' drinking bout, in a fit of melancholy, he had set fire to his own house; why had Mashenka of *Land and Factory*, after cuckolding her husband, taken up biokinetics; what sort of poetry did the White Guard Gorgulov, the French President's assassin, write; how did the old accountant seen once in the window of the *Pravda* office die; what was the Paris lady at the next table in the café carrying in her handbag; did Mussolini keep up his bluster when he found

himself alone with Ciano – in short, life's most trivial details. Everything interested him, and it was unimaginable to him that a writer
could be without an appetite for life. 'A great writer,' he said to me
about Proust's novels. 'But it's boring. Perhaps he himself felt bored
when he was describing it all?' Remarking on the promise shown by the
young *émigré* writer Nabokov-Sirin, Babel said: 'He can write, but
he's got nothing to say'.

He loved poetry and was on friendly terms with poets quite unlike
himself: Bagritsky, Yesenin, Mayakovsky. But he could not stand
literary circles. 'When I have to go to a writers' meeting I feel as if I'm
going to have to put down a mixture of honey and castor oil.' He had
friends of the most varied occupations: engineers, jockeys, cavalrymen,
architects, bee-keepers, cymbalists. He was capable of listening for
hours on end to someone else's happy or unhappy love affairs. He had
a way of attracting other people's confidences; perhaps they felt that
he not only listened to them but shared their feelings. While some of
his stories about other people's lives are told in the first person (for
instance, *My First Honorarium*) there are some which, purporting
to be about fictitious heroes, are in fact pages of the author's
biography (*Oil*).

In his short autobiography Babel related how in 1916 Maxim Gorky
'sent him out into the world'. He continues: 'And for seven years, from
1917 till 1924, I went out into the world. During that time I was a
soldier on the Rumanian front, then served in the Cheka, in the
Narkompros (People's Commissariat of Education), in the Food
Detachments of 1918, in the Northern army against Yudenich, in the
First Cavalry Army, in the Odessa *Gubkom* (Provincial Commissariat),
I was a printer in the Seventh Soviet Press in Odessa, a reporter in
Petersburg, Tiflis, etc.' And in truth those seven years gave Babel
much; but he was 'out in the world' even before 1916 and remained
'out in the world', too, after he had become a famous author: he could
not exist without people. *The Story of my Dovecote* was the experience
of a boy told much later by a mature master. During the days of his
adolescence and early youth Babel met the heroes of his Odessa tales:
bandits and profiteers, near-sighted dreamers and romantic rascals.

Wherever he found himself he immediately felt at home and entered
into other people's lives. He did not stay long in Marseilles but when
he spoke about the life there, his were not the impressions of a tourist:
he spoke of gangsters, municipal elections, the strike in the port, a

woman getting on in life – a laundress, I think – who, having suddenly come into a lot of money, gassed herself.

However, even in France, which he loved, he was homesick. He wrote in 1927 from Marseilles: 'Spiritual life in Russia is nobler'. In another letter to his old friend I. L. Lifshitz he wrote from Paris: 'Life in the sense of individual freedom is fine here, but we Russians pine for the wind of great thoughts and great passions'.

In the twenties there were many references in our papers to 'scissors'; this did not mean the tailor's instrument but the growing discrepancy between the price of bread and the price of cotton fabrics or boots. It makes me think now of another kind of 'scissors': the discrepancy between life and the meaning of art; I spent the whole of my life with these 'scissors'. I often discussed this with Babel. Passionately in love with life, involved in it at every minute, he had been devoted to art from his childhood.

It sometimes happens like this: a man has an important experience, he wants to relate it, it turns out that he does it with talent, and a new writer is born. I have heard Fadeyev say that in the years of the Civil War he never thought he would be drawn into literature; *The Nineteen* was a most unlooked-for outcome of his experiences. But Babel, even while he was fighting, knew that he would have to translate the reality into a work of art.

The manuscripts of Babel's unpublished works have disappeared. S. G. Hecht's memoirs reminded me of Babel's remarkable story *At the Troitsa*. He read it to me in the spring of 1938; it is the story of the destruction of many illusions, a wise and bitter story. The manuscripts of the stories have been lost as well as the chapters of an unfinished novel. Babel's widow, Antonina Nikolayevna, sought them in vain. The diary which Babel kept in 1920 when he was in the ranks of the First Cavalry Army has survived by some miracle; a woman in Kiev had preserved the thick exercise book with its illegible entries. The diary is very interesting: it not only shows how Babel worked, but also enables one to understand the psychology of creative art.

From the diary it appears that Babel shared the life of his comrades in arms: the victories and defeats, the attitude of the soldiers to the local inhabitants and that of the inhabitants to the soldiers; he was deeply impressed by what he saw of generosity and violence, rescue in battle, pogroms, death. Nevertheless, all through there are insistent reminders: 'Describe Matyazh, Misha'; 'describe the people, the air';

'for that day – it is most important to describe the Red Army men and the air'; 'remember – the figure, the face, and the joy of Apanasenko, his feeling for horses, how he leads them, chooses for Bakhturov'; 'must not fail to describe the lame Gubanov, the terror of the regiment, a dashing cavalry officer'; 'must not forget the priest in Luszkow, ill-shaven, kind, educated, possibly self-interested – but what self-interest! – a chicken, a duck'; 'describe the air-attack, the distant, almost slow, chatter of machine-guns'; 'describe the forests – Krivikha, the ruined Czechs, the buxom woman'.

Babel was a poet; neither the naturalism of the life he describes, nor the round glasses on his round face can conceal his poetical attitude of mind. He was set alight by a line of poetry, a painting, the colour of the sky, the sight of human beauty. His diary is not of the sort intended for publication: Babel was talking frankly to himself. That is why, when I refer to his poetical nature, I begin with notes taken from his diary:

'Cleared outskirts of forests, remnants of the war, wire, trenches. Majestic green oaks, hornbeams, many pines, a willow – majestic and gentle tree, rain in the forest, roads washed out, an ash.'

'Boratin – a solid, sunny village. Hops, a laughing daughter, a silent, rich peasant, eggs fried in butter, milk, white bread, gluttony, sunshine, cleanliness.'

'Magnificent Italian paintings, pink Catholic priests nursing the infant Christ, magnificent dark Christ, Rembrandt; Murillo-style (or perhaps Murillo) Madonna, saintly well-nourished Jesuits, a bearded Jew, a small shop, a broken reliquary, the figure of St Valentius.'

'I remember broken frames, thousands of bees buzzing and struggling beside a smashed beehive.'

'Aristocratic old Polish mansion, probably more than a hundred years old, mounted antlers, ceilings with ancient painting done in light colours, small butler's pantry, stoves, passages, excrement on the floor, small Jewish boys, a Steinway piano, sofas ripped open to the springs; remember white light and oaken doors, letters written in French dated 1820.'

Babel related his attitude to art in his short novel *Di Grasso*. An actor comes to Odessa from Sicily. His acting is conventional, perhaps even exaggerated, but the power of art is such that the unkind have a change of heart; the wife of a profiteer says to her shamed husband as they come out of the theatre: 'Now you see what love means'.

I remember when *Red Cavalry* was first published. Everyone

marvelled at its imaginative power; there was even talk of sheer fantasy. Yet Babel had described what he had seen with his own eyes. The proof of this is the evidence of the exercise book which was with him on the expedition and survived its author.

Here is the story *The Remount Officer*: '... Up to the very steps galloped Dyakov on his fiery Anglo-Arabian – Dyakov who had formerly been an athlete in a circus and was now a red-faced, grey-moustached remount officer with a black cloak and silver stripes down his wide red breeches'. Further on Dyakov tells a peasant that he will get 15,000 for the horse, and would have got 20,000 if the beast had been a little friskier. 'If a horse falls and gets up again, it's a horse; if, to put it the other way round, it doesn't, well then it isn't.'

And now here is the entry for 13th July 1920: 'The remount officer – fairy-tale picture, r(ed) breeches with silver stripes, a belt with silver trimming, from Stavropol, a figure like Apollo, sh(ort) grey moustache, forty-five years old ... was an athlete ... about horses.' 16th July: 'Dyakov arrives. Conversation short: for this sort of horse you can get 15,000, for another sort 20,000. If it gets up it's a horse'.

The story *Gedali*: here the author meets an old Jewish junkshop owner who sorrowfully expounds his philosophy: '... but the Poles shot because they were the Counter-Revolution. You shoot because you are the Revolution. But surely the Revolution means joy. And joy doesn't like orphans in the house. Good men do good deeds ... And I want an International of good people, I want every soul to be taken into account and given rations of the first category'. This is the description of Gedali's shop: 'Dickens, where was your kindly shade that evening? In that little old curiosity shop you would have seen gilt slippers, ships' cables, an ancient compass, a stuffed eagle, a Winchester engraved with the date 1810 and a broken saucepan'.

Entry for 3rd July 1920: 'A small Jew – a philosopher. Incredible shop – Dickens; brooms and gilt slippers. His philosophy: all of them say they are fighting for justice and all of them loot'.

In the diary you will find Prishchepa, and the little town of Beres-techko, and the letter written in French that was found there, and the killing of prisoners, and the 'pawn' in the battle for Lesznow, and the commander's speech about the Second Comintern Congress, and the 'furious sycophant Levka', and the house of the Catholic priest Tuzinkiewicz, and many other episodes and pictures which were later incorporated in *Red Cavalry*. But the stories are not like the diary. In his exercise book Babel described everything as it was. It is a list of events: advance, retreat, the ruined, terrified inhabitants of towns and villages that changed hands; executions, trampled fields, the cruelty of war. In his diary Babel asked himself: 'Why am I in the grip of un-relieved misery?' And he replied: 'Life is being destroyed, I am present at an endless funeral'.

But the book is different: in it, in spite of the horrors of war, in spite of the savage climate of those years, there is faith in the Revolution and faith in man. It is true that there were those who said that Babel had slandered the Red Army cavalrymen. Gorky intervened to vindicate *Red Cavalry* and wrote that Babel had 'embellished' the Cossacks of the First Cavalry Army 'better and with more truth than Gogol had embellished the Zaporozhye Cossacks.' The word 'embellish' that I snatch out of context and the comparison with *Taras Bulba* may cause bewilderment. Besides, the style of *Red Cavalry* is exuberant, hyper-bolic. (As early as 1915, when he made his début as a writer, Babel said that what he looked for in literature was sunshine, rich colours; he expressed his admiration for Gogol's Ukrainian stories and regretted that 'Petersburg had conquered the land of Poltava. Akaky Akakievich had unassumingly but with horrifying power put Gritsko in the shade.')

Yet Babel did not 'embellish' the heroes of *Red Cavalry*: he revealed their inner world. He ignored not only the workaday life of the army, but also many actions which at the time drove him to despair. It was as if he floodlit an hour, a moment when a man reveals himself. That is precisely why I have always looked on Babel as a poet.

Very different kinds of writers like *Red Cavalry*: Gorky and Thomas Mann, Barbusse and Roger Martin du Gard, Mayakovsky and Yesenin, Andrey Bely and Furmanov, Romain Rolland and Brecht.

In 1930 *Novy Mir* printed a number of letters from foreign writers, mainly German, in answer to a questionnaire on Soviet literature. In the majority of letters Babel's name topped the list.

But Babel criticized himself with the severity of a great artist. He often said to me that his style was too flamboyant, that he was trying to achieve simplicity and wished to rid himself of excessive imagery. One day, in the early thirties, he admitted that the Gogol of *The Over-coat* was closer to him than the Gogol of the early stories. He developed a liking for Chekhov. Those were the years when he was writing *Guy de Maupassant*, *The Trial*, *De Grasso*, *Oil*.

He worked slowly, painfully, and was never satisfied with himself. When we first met he said to me: 'Man lives for the pleasure of sleeping with a woman, of eating ices on a hot day'. One day I went to see him; he was sitting naked, the day was very hot. He was not eating ices, he was writing. When he came to Paris, there, too, he worked from morning till night: 'I toil here like an inspired ox, see nothing of the world (and in this world Paris is no Kremenchug'). Later he went to live in the country, a little way outside Moscow, renting a cottage room in the village, where he sat and wrote. Everywhere he burrowed himself away in seclusion to work. This exceptionally 'jovial' man laboured like an anchorite.

When at the end of 1932 and the beginning of 1933 I was writing *The Second Day*, Babel came to see me practically every day. I read out the chapters I had written, and he either approved or criticized: my book interested him, and he was a true friend.

He was very secretive, never said where he was going; his days were like the tunnellings of a mole. In 1936 I wrote of him: 'His own destiny is not unlike some of his writings: he cannot unravel it. On one occasion he was coming to see me. His small daughter asked: "Where are you going?" He had to give an answer and at once changed his mind and did not go. When in danger an octopus ejects ink; all the same they catch it and eat it – a favourite dish with the Spaniards is "an octopus in its ink".' (I wrote these words in Paris at the very beginning of 1936, and it horrifies me to copy them now: I could never have imagined how they would sound a few years later.)

Following Gorky's advice, Babel did not publish anything for seven years – from 1916 till 1923. Then one after another there appeared *Red Cavalry, Tales of Odessa, The Story of My Dovecote*, the play *Sunset*. Then again Babel fell into almost complete silence, publishing at rare intervals short (but remarkable) stories. 'Babel's silence' became one of the critics' favourite themes. At the First All-Union Congress of Soviet Writers I spoke against this kind of attack and said that a cow-elephant has a longer period of gestation than a doe-rabbit; I compared myself to the rabbit and Babel to the elephant. The writers laughed. And in his speech Babel made a joke, saying that he was the master of a new literary genre – silence.

But for him it was no joke. Every day he became more exacting with himself. 'For the third time I have started to re-write the stories I have written, and realize with horror that another, a fourth, version will be necessary.' 'My worst trouble in life,' he confessed in a letter, 'is an abominable capacity for work.'

I was not putting it on when I spoke about the rabbit and the elephant: I had the greatest admiration for Babel's talent and knew what high standards he set himself. I was proud of his friendship. Although he was three years younger than I, I often sought his advice and jokingly called him 'the wise rabbi'.

I had only two conversations with Gorky about literature, and on both occasions he spoke with tenderness, with confidence, of Babel's work; this pleased me as much as if he had been praising me. I was happy when Romain Rolland in his letter about *The Second Day* expressed his admiration for *Red Cavalry*. I loved Babel, and I loved and still love Babel's books.

There is something more I want to say about the man. It was not only in his appearance that Babel was unlike a writer, he also lived differently. He did not have mahogany furniture, or bookcases, or a secretaire. He even did without a desk and wrote on a kitchen table; and in Molodenovo, where he rented a room with the village cobbler Ivan Karpovich, he used a joiner's bench.

Babel's first wife, Yevgenia Borisovna, had grown up in a bourgeois family and found it hard to accustom herself to her husband's vagaries. For instance, he would bring his former army friends to the room where they were living and announce: 'Yevgenia, they're going to spend the night with us'.

His sensibility as an artist and his culture enabled him to be perfectly at ease with the most varied kinds of people. I heard him talk to Parisian snobs – putting them in their place – to Russian peasants, to Heinrich Mann, to Barbusse.

In 1935 a Congress for the Defence of Culture was held in Paris. The Soviet delegation arrived, without Babel. The French writers, who had organized the Congress, requested our embassy to include the author of *Red Cavalry* in the delegation. Babel arrived late, on the second or third day, I think. He was due to speak immediately. He reassured me with a smile: 'I'll find something to say'. This is how I described Babel's speech in *Izvestia*: 'Babel did not read his speech, he spoke gaily and in masterly French for fifteen minutes, entertaining the audience with several unwritten stories. People laughed, but at the same time they realized that under cover of those amusing stories the essence of our people and of our culture was being conveyed to them: "This collective farmer has bread, he has a house, he even has a decoration. But it's not enough for him. Now he wants poetry to be written about him"'.

Many times he said to me that the main thing was the people's happiness. He loved animals, especially horses; he said, when writing about his fellow soldier Khlebnikov: 'We were in the grip of the same passions. We both looked out on the world as on a May meadow where women and horses roam about'.

Life turned out to be no May meadow for him. But to the end he was faithful to the ideals of justice, internationalism, humanism. He understood the Revolution and recognized it as a pledge of future happiness. One of his best stories of the thirties, *Karl-Yankel*, ends with the words: 'I grew up in those streets, now it is the turn of Karl-Yankel, but they did not fight for me as they are fighting for him, few people had any thought for me. "It's not possible," I whispered to myself, "that you won't be happy, Karl-Yankel. It's not possible that you won't be happier than I." '

And Babel was one of those who paid with his struggle, his dreams, his books and, finally, with his life, for the happiness of future generations.

Late in 1937 I came to Moscow from Spain, straight from near Teruel. When I reach the narrative of those days, the reader will understand how important I felt it was to see Babel immediately. I found the 'wise rabbi' sorrowful, but his courage, his sense of humour, his story-teller's gift never left him. He told me once about his visit to a factory where books taken out of circulation were pulped to make paper; it was a very amusing and a very terrible story. On another occasion he told me about children's homes to which orphans of living parents were sent. Our parting in May 1938 was inexpressibly sad.

Babel always spoke affectionately of his native Odessa. After the death of Bagritsky in 1936 he wrote: 'I recall our last conversation. It is time to leave other people's towns, we both agreed, time to return home, to Odessa, take a small house in the Blizhniye Melnitsy, write stories there, grow old. We saw ourselves as old men, sly old men, warming ourselves in the Odessa sunshine, by the sea on the promenade, and following women steadily with our eyes. Our desires were never realized. Bagritsky died when he was thirty-eight, without having fulfilled even a small part of what he could have done. VIM, the Institute of Experimental Medicine, has been founded in our State.

May it find a way to prevent such insensate crimes of nature from ever being repeated'.

In our anger we sometimes call nature blind. Men, too, are sometimes blind.

Babel was arrested in the spring of 1939. I learnt about it some time later – I was in Paris. Mobilized soldiers were marching, smart women walked about with gas-masks, windows were being plastered with strips of paper. And I was thinking that I had lost the man who had helped me to stride not across a May meadow, but along the very difficult road of life.

Our kinship lay in our understanding of a writer's duty and our perception of the age: we wanted the new world to find room as well for some very old things: beauty, love, art.

At the end of 1954, perhaps at the same hour when the man with the funny name Karl-Yankel and his contemporaries – Ivans, Pyotrs, Nikolases, Ovaneses, Abdullahs – were leaving the University lecture rooms in a happy crowd, the prosecutor informed me of the posthumous rehabilitation of Isaak Emmanuilovich Babel. Recalling Babel's stories I thought vaguely: it isn't possible that they won't be happier than we.

16

A READER told me that she found *The Storm* heavy going: there was Valya reciting *Hamlet*, and the next moment it was someone called Hilda carrying on an intrigue with an Italian in a small German town, and then Sergey on the banks of the Dnieper, and Micky singing a partisan song in the hills of the Limousin: it was difficult to follow the events. The reader may have been right: a novel is a park where even the wilderness is landscaped. Whereas life is a forest, and it is hard to sustain a harmoniously connected narrative.

I have been writing about Protochny Lane, and now I jump immediately to Penmarch in the department of Finistère in France. (Between Moscow and Penmarch I visited Leningrad, Istanbul, Athens, Marseilles, Paris, Berlin; all this I now omit.) What's to be done: at the age of seventeen I started on my wanderings, for many years I spent my nights in casual rooms of grimy furnished lodgings, often changed my address, travelled uncomfortably in sooty green railway carriages, rested on ships' decks, slept in planes, covered hundreds of miles on foot, and never felt I was a tourist. The purpose of my wanderings over the wide world was not to collect material for the next book: I travelled voluntarily, and also because I was sent, with money or without; at first it was milestones that flashed past, then later the snow-drifts of clouds. I quickly wore out my shoes, and bought not bookcases but suitcases – that is how my life turned out. This must be a matter of natural inclination: there are stay-at-homes and there are 'wandering Jews'; it is nothing to be proud of, nor does it call for justification.

I was in Penmarch in 1927, and if I write about it now, it is not because I want to describe the grim beauty of the sea-lashed rocks or the character of ancient Breton sculpture; indeed, the Acropolis is more perfect, and the beauty of the ocean lies in that it does not lend itself to description. But I have undertaken to describe the journey of my life, and life is made up of more than historical events; sometimes a small happening, a trivial detail, a casual meeting impress themselves deeply on one's memory and shape many things to come.

Penmarch is a small town on one of Europe's western peninsulas; its inhabitants' occupation is fishing – they catch sardines. The women work in fish-canning factories. The smell of fish permeates Penmarch – the people, the clothes, the beds and the pillows all smell of fish.

When I saw this small town for the first time I was struck by the restlessness of the natural surroundings and of its people. Nowhere else had I heard such savage seas battering at the stone gates of the land. The wind blew you off your feet. Not a single tree to soften the landscape: stones, stones and among them the white cubes of the canning factories. In the main square fishermen in red sailcloth jackets and trousers stood about. In the port gaunt masts rose like a forest in winter. The women wore long black dresses, high white caps like mitres; they could be seen from a distance like tiny lighthouses. The factory gates were shut. The fishermen had been on strike for more than a day. Their demands would have astonished anyone who knew nothing about sardine-fishing: they wanted the factory owners to buy up the whole of the catch even at a low price. The sardine is fished only in the summer months when its shoals rise to the upper layers of the water quite close to the shore. The fishermen had to make enough money in summer to see them through the winter. The factory owners belonged to an association and refused to come to an agreement with the fishermen, saying that the equipment was inadequate; the truth was that they were afraid the price of the tinned stuff would fall.

The fishermen lost the strike, they had no money put by against a rainy day – all days were rainy ones. I observed the life of the people closely, it was a hard life. Large fish often broke the fine blue nets. Although French sardines were reputed the best in the world and were an item of export, the factories were, indeed, badly equipped, and the pay was low. Artists visiting Brittany liked to paint the Penmarch women, they were attracted by the old-fashioned clothes, the headdress, the beauty of the faces; but the women's hands were raw from the salt.

A fishing-boat came into port with a good catch. The wet, chilled men were pleased. But the factories refused the fish. In vain the men pleaded, insisted, swore. In another port – Audierne – there was a factory that did not belong to the factory owners' association, so the fishermen decided to try their luck there, although the wind was freshening into a gale. Those who remained on shore said sullenly: 'What else can they do? They've got large families'.

There are meditations on the 'thinking reed'; there are the fantasies of Villiers de l'Isle Adam, there are Gauguin's landscapes of Brittany.

But there is another thing – hungry children. One of the tragedies of our epoch is the contradiction between the soaring of man's genius and age-old animal need.

Women standing on the shore saw a huge wave capsize the boat. A human storm broke out: people hammered on the locked factory gates. The owners were away, probably taking a holiday. The frightened managers rushed to the telephone begging for a detachment of gendarmes to be sent.

A motorboat from the lighthouse went out and the drowning men were saved. Everything calmed down at once. In the morning the fishing boats put out to sea, the women neatly cut off the heads of sardines and packed the fish into tins.

So nothing had happened. Why, then, did the incident impress itself on my memory? That a well-fed man does not understand a hungry one[1] I knew not only from books but from personal experience. And the life of the Penmarch fishermen did not surprise me for I had long ago seen enough of human poverty. What had given me a shock was something else.

The fishermen of Penmarch fought the ocean daily in single combat. In the cemetery I saw many crosses over empty graves visited by the widows of men lost at sea. Man's struggle against nature always ennobles, and I do not think that there exists a more beautiful myth than that of Prometheus. Shortly before I came to Penmarch the young American flyer Lindbergh had been the first to cross the Atlantic, and in the fishermen's homes I saw his photograph cut out of newspapers. In my childhood I loved the book about Nansen's *Fram*, and later in the course of my life I lived through events, both great and small, which captured everyone's imagination: Blériot crossed the Channel, Russian seamen saved the inhabitants of Messina at the time of the earthquake, Calmette discovered the antituberculosis serum, the ice-breaker *Krassin* rescued the Nobile expedition, Amundsen perished, the men from the *Chelyuskin* held out on an ice-floe, Soviet airmen flew to America over the Pole, Fleming discovered penicillin, Englishmen climbed Everest, Norwegians reached Polynesia in a raft, the Soviet sputnik went circling the Earth, and finally the world held its breath in wonder: for the first time a man, Yuri Gagarin, had taken a look at outer space.

[1] Russian saying.

Side by side with these events which grip the imagination, ordinary men struggle day and night against blind nature – fishermen and doctors, miners and civil aviation pilots.

In 1929 I met the blind engineer Dalen in Sweden. He had been doing research on the unmanned working of lighthouses and was blinded in the course of an experiment: he had given his eyes so that others should see – ships' captains, pilots, fishermen. But in Penmarch it was something else that I encountered. There are heroic deeds and there are profits: that is what is so insufferable. There are men capable of sending not only three Breton fishermen but all 'thinking reeds' to their death, simply to prevent the price of sardines, oil or uranium from falling.

I may have strayed from my narrative, but, as I have said, nothing happened in Penmarch. The incident rated a tiny paragraph in one of the papers. The fishermen went on casting their nets. The shareholders of the canning factories got their dividends.

The respite continued. The year 1927 was poor in world events. Sir Henri Deterding, who could not forgive the Soviet Union for nationalizing the oil industry, engineered the breaking off of diplomatic relations between Great Britain and the USSR. The Americans executed Sacco and Vanzetti, and in Paris a noisy protest demonstration tried to make its way to the American embassy. André Citroën announced impressively that his factories were producing a thousand cars a day. In Warsaw a White *émigré* shot the Soviet ambassador Voikov. The first sound-film appeared in the Paris cinemas, I believe it was *Don Juan*. In Berlin Hitler held a meeting of his supporters; although Germany was going through a period of prosperity, speeches were made about 'living-space in the East'. In Moscow the RAPP group kept saying 'masks must be torn off', and with the masks they included many heads. (Though at that time this went no further than newspaper articles.)

In the winter I again went to Penmarch, this time with Moholy-Nagy whose ambition it was to make a film about sardines and the men who stopped at nothing for the sake of profits; he said he had his eye on a left-wing Maecenas. The fishermen told us about the factory owners, about gales. The ocean raged. The fisherman's wives sang mournful lullabies as they rocked their babies.

Moholy-Nagy did not find his Maecenas and did not make his film. And I, on my return from Penmarch, wrote: 'Terrible is the world in which Cain is the legislator, the policeman and the judge! This year will see the tenth anniversary of the end of the World War. If nothing changes in ten years' time we shall see another far more terrible war.' I do not know why I picked on this number but I was out by only one year.

17

AMONG Petrov's manuscripts there is the plan for a book he intended to write: *My Friend Ilf.* Chapter 5 of this plan contains the following lines: 'The Red Army. The only man who wrote to me was Ilf. The general attitude of those days was: nothing and nobody is worth a thought, it's silly to write letters, the Moscow Art Theatre is mediocre, read *Julio Jurenito.* Ehrenburg brought back from Paris strips of *avant-garde* films, in slow motion. *Paris qui dort.* Passion for the cinema. *The Cabinet of Dr Caligari, Orphans of the Storm,* Mary Pickford. Films with manhunts, German films. The first foxtrots. At the same time life was thin'.

The above-quoted lines belong, apparently, to the year 1926, when I showed in Moscow fragments of films given to me by Abel Gance, René Clair, Feyder, Epstein, Renoir, Kirsanoff. I did not yet know Ilf and Petrov at the time, but I was as enthusiastic about the cinema as they were and even wrote a pamphlet: *Realization of the Fantastic*; in point of fact, I did not like German films of the Caligari type and the people I really admired were Chaplin, Griffith, Eisenstein, René Clair.

A year later I was to become more closely acquainted with the 'realization of the fantastic', or rather with the fantastics of realization. Translations of my books were published in Germany by Malik Verlag. This firm had been founded by a friend of mine, the German Communist Wieland Herzfelde. He always came to the rescue of Soviet authors. (In 1928 Mayakovsky wrote from Berlin: 'All my hopes are in *Malik*'.) One day I received a letter from Herzfelde: UFA wanted to make a film of *The Love of Jeanne Ney*, to be directed by Georg Pabst, one of their best directors.

He was an Austrian who had never been attracted by the expressionist piling up of horrors. I knew his picture, *The Joyless Street*, about the desolation of the post-war years; I liked it and was pleased by UFA's offer. Soon Pabst asked me to come to Berlin where the film was being shot.

The success of *Battleship Potemkin* had given many film directors something to think about. The public's taste for the sinister antics of various 'doctors' had cooled off. Cowboys had also begun to pall. The exotic character of the Russian Revolution seemed attractive. Cecil de Mille hastily produced *The Volga Boatmen*, Maurice l'Herbier *Le Vertige*. Pabst decided to spice the plot of my novel with picturesque scenes: a battle between White Guards and 'Greens,'[1] a session of the Soviet of Workers' Deputies, a Revolutionary tribunal, a clandestine press. Although the Germans were aware that the scenario, hurriedly cooked up by someone, teemed with incongruities, they still tried, with typical pedantry, to achieve verisimilitude in the details. For this purpose they called at the Soviet embassy and at the same time invited General Shkuro, who was performing with a company of Cossack trick-riders, to be their adviser.

On the studio floor I saw sets of Feodosia streets with arcades, a frowsty Russian hotel, a Montmartre tavern, a fashionable French lawyer's study, a Grand Duke's armchair, bottles of vodka, a statue of the Virgin, dosshouse bunks, and a lot of other props. Moscow was only fifty paces from Paris; between them rose a Crimean hill; the White Guards' café was separated from the Soviet tribunal by a French railway coach. The film was silent, which allowed Pabst to use actors of different nationalities. Jeanne Ney's part was played by a pretty French actress Edith Jehanne, Andrey's by the Swede Uno Henning, the villain Khalibiev by the German Fritz Rasp, Zakharkevich by Vladimir Sokolov, a former actor of the Moscow Kamerny Theatre.

Of the actual shooting of the film I remember three scenes. First of all Jeanne's tears. The actress could not, however hard she tried, cry naturally. A very sad song was played on the gramophone. Edith Jehanne turned away, working up a tearful mood: possibly she was recalling an unhappy love affair, or possibly some unsuccessful professional engagement. Pabst, in a leather jacket, reminded one of a battery commander as he mercilessly rejected Jeanne's tears: they fell short or overshot the mark. In the end he drove the poor girl to perfectly natural tears and, satisfied at last, pulled a ham sandwich out of his pocket. He introduced me to the film star. She smiled: 'Oh, it's you who've written this terribly sad story? My congratulations'. Of course, I ought to have responded by congratulating her on producing first-class tears, but I was confused and only grunted in reply.

[1] Lawless bands operating during the Civil War against both sides.

The second scene concerns bugs. According to Pabst's idea the bugs were to crawl up the wall and Khalibiev was to hunt and squash them; the bugs were filmed in close-up. The props department of UFA delivered a jar of magnificent bedbugs; however, the creatures proved dim-witted: they either hastily left the field of operations, or else feigned death, evidently scorched by the overpowering light. Rasp, in Khalibiev's role, never managed to squash them. The assistant director told me that the bedbugs would cost UFA a pretty penny: four hours had been wasted on them.

The third scene was a White officers' carousal. Pabst had invited ex-officers of Denikin's army for that purpose. They had carefully kept their uniforms; it is hard to say what they had been expecting – a restoration or the shooting of a film. Epaulets glittered, tall, shaggy fur caps were in prominence, the skull of the 'death battalion' ornamented the sleeves. I recalled the Crimea of 1920 and felt ill at ease.

Eighty White Guard officers were junketing in the restaurant Feodosia. There were balalaikas, gypsy songs, vodka and, in the corner, a field telephone. I could hear the extras talking among themselves: 'Haven't seen you for ages . . .' 'I say, what regiment were you in?'

Pabst commanded: 'Interpret! Let them enjoy themselves! I want them to get really tight. See the idea?' A handsome colonel was supposed to undress a woman. She suddenly objected. Pabst shouted: 'Interpret! None of that nonsense! They'll let her keep her knickers. Tell her to imagine she's on the beach'.

The Whites were paid fifteen marks a day and were pleased.

(During an interval I heard a lieutenant say: 'I've heard that Chang Tso-lin is recruiting Russians. Two hundred dollars travelling expenses and the fare'.)

To get the extras to do better Pabst promised to employ them again: next week they would be Red Army men, UFA would supply the clothes. The poor fellows were delighted; this was far more real than China.

I cannot conceal that I found it far from easy to watch this shooting of the film. In Paris nightclubs I had seen White officers dancing, singing, quarrelling and weeping for the amusement of tourists; in the stews of Istanbul I had seen hundreds of Russian prostitutes; and now these officers, convinced that they had saved their military honour, were happily looking forward to playing the part of Bolsheviks. No, it was better not to see this sort of thing.

Of all the actors, I liked Fritz Rasp best. He looked a proper villain, and when he bit a bawd's hand and laid a dollar on the bite by way of plaster, I forgot that he was acting.

Rasp soon came to Paris: Pabst was shooting street scenes. Rain set in, the shooting was constantly put off, and Rasp strolled with me about Paris, whirled in roundabouts at fairs, danced himself to a standstill with gay shop-girls, daydreamed on the quays of the Seine. We quickly became friends. He played villains but his heart was tender, even sentimental; I called him 'Jeanne'.

We met again in later years, in Berlin, in Paris. When Hitler came to power in Germany things grew difficult for Rasp. He told me that during the war years he had lived in an eastern suburb of Berlin. SS men had entrenched themselves there and were shooting at Soviet soldiers from the windows. I have already said that Rasp looked like a classical murderer. What saved him was my books with inscriptions and photographs where we figured together. The Soviet major shook him by the hand and brought sweets for his children.

I go back now to the year 1927. I tried to protest against the scenario but Pabst said that I did not understand the special circumstances of the film world, that we had to take into consideration the producers, the distributors, the public.

Out of the blue a very real situation intruded on the fantasies of the scenario: UFA found itself on the brink of bankruptcy, the deficit amounted to almost fifty million marks. At that point Hugenberg, Germany's new king, owner of hundreds of newspapers, came on the scene; he hated Stresemann, Liberalism and the dove of peace, much preferring the lopsided Prussian eagle.

The new management of UFA told Pabst to alter the scenario. Pabst objected, but it was far more difficult to come to terms with the new UFA producer than with the White extras.

I have a friend, the American film-director Lewis Milestone, who in the early thirties produced a film of Remarque's novel *All Quiet on the Western Front*. He told me that during the shooting the producer Carl Laemmle came to him and said: 'I want the film to have a happy ending'. 'All right,' Milestone replied, 'I'll give it a happy ending: Germany shall win the war'.

Laemmle was a businessman with no firm convictions. But Hugenberg cut his stiff hair *en brosse* and subsidized the *Stahlhelm*. Pabst naturally had to comply. They showed me the film.

(Hemingway watched in silence the screen version of *A Farewell to Arms*. Only when doves appeared on the screen – the director meant to show that the war was over – Hemingway got up and walked out of the hall.

I was far more naïve and could not keep quiet as I watched the screen: one moment I laughed angrily, at another abused everybody – Pabst, Hugenberg, Herzfelde and myself.)

I have no intention here of defending the plot of my novel written in 1923; there are many artificial situations in it. When writing it I not only drew my inspiration from Dickens but directly imitated him (which, at the time, I naturally failed to recognize). In any case the times had changed; you cannot write about a Bolshevik involved in illegal activities in France in 1920 as you would about a Dickensian hero whose creditors have put him in prison where he drinks porter and jokes with the gaolers. My novel dripped sentiment. The hero, the Bolshevik Andrey, engaged in clandestine work, was accused of killing the banker Alfred Ney. Andrey could have replied that he had spent the night of the murder with the banker's niece Jeanne, whom he loved. He did not do so and perished. Jeanne, who until then had been a girl like any other, comes to realize many things and a new life begins for her: the struggle against the world of lies, money, hypocrisy. She goes to Moscow. That is what happens in the book. On the screen it all looked different, in details and in essentials. In the novel, for instance, there is a horrible French detective, Gaston, with a caved-in nose. In the film the detective has an aquiline nose and a noble heart. But Gaston is not the thing that matters. Pabst devised a happy ending. In the novel the lovers walk along the streets of Paris past an old church. Jeanne takes Andrey into the church: it is dark there and she wants to kiss him. This is probably one of the most realistic scenes in the novel which contains, as I have said, many incongruities. In the film Jeanne is a devout Catholic, she takes Andrey into the church to pray to the Almighty, the Bolshevik falls on his knees and the Virgin saves him from perdition. They will marry and beget children. All has ended well and one can go home to bed.

I protested, wrote letters to the papers, Herzfelde published my protest in the form of a pamphlet, but this could in no way ruffle either the distributors or the management of UFA. The replies I got were: 'The film must have a happy ending'.

In 1926, when I was in Tbilisi, an amusing case came up before the People's Tribunal. A girl had borrowed several books from a friend and did not return them. The judge asked: 'Why didn't you return the books?' 'Because I threw them into the river.' 'How could you throw away books that belonged to someone else?' The outspoken girl replied: 'And how could Ehrenburg write *Jeanne Ney* with such a horrible end? I read it and was so upset that I threw all the books into the Kura'. The judge fined her; I do not know what influenced his verdict: the defence of private property, respect for books, or the recognition of an author's right to a tragic ending.

I came to understand the nature of the 'factory of dreams', where films are mass-produced to lull consciousness to sleep, to blunt the intelligence of millions of people. In the course of one year, in 1927, spectators could see *Love on the Beach, Love among the Snows, Betty Peterson's Love, Love and Theft, Love and Death, Love Rules Life, Love Will Find a Way, Love is Blind, The Love of an Actress, The Love of an Indian Girl, Love Mystery, Love of an Adolescent, Love of a Bandit, Bloody Love, Love at the Crossroads, Love and Gold, Love Alone, An Executioner's Love, Love at Play, Rasputin's Love.* They were shown one more variant: *The Love of Jeanne Ney.*

I wrote: 'In my book, life is badly organized, therefore it has to be changed. In the film, life is well organized, therefore one can go home to bed'.

It makes me smile when I think of those angry tirades of an inexperienced author. It has all receded into the past now, both *Jeanne* and the Hugenberg concern. One thing, however, still remains: the fear of unhappy endings.

Some people think that happy endings are a sign of optimism; in my opinion they are a sign of a good digestion and calm sleep, and not of any philosophical outlook. We have lived through days that cannot be called anything but tragic. It is easy to understand that those who wish to lull millions of their fellow-citizens to sleep should demand a happy ending from the writer or the film director. One can suffer agonies and be very unhappy and retain one's optimism. One can also be a very gay cynic.

In the story of my life, of the people I knew, there are many unhappy, even tragic endings. This is not the morbid fancy of someone with a taste for gruesome literature, but the minimum decency of a witness. A film can be re-edited, an author can be persuaded to rewrite a novel, but an epoch cannot be repainted: it is great, but not rose-coloured.

18

We took a studio in the boulevard St. Marcel; it was a superstructure built over the usual slate-grey house. The landlord, hoping to get more rent, had had electricity laid on. The tenants were asked if they would like to have electric light put in their flats free of charge; nearly all of them refused: they did not want to have the meter-inspector knocking at their doors.

Of course, far more unpleasant than the meter-inspector was the unbidden guest – history; and people were glad that it had taken itself off. It is true that when they read in the papers that Briand and Kellogg had signed a pact banning war forever, it made them smile – they were Frenchmen, after all – but at least they firmly believed that there would be no war as long as they lived; such things did not happen twice in a lifetime.

Caricaturists began to occupy themselves with the new premier Tardieu; he was easy to draw because he always had an immensely long cigarette-holder between his teeth. Maurice Chevalier sang his ditties. For months on end the newspapers described how the jeweller Mestorino had murdered a broker and then buried his body. The Surrealist Buñuel made a fantastic film showing a cow instead of a lovely woman lolling on a double bed. When the Chamber was debating the Bill on the import of oil, a deputy remarked sarcastically: 'Previously, whenever some scandal broke out people used to say: *cherchez la femme*. Today we are entitled to say: *cherchez le pétrole*'. Another deputy interrupted him: 'Don't compare oil with woman, woman is divine!' And a third added amid general laughter: 'And what's more, woman is not inflammable'.

In a very old film by René Clair, *Paris qui Dort*, an amusing device is used: the film is transformed into a collection of stills, comical ones with tragic captions: raised legs, open mouths, arms thrown out. When I look back, that is how I see Paris asleep in the late twenties.

For me those were slow-moving, long years. Money was short; I had to live as best I could, not knowing what the next day would bring. Suddenly money would arrive from *Land and Factory*, suddenly the

Danish newspaper *Politiken* would decide to publish the translation of *Trust D.E.*, suddenly royalties on *Jurenito* would arrive from Mexico. Nevertheless, it all seemed to me enchanting, for I was not hungry as I had been in the pre-war years nor did I go about in rags.

Lyuba worked hard. Modigliani's friend Zborowski organized an exhibition of her pictures, and MacOrlan wrote an introduction to the catalogue.

Irina was at school; she had begun to speak French like a Parisienne, burring her r's; when she came home from school on a hot day, she drank white wine instead of water; one day I caught sight of her on the terrace of the Café Capoulade with other girls and boys in heated discussion; I passed on thinking: here is the new generation in the new Rotonde.

My handwriting became illegible, I could not make out what I had written the day before. One day when some unexpected money arrived I bought a typewriter. I lived in a room below the studio and tapped away there from morning till night. I wrote about the people's democratic leader Gracchus Babeuf, about the conveyor-belt in the Citroën factories, about the stormy life of the Gomel tailor Lazik Roitschwanz, who had involuntarily travelled all over the world.

One day I saw Paul Valéry. It was in the restaurant *Chez Vincent* which looked like a workers' *estaminet* but was famed for its cooking. Paul Valéry was sipping Bordeaux and reluctantly favouring his companions with mournful aphorisms. His outward appearance as a man of the world served to conceal bitterness and reserve. He seemed to me to have been born at the wrong time; he was no less gifted than Mallarmé, but the acoustics had changed. Valéry's fate was not that of the *poètes maudits*: at fifty he received an academician's sword and the title of 'immortal'; but he was not, like Mallarmé in his day, surrounded by devoted and disinterested followers.

In the days of which I am speaking, Paul Valéry considered the times favourable to art: 'Order invariably oppresses man. Disorder makes him dream of the police and of death. These are the two poles on which he feels equally uncomfortable. He wants an age in which he can feel at his most free and most secure. Between order and disorder there exists a charming interval; all the good that flows from the organization of rights and duties has been achieved. One can enjoy the first slackening of the system'. This is true: fruit ripens at the end of summer and it is useless to seek it in late autumn or early spring. But Paul Valéry had made a mistake in the calendar: the 'charming interval' was long past – at the end of the nineteenth or the beginning of the twentieth century. The golden September of France had had time to yield to November fogs. Paul Valéry lived to see the Second World War and to realize that one could be left both without freedom and without order. But he was created for a sunny day, for the light chirring of cicadas, for harmony.

I was introduced to André Gide. I often met him in the thirties and shall come back to him later. At our first meeting he puzzled me. He was like an Ibsen pastor, or perhaps an elderly Chinese surgeon. I had fairly recently read his books on his journeys to Africa in which he expressed indignation at colonialism. Today these are elementary truths, but in those days I admired his courage. I mentioned Africa to him. For some reason he changed the subject to an abstract one, explaining that beauty is linked with ethical principles. At his side sat the object of his affections, a young athlete, a German, I think, or a Dutchman, with a rather vacant face, wearing shorts.

Many entertaining light books were being published in France at that time. Maurois introduced a new genre: semi-fictional biographies of famous men. Writers began to produce books of this kind on the conveyor-belt system, gossiping about the amorous adventures of eighty-year-old Victor Hugo, about Voltaire's speculations in sugar, about Sainte-Beuve's despotic mother.

François Mauriac, to whom Francis Jammes had introduced me in 1913, wrote good novels about people's evil lives. He is a Catholic, but there is much more cruel truth than Christian charity in his books. A wife who has been unfaithful to her husband tries to poison him; he survives and, fearing publicity, shuts her up in a home-made prison where she is doomed to go mad. A numerous family is waiting for a rich lawyer to give up the ghost, while he, old and infirm, goes on living despite everything, kept alive by the desire to deprive his heirs of their inheritance. In reviewing this novel Edmond Jaloux wrote: 'Inheritances and Wills are the fundamental and traditional features of French life'.

I had often thought that the old world with its craftsmanship, its libraries and museums, lived like Mauriac's hero for one thing only: it did not want to leave anything to its heirs. But having read an article in the *Literary Gazette* or met the RAPP group I told myself that there were people who did not want any legacy, who were *bezprizorny*[1] endowed with the power of censors and prosecutors.

Duhamel and Luc Durtain, after visiting Moscow, wrote books about their experiences that were intelligent, tolerant, even, as they say today, progressive. I sometimes went to see Durtain; he spoke amiably about our country, with a shade of condescension, trying to justify what he had not liked partly by the special circumstances of Russian history and partly by the mystique of the *âme slave*. Olga Forsch arrived in Paris from Leningrad. One night we were dining together, the three of us: Olga Forsch, Duhamel and I. Duhamel was explaining to us that in the end everything would come right: Soviet Russia, having calmed down, would become a semi-European state; all that was needed was to translate more French books. For some reason he remembered *versts* in the old Russian novels and said that the French Revolution had given the metric system to the world and that it was a good thing that now the Russians had also adopted it. When Duhamel left, we broke into laughter. We liked his books, but his naïvety amused us: he was apparently convinced that he could measure our path with the metric yardstick.

I used to meet Barbusse in the office of *Le Monde*. He had just written a book about Christ. His friends attacked him: 'idealism', 'mysticism'. But to the Right-wing he remained an incorrigible Communist. He was frequently ill, spoke jerkily in a low voice while his thin, aristocratic hands sketched something in the air.

I remember a dinner arranged by the PEN club in honour of foreign writers. Jules Romains presided. He tried to say something pleasant in his speech to each of the guests. He called me a 'semi-Parisian', and to Babel he said: 'You are to be congratulated on the translation of your book into French'. He did not mean to be patronizing, he simply thought that we were still living in the days of Louis XIV, Richelieu and Corneille. (In 1946 I was returning from America on the *Ile de France*. There were refugees on board from many European countries returning home after long years of emigration; among them I caught sight of Jules Romains.)

I remember the PEN club dinner with gratitude: that was where I met James Joyce and the Italian writer Italo Svevo. They had long been friends: Joyce had lived for many years in Trieste, and Italo Svevo

[1] The lost, homeless children of the Revolution.

(whose real name was Ettore Schmitz) was a native of that city. They sat next to one another at table and talked with animation.

Joyce was already famous, his *Ulysses* seemed to many a new form of novel; they compared him to Picasso. His simplicity of manner surprised me: French authors who had achieved fame comported themselves rather differently. Joyce joked and told me almost at once how when, as a young man, he had come to Paris he had gone to a restaurant and, on finding that he had not enough money to pay the bill when it came, had said: 'I'll give you an IOU, everybody knows me in Dublin'. And the waiter replied: 'I know you all right, and you're not from Dublin, and this is the fourth time you've eaten here on tick'. And he laughed boyishly.

The man was as original as his books. His sight was bad, he had some eye-disease, but he said that he had a good memory for voices. He was fond of drink, suffering from a weakness long familiar to Russian writers. He worked frenziedly and seemed to have no interest in anything but work. I was told that when the Second World War broke out, he cried in horror: 'But how am I going to finish my book?' His wife did not take his work seriously and never read anything he wrote. He had left Ireland in his early youth, with no wish to return and lived in Trieste, Zurich and Paris. And he died in Zurich; but no matter what he wrote about, he always felt he was in Dublin. I thought him honest, fanatical in his work, a man of genius and at the same time limited by 'trying to be too clever': a sort of Irish Andrey Bely, but without the feeling for history, without either a Messiah or a mission, a great mocker, whom people took for a prophet, a Swift in his talents, but a Swift in the wilderness where there are not even any Lilliputians.

By contrast, Italo Svevo was little known; only a few Frenchmen appreciated his novel *The Confessions of Zeno*. He was twenty years older than Joyce, and I met him a year before his death. Svevo was often called a dilettante: he was an industrialist and he wrote very few books in his lifetime. But the part he played in the destruction of the old forms of the novel is unquestionable: his name must be set by the side of Henry James, Marcel Proust, James Joyce, Andrey Bely. He spoke to me at great length about the influence which the nineteenth-century Russian novel had exercised on him. Joyce's novels proceeded from his spiritual experience and from the element of music; he did not know men and did not wish to know them. Svevo told me that Stephen

Dedalus, the hero of Ulysses, should have been called Telemachus; Joyce liked symbolic names, and Telemachus means in Greek 'far from the struggle'. Italo Svevo, on the contrary, sought inspiration in life; he filled out his observations with his own experiences but never narrowed them down to his ego.

Occasionally I met Charles Vildrac, a kind fellow always upset either by events or by their absence. Jean-Richard Bloch kept asking himself and others how to reconcile Nietzsche with Tolstoy, and the Russian Revolution with Gandhi.

I met a number of young writers: Aragon, Desnos, Malraux, Chamson, Cassou; I shall speak about some of them later. At the time I did not know them well enough and, what is exceedingly important, did not understand them well enough.

The Surrealists were still busy with the interpretation of dreams, prophecies, the cult of the subconscious. They sometimes organized noisy evenings, produced ultra-revolutionary manifestoes and broke up parties, all of which was very reminiscent of our own Futurists.

Later I made friends among some of the French writers but in those years I found it difficult to communicate with them, for we had no common language. Many of them longed for the storm, but the storm was an abstract idea to them: for some an apocalyptic end of the world, for others a theatrical performance. For my part, I felt the kind of nausea on dry land that one sometimes gets after a rough passage.

André Gide was then sixty. André Malraux was about thirty, but they both seemed to me, by turns, adolescents who had not yet tasted grief, and old men poisoned not by alcohol or nicotine, but by book-addiction.

In André Chamson's small comfortable flat we talked about new novels, about the feeling of the city or the influence of the cinema on literature. All the writers whom I met admired the Russian Revolution, admired it as they would a remote and unusual phenomenon. They thought highly of *Red Cavalry*, but examined Babel himself with curiosity: this 'Red Cossack' spoke excellent French, he was intelligent, but in art he was a reactionary; for instance, he loved Maupassant! Sergei Eisenstein arrived. I was present the evening he lectured at the Sorbonne: *Battleship Potemkin* was to be shown, but the Prefect prohibited it, so for two or three hours Eisenstein spoke about everything under the sun, made sardonic jokes and deeply impressed the audience by his erudition.

A daily paper, the *Comœdia*, which came out in Paris, carried little political news and devoted its columns to the theatre, to books, to exhibitions. Yet politics made themselves felt in its appraisal of these plays or novels. One day I read in it a peevish review of my book *The Life of Gracchus Babeuf*, which had appeared in a French translation. The critic ended his review with these words: 'It would be better if Madame Ilya Ehrenburg, instead of writing about the French Revolution, would give us the recipe for making Russian *borshch*.' He had been misled by the name *Ilya*, taking it for that of a woman. This was not the reason, of course, why my book irritated him: not knowing who I was, he knew very well what kind of a man Babeuf had been. I decided to send the editor a humorous retort: I pointed out that I was a man, not a woman, but that nevertheless I could give the critic-gastronome the recipe that interested him. It is true that I did not know how to make *borshch* but Elsa Triolet came to my rescue. The critic was unperturbed; my letter was not published, but in a note to his next article the critic informed his readers that Ilya Ehrenburg had turned out to be a man — 'the Bolsheviks had muddled everything up, including the male and female sexes'. And in the cookery section the editor printed the recipe for making *borshch* with the note: 'Kindly sent to us by Monsieur Ilya Ehrenburg'. I am beginning to think that I talk too much about how critics have annoyed me, that is why I recall that at times they amused me.

In the evenings we used to go to Montparnasse. The Rotonde was occupied by American tourists; we sat in the Dôme or the Coupole. Some of the older artists – Derain, Vlaminck – used to come there; at one time they had belonged to the Fauves, annihilating classical art, but had calmed down towards the end of the twenties; to us they looked like old trees that had ceased to bear fruit. I made friends with the American sculptor Alexander Calder, a huge, jolly fellow; he was full of odd conceits and worked with tin and wire. He made a figure of my pet, the Scotch terrier Bouzou, out of wire. I sometimes saw Chagall; he no longer painted Vitebsk Jews flying over the rooftops, but nudes mounted on roosters, with the Eiffel tower or without. The Norwegian, Per Krohg, silently smoked his pipe. Pascin, surrounded by flashy, shrill women, drank whisky and sketched on scraps of paper.

Young artists would come and sit at our table. I heard conversations about technique, about the sky in a landscape being too heavy, or the left corner being unfinished.

The Petersburg art expert and producer K. Miklashevsky also used to come to the Dôme. He wrote a book called *The Hypertrophy of Art*. These words often recurred to me: art surrounded me, and even though it was and still is the greatest passion in my life, I sometimes went cold: I had a feeling as if I were in a waxworks museum and that all these were wax figures.

I do not know whether it is peculiar to me or is a common experience, but in Paris and in Moscow I looked at things in a different way. In Moscow I thought about man's right to a complicated spiritual life, about the impossibility of shaping art on a single model, whereas in the Paris of the late twenties I felt stifled: there was too much verbalistic complication, artificial tragedy, contrived originality.

Paul Valéry is right: the poles are unlike Parnassus, the Helicon or the ordinary little hill in a temperate zone. But what I saw in my mind were not Paul Valéry's poles: freedom without justice or justice without freedom, but the journal of the Parisian aesthetes *Commerce* or *Na Postu*. (Several years later Jean-Richard Bloch spoke at the Anti-Fascist Writers' Congress about the true and the illusory freedom of the artist: true freedom was in society's respect for his originality, his individuality, his creative activity; illusory freedom was the vain attempt to live outside society. When I speak of freedom, I am thinking, of course, not of freedom *from* society but of freedom *within* society.)

In the last century people knew about the aurora borealis; Russian poets published the *Polar Star*. The poles were explored in the twentieth century. Birches, oaks, olive trees, palms grow between the Arctic and the Antarctic, everybody knows this and everybody should be able to realize that one can reach the pole, that one can fly over it, but that it is difficult to live there.

19

I first got to know the poet Robert Desnos in 1927, and met him again later in 1929–30. He was never a friend of mine, but his passionate nature, his gentleness and humanity appealed to me; there was nothing of the professional man of letters about him. Then, too, he was unlike those Frenchmen I met who complicated everything or, as they say in France, *coupent un cheveu en quatre*. The cult of hermetic poetry still reigned supreme when Desnos pronounced that it was necessary to understand and be understood.

He was one of the youngest and most fanatical adherents of Surrealism in its early days. He had felt an immediate response to the doctrine of the 'automatism' of creative art, of the worship of dreams. In a noisy café he would suddenly close his eyes and begin to utter, while one of his companions would take down his words. At that time he was twenty-two, and I am speaking from hearsay.

But in 1929 Surrealism began to break up, and in spite of all André Breton's efforts – he was chaffingly referred to as 'the Pope of Surrealism' – to preserve the unity of the group, the poets dispersed, each going his own way. Contrary to the suggestion of its name, Surrealism was not a soaring flight but a good launching ground, and despite the vociferous naïvety of its early pronouncements it produced such poets as Eluard and Aragon.

In 1930 Desnos declared: 'Surrealism, as Breton presents it to us, is one of the dangers to free thought, a cunning trap for atheism, the finest auxiliary in the revival of Catholicism and the pro-clerical outlook'.

What was it that appealed to me in his poetry and his personality? The answer is in Eluard's words: 'Of all the poets I have known, Desnos was the most spontaneous, the most free, he was a perennially inspired poet, who could talk as few poets can write. He was the bravest of men'.

I have said that we met occasionally, but he came to see me several times in the boulevard St. Marcel (the concierge, who regarded both me and my visitors as suspicious characters, shouted to Desnos to wipe his feet; he calmly replied: '*Madame, vous êtes un con*'.) I once went to his studio in the rue Blomet, near a Negro dancehall. The place was cluttered up with indescribable junk which, for some reason, he kept on buying at the Marché aux Puces. I can still remember a hideous wax siren. Desnos liked it very much. (Many years later I read his poem *Youki*: he called the woman he loved a siren and himself a sea-horse.)

Desnos tried to make a living by journalism; he worked as a reporter for Merle's *Paris-Matinal,* and later for other papers. He found out what the power of money means and wrote: 'Is it true that a newspaper is printed in ink? Perhaps so, but the articles are written in oil, margarine, coal, cotton and rubber, if not in blood.'

He wrote a good deal about love, and one of his best books he called *The Night of Loveless Nights*. He found his siren. I knew Youki; she was beautiful, very lively, and often came to Montparnasse with her husband, an old habitue of the Rotonde, the elderly Japanese painter Foujita. Foujita went back to Japan, and Youki married Desnos. He was touching in his love, with that light irony which is inseparable from Romanticism. When, in 1944, he was arrested by the Gestapo and sent to a transit camp, he wrote to Youki: 'My love! Our pain would be unbearable if we did not take it as a disease that will pass. Our meeting after our separation will add beauty to our lives for the next thirty years. I do not know whether this letter will reach you for your birthday. I should like to give you one hundred thousand cigarettes, twelve glorious dresses, a flat in the rue de Seine, a car, a cottage in the Bois de Vincennes, a house in the island of Belle-Ile and a fourpenny bunch of lilies-of-the-valley'. If you think of where he wrote this and how he must have felt at heart, you will understand what I mean by 'romantic irony': it was no literary trick but purity of spirit. His last poem, written in the death camp, is addressed to Youki:

> *J'ai rêvé tellement fort de toi,*
> *J'ai tellement marché, tellement parlé,*
> *Tellement aimé ton ombre,*
> *Qu'il ne me reste plus rien de toi.*
> *Il me reste d'être l'ombre parmi les ombres,*
> *D'être cent fois plus ombre que l'ombre,*
> *D'être l'ombre qui viendra et reviendra dans ta vie ensoleillée.*

In 1931 Desnos, fed up with newspapers, took a job with an estate agent. His history contains few picturesque episodes: his conduct was censored by modesty.

At the time when he was still working on the paper, he was sent to Cuba where some kind of congress was being held. Desnos fell in love with the folk-music and when talking about it would hum and drum the table with his fingers. In imitation of the anonymous Cuban poets he began to compose little songs.

In 1942 he wrote *Couplets de la rue Saint-Martin* (where he was born). It was a period when the people of Paris had learnt the meaning of a ring or a knock at the door before dawn.

> *Je n'aime plus la rue Saint-Martin*
> *Depuis qu'André Platard l'a quittée*
> *Je n'aime plus la rue Saint-Martin*
> *Je n'aime rien, pas même le vin.*
>
> *Je n'aime plus la rue Saint-Martin*
> *Depuis qu'André Platard l'a quittée.*
> *C'est mon ami, c'est mon copain.*
> *Nous partagions la chambre et le pain.*
> *Je n'aime plus la rue Saint-Martin.*
>
> *C'est mon ami, c'est mon copain.*
> *Il a disparu un matin,*
> *Ils l'ont emmené, on ne sait plus rien.*
> *On ne l'a plus revu dans la rue Saint-Martin. . . .*

I met Desnos for the last time in the spring or summer of 1939; it was very hot, we sat on an empty café terrace and naturally spoke about the same thing that everybody else was talking about: will it be or won't it? Desnos was depressed. And as we parted, he swore: '*Merde! C'est de la pure merde!*' I do not know to what the words referred – to Hitler, to Daladier or to the war.

When I came back to Paris after the war I was told that Desnos had died in a concentration camp. Later I learnt the details. He was in the Resistance, and not only wrote political verse, but collected information about German troop movements. On 22nd February 1944 he was warned by telephone: 'Don't spend the night at home'. Desnos feared that if he went into hiding they would take Youki. When they came to arrest him he calmly opened the door.

At the Sûreté in the rue des Saussaies, where he was taken, a young fascist barked: 'Take off your glasses!' Desnos knew what this meant and said: 'We're the same age. I should prefer no face-slapping – use your fists'.

A high-up Gestapo man, who was dining with some French writers and journalists, referred to the latest arrests: 'At the Compiègne camp, just imagine, we've got a poet! Wait a minute . . . Yes, Robert Desnos. But I don't think they'll deport him'. Then a journalist friend, who was well known to us (he later fled to Spain), cried: 'It's not enough to deport him! He must be shot! He's a dangerous character, a terrorist, a Communist!'

From Compiègne Desnos was sent to Auschwitz. Some of the prisoners miraculously survived; they say that Desnos did all he could to cheer the others. In Auschwitz, seeing his comrades succumb to despair, he announced that he was a fortune-teller and foretold a long life and happiness to all. He used to mumble to himself – he was composing verses.

The Soviet armies were swiftly advancing westwards. The Hitlerites drove the prisoners first to Buchenwald and then to the Terezin camp in Czechoslovakia. The emaciated men could barely walk; the SS men killed those who fell behind.

On 3rd May the Soviet army liberated the Terezin camp prisoners. Desnos was down with typhus. He struggled for a long time with death, he loved life and wanted to live. A young Czech, Jozef Štuna, who worked at the hospital to which he was taken, saw the name of Robert Desnos on the lists. Štuna knew French poetry and wondered: perhaps this was the same man? Desnos confirmed his guess: 'Yes. Poet'. During the last three days Desnos was able to talk to Štuna and to a nurse who knew French, recalling Paris, his youth, the Resistance. He died on 8th June.

I should now like to recount a talk I had with Desnos and which I have kept alive in my memory. This conversation took on a new meaning after I read the poetry he wrote in the concentration camp and learnt about the last months of his life.

We had met by chance in the boulevard Port-Royal. At that time I was living in the rue du Cotentin near the Montparnasse station. But for some reason we went in the direction of St. Marcel and found ourselves in the coffeehouse attached to the mosque. It was dark and empty inside. This was in 1931 when Desnos was happy: he had found Youki, was writing a lot, and was also outwardly much calmer.

I do not know how we got on to the subject of death. People usually avoid talking about it, each preferring to keep such thoughts to himself.

I have admitted that I shall pass over in silence many of the experiences of my mature years, those which in students' hostels are called 'woman trouble'; I also find it difficult to speak of certain thoughts which by their very nature command silence. But when I started on this volume I thought: shall I really be writing only about the 'grimaces of NEP' and the struggle for rubber? Of course, all these things stirred me, but life is broader and a good deal more complex. I had thought about death when I was a child and it frightened me; and I thought about it again as a young man, with a mixed feeling of horror and fascination, but always with romantic embellishments. Later I suddenly realized that one has got to think courageously, connect death with life.

And yet I should never have started this conversation; it was Desnos who began it out of the blue, not with reference to his own end, but with lengthy reflections about the cosmos and matter. He seemed to have found a new faith: 'In us matter becomes capable of thought, then it returns to its original state. Planets perish, certainly life on other celestial bodies also perishes. But for all that, does thought lose its value? Does impermanence deprive life of meaning? Never!'

A short while ago I was sent a book on Desnos' poetry, published by the Belgian Academy. The author, Rosa Buchole, quotes an unpublished sonnet by Desnos written by him in the concentration camp:

> . . . Sur le bord de l'abîme où tu vas disparaître,
> Contemple encore la rose, écoute la chanson
> Qu'autrefois tu chantais au seuil de ta maison
> Vis encore un instant consenti à ton être.
>
> Et puis tu rejoindras, dans l'oubli, tes ancêtres,
> Ô passante, et passée avec tant de saisons
> Tu te perdras dans la planète et ses moissons.
> Ne va pas espérer, pourtant, un jour renaître.

Une étoile filante, au fond des temps rejoint
Maintes lueurs, maints crépuscules et maints points
Du jour au bord d'un fleuve où tu te désappris.

La matière eut, en toi, conscience d'elle-même,
Au loin l'écho se tait qui répétait 'je t'aime'
Et le pur mouvement n'émeut plus nul esprit . . .

The sonnet was written in surroundings where a lie or a pose is pointless. Desnos saw the gas-chambers to which groups of prisoners were taken daily. Thinking in verse about approaching death he repeated what he had said to me in the days of his happiness. How he loved life! And his friends, and Youki, Paris, the red flags in the Place de la Bastille, and the grey houses.

The echo is silent. But nothing passes without leaving its trace: not poetry, not courage, not the shadow among shadows, not the fugitive light of a flaming star. I am no good at philosophizing, I seldom think in generalizations; this is perhaps one of my greatest weaknesses. But sometimes, railing against wasted time, I try to apprehend whatever it is that people call the sense or meaning of life: this includes, of course, the murmur of the 'thinking reed', and the echo that Desnos heard until the last moment: words of love, the glowing throb of the heart.

20

AT the age of seventeen I studied assiduously the first volume of *Capital*. Later, when I wrote *Verses about the Eves* and worked at night in the Vaugirard goods yards I developed a hatred for capitalism; it was the hatred of a poet and of a lumpen-proletarian. In the Soviet newspapers I read about 'monopolists', 'imperialists', 'the sharks of capitalism'; such were the names of the familiar yet inscrutable devil. I wanted to take a closer look at the complicated machine that went on producing plenty and crises, weapons and dreams, gold and apathy; to understand what kind of men were these 'kings' of oil, rubber and shoes, what passions inspired them; to trace their mysterious ways on which depended the destinies of millions of mankind.

I began this work in 1928 and finished it in 1932; I spent four years on what I called *A Chronicle of our Times*. I wrote *10 H.P.*, *The Single Front*, *The Shoe King*, *Factory of Dreams*, *Our Daily Bread*, *Barons of the Five Main-lines*.

I was obliged to study production statistics, reports of joint-stock companies, financial surveys; to talk to economists, businessmen, all kinds of fishy customers who knew the ins-and-outs of the world of money. This was far from enjoyable, and I realized that the work I had embarked on would bring me neither fame nor the readers' affection.

Things were happening in my private life about which I should rather not talk – except to say that I often wished I were writing about great human feelings instead of about the Stock Exchange and had to pull myself up angrily. An intelligence man is sent into enemy territory to reconnoitre, it is an unrewarding and sometimes dangerous task, but it is part of the man's profession. Nobody sent me anywhere, nobody commissioned me to write a book on the warfare between trusts: I had condemned myself to this job.

The papers wrote about the famous film-star Pola Negri's divorce from her husband, a Georgian prince; about the Prince of Wales being thrown from his horse; about Maurice Bedel's story of how sportingly, without unnecessary emotion, Norwegian *fröckens* spend a night with a gallant Frenchman; about Primo de Rivera's chilly conversation with the King of Spain; about the Smith couple, who won the Charleston marathon after dancing for twenty hours without a break.

Far more important events were developing behind the scenes. There was, for instance, the war between England and America, a war without tanks, without bombings, but with a large number of casualties. The price of rubber, a commodity chiefly derived from the British colony of Malaya, had fallen catastrophically. Then Winston Churchill, Britain's Chancellor of the Exchequer, gave battle; experts called it the 'Stevenson Restriction Scheme': the area planted with hevea was extended or reduced according to rubber world-prices. In vain did Stuart Hotchkiss, vice-president of the U.S. Rubber Co., try to reach an agreement with Churchill. In vain did the American President Hoover exclaim: 'To begin with, State intervention is immoral!' The plantations shrank, and the price of rubber rose. Hundreds of thousands of Malays starved, deprived of their beggarly earnings. The Americans exercised pressure on The Hague; the second most important rubber-producing country was Indonesia, which at that time belonged to Holland.

Hevea will not grow in the USA, but hevea trees were found in tiny Nicaragua. This small Republic was unlucky enough to try and defend its independence. Times change. In 1961 the attack on Cuba aroused the indignation of the entire world. It was different in 1922. General Sandino appealed in vain: 'Yesterday planes bombed four villages. The Yankees dropped over a hundred bombs. Seventy-two people were killed, among them eighteen women. Shame on the killers of women! The Yankees want to swallow up Nicaragua as they have swallowed Panama, Cuba, Puerto-Rico. Brothers, remember Bolivar, San-Martin! The fatherland is in danger!' The Americans laconically announced: 'Our marines corps has surrounded one of Sandino's gangs. The bandits have been wiped out with insignificant losses to the marines'.

There was also another war going on: the war for oil, between Royal Dutch and the American Standard Oil trust, between Sir Henri Deterding and Mr. Teagle. The opponents concluded a truce for common action against the Soviet Union.

The Swede Ivar Kreuger, a gifted adventurer, a romantic swindler, the Match King, having crushed his rivals, threw out a challenge to Moscow; he had the temperament of Charles XII.

Ford was at war with General Motors; General Electric with

Westinghouse. Railway magnates threw out French governments. The Shoe King, Bata, looked down on the President of Czechoslovakia.

I saw how French brokers engineered a Stock Exchange panic; in Sweden I visited Kreuger's factories; in London I took a look at Sir Henri.

Deterding was a Dutchman. He went to Java to seek his fortune and vegetated in a bank as a junior clerk. But fortune knocked at his door: he was given a job in the Royal Dutch office. Five years later Deterding became a director, ten years later he was an oil magnate. He penetrated into Mexico, Venezuela, Canada, Rumania. The English made him a baronet, and he became Sir Henri. The University of Delft elected him doctor *honoris causa*. Every year he returned to his native country for the Queen's birthday, and the Queen smiled on him with admiration. He had a hand in the *coups d'état* in Mexico, Venezuela and Albania.

He must have seen himself as the Napoleon of oil: more than once he declared that it was his mission to bring refractory Russia to her knees. He bought up the shares of the former owners of the Baku oil-fields for a song and called Soviet oil 'stolen' oil. He was behind the Arcos raid in England and the breaking-off of diplomatic relations between Britain and the Soviet Union. He succeeded in getting Rakovsky, the Soviet ambassador in Paris, recalled. He gave money to Hitler, approved of Rosenberg's books, engineered the raid on Derop (German-Russian Oil Products) which traded in Soviet oil, set up a printing shop in Berlin where Soviet paper currency was forged; he did not disdain any means. He met Krassin and offered him peace. He met Hitler and offered him war. He advised Chamberlain to come to an agreement with Ribbentrop.

He was a strong, energetic man; almost to his last day he skated and smoked sailor's shag in his pipe. He married a Russian *émigrée*. In Paris there was a 'Lady Deterding School' for the children of former oil-kings. He had steady nerves; when the world crisis broke out, he did not lose heart. On one occasion a journalist asked him what was the most important thing in life. Sir Henri replied briefly: 'Oil'.

Ivar Kreuger built up an empire out of matchboxes. He gave Poincaré advice on how to stabilize the franc, helped the Poles to put through monetary reform. In Wall Street he was regarded as a highly shrewd financier, as well as a gentleman and a model of integrity, cool-headedness and honour. In Chile he closed down the match factories and threw the workers on to the street; in Germany he persuaded the Social Democrats to prohibit the import of matches to protect the workers from unemployment: in the years of inflation he had bought up the German factories. He rather liked the Greek dictator Pangalos, but Pangalos would not give him the match-monopoly, so Kreuger lent a hand in the next *coup d'état*. He helped to overthrow the government in Bolivia. He hated the Russians: not only did they dare to make their own matches but they exported them. He was quite a man of the world and could talk about Freud and Oscar Wilde.

My book about the Match King appeared in 1930; unlike my other books of those days (which were documentary), *The Single Front* was a *roman à clef*. In the novel Ivar Kreuger was called Sven Olson. For some reason I decided to bury the Match King; he died after talking about the French premier Tardieu. The novel was translated into several languages. The year was 1931; the world crisis was mounting. Kreuger was nervous; he tried to explain to the public that the fall in share prices was caused by 'Bolshevik intrigues'; a small paragraph appeared in a paper stating that I was out to destroy the Match King. This was so silly that it did not even flatter my vanity.

French governments followed each other in rapid succession, but Tardieu was still premier when, in 1932, Ivar Kreuger shot himself. His secretary, Baron von Drachenfels, wrote in his reminiscences that on the eve of the suicide he had seen my book on the Match King's bedside table.

Kreuger was buried with full honours; the papers called him 'an innocent victim of the world crisis'. The Swedish parliament declared a moratorium. Suddenly it came to light that Kreuger had forged Italian bonds; the noble gentleman turned out to have been a crook.

I also wrote about the head of the American Kodak firm, George Eastman. His career began with the slogan: 'You press the button, we do the rest'. He advertised cameras for amateurs. In 1896 he drew a lucky number; he wrote to Edison: 'We have had some inquiries about so-called animated photographs.' He began to produce ciné-film. He became fabulously rich but trials awaited him: Agfa, a branch of I. G. Farben, put a spoke in his wheel. The Germans took the offensive, they made sure of Ford's support and of that of the National City Bank, and began to put up factories in the USA. Undismayed, Eastman accepted the challenge. His capital increased.

He was very fond of music and gave away millions to various musical institutions. His workshop conditions were harsh.

He was fifteen years old when he opened a bank account, seventy-seven when he decided to close it. He was giving a party, the conversation was about music and, of course, about the crisis. George Eastman went into the next room and shot himself. Perhaps he had remembered the aphorism of his youth: 'You press the button, we do the rest'.

Many of the real-life heroes of my books ended in suicide, as if they were not grey-haired, experienced tycoons but poets or young men in love. Capitalism survived the world crisis but some capitalists proved a great deal more fragile: they were human after all. Kreuger opened the series in March 1932. A month later the Sheffield Razor King killed himself. He boasted that he shaved the entire world, but he himself wore a beard and shot himself with an ancient sporting-rifle. In May of the same year Donald Pearson, one of the Steel Kings, committed suicide. During the war he had presented the American government with a cruiser; he was studying the means of combating submarines. He left a note saying he was tired of life.

In the same month of May, in Chicago, the Meat-canning King, Swift, jumped out of a window on to the pavement below. The Meat Trust shares had fallen in a week from seventeen dollars to nine. His family, concerned for the financial reputation of the Trust, insisted that the affair had been an accident.

Bata's personal plane stood ready to take off. The weather was unsuitable for flying, and the pilot tried to persuade the Shoe King to wait. Bata was nervous. The plane rose over Zlin and crashed.

I must say something about Tomas Bata; I spent a lot of time on him.

The Shoe King was the son of a cobbler; he drove round the villages selling shoes, then later went to America where he learnt quite a lot. War broke out. Bata began to make boots for the Austro-Hungarian army. The town of Zlin resembled a prison: reservists and prisoners of war worked in his factory. Peace came, and Bata said: 'We must dry the tears of the mothers who want to see their children shod'. He loved aphorisms, and when he became the Shoe King he adorned the walls of his factories with such slogans as: 'Let's be cheerful', 'One must work, one must have an aim', 'Life is not a romance'. On the pay-packet envelopes it said: 'Teach yourselves to make money'. Some of

Bata's saws were meant for the customers; I remember two of his maxims side by side: 'You never get corns from my shoes', and: 'Don't read Russian novels, they rob you of the joy of life'.

When I asked his permission to inspect his kingdom, he replied: 'I don't show my factories to representatives of a hostile power'. (I nevertheless saw over his domain.) Bata suffered from megalomania; he scratched his name on the skeleton of a mammoth; he announced a 'Tomas Bata Five-Year Plan'. He refused to recognize trade unions and had his own police force. He underpaid his workers and flooded the world with cheap footwear. There did not seem to be any town without the four-letter sign: 'Bata'. He was a Catholic and hated Communists.

After reading my article describing the state of things in Zlin, Bata was furious and sued me. The article had been printed in Germany, and German judges were to hear the case. Bata succeeded in getting sequestrated the royalties due to me for translations of my books and for the film.

Bata loved litigation; he entered proceedings against me in two courts. In the Civil Court he demanded costs of half a million marks (I had never seen that much money in my life). In the Criminal Court he tried to get me sentenced to prison for defamation.

Bata engaged a good counsel. I was obliged to engage one too. The Zlin workers came to my rescue: they sent me documents and photographs that proved the veracity of my article. The workers were publishing an illegal journal, *Batorok*, in which they described the Shoe King's harsh methods and the arbitrariness of the police he had organized. I produced in court a complete file of this journal too.

Bata's counsel appeared at the trial with a translation of *Julio Jurenito*; he quoted from the novel to prove my cynicism, and asserted that I not only trained rabbits but had worked as a cashier in Mr Cool's brothel. He also put in evidence articles by various Moscow critics: 'Even in Communist Russia people are revolted by the immorality and lack of principles of this man who has dared to calumniate the respected Tomas Bata'.

The court asked for additional evidence from both parties. Tomas Bata's plane crashed. Hitler came to power in Germany. The Nazis burnt my books and closed Bata's shops. As for my very modest royalties which had been sequestrated, the money went not to Bata's heirs but to the Third Reich.

I had begun to write about trusts and various tycoons in the last year of the 'fat-fleshed kine'. The world crisis suddenly broke out, and in my subsequent books I had to describe the years of the 'lean kine'.

I now want to speak about cows, not figurative ones, but real Führen red cows, though the end of this story belongs to the year 1933 and I shall have to anticipate once again.

In the summer of 1929 the Americans were disturbed by a small newspaper item: in the U.S.A. the surplus of wheat exceeded 240 million bushels. It soon became apparent that in Canada, Australia, Argentina and Hungary there was also too much wheat. The price of wheat was falling rapidly. Farmers were ruined and reduced to beggary.

The words about a world surplus of wheat should not be taken literally. Whole continents were starving. There were forty million registered unemployed in the world. The import of wheat into West European countries decreased sevenfold.

Representatives of forty-six countries assembled in Rome for a conference to discuss what was to be done with the wheat surplus. That was in the spring of 1931. People seemed to have gone mad. In Brazil they burnt coffee. In the USA they burnt cotton. It was suggested at the conference that wheat should be de-natured by means of eosin: the red grain could be used as cattle-fodder.

The propaganda began: 'Feed cattle on wheat, it is cheaper and more nourishing than maize'. Banks went on failing. Hungry peasants abandoned their fields and went to the ends of the earth in search of bread.

Cows ate wheat of the best quality – from Manitoba or Barletta. But a few months later the newspapers carried the information that there was too much butter and meat in the world; and for precisely that reason men died of hunger.

I went to Denmark in 1933. I already knew this country – quiet, green, prosperous. The Danes sold butter, meat and bacon to the English and the Germans. On the island of Laaland, in the small town of Nakskov I saw an unusual machine which turned cows into round flat cakes used as pig-food. The machine ground bones and mixed them with meat into an earth-coloured mass. (England was still buying bacon, but it was already clear that there was too much fat in the world, and if the general situation did not improve pigs would have to be done away with soon.)

The man who showed me the machine was the local vet., fair-haired honest, shy, and very depressed. All his life he had treated cows and he could not bear to see them being destroyed.

In Copenhagen I saw the hungry unemployed. I knew what hunger was and when I ran into them, I looked away.

The ancient Greeks had a legend about Sisyphus, a bandit and the King of Corinth. After his death the gods found a terrible punishment for him: he had to roll a huge stone up a hill, and then the stone rolled down again. Sisyphus robbed and murdered. But for what sins are hundreds of millions of men doomed to Sisyphus' labour? At first the area under the plough was extended; then they dyed wheat with eosin and fed it to the cows; then they began to destroy the cows and feed them to the pigs.

These four years did not pass without leaving their traces on me. I do not know whether I have succeeded in showing my readers anything, but I myself saw a great deal. Long before then, I had hated the world of money and greed, but hatred alone is not enough. I realized that it was not the character of the men that mattered: among the factory owners, the financiers, the kings of industry and the financial magnates there were both kind and cruel men, intelligent and stupid ones, pleasant and repellent ones. The matter lay not in some devilish quality of theirs but in the senselessness of the system itself. In Balzac's day capitalists were greedy, obtuse, sometimes vicious, but they built factories, bred pedigree cattle, raised the standard of living. They could be accused of heartlessness but not of folly. A hundred years had passed and the grandsons of Balzac's characters seemed to be seized by violent insanity.

I am glad I realized this and gave it thought at the onset of the thirties. Looking back on the past I think of Hitler's Germany, of the years spent in Spain, of the war. One of my most bitter experiences was at the end of 1937, when I came straight from below the walls of Teruel to Moscow. I shall describe this in the next part of my memoirs, but I should like to say here that if I could not foresee very much of what, in 1956, is common talk at the Party Congresses and in any Moscow flat, I had thoroughly grasped the obtuseness, the barbarity, the savage fanaticism of the hostile world in the days before Hitler, before Guernica, before villages were burnt down and cows shot in the fields of Byelorussia.

21

WHEN I was working on the books about the struggle between the various trusts, Eugène Merle introduced me to representatives of the business world and provided me with confidential material. He published a French translation of my novel *The Single Front*. 'Let's call your book *Bon appétit, Messieurs*,' he suggested impulsively. I was against this; in the end the novel appeared under another title invented by Merle: *Europe, Société Anonyme*.

It must not be thought that Merle was a professional publisher. He occasionally published books; he put out now a large daily paper, now a satirical journal, now financial bulletins; he wrote articles and was in business.

In his early youth he had been an anarchist and associated with Bonnot, a bandit with political convictions. I remember how some three years before the World War, Paris was roused: huge police forces surrounded the house from which Bonnot was shooting. The anarchist newspaper *Le Libertaire* wrote at the time: 'A thief, a swindler, a blackmailer invariably rebels against the established order, he understands correctly his role in society'. Many of the young Merle's friends perished. He happened to survive, sobered down, and became an integral part of political, financial and literary Paris, although he was not a deputy, a banker or a writer.

Merle had no firm political convictions but to the end of his days he was attached to the anarchists and hated the Right wing. Nor did he have those moral principles with which French schoolboys are imbued from their tenderest years. Merle had an offhand way with the great ones of this world, but with people to whom fate had been unkind – whether it was an unsuccessful poet or the messenger-girl in the office – he was good and considerate. There was something about him of the highwayman who shared his loot with the poor. What I liked about him was not only his vivacity, his gaiety and his extraordinary imagination, but also his warm heart.

He came from Marseilles where his father, who was called Angel, sold oranges. I think his father's surname was Merlo. In French *merle* is a blackbird, and when they speak of an extraordinary fellow, they use the term *merle blanc*. At one time Merle published a satirical paper *Le Merle Blanc*. He himself was rather like a bird, and a very rare one at that: between the two wars, when people were trying to establish themselves as firmly as possible on this earth, when even crooks talked philosophy, religion and lofty political ideas, Merle fluttered about, picking up an occasional seed, becoming rich for a month or a year, and at other times scouring Paris for someone likely to pay for his dinner; he gave and took away money as freely as if he were distributing smiles or picking flowers.

Some time before I met him Paris had been shaken by the brief episode of *Paris Matinal*: Merle had decided to publish a frivolous paper of a new type. He got together the best journalists. In a glass cage, in full view of the passers-by, Georges Sim sat writing a detective novel; each finished page was immediately whisked away to the printer (Georges Sim later became the famous author Georges Simenon who raised his particular genre to a genuinely literary standard). Merle threatened politicians with sensational revelations, promised the subscribers valuable prizes; then suddenly the paper ceased.

At one of our first meetings Merle said to me: 'My friend, you are too modest; in France talent isn't enough'. He made up his mind to push me, arranged a dinner in the private room of a luxury restaurant and invited the authoress Germaine Beaumont, literary editress of *Le Matin*. He also invited Desnos who was one of his protégés.

After Desnos had eaten, and more particularly after he had drunk, he started to revile *Le Matin*, turning to Mme Beaumont all the time to say: 'Of course, I don't mean you'. As befitted an early Surrealist, Desnos was fond of rather unprintable words and in characterizing *Le Matin* brought in every part of the human anatomy. Finally Germaine Beaumont could stand it no longer and left. Merle was disappointed; he had not managed to win world fame for me: 'At heart Madame Beaumont may agree with Desnos but she couldn't let her bosses be reviled, especially in the presence of a Soviet writer'.

Merle had a delightful country place not far from Paris. When he entertained, he liked to impress people, but personally he retained the simple habits of his youth. In the morning he breakfasted in the kitchen off well-salted tomatoes, then he took the train to Paris. Usually he had no money in the morning but in the train evolved grandiose plans.

He liked to dine in restaurants where they went in for Provençal cooking, was particularly fond of *ailloli* (mayonnaise with garlic) and often went to Nina's: she kept a small restaurant, outwardly very modest but in fact very expensive. Nina was both proprietress and cook, and catered for only a narrow circle of gourmets. And what people I met at Merle's table: anarchists and industrialists, Laval and Daladier, the poet Saint-Pol-Roux, Tristan Bernard, the 'prince of gourmets' Kurnonsky, Blaise Cendrars, deputies, brokers, successful lawyers, film stars.

When Laval went to Moscow Merle said to me: 'He's the most gifted crook in France, I'd like him to come to terms with Moscow because it would cost him nothing to come to terms with Hitler'. In those days Daladier was referred to as 'the Bull of Vaucluse': he was bold and assertive in his speeches. Merle said unhappily: 'The French aren't able to distinguish any longer between things that were considered their speciality. Now how can one call Daladier a bull? He's a typical steer! Ask any heifer'.

In 1933 another 'Panama' was exposed: Stavisky, who had been through the courts in 1917 for some small theft and who, fifteen years later, figured as an expert at diplomatic conferences, pocketed 650 million francs. Tardieu claimed that the swindler was protected by the Radicals. Merle chuckled: 'If they dare touch me, I'll produce stubs from Stavisky's cheque-book: Tardieu's friends also accepted bribes from him'.

Merle naturally had many enemies who were out to destroy him. The pigs he kept at his country place were named after his enemies. He was the particular target of Carbuccia, the editor of the fascist paper *Gringoire*, and a huge fat hog bore his name. One day Merle sent me a ham with the note: 'Please accept as a gift a leg of my unforgettable Carbuccia'.

I was once staying with him on 14th July. Peasants came to greet him on the National Day. He brought out ten cases of champagne and solemnly said, raising his glass: 'Long live France!' The peasants replied in chorus: 'Long live Monsieur Merle!'

He loved pathos: 'When I die, I want no sumptuous funeral, no speeches, only a standard flying at half-mast from the tower of my château.'

When guests came to his place, Merle put on an apron and cooked the dinner, but in the kitchen, too, he gave free rein to his imagination, lacing common onion soup with dry port. He was very super-stitious. The French say you must touch wood to avert the evil eye. Merle complained: 'I used to feel safe – all the café tables were made of wood. Now they're made of marble and I've got to carry a pencil stub in my pocket'. He bought some peacocks, and this coincided with a run of bad luck. He ascribed all his troubles to the peacocks: at night they came close to the house and dropped feathers on which there was an evil eye. He could not make up his mind to kill the birds or give them away: 'It's no use going against Fate'. One day some peasants came looking very upset: dogs had worried the peacocks to death. Merle brightened up and immediately set off for Paris with new magnificent plans.

I was wrong in saying that Merle had no moral principles; it would be more correct to say that his principles did not happen to coincide with those generally accepted. For instance, he did not recognize contracts and did not pay his authors; but Desnos told me that it was enough for him to hint that he was in difficulties for Merle to pay him more than had been agreed. To the end of his life he helped the children of his anarchist comrades.

When Bata sued me, Merle asked Lyuba what size shoes she wore: 'Tomorrow you'll receive twelve pairs of shoes from the association of French manufacturers'. Lyuba scolded him, then told me about it; I was angry, and strictly forbade Merle to talk about me to Bata's French rivals. Merle looked at me with a mixture of pity and admira-tion: 'My God, how simple you are! But I respect you for it.'

After visiting Moscow, Panait Istrati began to revile the Soviet Union. Merle was disgusted: 'When I first started working on a paper, we had a fine chap there, a reporter called Gustave. He had a girl-friend, beautiful, very tall and very temperamental. She made jealous scenes, and he often came to the office with bruises. One day he arrived with his face covered in blood, he was a pitiable sight. His other colleagues and I decided to talk to the lady: "Why have you hurt our Gustave?" She threw up her hands: "You want to know why? Because it's I who paid for his false teeth, and now he smiles at other women with my teeth". I'll tell you why I've recalled this story. It's not an allegory. Istrati told me that in Moscow they fitted him with lovely false teeth, and now he smiles with Soviet teeth at Poincaré and Briand.'

Merle introduced me to Madame Hanaut. She was arrested, then released, the case created rather a stir. Merle respected her and often said: 'A wonderful woman!' She told me many interesting things about the tricks of the financial magnates. As for Merle, he said over and over again: 'In ninety-nine cases out of a hundred the crook or the thief is a better man than the prosecutor or the judge'.

The Civil War started in Spain, and I left for Madrid. In the autumn I returned to Paris to pick up a van and a mobile cinema; meeting Merle I told him I was going to the Aragon front and wanted to buy a printing press but did not have enough money. Merle embraced me: 'I think of nothing but Spain now'. Next day he brought me the press and the type. He was short of money at the time, and I do not know where he got the press, but it worked excellently.

At our last meeting he looked tired and wilted: he always had a hoarse voice, and now he spoke with difficulty, though he loved to talk. He died of cancer of the throat.

Why have I written about him? After all, we did not meet very often, and the whole story has no moral; it is simply the story of a man who was like no one else. Merle was a poet at heart. Even good poets sometimes write less than good poems; Merle sometimes made out bad cheques. But he lent animation to the Paris of those years. And besides, one cannot always be writing about heroes or historical events: in life *merles blancs* are also necessary.

22

In 1927–8 the French eagerly read Panait Istrati's books. His works were translated into various languages; he was particularly popular in the Soviet Union: in two or three years no less than twenty editions of his books were published. Romain Rolland, in his admiration for the young author, called him the Balkan Gorky.

Nowadays few remember Istrati's books. Meeting him was only a casual episode in my life. I willingly listened to his highly-coloured stories; I rather liked him: he seemed kind, happy-go-lucky and at the same time cunning, something like a night club fiddler, or an anarchist fingering bombs as others tell their beads. When he was out of sight I did not think about him. Still, I should like to dwell upon his life a little: one understands a period not only through engineers who build *autobahns*, but also through smugglers who slink about in the night.

Near the Grands Boulevards in the rue de Châteaudun, there used to be an oriental restaurant kept by an obese oily Syrian. It was frequented by Greeks and Turks, Rumanians and Egyptians, Lebanese and Persians. Kebabs were served there, meat wrapped in vine-leaves, honey cakes dripping grease, fragrant kodar, aniseed vodka with water – the Arabs call this drink 'lion's milk' – Greek wine smelling of resin. I was taken there by Panait Istrati; he delighted in the dishes which had tempted him as a child; the sweetmeats, the spices, the aroma of mutton intoxicated him and he would begin to tell fantastic stories.

By nature Istrati was not a writer but a story-teller; he was an excellent raconteur, and got carried away, quite uncertain himself whether what he was saying was true or not. This often happens to gifted yarn-spinners; others listen to them with bated breath, they do not even give you time to think about the funny or sad tales; only later the listeners, according to what they feel about the narrator, say either: 'What a liar!' or 'What a rich imagination!'

Why did Istrati become a writer? He had followed a number of professions: he had served wine in a Rumanian tavern and loaded cargo on to steamers, he had decorated houses and baked bread, he had painted shop-signs and worked as a locksmith, he had been a navvy and a street photographer, taking pictures of tourists on the promenade at Nice; for many years he wandered about the world, visited Egypt, Turkey, Greece, the Lebanon, Italy, France; he could speak many languages, none of them correctly. He regarded Rumania as his homeland; his mother was a Rumanian peasant, his father a Greek smuggler. His whole life was so fantastic that probably no writer would dare to describe it. Besides, Istrati himself had no ambition to make a literary career. He liked reading and he read indiscriminately: Eminescu and Hugo, Gorky and Romain Rolland.

Finally he became disgusted with it all: the hunger, the imagination, the books, the palm-trees in Nice, the police. He tried to cut his throat with a razor. He was taken to hospital and survived. From the hospital he wrote to Romain Rolland: he wanted to tell an elderly intelligent man about his despair; being a gifted story-teller and a child at heart, he digressed and went on to recount amusing incidents. After reading the long missive Romain Rolland was delighted with the talent of the young Rumanian, and Panait Istrati found a new profession: he became a writer.

Fame and money came to him quickly. When I met him he was at the zenith of his success. He seemed to be trying to make up for lost time when he re-read enthusiastic reviews or selected unusual hors d'œuvres from the trolley at the Syrian restaurant; he had a great naïvety, a childish guile, the charm of the gypsy in Pushkin's poem, of an oriental story-teller, of a Levantine braggart and of an ordinary dreamer who, despite hunger and blows, had retained a longing for love, for the stars, for justice. He once said to me: 'I'm no writer. It's just that I've had a varied life, and I'll soon write myself out'. He said this without bitterness, like a tramp who happens to find himself in a good hotel and knows that a beggar's knapsack and a dusty road await him.

Istrati's first books which brought him fame are romantic and read like a fairy-tale. The French were amazed to find a Scheherazade in coat and trousers. Istrati wrote about his childhood, his wanderings, about Turkish harems, Rumanian *haiduks*. The *haiduks* particularly attracted him: they defended the oppressed, they had no party discipline, and noisy but weak-willed Istrati, who had been an anarchist all his life, saw them as his teachers, his elder brothers. He once told me that there had been a time when he had been enthusiastic about politics and had organized strikes; this was probably true, but one has to remind oneself that he had taken up almost everything under the sun in the course of his life.

Had he been living in the nineteenth century all would have ended well; he would have written another ten or twelve books; he would have been elected to the French Academy or he would have returned to his own country where the sentimental authoress Carmen Silva, *alias* the Queen of Rumania, would have shed tears over his novels. But this was a different century.

In 1925 Istrati went to Rumania and saw how the gendarmes brutalized the peasants, how those who had taken part in the Bessarabian rising were being shot. He returned to France full of indignation, spoke at meetings of the *Ligue des Droits de l'Homme* and wrote several angry articles. He wondered what he ought to do. There were no *haiduks*. There were Communists, and Panait Istrati directed his dreams to the Soviet Union.

He did not like to reason, nor did he know how to; he thought in fairy-tale images; he saw the world divided into two – the evil-doers and the just, the slums of beggarly Naples and a land of milk and honey. I sometimes found it difficult to talk to him: he could not believe that in Soviet Russia there could be stupid or heartless people. Scheherazade told stories in the night; as for Istrati, he began to inveigh against the modern caliphs.

He went to Moscow where he loudly admired everything and declared his intention of settling in the Soviet Union. On his return to Paris he wrote a book full of sharp, and for the most part unjust, attacks on the country which he had only yesterday glorified. The volte-face was so complete that everybody was stunned. Some spoke of 'perfidy' and 'bribery', others of 'miraculously seeing the light'.

The book on his visit to the Soviet Union is quite unlike all Istrati's other books, and it was suggested that someone else had written it. I do not know if this is true. Perhaps it was the effect of Istrati's ineradicable frivolity. The pilgrim was resentful: reality was unlike the oriental fairy-tale he had invented. He was immediately surrounded by journalists and political dabblers; before he could come to his senses he had become a card in a gambling game.

He had once told me how, in his early youth, he had travelled as a stowaway in trains and on boats; it was an exciting game to travel from the Piraeus to Marseilles without a *drachma* in his pocket. Perhaps he had wanted to cross the century as a stowaway? Anyway, he was pushed out at a strange, unfamiliar station. There were no longer any old friends or fairy-tales. He tried to justify himself, he accused, he wrote hysterical articles. Soon after, he left for Rumania. I know little about his last years. His tuberculosis grew worse, and he spent some time in a mountain monastery; he called himself an anarchist, tried to join the Nationalists, wrote about God and was overjoyed when Mauriac remembered him. He died in Bucharest in 1935. A few French newspapers carried short obituary notices; he had already been forgotten.

Many years later, at a wedding in a remote Rumanian village, I met Istrati's heroes – mutinous, gentle, they sang restless, mournful songs. They brought back to me the dreamer, the hothead, the rake who told stories in the semi-darkness of the restaurant in the rue de Châteaudun, and once again I thought about the terrible responsibility of a writer. There are no easy trades, but the hardest one is perhaps that of putting pen to paper: it is sometimes well paid but it has to be repaid with one's life.

23

In the years of which I am now writing I travelled a great deal about Europe: all over France, Germany, England, Czechoslovakia, Poland, Sweden, Norway, Denmark; I visited Austria, Switzerland and Belgium. From 1932 I became *Izvestia* correspondent and many of my trips were at any rate partly connected with newspaper work. But in 1928–9 I had not yet become a professional journalist. *Vechernaya Moskva* (Evening Moscow) sometimes published my travel notes. Nor was I a proper tourist. When I found myself in Norway, instead of admiring the picturesqueness of the fjords, I travelled to the remote island of Röst where even the pillows smelt of cod, and then to the small port of Moss where there is nothing of interest to look at and where I discussed the events of our age with a shipping agent at night; in England I visited smoke-blackened sombre Manchester and went down the antediluvian coalmines at Swansea; in Sweden I made my way to the new Arctic town of Kiruna where iron ore is mined.

I was very short of money. I was taken to Poland by a literary agent and gave lectures on literature; I was invited to England by the PEN club and by a publisher; to Vienna I went for a meeting of some cultural organization. Everywhere I found my way to cheap hotels and relied more on my legs than on taxis.

Pushkin wrote about Onegin: '. . . And started travelling without aim, accessible to only one emotion; and travel bored him, like everything else in the world'. I had no 'aim', but travelling did not bore me. One cannot, of course, travel away from oneself, and no matter where I happened to be my thoughts never left me. That may be precisely why I liked (and still like) to travel: sometimes, in some distant land, taking a close look at an alien life, you find the solution that you have been vainly seeking at your desk. I was then in my late thirties, so I can be said to have left behind me the age which is usually connected with the notion of maturity; nevertheless, I still felt myself a pupil.

Sooner or later people find themselves surrounded by those with whom they have interests or a profession in common. One cannot get away from oneself but one can, for a time, break out of the circle of habitual associates. Of course in other countries, too, I often found myself among writers; I met Maierova, Novomesky, Antoni Slonimski, Broniewski, Andersen Nexö, Nordahl Grieg, Josef Roth.

On one of the Danish islands I met Karin Michaëlis by chance. She took me to see the peasants, showed me excellent farms; she was known and respected everywhere. In early years in Russia we read her novel *The Dangerous Age*. I thought she was only interested in the problems of the female heart, but she talked about quite different things: about the unavoidable catastrophe, about the Danish farmers who had not been willing to help starving German children but now turned away when she spoke of fascism; about the threat of war, about the terrible fat sluggishness, the indifference. (Eight years later in Madrid at a writers' congress, amidst the shell explosions, someone read out a message from Karin Michaëlis from her sick-bed, and it brought back to me our conversation on a quiet green farm.)

However, when I think of moving outside the familiar circle, I recall other encounters: with an old shepherd in Tiszovcze, with Lodz weavers, with a lighthouse-keeper on the Lofoten Islands, with a Zaddik's grandson from Gora Kalwarija, with Berlin workers. Here is one of these oddly assorted meetings. In Kiruna I met a miner, a Communist, who had a Russian wife, Nusha. She gave me coffee, showed me with proud delight her refrigerator, her electric cooker, her washing-machine. The miner spoke to me in German, but he hardly talked to his wife: he knew about a hundred words of Russian, and Nusha had not yet mastered Swedish. He told me he had been to the Soviet Union with a delegation, had caught pneumonia in the Caucasus and fallen in love with his nurse. He believed that Nusha was 'the soul of the Russian Revolution', and regretted that he was unable to ask her advice on this or that occasion. But Nusha was happy to have come to a quiet, prosperous country, and said with dismay about her husband's comrades: 'They don't know what they want!' I did not want to judge her harshly, for she had experienced both grief and hunger, her brother had been shot by the Whites, her mother had died of typhus, I liked her husband, a fine and courageous man. Nusha was very sad because she had not yet learnt Swedish. A fat dictionary lay on the table but the newly-married couple seldom opened it. They both cursed their inability to communicate, never suspecting that it was to this that they owed their happiness.

This is just a rather pathetic and funny story from which no conclusions should be drawn; and I did not draw any. Industriously I noted my impressions.

Some of my trips I described and I called the book of sketches *Visa of Time*. It can easily be imagined that, for the holder of a Soviet passport who wished to travel in those days, a visa was a magic symbol. Yet in choosing this title for my book I had in mind not so much exacting consuls as the far more exacting age: I wanted to make sure which of our former ideas time would visa. My travels helped me to get rid of a number of preconceived ideas, old and new, and to see life as it really was. By talking to a Danish farmer I tried to discover the path of a Soviet writer.

The representative of the Soviet Union at the League of Nations, Maxim Litvinov, had impressed everyone with the brief axiom: 'Peace (*mir*) is indivisible.' Wandering about foreign countries I realized that the other *mir* ('world') is also indivisible.

I realized, too, that all the peoples are different, as unlike each other as individual men. The author of the preface to one of the editions of *Visa of Time* warned the readers: 'Ehrenburg holds to the outdated theory of national character. He thinks that every nation has its own "soul" which depends on its national character. In this respect Ehrenburg has a brilliant forerunner in Stendhal who, in his *Chartreuse de Parme*, also vainly tried to solve the problem of the Italian national character. This mistaken notion of a national "soul" follows logically from the whole idealistic system of Ehrenburg's outlook. Like Stendhal he is an idealist, not a materialist. He prefers not to study but to apprehend through intuition'.

(This was written in 1933. Ten years later Alexey Tolstoy published the story *The Russian Character*, various poets sang of 'Russian customs', 'Russian love' and, of course, of 'the Russian soul'. No one upbraided them, they won unanimous applause. Since the Russians were found to possess a 'soul', that is, certain national characteristics, it is evident that other peoples must have one too. I have often read how I and other writers 'overcame their former errors'. What about those who took us to task? No one writes about them. Yet they, too, disavowed many things and began to understand a great deal.)

I have never thought that the 'soul' of a people is connected with blood – I have suffered from many diseases but not from racialism. The soul of a people, that is, its character, is formed in the course of centuries, and its traits are influenced by geography, by the special conditions of social development, by the twists and turns of history. I got to know other continents later, after the Second World War, but even in the years of which I am writing I was able to make a number of comparisons. Of course, I saw that a Swedish worker reasons differently from Kreuger or the banker Wallenberg, but this did not prevent me from observing that the character of a Swedish worker differs from that of an Italian worker. There is no idealism in this; it is perfectly consistent with the existence of the class-struggle and with the principles of internationalism.

How can anyone, visiting England, fail to notice that the English like a certain seclusion, that they prefer uncomfortable cold houses with narrow stairs to a modern flat in a many-storeyed block; that, unlike the French, they do not live in the street and do not happily plunge into a crowd? Any tourist, even a not very observant one, sees that in Paris there are heaps of shops selling paints, artists' materials, many small picture galleries, while in Vienna there are hundreds of shops where they sell music and the walls are plastered with concert bills. The bourgeoisie of different countries takes its pleasures differently. An Englishman is bound to be a member of some club, and his choice of club is seldom influenced by his political sympathies; in every club there is a library with comfortable armchairs in which the members sleep, some quietly, some with gentle snores. The Spaniards also like clubs, yet they sit not in half-dark rooms but by wide windows or in the street, looking at the passers-by, and when a more or less young woman comes into view, they smack their lips. The German bourgeois loves scientific and exotic novelties; in a Berlin restaurant there was a menu showing the number of calories contained in each dish (vitamins came in later); in another the customers lay in hammocks and tropical birds fluttered above them. This would never have suited a Frenchman, who does not want to pay for frippery and prefers to have a good meal in a small, unpretentious bistro. In the English House of Commons people argue politely, while in the French Chamber I more than once saw them come to blows. I could cover hundreds of pages enumerating peculiarities of character and ways of life, but I do not intend to describe all the various countries here, and merely want to make clear what influence my travels had on my subsequent road.

I saw that people live in different ways, but the diversity of the forms of life did not hide from me what was common to them in human terms, what enables one to believe in the unity of the world. Of course the Swedes seemed to me too formal (now they have become simpler): one could not just drink a glass of vodka – a complicated ritual had to be observed. The Swedes looked cold and reserved. But then I met Axel Claussen, a former military attaché in Petersburg. He knew Russian and, after his retirement, took up translating; among other books he had translated two of mine. He was a true Swede of the old school, he loved to dine by candlelight, he pressed his small glass to his heart and never failed to recall what a pleasant evening we had spent together, even if that evening was two years ago. We saw quite a lot of each other, and I found him a warmhearted man and loyal friend who could talk well, and, what is more difficult, keep silent.

Slovakia had at first struck me as a country of the distant past: the peasant women wore charming brightly-coloured baroque costumes, in some districts the men wore aprons. The crosses in the cemeteries were painted in vivid colours like gay toys. Later I saw that the Slovak writers were preoccupied with the same problems as myself; I made many friends there, including the poet Novomeský and others.

The English seemed creatures from another planet, to everything one said they answered: 'You've got Continental tastes', or: 'That doesn't happen here though it may on the Continent'. I soon detected that the intelligentsia was unhappy; they admired Chekhov and performances of the *Three Sisters* reduced the audience to tears. I found that it was possible to have heart-to-heart talks with many Englishmen.

I have said that my meditations and doubts accompanied me everywhere: they were born long ago, in the years of the First World War when I began to think independently. Seeing the huge military organization, the speed with which people renounced thinking, the mechanization of love, the killings, death, I realized that the very conception of mankind was in danger. In the late twenties there was still no applause by command, no machine capable of turning out verse, no Auschwitz statistics, no hydrogen bombs. And I was ceaselessly, painfully thinking not about the characteristic features of this or that people, but about the character of the times.

I would not like to overburden this book with quotations from my own writings, to refer to old sketches or notes, but if I were to relate my impressions of Western Europe in 1928–9 I might unwittingly alter or supplement them in the light of experiences in later decades. This is what I wrote at the time about Germany:

'One man works out the most economical way of seating passengers in planes, another produces a lighter which lights at the slightest touch. I went to see Maximilian Harden. Apparently he is not the kind of man to manufacture improved lighters. We talked about the Russian Revolution, about the streets of Berlin. He said to me: "I'm afraid of this even tenor of life, of the absence of the unforeseen". In the public conveniences in Berlin there is a notice: "Not later than two hours after intercourse with a woman hasten to the nearest sanitary post". Berlin is the apostle of Americanism, and lighters here are objects of special veneration. Alfred Doeblin, the author of *Alexanderplatz*, invited me to his place. Mechanical civilization depressed him; he said he had been to Poland, talked to the peasants, and in backwoods villages found more humanity than in Germany.

'I went to Dessau, where the Bauhaus, the school of modern art, is now situated. A glass house; the style of the epoch has been discovered: the cult of dry reason. The dwelling houses built in this style are terrifying; they are all so alike that children get lost. They say that the new style is suitable for factories, railway stations, garages, crematoriums, but that the style for dwelling houses has not yet been found. It is hardly likely to be found: people now live at their jobs, not at home. In the architect Gropius' house there are lots of buttons and levers, household linen swoops along pipes, like *petits bleus*, plates crawl from the kitchen into the dining-room; everything has been thought out down to the last slop-pail. All is perfect and inexpressibly dull. Did we ever think when we were championing Cubism and, later, Constructivism, that one decade would separate the philosophic cubes from the completely utilitarian slop-pail? In the house of the painter Kandinsky there are numerous concessions to art: Novgorod icons, landscapes by the Douanier Rousseau, a volume of Lermontov. One of the pupils said to me: "Kandinsky is a muddlehead and a bit of a conservative".

'At the Stuttgart railway station or in a Leipzig printing works one can understand how well America has fitted in here. At an exhibition in Cologne I saw an ultra-modern church with every comfort and Cubist stained-glass windows, Christ looks like a piece of complicated machinery.'

And this about England:

'Contempt for America and the Americanization of the way of life American films, American architecture, American shops.

'Hampstead. Long streets. Cottages. All the houses alike. The English like individualism yet they are not worried by this barrack-like conformity.

'In London one keeps wondering how this immense city came into existence – on an island, isolated from the mainstream of life, among damp and spleen? How did it come to rule and oppress? How did it sway, shudder, fill cupboards with peace treaties and entertaining novels? How does it live with its ancient periwigs, the "Great Power" tone of its diplomatic notes, still confusing the issues, bluffing, but afraid of the dawn? How did it come to know American colonizers, continental disorders, unemployment, suicides? The English are conquerors, seafarers, excellent sportsmen. This does not prevent them from being extremely shy. Hence the conservatism, the attachment to ridiculous ceremonial.

'They stand confused before young and arrogant America.

'There is something here that exceeds all measure. Piccadilly and Poplar. Ostentatious luxury and the indescribable poverty of the dock area. The mines in South Wales have primitive equipment; they frequently cave in; I saw children in the pits, I was told that recently children under fourteen were forbidden to work there, these were in their fifteenth year. There is still corporal punishment in the schools. The hell of David Copperfield, but no Dickens.'

And here is Scandinavia:

'Sweden is trying to preserve her way of life, her habits. The whole of Europe is busily adopting the mechanical convulsions of a New York businessman, the Swedes resist. Probably not for long – there are only seven million people in Sweden, the rest is forest. The forests will be felled, and the people will be re-educated.

'68° N.lat. Night for three months in the year. Two hills and between them the town of Kiruna. They are still building it, the streets have not got any names yet, the number of the house serves as address. The miners live well. Many of them are Communists, Lenin's portrait hangs in the newspaper office. The miners have cars. And all around is the tundra. A luxurious church: gold statues (modern style) represent the several virtues. The newspaper says: shares of Luosvaara-Kirunovaara are rising. One of the biggest shareholders is Ivar Kreuger.

'Röst is a tiny island (Lofoten Islands). Norway has a king, he trades in butter. The mayor of Röst is a fisherman and a Socialist. However, the real rulers of the island are the cod merchants; the houses, the canning factories belong to them. The refuse is boiled and glue is extracted. The merchants own the shops, they are also the local bankers, they hire out the boats to the fishermen, they insure them; the whole life of the island is dependent on them.

'The chocolate factory Freia. The women workers are given manicures, and there are paintings by Edvard Munch in the factory canteen. Incredible noise. The owners of Freia pay low wages and have refused to recognize the trade union.

'Fogt told me that Norway has a way quite her own. I replied that on a desert island it is easy to save one's soul – that is, of course, till the first American ship arrives.

'Danish farmers live in greater comfort than the French bourgeoisie. On the walls hang old peasant plates: they have become ornamental objects. A farmer told me that in the previous winter he had read *War and Peace*: "An interesting book". After a moment's pause he asked me: "And how much would they have paid this Tolstoy?" Another farmer had had frescoes painted – the history of his life. First his father's poor cottage in the north of Jutland. Then his own house and, of course, pigs. His wife's house – her dowry. More and more pigs. Finally a luxurious two-storeyed farmhouse, trees, a legion of pigs.

'The artist Hansen, young poets, the sceptical journalist Kirkbø who writes in *Politiken*. They drink a lot, try to revive bohemian life, complain: not only are the pigs more numerous than the people, but they live better. They say that Copenhagen is fast becoming Americanized; this is not just a whim of a handful of snobs but a state of mind: no one reads poetry; painting, even the most extreme, is regarded as furniture or as stock and shares; everything has been reduced to mechanical techniques.'

But enough of this copying from old notes. Today I realize what it was that depressed me in those years. This was still before the world crisis. Hitler was making a stir in various beerhalls, but for some reason people believed in the solidity of Müller or Brüning, in the magic of the Young Plan; they believed that Remarque's novel *All Quiet on the Western Front* showed the peaceableness of the ordinary German. I saw the rebuilding of Rheims, of Arras. People were beginning to forget the war. For those who were in their thirties, stories about the Somme or Verdun were like boring ancient history; I remember someone remarking: 'There was a Trojan war too'. Peace seemed solid. In fact it was illusory. The towns had been rebuilt, but life had not.

Until 1914 certain concepts, standards, ideas still held good. Anatole France with his scepticism, his love of beauty, his slightly frigid humanism was part of the Paris landscape in 1909. In 1929 Paul Valéry seemed an anachronism. The old concepts of good and evil, of beauty and ugliness had been destroyed, and no new ones successfully created.

The influence of America is usually ascribed to her economic power: the rich and energetic uncle instructs his feckless, penurious nephews. But the Americanism which I noticed everywhere was not only concerned with economics. After the First World War people's mentality had altered. They delighted in Broadway attractions, in the silliest American films, in detective novels. The growing complexity of mechanical technique went hand-in-hand with the simplification of the inner world. It was a preparation for all the events to come: little by little resistance was being paralysed. The dark years were approaching when, in different countries, human dignity would be trampled underfoot, when the cult of force would be taken for granted; the era that loomed was that of nationalism and racialism, of torture and unheard-of legal trials, of simplified slogans and perfected concentration camps, of portraits of dictators and epidemics of denunciations, of the accumulation of first-class armaments and of the growth of primitive savagery. The post-war years had somehow, imperceptibly, become pre-war years.

24

I was sitting in the sumptuous office of the *Frankfurter Zeitung*'s editor; he wanted to publish my German sketches in his paper. He was rotund and good natured. At his side sat a thin, nervous man with mild but ironic eyes; suddenly he said to me in broken Russian: 'Tell him cutting is out of the question, and ask more – they've got plenty of money'. That was how I first met the Austrian writer Josef Roth; this was in 1927. A few years later he became known to a wide circle of readers.

Here was someone whose *curriculum vitae* would have delighted the cosmopolitan-hunters. His father was an Austrian civil servant, an intermittent drunkard; his mother a Russian Jewess. He was born in Galicia in a frontier settlement; he was regarded as a German writer, but he told everyone that he was an Austrian; when the Germans voted for Hindenburg he said: 'Well now, that's quite clear', picked up his hat and stick and went to Paris. He always lived in hotels, sometimes in good ones, but mostly in shabby and rather smelly ones. He had no furniture and no personal luggage. An old-fashioned leather bag was crammed with books, manuscripts and knives: he had no intention of cutting anyone's throat but he had a passion for knives. The *Frankfurter Zeitung* sent him as their reporter to various countries; he wrote travel notes, suffering torments over every line – he hated not to write well. He walked very fast, always with a stick that he used to trace something vaguely in the air rather than for support.

He never wrote poetry but all his books are wonderfully poetical, not with that light poetry which some prose-writers insert to embellish empty passages; no, Roth was poetical in his involved, detailed, profoundly realistic descriptions of humdrum life. He noticed everything, he never withdrew within himself, but his interior world was so rich that he could share much of it with his characters. When depicting coarse scenes of drunkenness, debauchery, of dull garrison life he endowed the people with humanity, he neither accused nor defended them, perhaps he pitied them. I shall never forget the slight, faintly rueful smile which I often saw on his face.

In 1932 I was entranced by his novel *The Radetsky March*. Thirty years later I re-read it and thought it was one of the best novels written between the two wars. It is a book about the end of Austro-Hungary, about the sunset of a society and of a people.

The twilight of the Hapsburg Empire formed and inspired many authors writing in different languages. When the empire collapsed, Italo Svevo was fifty-seven, Franz Kafka thirty and Roth only twenty-four. And yet, no matter what he might be writing about, Roth invariably returned not only to the way of life but also to the spiritual climate of the last days of Austro-Hungary.

Writers who tried to find new forms to reflect the disintegration of society between the two wars shook the structure of the novel; for example, Joyce's *Ulysses*, Kafka's *The Trial*, Italo Svevo's *Zeno*, André Gide's *Les Faux Monnayeurs*. These books are not at all alike and, besides, they are of different calibre, but they all remind one in some way of early Cubism, perhaps in their aim to dismember the world. At the same time excellent novels written in the old manner still appeared, novels about the new life told in the way of writers of the past century: Roger Martin du Gard's *Les Thibault*, Galsworthy's last novels about the Forsytes, Dreiser's *American Tragedy*. *The Radetsky March* is written in a new way, but it is a novel and a soundly constructed one. To use another comparison with painting, it recalls the Impressionists; there is much air and light in Roth's novel.

I was amazed by his feeling for people. Now what could be more commonplace or silly than the love affair of a good-for-nothing young officer with the frivolous wife of a military police sergeant? But Roth succeeded in raising it, in illuminating it from within, so that together with his hero I find myself standing, deeply moved, by the graveside of an imaginary woman whom the author was able to endow with reality, with material being.

Roth put his whole heart into his writing. The *Frankfurter Zeitung* sent him to Paris as their special correspondent. He could write novels. He loved Paris, and there I saw him in joyful mood. He came to me with his young, very beautiful wife, and I thought: now Roth has found happiness.

Soon the paper sent another correspondent to Paris, and Roth lost his job. (I should like to say a few words about this other correspondent. His name was Sieburg, he was regarded as left-wing, and he called himself Roth's friend. Sieburg wrote a book called *Like God in*

France – this is a German expression for good living; the French say *comme un coq en pâte*, and the Russians *like cheese in butter*. In this book Sieburg sang France's praises. I was still in occupied Paris when Sieburg arrived there with Abetz: his job was to keep an eye on the French journalists.)

Roth had no money. And then a terrible misfortune occurred: his wife developed a mental illness. For a long time he would not part with her, but her condition became acute, and she was taken away to a home.

I heard then from mutual acquaintances: 'Roth, poor fellow, he's off his head. He sits in the café opposite the hotel, drinks and doesn't say a word. He's become a partisan of the Hapsburgs. In fact he's in a thoroughly bad way'.

It is difficult to speak of Roth's political opinions. There were critics who saw in *The Radetsky March* an apotheosis of the patchwork empire. But it is no apotheosis, it is its funeral dirge. Roth depicted obtuse civil servants, spiritually degraded officers, the outward glitter and the poverty, the shooting of strikers in a Ukrainian village, smugglers, money-lenders, and lording it over all this an old man who is still styled 'His Imperial Majesty' and whose nose runs.

On one occasion Roth mentioned the Hapsburgs to me too: 'But you must admit, when all's said and done, that the Hapsburgs were better than Hitler'. His eyes held a nostalgic gleam. None of this was a political programme, it was merely memories of long-past youth.

He was good at describing sorrow, old age, the simple-heartedness of adolescents, age-old trees, the love of Ukrainian peasants for the land, spiritual calm, bearded Jews, death and skylarks, frogs, sunbeams piercing green shutters on a summer's day.

Terrible years set in. The Hitlerites burnt books. The *émigrés* in Paris quarrelled among themselves. Roth lived in the old Hotel Foyot in the rue de Tournon. It was decided to pull the hotel down; Roth was the only person left living in a small room on the top floor. Then he moved to another small hotel in the same street.

In 1937 I came from Spain to Paris for a few days; walking down the rue de Tournon I caught sight of Roth in a café. He called out to me. He looked ill, and one could sense that he found it an effort to go on living; but he was, as always, very courteous, and wore a neat bow-tie. A stack of saucers stood before him; he spoke quite coherently but his hands were trembling. He asked me how things were in Madrid, then said: 'I envy everybody now. Because you know what you have

173

to do. As for me, I no longer know anything. Too much blood, too much cowardice, too much treachery . . .' He ordered another glass. I was in a hurry but he would not let me go. 'Your friends take me to task. I've written a novel about an inspector of weights and measures. Perhaps it's a bad novel; I often think how devoid of talent we are. But there's something else I want to tell you. My inspector doesn't live a good life, he loses his bearings, like me. In the end he dies. He's delirious before his death and he fancies that he's not an inspector but a shopkeeper; the chief of all the inspectors, a terrifying one, comes along, and all his scales are wrong: he's been giving short measure, short weight, he's been swindling. He'll be sent to prison at once. He says to the chief inspector: "Of course my weights are lighter than they should be. But it's the same as everybody else – without that there's no making a living in our town". D'you know what the chief inspector replies to him? He says there are no true scales. Your friends say I want to justify Schuschnigg. But I was thinking about people like myself. You'll ask: "Well, why publish your novels?" I've got to live, though there's no point in it'. He ordered another glass. Then we parted and I never saw him again.

Ernst Toller committed suicide. German divisions marched through the streets of Prague. Josef Roth, dangerously ill, was taken from the café to hospital. He was forty-five but he could not go on living.

His manuscripts and his walking-stick were handed over to his friends.

25

I⊤ was MacOrlan who introduced me to Pascin; I think it was in 1928. We were dining in a small restaurant in Montmartre. I knew and liked Pascin's drawings and looked at him with unconcealed curiosity. He had the face of a southerner, perhaps an Italian; he was too correctly dressed for an artist: a navy-blue suit, black patent-leather shoes and, although by then bowler hats had practically disappeared, Pascin often wore an old-fashioned bowler. During dinner he said nothing. Mac-Orlan was talking; he spoke about the last war, about the gigantic growth of towns, about the night illuminations in the Place Pigalle, about the wandering shadows under the black bridges, calling it all 'the new romanticism'. Pascin listened at first, then he began to make drawings on the menu of MacOrlan, me, naked women. Coffee was served and brandy; he swallowed a glass as we do vodka, at one gulp, and suddenly came to life: 'Romanticism? Rubbish! It's a calamity. Why build art schools out of muck? There are a hundred brothels in the Place Pigalle. There are people sleeping under bridges; give them beds, and they'll vote and go to church on Sundays. No use dressing people in suits, fashions change. Better strip them. A naked navel tells me more than all the dresses. Romanticism? I think it's just beastliness'. He drank another glass, and then I saw a different Pascin: uproarious, restless, the Pascin who was famous for his dissipations. I was suddenly reminded of the friend of my early youth, Modigliani.

At later meetings with Pascin I found him serious, sad, even diffident, and sometimes violent, and I saw that I had not been mistaken at our first meeting: there *was* something like Modigliani about him. Perhaps it was the sudden switching from reserve, silence, concentrated work to riotous behaviour? Perhaps his mania for drawing on scraps of paper? Perhaps because both of them were always surrounded by people, and both came to know the full measure of loneliness?

Pascin had come to Montparnasse when that tragedy had already been played out. Other tragedies were being enacted far from the Rotonde. He came suddenly and too late, like a star that has lost its way. He should have been sitting with Modi, they would have understood one another. But in those days Pascin had been far away – in Vienna, in Munich, in New York.

He lived like a vagabond. In Paris he had various circles of friends; now he would spend his time with writers, artists, Derain, Vlaminck, Salmon, MacOrlan, the Surrealists; now he would dive into another world, drinking with circus people, prostitutes, crooks. Everyone knew that he was a famous artist, that his works hung in galleries: yet he tore up his drawings, he drew and he tore up; and there were few who knew where he had come from, where he had spent forty years of his life, and whether he had a native land, a home, a family.

Pascin's name was Julius Pinchas, and he was born in Vidin, a small Bulgarian town on the Danube. He was the son of a merchant, a Sephardic Jew (like Modigliani). Pascin's ancestors had originally lived in Granada until they were expelled by Ferdinand the Catholic in 1492. It is therefore very ancient history. And yet, when in 1945 I was in Sofia, I found myself sitting at table next to a former partisan who did not speak Russian and it suddenly turned out that we could converse in Spanish: the partisan was a Sephardic Jew. In his childhood Pascin spoke Spanish at home and Bulgarian with the children in the street. A short while ago I received a letter from Bulgaria, from a schoolfellow of Pascin; he sent me a photograph of the house where the small Pinchas had gone to school.

Pascin went to Vienna to study painting; in Munich he did drawings for *Simplicissimus*; he then made his way to America where he suffered great poverty. Later, money came pouring in; he spent all of it at once, giving it away to casual drinking companions, arranging wild parties, heaping presents on his models. It was as if he did not trust his fame, or trust himself; he often spoke angrily about his work.

One day he invited me to his place: 'There'll be a few friends'. Even before I reached the house I heard a roar bursting from the windows. There were too many 'friends'; people were standing on the stairs with glasses in their hands. The guests sat or lay on the drawings. A rumba blared out: it was more or less a ball in the street.

I remember that same studio in the boulevard de Clichy on an ordinary day; sofas and pouffes, dusty, lustreless – Pascin seated his models on them; disorder, empty bottles, withered flowers, books, women's gloves, caked palettes; an unfinished painting on an easel: two nude women. Pascin's colours were always toned down; the unfinished canvas seemed to have faded.

What were the grounds for the widely held belief in Pascin's licentiousness, his eroticism? Perhaps what struck people was the fact that he was always drawing or painting women's bodies; or perhaps it was Pascin's mode of life that was misleading: he would suddenly appear surrounded by a dozen women. But he was a Romantic, he fell in love in the good old-fashioned way, disarmed, defenceless before the loved one; and when one stops to reflect on his drawings, what one finds in them is not sensuality but despair; all these short-legged, plump girls with hurt eyes look like broken dolls, like that curious dolls' hospital I saw in Naples.

It is strange: he was always in the thick of discussions about art, schools, currents, yet he did not seem to notice anything: not the *Blaue Reiter*, not Cubism, not the loud Surrealists. When he read an article in a magazine where he was referred to as the leader of the 'Paris school' and where it pointed out that those who had created the 'Paris school' were neither Parisians nor Frenchmen, Pascin laughed and suggested that the critics should create a new movement – *Pentoorthoxenophagism*, that is, a fivefold devouring of foreigners.

I pored over books on economics, and in the evening went to the Coupole bar; Pascin often came there. He was becoming more and more glum; there was talk about trouble in his private life; he drank a great deal, but would suddenly shut himself up in his studio and work furiously.

He knew that I liked his work and one night he said to me: 'I've got to talk to you. We must do a book together. You write letters to me and I'll reply with drawings, I can't reply like you with caustic phrases, I'm no writer. It'll be a splendid book. We'll tell the whole truth frankly, without dressing it up. Why do I have to do illustrations for other people's books? It's silly. I illustrated Paul Morand's stories, they don't interest me. I illustrated the Bible. What for? I don't know the Queen of Sheba. You write to me about whatever you please, and I'll answer you. It'll be a book about people; today they talk about all sorts of things and they've forgotten about people. But don't put it off. It might be too late'.

I agreed, but I did keep putting it off because I wanted to finish my novel about Ivar Kreuger. (This was at the beginning of 1930.)

One bright spring morning I opened the newspaper: there was a brief report: 'The poet Vladimir Mayakovsky has committed suicide'. At the time we had not yet become inured to bereavements, and I was stunned. I did not ask myself why, I did not try to guess, I simply saw before me the huge, living Vladimir and could not believe that he was no more.

Perhaps a fortnight later – I cannot exactly remember – I saw Pascin at the Coupole. He was shouting something, but on seeing me calmed down and greeted me quietly. I was told that he was working hard in preparation for an important exhibition.

Several weeks passed, then Fotinsky dashed into the Coupole, barely able to speak: 'Pascin . . . No one knew . . . On the fourth day they broke down the door . . .'

Like Yesenin, Pascin had tried to slash his veins with a razor. He also wrote in blood, not on paper, but on the wall: 'Good-bye, Lucy!' Then, like Yesenin, he hanged himself. On the table lay a neatly written will. Pascin killed himself on the very day when the exhibition of his works was due to open.

He was buried in the remote cemetery of St. Ouen; his hearse was followed by famous artists, writers, models, itinerant musicians, prostitutes, beggars. Later we filed past the grave, each throwing a bright summer flower on to the coffin. And again it was impossible to believe that there would be no more of this melancholy man in an untidy studio, no pathetic grey-pink women on an unfinished canvas, no shouts in the Coupole, no bowler hat, no book together – nothing but the cold rooms of picture galleries.

In the autumn of 1945 I was in Bucharest. The porter told me that a Mr Pinchas wished to see me. I recalled that Pascin had a rich brother who had settled in Rumania; the brothers did not meet nor, so far as I know, did they correspond.

Mr Pinchas arrived in a carriage drawn by two small horses and took me to the restaurant Kapsha. Rumania was then in a period of transition: King Michael was still living in his palace, in the Kapsha there were still dusty bottles of *kotnar* reserved for old customers, and Mr Pinchas could drive about in his own carriage.

He told me the story of his life: 'I thought that my brother was mad, he took to art and then hanged himself. And I was rich. A pity I can't show you what trees, what birds I had in my park. I married a Rumanian aristocrat. And then fascism came. I wanted to save my property, so I transferred it all to my wife's name; she was not only a pure Aryan but also belonged to a well-known boyar family. No sooner had she got all the papers than she left me. I've no money now'. I've got a flat, furniture and the carriage. I know they'll soon take all this away from me too. Yesterday they wanted to destroy me as a Jew, tomorrow they'll want to destroy me as an exploiter. Yes, I now see that my brother was far cleverer. I read in a French newspaper that his drawings are sold at auctions, he made real money. Then he hanged himself at the right time. No, I'm the lunatic!'

Pinchas knew that I was Pascin's friend, he recalled his childhood, grew quite emotional and presented me with two of his brother's drawings: 'I've got quite a number of his things. I don't want to make money out of them. I want to give them to a museum'.

The story of the two brothers sounds like an edifying parable for commercially-minded young men. But what fills my thoughts now is the question why so many of my acquaintances, of my friends – writers, artists – voluntarily parted with their lives. They were all different and they lived in different worlds; their destinies were unlike, one cannot compare either the underlying reasons that led to the fatal act, or the immediate reason: each had his 'last drop', which, according to idle conjecture, makes the cup overflow. And yet, what is the key to the puzzle? (I do not want to list them all just now, it is too painful.)

During his last years Pascin did not know want. Critics, picture dealers, publishers came to him cap in hand. He committed suicide at the age of forty-five; he could have gone on enjoying life for a long time. Perhaps hardships and injuries had undermined his resistance. But this is not the whole story. Pasternak once said that 'lines, when mixed with blood, do murder'. I hardly think he meant the fatal reckoning to which so many genuine artists came, but simply knew from his own inner experience that poetry does not come easily. Without an acute sensibility there can be no artist, no matter how many dozen Unions or Associations he belongs to. To rouse emotions with commonplace words, to bring canvas or stone to life there must be breath, passion; that is why the artist burns out more quickly than others – he lives twice as hard for, besides his creative life, he has his own woolly, tangled life like everyone else – no whit less, believe me.

There is a recognized conception of 'hazardous occupations'; workers engaged in processes harmful to health are issued with special clothes, milk, their working hours are reduced. Art is also a 'hazardous occupation', but no one attempts to safeguard poets or artists; it is generally overlooked that, by the very character of their profession, a scratch may prove mortal.

And then you file slowly past a grave and throw a flower.

26

THE year 1931 in Paris was not gay: the economic crisis was spreading; shopkeepers went bankrupt, factory workshops closed down. All kinds of fascist organizations began to make their voices heard: the 'Croix de Feu', 'Jeunesses Patriotes', 'Solidarité Française'. Pierre Laval, the cunning Auvergnat, headed the government. The Minister of Colonial Affairs, Paul Reynaud, toured the overseas demesnes, and the cinemas showed him drinking tea with the Emperor of Annam in his palace. Presidential elections were held; Briand's candidature was unsuccessful, he was too notorious a figure, the members of parliament preferred the little-known Doumer. Joffre was buried with great pomp, and the newspapers recalled the victory of the Marne. Incidentally, the papers gave far more space to a new victory, for a French girl had won the title in the 'Miss Europe' contest. Germany continued to rearm. The film-star Marlene Dietrich won the hearts of Paris. The Royalists, assembled in the Place de la Concorde, welcomed King Alfonso XIII whom the Spaniards had chased out of Spain. Unemployment caused an increase in the number of suicides.

The International Colonial Exhibition opened. The Bois de Vincennes was crammed with visitors. Pagodas, palaces, whole villages had been built. Negroes had to work, eat and sleep in full view of the onlookers; the women suckled their babies. Sightseers crowded round them as at a zoo.

The Dutch pavilion impressed me by its businesslike candour. On the walls hung diagrams: the Indonesians worked, and money flowed through the window into a savings-bank, over which ran the inscription: 'The Netherlands'. Another map showed how the colonials held Indonesia in submission: red lights indicated military posts, green ones police posts.

The French boasted of Indo-China, Tunisia, Morocco, Senegal, Algeria.

I published an article suggesting that a native 'white village' should be built where Europeans could be shown leading their normal life: 'The Chamber – a deputy makes an impassioned speech; the Bourse –

roar of the brokers; Beauty Parlour – a lady has her buttocks massaged; a brothel – a customer stands on all fours and barks; the Academy – the "Immortals" in musical comedy uniforms greet one another'. I said that such a town was bound to have a great success in Asia and Africa, and ended with the rather sensible reflection that the colonial empires were nearing their end. Later I learnt that this article nearly got me deported from France.

But unaware of the wrath I had caused, I calmly walked about the streets of Paris with my Leica, taking pictures of houses, street scenes, people. It had become a real passion with me.

I like neither paintings that resemble coloured photographs nor photographs that try to pass for works of art: both seem to me substitutes, charlatanism.

Yet I had taken up photography with zest. I said at the beginning of these memoirs that in our day diaries and frank, informative letters have become rare. This may be exactly why readers turn so eagerly to human documents, such as Anne Frank's diary, the notebooks of Ena Konstantinova, the schoolgirl who later became a partisan, and the letters written by French hostages before their death (Babel's words come back to me: 'The most interesting things I have ever read are other people's letters').

The artist studies his model, and when he paints the portrait he is not out to reproduce the misleading external likeness but to disclose the essence. When a man sits for his portrait the fleeting changes gradually disappear from his face and it loses what we usually call 'expression'. More than once in the métro, on the last trains at night, I have watched the faces of the tired people: they held nothing fleeting, the characteristic features emerged.

Photography is quite a different thing; its value lies not in any deep disclosure of the essence but in the treacherous catching unawares of a fugitive expression, of a pose, a gesture. Painting is static, whereas photography seizes the minute, the instant, that is why it is called 'instantaneous'.

A man who is being photographed is, however, unlike himself: when he notices the camera pointed at him, he immediately changes. This is what makes the wedding couples in the show-windows of provincial photographers so unnatural. On photographs where people have tidied up their faces, as a room is tidied up for guests, there is none of the permanent character of the model or of the moment of truth.

I am very fond of Gorky's reminiscences; they contain a great deal of secret observation: it is impossible to forget the picture of Chekhov trying to catch a sunbeam in his hat. It is clear that had Chekhov noticed Gorky he would have stopped his game at once.

The photographs in which I delighted were human documents, and had there been no such thing as a right-angle viewfinder I should not have started to wander about the outskirts of Paris with my camera.

The right-angle viewfinder is built on the principle of the periscope. People did not realize that I was photographing them; at times they wondered why a blank wall or an empty bench interested me, for I never turned to face the people I was taking. A strict moralist might take exception to this, but it is part of a writer's profession – we do nothing but try and peep through a chink into other people's lives.

I had no ambitions as a press-photographer. In my book *My Paris* in which the photographs I took are reproduced, there is not a single topical one. (The date is betrayed only by a huge poster on a wall: 'Seventeen years after the aggression. Great breast-beating. Twice now the victors have been robbed. In reply to Hoover's offer we present our Five Year Plan'. This appeal was signed by the perfumer Coty who published the fascist paper *Ami du Peuple*.)

Tourists are taken to the Champs Elysées, the Place de l'Opéra, the Grands Boulevards; I did not go there with my Leica, but photographed the workers' districts: Belleville, Ménilmontant, Italie, Vaugirard – the Paris which I had grown to love in my early youth.

They are sad scenes, at times tragic, and always lyrical: old houses, old women knitting on benches, beside them couples of lovers kissing, *pissoirs*, flower-girls, workers' bistros, mothers with children, artists, concierges, tramps, lunatics, anglers, booksellers, stonemasons, dreamers.

Ten years later I wrote the novel *The Fall of Paris*; there is plenty of love and bitterness in it. And this is what I wrote in 1931: 'I do not think that Paris is more unhappy than other cities. I am even inclined to think that it is happier. How many hungry people are there in Berlin? How many homeless in dark, damp London? But I love Paris for its unhappiness, it is worth more than some happinesses. My Paris is crowded with grey slimy houses in which there are winding staircases and a jumble of strange passions. People here love uncomfortably, fully aware of the insincerity of their love, like Racine's heroes; they know as well as old Voltaire did how to laugh; they piss anywhere with unconcealed pleasure; they are immune after four revolutions and four hundred loves. I love Paris because everything in it is invented. You can become a genius: no one will help, no one will be revolted, no one will be greatly surprised. You can also die of hunger, that's your own affair. You can throw cigarette ends on the floor, keep your hat on wherever you are, revile the President of the Republic, kiss anywhere you please. These are not the articles of a Constitution but the morals of a theatrical company. How many times has the human comedy been staged here, and it invariably plays to a full house. Everything is invented in this city except its smile. Paris has a strange smile, barely perceptible, adventitious. A down-and-out sleeps on a bench; he wakes up, lights a butt-end, inhales and smiles. It is worth while tramping over hundreds of towns for the sake of a smile like that. The grey houses of Paris can smile just as unexpectedly. For this smile I love Paris, everything in it is invented except the make-believe, and the make-believe here is understandable and justified.'

The people of Paris live in the street and this facilitated my work: I photographed lovers, people gossiping, dreaming, quarrelling, writing letters, dancing, falling senseless to the ground. In those days the unemployed slept in the streets, and I took photographs of many of them. Here is one stretched out on a public bench, above him are two shop-signs: 'Undertaker's Establishment' and 'Carriages for Weddings'.

The illustrated weekly *Vu* published a page of my snapshots of concierges. I should say that many concierges are distinguished by their ill-temper. I took a very angry one on her doorstep with her scrubbing broom at the ready to beat off any attacks. This woman was infuriated; she demanded my address from the editor's office and threatened to put her broom into action. (I should also say that there are exceptions. After some passages from the first part of this book had been translated into French I received a letter from the husband of my concierge in the rue du Cotentin, where I lived for many years, saying that he read the journal of the USSR-France Friendship Society and remembered us all with affection, including my dogs.)

An album of my photographs, with some text I had written, was published in Moscow. Lissitzky designed a photomontage for it: I am taking a photograph with the aid of the right-angle viewfinder, and I have four hands – two holding the camera, the other two typing. The book was published by Boris Malkin of whom Mayakovsky had written:

'When, frightened by the futuristic pace, they put spokes in our wheels, we implored: "Save us, Father Boris!" And the enemies dispersed before the furious Malkin.' Unexpectedly I found myself among the 'left-wing' of the early twenties.

But I soon neglected my Leica, there was no time for it. During the 'phoney war' an inspector of the Security Police came and said to me: 'You have in your possession an apparatus for signalling to enemy planes'. He went to the corner where there was an ordinary apparatus for enlarging photographs and examined it for a long time.

The reason why I have been talking about *My Paris* is not that I fancy myself as a photographer or that I want to gossip about myself. When I look at the photographs I took thirty years ago, I think about my profession – literature. Of course my book of photographs is narrow in scope, it is not the whole of Paris, it is only my Paris of those days. There is a multitude of Parises. It is easier to press a button than to write, and I could have taken pictures of everything within sight, but I took only those which expressed my thoughts and feelings. I photographed a city that was not strange to me and I was not giving a tourist's impressions as a substitute for real life: I knew by heart all the streets, all the benches, all the people I was photographing.

Zaslavsky wrote: 'Ehrenburg's book discloses Paris but it also discloses Ehrenburg himself. Ehrenburg is attracted by backyards . . . The right-angle viewfinder has rendered Ehrenburg a disservice. He does indeed photograph what is "angular" '.

Some Frenchmen who studied the photographs also said that I was tendentious. I told them that there were countless books by experienced photographers showing the other Paris.

I believe that all I have said here applies not only to photography, but to literature as well; not only to Paris but to other cities too. This seems obvious to me, but here I have been writing for half a century and still keep hearing: 'You're not photographing the proper thing, comrade. Turn to the left, there's a suitable model for you with a smile of excellent quality'.

27

In the autumn of 1931 an important event occurred in my life: I saw Spain for the first time. My visit to that country was not just one among my many travels but a discovery; it helped me to understand much and to reach many decisions.

Spain had long attracted me. As so often happens, it was through art that interest became understanding. In the art galleries of various towns I had stood gazing at the paintings of Velasquez, Zurbaran, El Greco, Goya. During the First World War I taught myself to read Spanish and translated passages of the *Romancero*, the poems of Gonzalo de Berceo, Juan Ruiz, archpriest of Hita, Jorge Manrique, Quevedo. What attracted me in the writings of these dissimilar poets was some strain common to them all and inherent in the national genius of Spain (it is to be found in *Don Quixote*, in Calderòn's plays and in Spanish painting): a grim realism, an ever-present irony, the austerity of the rocks of Castile and Aragon and, at the same time, the dry heat of the human body, grandeur without magniloquence, thought without rhetoric, beauty in ugliness, and also the ugliness of beauty.

Of course, as I myself changed with the years, so did my perception of poets and painters change. When I was twenty El Greco's pictures came as a revelation. The explanation lies not only in his closeness to the painting of the turn of the century but also in his vehemence, his wonderful rendering of human suffering, of soaring and of helplessness; in those days I was absorbed in Dostoyevsky. El Greco's destiny was a strange one: he was born in Crete where the passion of robbed and humiliated ancient Greece lived on, shackled by Byzantine dogma. He was thirty-six when he went to Spain and there he found himself: the Cretan gave expression to one of the essential features of the Spanish character. At forty my admiration for him cooled; his elongated saints and martyrs began to seem to me effeminate, mannered, and the harsh juxtaposition of colours jarred on me. In the autumn of 1936 I was again in Toledo during the street fighting there. I felt I wanted to check my impressions and asked one of the soldiers to take me to the church to see the *Burial of Count Orgaz*. We found the church sealed, but the soldier let me in, and then locked the door, saying he would be back in three hours' time. It was then that I understood why I had lost my admiration for El Greco: there was too much genuine human distress about. Certain of Dostoyevsky's pages which used to move me profoundly in my youth seem to me affected today. All this, of course, belongs to my biography and not to the history of art or literature, and I recognize that both El Greco and Dostoyevsky are very great artists; but apparently one's perception of them is better in externally peaceful times when men seek fury and exaggeration in art. By contrast, I came to admire Goya when I was mature, and this again must have been partly owing to the period. There was a time when he had seemed to me a fantasist, a creator of the improbable, an Edgar Allan Poe of painting. Life, however, upset my naïve conceptions of the bounds of probability, and I suddenly realized that Goya was, above all, a realist. I am convinced that the kings, queens, counts and countesses were exactly as he depicted them. His visions of war stagger me, although I have seen wars far more terrible than the Napoleonic wars; for what interested Goya was not uniforms, not banners, not generals, but the distorted faces, the convulsions, the madness. In depicting Napoleon's soldiers shooting the rebels he conveyed not only the full measure of human suffering but also the artist's sense of outrage. He called his nightmares *Caprices*, but his phantoms stalk, kill, devour, belch and burden the earth to this day. He was not afraid of being thought tendentious; but he never simplified the world, nor did he narrow it down. I often think of his diptych in the Lille museum: a pretty young girl is reading a letter from an admirer brought to her by a maid, and then, fifty years later, there are two old women, and above them death with a broom waiting to sweep away the human refuse, simply and in a businesslike manner. Goya often pondered on death and, in a way, his pictures echo the poem of the fifteenth-century poet Jorge Manrique written after his father's death: 'Our lives are rivers, and death is the sea, into it pour so many rivers, into it flow forever our joys and sorrows, all by which man has lived . . . And so, having moved so many pawns on the chessboard and satisfied his passion; and so, having overthrown so many lords, fighting of his own free will for the King; and so, having experienced various trials, he shut himself up in his castle of Ocaña and death knocked at the door'. (How can one help being reminded of Tvardovsky's 'little old woman' who entered the Kremlin without a pass?)

People often speak about Spain's aloofness, her isolation, yet the Spanish genius, for all its singularity, has invariably tackled the problems which torment people the world over. Much has been written to prove that *Don Quixote* is a scathing satire on a long-forgotten literary genre. But centuries have passed, and the Knight of the Sorrowful Countenance rides through the world on his wretched Rosinante with greater ease than the heroes who have been flying in fast planes before they were out of their cradles.

Everyone knows Cervantes' novel but few know Juan Ruiz, the archpriest of Hita. He is a remarkable poet; he lived a hundred years before François Villon and expressed all the complexity, all the scissions of the long day to come. It is difficult to make out where he is blaspheming and where making his confession, where mocking and where weeping bitter tears. He describes everything frankly, calling a spade a spade and at the same time there is always a second level, a fourth dimension: poetry; it is precisely in this that I recognize the originality of Spanish realism, and also the very character of Spain.

It looks as though I had started at the end, but it will be easier now to explain the role Spain has played in my life.

Alfonso XIII was ousted in April 1931, but we were given our visas only in the autumn: the Spanish consul liked neither Soviet passports nor my books.

The authorities did not know what to do with us: offer us a glass of manzanilla or put us in jug. The Ministers were new to their jobs, whereas the police could claim long professional experience. The Republicans were renaming everything – institutions, streets, hotels – but the men who had served the king remained at their posts. At the railway station in Madrid we were detained and taken to the police station where they examined our meagre luggage at great length, looking for bombs, revolvers, leaflets. After that, policemen followed us everywhere; from time to time they dropped all attempts at camouflage and pulled badges out of their pockets, testifying to their official function.

The Deputy Minister of the Interior received me amiably and after a few smiles asked me to produce a list of the towns we intended to visit. Whenever we arrived in a town, police and representatives of the left-wing intelligentsia would be waiting for us at the station. The latter learnt of my coming from the police who were eager to share the sensational news, for I was the first Soviet citizen to reach Badajoz,

Zamora and San Fernando. In Madrid I had collected almost a hundred letters of introduction to enable me to find someone to talk to wherever I went. The letters were from Spanish writers, my publisher, Radical journalists, deputies, casual acquaintances.

I arrived in the small provincial town of Caceres in Estremadura and sent off several of my letters of introduction. Soon the hotel proprietress told me that there were visitors for me. I saw two elegant gentlemen looking like provincial lawyers (for some reason most of the letters were addressed to lawyers) and held out my hand; they looked embarrassed and produced badges from their pockets: 'We are the police'. An amusing conversation ensued: the policemen asked me in some alarm whether I intended to settle down for good in Caceres, and when they learnt that I would be leaving in a few days they were much moved and thanked me profusely.

Revolutions nearly always have a jubilant beginning: people sing, flock to meetings, embrace one another. I arrived when the era of embraces was over. Every day the Civil Guard shot at 'disturbers of the peace'. Strikes broke out. When I was in Badajoz there was shooting. In Madrid, too, they fired to disperse a demonstration. In Seville I met the Governor who said: 'It's time to curb the workers'. I was present at a session of the Cortes; Miguel de Unamuno made a speech; he spoke beautifully about the soul of the people, about justice. On the same day in Estremadura guards shot some poor wretch who had dared gather acorns on the land of an absentee marquis.

In Madrid, in Malaga there were blackened ruins of churches and monasteries burnt down during the spring; the people were taking vengeance for the oppression, the extortions, the payment for Masses, for the heartless stifling of the confessionals, for ruined lives, for the fog that had hung over the country for centuries. Nowhere had the Catholic Church been so omnipotent and so ferocious. In Malaga Cathedral women crawled along the stone flags praying for forgiveness, and a narrow-faced monk with cruel black eyes kept on about retribution. Catholic newspapers gave much prominence to miracles: the Virgin appeared almost as often as the Civil Guards and invariably condemned the Republic.

I visited the mountain region of Las Urdes where the people were completely cut off from the world and had never in their lives eaten their fill. Young mothers looked like ten-year-old girls, those of thirty like decrepit old women. It was difficult to imagine that within a hundred miles well-to-do drones were making smacking sounds with their lips as they stared at the beautiful women of Salamanca. In a school exercise book I saw a dictation: 'Our benefactor, the King', and on the next page: 'Our benefactor, the Republic of Workers'.

Spain was officially styled 'The Republic of All the Workers'. This title was not invented by a humorist but by the perfectly grave deputies of the Cortes. The workers of different classes worked in different ways. I travelled over vast estates in Estremadura and Andalusia. The land was largely uncultivated. The aristocratic landowners lived in Madrid, Paris or Biarritz. The stewards engaged labourers, the contract stated that they were to work from sunrise to sunset. The bourgeoisie was lazy and lived as in the old days. I saw antediluvian factories. Young dandies in gleaming shoes did not know what to do with themselves; a popular expression was 'to kill time'. The Republic had not brought about many changes: the hungry remained hungry, the rich enjoyed luxury in a stupid provincial way. Salvador de Madariaga, the Liberal writer, was a professor, a deputy, an ambassador and the Spanish representative at the League of Nations; he received 470,000 pesetas a year. I talked to Andalusian labourers who could not earn so much as 1,000 pesetas a year. The 'working' duke Ornachuelos owned 150,000 acres of land; he was fond of hunting and came to his estate for one week in the year. In Murcia there lived a gentleman who owned land valued at 25 million pesetas. He took an interest in politics and participated in the shooting of strikers. After the Revolution he went abroad leaving a steward in charge, who continued to collect the rent. Everyone was declared to be a worker: shareholders, monks, pimps.

I travelled to Sanabria, in the backwoods, with a doctor from Zamora, a kind and just man. We came to a lake where the road petered out and we had to take to donkeys. The small village with the long name of San Martin de Castañeda struck me by its extreme poverty, rare even for Spain. Among the huts we saw the ruins of a monastery. There had been a time when the peasants paid the monks quit-rent – *foro*. The monks had long ago moved to more comfortable quarters, but the peasants continued to pay 2,500 pesetas to the 'working' parasite, the lawyer José San Ramon de Bobilla, whose great-grandfather had bought from the monks the right to mulct the peasants. Later we went to another village – Riva de Lago. The villagers did not pay any *foro* but they had no land; they huddled in smoky huts and ate dried peas. The village stood on the shore of a lake well-stocked with trout, but the lake belonged to a rich woman who also owned property in Madrid; the steward kept a sharp watch that the peasants should not steal even a single little fish. A peasant woman said bitterly to the doctor: 'Well, Don Francisco, the Republic hasn't reached here yet, has it?'

(After my trip to Spain I wrote a book about what I had seen. Even before it came out in Moscow it was published in Spain under the title *Spain – Republic of Workers*. The doctor from Zamora went with my book to Riva de Lago and read out to the peasants my chapter on the hunger, the lake and the Madrid lady. On the next day the peasants flocked to the steward's house demanding that he renounce all the fishing rights immediately. Telegrams went off to Madrid, and the frightened landowning lady gave in. The peasants sent me a letter of thanks, inviting me to come to Riva de Lago and promising me a dish of trout. I may as well admit that this letter gave me great joy, for it is not often that a writer knows a book of his has brought about a change in the world. Usually books alter people, but it is a long and unseen process. While here, I realized, I had helped the peasants of Riva de Lago to do away with an age-old injustice. No matter if my part in this was fortuitous, no matter if the village was a small one and the victory short (the fascists are not likely to have left the trout to the rebels); all the same, I think of this incident from time to time and it affords me a good deal of pleasure.)

The Civil Guard went on shooting. The deputies went on making fine speeches. The people were unarmed. The Socialists hesitated. The Anarchists threw bombs. In a small Andalusian village I was present at a heated dispute between the mayor and the schoolteacher: the teacher was in favour of the Third International, the mayor of the Second. Suddenly a labourer broke into the discussion: 'I'm for the First International, for Comrade Miguel Bakunin'. In a tiny newspaper published by the workers of Jerez I read that the Spaniards should take their inspiration from Kropotkin's principles. In Barcelona I met the leader of the FAI (*Federación Anarquista Ibérica*), Durruti. We were sitting in a café. Durruti showed me a revolver, hand-grenades: 'They don't frighten you, do they? I won't be taken alive'. His opinions were utterly fantastic, but he impressed me by his courage, his integrity, his nobility of outlook. I did not know that five years later, on the Aragon front, he would aim his revolver at me – 'Now I'm going to shoot you' – nor that in the end we should become friends.

There was much I did not know in those days, but one thing was clear: this was the first act of a tragedy, others would inevitably follow. I remember a sullen-looking officer being pointed out to me in Madrid: 'There's Sanjurjo'. Of course, I could not foresee that, five years later, together with Franco and Mola, he would drown Spain in blood, but in 1931 I wrote: 'The commander of the Civil Guard, General Sanjurjo, works in silence. Forty-eight thousand guards shoot from time to time, they are preparing for a general massacre'.

Speaking of the autumn of the year 1931, about the farce and the tragedy, I have still not said anything about the most important matter: the people. In these memoirs I sometimes try to show the people I have met in the course of my life; I try to do this with love, with loyalty, I try to write less as a detached chronicler than as one who recalls those friends of his who are no longer among the living. I speak of people whom the reader knows something about – writers, artists, public men. (There are, of course, in my heart other cherished images, but they are known only to an intimate circle and I would not be able to illustrate my descriptions by reference to books or pictures.) But about Spain I should like to speak as I would about a person close to me and dear.

I spent the years of the Civil War in Spain, and at that time got to know its people really well; but I liked them straight away, in 1931. Pablo Neruda called one of his books *Spain in the Heart*. I should like to echo these words: Spain is, indeed, in my heart, and not casually, not temporarily, not as a guest, lit up by the Bengal lights of historic events, not as a visitor surrounded by photographers and reporters, but something that is my own, dear to me both in the loud years and in the voiceless ones, forbidden, shackled. I have the right to say it now: Spain is in my heart till death.

Quite a few of my pages will be devoted to the Spanish war. But just now I am relating my first meeting with Spain. In 1931 I wrote: 'I have a scratchy pen and a bad temper. I am accustomed to write about those phantoms – as contemptible as they are pitiful – who rule our world, about fictional Kreugers and living Olsons. Poverty, humiliated and envious, I know well, but I have no words with which to speak fittingly of the noble beggary of Spain, the peasants of Sanabria, the labourers of Cordova and Jerez, the workers of San Fernando and Sagunto, the paupers in the south who sing melancholy flamencos, and in Catalonia dance the *cerdana*; about those who face the Civil Guards unarmed, those who are now held in the gaols of the Republic, those who struggle, and those who smile; the stern, courageous, gentle people. Spain is not Carmen and toreadors, not King Alfonso and Lerroux's diplomacy, not Blasco Ibañez' novels, not any of those things that are exported abroad, together with pimps from the Argentine and Malaga from Perpignan; no, Spain is twenty million ragged Don Quixotes, it is barren rock and bitter injustice; it is songs as mournful as the rustling of the dry olive-tree; it is the deep roaring of the strikers among whom there is not a single blackleg; it is kindness, compassion, humanity. A very great country, it has succeeded in preserving its youthful ardour despite all the efforts of inquisitors and parasites, despite the Bourbons, the sharpers, the pettifoggers, the English, the hired assassins and the titled scoundrels'.

Many things struck me in Spain during my first fleeting encounter with that country, and what impressed me above all was the feeling of personal dignity in a poverty-stricken, perpetually hungry and largely illiterate people. On a bench in Seville I saw a respectable bourgeois and an unemployed man; the poor fellow took a pea-sausage out of his bag and offered it sociably to his neighbour. Idlers lolled on the terrace of an expensive Madrid café. A woman with a baby was trying to sell lottery tickets (one form of begging). The baby started to cry; the woman sat down calmly at an empty table and gave her breast to the baby. No one evinced the smallest surprise at her behaviour. I thought involuntarily: they would have turned her out, not only at the Café de la Paix in Paris, but even at the Metropole in Moscow.

In a poverty-stricken hamlet in Sanabria I wanted to pay a peasant woman for some apples; she absolutely refused to take my money. My companion, a Spaniard, said: 'You could give it to the baby, but I'm afraid he'll put the coin in his mouth and swallow it. And the older children won't take it'. A young boy, a shoeblack, seeing me standing outside a tobacconist's closed for the dinner hour, pulled a cigarette out of his pocket: here, have a smoke. Near Murcia a peasant whom I wanted to pay for some oranges shook his head: 'A smile is worth more than pesetas'.

(The disinterestedness of the Spanish peasants has always impressed foreigners. Martin Andersen Nexö told me that he had spent his early years in Spain; he had no money, and the peasants invariably set a plate of soup before him: 'Go on, eat!')

A porter at a railway station said to me: 'I've earned something already today. I'll go and fetch my mate'. I took a pair of shoes to a cobbler; he asked his wife if they had enough for their dinner, and when she said yes, he directed me to another cobbler. The unemployed received no dole. I asked them how it was that they did not starve to death and they said: 'The comrades . . .' An Andalusian labourer cut a loaf in two and gave half to his neighbour who was out of work. The workers of Barcelona paid part of their wages to their trade union for the unemployed, without appeals, without phrasemongering, just simply, humanly.

I have said that Spain was twenty million Don Quixotes in rags. I return to this image, not only because I love Cervantes' novel, but also because in the Knight of the Sorrowful Countenance the whole spiritual charm of Spain can be found. Here are some lines I wrote in 1931: 'This is a country where you can persuade people that a windmill is an enemy and they will go and fight it – that is the history of human error. But you cannot persuade them that a man is a windmill: he will not obediently wave his arms as sails. In this country live people – real, live people.'

Several years later, when great, advanced, well-organized nations were preparing, one after the other, to capitulate to fascism, the Spanish people accepted the unequal battle: Don Quixote remained true to himself and to human dignity.

Spain helped me to overcome many doubts. I knew that I should more than once fall into error, sometimes along with everyone else, sometimes on my own. Very well. So long as one does not become a small screw, a robot, a stage-windmill!

28

BEFORE me lies a faded photograph. A wine cellar in the small town of Montilla, not far from Cordova. Our stout host, Lyuba and Ernst Toller. The day was cheerful and full of light. We stayed for a long time drinking wine in the cool cellar. Toller told amusing stories. And the host told us that there was no better wine in the world than Montilla: 'It's no accident that they make Amontillado in Jerez, but in Montilla no one would think of making Ajerezado'. This sounded convincing, and it was an occasion to recall Edgar Allan Poe's story about the cask of Amontillado. There was also another type of Montilla to be tasted; for a few hours one could forget what lay behind and ahead of us. We were in no hurry to leave. Toller said: 'One doesn't leave Paradise, one's turned out of it', and we went back to Cordova late that night.

(During the war Loyalist forces were stationed near Montilla. A copy of the army sheet had to be printed; there was no newsprint and the sheet appeared on the thin wrapping-paper the stout wine-merchant used for his bottles; through the military communiqués one could read the words: 'Montilla is the best wine in the world'.)

It seems odd that I should have begun my story about Toller with Montilla. After all, I had first met him in Berlin in 1926 or 1927; we also met in other cities – in Paris, in Moscow, in London – and had many serious talks. But my memory brings back the few days we spent together in Andalusia (we met in Seville and parted in Algeciras) when Toller was happy. He had had a hard life; he argued, persuaded, cursed, believed, despaired, and at the same time he was a dreamer, a joker, even a sybarite, and when speaking of this poet-fighter the first thing I recall is that briefly snatched 'break'.

Toller was handsome; he looked like an Italian, gay and melancholy, like the perpetually unlucky heroes of Neo-Realistic films. His main quality was, I think, an exceptional gentleness, though his life was a very troubled one. People are made of different stuff: some are moulded out of wax, others are hewn out of rock; this is not a matter of their convictions but of their nature, and a man often chooses a path that is

195

at variance with the stuff of which he is made. I have known men of strong will, iron nerves, bold in a sort of way, who settled down happily in a backwater; the steel rusted. Toller was made for meditation, for producing tender lyrics, yet from early youth he chose the strenuous path of action, of struggle.

He did not live very long – only forty-five years – but there does not seem to have been a single day when someone did not write about his mistakes. He made no protest and once he said to me: 'Actually I've made a hundred times more mistakes, but they don't know half of them. Besides, all they count are those idiotic things I did on my own. But what about the times when everybody made mistakes together?'

Some of Toller's mistakes were dictated by his age, and also by the times; he not only recognized them but redeemed them in action. When the First World War broke out he was not yet twenty-two; he was delicate and was rejected by the army, but finally he managed to get sent to the front, in France: he believed that Germany was defending a just cause. Barbusse was forty at the time, and he believed that France was defending a just cause. Toller very soon realized that he had believed a lie, had yielded to the general psychosis, and he began to denounce the instigators of the war. He was arrested, sent to a military prison and later to a lunatic asylum.

He was a young and gifted poet: Rilke and Thomas Mann praised his work. He could have gone on writing, glorifying the Revolution in verse. But he elected to do something else. He became one of the leaders of the Bavarian Revolution, the Deputy Chairman of the Central Committee of Workers' and Soldiers' Deputies. Critics have often said, and still say, that Toller was not politically experienced enough. That is certainly true. But he happened to have an enlarged conscience, a burdensome quality for which its owners always pay the price.

The Bavarian Soviet Republic lasted a bare few weeks; the Whites broke into Munich. A large reward was set on Toller's head, and he was denounced. At the trial he said: 'The fight has started and will not be stopped by the bayonets or the courts martial of the combined capitalist governments of the entire world.' He was twenty-six, and he spent five years in the Niederschönenfeld prison. I remember the emotion with which in Berlin we watched the play he had written in prison: it was like a letter smuggled out into the free world.

In those years German reaction triumphed everywhere: not only in

Bavaria, but in Berlin, in Saxony, in Hamburg; no doubt the White General von Epp knew how to conduct military operations better than the poet Toller. One may regret that the Bavarians did not have their Shchors or their Chapayev, but it is silly to blame Toller: he knew that the battle was unequal and that what lay ahead was not honour, not power, but the violence of the suppressors. He was called a 'sentimental revolutionary'; but then he had not come into the revolution from the underground groups, where for years tactics had been thought out and plans elaborated, but from poetry; in politics he remained to the end of his days a self-taught man.

When he came out of prison in 1924 he already had a name in literature; his plays were produced in various countries. Perhaps their success is to be explained not only by their intrinsic merit as art but also by their burning themes; perhaps the audiences' applause was at times not so much for the play as for the author's own qualities. Nevertheless, Toller was neither an impostor nor a casual guest in the literary world. Writers as dissimilar as Thomas Mann, Gorky, Romain Rolland, Sinclair Lewis and Feuchtwanger were warm in their tributes. He could have set to work and become an established, recognized author. But he was permanently restless. He did not, and indeed could not, become a soldier of the revolution, but he carried on partisan forays; his conscience proved stronger than his fondness for the thousand trivialities that go to make for a lighthearted, carefree life.

He had a very complex personality; had it not been for his rare charm, he would probably have set everyone against him; as it was, his opponents suddenly relented. One very exacting critic said in my presence: 'Well, you see, it's – Toller. What can you do about him?'

I recall a muddled but satisfying conversation we had in Cordova. Before that we had been strolling about the town for a long time; a local town-planner explained to us that the meandering streets of Cordova had been planned by experienced architects, Arabs and Jews: even on a hot July noon there was always shade on one side of the street. Our conversation started from there. Toller was full of admiration: 'They gave some thought to the ordinary pedestrians, fancy that!' Then we passed on to the relations between man and society. Toller smiled: 'I've written several mediocre plays about that. Perhaps I'm not a real dramatist, but I feel drawn to the theatre, the illusion of action. It's easy to make a reputation. Ibsen demonstrated this in a masterly fashion: the "Enemy of the People" is a profoundly honest man. But look at all the careerists, egotists, nonentities who shout about the "rights of the individual". They confuse the issue. The struggle ought to be for the kind of society where all men have the right to sunshine and shade. I've seen how power, even if it's ephemeral, distorts a man'. He told some amusing stories from his past, about German writers, and suddenly his face clouded over: 'I'm afraid the Nazis will get the upper hand. You know what that means? War . . .' He recalled the book about swallows which he had written in prison: 'No, I'm not talking about my verses. But do you remember the letter from the worker, a stonemason? The prison governor gave orders to destroy the swallows' nests, and the worker, occupying the next cell, wrote that the swallows took a lot of trouble making their nests and were, in general, honest, hardworking birds. Of course the letter didn't make the prison governor change his mind. It's a thumbnail sketch of the war: the destruction of nests . . . It's frightening to think of the future.'

In Spain he told me that he wanted to write a play about a modern Don Quixote and Sancho Panza in the world of money, arrogance and stupidity. He did not write the play. He told Feuchtwanger that he was writing a novel about Demosthenes, the man who wanted to protect Greek culture against barbarity. He did not write the novel either. He was always in a fever, beginning things and then abandoning them: they were troubled times and his heart was too responsive.

Abroad, Toller always defended the Soviet Union, even the things he did not like about our country. He had friends in Moscow with whom he had long, frank talks. At our last meeting he said to me that the one hope he had was Moscow.

In the book about his youth, written in 1933, after Hitler had come to power, Toller wrote about his love for Germany; his expressions of feeling are not unlike those of Tuwim: 'Do I not love this country? Did I not amid the luscious landscapes of the Mediterranean long for the sparse sandy pine forests, for the beauty of the quiet, hidden lakes of the German North? Was I not moved to gratitude for the poetry of Goethe and Hölderlin when, as a lively youth, I read it? The German tongue – is it not my tongue, the language in which I think and feel, speak and act, part of my being, motherland that reared me, in which I grew up? . . . In every country blind nationalism and absurd racial arrogance raise their heads. Must I take part in the madness of our time, in the patriotism of our epoch? . . . The words "I am proud to be a

German", or "I am proud to be a Jew", seem to me as senseless as if a man should say: "I am proud of having brown eyes." '

No, he did not give way to the madness of our time; he remained a genuine internationalist. Not long before the tragic end, sick, in despair, he was collecting money for the famished children of Spain in a kind of frenzy, wresting pounds and dollars from selfish, indifferent people and, in a short time, he had collected over a million dollars. Even harsh men softened when Toller spoke to them – he exuded kindness.

A short time before the Spanish War, in June 1936, I was in London at the meeting of the Congress of the International Association of Writers for the Defence of Culture. After the meeting Toller took me home with him; he lived in a small house in the suburbs. As usual, he was busy with a number of urgent, troublesome jobs; as usual, he was surrounded by people, yet lonely, more lonely than in his prison cell, a fact that he confessed to me at once. He looked to me thinner and more despondent. He was irritated by what he regarded as the callous attitude of the English and French to the German refugees. The papers spoke about Hitler if not favourably, at any rate with restraint, and Toller angrily marked articles in red pencil and then threw the papers on the floor. Suddenly, in a childish way, he complained that London was cold in winter, that one could not get warm. I remember his words: 'Now we are in for a winter longer than Moscow's, longer than Lapland's – a winter for the next ten or twelve years. There are people with strong roots, they'll endure. But the others are being killed by the frost, one by one'.

Toller held out for another three years. I saw him for the last time in Paris. For a moment I thought he seemed better; he even tried to joke. That was when he was collecting money for the Spanish children. When we were saying good-bye, he asked me: 'Can you sleep without taking something? It's terrible at night – you see everything so much more sharply than by day. Ah, well . . . We'll probably be meeting again soon. I've decided to give up living in America, it's too far, you can't even open your mouth about what's going on in the world without someone being shocked and advising you to see a psychoanalyst. *Au revoir!*'

We did not meet again. In the spring of 1939 there was a PEN Club congress in New York. At the gala dinner Toller tried to rouse the others by reminding them of Mühsam's fate, of Ossietzky's, of

Tucholski's. A few days later, on 22nd May, he hanged himself in his bathroom.

I think of Toller and smile gently to myself: a kind man, a friend, a poet not only in literature but in life. I love his book of poems written in prison, *The Swallow-Book*.

> *O Master Masons of the Gothic churches,*
> *Curb your pride!*
> *You needed quadrants, rarely chiselled stones,*
> *Pilasters, shafts and capitals and painted glass.*
> *Your mortar was*
> *The misery of multitudes who spent themselves*
> *To dedicate your pile*
> *To worlds to come,*
> *to Death.*
>
> *But see the swallows:*
>
> *From dust and slime, from blades of grass and horsehair,*
> *Religiously they build their vaulted nest,*
> *And dedicate it*
> *To this earth,*
> *To Life.*

Toller himself was like a swallow, perhaps like the 'one swallow' that comes too soon and does not make a summer.

29

In 1931 I visited Berlin twice, at the beginning of the year and again in the autumn. Nothing exceptional was happening at the time. The Catholic moderate, Brüning, was Chancellor; despite the crisis life went on as before. Yet in my memory these visits have remained like the kind of dream, senseless and at the same time full of significance, one vainly tries to unravel on waking up in the middle of the night. I find it difficult to give a connected account of Berlin in 1931; it would be more honest if I were to reconstruct disjointed pictures, not particularly noteworthy in themselves, but which have stayed in my mind; they will explain why I mention these visits at all.

In the train there is an elderly German with a shaven neck and a stiff collar, he is reading a bulky newspaper. I already know that he is a commercial traveller, that he sells some kind of patent writing-pads. I ask him when we are due in Berlin. He takes a timetable out of his briefcase: 'At eleven-thirty and thirty seconds'. Then he picks up his paper again and says quietly and without emotion: 'This is the end. The end of absolutely everything'.

The editor of the Radical *Neues Tagebuch* is entertaining writers for dinner. All is as it should be: lots of expensive glass, good wine, flowers, talk about Feuchtwanger's latest novel, about Hoover's moratorium, about the insidious quality of Rhine wine. And suddenly the host says, exactly like the commercial traveller: 'You know, everything's coming to an end quite soon'.

They are showing the film of Remarque's novel *All Quiet on the Western Front*. The Nazis are indignant: 'German soldiers died without a word, but the hero of the film yells like a Pole. It's libellous!' I have already seen the film in London, but a friend insists: 'Today the Nazis mean to have a go. They'll be properly dealt with'. We watch the film. Suddenly hysterical screams break out. The lights go on. No one is beating up anyone, but the screaming continues. The spectators leave. What happened was that the Nazis had released a hundred mice in the cinema.

The owner of a tobacco factory says to me: 'I don't know who'll come out on top – the Nazis or your friends. By and large it's all one to me – I've long ago transferred my money to Zurich. I'm very much taken by Gandhi at the moment. I like Tolstoy. But it's the wrong time for it. The Germans want a dictatorship, grandeur, what's under the surface doesn't matter. When you buy a packet of my cigarettes half of what you pay is for the packing. Hugenberg gives money for propaganda against capitalism. A farce? No, he understands the German character. In Zurich I've opened a small branch. The air's good there, it's quiet. Romain Rolland wrote about Gandhi in Switzerland, I can understand that.'

I spend several evenings with Rudolf (I have forgotten his surname). He works for the *Rote Fahne* and knows the northern districts of Berlin well; he has shown me quite a lot. Rudolf is the son of a monarchist customs' official; he was a student but did not finish his studies; his wife left him. He took to politics as a boy, as early as 1919; he told me how he thrashed a big bully who tried to shout down Karl Liebknecht. Rudolf is very tall, lean, with a large Adam's apple and soft blue eyes. He speaks in newspaper phrases, constantly says 'Let's get down to facts', but his voice touches me: he believes in what he is saying.

Rudolf explains to me: 'Let's get down to facts: seven million unemployed. Capitalism's disintegrating under our very eyes. They all know they're done for. You know what they're after now? To meet some member of your Trade Delegation: perhaps Moscow'll buy something. In fact, all eyes are on Moscow. Have you noticed all the Russian translations? Yesterday I could only get a seat to see the *Road to Life* with the greatest difficulty. The audience were very bourgeois; that's understandable enough – the workers haven't got any money. Emil Ludwig's going to Moscow in a fortnight's time, he's decided to write a book about Stalin. I've been given the job of making an inquiry; I've talked to writers, they're all coming to us – Ernst Glaeser, Plivier, Oskar Maria Graf. Let's get down to facts: last year we polled 4,600,000 votes, the Nazis 6,400,000. But how many of those who voted for them will follow us? Three-quarters. After all, they're workers, they vote for the Nazis because they hate capitalism. It's a good thing our leaders have taken the mood of the masses into account. We're now putting forward a programme for the national liberation of Germany. The Nazi workers have begun to listen to us. Of course, there are some crazy ones, but I'm convinced that healthy instinct will tell in the end. No, this isn't 1919. When you next come to Berlin you'll find a different Germany'.

Oskar Maria Graf is stout and goodnatured; he has the naïve eyes of a child. He listens to discussions and says nothing. Maria Grosshenner had introduced me to Malik's new author who is called Domela. He posed as a Hohenzollern prince, landed in prison and wrote a book about it all. Maria tells me what a success this book, *The False Prince*, is having. The author laughs gently. He is garrulous; he likes literature, the revolution and men; to women he is indifferent.

The Kurfürstendamm is ablaze with lights; here you would never think that there is a crisis. The shop windows display the most luxurious goods. The expensive restaurants are packed. The writer Walter Mehring, a melancholy humorist, takes me to the restaurant Kakadu. Small tables under palms. Parrots briskly let their droppings fall on the plates; the snobs are happy: they think they are in Tahiti. Seeing my embarrassment Mehring laughs: 'You can see now, can't you, that the Germans have gone mad? You needn't eat here, we'll have dinner in an ordinary restaurant. The parrots are really nothing. I'm thinking of the time when there'll be bombs dropping on us. But what can one do? They break windows, they deface walls, and they're not tramps – they're philosophers, every housebreaker quotes Nietzsche. The parrots are philosophers too'. All round us there is talk of business, first nights, society scandals, anything you like except politics. Mehring taps his glass with his knife – it is time to go; and a parrot peevishly squawks in an old man's voice: 'The bill! The bill!'

By chance I come across a left-wing journalist whom I had first met four years ago at the time of the shooting of *Jeanne Ney*. He was then cruelly satirizing the Nazis, calling Hindenburg 'a stupid mammoth'. He has risen in the world: now he is the literary editor of a big newspaper; he has aged, he has acquired a limp. We touch upon politics: 'It's not all that simple. We underestimated a great deal. Of course there are sinister elements among the Nazis, but on the whole it's a healthy movement'. A friend of mine tells me later that the journalist is in trouble: there was a paragraph in a Nazi newspaper about his past: it was no accident that he had slandered Ludendorff, his mother was a Jewess and he had weak legs, which was a true sign of Jewish ancestry. He was now busy with genealogy, collecting documentary proof of the purity of his ancestors' 'Aryan' blood.

The northern part of the city is unlike the Kurfürstendamm: here the crisis is manifest in the houses, in the people's clothing, in their faces. Cold winds are blowing from the Baltic; winter is on its way. There are many homeless; they sleep in all kinds of dosshouses, some sleep in the streets; this is in fact forbidden, but there are little-used paths in the Tiergarten, waste plots, cellars. The huge window of a snack-bar near the Alexanderplatz: a variety of tempting dishes is displayed: potatoes with bacon, sausages, a leg of pork. (*'Kolossal! Nur 50 Pfennig'!*) People stand for a long time gazing at the window. Some go in and gobble something hastily.

An unemployed man tells me that he is getting a dole – nine marks a month. Fortunately he is single. A bunk in a dosshouse costs fifty pfennigs; generally he has to spend his nights in the street. 'The Nazis give meat soup free, my pals say it's good there, but it turns me up.'

Berlin has become the paradise of international homosexuals: it costs nothing to find a good-looking youngster here. At night under the Unter den Linden arcades, in the Tiergarten, near the Alexanderplatz unemployed boys stroll about, many of them in shorts; they simper coquettishly. They get paid one or two marks. I got into conversation with one of these boys in a snack-bar. He said that in Berlin there lived a Hohenzollern prince, a real, not a phoney one. When the prince saw a boy whose looks he liked, he beat him with a whip, and after that gave him ten marks. Young fellows loitered round the house where the prince lived, hoping to be lucky.

I went to a Nazi meeting; it was held in a beerhall. The smoke from cheap cigars made one's eyes smart. A Nazi, waving his large hands, shouted for a long time that the Germans were tired of going hungry, that only the Jews lived well, that the allies had robbed Germany, that the French and the Poles should be smashed. In Russia Jews were the masters, so the Russians would also have to get a drubbing. Hitler would show the world what German Socialism was. I took a good look at the customers. Some drank beer, others sat at tables drinking nothing. Many of them were workers, and this was unbearably painful. Of course I already knew that there were many workers among the Nazis, but it was one thing to read about it in the press, and another to see it for oneself. How could one believe that this elderly worker was a fascist? A good, sad face; one could see that things were not going too well for him. And that other, a young fellow, was like the comrade to whom Rudolf entrusted the distribution of leaflets.

The headquarters of the Nazis was in the Berliner Kindl beerhall.

In the next street was another beerhall where the Communists used to meet. I was taken there by Rudolf. Threadbare plush benches, antlers on the walls; an ordinary beer saloon.

I was walking with Rudolf along a deserted street in north Berlin. He was just finishing telling me something: 'Let's get down to the facts . . .' Suddenly shots rang out. Rudolf ran to the spot and cried: 'Weber!' The Nazis had shot a Communist worker. Then a policeman came up hurriedly. A call was sent out for a police car. Then much time was spent on taking down the particulars. I stood aside waiting for Rudolf. An old woman came running up, sobbing loudly. The night was dark; the wind snatched at caps, at the last leaves on the trees.

I returned to Paris in a black mood: the storm was blowing up. In a newspaper article I wrote: 'Capitalism is decomposing for too long, in too revolting a fashion. The gangrene has had time to spread to the living parts of the body. History has seldom known a tragedy equal to that of the German proletariat. Gritting its teeth in disgust, it forged guns and died at Verdun. Women gave birth to degenerates, blind babies, mental defectives. When the proletarians demanded a right to live, means were found to sow disunity and to corral them. Once again the workers became accustomed to need and frustration. Seeing that they no longer trusted the Social-Democratic police, fascist rowdies were recruited from among them. Not only their bodies have been defiled, but their very souls. The reckoning has been postponed, but it will be a cruel one – history knows how to take its revenge'.

30

A QUARTER of a century ago, in *A Book for Adults*, I wrote: 'In 1931 I reached the age of forty. The year seemed to me quite ordinary. Now I see that it gave me the possibility to live on. It was a preparatory class in a new school of which I became a pupil in my fifth decade'.

I have talked about Spain and my visits to Berlin, of long wanderings with a camera in the northern districts of Paris. I can add that I visited Prague, Vienna, Switzerland, attended a session of the League of Nations, took a look at Briand, who kept lowering his heavy, fleshy eyelids from time to time, listened to an argument between the German Foreign Minister Curtius and the Pole Zaleski. All spoke about disarmament, and all realized that things were moving towards war.

We went to live in the rue du Cotentin, opposite the Vaugirard goods yard where, during the war years, I had unloaded ammunition trucks. The flat was on the ground floor and it was noisy at night: lorries carrying milk drove past the windows with a clashing of churns.

At the beginning of the year I finished my book on the film industry, *The Factory of Dreams*. In short, the year was, as I have said, rather ordinary. Yet it certainly changed much in my attitude to people and life in general.

The respite granted to me, as it was granted to others of my generation, was coming to an end. There were no storms yet, but the calm seemed unnatural. Friends arriving from the Soviet Union told me about the liquidation of the kulaks, about the difficulties over collectivization, about the famine in the Ukraine. After my Berlin visits it had become clear to me that fascism was on the offensive and that its opponents were disunited. The crisis was looming larger all the time. Hardship, humiliation, hunger are not the best guides to wise decisions; the fascists recruited into their ranks not only ruined shopkeepers and young toughs but also desperate, bemused, unemployed working men.

I had not studied the oil, steel and match kings in vain; I knew that, though more or less enlightened and feeling somewhat squeamish about having open relations with the fascists, they generously supplied various fascist organizations with money. Fear of the revolution proved stronger not only than traditional liberalism, but even than plain common sense. Some of the maniacs were brought to trial at Nuremberg, but the responsibility was also that of the entire ruling circle of society. It may be that some of those who aided and abetted the fascists later wept over the burned books, shattered towns, lost relatives. The attempt has been made to present fascism as a stranger who accidentally intruded on decent civilized countries; but fascism had generous uncles, loving aunts, who to this day enjoy good health.

The battle was inevitable: diplomats know disengagement zones, neutral and buffer states; but I realized that between us and the fascists there was not even a narrow strip of no-man's-land.

In the past there may have been periods when an artist could stand up for human dignity without leaving art even for an hour. Our time demanded from all men not the fire of inspiration which may easily consume them, but daily renunciation.

Dear God, how many times I have answered the standard questions set out on forms! Now I want to talk not about actions, or travels, or even books, but about myself. Up to the age of forty I never found myself, I turned and tossed this way and that.

I am probably wrong in putting it down entirely to the times. After all, I did meet writers who gave full expression to their thoughts, their hopes, their passions – Thomas Mann, James Joyce, Vyacheslav Ivanov, Valéry. Of course they did get carried away by many things in life and recoiled from many others, but their weapons were their books. This was true of Balzac too, for though he dreamt of becoming a deputy, wrote political pamphlets and worked out plans for financial undertakings which would free him from his permanent burden of debt, none of it was more than so many ripples on the surface, and he really came to life only through his characters. And though for his contemporary Stendhal, literature was one of the possible forms of participation in life, he fought, he took a lively interest in politics, he fell passionately in love, and lived not in order to learn more about the passions of others, but for the sake of life itself.

It is not only great writers who are cut according to different patterns. After *Julio Jurenito* I became a professional man of letters. I wrote a lot; I have just totted it up and find it quite embarrassing to confess that between 1922 and 1931 I wrote nineteen books. This haste was dictated by inner confusion and not by ambition: in using up paper I used up myself.

Contemplation has never satisfied me; I wanted to reflect on the destinies of invented characters and to become like them myself. And yet, during the decade to which the third part of these memoirs is devoted, I found myself all too often in the role if not of an idle spectator, at most of a passive supporter.

In 1931 I felt that I was at odds with myself. I began to think about the recent past and, as the night lorries rumbled and clattered, I insistently asked myself how I ought to shape my days to come.

It may seem odd that the individual now questioning himself was not the callow young man who, ragged and hungry, roamed the streets of Paris and wrote poems about the end of the world, nor the perplexed but cocky young intellectual whom Alexey Tolstoy used to call a 'Mexican convict' and who entertained young girls with descriptions of the still unwritten adventures of *Jurenito*, but a forty-year-old man of letters whose hair was turning grey. But I have already said that in our times, while historical events developed with bewildering speed, many individuals developed slowly. Herzen was forty when he sat down to write *My Past and Thoughts* and to sum up his life: he never looked at events from the auditorium but took his part as an actor in all the tragedies that were played out in his time.

Perhaps such a long search for myself could also be explained by the fact that I had lived in two worlds, had spent my youth in Paris, and that at the beginning of the Revolution my tastes, my attachments and aversions were already formed. My nature, too, may have had something to do with it: I have always felt the necessity to verify what to many seemed a simple multiplication table.

When I speak of my path as a writer, it is clear I did not alter course in the space of a year. In the twenties it was always pointed out in the forewords to my books that though I was a 'played-out cynic' and a 'Nihilist', my books were worth publishing because I gave a good picture of the 'decay of the capitalist world'. In *Jurenito* I did, indeed, ridicule Clericalists, Radicals, fanatical Communists and tame Socialists, French hedonists and Russian intellectuals with their pangs of conscience, but I gradually abandoned this approach to people. Age must have had its effect: the ruthlessness natural to youth had disappeared. I found it more and more difficult to live by negation alone: I wanted to find at the back of the stupid or evil actions of men something genuine, something human. (I did not often succeed in this, but what I am talking about is not literary values but my intentions.)

However, it was not the approach to fictional characters that was most important for me in the year 1931. I gave little thought to how I was going to write my next book; I was asking myself how I ought to shape my further life so that the years ahead should not be mere notes in the margin of life, but life itself.

Everyone takes keenly to heart questions that are connected with their work and, of course, I was deeply concerned about the fate of literature and art. Mayakovsky was no more. Loudest of all were the voices of the RAPP group. The exhibitions were crowded with huge paintings of the AKRR (Association of Artists of Revolutionary Russia). The days of experiments and eccentricities had been left behind.

The Revolution had initiated the people into art, and of course those who held a novel in their hands or visited an exhibition for the first time did not understand much about craftsmanship; often a clever imitation of art won their admiration. The new readers, the new gallery-visitors could be educated, but they could also be flattered by being told that they were the supreme judges. Flatterers, naturally, did not fail to appear.

Versifiers wrote *ad hoc* poems. The *Literary Encyclopedia* explained that the trend was now towards the 'production' novel which would supersede all other kinds. The style that was to prevail for a quarter of a century was coming into being: the style of ornamented architecture, of those metro stations crammed with statues, of incessant panegyrics, and of satire modestly pillorying the careless house-manager or the tipsy music-hall artist. Of course in 1931 all this was still in the embryonic stage. There had, however, appeared the first portraits and statues of the man who perhaps did not suspect at the time that he would become both the object and the begetter of the 'cult of personality'. All this was accompanied by conscientious over-simplification; the *Literary Encyclopedia* stated that 'Hamlets are useless to the masses' and that the proletariat '. . . was throwing Don Quixote on to the rubbish heap of history.'

At the beginning of 1932 I wrote a not very important short novel called *Moscow Does Not Believe in Tears*. One of the heroes, a Soviet artist, a veteran of the Civil War, reads a review of an exhibition signed O.B. in a Moscow newspaper: ' "Chuzhakov's landscapes show that he has definitely lost contact with the masses. It is art typical of the declassed renegade and will appeal only to some ten or twenty bourgeois bohemian degenerates" '. The artist reflects (and his thoughts were those of the author): 'To ten or twenty. Let's admit that it's so. And AKRR – to ten thousand? So one ought to be doing potboilers? But take, say, Rembrandt – how many people admired his work in his lifetime? Yet today excursion groups are shepherded to see his pictures: stop and be enlightened. Citizen O.B. – or perhaps you are a citizeness? But that's not the point. I know too well – you keep things nicely separate: in an affair with a woman you don't care how you behave, but when it comes to writing articles you watch your step pretty carefully. Expense and income – not to be confused, please. Naturally you don't paint pictures – it's an outdated business – and in point of fact you can't give pleasure to anyone. If you are a citizen, I doubt whether you could give any pleasure to citizeness O.B. or B.O. But that's not the point. Let's listen to the siskins. They sing like degenerates. Would you say they'd lost contact with the masses? And what about vocal cords? You see, O.B., they sing because they like singing. It's gayer for them and for me, nobody needs listen who doesn't wish to. I don't want to impose my pictures. I'm quite ready to make room for others once again. If you, O.B., have worked out that my pictures aren't wanted, all right, I could whitewash walls, for instance. I'm amenable. But leave painting alone. That's quite another matter. The siskins will understand, but for you there's no hope of it. Fools think: twice two, a beefsteak for everybody, and to hell with the arts. But that's just where art will begin – after the beefsteak, and then it'll get its teeth into not four, my dear chap, but five. Or twenty-five. An O.B. may understand nothing about painting, there may be hundreds, even millions of O.B.s – well, I'll have to lay down my paintbrushes, that's all. I'll find myself another job to suit the times. We'll manage to live without pictures. But ten years will pass. Well, perhaps not ten – a hundred, what's the difference? Then they'll understand.'

I remember a conversation with the young French actress Denise. We were talking about Meyerhold's tour, about Renoir's portrait of Denise's grandmother, about Desnos' poetry, about art: there was nothing for it, fish needed water. And suddenly I admitted: 'It's all very well, Denise, but just now art's not the point. Ten years ago I argued that art was dying; we believed then that the old forms were worn out – novels, easel-painting, footlights. It was all nonsense.

Today the reaction's setting in. But there's no need to write novels. I've made my choice long ago. Besides, it's not I who made the choice – there is no choice'.

At night I pondered over many things: humanism, the end and the means. It was not the bad paintings that worried me and, in fact, art was only a tiny part of the enigmas of the future – it was not a matter of the trends of art but of man's destiny.

When you go to a library you do not have to take a book that you do not like; you might take one out by mistake and return it without having read it. But life is not a library. In 1931 I came to realize that a soldier's fate is not that of a dreamer, and that one ought to take one's place in the fighting ranks. I did not renounce what I held dear, nor did I repudiate anything, but I knew that I would have to grit my teeth and master that most difficult of disciplines – silence.

Critics who wrote about me said that the year 1933 was the turning-point: they knew the book *The Second Day*. But I knew well enough why I had gone to Kuznetsk: I had thought it all out in 1931, not as I stood by the foundation trenches of a construction site, but in the rue du Cotentin to the nightly clatter of milk-churns.

31

In the spring of 1931 the playwrights Vladimir Kirshon and Alexander Afinogenov arrived in Paris. I took them round and explained the sights. They on their side informed me about the highlights of our literature. They were both elated with success: Kirshon's *Bread* and Afinogenov's *Fear* were being played in dozens of theatres. However, they took more pride in the victories of RAPP than in their own plays. According to them RAPP had united all the 'real' Soviet writers. Kirshon kept saying: 'We are the main road of our literature.' (I did not know at the time that this expression was originally Fadeyev's.) Afinogenov, a very tall and modest man, smiled and concurred with what Kirshon was saying. Kirshon sermonized, denounced, smiled sarcastically. 'It's time you shifted your position,' he said to me. I confessed that I had shifted my position. 'Then make an application to join RAPP.' I said that RAPP's literary principles did not greatly appeal to me, and that people drove along main roads – formerly in carriages and now in cars – while writers were by nature pedestrians; everyone could approach the common goal in his own way. 'Leave him alone,' Afinogenov smiled. 'He may be right.'

We were sitting on the stones of the old Arènes de Lutèce. It was a hot day and despite the morning hour we had sought the shade. I opened the paper: 'Moscow reports: RAPP has been dissolved.' This news seemed to me quite immaterial, for the signboards of various writers' organizations had been changed time and again; and, besides, what interested me was writing, not writing about writing; at that time I did not yet know what 'practical conclusions' meant. Kirshon jumped up: 'It can't be! It's a lie! What paper is it?' I said: 'It's *Humanité*'. We were planning to have a look round the working-class districts, but Kirshon said they would have to go to the embassy. A day or two later they left for Moscow, although they had meant to stay longer. (Later I often used to meet Afinogenov and we became friends; I shall have more to say about him when I come to the year 1937.)

It was clear to me that the liquidation of RAPP was a serious matter, and I took heart: perhaps, after all, they had realized in Moscow that a metalled road has got to be built for motorized traffic, while leaving the writers free to follow their own path.

However, I was faced with the question: how was I to get closer to life, to action, to the struggle?

In May a journalist on *Izvestia*, Rayevsky, called on me; he told me that the editor and P. L. Lapinsky, whom I had often met in the war years, were offering me the job of regular Paris correspondent. They had one correspondent already – Sadoul, who had been a member of the French military mission in Russia in 1917 and had gone over to the Revolution. Rayevsky told me that Sadoul would keep his job but that, being a Frenchman, he did not know enough about Russian readers. I would have to write feature articles and, if the occasion required it, telegraph information.

The offer caught me off my guard: I had been living for quite a long time unfettered by regular employment and was accustomed to dispose of my time as I pleased. Of course journalism attracted me: I wanted to do something active, but I was afraid of being unequal to the task.

I called on our ambassador, V. S. Dovgalevsky, with whom I was on friendly terms. He was a kindly, considerate man; talking to him I forgot that he was a high official, an ambassador, and I a writer, a 'right-wing fellow-traveller' perhaps, or a 'rotten cynic'. Dovgalevsky knew France well; an old Bolshevik, he had been a political exile and had studied in Toulouse. The French thought highly of him; more than once I met Herriot at the embassy, he used to come to talk to Dovgalevsky, and sometimes to ask his advice. (Dovgalevsky died of cancer at the age of forty-nine. I grieved at the time, but later thought more than once that death had spared him many trials.)

Dovgalevsky knew about *Izvestia*'s offer and said at once: 'That's very good, you shouldn't hesitate.' It was not difficult to persuade me: I had been longing to take part in the battle.

For about eight years I carried out the duties of *Izvestia* correspondent – in Paris, then in Spain, then back in Paris – up to the pact with Germany; I wrote hundreds of essays and articles, sent information; sometimes the contributions were unsigned, sometimes I used a penname (one was 'Paul Jocelyn'). I learnt to type telegrams in Latin lettering; I became hoarse or lost my voice completely dictating articles over the telephone. I shall have to refer again later to my journalistic work; at the moment I want only to say that I look back on it with gratitude. Naturally it took up much of my time but, on the other hand, it enabled me to see a great deal and to come in contact with many people. Besides, it was good training for my trade as a writer: I learnt to write succinctly, for I had to remember to keep down the paper's expenses: letters took a long time, I sent almost all my articles by telegraph or telephone. (Conciseness, short phrases had always appealed to me. I wanted to write exactly as I thought, without subordinate clauses. Critics took me to task for my 'telegraphese', but I found that this style corresponded both to my feelings and to the rhythm of the times.)

Hardly any of my comrades on *Izvestia* of that period are alive today. During the war years, in the Seventh Staff Department of one of our armies I was struck by the voice of a woman – a lieutenant: it sounded very familiar but I did not recognize her face. We fell into conversation. The lieutenant had worked as a stenographer on *Izvestia* when I was transmitting daily articles or reports from besieged Madrid. The line was bad, and the stenographer kept saying: 'I can't hear . . . spell it out . . .' I would yell: 'Boris, Olga, Ivan . . .' Sometimes the foreign editor wished to speak to me, and the stenographer, to avoid our being cut off, said: 'The weather's lovely in Moscow', or 'Your daughter sends you her greetings'. All this went on to the accompaniment of artillery fire. And here, near Briansk, I had met a familiar stranger with a charming, warm voice, and an artillery battle was again in progress.

Let me return to the year 1932. I began to take steps to get my credentials as *Izvestia* correspondent from the French authorities. I was summoned to the Ministry of Foreign Affairs. I thought the officials in charge of relations with the foreign press wanted to talk to me; but I was sent to the 'Control of Aliens', familiar to me from my grim visa pilgrimages. It was the police, not diplomats, who worked there and they treated me with scant civility. I noticed on the table a huge file bearing the name: 'Ilya Ehrenburg'. The official told me without wasting words that I was well known to him and in the worst light, that the correspondent of a Bolshevik newspaper would be under special observation and that any attempt to break the rules would lead to my expulsion.

Some two months later I had occasion to talk, not to policemen working in the Ministry of Foreign Affairs, but to genuine diplomats. This was in Moscow; the French ambassador Dejean invited me to lunch. Among the guests was an attaché of the Polish embassy. Dejean seated Lyuba next to him and carried on a perfectly peaceful conversation with her about the character of various French cheeses. And the counsellor of the embassy (I do not remember his name) began to question me about what I had seen on my trip (I had just returned from Bobriki). He was patently dissatisfied with my account: 'You're giving me official answers, but we'd like a frank talk. After all, everybody knows that the Five Year Plan has failed'. The Polish attaché chipped in: 'Especially the construction works in Bobriki'. This made me angry: where was diplomatic courtesy – to invite one to lunch and then start provocative conversations! I could not even do justice to the wines and the cheeses. Coffee was served in the drawing-room. The counsellor suddenly opened a volume of the *Shorter Soviet Encyclopedia* and triumphantly began to read out (halting syllable by syllable, but quite distinctly) what was said about me. Having recalled this episode, I have now got hold of the book and here is a short quotation: 'Nurtured by the declassed bohemia, Ehrenburg wittily satirizes Western capitalism and its bourgeoisie, but he does not believe in the creative power of the proletariat. Asserting that Scientific Socialism is incapable of planning life in face of the basic biological nature of man, and prophesying that Communist plans are helpless in face of private property, Ehrenburg is revealed as one of the outstanding exponents of the neo-bourgeois wing of literature.' The article was signed by one of the leading spirits of RAPP.

It suddenly dawned upon me why the counsellor of the embassy had expected me to tell him about the failure of the construction works, and I burst out laughing. I did not try to explain that the author of the article belonged to the RAPP group and that RAPP had been dissolved shortly before: for the French, an encyclopedia is a reference book which states that Joffre won the battle of the Marne, that the cow is a ruminant, that Anatole France has an excellent style as well as irony, and all this holds good for at least one generation. The counsellor, having read that I was a representative of neo-bourgeois literature, had concluded that it would be easy for a representative of old bourgeois diplomacy to come to an understanding with me. How was he to know that the Encyclopedia revised its judgements from one volume to the next?

In 1932 I supposed that, along with RAPP, a certain style of literary criticism had also been eliminated. This was simple-minded, particularly for the author of *Jurenito* who had now entered his fifth decade. I soon realized my mistake: one of our critics wrote that in my books 'one detects the features, distorted by fear, of a class enemy', and called me 'a literary lackey of the bourgeoisie'. In 1934 the up-to-date volume not of the *Shorter* but of the *Great Soviet Encyclopedia* appeared, and I read: 'Ehrenburg is a typical exponent of the moods of that section of the bourgeois intelligentsia which followed in the steps of the ideologists of the *Change of Landmark* group'. As I have said, susceptibility becomes blunted: the first time I felt totally taken aback, at the tenth I was angry, at the hundredth the familiar labels left me cold. I realized that haphazard sniping was one of the peculiar features of a war which had not begun yesterday and would not end tomorrow: gunfire often hit one's own side. This is rather unpleasant, of course, but it cannot be helped; a man may die from a bullet, but a moral hurt merely steels him; you do not change your convictions because of a wound, even a most painful one, and you do not cross over to the enemy.

I also realized that the crux of the matter was not in my muddled life, nor in the fact that I had lived for a long time in Paris; obloquy was heaped in the same random, groundless and unjust fashion on other writers who had never been enthusiastic about the Middle Ages, who did not know Picasso and who lived not in the rue du Cotentin but in Moscow side-streets. That is why at the First All-Union Congress of Soviet Writers I could say in all sincerity: 'I find it difficult to visualize the path of a writer as a smooth macadamized road. But one thing I know beyond all doubt: I am a rank-and-file Soviet author. That is my source of happiness, that is my pride'.

32

In May 1932 Paris was shaken to its foundations by a horrifying event: a certain Pavel Gorgulov, who had been born in the Cossack village of Labinskaya, shot at and killed Paul Doumer, the President of the French Republic, in full daylight. The murder was committed on the eve of the parliamentary elections, and the right-wing newspapers hastened to report that Gorgulov was a Bolshevik. Another Cossack, Lazarev by name, immediately appeared to confirm that he knew Gorgulov, under the name of 'Mongol', to be a member of the Cheka.

Izvestia told me to cover the case. I still did not have a press-card. Semyon Chlenov, who knew everybody, came to my rescue. The presiding judge Dreyfus, one of the outstanding French jurists, allowed me to attend the trial as his guest. I went in through the official entrance and did not sit in the body of the court but behind the judges.

In the evening as I was leaving the law courts I was arrested: I could produce no document to justify my presence at the trial. I was taken to the préfecture, where I had to submit to a humiliating cross-examination and was locked up. I was furious: there would be no time to telegraph to the paper. And, sure enough, I was not released till the middle of the night and the report appeared in *Izvestia* one day late.

The trial lasted three days: the whole thing seemed an incredible and terrifying nightmare. I have said that there were people who alleged that Gorgulov was a Soviet agent: 'Moscow was trying to plunge France into anarchy'. There was also another version: Gorgulov was an agent of the French police: the assassination had been planned to ensure the success of the right wing at the elections and to wreck the prospective talks with Moscow. In reality it was both much simpler and more complicated. The crime was committed by a deranged, desperate *émigré* who was on the borderline of insanity. For three days I watched Gorgulov and heard his impassioned and senseless cries. Before me was a man whom Dostoyevsky could have invented in his sleepless hours.

Gorgulov was tall and powerfully built; when he shouted confused, inarticulate curses in unintelligible French, the jury – who looked like notaries, shopkeepers, rentiers – flinched nervously.

In the first place, it was impossible to explain his act. In the twenties Kaverda had assassinated the Soviet ambassador Voikov, Conradi had assassinated Vorovsky. Now Gorgulov had shot the French president Doumer, a man of right-wing views, and an old man of seventy. However, the affair had its own inner logic, the logic of hatred and despair.

At the trial the assassin's history came to light. He had taken his degree in medicine at Prague University and had practised in a small Moravian town. He was lucky indeed – how many Russian *émigrés* had been forced to become navvies or were driven to begging! But Gorgulov was incapable of adjusting himself to a modest way of life in a foreign country. He detected slights and intrigues everywhere. He thought his Czech colleagues were pushing him to one side; he took to drink, became violent and introduced the squalor of a Russian tavern into the life of the respectable little town.

Also his heart was not in medicine. Even in his early days at the University of Rostov he had frequented literary circles. He took up poetry. An elderly quixotic Czech woman whom he met by chance believed in his talent and paid to have his book published. Gorgulov chose the significant pseudonym *Bred* (Delirium). I have read his books; they showed a certain amount of talent, but he did not know how to work, and in any case this delirium of his was uninteresting and repetitive; his verses sounded like echoes of something very familiar.

At the same time he did not abandon politics; at first he called himself a Socialist, he even told one of the Czechoslovak Ministers how to defend democracy. Later he became a fascist; he founded a 'National Peasant Party'; it had no members but there was a handsome banner embroidered by two Russian dancers who worked in a cabaret.

After several scandals the Czechs struck Gorgulov off the medical register and he went to live in Paris; here he met one Yakovlev who traded in ladies' stockings and published the newspaper *Nabat* (The Tocsin). Hitler's successses in those years inspired quite a few people. Yakovlev and Gorgulov gathered a dozen adherents in a workers' café in Billancourt, raised their arms and shouted: 'Russia, awake!'

Gorgulov soon quarrelled with Yakovlev and published the programme of his new party. He also invented a new religion: 'Naturism', which was based on kindness and the love of Nature. At the same time he called for the killing of all Communists and Jews. He had no money and secretly treated fellow-Cossacks who had caught gonorrhea, spending the money he earned this way on publishing books of verse and political leaflets.

He did not know what to do next. Here is a list of his plans: live in Harbin; make an interplanetary rocket flight: kill Dovgalevsky; join the Foreign Legion; go to the Belgian Congo; join Hitler's storm-troopers; find a rich bride.

The French police discovered that Gorgulov was treating patients illegally; they took away his residence-permit. He went to Monaco. At first he tried to win at roulette. Then he decided that Russia must be freed from the Bolsheviks – there was no other way out. He wrote to the writer Kuprin: 'I am a lonely Scythian returned to savagery.'

He hated the French for negotiating with the Bolsheviks while he, an honest Cossack, a faithful ally, had been expelled from France. He had read somewhere that Kolchak 'had been betrayed by the French'. A portrait of Kolchak hung in his room. Gorgulov wrote two dates on it: the date of the Russian admiral's death and the date of the forth-coming death of the French president.

What followed was indeed like delirium. Gorgulov came to Paris with two revolvers; he went to the cathedral and prayed; then he drank a litre of wine; fearing the police, for he had no residence-permit, he chose an obscure hotel of the kind where you can take a room for a night or for an hour, bringing with him a prostitute as a blind; he soon sent her away and spent the night writing curses on the Communists, the Czechs, the Jews, the French. Then he went out of the hotel and killed Doumer.

It was painful to watch him, he was like a hunted animal. Both Yakovlev and his other associates repudiated him.

I recall a terrible scene. At night, by the dim light of dusty chande-liers, the courtroom seemed like a stage set: the judges' imposing robes, the black gowns of the counsels, the face of the accused, green and deathlike – the whole thing had an unnatural quality. A judge read out the verdict. Gorgulov jumped up, tore off his collar, as if in a hurry to put his head under the guillotine, and shouted: 'France has refused me a residence-permit!'

As I walked that night along the deserted streets my thoughts dwelt on this man's destiny. Of course Gorgulov did not inspire compassion: a bad life, a savage, senseless crime. But I was thinking that there must have been a time when he was an ordinary Russian boy, who played skittles in a hot, dusty street. It was appalling that before his death he

219

could find no words other than 'residence-permit' – a trivial, common-place *émigré*'s complaint! Why did he write about loving tiny insects and want to kill millions of people? Why had he murdered Doumer? Why did he have to play someone else's role in a fatuous but bloody melodrama? Why had he written to his friend Yakovlev three months before the crime: 'I have only one emotion left – the thirst for venge-ance'. He lived by the hope: 'War alone will save us!' I recalled that Yakovlev traded in women's stockings. Under the peaceful ripples of European life terrible currents were flowing.

Gorgulov's trial was my psychological introduction to a grim decade. The word 'war' became familiar. Everywhere people began to be drawn into a new, cruel business. There was a smell of blood.

33

IN the summer and autumn of 1932 I travelled a great deal all over the Soviet Union: I visited the construction works on the Moscow–Donbas trunk-line, those at Bobriki which later became Stalinogorsk, at Kuznetsk which later became Stalinsk, at Sverdlovsk, Novosibirsk, Tomsk.

Those were extraordinary days; for the second time our country was shaken up by a tornado; but if the first one – during the Civil War years – had seemed elemental, bound up with the struggle between classes, with wrath, hatred and heartsickness, this time collectivization and the laying of the foundations of heavy industry, which churned up the lives of tens of millions, were determined by an exact plan, inseparable from columns of figures, subordinated not to explosions of popular passion but to the iron laws of necessity.

Once again I saw railway stations crammed with people and their belongings; a great transmigration was taking place. Peasants from Orel and Penza abandoned their villages and made their way eastwards where, they had been told, bread, smoked fish and even sugar were distributed.

Komsomols, fired with enthusiasm, set off for Magnitogorsk or Kuznetsk; they believed that it was enough to build huge factories to create an earthly paradise. In freezing January metal scorched the hands. People seemed to be frozen to the marrow; there were no songs, no flags, no speeches. The word 'enthusiasm', like many others, has been devalued by inflation, yet there is no other word to fit the days of the First Five Year Plan; it was enthusiasm pure and simple that inspired the young people to daily and unspectacular feats.

Many workers felt a real affection for their factories; they called a blast-furnace (*domna*) 'Domna Ivanovna', an open-hearth Martin furnace 'Uncle Martin'. I asked a student at a technical school how he visualized Paris. He answered: 'In the centre there must be huge factories, and people living all round them in big houses, and the transport's good – hundreds of trams'. He had come to Novosibirsk from the country and it seemed to him that towns grew round factories;

however, he had read Victor Hugo and asked me: 'But where is the Notre-Dame Cathedral over there?'

There were, of course, different types of men among the construction workers. Cynics came and adventurers and drifters who moved from one site to another in search of what was called a 'long rouble'. Peasants looked mistrustfully at the machines; when a lever would not work they grew angry and treated it like a baulking horse, often damaging the machine. If some of the men were spurred on by noble feelings, others exerted themselves in order to get a pound of sugar or a length of material for a pair of trousers.

I saw parties of special deportees: they were former kulaks who were being taken to Siberia. They looked like the victims of a village fire. Others being taken the same way were traders in garden produce from the Moscow suburbs, petty speculators from Sukharevka, religious dissenters, embezzlers.

In Tashkent and Ryazan, in Tambov and Semipalatinsk recruiting agents were taking on navvies, bridge-builders, peasants who had fled from the villages after collectivization.

I came across villages where it was hard to find an able-bodied man, there were only women, old men and children. Many cottages had been abandoned. The women buzzed like a disturbed hive of bees.

Tomsk was poor and neglected. The fences had been broken up for fuel; there were no pavements. The more active members of the population had left for Novosibirsk, Kuznetsk. The *lishentsy* (people deprived of civic rights) screened from the sight of passers-by the small oil-lamps that usually burnt in front of icons. Tea was drunk without sugar. At the station buffet they sold mineral water and empty cardboard sweet-boxes.

Some towns were growing at a tremendous pace. Stagnant Novonikolayevsk had been transformed into noisy Novosibirsk. The houses were like pavilions in an exhibition. In the hotel restaurant men swilled vodka all night long. On the outskirts newcomers put up shacks, built mud-huts; they were in a hurry – the severe Siberian winter was on its way. The new settlements were called Nakhalovka[1]. The inhabitants joked: 'In America they have skyscrapers, here we've got earthscrapers' – this was long before our multi-storey buildings.

Life was hard; everybody talked about rations, about distribution

[1] From *nakhal*: 'insolent fellow'.

centres. In Tomsk the bread was like clay; it reminded me of the year 1920. In the market they sold minute grubby lumps of sugar. Professors took their place in the queues between lectures. The *Torgsin*[1] shops stocked tempting flour, sugar, shoes, but there you had to pay in gold – wedding rings or hoarded Tsarist coins. In Kuznetsk new arrivals immediately asked: 'Do they issue meat?' The typhus isolation building of the hospital was overcrowded: typhus was again taking a heavy toll. In Tomsk I saw a professor's wife boiling soap. It all reminded one of the rear in a war, but this rear was the front: the war was on everywhere.

This vast canvas was painted in two colours: rose and black; hope lived side by side with despair; enthusiasm with dark ignorance – some were given wings, others were destroyed by the experience.

A meeting was held on the construction site of the Moscow–Donbas trunk-line. A navvy in a lambskin cap with a weatherbeaten face said 'We're a hundred times happier than the capitalists. They stuff themselves and die – they don't know what they're living for. When one of them makes a bad deal, he hangs himself from a hook. But we know what we're living for: we're building Communism. The whole world's watching us'. I went with him to the canteen. At the door of the canteen hut the men had to give up their caps which were returned to them when they handed back their spoons. The caps lay in a heap on the ground; everyone spent a long time finding his own. I tried to make the manager see that this was both irritating and silly: the men wasted time unnecessarily. He looked at me with vacant eyes: 'You're not responsible for the spoons, I am'.

In Kuznetsk I met a foreman. He told me that eight years ago he had been a village gooseherd. He was considered a gifted engineer. He had read Paustovsky's *Kara-Bugaz* and spoke passionately about style.

For a long time I sought in old Kuznetsk the house where Dostoyevsky had lived, and at last found it; the women answered me crossly: 'There's no one here of that name.' Schoolboys assured me that they knew many authors: Pushkin, Gorky, Demyan Bedny but had not 'done' Dostoyevsky.

A peasant in a village near Tomsk said to me: 'A fellow came here

---

[1] *Torgovlya s inostrantsami* – 'for trade with foreigners' (who paid in foreign currency).

and said: "Anyone who wants to build Socialism, he's welcome to join the collective farm voluntarily; and anyone who doesn't want to, he's welcome, it's his own full right. But get this clear: to chaps of that sort all we have to say is to hell with his soul, and string his guts on the nearest telephone pole" '.

In the same village I met a girl; after work she read *Cement* and commented: 'It's very difficult to understand it all, but I'm learning. I'll go to the town. Today if you want to learn, every door's open to you. I'm so happy, I can't tell you!'

New cars bounced over the potholes of Novosibirsk. Wonderful machinery was brought to Kuznetsk. And yet the gigantic factory was being built practically by hand. There were powerful excavators but I saw men humping loads of earth. There were not enough cranes, and a young worker built one of wood. A short time before I arrived some scaffolding collapsed; the men fell into the wreckage and were smothered. They were buried with military honours.

Two hundred and twenty thousand builders were working in Kuznetsk. The man in charge of the construction works, the old Bolshevik S. M. Frankfurt, was possessed – there is no other word for it: he hardly slept, snatched bites of food when he could; now it was investigating the reasons for the latest breakdown, now it was the migrant workers who had knocked off work with cries of: 'We want specialists' rates and conditions!' and had to be placated, and now it was housing that had to be found for some Kazakhs who had arrived without warning. I noticed a watercolour in his room – Paris by twilight (Frankfurt had been a political exile before the Revolution). This man was much in the news in those years; after 1937 the name of Frankfurt disappeared. The chief engineer, I. P. Bardin, was a man of great culture; as a young man he had worked in America and had kept up with developments in technology. He realized that the task entrusted to him was difficult, practically impossible to carry out, but he knew that he would carry it out. During one of the many accidents he broke a leg; but he was out of hospital and back at work in no time. He struck me as a gentle and reserved man.

There was no town yet, but it was growing. Films were shown in huts. Supply centres were started, as well as canteens for foreign specialists. Artists were coming from Moscow.

The opening words of my book on Kuznetsk were: 'The people had the will and desperateness – they held out. The wild beasts retreated.

Horses panted and fell. The foreman Skvortsov brought a pointer with him. At night the dog howled with hunger and wretchedness and shortly died. Rats tried to find a home, but they could not stand the grim existence. Only the insects did not desert man: lice moved in thick hordes, fleas hopped briskly, bedbugs crawled in a purposeful way. The blackbeetle, having discovered that it could not find any other food, began to bite man'.

Foreign specialists who worked in Kuznetsk said it was impossible to build like this, that roads had to be made first and houses put up for the builders; besides, the workers were a floating population, and anyway they did not know how to treat the machines; the whole undertaking was doomed to failure. They formed their judgements on the basis of textbooks, of their own experience, of the mentality of people living in tranquil countries, and were totally unable to understand the spiritual climate and potentialities of this, to them, alien land. Once again I realized how great was our people's fortitude in years of sore trial. Factories were built under conditions in which success was nothing less than a miracle, just as an older generation had seen the miraculous victory in the Civil War, when blockaded, hungry, barefooted Russia defeated the Interventionists. I do not know whether this is a universal human trait, but Soviet people have invariably shown themselves at their best in the worst times.

In spite of almost insuperable difficulties factory buildings went up swiftly. Cinemas were opened, schools and clubs organized among the foundation trenches. In 1932 one could not take a step in Kuznetsk without stumbling into some hole, but the first blast-furnaces were blazing and in the literary club young people discussed the rival merits of Mayakovsky and Yesenin.

The young people never saw the earthly paradise which they had dreamt of, but ten years later the blast-furnaces of Kuznetsk enabled the Red Army to save their country and the world from the yoke of the racialist madmen.

A new generation was coming into being – young men and girls born on the eve of the First World War: to them the Tsar, the factory owners, the policemen were abstract notions. Of greater interest to me than blast- and open-hearth furnaces were the new people – the future of our country. Observing them closely, I detected many contradictions. The process of the democratization of culture is slow and complicated. During the first twenty-five years culture was broadened at

the expense of depth; at the outset universal literacy led to an intellec
tual semi-literacy, to over-simplification. It was only in the years of th
Second World War that the new stage began and there was a deepenin
of culture.

I remember how surprised French writers were at the huge edition
of Balzac, Stendhal, Zola, Maupassant, translated into the languages o
the Soviet Union. Of course the size of editions is no indication of
rich harvest, but it shows the increase of the area sown. The thirst fo
knowledge was unquenchable in those years. I felt this particularl
acutely having come from the country of Valéry, Claudel, Eluard
Saint-John Perse, Aragon, Supervielle, Desnos, and many other fin
poets whom everybody recognized but few read.

In the summer of 1932 in Moscow I received a letter from a smal
Ural town; a young teacher wrote to me: '. . . By the way, ask th
French writer Drieu la Rochelle what evil spirit whispers to him such
ridiculous things as: ". . . It was of no interest whatsoever, but tha
was what life was like. . . . There is no such thing as intelligence, since
there is nothing to understand." (His novel *Le Feu Follet* as rendered
by our *Literary Gazette*.) Tell him, too, that one of the millions o
people, living in our country and trying, not without success, to
reshape the world to a new way of life, assures him on his honour that
this life is full of "absolute" interest and that in addition to his morbid
intelligence there are the untouched layers of the intelligence of millions
who have yet to learn to understand a number of things. Tell him also
that in the opinion of his adversary in the distant Ural, human intelligence is only now getting ready to fulfil that great mission history has
assigned to it: the mission of literate interpreter of the great language of
emotions − made up of love, hatred, courage, daring, willing self-
sacrifice, etc. − into its own new language which gives them new life by
freeing them from the shackles of dogma.'

(Drieu la Rochelle was at that time frequenting left-wing circles, and
I used to meet him occasionally. When I translated the Ural teacher's
letter to him he made a gesture of dismay: 'Why does he take every
single word of mine so seriously? It's splendid of him but also very
silly.')

Of course the teacher who wrote that letter was head and shoulders
above the average young man of those times; I have not quoted his
point of view as an indication of the intellectual development of the
young in those years of the First Five Year Plan; but his letter

does contain some very good things about the untouched layers of intelligence. It was precisely in those years that the virgin soil was upturned.

A young Tungus saw a bicycle in Kuznetsk. He examined it for a long while and then asked: 'But where's the motor?' He knew that people drove about in cars, flew in planes, but had never seen a bicycle. In the remote villages of Siberia people knew about wireless telegraphy and when they saw telegraph poles with wires they were astonished – what were the wires for?

I met a young girl, a Shor, in the Tomsk museum; she was a medical student and had come to present to the museum a small carved wooden figure, a talisman against fever and evil spirits, which her parents had given her. She knew that the museum was collecting objects that belonged to the old way of life. She asked me a lot of questions about life in France, whether there were many hospitals, how they were combating alcoholism, whether the French liked going to concerts and Romain Rolland's age. She had trusting and eager eyes. Her parents had no doubt asked the shaman to exorcise the evil spirit that possessed their headstrong daughter.

A literary evening was held in one of the Kuznetsk clubs; Mayakovsky's poems were recited, there was applause. Then an engineer began to recite: 'For the shores of the distant fatherland . . .' My neighbour, a Bashkir girl, sent up a note: 'Who is the author?' Later we fell into conversation and she confessed: 'Of course I know Pushkin – he wrote *Eugene Onegin* – but I've never read poems of that sort. I suppose I'm not cultured enough, but I enjoyed it very much, even better than Mayakovsky. I didn't know people wrote things like that'.

In those days it was difficult to get from one place to another; at the Taiga station I was held up for several days. The stationmaster at the junction sought me out, told me that he liked *Julio Jurenito* and put an official coach at my disposal. It is true that things even with this coach were not too easy: at night it would suddenly be uncoupled at some station and shunted on to a siding. But it is not the coach that I want to talk about, it is the guard, a young Siberian girl, Valya. She was afraid to leave the coach even for an hour: 'They'll smash the glass, rip the seats'. She told me an extraordinary story. She had come to Kuznetsk from a village and worked as a cleaner. She kept the hut so clean that someone in authority noticed it and Valya was transferred to the official coach. She had plenty of leisure, and she started reading. Some railwayman had left behind a *Traffic-controllers' Manual on the Movement of Trains*. Valya showed me the book. I had a look at it and could not understand a thing. Valya laughed: 'I couldn't make head or tail of it either at first. I must have read it a hundred times, and in the end I began to find my way about. I got hold of some textbooks on mathematics. Now I've got through the preliminary course and they've promised to let me go to the *Rabfak*'.

I must confess that such encounters moved me deeply. I began to envisage the future with more confidence.

I have said a good deal about the difficult conditions of life, but it would be impossible to tell the whole story. In the huts newly-married couples tried to curtain off their bunk with rags. I happened to be in a hut when a young navvy brought a girl in with him (it was already freezing hard). They had no curtain, and he covered up their faces with his coat.

In spite of such grim conditions, new feelings, new thoughts were born; young men and girls often discussed in my presence whether there was such a thing as eternal love, whether jealousy was defensible, whether it was undignified for a Komsomol to feel melancholy, whether Lermontov's poetry, music, hours of solitude were necessary for construction workers.

I mentioned that I wanted to write a book about young people and they produced their diaries and letters; they told me about their work, about their troubled love affairs. Sometimes I asked them questions and made notes of the answers.

Even before I wrote *The Second Day* I published some of the documents I had collected in *La Nouvelle Revue Française*. In the preface I said: 'A writer does not usually disclose the source material which has gone into the writing of his book; but in my view these documents have a value quite independent of my work. Many readers will find them more convincing than the most successful novel'.

I have now unearthed in the library an old copy of the *Nouvelle Revue*, have re-read the passages from diaries, letters and shorthand notes, and it makes me feel that life has changed, but many of the questions that the new generation was asking for the first time in those days are still stirring our youth: discussions about how to avoid narrow specialization, disgust at double-dealing and hypocrisy, the problems of true friendship and condemnation of indifference.

In the twenties old peasant Russia was still living out her days. In the factories and in various institutions people formed before the Revolution still predominated. The beginning of the thirties marked the break. I recall the construction of Kuznetsk with awe and admiration; it was all unbearable and magnificent.

I have said that the steel of Kuznetsk helped our country to defend itself victoriously in the years of the fascist invasion. And what about the other steel, the human one? The builders of Kuznetsk, like all their contemporaries, did not have an easy life. Some died young – either in 1937 or at the front. Others became prematurely bowed down and silent – there were too many sudden turns, there were too many things to adapt oneself to, to get used to. Now those heroes of *The Second Day* who have survived are on the wrong side of fifty. That generation had little time for reflection. Its morning was romantic and cruel: collectivization, the liquidation of the kulaks, the scaffolding of the construction. What followed, everybody remembers. The courage demanded of those who had been born on the eve of the First World War would have been more than enough for several generations: courage not only in work and in battle, but also in silence, in dismay, in anxiety. I saw these people given wings in 1932. Later, wings were no longer in fashion. The wings of the First Five Year Plan were inherited by the children, together with the gigantic factories paid for at so high a price.

34

BEFORE I went to Kuznetsk I read sketches and stories about the construction works. What I saw was not at all like what I had read. I cannot exactly say when the term 'to varnish' appeared for the first time in articles on literature; I think it was later. The dictionary gives the following explanation of this neologistic use of the term: 'to embellish, to present in a better light than the true one'. As a matter of fact, reality was both more terrible and more beautiful than those bland and instructive pictures which were and still are produced by the 'varnishers'.

We can all think of the novels and films where war is depicted as though it were manoeuvres, with cheery soldiers in smart uniforms, with songs and slogans, with a parade-ground march to victory. Was not the richness of the colour lost beneath the varnish? How could anyone, watching the screen where the fall of Berlin was shown as a pantomime, have an inkling of the great exploit of the Soviet people who had stood to the death before Leningrad, before Moscow, on the narrow strip with their backs to the Volga?

And it was the same with the construction of Kuznetsk and Magnitogorsk. Men built the factories in conditions of unheard-of severity. I think no one anywhere has built or ever will build like that again. Fascism had interfered with our life long before 1941. In the West feverish preparations were being made for a campaign against the Soviet Union; and the foundation trenches of the new construction works were the first battle trenches.

I witnessed the self-sacrifice of some, the greed, the crassness of others. Everybody was building, but they built in different ways: some for the idea, others out of need, and others because they were forced to. For many this was the beginning of the building up not only of industry but of human consciousness. I called my novel *The Second Day*. According to the biblical legend the world was created in six days. On the first day the light was divided from the darkness, the day from the night; on the second day, the firmament from the waters, the waters from the dry land. Only on the sixth day was man created. It seemed to me that in the creation of the new society the years of the Five Year Plan were the second day: the dry land was gradually separating from the waters.

And there were many waters (there are always more of them than of dry land, as on the terrestrial globe there are more seas than land). I did not want to pass this over in silence, so side by side with Kolya Rzhanov, Smolin, Irina – the finest representatives of the younger generation – I showed cynics, egotists, people who care nothing for what does not affect their personal life.

I made no attempt to be an uninvolved observer; the novel was dictated by admiration, by love, by eagerness to fight for the protection of the tender shoots of new consciousness. And that is precisely why I tried to be honest: reality needed no varnish. I knew, of course, that many readers would think my story slanderous and would once again remind me that I was an 'incorrigible sceptic'; they would say that I had tried to distort the glorious reality, that, in other words, I had not produced one more oleograph on the established and approved pattern. But while I was writing I thought neither about the critics nor about the publisher; I did not even ask myself whether the book would be published; I simply wrote for days and nights on end filled with emotion.

I began the novel in November and finished it in February; some of the chapters I re-wrote several times.

I have already said that Isaak Babel used to come and see me nearly every day; he read pages of the manuscript, sometimes approving, sometimes saying: this ought to be re-written, there are gaps, unfinished corners. Occasionally, taking off his glasses when he had finished reading, he would grin mischievously: 'Well, if it ever gets into print, it'll be a miracle'.

The novel also included some of the results of my prolonged ponderings. Volodya Safonov is a good, honest young fellow; he is studying at the University of Tomsk; then he goes to Kuznetsk; he is well-read, he is sensitive, he loves Irina with a pure love. But he does not believe in the birth of a new consciousness; he admits that he is poisoned by the wisdom of old books and is aghast at the simple-mindedness, the childishness of his comrades. He writes in his diary: 'I am working at the factory. Learning. I shall probably become a decent technician. But all this has been imposed on me from outside. In my heart I take no part in the life that goes on round me. I am no good for the work of construction. In mining I think this is called "worthless mineral". You have emptied life of recusants, dreamers, philosophers, poets. You have established universal literacy and equally universal ignorance. That done, you come together and start babbling from a prompt-book about culture. An ant-heap is a model of commonsense and logic, but this ant-heap has been in existence for over a thousand years. There are ant-workers, ant-experts, ant-managers. But there has never been an ant-genius in the world. It was not of ants that Shakespeare wrote. The Acropolis was not built by ants. It was not an ant that discovered the law of gravity. The ants have no Senecas, no Raphaels, no Pushkins. They just have their ant-heap and they work.'

Volodya meets a French journalist, questions him closely and realizes that in the West, too, there is no such culture as the one he dreams of. He goes to a students' meeting with the intention to show up the naïvety and the ignorance of his comrades, but instead, still impressed by his conversation with the Frenchman, he says: 'Can anyone doubt in whose hands the future lies? I feel this particularly keenly because I myself am most probably doomed. I want to join in with everybody else, I try to work well. The matter doesn't rest with me, it rests with all of us. I use the word "us" deliberately. We must conquer. Culture is not an unearned income. You can't keep it in a cupboard. It's being created every hour, by every word, by every thought, by every action. I've been listening to you talking – you talked about music, about poetry. And that's the birth of culture, its growth, a painful and difficult growth.' When he gets home he notes in his diary: 'What is particularly odd is that I spoke sincerely. Certainly not from fear. But what I said was not what I was thinking. Or rather, it was the same, yet not the same. It was as if others were speaking in my stead'.

In an unposted letter Irina argues with him: 'You are more intelligent than the others, you know more. But you do nothing to make life better. You only see what is wrong and mock at it. Do you think I myself do not notice all the beastliness about? Our building work is taking place not in a fine, clean laboratory, but, let's be blunt, in a pigsty. Cowardice, cheating, petty self-interest. There are moments when I am frightened for everything, for everybody. But that is the very reason why I believe that we must struggle and not merely sneer and tell jeering anecdotes on the quiet. You said to me: "Today a man cannot love". My dear Volodya, that is simply not true. Life today is so hard, so tense, so great, that love, too, gains in stature. It is difficult,

232

very difficult to love today. And you said: "Today it's not love, it's pig-iron", and you kept on repeating "pig-iron, pig-iron" – and for some reason you found it funny. But it is not funny at all. Tell me this, which is more important just now: to read your Anatole France or to forge rails, so that at last the country can have more bread and more cloth? But people today are not only smelting pig-iron, or rather they smelt pig-iron, but it contains something more than coke and iron ore. In the same way as Senya "is straining into the darkness of melody" others are straining too – higher and higher. It is all there – the blast-furnaces, and the poetry, and love'.

Irina preferred the much alive Kolya to the doomed Volodya. But that was not why Volodya committed suicide. No one gave him the rope – not his comrades, not the old professor to whom he went for advice on his last day, and not the author of the novel. It was his own quickened conscience that brought him to despair. And if anything condemned him it could only be the epoch, the epoch which visited the rue du Cotentin at night and endlessly discoursed with me.

I have dwelt at some length on Volodya because a number of critics tried to present him as an enemy. The latest edition of *The Second Day* (1953) has notes by V. Yemelyanov who claims that Volodya is a fascist: did he not say to the old lady in charge of the library that he would have liked to burn all books? Yes, Volodya did confess on one occasion that he hated books as a drunkard hates alcohol. But this bookish man could hardly be likened to one of Hitler's storm-troopers. Volodya was entangled in his own contradictions. If he had had a less tender conscience and a little more stamina, he would not have hanged himself but would have become a respected technician.

In my novel I portrayed not only Kolya and his friends but also migrant workers, speculators, ignorant men who ruined the machines; I tried to present the whole truth. If the novel seemed optimistic to me then – as it does now – it is not because, as a result of this great ordeal, the plants went into operation, but because the embryos of men were gradually becoming real human beings.

The novel ends with the words of a former partisan: 'Look at Kolya Rzhanov, look at the other fellows. I fought with them in Kuznetsk when the coffer-dams gave way. I fought with them for this dam. As an old partisan I don't mind saying that I can now die in peace, because, comrade, we've got real men today!'

There is no main hero in the novel; it is, as we say, kaleidoscopic –

a number of characters slide past in quick succession. I was very keen at the time on short sentences, rapidly shifting scenes, swift sequences. I wanted to find a new form for the new content.

In June 1934 the journal *Literary Critic* organized a discussion on *The Second Day* in Moscow. For the first time in my life I was present at a meeting where a book of mine was discussed and where I myself had to speak. In my reminiscences I have often referred ironically or with vexation to my past judgements. But now, having re-read the shorthand account of the discussion on *The Second Day*, I find myself, oddly enough, agreeing with almost everything I said twenty years ago. 'I feel today like one of the builders of the White Sea canal: I have sinned, but I have redeemed my sins. I have been admitted into the ranks of conscious citizens who are building their Socialist country. The smug opinion that we writers must be put on trial and that we should repent is, in my view, entirely wrong. I have written many mediocre books, I did not know how to let a book ripen, I was not mature enough, but I have never slandered Soviet reality. Today some comrades say that in *The Second Day* I have given undue weight to the difficulties because I am used to comfort. Comrade Frankfurt, who was in charge of the construction works, and the Secretary of the Town Committee do not think that I have exaggerated anything but that I have shown the difficulties as they really were. Some comrades here have said that Volodya is a clever fellow but that I have not shown him in relation to an honest, equally knowledgeable Komsomol. But, comrades, we are not at the sixth day, only at the second. I don't want to anticipate. My books are written in a still unformed hand. We are all to some extent Tredyakovskys[1]. But Tredyakovsky did play a useful part. Better to turn out a poor book that is one's very own than to take a little from Zola, a little from Leo Tolstoy and a little from Soviet reality.'

And even now, in 1961, I am not sure whether I succeeded, even if only partially, in embodying my idea. *The Second Day* may not be a particularly good novel but it is not derivative and it was written out of an inner urge.

When he finished reading the last page Babel said: 'You've done it!' which, coming from him, was praise indeed. (When the book was

[1] Mediocre eighteenth-century poet but a pioneer in revolutionizing Russian prosody.

translated into French I received a long letter from Romain Rolland; he wrote to say that *The Second Day* had given him a better insight into Soviet youth.)

I sent the manuscript to Irina and asked her to submit it to *Soviet Literature*. Shortly after, Irina informed me that the manuscript had been returned: 'Tell your father that he has written a bad and harmful book'.

I resorted to a desperate measure: I had several hundred, numbered, copies printed in Paris and sent to Moscow – to members of the Politbureau, to editors of newspapers and journals, to writers.

In the thirties and forties the fate of a book often depended on chance, on the opinion of one man. It was a lottery, and I was lucky: a few months later I received a long telegram from a publisher informing me that they were sending me a contract, and congratulating and thanking me.

The Second Day appeared in Moscow in April 1934. *Izvestia* wrote: 'This is no "sugary novel". It is a novel honestly depicting our reality, without concealing the hard conditions of our existence'. On the same day the *Literary Gazette* printed an article by A. Garry: 'The author sings the praises of a violent primordial force which, in this case, happens to be creating one of the largest metallurgical plants in the world. Against the background of the chaos of construction there live, love and suffer tiny human beings. And these tiny human beings unfortunately also think. This is very bad because their thinking is extremely helpless. In I. Ehrenburg's novel the people are lost in the chaos of the new construction, they have lost their way among the ditches, the excavators, the cranes. This strange thing has happened in the novel not only to the "negative" characters but also to the "positive" ones. And that is in itself a slander. In fact, if one were to judge I. Ehrenburg's novel sharply, one could easily show that it is an apology of Austro-Marxist nonsense about the "Five Year Plan built on the bones of the shock-workers".' *Izvestia* retorted: 'What does Garry think – that Socialist Realism consists in an artist producing cheap popular prints to show what an easy job it is to build Socialism?' This controversy, it seems to me, could have been taken from any recent newspaper.

All this happened more than a year after I had written *The Second Day*. On the very same day I heard from Irina that the book had been rejected, I saw a German newspaper which carried a description of the

May *auto-da-fé*. Berlin students incited by Goebbels had made a bon-fire in front of the University and burnt the books that were anathema to them, listed in the Nazi Index. Among those books were the transla-tions of my novels.

The papers were full of horrifying news: Jewish pogroms, shooting of Communists, concentration camps.

Dovgalevsky, on his return from Geneva, described how the dis-armament conference had been wrecked; Rosenberg made a trip to England; some British politicians were all for the rearmament of Germany, counting on the Nazis to attack Russia. That was the reason for the signing of the Four-Power Pact.

I went with Jean-Richard Bloch to an anti-fascist meeting in the Palais de la Mutualité. The audience was jumpy, people leapt to their feet, clenched their fists. A German who had escaped from a concen-tration camp made people weep as he told his story.

Later we sat in a small café with Professor Langevin. He said with a rueful smile: 'How stupid it all is! Humanity hasn't yet emerged from infancy – it has a mere two billion years behind it'. I asked: 'And how many are there ahead of it?' 'Ten billion if it doesn't put an end to its existence by suicide out of sheer stupidity.'

Jean-Richard Bloch spoke heatedly about the need to organize committees everywhere, to act before it was too late. Workers went past singing: 'The last fight let us face . . .'

A new chapter was beginning, not only in history but also in the life of every man of my generation, perhaps the most difficult chapter of all.

1961.

EVE OF WAR: 1933-1941

1

I N 1933 I met the American film-director Lewis Milestone and we soon became friends. He is a very stout and very kindly man. In his early youth, before the First World War, he left Bessarabia to seek his fortune in America; he knew poverty and hunger, worked as a labourer, as a store-clerk, as an itinerant photographer, and in the end became a film-director. The film *All Quiet on the Western Front* brought him fame and money, but he remained simple and jolly or, as Babel would have said, jovial. He loved everything Russian, retained the colourful southern modes of speech and was happy when offered a small glass of vodka and some pickled herring. When he came for a few weeks to the Soviet Union he was at once on the best of terms with our film-directors and kept saying: 'I'm no Lewis Milestone, I'm Lenya Milstein from Kishinev'.

He once told me that when America decided to enter the war, army men were asked whether they wished to go to Europe or remain in the USA; two lists were drawn up. Milestone was among those who wanted to be sent to the front, but it was only those who had said they wanted to stay behind that were sent. Milestone added with a laugh: 'On the whole, that's what always happens in life'. He was a cheerful pessimist: 'In Hollywood one can't do what one wants. And that goes for more places than Hollywood'.

He decided to make a film out of my novel *The Life and Death of Nikolay Kurbov*. I tried to dissuade him: I did not care for this old book and besides, it would have been ridiculous in 1933 to show an idealistic Communist aghast at the sweeping tide of NEP. Milestone pressed me to write a scenario in any case, suggesting that I alter the story and describe the construction works and the Five Year Plan: 'Let the Americans see what the Russians are capable of achieving'.

I had great doubts about my ability to do the job. I am no playwright and I was not sure I could produce a decent scenario, while a rehash of several books combined seemed to me silly. But I liked Milestone and agreed to try and write the script with his collaboration. He invited me to the small English seaside place where he was engaged on a difficult task – slimming. He weighed almost sixteen stone, and every year starved himself for three weeks, losing some three stone; after that he would naturally start stuffing with a vengeance and very soon look as he had done before. To do his fasting he would choose a comfortable hotel where the cooking was so bad that he did not envy the people who lunched and dined.

He lay supine and slimmed while I sat at his side, ate indifferent food and wrote. Milestone had a wonderful feeling for the rhythm of a picture and would say: 'Here we must have a break . . . Maybe it starts to rain? Or a little old woman with a shopping bag comes out of the house?'

I have not kept the script; I remember it vaguely; I think it represented a mixture of Hollywood and the Revolution, of some of Milestone's bright inspirations and film routine, a melodrama seasoned with the irony of two adults.

We managed to fill a fat writing-pad. Milestone had grown thinner, his suit hung on him in folds, and at long last we left for Paris. In Montparnasse Milestone met the artist Nathan Altman and asked him to prepare sketches for the sets and costumes.

Milestone's pessimism was justified. Harry Cohn, the president of Columbia, said after reading the scenario: 'Too much social stuff and not enough sex. This is no time for throwing money down the drain'.

Milestone was naturally upset: he had wasted almost a whole year, but he managed to make Columbia pay both Altman and me.

(Shortly before the Second World War I met Milestone in Paris. He had not grown thinner but had become less jolly. During the war years he produced a Hollywood film about the Soviet people in a desire to do what he could to help us. When I went to the USA I spoke to him over the telephone and he invited me to Hollywood, but I went to the South instead. I do not know what he did in the post-war years or how often he has been forced to do things he did not want to.)

Altman and I rejoiced at the unexpected windfall. In those days the papers were full of stories about two lucky men who had won five million francs each in the State Lottery: one was a coal-merchant, the other a baker. Although our wealth was far more modest we called ourselves coal-merchant and baker. We decided to celebrate the coming New Year 1934 in style.

In the rue de l'Ecole-de-Médecine there was a small Polish restaurant where we sometimes went when we felt homesick for Russian food.

The owners were friendly people and the Soviet-Polish conflicts, frequent in those days, did not affect the quality of the *bigos*-hash or the jam puffs. On New Year's Eve the Pole closed his restaurant and moved into the rue du Cotentin. Our flat consisted of two rooms; we opened the connecting door wide and set out ten small tables brought from the restaurant. At the entrance hung a notice drawn by Altman: 'The coal-merchant and the baker welcome you'.

From old photographs I see that by this time I had put on a good deal of flesh; I had not, however, become good-natured, like Milestone but, on the contrary, was eager to join battle, fought both windmills and some very real millers, taunted police-agents and Paul Valéry, harshly criticized the Surrealists and Russian painting of the last century, prodded sleeping dogs, wrote all sorts of pamphlets almost every day, sent pugnacious articles to *Izvestia* – in short, I behaved more like a young poet than a respectable forty-two-year-old prose-writer.

It seemed to me that in 1933 Europe had touched bottom and was now beginning to surface again. A few days before our New Year celebrations the papers carried the news that the Leipzig judges had been forced to acquit Dimitrov. This was Hitler's surrender to public opinion. I often met German émigrés; they said that the Fascist régime was bound to fall any day – it was wishful thinking in which I shared, believing that the year 1934 would prove fatal to Hitler.

The wild fanaticism and cruelty of the Nazis roused furious indignation and a longing to retaliate. I remember how in the Closerie des Lilas the head of Hungary's first revolutionary government, Count Károlyi, an exceptionally mild man, said to me: 'D'you know my fondest dream? A fine summer morning. I come out on the veranda. I drink my coffee. And on every tree there hangs a Fascist'. I could not help smiling as I listened to him.

I still have a vivid memory of one of the first anti-Fascist meetings in Paris. Among the speakers were Langevin, André Gide, Vaillant-Couturier and Malraux. André Gide reminded me of a pastor out of Ibsen; he preached, arguing that Communism alone could vanquish the evil, and frequently took drinks of water; his spectacles gleamed. The workers in the audience had never read his books but they knew that they were listening to a famous writer, and when Gide said: 'I look with hope towards Moscow', there was a loud buzz of pleasure. Malraux spoke unintelligibly; a nervous tic constantly distorted his features; suddenly he stopped, raised his clenched fist and shouted:

241

'If there is a war, our place is in the ranks of the Red Army'. There was a thunderous echo of applause.

All this may seem surprising. As times changed, so men changed too, each in his own way. When a man dies we can understand more clearly the internal consistency of his varied, sometimes contradictory phases, but while he is alive, today veils yesterday.

In 1933 Paul Eluard was a firm supporter of Surrealism; hardly anyone could have foreseen at the time that his poems would be recited by the *maquis*. Langevin remarked once with a deprecating smile that Joliot-Curie did not realize the full danger of Fascism.

André Malraux is now a Minister in de Gaulle's government. But during eight years, in Paris and in Spain, he was invariably at my side, he was my close friend. Some people who write memoirs enjoy denigrating their former friends; this does not appeal to me. I have warned my readers that when speaking about the living I shall not feel entirely free and shall pass over a good deal in silence. But I cannot speak about the thirties without mentioning Malraux.

In 1933 his novel *La Condition Humaine* appeared. This is what I wrote about him: 'His journey into the past has enriched Malraux not only with a collection of sculpture; it has also cluttered up his understanding with that complexity, that inevitable profundity, those infinitely subtle contradictions with which every culture that has passed its heyday and is doomed to death still teems'. I saw, however, that Malraux was moving towards real life, and I was glad when rather conventional writers awarded him the Prix Goncourt: the committee was influenced by the circumstances of the day – France was shifting to the left.

Malraux introduced me to many young writers – Jean Cassou, Claude Aveline, Eugène Dabit. I struck up a friendship with one of his admirers, Louis Guilloux. A year or two later Guilloux published his book *Le Sang Noir*, one of the best novels written between the two World Wars. He was a teacher in the Breton town of St Brieuc and was quite unlike the usual run of literary men: he was simple, unassuming and had no urge to philosophize or, as the saying goes, to split hairs. (Not so long ago I met him in Rome and we warmly recalled the years long past.)

I also met German writers, including Brecht, sensitive and astute. He talked about death, about Meyerhold's productions, about agreeable trifles. The ex-sailor Turek assured me that before a year was out Hitler would be thrown into the Spree; I liked him for his optimism and gave him a pipe. Toller kept falling in love and into despair, making plans for plays and for the liberation of Germany; he made one feel that his pockets were full of playing cards with which he was forever building houses. I was attracted at once to Anna Seghers, erratic, very lively, shortsighted, though nothing escaped her notice, and absent-minded, yet with a retentive memory for every casually dropped word. We met, we argued, we speculated about what was going to happen next. Some were convinced that German Fascism would shortly collapse while others were equally sure that the brown plague would spread to France.

Colours, by the way, changed, and the plague in France was blue. On several occasions I watched demonstrations of the Solidarité Française: young Fascists in blue shirts marched and raised their arms in salute to their Führer. The Croix de Feu and the Jeunesse Patriote issued their appeals everywhere. Unlike in Germany, there were few workers among the French Fascists, and I watched sardonically as pampered young men swore to exterminate all Communists.

I intended to go to Moscow in the spring. The Congress of Soviet Writers was due to be held in the summer. I was as nervous as a girl going to her first dance: all the writers would be there and an out-spoken and serious discussion about art would take place; it was bound to be a great event.

In 1933 I read *Virgin Soil Upturned*, Bagritsky's latest poems, Pasternak's *Safe Conduct*, Babel's new stories, Selvinsky's poems. Our literature seemed to me to be airborne.

In 1933 many French writers turned hopefully to the Communists; this was probably owing to the horror and anger which millions of people felt when they read of the burning of books by the Fascists, of the executions and pogroms. Among the signatories to the appeal of the Association of Revolutionary Writers were Jean Giono and Pierre Drieu la Rochelle.

Giono I met in the late twenties; he was dreamy, faintly smiling, and wrote sound novels about village life. In 1933, in common with a great many others, he condemned Fascism. After that I did not meet him for a long time and was astonished when I came across an article he had written saying that one should be reconciled to Hitler. When the time came he also reconciled himself to the occupation; but by then I was no longer astonished.

Drieu la Rochelle was a more important figure: talented, sincere in a way, but with a spiritual canker. We both made speeches in the

Maison de la Culture, where the anti-Fascist intelligentsia used to forgather, and had friendly talks. On returning to Paris from one of my journeys I caught sight of Drieu at the entrance to a café in the boulevard St Germain. He hastily turned away. Somebody gave me his last book; it contained strange admissions: 'We shall fight everybody. This is the essence of Fascism ... Freedom is exhausted. Man must immerse himself in his own dark depths. So say I – an intellectual and an unshakeable lover of freedom'. He was seduced by Fascism when the Nazis occupied France, he collaborated with them and shot himself in 1944 realizing that he had backed the wrong horse.

A gifted essayist, Jean Guéhenno, a Breton, the son of a worker, used to come to our meetings. I still have the book he gave me: *Journal d'un Homme de Quarante Ans*; just now I opened it: 'Towards the end of the war, a great fire blazed up in the East. Its light has helped us to live during the past twenty years ... We did not follow that example. The battle did not spread. We watched the sparks from that fire, wafted to us by the wind, disappear and sink in the morass of the West ... In that battle and in that example lie all our hopes, all our happiness ...' Today Guéhenno thinks differently. But what has been done cannot be undone. You can tear pages out of a history book, but history itself cannot be rewritten.

At the end of 1933 the French Fascists raised their heads. Paris buzzed like a disturbed beehive. People argued until they were hoarse, in cafés, in the *métro*, at street corners. Families were divided. In a way it reminded one of Moscow in the summer of 1917.

Even the Montparnasse artists began to take an interest in politics.

For the first time in my life I developed a passion for that box, the wireless set.

In one of his articles Konstantin Fedin recalled an evening spent at my place in the rue du Cotentin, when Malraux questioned him about the Soviet Union and when he got into an argument with Leonhard Frank. We often argued, both at the Coupole and in my flat.

Now and then I used to meet André Chamson; he was a fiery southerner, pleasant and easygoing, but to hear him was to believe that he would execute anyone even suspected of Fascism; he called himself a Jacobin. Today he is an academician; we meet once every five or ten years and peacefully recall the past.

At the bar of the Coupole one met Semyon Chlenov, Elsa Triolet, Aragon, Desnos, Roger Vaillant, René Crevel and other former and actual Surrealists. René Crevel's expression was gentle but haunted: he was taking the break between the Communists and the Surrealists very badly. All my attempts to reassure him failed.

Sometimes the fiery Vogel, publisher of the weeklies *Vu* and *Lu*, invited me to his country house La Faisanderie. He was a snob, not by deliberate intention, but by nature – he did not notice it himself. He admired the Soviet Union, made a trip to Moscow with Ignatyev, entertained Communists but was somewhat taken aback when his daughter Marie-Claude married Vaillant-Couturier. At the Faisanderie heated arguments were constantly going on, and the loudest voice was Vogel's, benign in life and ferocious in his opinions.

There is no need to conceal that I was pleased with my success: despite gloomy predictions, *The Second Day* was being printed in Moscow. This fact may have influenced my assessment of events. In the course of my life I have often noticed how strongly people's judgments are coloured by their private affairs, successes or failures in their work, and even by their state of health.

Be that as it may, I looked towards the future with confidence.

At the end of December I received a telegram from Moscow: 'Married Boris Lapin old surname and address good wishes New Year Irina'. I had met Boris Lapin the year before; what attracted me about him was the unusual combination of his taste for literature and for difficult and dangerous adventures; and I had liked his book. I shall have more to say about him later on. I came to know him better when we shared a flat in Lavrushensky lane. But the telegram surprised me: my daughter Irina had never mentioned Lapin in her letters. The words about the surname and the address amused me – they were typical both of Irina's character and of the times.

We drank to her happiness. The New Year celebration was successful not only because the Polish cook produced a wonderful supper: nearly everybody – and there were a lot of people – was in excellent spirits and we enjoyed ourselves till the early hours of the morning.

I was forty-two; that is not very young but apparently still not mature. I believed in the speedy collapse of Fascism, in the triumph of justice, in the blossoming of art. The past year seemed to me too long a prologue, and I called the volume of articles written in 1932–3: *The Protracted Dénouement*. I shall say nothing to justify myself; I shared the illusions of many and could never have believed that I should reach old age without having witnessed the denouement.

2

I FIRST met Ilf and Petrov in Moscow in 1932, and we grew to be friends a year later when they came to Paris. In those days the travels of our writers abroad were rich in unforeseen incident. Ilf and Petrov went to Italy in a Soviet warship in which they intended to return, but instead they went to Vienna hoping to collect their royalties for the translation of *The Twelve Chairs*. With great difficulty they extracted a small sum from the publisher and left for Paris.

I knew a lady of Russian origin who worked for an ephemeral film company, a very genial creature. I convinced her that no one could write a better comedy film scenario than Ilf and Petrov, and they were given an advance.

Naturally I immediately told them the story of the coal-merchant and the baker, the lottery winners. Every day they asked: 'What have the papers got about our millionaires?' And when it came to writing the scenario Petrov said: 'We've got the beginning – a poor man wins five million'.

They sat in their hotel busily writing away and in the evening came to the Coupole. There we invented various comic situations; others joined in helping the authors of the scenario to find gags: Savich, the artist Altman, the Polish architect Senior and myself.

The film comedy fell through: no matter how hard Ilf and Petrov tried, the script showed the lack of any real knowledge of French life. But the purpose had been achieved: they had had their stay in Paris. I, too, had gained something: I had got to know two delightful people.

In one's mind the two names run into one: Ilfpetrov. Yet they were quite unalike. Ilya Ilf was shy and taciturn, his jokes were caustic but infrequent and, like many writers who have made millions of people laugh – from Gogol to Zoshchenko – he was melancholic. In Paris he found his brother, an artist, who had long before come from Odessa and who now tried to initiate Ilf into the mysteries of modern art. Ilf liked spiritual turmoil and havoc. Petrov, on the contrary, liked snugness; he made friends easily and at gatherings he spoke both for

246

himself and for Ilf; he could make people laugh for hours on end and himself joined in the laughter. He was an exceptionally warm-hearted man; he wanted everyone to have a better life and was always on the look-out for things that could ease or enrich their existence. I think he was the greatest optimist I have ever known: he said of an indubitable scoundrel: 'Perhaps people have got it wrong? You can't believe everything they say'. Six months before Hitler attacked us Petrov was sent to Germany, and on his return assured us: 'The Germans are sick and tired of war'.

No, Ilf and Petrov were no Siamese twins, but they wrote together, tramped the world together and lived in perfect harmony. They, as it were, complemented one another – Ilf's caustic wit was a good spicing for Petrov's gentler humour.

Despite his taciturnity Ilf somehow put Petrov in the shade so that I really got to know Petrov only much later, during the war.

The fate of the Soviet satirists – Zoshchenko, Koltsov, Erdman – comes to my mind. Ilf and Petrov were lucky in every way. With their first novel the readers took them to their hearts. They had few enemies and they were seldom criticized adversely. They went abroad, travelled all over America and the book they wrote about this trip was clever as well as amusing – they knew how to use their eyes. It was in 1936 that they wrote about America, and this, too, was a piece of luck: what we all call 'the cult of personality' was not favourable to satire.

Both of them died young. Ilf contracted tuberculosis in America and died in the spring of 1937 at the age of thirty-nine. Petrov was thirty-eight when he was killed near the front-line in an air crash.

Even before his American journey Ilf said more than once: 'Our repertory's exhausted', or 'The tree's bearing no more fruit'. But after reading his notebooks one realizes that, as a writer, he was only just getting into his stride. He died with the rank of Chekhonte[1], and he once said to me: 'I wish I could write a story like *Gooseberries* or *The Darling*'. He was not only a satirist but a poet (in his early youth he wrote poetry but this is not the point – the entries in his journal are permeated with genuine poetry, laconic and restrained).

'How are we to write now?' Ilf asked me during his last stay in Paris. 'The "great fixers" have been withdrawn from circulation. In

[1] Chekhov's *nom de plume* in his early days.

newspaper articles one can show up despotic bureaucrats, thieves, scoundrels. If there's a name and address, it's an "ugly case". But if you write a story, a howl immediately goes up: "You're generalizing, it's not a typical case, it's slander".'

One day in Paris Ilf and Petrov were discussing what should be the subject of their third novel. Ilf suddenly looked glum: 'Do you really think it's worth while writing a novel? All you want to do, Yevgeny, is to prove, as usual, that Vsevolod Ivanov was wrong and that palm-trees grow in Siberia'.

Nevertheless, among his numerous notes Ilf left a plan for a fantastic novel. The story is that for some unknown reason there is a plan to build a ciné-city 'on the ancient Greek pattern but with all the latest American technical improvements' in a small Volga town. 'Two expeditions were to be sent out simultaneously – one to Athens, the other to Hollywood – after which their experience was to be, so to say, merged, and the place built'. Those who go to Hollywood receive insurance money on the death of one of their members and take to drink. 'They wandered knee-deep in the waters of the Pacific[1] and the magnificent sunset lit up their radiantly drunken mugs. They were fished out by Molokane[2] commissioned by Mr Aberson, representative of the American cinema.' In Athens the members of the expedition fare badly: their drachmas soon give out. Both expeditions meet in Paris in the Sphinx brothel and, horrified, return home, fearing retribution. But everybody has forgotten them and, besides, no one intends any longer to build the ciné-city.

They did not write the novel. Ilf knew he was dying. He wrote in his notebook: 'Such an ominous, icy spring evening that one's soul is filled with cold and fear. I've had awfully bad luck'.

After Ilf's death Petrov wrote: 'In my opinion his last notes, typed straight out in close spacing, are a remarkable literary work. Poetical and sad'.

I, too, think that Ilf's notebooks are not only a remarkable document but also splendid prose. He succeeded in expressing his loathing of vulgarity, the repugnance it aroused in him: 'How I love the conversation of office-workers. The calm, solemn talk of the messenger-girls, the clerks' unhurried exchange of thoughts "and for the sweet

[1] Russian saying: For a drunkard the sea is only knee-deep.
[2] Sect of Old Believers, particularly abstemious.

there were stewed cherries" ' . . . 'We were sitting in silence under the Ostafyevo colonnade basking in the sunshine. The silence lasted some two hours. Suddenly one of the holiday-makers appeared on the road carrying a chromium kettle. It shone blindingly in the sunlight. All at once everybody became extraordinarily animated: "Where did you buy it? How much did it cost?" ' . . . 'A new shop has opened. Sausage for anaemics, pies for neurasthenics'. . . . 'The land of serene idiots'. . . . 'Those were the proud offspring of small responsible workers.' . . . ' "There is no God! – And is there any cheese?" the teacher asked sadly.' He wrote about circles he knew well: 'The composers did nothing but write denunciations of one another on music-paper.' . . . 'In all the journals they come down on Zharov. For ten years they have been praising him, now they will attack him for another ten. They will criticize him for what they formerly used to praise him. It is difficult and boring to live among serene idiots.'

There is something about Ilf's notes that remind one of Chekhov. But Ilf never came to write either *The Darling* or *Gooseberries*: he did not have the time, or perhaps, out of sheer modesty, he could not bring himself to do it.

Petrov took his bereavement very hard: it was not only grief at the loss of his closest friend – he realized that the author whom people called Ilfpetrov had died. When we met in 1940 after a long separation, he said with a sadness unusual in him: 'I'll have to start all over again'.

What could he have written? It is hard to tell. He was highly gifted and had a strong personality of his own. There was no time for him to show what he could do – the war broke out.

He did unrewarding work. S. A. Lozovsky was the head of the Sovinformburo which was responsible for sending information abroad. Things were difficult for us, many of our allies were giving us up as lost. The Americans had to be told the truth. Lozovsky knew that few of our writers or journalists understood the mentality of the Americans or could write for them without Marxist quotations and clichés.

So Petrov became war-correspondent for NANA (The North American News Agency, which had also sent Hemingway to Spain). Petrov did his job manfully and patiently; he also wrote for *Izvestia* and *Red Star*.

We lived in the Hotel Moskva; it was the first winter of the war. On 5th February the lights went out, the lifts stopped. On that same night

Petrov returned from near Sukhinichi suffering from shell shock. He concealed his state from his travelling companions; painfully he crept up the stairs to the ninth floor and collapsed. I came to see him two days later; he had difficulty in speaking. A doctor was sent for. As he lay in bed he wrote about the fighting.

In June 1942, at a time when things were pretty bad, we were gathered in the same hotel in K. A. Umansky's room. Admiral Isakov arrived. Petrov asked the admiral to help him to get into besieged Sevastopol. The admiral tried to dissuade him. Petrov insisted. A few days later he managed to make his way into Sevastopol. There he was caught in a fierce bombing attack. He was returning in the destroyer *Tashkent*; a German bomb hit the ship; there were many casualties. Petrov reached Novorossiysk. There he was involved in a motor accident, but once again he escaped unhurt. He started writing an article about Sevastopol and was in a hurry to get back to Moscow. The plane was flying low, as ours generally did near the front-line, and hit the crest of a hill. Death had been pursuing Petrov for a long time and had caught up with him at last.

(Soon after, Admiral Isakov was gravely wounded, and later Umansky died in a plane crash in Mexico.)

Ilf and Petrov stood out in the world of letters: they were both good men, they were not conceited, they did not pontificate, did not try to push themselves regardless of others. They undertook any job they were asked to do, even the hardest, diverting much of their energy to newspaper work; and this does them honour for they did it to combat callousness, boorishness, conceit. They were good men; there is no more fitting word. They were good writers: at a very difficult time people laughed when they read their books. The happy rogue Ostap Bender amused and still amuses millions of readers. And I, not being spoilt by the friendship of my fellow writers, will add this about Ilya Ilf and Yevgeny Petrov: they were good friends to me.

3

ONE DAY in 1931 or 1932 I was lunching with Merle in a Marseilles restaurant. At the next table sat a handsome dark-haired man who looked like an Argentinian dancer; he was paying court to a lady; when a flower-girl offered her a rose he threw a banknote to the girl and said too loudly: 'Keep the change'. Merle leant forward and said: 'That's Alexander, one of the most gifted Paris swindlers. By the way, he's a compatriot of yours'. I did not press him for details: Paris had plenty of gifted swindlers of every nationality.

But in January 1934 I saw in all the papers photographs of a sleek dark-haired man. Alexander Stavisky had indeed been born in Kiev, in the Slobodka. The journalists called him 'handsome Sasha'. It emerged that the handsome fellow had dishonestly pocketed in no time at all six hundred and fifty million francs. The papers said that he had already been had up three times, that he enjoyed the confidence of diplomats and was working for the police and that he distributed cheques as nonchalantly as roses, not only to deputies but also to certain Ministers.

A paper war started: the right-wing asserted that Stavisky bribed the Radicals, the Radicals retorted that cheques also came the way of Tardieu's friends.

Suddenly headlines reported that handsome Sasha had shot himself. The papers gave touching details; the swindler became a kind of Werther. The melodrama did not last long; it turned out that Stavisky had been shot by the police agent Voix. The police feared that, once cornered, Sasha would talk too freely, and men in high places were involved.

The whole thing reminded one of Ostap Bender's adventures. The investigation disclosed that the deputy Bonnaure had accepted large bribes. I do not remember to which party he belonged, but during the election campaign he had written: 'My programme is: enough of political principles! Honesty before all else!'

Financial scandals were an everyday occurrence in France and every year some gigantic swindle came to light: Oustric, Péret,

Baghdad, 'Ngoko-Sanga'. This seemed just one more of them. I never thought that handsome Sasha would open a new page in history.

The right-wing papers raised the question of morality; a matter of political calculation on their part: the government in power was a left-wing bloc. The Minister of Foreign Affairs, Paul-Boncour, was in favour of a *rapprochement* with the Soviet Union. As for the various Fascist organizations, they derived their inspiration from Germany's example; the Stavisky scandal, in which deputies and several Ministers were involved, furthered the campaign against the parliamentary system for 'a healthy State under a firm authority'.

A ministerial crisis ensued; it brought little change, for the Radicals and Socialists held a majority in the Chamber. The new Premier, Daladier, taking courage, decided to replace the prefect of police, the all-powerful Chiappe, who protected the Fascist organizations. Chiappe, despite his short stature, suffered from megalomania; he was a Corsican and apparently saw himself as another Napoleon. On hearing of his dismissal, he said that if need be he would 'go to the people'.

And indeed, two days later, on 6th February, I saw a Fascist riot in the Place de la Concorde itself. The supporters of the Croix de Feu, Solidarité Française and Jeunesse Patriote tried to break through across the bridge to the Chamber of Deputies where the terrified members of parliament were in session.

The singing of the *Marseillaise* by the Fascists was punctuated with yells. The police behaved with uncommon mildness: many of them, also from Corsica, were devoted to their chief and fellow-countryman and, besides, they were dealing not with workers in caps but with well-dressed young men. The Fascists set fire to buses, tore down statues of nymphs in the Tuileries, slashed the horses of the mounted Garde Républicaine with razor-blades. Shots sounded from time to time. Shady types arrived on the scene and started looting the shops. Towards morning everyone got tired and went home.

The Radicals liked to call themselves Jacobins; but these Jacobins lost courage and Daladier resigned. The usual parliamentary shuffle began and a new Cabinet was scraped together by Doumergue, who brought into it such respectable Frenchmen as Pétain and Laval.

All this seemed very much as usual, but in fact the times had changed. The Communists issued a call to the workers to demonstrate against the Fascists on 9th February. The night was foggy. I walked towards the Gare de l'Est where clashes between workers and police were said to be going on. An elderly worker, walking beside me, asked for a light and said: 'It's a disgrace'. At this moment a police car dived out of the fog; a policeman jumped out and struck the worker over the head with his truncheon.

They were building a barricade in a narrow street, dragging up barrels, tables, handcarts; the *Internationale* was sung. I tried to push farther on. Shooting began. It was impossible to see anything. When I ran to the street corner there was no one there; all I saw was blood on the pavement.

Day was already dawning when I made my way to the telegraph office which stayed open all night in the Bourse building: I wanted to send off an account of the events as soon as possible. On the way I was stopped several times and searched.

This happened on Friday. The next two days brought about many moves: the various trade union organizations – those who followed the Communists and those led by the Socialists – succeeded in reaching an agreement; a general strike was called for Monday, 12th February. The workers' organizations appealed for everyone to assemble in the Place de la Nation.

The day before, the papers said that the strike was doomed to failure; however, on the next day no paper appeared: the printers had come out. Life was at a standstill: there were no buses, the shops were closed, the postal service did not function; even the teachers joined in the strike.

I went to the Place de la Nation. This was the first general popular demonstration in Paris and the most striking thing about it was the combination of stern determination and irrepressible gaiety, typical of the Paris crowd. Hundreds of lorries packed with police and Gardes Républicaine were stationed in the side-streets. But in the square people were joking and singing. Someone had the idea of decorating the statue of the Republic with a red flag; the statue is large and stands on a high pedestal; immediately a pyramid of human bodies was formed. The demonstration warmly greeted foreigners – refugees from Italy, Poland, Germany. I thought of the maniacal Fascists in the Place de la Concorde. Two worlds . . .

12th February was to become a memorable date for France. It might have been thought that nothing had happened, for the next morning Paris looked its usual self. The Fascists' demonstration of 6th February had brought the Government down, whereas now all the Ministers retained their posts. But it was precisely 12th February that produced a real change – not in the composition of the Cabinet but in France. Almost overnight speculations about when the Fascists would demonstrate again and whom they would set up as Führer came to an end. Everybody realized that the power was with the people. 12th February was the first rehearsal of the Front Populaire which, two years later, was to shake up France.

All day I wandered through the streets, happy and excited, and in the evening I wrote an article and took it to the telegraph office. On the next day I received a telegram from my newspaper: armed clashes between workers and police had occurred in Vienna; I was to apply at once for an Austrian visa and set out with all speed.

12th February had lent me wings: I saw victory everywhere. After Paris – Vienna. It looked as though that 'last fight to be faced', of which the workers had been singing in the foggy night, was approaching. It was frustrating that a man with a Soviet passport could not take part in the shooting: all I could do was to carry out a war correspondent's job.

4

I REALIZED that the Austrians would not give me an entry visa and decided to use strategy: I said I was going to Moscow by way of Vienna and asked for a transit visa. Secretly I thought: 'I'll stay in Vienna as long as necessary; besides, there's no telling who'll come out on top'. But the Austrians took two days to give me a transit visa.

When I arrived in Vienna, snow was falling in large flakes as if trying to cover the fresh wounds; holes showed black in the walls of the houses smashed by the Heimwehr's artillery. In Floridsdorf a smell of burning hung about. Strips of sheets and handkerchiefs – the white flags of surrender – fluttered from the windows. I saw the dead body of a woman abandoned on a pile of rubble. Heimwehr men stopped passers-by in the streets and occasionally searched them. It was all very much like Presnya in December 1905.

A journalist told me that the day before, when fighting was still going on, a worker was brought to trial; he had been severely wounded and was carried into court on a stretcher. Three hours later they hanged him. This first death sentence was followed by others.

I tried to find people I knew and make inquiries; everybody was frightened and answered my questions reluctantly. I learnt that many members of the Schutzbund had managed to reach the Czechoslovak frontier.

I saw victory in Paris, but in Vienna I saw defeat. I did not realize the nature of the epoch that we were about to enter and the crushing of the Schutzbund staggered me.

I recalled that when I had been in Vienna in 1928 I had been invited to visit the workers' estate; the invitation was on handsome paper bearing the city's crest and was signed by the burgomaster, a Social-Democrat. I was shown round by a municipal councillor, also a Social-Democrat. I saw excellent houses with gardens, sports grounds, spacious reading-rooms. The admiration I expressed pleased my guide. He invited me into a café where workers were sitting poring over dozens of newspapers of different political trends. I remember imparting my doubts to the amiable Austrian: 'The houses are magnificent. But aren't you building them on land that belongs to somebody else?' My companion launched into explanations that Socialism would conquer by peaceful means – after all, at the last elections in Vienna seventy per cent of the electorate had voted for the Social-Democrats.

Now these lovely houses, named after Marx, Engels, Goethe, Liebknecht, stood blackened and mutilated by shells.

I heard a shot: a Heimwehr man fell. This was the last feeble peal of the past thunderstorm. In the Ring the cafés were crowded with elegant customers. Theatre posters were being pasted up: *Ball in Savoy, The Temperamental Maiden, Let Us Dream.*

I travelled to Bratislava and found Schutzbund men there. One of them said he had saved a number of documents. He was a Social-Democrat, a worker. He spoke to me for a long time about the tragic events, showed me minutes of meetings which preceded the February days and the reports of regional leaders. He said: 'I don't mind your being a Communist. I've read your books. Write the truth. Tell everyone that we weren't cowards. Of course there were traitors like Korbel, but there weren't many of them. What's terrible is that our leaders hesitated too long. They're good men, I've been working with them for twelve years. But when the fighting began they lost their heads'.

I read the documents carefully and recorded what rank-and-file participants in the fighting told me. I could have got down to work at once, but was told that a Schutzbund leader, Julius Deutsch, was in Brno. I went to Brno. Deutsch frowned and then began to tell his story. He was revolted by the fact that Dollfuss and Fey had provoked the rising. I was struck by the discrepancy between the political opportunism of his arguments and the nature of the man: hard and, one would have said, unyielding. He behaved better than he reasoned. (His subsequent fate was also full of contradictions: he was in Spain during the Civil War; he was promoted to the rank of general, and the Social-Democrats cold-shouldered him – he had the reputation of being left wing. Later, too, he often quarrelled with his comrades and was constantly being expelled from the party and readmitted.)

Here was a man disheartened by the events; his resentment made quite a lot of things clear to me.

Brno is close to the Austrian frontier. All the time people who had escaped from the reprisals were crossing over; they spoke about the gallows, the barracks into which 3,000 workers had been herded. I read in the paper that among other 'Marxist organizations' the 'Union of Allotment-Holders and Rabbit-Breeders' had been proscribed. It was funny but I could not summon up a smile.

In Brno I wrote some articles for *Izvestia*; they formed a little book and came out in the paper in serial form.

What I wanted to do was not only to describe the events but also to try and understand what had happened. The Austrian workers were well organized. Perhaps because the Communists were much weaker here than in Germany, the Austrian Social-Democrats appeared different from their German comrades; they had, for instance, formed fighting units – the Schutzbund – and even concealed rifles and machine-guns from the authorities. Why, then, had they been put down in two or three days?

In our press the Social-Democrats were in those days called Social-Fascists; this was caustic but did not carry conviction. Of course there were traitors among the German Social-Democrats who quickly adapted themselves to the Nazi régime. But the Social-Democrats were no fascists; this was clear at the time to anyone familiar with life in the West. The Fascists did not fear the Social-Democrats, but the Social-Democrats were mortally afraid of the Fascists, and if they did not come out against Fascism it was simply because they feared the Communists as much as the Fascists and tried to constitute a 'third force', whereas in fact they lost all power and led the workers from capitulation to capitulation.

The events in Vienna were a healthy lesson for me. I saw several Austrian Social-Democrats, perfectly honest men, personally courageous but politically timid who, without intending to, did everything to ensure victory for Chancellor Dollfuss and Prince Starhemberg, the leader of the Heimwehr.

At the beginning of February the Vice-Chancellor of Austria, Major Emil Fey, declared: 'Within the coming week we shall clear Austria of Marxists'. What did the leaders of the Social-Democrats do in reply? They tried to persuade the left-wing Christian-Socialist deputies to join in their protest. In the meantime the police arrested the regional leaders of the Schutzbund one after another. The general strike was postponed from day to day. When the Linz workers refused to give up their rifles and fought back, a telegram arrived from Vienna about 'Aunt Emma's health'; this was a code message – Vienna advised that the demonstration should be put off. Only when the

Floridsdorf workers went on strike and dug out their concealed weapons did the Schutzbund leaders send the telegram 'Karl has fallen ill' – which meant that the general strike was on.

This is what I wrote in *Izvestia*: 'The Social-Democratic leaders are right in declaring that the fight was forced on them against their will . . . They were ready to yield their arms – so long as they might keep their stripes: the right to call themselves Social-Democrats in a Fascist State. Dollfuss refused them this right. So they were left with only one alternative: either to throw in the towel, as their German comrades had done, or to put up a fight. I know that in the February days many Social-Democrats gave proof of real heroism. They were not afraid of death. But they were afraid of victory'. In the newspaper office these lines made rather a confused impression but were nevertheless printed.

The events in Vienna made me pause to think about the political helplessness of the Social-Democratic leaders. I asked myself how they had managed to render sections of the working-class so placidly content and even docile. The printers in Vienna did not strike. You could not accuse them of ignorance. They knew well enough that the Chancellor, Dollfuss, would do nothing to make their lives happier, but, though sympathizing with the Schutzbund, they set up and printed newspapers where their fellow-workers were called rapists, murderers, paid agents; they knew this was not true but, dubious about the success of resistance, were afraid of losing their jobs, and, as a matter of fact, they earned good wages. The railwaymen also refused to join in the strike; this allowed the government to move military units and crush resistance in the provinces. On the first day some twenty thousand workers took part in the armed struggle; on the second and third days only seven or eight thousand still resisted. This did not astonish me; it has happened time and time again throughout history. What was astonishing was the fact that the general strike collapsed at once and that the fighters of the Schutzbund found themselves without a rear.

I realized now that Hitler's triumph was no solitary, isolated incident. Everywhere the working-class was disunited, worn out by the fear of unemployment, confused in its thinking, tired of promises and paper wars. I asked myself what would happen next – Paris or Vienna? Resistance or surrender?

The year 1934 which I had entered with such high hopes became a

258

year of disillusionment. Fascist risings and *coups d'état* followed one another – from Latvia to Spain. In the autumn Asturian workers tried to head off the course of events and were beaten.

I cannot say that the Austrian bourgeoisie was happy in February 1934 about the Heimwehr victory. Of course they were glad that the Schutzbund had been defeated, but at the same time they feared Fascism. They naïvely longed to bring back the distant past: the care-free and lighthearted Hapsburg years, the witty articles ridiculing the régime, the Ministerial crises, the musical-comedy officers in the Ring. But the century refused to stand on ceremony. In February Dollfuss crushed the workers and declared a new Constitution which reeked of Berlin militarism and Vatican incense. I saw Dollfuss in Vienna. He looked like a dwarf; Velasquez would have made a good painting of him. He wore a self-satisfied smile. Soon after, he went to Italy where he signed an agreement with Mussolini in the hope of saving Austria from Hitler. And in July he was killed by an admirer of the Führer. When, two years later, I was back in Vienna the February victors looked pretty miserable. Prince Starhemberg had taken up physical training, the former Vice-Chancellor Fey was working in a shipping office. The Chancellor was the supremely cautious Schuschnigg who knew that one must not incur the wrath of either God or Hitler. When in May 1938 the Nazis broke into Austria, Schuschnigg counselled the Austrians to offer no resistance.

Nevertheless the Nazis put him into a concentration camp. The gay Viennese bourgeoisie had to die for Greater Germany on the Don and on the Volga. Such was the outcome of the tragedy which began in February 1934.

5

To GET out of Czechoslovakia proved rather difficult. When I arrived in Prague snow was still lying about. The gardens had time to break into leaf. Nezval wrote a dozen poems and in various cafés tried to persuade me that Breton's Surrealism was little different from Socialist Realism.

I met Karel Čapek. Some left-wing critics were attacking him: the times were menacing yet he was writing about lapdogs. Outwardly Čapek was like a London clubman; he was polite and reserved, but I immediately sensed the bitterness behind the mask. An hour later Čapek said: 'In the past people used to speak about an old man with his back bent under the burden of years. We can say: under the burden of centuries. The epoch of aggressive stupidity is upon us'.

Mayerova told me funny stories about Hašek's life. Only sixteen years had passed since the end of the war and already the days of Schweik seemed idyllic.

Hofmeister began to draw me from memory – with or without my pipe, with or without my suitcase; this object, I must confess, worried me and, out of superstition, I did not unpack my suitcase although my friends had long ceased asking me when I intended to leave. They had got used to me. But I myself could not get used to the situation; much as I liked Prague my one wish was to get out of it.

My articles had appeared in *Izvestia* before I had asked the Austrians for a transit visa; it was refused. The Germans also refused. The Prague–Paris plane touched down at Nuremberg and a transit visa was necessary.

Herzfelde transferred his 'Malik' publishing house to Prague. When I saw books of mine there that had been published in Berlin I was surprised that they had not been burnt. It appeared that the Nazis were selling proscribed books abroad, and selling them at a discount. They needed the *auto-da-fés* as a demonstration of the purity of their motives and of their inflexibility, but they did not despise Czech kronen.

There were many visitors at the publisher's: various German writers had moved to Prague. One of them told me that at the German embassy there was an official who enjoyed von Papen's favour and that he was a great amateur of letters who collected all the proscribed books and had had *Julio Jurenito* bound in *de luxe* covers. The man might prove generous and let me have a transit visa.

I went for the second time to the German embassy. The bibliophile was tall and very fair with a military bearing but shortsighted, kindly eyes. He received me amiably enough, praised my books but refused to give me the visa: 'I don't want any incidents'. I did not understand what incidents he meant and started to assure him that while in Nuremberg I would not open my mouth. The diplomat smiled: 'An incident might occur through no fault of yours. You appear to be insufficiently informed. Read Ilya Ehrenburg's articles on Germany'.

I wanted to travel through Hungary and Yugoslavia. The Hungarian embassy asked Budapest for instructions; I paid for a long telegram. The reply was brief. The secretary of the embassy rang me up at my hotel: 'You will have to choose another route'.

The Czechoslovak Minister of Foreign Affairs, Eduard Beneš, invited me to come and see him. In a very large study I saw a small, extremely lively man. He spoke at first about literature, then said with a smile: 'I know you like Slovakia and criticize our attitude towards Slovak culture'. He then proceeded to prove to me that the policy of the government was not so bad after all. I knew that negotiations were going on between Moscow and Prague and that it would be better to hold my tongue, but could not help myself and began to argue.

Finally Beneš said: 'Perhaps I can help you in some way?' I hastily replied: 'Yes. Help me to leave your delightful country. I must get to Paris, all my plans have been upset'. And I told him about my unhappy experiences with transit visas. Beneš led me up to a map of Europe that hung on the wall: 'You can see for yourself how surrounded we are. Czechoslovakia is in mortal danger'.

After some reflection Beneš said that he would try to get me a Rumanian transit visa and that if he succeeded I could travel by way of Rumania, Yugoslavia and Italy. I took another look at the map and smiled: I had to go west but would travel eastwards. Yet I had no choice and could only thank Beneš.

Sure enough, two days later I was invited to the Rumanian embassy. Everybody examined me for a long time and then my passport even longer – they had never seen a Soviet passport before. (This was before diplomatic relations were established.)

The journey was lengthy. I was obliged to spend the night in the Rumanian town of Oradea. I was fascinated by the shabby but rather dashing cabbies who drove overdressed ladies about, by the barefooted peasants and the smart policemen, while the journalists were no less fascinated by me: my Soviet passport seemed to them like the first swallow. From Oradea in an abbreviated and leisurely train I reached the town of Timisoara and there saw two remarkable personalities: the Minister of Education Angelescu and the Führer of the local German colonists, Fabricius. The Minister spoke of 'Greater Rumania', the *Führer* of 'Greater Germany'.

On leaving Rumania I was searched and my fountain pen was taken from me as contraband, but when the customs officer learnt that I was a writer he returned it to me with a sigh. The Yugoslav customs officer, to my surprise, asked me for my autograph and said that he had liked my book *Thirteen Pipes*. It turned out that he was a Russian who had come to Yugoslavia with the remnants of Wrangel's army and was now very homesick. There were armed guards on board the train. Some said that trains were blown up by Croat separatists, the Ustashi; others that the dynamiters were acting on instructions from the Belgrade police.

In Trieste I sought out an acquaintance, the wife of a doctor; she told me a long story about the stupidity and humiliation of life under the Duce. When she was seeing me off she asked the station-master at what time the train was due to leave and raised her hand in the Fascist salute. Afterwards she said: 'Forgive me for doing that. One's got to do it'.

I arrived in Venice. The platform was spread with red carpets; along them the Austrian Chancellor Dollfuss had solemnly passed. In St Mark's Square there was a parade of blackshirts. Loudspeakers were relaying Mussolini's speech: 'Fascist and proletarian Italy, forward!' The blackshirts shouted joyfully and indeed marched forward – across the square glistening with the spring rain.

In Milan I was invited to his house by the publisher who had recently brought out the Italian translation of *The Second Day*. The book had been provided with a foreword which said that the novel teemed with faulty judgments – for instance, the author glorified Communism – but the Italian reader would be able to separate the chaff from the grain: *The Second Day* glorified labour, and everybody knew that only Fascist Italy had succeeded in assuring the freedom and happiness of the workers. After closing all the doors the publisher began to explain to me in a half-whisper that it would have been impossible to publish the book without the foreword. Then his daughter, a student, came in and said loudly: 'When I see "Duce, Duce" on the walls I could howl with shame'.

I brought back to France unhappy impressions: fascists and semifascists had swiftly transformed Europe into an impenetrable jungle. At the frontiers all the trees had been cut down and in their stead rose thickets of barbed wire. Travellers were searched for newspapers, revolvers, foreign currency, bombs. Croat Fascists attacked Serbs who shared their opinions. In Rumania the Iron Guard looted shops and threatened the Magyars, while in Hungary Horthy's followers killed peasants and swore they would reconquer Transylvania. Italian blackshirts shouted about the Austrian Tyrol and French Savoy. The Fascist plague crossed frontiers without any visas.

In the description of my journey across the European jungle I wrote: 'As one travels through Europe, it feels as though it were at war. Who is fighting whom it is hard to say. In all probability everybody is fighting everybody else'.

Before my eyes rose the pictures of defeat: Floridsdorf, white rags, charred façades, Heimwehr men.

However, what I saw in France raised my spirits once more. During my absence hundreds of vigilance committees had been formed. Peasants came to the towns armed with shotguns and asked where they could find the Fascists. I went to one of the innumerable meetings in the Italie quarter; the temper of the people was such that if they had been told: 'Here are the Fascists', they would have attacked tanks with their bare hands.

Professors Langevin and Alain organized a vigilance committee in which writers, scholars and university teachers joined; among them were men who until recently had refused to take part in political life: Roger Martin du Gard, Julien Benda, Léon Paul Fargue and many others.

Jean-Richard Bloch arrived, gay and excited, saying that the February days had transformed France and that things were moving towards a revolution.

In the beginning of June I set out for Moscow. Once again I had to give some thought to my itinerary; I chose to go by sea: London–Leningrad. Malraux came with me – he had a number of plans: *Mezhrabpom* (International Workers' Aid) wanted to make a film based on one of his novels, and Malraux hoped to discuss the production with Dovzhenko; further, he had started to write a novel about oil and intended to visit Baku.

The Soviet boat passed through the Kiel canal. I eagerly observed the banks: here was Fascist Germany. People with long-handled nets offered chocolate, cigars and eau-de-cologne to the passengers.

Suddenly I caught sight of a worker; he raised his clenched fist in salute to the Soviet flag. It is hard to describe how fervently I wanted to believe in that token, and not I alone. I raised my fist in reply, saluting not only the courageous man but also the revolution which did not happen the next year, nor ten years later.

To see the truth before others see it is gratifying even if one is abused for it. It is far easier to be fooled along with everybody else.

6

In Moscow I had no flat. Lyuba went to live with her mother in Leningrad, and I, with the help of *Izvestia*, managed to get a room in the Hotel National. It was small, unattractive and expensive, but I had no choice.

One morning when I ordered tea, the waiter returned empty-handed: I would get no tea, from today the restaurant served only those who paid in foreign currency. This angered me but I kept my temper and asked the man to bring me some boiling water and a teapot to make tea in – I had both tea and sugar. Again he came back empty-handed: 'They wouldn't give me the hot water, they say they don't cater for Soviet citizens'.

I decided to go and see the manager. Potted plants were set out all along the staircase. Floor-waiters in bright green tunics and chambermaids in rustling aprons and smart caps stood in rows; at a word of command they bowed, turned to the right and to the left, smiled, then bowed again. It reminded me of a rehearsal for a film about the life of merchants in the old days.

I made my way into the restaurant and found it transformed: they were selling salt-cellars with carved cockerels, very inferior icons produced by Suzdal icon-painters, and boxes, brooches and saucers adorned with Vasnetsov's[1] paladins. The orchestra was rehearsing *Down Mother Volga*.

The manager explained that I must immediately vacate my room: in an hour's time a large group of American tourists was due to arrive from Leningrad.

I hung about to have a look at the important travellers; they were all very rich people. The floor-waiters panted as they lugged their heavy suitcases. The chambermaids, remembering their lesson, smiled coquettishly and the tourists nodded condescendingly. I spoke to one of them who turned out to be a broker from Buenos-Aires. He told me that people had tried to dissuade him from going to

---

[1] Famous painter of religious frescoes and folklore pictures.

Moscow but that now he was quite reassured: the hotel was like any other: 'Of course, it's less smart, but on the other hand one feels the Russian atmosphere. I've been to Paris, there's an excellent restaurant there called the Troika'.

(I was angry but not surprised. Shortly before I had been in Ivanovo. I went into a restaurant. Dusty palms cluttered up the dining-room. The tables were covered with grubby tablecloths bearing the dried traces of yesterday's sauces and the day before yesterday's *borshch*. I seated myself at a table that looked cleaner than the rest. The waitress shouted: 'Can't you see this table is for foreigners?' It appeared that two young Turks were studying at the local Textile Institute. They were looked upon with respect and served at a clean table.)

I went off to the newspaper office, asked for a typewriter and wrote an article which I called *Plainly Speaking*. I described all I had seen at the Hotel National and said that it was ludicrous to present the Soviet country as an old Russian hostelry with well-drilled servants and bogus sentiment. 'Were I your guide, citizen tourists, I should show you not the past but the present of my country. I should not prevaricate and should not conceal from you many harsh facts. I should not say to you: "Look to the right – there's a little old church there", because on the left there is a queue lined up. There is plenty of want, crassness, ignorance in our country, for we are only now beginning to live. You have heard for yourselves the nasty story of our hotel, it will enable you to understand how hard it is for us to throw off the cruel heritage from the past. Besides the story of the floor-waiters in green tunics I could tell you many other unpleasant things. We hear a great deal about respect for man, but not everyone has yet learnt how to respect him. I have told you some nasty facts, now let me speak of some admirable ones'. I described the builders of Kuznetsk, peasants in a rest-home, the literary circle at the ballbearing factory. I knew the capitalist world, where they were still burning cotton and books, where the unemployed slept under bridges, where Fascists organized pogroms; in short, it was not only despicable but stupid to be ashamed of our poverty before some hundred American tourists.

Let me recall the date: June 1934. People lived austerely but one could feel that things were easier in comparison with the two preceding years. The cult of personality was already beginning to make itself felt in articles, portraits, in exaggeratedly strident 'hurrahs' which revived dying applause. At times this offended my taste but not my conscience – how could I have foreseen the turn events would take? That summer people argued a lot and dreamt about the future. There was still no shackling and *Izvestia* printed my article.

I received many letters: readers thanked me for reminding people of the dignity of Soviet man. But a cloud was gathering over my head. Foreign newspaper correspondents reprinted my article abroad. *The Times* said that a Soviet writer had disclosed how Intourist 'misled foreign tourists'. The Intourist people claimed that after reading my article several English and French tourists who had intended to visit the Soviet Union had changed their minds and that I had thus caused financial loss to the State. The newspaper stood up for me. (I knew nothing about all this to-do: I was at a lumber camp near Archangel.)

In describing this comic and not particularly important episode I had no intention of making the readers laugh. Recalling the ridiculous play-acting at the National has started me on another train of thought.

The floor-waiters bowing low to the Intourist travellers came back to my mind for the first time in 1947 when one of the then leading members of the Writers' Union told me that from now on and for many years to come the task of our literature would be to fight servility and sycophancy. I plied him with questions: I hoped he was thinking of the humiliating behaviour of people like the Intourist manager whom I had described, of the blind admiration Moscow women of fashion felt for any sort of foreign rubbish, of the people, not very numerous but still to be found, for whom the world of money, free competition and shady deals remained attractive. But I was mistaken: the comrade who was speaking to me explained that it was imperative to struggle against servility in relation to the scholars, writers and artists of the West.

I could not grasp at all what 'West' meant: for me the countries of Western Europe and America were not of one hue: Joliot-Curie lived in a different world from Bidault, Eluard was quite different from Guy Mollet, Hemingway distinctly unlike President Truman. 'The West?' But was not Marx born in Trier, was not the October Revolution preceded by the days of June 1848, by the Paris Commune, by the struggle of the workers in various western countries?

Very soon I came to see what combatting servility and sycophancy boiled down to. The directors of the Food Industry renamed Camembert '*zakusochny* cheese' and called Leningrad 'Nord' coffee '*Sever*'. One newspaper announced that the palaces at Versailles were imitations of

267

those built by Peter the Great. The *Great Soviet Encyclopedia* printed an article on Aviation attempting to prove that Western European scientists and engineers had made a very feeble contribution to the development of aerodynamics. In one article of mine the editor deleted a sentence saying that Edouard Manet was a great twentieth-century artist: 'This is sheer sycophancy'.

In 1949, during the First Peace Congress which met in Paris, the French insisted on my holding a press conference. One of the journalists asked me what I thought about an article that had appeared in a Soviet paper in which Molière was said to be a poor dramatist, as was quite clear from seeing Ostrovsky's plays. The journalist held up a Russian newspaper whose name I could not see. I replied that I did not know whether the translation was correct and that I had not seen such an article; if it had indeed been printed it only proved that its author was not well informed about literature, nor could he boast of much intelligence. 'We say that we have done away with exploiters in our country, which is true, but we have never claimed to have done away with fools'. The journalists laughed and began to listen with greater attention to my answers about the cold war, Truman's policy and the aims of the Friends of Peace. But I was sweating freely, trying to guess which paper the man had been quoting. When the press conference came to an end, the journalist who had put this poser to me came up and showed me the paper. I sighed with relief – it was only the *Vechorka*[1].

Since then much has changed, but genuine servility – not that which the critics wrote about in 1947, but that which inspired the Intourist manager in 1934 – is still in evidence. Not far from the house where I live, in the town of Istra, there stands a small bust of Chekhov (he had worked at the hospital of Voznesensk, as Istra was called before the Revolution). The memorial was set up in 1954. During the next few years it was smothered in burdock, nettles, thistles. All my efforts to persuade the local authorities to clear the ground surrounding the bust and plant some flowers proved vain. Two French women, correspondents of *L'Humanité*, came to see me; one of them spoke Russian. On the way they stopped at Istra and took photographs of Chekhov's bust. A member of the Regional Council was surprised: 'It appears that in France they know about Chekhov'. The Frenchwoman replied:

[1] *Vechernaya Moskva;* a gossipy evening paper.

'Of course. But I thought they knew about him in the Soviet Union', and she pointed to the tangle of weeds. On the next day I saw pansies planted round the memorial.

An inferiority complex is often coupled with a superiority complex, and a man unsure of himself frequently behaves with arrogance. Our people was not only the first to undertake the difficult task of building a new society but has also played a leading part in various fields of science. Of course we have many bad roads, communal flats and short-ages of household goods; there is no need to be ashamed of this in relation to foreigners; we should be ashamed in relation to ourselves and work to raise the standard of living. No one can be humiliated by a respect for the culture of other countries, including those where a system living out its last days still prevails. The peoples of those countries are alive; they have not only produced in the past but are still today producing great scientists, writers, painters. Slavishness is for those people who have not yet rid themselves of the mentality of slaves. And a sense of self-respect has nothing in common with that arrogance which is part servility, part conceit.

7

I HAVE said that I was preparing myself for the Congress of Soviet Writers like a girl for her first dance. It is true that many of my naïve expectations did not materialize, but the Congress has remained in my memory as a great and marvellous festival. The walls of the Hall of Columns were adorned with portraits of our great predecessors – Shakespeare, Tolstoy, Gogol, Cervantes, Heine, Pushkin, Balzac and others. Opposite me was Heine – youthful, dreamy and naturally mocking; I automatically repeated: 'The scenery was brightly painted and I declaimed so passionately. The shining mantle, the feather in my hat, the feelings – all was admirable.'

The opening of the Congress makes me smile in retrospect: the orchestra suddenly began to play deafening fanfares as if toasts were about to follow.

The Congress lasted fifteen days and every morning we hastened to the Hall of Columns, while Muscovites crowded the entrance to see the writers. Towards three o'clock, when a break for lunch was announced, the crowd would be so dense that we had difficulty in making our way through. Autographs had not yet come into fashion, people just stared, recognized some of the personalities and greeted them. The members of the general public who came to the Congress were different each day so that, in all, 25,000 Muscovites attended it.

Various delegations came: from the Red Army and the Pioneers – the 'Nippers' Camp' – from the women-workers of the Tryokhgorka factory and the metro builders, from Uzbekistan collective farmers and Moscow teachers, from actors and former political convicts. The railwaymen lined up to the sound of a signal-whistle; pioneers blew their trumpets; women from collective farms brought huge baskets of fruit and vegetables; the Uzbeks presented Gorky with a robe and a skull-cap, sailors with a model of a launch. It was all very sincere, naïve and touching and like an extraordinary kind of carnival; accustomed as we were to arduous hours at a desk we now found ourselves in a public square, smothered with roses, asters, dahlias, nasturtiums – all the flowers of an early Moscow autumn.

I have opened a book which is now a bibliographical rarity – the transcript of the Congress proceedings – and have looked through the list of delegates; those who took part in the First All-Union Congress of Soviet Writers have also become rarities: out of 700, possibly fifty are still amongst the living. Twenty-seven years have passed since then, and those were very difficult years.

I presided at the session at which Gustave Isnard, a veteran of the Paris Commune, spoke; he was eighty-six.

The delegates who came to bring their greetings to the Congress were the characters of unwritten novels. I remember a tall, strongly built woman, a collective farmer from the Moscow region. She said: 'I'm a married woman. For over three years now I've been the chairman of our *kolkhoz*. You know that the chairman of a *kolkhoz* is much the same as the director of a factory, and my husband is a rank-and-file collective farmer. But he's learnt to put up with it. When he's given a job, he's got to do it. If he doesn't do it well, I bring it up at the board meeting. If he doesn't reform – I'll dock his work-days[1]. If he still doesn't reform, I can expel him from the *kolkhoz*. I'll set an example to the other men: people will say she dealt properly with her husband. It'll make things easier for us'. At her side stood a short man wincing apprehensively.

All the delegations 'presented claims': the women textile-workers wanted a novel about weavers, the railwaymen said that writers neglected transport problems, the miners asked for a description of the Donbas, inventors insisted on inventor-heroes. (People do not always realize what precisely they do need. Some writers hastened to meet these claims: hundreds of novels about production appeared. Meanwhile the readers' minds matured. Twenty-seven years have not passed without leaving their trace. Librarians say that railwaymen pore over Chekhov's stories, miners enjoy Alexey Tolstoy's *Peter the First*, women textile-workers weep over *Anna Karenina*, inventors prefer novels without any inventions, from *Quiet Flows the Don* to *The Old Man and the Sea*.)

The old *ashug* (poet-singer) Sulayman Stalsky instead of making a speech decided to recite, or rather sing, a poem about the Congress: 'A welcoming sign was given to the *ashug*, and now I, Stalsky,

[1] Collective farmers are paid according to the number of work-days to their credit.

271

Sulayman, have come to the glorious meeting of singers'. Gorky wiped his eyes with his handkerchief. I noticed more than once tears of emotion fill his eyes; Andersen Nexö was also moved to tears when Pioneers surrounded him.

Pasternak sat on the platform beaming all the time. When the metro builders' delegation arrived he jumped up to take a heavy tool from one of the girls; she laughed, and the entire audience laughed with her. As for Pasternak, he tried to explain his gesture in the speech he made: 'And when an unconscious impulse made me try to take off the shoulder of the metro worker a heavy tool, whose name I don't know, how could the comrade on the platform who ridiculed my intellectual's sensibility know that at that moment this metro worker was in some immediate sense my sister, and I wanted to help her as someone close and familiar to me'.

The crowded hall was like a theatre: ovations greeted favourite authors; felicitous speeches excited applause. Olesha moved the audience deeply with a poetic confession of faith, Vishnevsky and Bezymensky with rousing speeches, Koltsov and Babel drew laughter.

All spoke with sincerity, even though the content of the speeches did not always accord with the spiritual state of this or that writer. Olesha said that, having freed himself of recent doubts, he had experienced a revival: 'For some unknown reason youth has suddenly returned to me. I see the young skin on my hands, I am wearing a sports shirt, I have become young – I am sixteen. There is nothing I want. All doubts, all sufferings are past. I have become young. A whole life lies before me'. It may have been that day, or perhaps a day or a week later that I lunched with him and he said regretfully: 'You know, I can't write any more. If I write "the weather was bad" they'll tell me it was good for the cotton crop'. Olesha was very talented. His book *Zavist* (Envy) written in 1927 has stood the test of time. The fragmentary notes of his last years show great literary power. But youth did not return to him; it had been an illusion, a dream induced by the festival.

Gorky listened attentively to the speeches. He wanted the Congress to take practical decisions. He made many suggestions: a *History of Factories and Works*, a book to be called *One Day of Peace*, the history of the Civil War, histories of various towns, literary schools, collective work, a journal devoted to the professional training of would-be writers. Some of his projects were later realized. But the

Congress was not and could not be a business congress: it became a political demonstration. The smoke of the Fascist book-burnings reached us from Germany. Everyone was acutely aware of recent events: the Fascist riots in Paris, the crushing of the Schutzbund. The presence of foreign writers expanded the walls of the Hall of Columns, we were conscious of the looming menace of war.

Gorky invited the foreign guests and some Soviet writers to his *dacha*. I remember the horrifying story of a Chinese authoress about the young writer Li Wei-sun who had been buried alive. A Japanese guest told the Congress how the police tortured and killed the writer Kobayasi. We gave Willi Bredel a rousing reception – he had spent over a year in a Fascist concentration camp. He told us about the fate of Ludwig Renn and Carl von Ossietsky. How could one listen calmly to such things? To re-create the mood of those days let me record that a man as far removed from politics as Pasternak, recalling in his speech the greetings from the representative of the Red Army who had spoken of the defence of the fatherland, said: 'You heard the sound of your own voice in the words spoken by the cadet Ilyichev'.

I have said that history cannot be rewritten. In one of its resolutions the Congress welcomed those present: Andersen Nexö, Malraux, Jean-Richard Bloch, Yakub Kadri, Bredel, Plivier, Hu Lang-chi, Aragon, Johannes R. Becher, Amabel Williams-Ellis, and sent greetings to the absent: Romain Rolland, Heinrich Mann, Lu Hsun (I keep to the order of the resolution). Some of those enumerated here have, in various circumstances, at various times and in various ways, abandoned the ideas which they shared in 1934; but I am speaking now about the Congress and not of what happened to these people later.

Andersen Nexö begged Soviet writers to be broader: 'You must set before the masses ideals not only for days of struggle and work, but also for those hours of quiet when a man is alone with himself. An artist must offer asylum to all, even to lepers, he must possess a mother's heart so that he can come out in defence of the weak and the unfortunate, in defence of all those who, no matter why, cannot keep pace with us'.

Radek in his speech mentioned certain hesitations on the part of Jean-Richard Bloch. Bloch spoke about the necessity of a broad anti-Fascist front: 'Comrade Radek, if you persist in condemnation, if you go on showing mistrust, I personally warn you that this will only push the broad masses in the West towards Fascism'. Aragon, youthful and inspired, with his head thrown back, spoke about the heritage of 'Rimbaud and Zola, Cézanne and Courbet'.

Malraux spoke twice. His first speech was about the role of literature: 'America has demonstrated that while a literature can express a powerful civilization, that does not in itself mean that it is a powerful literature, and the photograph of a great epoch is not tantamount to great literature. You, who are like one another and yet as unlike as seeds, are inaugurating a culture from which new Shakespeares will emerge. May the Shakespeares not be stifled by a heap of beautiful photographs'.

He asked to be allowed to speak a second time in order to refer to his political position: 'If I had thought that politics were inferior to literature, I should not, with André Gide, have led the campaign in France for the defence of Comrade Dimitrov and, in the last resort, should not be here'. As I have said, Malraux suffered from a nervous tic. Radek thought he was grimacing in displeasure at the discussion: 'he often made a wry face when he considered that a question was too strongly put'. He hastened to calm Malraux but naturally he could not cure his tic.

Among the speakers were my old friends Toller, Nezval and Nowomieski. Rafael Alberti behaved with great modesty and was not even included in the list of distinguished guests.

What then did we talk about in the course of those fifteen days? There did not seem to be any Pushkins or Gogols among us, but many were already more than seeds: they were trees or shrubs. Alexey Tolstoy was not like Serafimovich, Babel like Panferov, or Demyan Bedny like Aseyev, and political speeches alternated with literary disputations. The poets made the most noise. When Mayakovsky's name was first mentioned the audience broke into wild applause. However, here too there was no unanimity. In his concluding speech Gorky, after calling Mayakovsky 'an influential and original poet', said that his inherent 'hyperbolism' was having a detrimental effect on some young poets. There were arguments about whether lyricism had any justification, whether political pamphlets were outdated or not, about 'accessibility' and much else.

Genuine writers have always tried to express not their own personalities but, through themselves, the thoughts and feelings of their contemporaries; but the writer's work is not done in a workshop, nor on a stage: he works behind closed doors. One can help a budding author to overcome his literary ignorance, improve his taste, show him how to read, but it is impossible to teach him to become another Gorky, Blok or Mayakovsky. Even a great master cannot teach another master: different keys fit different locks. Stendhal tried to take Balzac's advice and nearly ruined his *Chartreuse de Parme*, but he realized this in time and refrained from altering his novel. Turgenev, in an attempt to amend some of Tyutchev's poems – which, in his opinion, suffered from certain defects – crippled them mercilessly.

At times (though not very often) writers talk to each other about literary problems; such talks or arguments can help to clarify quite a lot of things. But how can one discuss technique in a vast hall amidst loud music and ovations? Besides, the Congress had a different purpose. The readers saw that we were at one with them, that we had a common aim. We, on our side, realized that millions of people were interested in our work; this compelled us to give even more serious thought to the writer's responsibility. The Congress met on the eve of an extremely difficult decade. We saw the bared teeth of Fascism. However great our aesthetic dissensions and, at moments, the hostility they engendered, we demonstrated to all those who were willing to comprehend that standing shoulder to shoulder in battle was for us no abstract notion. That is what the Congress achieved, and I do not believe it could have done more.

All the same, out of naïvety or because such was my nature, I, like several others, joined in literary disputes. For instance, I ventured to express my doubts about the value of collective work. Gorky, in his reply to me, said that I was talking 'out of misunderstanding, out of ignorance of its technical meaning'.

Later Gorky said to me: 'You're opposed to collective work because you're thinking of accomplished writers. You probably don't read much of what's published today. I'm far from advocating that Babel should collaborate with Panferov. Babel knows how to write, he has his own themes. I can think of others too: Tynyanov, Leonov, Fadeyev. But the young ones – they not only don't know how to write, they don't even know how to get started'. I must admit that Gorky did not make me change my mind. I was thinking in the first place of Gorky himself: he had learnt how to write, had found his own themes, no one predigested things for him. Besides, in 1934 there were writers who had been through the hard school of life and had discovered their own path. The works of our great predecessors provided those lessons which one could never learn from foremen of literary teams or professors of the projected Literary Institute. But it is something else that saddens me: the fact that I got to know Gorky too late. I talked to him twice and watched him constantly during the Congress. What struck me about him was his inherent talent which made itself felt in every gesture. During a speech he suddenly began to cough, the fit lasted a long time and the audience sat hushed: everyone knew he was ill. The harsh glare of the arc-lights irritated him. When we were dining at his *dacha* he suddenly got up and with an apologetic smile asked us to excuse him – he was tired and must go and lie down. Babel, who knew him well, said to me: 'He's in a bad way. His son Maxim's death has got him down. He's not the same Gorky'. Babel was probably right, and I never had the chance to know 'the same' Gorky.

I made a long speech at the Congress. Here are some passages from it:

'Can one rebuke an author for not being universally accessible? Songs to the accompaniment of an accordion are much more easily understood than Beethoven . . . Every true artist seeks simplicity, but there are different kinds of simplicity. The simplicity of *Mozart and Salieri*[1] is not the same as that of Krylov's fables. There is the kind of simplicity that cannot be understood without some training. We can be justifiably proud that some of our novels are already accessible to millions. In this respect we have far outstripped capitalist society. But at the same time we must care for and protect those forms of our literature which today still seem to be the preserve of the intelligentsia and of an élite amongst the workers, but which tomorrow in their turn will become the property of millions. Simplicity is not primitiveness. It is a synthesis, not babbling. I feel obliged to say this only because our literature is still to some extent intrinsically provincial. Our country today has achieved hegemony. But in our books one often senses the arrogance and at the same time the subservience of the backwoods.

'The great writers of the last century have bequeathed us their experience. But instead of studying this experience we rely on

[1] A short tragedy by Pushkin.

imitation. That is how epigones come into being, how novels and stories that blindly copy old naturalistic fiction come to be written. . . . We often find the cult of the most reactionary artistic form being imposed under the guise of a struggle against formalism . . . The worker rightly protests against houses that look like barracks. But does this mean that one can take a pseudo-classical portico, add a little Empire, a little baroque, a few Old Moscow features and try to pass it off for the architectural style of the great new class? Who would dream of tracing the history of painting purely in terms of subject matter? Seventeenth-century Dutch masters painted apples, so did Cézanne, but they painted apples in different ways and the whole crux lies in *how* they painted apples . . .

'Instead of serious literary criticism we have a red and a black list of authors, and what is truly fantastic is the ease with which they are transferred from one list to the other. You cannot, after all, put an author on a pedestal one moment only to throw him off the next. We are not dealing with physical culture. It is inexcusable that literary criticism should have a direct effect upon an author's position in society. The distribution of material benefits should not depend on literary criticism. In the last analysis one cannot treat an artist's failures as crimes and his successes as a form of rehabilitation.'

Usually when I recall the past I am astonished that I could have written this or acted like that. I find it hard to recognize myself on faded photographs. But my speech at the Congress astonishes me in a different way: it seems like a quotation from some recent article of mine. Yet twenty-seven years have elapsed since then. The world has changed out of all recognition. At the Congress Professor Otto Schmidt spoke to me about the wonderful prospects for aviation: within the next few years our airmen would succeed in flying over the North Pole. I listened to him as to a magician. Could anyone in those days have imagined that twenty-seven years later a Soviet cosmonaut would calmly go to sleep in outer space while endlessly circling our planet?

At that time I was shaggy-haired and full of fight; I have withered and gone slightly bald, and I have also mellowed. But here I am repeating in my articles, in this book, the thoughts I expressed in 1934. Perhaps I am senile and like an old man who tells you, as though it were a bit of news, that a policeman insulted him for no reason in Troitskaya street near the Governor-General's house? I do not think so. People ignore such old dotards, whereas I am often attacked. Unfortunately it looks as though I shall not live to see the day when the questions I raised at the Congress will have become outdated.

In 1934, after *The Second Day*, my name stayed on the red list and no one abused me. In general, it was a good period and we all thought that in 1937 when, according to the rules, the Second Congress of Writers was due to meet, we would be living in a paradise. Schmidt spoke at the Congress. He referred with bitter irony to one of the films about the *Chelyuskin* epic: 'And then you hear a voice suspiciously like that of the leader of the expedition – though I never said any such thing – which keeps shouting: "Forward! Faster! Still faster! Forward, forward!" Those were certainly not our methods of leadership. Our work needs no spurring on, our leaders no pressure or shouting, there is no need to make distinctions between the leader and the rest of the masses. These are not our methods at all'. We heartily applauded his sensible words. Otto Schmidt was a fine scholar; but he was no oracle.

The governing committee was elected, the rules approved. Gorky declared the Congress closed. On the next day porters were hard at work with their brooms at the entrance to the Hall of Columns. The festival was over.

8

BEFORE THE Congress I had made a trip to the North with Irina. We visited Archangel, Kholmogory, Ust-Pinega, Kotlas, Solvychegodsk, Syktyvkar, Veliky Ustug, Nyuksenitse, Totma, Vologda. We travelled on steamers bearing such proud names as *Ferocious*, *Marxist*, *The Agitator*, *Sturdy*. The steamers were slow; passengers told stories, argued, dreamed, sang, swore. At the jetties they bought milk, bilberries, they bathed, struck up friendships, the women did their washing. The banks were green and mysterious; it seemed as though the ship was breaking into the age-old sleep of nature with hoots of surprise. Here and there human habitations came into sight – strongly built two-storied log houses. Huge tree-trunks drifted slowly downstream – the timber floated down the placid Sukhon, the wayward Vychegda, the broad Dvina – to the sea. The nights were light and the beauty of it made you catch your breath. I was seeing the Russian North for the first time and was immediately conquered by its tenderness and sternness, its ancient art and the youth of its tall, taciturn people.

I visited the lumber camps in the backwaters where men standing on rafts and armed with boat-hooks lined up the trunks of pine and fir. Occasionally the log dam would creak and it seemed as if at any moment it would give and the timber would break its way out to sea; but the men worked day and night. The logs were lashed together; tugs hauled the rafts to Archangel where the timber was loaded on to English, Norwegian and Swedish ships. This meant hard currency; it went to buy machinery for the factories.

I had long conversations with workers and with young men and girls who had recently come from their villages. It is not only trees that grow unevenly, but people too. I met workers who in their leisure studied mathematical textbooks, read poetry, keenly felt the tragedy of the German Communists. I also met callous people, smart operators, swindlers.

Naturally I was glad to see the new communities round Archangel, the bristle factory in Veliky Ustug, the tractors; but above all I was struck by the growth of consciousness. Human relationships were becoming deeper and more complex. At the lumber camps, the backwaters, in the ports I met people with a broad outlook, a rich spiritual life – not permanently smiling shock workers from the honours boards, but complicated, inwardly mature people, and no matter how cruel the conditions of life were, how revolted I was by the soulless administrators who had made their appearance by then and whose only concern was figures – sometimes imaginary ones – I rejoiced to see how our society was growing up.

A short time ago, looking through old sets of *Krasnaya Nov* (Red Virgin Soil) I came across these lines: 'Ehrenburg sees the world as a series of contrasts. This is a peculiarity of his eyes'. The author was writing, as it happened, about my impressions of the North in 1934. I paused to think: was it true that I had peculiar eyes that ought to be examined if not by an oculist then by a psychiatrist? I read old notes and try to call to mind the summer of 1934: it was not so very long ago, but it was not just yesterday either. Yes, I frequently gave vent to admiration and to anger, I frowned, then once again felt happy. However, when I talked to other people I found that they, too, praised some things and disapproved of others. It was not my eyes that were at fault but the epoch that was so lavish with its contrasts.

Moscow had never before known such a fever of construction; there was a smell of mortar, and this gladdened the heart. I saw the first section of the Metro being built and shared the joy of all the Muscovites. Huge factories rose round the Simonov monastery. There were many familiar streets I no longer recognized; in place of crooked little houses there were scaffolding, rubble and building sites. At night an orange mist hung over the city; for the first time the provincial Moscow of my childhood was taking on the appearance of a capital.

Side by side with all this one could see ancient monuments being pulled down: Kitay-gorod, the Sukharev tower, the *Krasnye Vorota* (Red Gates). They were destroying the green belt of the Zubovsky, Smolensky, Novinsky boulevards with their age-old trees. It is hard to explain why seventeen years after the Revolution a number of treasures were destroyed, and this not accidentally but in an organized way. I remember a conversation I had with Igor Grabar. He told me that many architects had protested against the pulling down of the *Krasnye Vorota*, saying in their report that the arch did not hinder traffic because in any case cars would have to go round the square, and a militiaman would be stationed on the site of the arch; their arguments had no effect.

In the North I saw with what frenzy people were destroying things that were eminently worth preserving. There were still quite a few sixteenth and seventeenth century wooden churches in which the creative genius of the Russian people had expressed itself. People kept potatoes or hay in these churches and, after standing for three or four hundred years, they caught fire and were destroyed, one by one. When I was in Archangel they were exerting themselves tremendously to blow up the handsome Customs building of Peter I's times. (In the wall they found a casket containing a wooden Venus; the 'doll' was broken to pieces.) I saw one of the oldest churches in Veliky Ustug being dismantled brick by brick; people explained to me: 'We're building a bath-house'. In another church, washing was hung up to dry, and figures of Christ sat under the shirts. In the North painted wooden baroque carving was very common; mostly the craftsmen represented Christ in prison. (In the Spanish town of Valladolid I saw carvings very similar to those of Veliky Ustug.) We are accustomed to seeing solitary figures of Christ, but in the warehouse I saw a whole assembly of Christs, some without arms or legs; they sat in sombre meditation.

The places I visited that summer had played an important part in the development of Russian art. Veliky Ustug, the Sophia at Vologda, the tent-roofed wooden churches, the Stroganov icons; legends, songs, incantations, local sayings; popular creations: black and white clay toys, Vologda lace, carved bone, niello on silver. There was none of the southern colourfulness, everything had a clear-cut sober look.

It was suggested to the Vologda lacemakers that they replace the traditional designs – '*chistyanka* (dainty)', 'little spider', 'little river', 'mole-cricket' and so on – by tractors. In Veliky Ustug I got to know an old craftsman, Chirkov, an expert in niello work. He told me how at first they had said that nobody needed niello work, and how later people had come from the Town Soviet asking him to tell them the secret of his craft. In vain Chirkov explained that there were no secrets, that what mattered was not technique but inventive skill, imagination. An *artel* (working team) was organized which started making niello bracelets in wretched taste. (I told Gorky about what had happened to Chirkov, about the bone-carver Guryev, about the peasant-woman Mezrina who was instructed to take the epaulettes off the clay hussars, about Mazin, who came from the same district as Gorky and who painted benches, stools and walls. Gorky was distressed, he asked me to write it all down and kept wiping his eyes. Chirkov was summoned to Moscow, but the *artel* went on making the same kind of bracelets. And then Chirkov died.)

1934 was an historic year. Courageous men who had explored the stratosphere perished. Airmen rescued the passengers and crew of the ship *Chelyuskin*. I shall never forget how Moscow welcomed them: sunshine, coloured transparencies, flowers and the public emotion – there is no other word for it – excited by the courage and the comradeliness of the heroes.

A member of the *Chelyuskin* crew told me that on their ice-floe they had had a small volume of Pushkin; they read the poems aloud and it kept their spirits up. No writer could hear such a thing without feeling deeply moved.

In the Red Forest Club a Komsomol recited Tyutchev's poems. Involuntarily it brought to my mind a line by Fet: 'Tyutchev will not come to the Zyriane'. But this was Syktyvkar, the capital of the Komi[1] who were formerly called Zyriane.

Some people grasped Tyutchev with all his difficulties. Others lost ordinary human feelings. A party purge was in progress. At the meeting they discussed the work of Krasnov (this name, as the others that follow, is fictitious). His colleague Smirnov said: 'And what's more, comrade Krasnov sleeps with Shelgunov's wife'. Shelgunov was present at the meeting; he poured out a glass of water but did not drink it. Krasnov started to justify himself: 'She threw herself at my head'. He was demoted from membership of the party to the the status of a party candidate.

In Totma they were establishing a health resort for patients with nervous diseases. The social club was in a church where under a faded Virgin hung a notice: 'A healthy body is necessary for carrying out the Second Five Year Plan'. The graveyard attached to the church was dug up. I caught sight of some human remains. The official in charge, with perfectly expressionless eyes, stroked his flabby cheeks and

---

[1] People of the Autonomous Soviet Socialist Republic in the extreme N.E. of the European part of the RSFSR.

remarked phlegmatically: 'We'll clean it up when we can get down to it. Anyway, when they start kicking a ball about, they won't notice anything'.

In the press, critics were still giving favourable accounts of Shosta-kovich's new opera *Katerina Izmailova*. At the first night of *La Dame aux Camélias* Meyerhold received an ovation. I was shown Zabolotsky's poem *The Triumph of Agriculture*; it astonished, then captivated me; for a long time I used to recite it to myself. In Moscow I spent several evenings with Alexander Dovzhenko; he was always excited and glowing with passion, and was now in torment over his film *Aerograd (Frontier)*. But the model they set before him was a thing called *Vstrechny* (The Down Train) in which saccharine shock workers achieved easy successes. The exhibitions were already teeming with huge paintings that made one think of coloured photographs: Stalin on the Tribune, Stalin on a Garden-bench, 'A Session of the Village Soviet', 'Workers' Meeting in the Foundry'. A house in pseudo-classical style had been built next to the Hotel National; it was said: 'This is our own Soviet style, no formalistic nonsense'. In the Mostorgs[1] they sold flower-pots, china pussy-cats and owls like those I had seen in my childhood on chests-of-drawers in merchants' houses. The popular song 'Masha and I by the samovar' came blaring out of the windows. There were many more Mashas than samovars, but 'Masha by the samovar' suited the members of boards, the chairmen of Town Soviets, the clerks: the petty bourgeois tastes of pre-revolutionary times seemed to them the criterion of beauty.

Life contained many more contrasts than did my books, though not because I wanted to keep silent about the gigantic weeds, the thistles as sturdy as baobabs, the nettles left uprooted and, on the contrary, carefully tended. I did speak about the weeds; they angered but they did not particularly surprise me. It was a quite different thing that caused me surprise: the first shoots of a new consciousness pushing up, the young people who were opening the book of life and were seized by the feverish desire to construct not only factories and houses, but also their own spiritual world. By then I had long since left the North; I was not amidst the green forests but in grey Paris luminous under autumn rain, yet I still kept seeing the young men and girls who, in the distant lumber camp, had spoken about friendship, about

[1] Moscow State Shops.

283

the sorrows of love, about the struggle for timber, for their country, for happiness.

Six months later I wrote the short novel *Ne Perevodia Dykhaniya* (Without Taking Breath) where the action is laid in the North.

The critics received this book far more favourably than my previous ones. Personally I do not think it very good: I put into it a lot of what had found no place in *The Second Day*, and, without noticing it, I had repeated myself.

Still, the novel was useful to me: it contained sketches of characters to whom I later returned more than once. The botanist Lyass, buoyant, intelligent, occasionally grumpy, is the first rough sketch for Professor Dumas in *The Fall of Paris* and Doctor Krylov in *The Storm*. The ill-fated actress Lidya Nikolayevna, who finds comfort in an ephemeral success, later became Jeannette and Valya. The unrecognized artist Kuzmin, keenly interested in reconciling the times with his aesthetic outlook, is the twin of the Frenchman André and of the hero of *The Thaw*, Saburov.

There was one other character in the novel who expressed my anxiety. He appears in the book as a fleeting shadow: the German Strem. He came to Archangel on a dubious mission. Life held little attraction for him, he was possessed by thoughts of death. After a few drinks with a Swedish captain in an Archangel restaurant, he held forth: 'Death's a serious business. As a matter of fact, it's the only reality. Last winter in Berlin I met a journalist. Today he's got some important job. He invited me to his house. A wife, a cosy home, you couldn't find a kinder fellow. And then he told me how he had killed sixteen people – just like that. It isn't a matter of sadism. When you come to think of it, we have no power over our own lives. But if you have power over other people's lives – "shoot them!" – somehow you gain stature in your own eyes. It's a sort of substitute for immortality'.

Strem's reflections were not empty chatter, not drunken bluster; behind them was the terrible reality of what was going on in a great civilized country. After re-reading *Without Taking Breath* I realize that as far as the content goes, Strem got into this book by accident, without a ticket, as it were, without a visa. His character is only roughly outlined; the only justification for his suicide was the author's desire to sweep a nasty person off the stage, the important thing was the world which brings such people into existence. Why did the German Strem turn up in Archangel, why did he talk so long in the public garden to the nice bewildered actress? Just because I could not get Strem out of my mind. A writer's book is hardly ever confined within the framework of the story. In the novel about life in the lumber camp, about the Komsomol's love, about the grief of the young woman who had lost at one and the same time her child and her faith in her husband, other things found expression: the author's thoughts and experiences, the Berlin *auto-da-fés*, the night of the Fascist rising in Paris, the ruins of Floridsdorf, the anxiety about the future. There was a great deal I still could not foresee but I already realized that coexistence with Fascism was impossible. These are the contrasts which to me seemed intolerable.

9

JEAN-RICHARD BLOCH had said at the Congress that dogmatic inflexibility could easily antagonize the waverers. Many western writers could not understand the methods of Socialist Realism, but fascist methods were easily understood by all: they meant bonfires of books and concentration camps for authors. During the Congress we said more than once that an anti-Fascist front of writers ought to be set up.

I went back to Paris in a roundabout way: I took a Soviet ship to Piraeus. Travelling with me were the Greek writers Glinos and Kostas Varnalis with whom I made friends. Varnalis' character was a blend of fighting vigour, gentleness and dreaminess. In Salonica the Greek police did not allow Glinos and Varnalis to go ashore – they were to be searched when they reached Piraeus. Everybody in Greece spoke about the growing menace of Fascism. Everywhere there were Germans who behaved like instructors. 'They're out to devour us,' Varnalis said. A year later he was arrested.

From Athens we went to Brindisi and crossed Italy; once again I heard the yelling of the blackshirts.

The papers said that Moroccan mercenaries were being used to put down the Asturian miners. Spain was no longer just another European State to me. I thought of her proud and kindly people; I asked myself unhappily: is it possible that even people like that can be beaten to their knees?

Newspaper boys rushed shouting through the Paris streets: in Marseilles the King of Yugoslavia and Barthou, the French Minister of Foreign Affairs, had been assassinated. I did not know anything about the king and did not understand who had killed him or why. Barthou I had once met at a Foreign Press dinner; he surprised me by the youthfulness of his outlook – he was over seventy. He spoke brilliantly about Mirabeau, Danton, Saint-Just. He was a passionate bibliophile and more than once I caught sight of him on the quays of the Seine browsing at the bookstalls. The German Fascists hated him: although a man of right-wing opinions, Barthou was strongly in favour of a rapprochement with the Soviet Union, for a defensive alliance that would have checked Hitler. Everybody interpreted Barthou's murder as a symptom of the Fascist offensive. I remember a big meeting in the Palais de la Mutualité to report on the Congress of Soviet Writers. Vaillant-Couturier, André Gide, Malraux, Andrée Viollis and Communist workers sat on the platform. In the audience were people who had also long ago made their choice; they shouted rhythmically: 'Les Soviets partout!' Andrée Viollis who sat next to me whispered: 'Soviet writers must show that they're ready to work with everybody in the struggle against Fascism'.

I had a talk with Jean-Richard Bloch. He said he had come to Communism by a tortuous path, that at this juncture it was necessary to unite for the most pressing task – the struggle against Fascism – otherwise Communist writers would find themselves isolated.

I sent a long letter to Moscow reporting on the mood of the Western writers and the scheme for an anti-Fascist union.

Today it may seem strange that I attached so much importance to the writers: much has changed in the last quarter of a century and, among other things, the role of literature and its place in the life of millions of people. At the Congress of Soviet Writers Otto Schmidt, after speaking about the achievements in physics and astronomy, had added: 'A writer is a lucky man. I deeply envy him. A scientist has to think things out long and carefully, whereas writers have, as it were, sudden insight'. In that very same year, when we met our readers in the Hall of Columns, Frédéric and Irène Joliot-Curie discovered artificial radiation: the epoch of nuclear physics had begun. I (and probably the majority of writers) had no inkling of the fact.

Twenty-five years later millions of people began to follow the work of the scientists now with hope and now with terror. The poet Slutsky wrote half jocularly: 'The physicists seem to be in high favour, the lyricists in disrepute'. The lyricists did not smile when they read these lines.

Between the two world wars the social role of the scientist was circumscribed. Ordinary people saw the scientist as someone shut up in his laboratory, looking down with a mixture of contempt and uneasiness at the restless life of the streets. The scientists did little to dispel this myth. Langevin was an exception. It was Gorky's articles, Romain Rolland's appeals, Barbusse's speeches that carried on the war against Fascism. Writers still enjoyed tremendous authority. I remember how in the Paris working-class suburb of Villejuif one of the streets was being re-named after Gorky. Thousands of workers gathered for the ceremony. Vaillant-Couturier announced that André Gide would speak. The workers who had probably never read a word of André Gide gave him such an ovation that he was quite overcome. This exemplified the quite paradoxical veneration in which the calling of 'writer' was held. Perhaps the respect enjoyed by writers in 1934 was partly derived from the interest on the capital earned by literature a hundred years previously, when Pushkin, Victor Hugo, Balzac, Gogol, Stendhal, Heine, Mickiewicz, Dickens and Lermontov were alive.

Yes, much has changed since then. After Hiroshima the scientists realized their responsibility. Joliot-Curie took the lead in the Peace Movement. Today people are far more interested in international scientific conferences than in PEN Club congresses. I do not know whether the writers have begun to forget their role of 'teachers of life', or whether the pupils have opted to attend other classes, but today I (and not only I but responsible politicians) find the importance I attached to the Anti-Fascist Association of Writers highly exaggerated.

(The clue to the change that has taken place is to be found less in the indisputable achievements of science or in the equally obvious eclipse of literature than in factors that do not properly belong to the sphere of whether poetry has a right to exist or not – namely, the threat of nuclear war. Neither the lyricists nor the physicists decide questions of peace and war, but by the nature of their work the lyricists can only contribute to the enrichment of their readers' spiritual life, whereas the physicists are capable of improving life and of perfecting death as well. A spiral is one of the most common forms of development both of living organisms and of human society; lyricists will probably be held 'in high esteem' when people are again able to look calmly at the sky – at the moon which, thanks to the physicists, has been investigated by men, and at the lovers' moon no longer threatened by the physicists' moon.)

These are reflections about the present and the future, and I am not now talking about the importance of the writer's status in the past merely to sigh for what is gone. I want to make clear what subsequently happened. I was working in the rue du Cotentin on the fifth or the sixth chapter of the novel *Without Taking Breath* when our ambassador, Potemkin, rang me up and asked me to come to see him on urgent business. He told me that in connection with my letter about the mood of the western writers they wanted me to come to Moscow: Stalin wished to speak to me.

I arrived in Moscow in November. The weather was foul, wet snow was falling, but I was in excellent spirits. I found Irina in a happy mood. She had never told me that she had taken to literature and had written the *Reminiscences of a French Schoolgirl*. And now she mentioned, quite casually, that it had been printed in a journal edited by Gorky and was soon to appear in book form. I read the *Reminiscences* in the course of one night. Naturally I read them with particular interest: Irina described her school years, her first emotional storms. I recognized her girl-friends, the boys who sometimes came to our place and discovered a lot of things I did not know: Irina was secretive.

While waiting for my meeting with Stalin I saw many old friends. Young writers also came to see me – Lapin, Slavin, Levin, Gabrilovich. The Vasilyev brothers showed me *Chapayev*. I spent my evenings at Meyerhold's; he was holding his own and spoke about the production of *Gore Umu* (Woe to Wit)[1]. The general mood was good. People said that at the forthcoming session of the Soviets the draft of the new constitution would be discussed. December felt like May and I saw everything in a rosy light.

One day I called at the office of *Izvestia* and went in to see the editor; he looked ghastly and could barely stammer out: 'A terrible thing's happened. Kirov's been killed'. Everyone was stunned; Kirov had been well liked. Grief was mixed with apprehension: who? why? What would happen next? I have noticed that great trials are almost always preceded by weeks or months of unclouded happiness – both in the life of individuals and in the history of nations. Perhaps it only seems so afterwards when people recall the days before the calamity. None of us could guess, of course, that a new epoch was beginning, but everyone became subdued and watchful.

A few days later the director of the cultural section of the Central Committee, A. I. Stetsky, told me that in view of the situation my meeting with Stalin would not take place; they did not want to detain me needlessly. Stetsky asked me to dictate to a typist my ideas on the possibility of uniting the writers who were prepared to fight Fascism.

[1] Pun on Griboyedov's famous play *Woe from Wit*.

In Paris I managed to get a few more chapters of my novel written. I had talks with Malraux, Vaillant-Couturier, Gide, Bloch, Moussinac, Guéhenno. After long discussions a group of French writers decided to convene an international congress in the spring or early summer. Writers are not like workers: it is very difficult to get them to combine. André Gide proposed one thing, Heinrich Mann another, Feuchtwanger something else. The Surrealists shouted that the Communists had become high priests and that the congress ought to be sabotaged. Writers close to the Trotskyists – Charles Plisnier, Madeleine Paz – gave warning that they would speak and 'unmask' the Soviet Union. Barbusse feared that the congress would be politically too broad and therefore unable to take any decisions. Roger Martin du Gard and the English writers E. M. Forster and Aldous Huxley, on the contrary, thought that the congress would be too narrow and that only the Communists would be allowed to speak. Much patience, restraint and tact were needed to reconcile what seemed irreconcilable attitudes.

But all these difficulties arose only at the beginning of 1935. On my arrival from Moscow I had hardly time to get my bearings when a telegram arrived from the editorial office: a plebiscite was being held in the Saar and would I please go there. I left an unfinished chapter of my novel on my desk and rang up Malraux to say that I would be unable to come to the meeting of the organizing committee.

In the train, during the night, I indulged in dreams or, as red-haired Romka used to say, in 'working hypotheses'. The congress would force the doubters to choose the path of struggle. After all, Fascism was not as strong as it seemed: it derived its power from the general helpless state of hypnotism. Perhaps the Germans in the Saar would vote against Hitler?

The compartment was overheated. With difficulty I lowered the window. Smoke poured in – yellow, thick, pungent.

10

I ARRIVED in Saarbrücken in the evening. Small festive lights flickered in the fog. A shop-window in the main street displayed a swastika of sausages; the passers-by gave it approving smiles. The proprietress of the hotel, a stout apoplectic woman, shouted in the passage: 'Don't forget I'm a German!' In the street loudspeakers broadcast military songs: 'We are marching, left, right'. I slept badly. There were shots in the night. I opened my door and the bootboy who was collecting the shoes to be cleaned explained: 'They've probably done away with another traitor'. In the morning the proprietress said to me: 'You must vacate your room immediately. I let it to you by mistake. I'm a German, sir. D'you understand me?'

I understood everything; but perhaps a young reader may not realize what was in fact going on in the Saar. Let me remind him. In 1919, when they drew up the Versailles Treaty, the Allies had a long argument over the Saar basin. Clemenceau wanted France to get the Saar coal. Wilson objected. It was finally agreed that in fifteen years' time a plebiscite would be held for the population to decide whether their province should be united with Germany or not. Before Hitler came to power it was quite straightforward: Germans lived in the Saar, therefore they would vote for reunification.

The fascist terror gave some people pause. The voters were offered the choice: union with Germany or the *status quo*, that is, autonomous self-government and economic union with France. Apart from a small group of autonomists it was only the Communists who appealed to the people to vote for the *status quo*. On arriving in the Saar I realized at once that a huge majority would vote for reunification; the Nazis made great play with patriotism. Posters, songs, banners proclaimed, like the proprietress of the hotel where I had spent my first night: 'We are Germans, our place is in Germany!'

The 'free expression of opinion' degenerated into a tragic farce. In theory there was freedom of speech, of assembly, of the press. British soldiers were supposed to ensure order. In actual fact the Fascists wrecked the Communist meetings. There was not a single newspaper kiosk where I could buy a paper that came out against reunification: the newspaper sellers told me nervously: 'They warned us that they would burn down the kiosks'. People were killed from ambush. Even I received an anonymous letter stamped with a swastika: if I did not quit the Saar immediately 'a good German bullet' would be found for me.

The real master of the Saar, Hermann Roechling, promised rewards to those who obeyed and death by starvation to those who did not. The unemployed who refused to join the 'German Front' were forthwith disallowed the dole.

(Today when I read in the Western press that the German problem could be solved by 'free elections' I think back to the plebiscite in the Saar.)

In one village I witnessed a funny episode in this unfunny campaign. There were two bulls there, legally recognized breeders. One of these was considered the better of the two, and its owner, a poor peasant, lived more or less on the earnings of his bull. This man was suspected of intending to vote for the *status quo* and his bull was stigmatized as a '*status quo* bull'. No one dared let their honest Aryan cow be mounted by him.

It was the German writer Gustav Regler who helped me to find my way to this and other remote villages. I had first met him in Paris and later saw him in Moscow during the Writers' Congress. He was a nervous, impressionable man. The Saar Fascists threatened to kill him. He spoke out boldly everywhere about the terror in Germany. He took me to the miners' homes where I heard the truth about what was going on.

Even before the plebiscite took place I wrote some articles for my paper and ended the last of them with the words: 'The battle may be lost. But the war – never'.

On returning to Paris I finished writing my novel, attended a meeting of the organizing committee of the Writers' Association and was again obliged to leave: an Extraordinary Session of the Council of the League of Nations was due to be held in Geneva.

The Swiss procrastinated over my visa. Finally the counsellor of the embassy showed me the following telegram from Berne of which I made a copy: 'The Soviet citizen Ilya Ehrenburg is authorized to remain ten days in Switzerland as *Izvestia* correspondent to attend the Extraordinary Session of the Council on condition that the above-named Ilya Ehrenburg refrains from any activity disturbing to the internal order of Switzerland or harmful to her good relations with neighbouring States'. The diplomat explained to me that while on Swiss territory I must neither say nor write anything against Germany – neutrality demanded this.

Well, neutrality – like everything else in the world – can be interpreted in various ways. Shortly before I arrived in Switzerland Hitler's agents kidnapped the German anti-Fascist émigré Jakob in Basel and whisked him off to Germany. The Swiss authorities pretended that nothing out of the way had happened. Geneva was packed with Nazis; they were not asked to sign any conditions; they had their own newspapers in Switzerland and wrote without interference that 'to remove the malignant tumour of Communism it is necessary to use surgery and to start with Russia'.

By now I am accustomed to all kinds of international conferences and know that they are very much like the court described in *Reineke-Fuchs*. But in those days I was new to the business and was often startled. The League of Nations was a rough draft of the UN; the Americans did not take part and the French and English were looked upon as the leading powers. Germany had left the League as far back as 1933, but everyone gave way before Hitler. In Danish Schleswig I had seen how the Danes feared the German divisions. Yet at Geneva the Danish delegate made a long speech to prove that Hitler's policy was the embodiment of peace; and the worst of it was, this advocate of Fascism was a Social-Democrat. Negotiations were carried on behind the scenes in various restaurants outside the town. The Germans promised Spain a trade agreement, and Lerroux suddenly developed an affection for the Third Reich. The Portuguese and Chileans were promised various titbits. The alarm that was spreading like wildfire over the world was to be allayed by Articles, clauses and annotations.

Litvinov took the floor; he spoke calmly and looked like a good-natured *paterfamilias*. He reminded the diplomats that appetite grows by what it feeds on and that one should not rely on Hitler's smiles: 'One could hardly accept on good faith the promise of the truculent citizen to spare certain city quarters and to reserve to himself and his weapons freedom of action only in the other parts of the city'.

In the Café Bavaria where journalists foregathered, the *Figaro* correspondent exploded: 'Emile Buré's mad! Why should France fear the German army? Even a child can see that Hitler intends to move against the Ukraine'.

In the show-window of a German travel agency near the Café Bavaria there was a large map of Europe showing Alsace and Lorraine as part of Germany.

The spring was cold and stormy; but the papers said that France was expecting more tourists that summer than in any previous year: 'Peace has triumphed'. Germany continued to rearm. The League of Nations considered various disarmament plans. The French discussed the coming holidays.

I went to the Belgian town of Eupen which had belonged to Germany till 1918. Again there was a long delay over the visa. At the time Belgium had a coalition government which included the Socialists Vandervelde and Spaak. Until quite recently Spaak had been regarded as 'red'. I remembered how he shook his fists at a miners' meeting in the Borinage. Any of Meyerhold's actors might have envied the speed with which he changed his roles. He became an important political figure in post-war Europe. I saw him in Brussels in 1950; despite his obesity he behaved in a most violent manner. He defended ideas which, according to him, were 'moderate', but he defended them without moderation. I always feel a bit uneasy about such men: they are capable of setting fire to the world merely because they think themselves good firemen. Vandervelde was a man of the past century and he did not try to keep up with Spaak; he was then seventy. He wrote a review of my novel *The Second Day*. I do not know what influenced him – my style or Hitler's – but the article contained some unexpected sentiments: 'So, despite everything, this people is trudging through mud and snow towards the stars. The most justifiable of all revolutions brought it faith and hope – a miraculous renovation of the whole of social life'. However, Vandervelde's ideas found no reflection at all in day-to-day politics: in Eupen I found a scene very like the one in the Saar. Nazis came by tram from Dortmund or Düsseldorf; they were not required to have visas. They behaved without ceremony. The paper *Eupener Zeitung* said that the Germans would soon liberate the town. I went into a bookshop that belonged to Giretz, the local Führer. He smiled politely and offered me Alfred Rosenberg's works.

While I was in Eupen a German Communist who had managed to escape from a concentration camp arrived there. The Eupen police arrested him and threatened to hand him over to the Nazis. Four days later he was deported to France. I went with him to the frontier – he was in a terrible mental state and gave incoherent replies to the frontier guard's questions.

Paris once again. Writers, talks about the congress. Malraux was pleased that Benda had promised to speak. Waldo Frank wrote a long letter from America; he was coming to the congress. Joyce would send greetings.

The Parisians were discussing where to spend the summer months – on the Normandy coast or in the Savoy. Everything was as usual. But I could not forget what was going on across the Rhine.

I went to Alsace. It was like everywhere else: the Nazis grinned and talked about the coming 'liberation'; the 'autonomists', inspired by the Saar, demanded a plebiscite; people sighed, shuddered, extracted promises from local Fascists to rescue them in the hour of 'liberation'. One night in a deserted street I met a dozen young fellows truculently bawling the *Wacht am Rhein*.

This is what I wrote at the time: 'These last few months I have been doing an exhausting job: travelling from one region to another bordering on Germany. One can look at a snake for a long time and retain one's sanity; if a snake swallows a rabbit, it is, when all is said and done, a dinner. But one cannot bear to look at the rabbit for long: its glassy staring eyes can infect even a human being of steel nerves with insanity'.

Not so long ago there was a Round Table conference in Rome. We tried to convince our western colleagues that yesterday's SS men should not be re-armed. One evening our Italian friends showed us a documentary film: the history of Fascism. On a balcony the Duce raised his arm and hammed like a bad provincial actor. Men died in Abyssinia. Houses crumbled in Madrid. Dead children were carried away. Nazis marched through the streets of Prague. Hitler, on learning of the capitulation of France, patted his stomach. Russian prisoners of war died in concentration camps. Jewish girls were herded into gas-chambers. Then came victory, and once again the screen showed the surviving Fascists running riot, again a young Italian boy was dying. The telling of the tale is not yet finished. As I watched the film the thought suddenly came to me: Good heavens, this is the story of my life! Forty years have gone by to the accompaniment of atrocities, wars, pogroms, concentration camps. In his time Pushkin wrote: 'We are born for inspiration, for sweet sounds and for prayers'. Even at that time this must surely have been merely a dream: Ryleyev was hanged, Küchelbecker languished in exile, and Pushkin himself died a premature death that was forced upon him. But at least he could dream.

In the spring of 1935 the last thing I thought of was 'sweet sounds'. We spent days and nights preparing for the Writers' Congress. Others may have been unruffled but I could not go on living as I had done before: the very air had changed. There were no practice mobilizations, no air-raid rehearsals, no black-out exercises so far. But the war was already on. I know now that war always arrives long before the performance starts; it comes through the stage-door and waits patiently in the dark wings.

11

THE FRENCH writers engaged in the preparation of the Congress –
André Gide, Jean-Richard Bloch, Malraux, Moussinac, Nizan and René
Blech – often gathered in my small flat in the rue du Cotentin.

I had a dog, Bouzou, affectionate and cunning, a cross between a
spaniel and a Scotch terrier; he could not have been entered at a dog-
show, but he was intelligent – he would go by himself to the horse-
meat butcher's and perform circus tricks there. Bouzou loved André
Gide but it was cupboard love: Gide would take a biscuit and launch
into a long tirade gesticulating with his hand; Bouzou would jump up
and snatch the biscuit. Without noticing what had happened Gide
would take another, and the whole thing would be repeated a dozen
times.

In those days I often met Gide, at his home in the rue Vaneau, at
literary gatherings, at workers' meetings. When we were alone together he nearly always talked about himself. It might have been
thought that I would get to know him well, but I never did: as far as
I was concerned he remained a man from another planet.

When he manifested an enthusiasm for politics and declared himself
a supporter of Communism, I regarded it as a victory: André Gide
was the idol of the Western intelligentsia. I was glad that he should
be taking part in the struggle against Fascism, but even in those days I
entered the reservation that up to the age of sixty André Gide 'had seen
nothing before him except the reflection of his own passions'. He
called only one of his books a novel – *Les Faux Monnayeurs*. In 1933
I wrote about it: 'Of course no one can feel involved in the fate of the
characters in the novel *Les Faux Monnayeurs*. But then do these
characters actually exist? This is a novel about a novelist and his novel.
and not about people at all . . . It is a book about a book: the desert
turns out to contain no life'.

I was not alone in my delight over Gide's 'conversion'. At the
Moscow Congress of Writers, Gorky said: 'Romain Rolland and
André Gide have every right to call themselves "engineers of souls"',
and Louis Aragon ended his speech with these words: 'It remains for

me to convey to you the greetings of our great friend André Gide'. A year later, at the Paris Anti-Fascist Writers' Congress, no one got so warm an ovation as André Gide.

In 1936 he went to Moscow, unreservedly admired everything, yet on his return to Paris just as unreservedly condemned it. I do not know what affected him; another man's heart is a dark continent. In 1937 when I was in Spain I read an article of his in which he accused the Republican authorities of oppression. I lost my temper and called him 'an old man suffering from a renegade's malice and an uneasy conscience'. All this is now long past. I want to reflect calmly on this man who crossed my path.

Of course I was at fault both when I extolled his adherence to Communism and when I called him a renegade: I had taken the erratic flutterings of a moth for a set pattern. I have frequently admitted to various errors in these memoirs; too often I mistook my wishes for the reality.

Can a man, after living sixty years in a desert, absorbed in himself to the exclusion of all else, suddenly be transformed, become involved with humanity and a defender of justice? André Gide told me more than once that a man surrounded by unhappiness could feel no joy; these words touched me. He talked with sincerity and he had great charm. All the same, I could believe in the firmness, in the enduring quality of such sentiments only because I very much wanted to. I did not give any thought to Gide's previous career. During the years of the First World War he was overjoyed when a friend of his became a militant Catholic: 'You have outstripped me'. Fifteen years later he proclaimed everywhere that religion was man's worst enemy. He looked like a parson, he had intelligent eyes and fine expressive hands; he was surrounded by books and manuscripts; he always carried a small volume of Goethe or Montaigne in his pocket; he said he was studying Marx. His most consistent trait was supreme inconsistency. There were people who admired his audacity, while others, on the contrary, accused him of exaggerated caution; but the moth does not fly towards the flame out of audacity nor does it fly from man out of caution; it is neither a hero nor a self-seeker, it is simply a moth.

I do not want to be misunderstood: when I use the term 'moth' I have not the slightest intention of denigrating Gide's talent or intelligence. He once noted in his diary: 'I doubt if a butterfly after having laid her eggs still gets much enjoyment out of life. It flutters hither and thither at the mercy of the perfumes and the breeze'. Gide was seventy-two when he wrote this; he considered that he had fulfilled his task. Perhaps his words about the butterfly are purely accidental; I cannot tell, but the image is a happy one: he was a magnificent night moth of that extremely rare colouring that dazzles both the expert entomologist and the small boy with a butterfly-net. (Gide said that he liked to catch brightly-coloured butterflies.)

No matter how often I saw him, he always talked about his health: he was afraid of catching cold – there was 'flu about – he could not lunch at a particular bistro because of his liver. In the immense world, meeting innumerable human beings, André Gide really only noticed one: André Gide. When he was dying, his old friend Roger Martin du Gard was at his flat in the rue Vaneau. Martin du Gard has published *Reminiscences of André Gide*; the book is lovingly written and I found in it confirmation of my far more fleeting observations: 'He lives absorbed in himself, deeply preoccupied by his small troubles . . .' 'He is still more concentrated on himself.'

Whatever he wrote about – Nietzsche or Dostoyevsky, imaginary characters or intimate friends, homosexuality or the tragedy of France – he saw himself, admired himself or was horrified at himself.

He had a wonderful style: lucid, precise and at the same time original. His style undoubtedly contributed to his success, for he began to write at a time when everyone was sick and tired of the artificial turgidity of the epigones of Symbolism; others imitated Mallarmé, Gide was captivated by Montaigne.

A brilliant stylist, a writer of great erudition – all this is beyond doubt; and yet it is difficult to credit that between the two world wars many people regarded Gide as a teacher, as the conscience of the epoch, almost as a prophet.

He was at one time attracted by unusual criminal cases. In the late twenties he began editing a series of books devoted to various crimes; I vaguely remember one of these – the story of a woman incarcerated by her relatives.

It is common knowledge that there are people whose sexual life is aberrant. André Gide transformed a pathological condition into a militant programme. He braved the loss of many friends, unpleasantness, a press hue and cry.

Shortly before his visit to the Soviet Union he invited me to his place: 'I shall probably be received by Stalin. I've decided to raise with him the question of the treatment of my fellows'. Although I was aware of Gide's abnormality I did not immediately grasp what he meant to speak to Stalin about. He made it quite clear: 'I intend to raise the question of the legal position of pederasts'. I could hardly refrain from smiling; I tried politely to dissuade him but he was adamant. He was a Protestant, even a Puritan – not only by upbringing but by nature – and yet he had become a fanatical moralist of immorality.

No, it was not to his style alone that he owed his success; it was also to his ruthless exhibitionism. He criticized very superficially the shortcomings both of Soviet society which, as a tourist – albeit a very important one – he had barely glimpsed, and the bourgeois *milieu* which he knew well; but though wholly self-centred he was pitiless in analysing himself.

In the summer of 1936, when I was in Moscow, he said to the students: 'As my health is frail and I cannot expect to live long, I was content to leave this earth without having known success. I saw myself as a writer to whom fame comes only posthumously, as it came to Stendhal, Baudelaire, Keats and Rimbaud . . . Now you understand, young people of new Russia, why I turn to you: it is for you that I have been waiting, it is for you that I have written my new book'. How strangely that reads today! André Gide had a long life: he died at the age of eighty-two. What is more, he was not one of those who are discovered by later generations: he was read and appreciated in his lifetime. The Swedish Royal Academy awarded this 'immoralist' the Nobel prize. Today even in France readers seldom pick up his books. He saw himself as a lasting monument, but he was, for all his talent, his craftsmanship, his artistic boldness, merely a mayfly that beats its wings against a clouded window-pane.

I have said that time puts everything in perspective. As my memory evokes André Gide discoursing in my flat about 'Communist brotherhood' while Bouzou snatches the biscuits, I somehow feel sorry for him. He was very lonely: he was highly esteemed but not loved. Did he himself love anyone? After his death some pages of his diary that he had not wanted to be read during his lifetime were published. He wrote that he loved his wife. He had married at an early age a mild, God-fearing girl and at the time of his marriage was aware of his perversion. His wife lived separated from him in the country, and he wrote her letters about his love for her. At one point he wanted those letters for the first volume of his memoirs but found that his wife had burnt them. He made the following entry in his diary: 'I wept for a whole week from morning till night . . . I compared myself to Oedipus'. I do not doubt the sincerity of those tears; what he wept over was not his love but his own avowals of it – he was a man who, to recall Bryusov's words, 'from cloudless childhood' sought 'the combination of words'. No one could have described him more cruelly than he did himself.

During his lifetime he published his journals of the war years. They contain some terrible pages. On 5th September 1940, soon after the Nazis had occupied France, he wrote: 'To come to terms with one's enemy of yesterday is not cowardice; it is wisdom, and accepting the inevitable . . . Whoever baulks at fate is caught in a trap. What is the use of bruising oneself against the bars of one's cage? In order to suffer less from the narrowness of the jail, there is nothing like remaining squarely in the middle . . .' Three weeks later he comforted himself: 'If tomorrow, as I fear, all freedom of thought or at least of expression of that thought is denied us, I shall try to convince myself that art, the thought itself, will lose less thereby than through excessive freedom. Oppression cannot debase the best; and as for the others, it matters little. Hurrah for thought held in check! . . .'

I am convinced that in the years 1930–5 he was genuinely attracted to Communism. He felt the world as a chill place and was drawn to the warmth of the workers' meetings; like a tramp he warmed himself at another's campfire. I remember him speaking at a street meeting in the suburb of Villejuif; he raised his clenched fist with a shy smile. He was not trying to deceive anyone, except perhaps himself.

Roger Martin du Gard noted in 1934 after a conversation with him: 'How incautious to attach so much importance to the adherence of a man who, by his very nature, is unfitted to hold firm convictions, who is never to be found where one thought he had settled down the day before. Despite sincere goodwill, I greatly fear that his new friends will soon be disappointed in him'. Martin du Gard knew the man well, but I was taken in. I say this without bitterness: time, as they say, is a great healer.

In 1935 André Gide often came to see me; together we prepared the Anti-Fascist Congress of Writers. It would be stupid cowardice on my part, in evoking these years, to ignore the shade of that sixty-six-year-old moth in a cape with *Capital* or a small volume of Euripides in his hand.

12

A T   T H E   Congress of Writers in Moscow I was merely an ordinary delegate, but I was one of the organizers of the Paris Congress and was as excited as a boy. Till the last day we feared that it would all come to nothing; prominent writers were being dissuaded: it was said that the Congress was a Communist affair, that those who took part in it would antagonize not only critics, editors and publishers but the reading public as well.

The Congress was organized in a very primitive way – without much money, or any premises, and with neither a secretary nor a typist – and we had to do the typing ourselves, make the telephone calls, persuade, pacify and appease. Those who worked hardest were Jean-Richard Bloch, Malraux, Guilloux, René Blech and Moussinac.

In his speech to the Congress Mikhail Koltsov recalled that the first international meeting of writers had also taken place in Paris – in 1878. He added that today Russian writers could speak to their Western fellows very differently: the convict prisons, the general illiteracy, Saltykov-Shchedrin's despotic governors no longer overshadowed them.

The writers' meeting mentioned by Koltsov had been attended by Victor Hugo and Turgenev. There were no writers of such stature at our Congress, but I do not think any such were alive in 1935. Yet we succeeded in assembling the most widely-read and recognized authors: Heinrich Mann, André Gide, Alexey Tolstoy, Henri Barbusse, Aldous Huxley, Bertolt Brecht, André Malraux, Isaak Babel, Louis Aragon, Martin Andersen Nexö, Boris Pasternak, Ernst Toller, Anna Seghers. Greetings were sent from Ernest Hemingway, Theodore Dreiser and James Joyce. The presiding committee of the Association elected by the Congress included André Gide, Heinrich Mann, Sinclair Lewis, Rámon del-Valle-Inclán and Henri Barbusse.

The Congress was very mixed: Vaillant-Couturier sat next to the liberal critic Julien Benda; the speech of the sceptical English novelist E. M. Forster was followed by that of the fiery Aragon; the Spanish individualist Eugenio d'Orz conversed with Johannes R. Becher; the seventy-year-old German critic Kerr talked about the importance of the literary heritage with the youthful Korneichuk; Kafka's friend and closest sympathizer, Max Brod, discussed the draft resolution with Shcherbakov, while in the refreshment room Galaktion Tabidze drank the health of Karin Michaëlis, who was deeply touched.

The Congress lasted five days and the immense Palais de la Mutualité was packed the whole time; loud-speakers relayed the speeches to the lobbies; people stood listening in the street. The newspapers that had intended to ignore the Congress were forced to give it a lot of space. Even Hitler was moved to declare angrily: 'Bolshevist writers represent the murder of culture'.

Another congress comes involuntarily to my mind – the one that took place thirteen years later in Wroclaw; it was not as mixed as that in Paris, yet the few Liberals and Socialists who attended it kept taking offence, making venomous remarks, threatening to leave the hall. The Paris Congress was held under the slogan: 'In Defence of Culture', the one in Wroclaw: 'In Defence of Peace'. Of course Fascism aroused fear in everybody, but in 1948 war was not an abstract notion.

The political atmosphere in 1935 was favourable to the success of the Congress. The Popular Front was emerging in France. André Chamson, one of the organizers of the Congress and a Radical-Socialist, was the curator of the Versailles museum; he, too, spoke admiringly of the Soviet Union and shook hands with Vaillant-Couturier. This was quite in the order of the day: three weeks later, in the Place de la Bastille, Daladier embraced Thorez. Fascism was on the offensive. While the Congress was on we learnt from the papers that 15,000 French Fascists had marched through the streets of Algiers, while Fascist planes circled overhead and their leader exclaimed: 'I swear that within a month we shall seize power in France'. In Germany they were beheading the recalcitrant. Gil Robles dealt ruthlessly with those who dared to think for themselves. Italy was openly preparing to attack Abyssinia. All this is beyond question, and I do not deny for a moment that after the Second World War the situation was far more complicated: fear of Communism had grown and in America witch-hunting was only just beginning. All the same, that is not the whole story.

Aldous Huxley did not attend the Wroclaw Congress, but his brother, Julian, the biologist, was there; honestly speaking, he was no more right-wing than his brother had been in 1935, but people talked to him differently and he felt as if he had wandered into a strange house by mistake.

In Wroclaw there were not many who had taken part in the Paris Congress: Andersen Nexö, Benda, Marchwitz, Stoyanov, Korneichuk and myself – I do not think there were any others. Benda, a devout rationalist, said to me on one occasion: 'You see, I've come after all. But I don't understand anything any longer. Tell me, what's become of Babel, of Koltsov? When I ask I get no answers. One of your comrades in his speech referred to Sartre and O'Neill as "jackals"? Is that fair or, to put it at its lowest, wise? And why do we have to clap every time Stalin's name is mentioned? I'm against war. I'm against the policy of the USA. I'm all in favour of co-operation, but what I'm being asked to do is to swear allegiance. I'm seventy-eight, you know – a bit too old for an elementary school'.

But to return to the Paris Congress. The behaviour of the Soviet writers helped to contribute to its success, I believe. It would have been absurd to do nothing but denounce Fascism for five days on end. The speakers touched on the role of the writer in society, on traditions and innovations, on the national foundations of culture and on common human values. Naturally Soviet life interested everyone. I can recall some of the speeches of our writers. Koltsov's contribution was lively and amusing; he spoke about the importance of satire in Soviet society: 'Our readers are disgusted with the kind of administrator who, distorting the principles of Socialism, forces everybody into the same pattern, making them eat, wear, say and think the same things'. Lahuti said that long before the yellow star was introduced by the Nazis, Jews in pre-revolutionary Bukhara had been made to wear the *nakhi-danat* – the 'accursed sash' – and that today all the people of the Soviet Union were united by a *nakhi-vahdat*: the sash of brotherhood.

A few days before the Congress opened the French writers, who were amongst the organizers of the Congress, approached our ambassador: they would like Babel and Pasternak, who had not been included in the delegation, to come. Babel did not prepare a paper but spoke easily and humorously in excellent French about the Soviet people's love for literature. For Pasternak things were more difficult. He told me that he was suffering from insomnia, that the doctor had diagnosed nervous debility, that he was in a rest-home when he heard that he would have to go to Paris. He wrote a draft of his speech – chiefly about his illness. It took a lot of persuasion to get him to say a few words about poetry. We hastily translated one of his poems into French. The audience applauded enthusiastically.

Nikolay Tikhonov, gaunt and inspired, spoke about poetry: 'Take Mayakovsky. There you have a master of the Soviet ode, of satire, of farce and comedy in verse. Or Bagritsky. Here is passionate and simple verse. Verse full of telling imagery and of genuine emotion. Hunter, angler, a partisan fighter – he loved nature. In Boris Pasternak we are presented with the complex world of psychological expanses, with ebullient poetry, headlong and tense, with a breathless art. Here is a poetical and deeply sincere striving to perceive and to combine various intersecting attainments'.

(My piece for *Izvestia* at the time contained the following sentence: 'When Tikhonov passed on to the evaluation of Pasternak's work, the poet who had shown that sensitive skill and a sensitive conscience are not incompatible was greeted with prolonged applause'. Six months later a Moscow writer who, in his own words, enjoyed 'smearing' his comrades, stated that in Paris I had saluted Pasternak by saying that 'only he possessed a conscience'. This myth gained ground and *Komsomolskaya Pravda* denounced not Tikhonov, not the members of the Paris Congress who has so lightheartedly applauded Pasternak, and not Pasternak himself, but me. A short paragraph appeared in the French press: 'Moscow disclaims Ehrenburg'. I wrote to Shcherbakov, to Koltsov, asking them to refute the slander, but with no result. The French writers asked me what was up. This was a quarter of a century ago, before 1937, and I was simple-minded enough to believe that there was an answer to every question.)

In the West they were saying then – as they are still saying – that the whole of our literature is propaganda. In my speech I said: 'We have lived through difficult times, our days were battle-trenches. People's feelings do not change all at once. Our propaganda literature is linked with the memory of the past. Well aware that our enemies might attack our country we created the Red Army. But no matter how perfect its weapons, we shall never claim that its guns are examples of Soviet culture. The Fascists, too, have guns. But they cannot have our Red Army men. Propaganda literature is military equipment; it was forged in the arsenals of the bourgeoisie. While insisting on "pure art" the bourgeoisie cold-shouldered authors in revolt and pampered tame ones. It is not the *poètes maudits* but the tame ones who created functional literature. Genuine, disinterested art, whose aim is not the preserving of social hierarchies but the development of man, is possible only in a new society. We have come here not proud of ourselves but of our readers'. The two oldest writers on the platform – Heinrich Mann and André Gide – came up to shake my hand; this gesture was, of course, intended as a tribute to Soviet readers. I was deeply moved and mumbled something.

Frequently I was obliged to leave the hall and see to a number of tedious jobs. On returning to my seat I invariably heard friendly and at times enthusiastic words about Soviet society from all kinds of Western writers: Chamson, the Catholic Mounier, Heinrich Mann, Gide, Guéhenno and others.

There were some highly dramatic moments. A man in dark spectacles and a rather obviously false beard suddenly appeared on the rostrum: he was a German Communist working in illegality. It is not only the young who respond to the romance of great courage: the hall was seized with frenzy; André Gide, who translated the anonymous speaker's words into French, stammered with emotion.

The weather was exceptionally torrid – it was close and thundery. One could hardly breathe in the packed hall and there was not a moment's respite. At night I had to translate speeches, write reports for *Izvestia* and even occasionally mollify some writers who had not been given the chance to speak.

In my description the whole thing seems duller and more arid than it really was. We lived on a dozen different planes. In the corridors during the debates Marina Tsvetayeva recited poetry to Pasternak. On one occasion we spent half the night in a small café arguing about Socialist Realism; Shcherbakov who was with us, trying not to fall asleep, suddenly said: 'But why argue? It's all in the rules'. Lahuti presented André Gide with a Tadjik robe and skullcap and, seeing the author of *Corydon* in this unusual attire, we suddenly realized that he ought to be sitting in an Oriental tea-house measuring eternity instead of speaking at meetings. Babel talked enthusiastically to André Triolet about some remarkable stallion. Galaktion Tabidze bought rare editions of Baudelaire and Rimbaud; he could not read French but lovingly stroked the pages. Brecht and Malraux discussed whether death could enter into life. In a small bar near the Mutualité where we went to drink iced lemonade, lovers were kissing; in the meantime the loud-speaker announced that the playwright Lenormand would be the next to speak; as for myself, I looked at the couple and recalled the words so often used by my uncle Leo, who ran a travelling circus: 'Do not live as you want but as God commands'[1].

Suddenly the chattering in the corridors ceased: the Surrealists were going to speak – they had decided to wreck the Congress.

On the eve of the Congress we learnt of the suicide of the young Surrealist René Crevel. I sometimes met him and knew that he had strong feelings about the break between the Surrealists and the Communists. They said he had taken poison, leaving a short note: 'I am fed up with everything'.

Afterwards, from his friends Klaus Mann and Moussinac I learnt that quite unwittingly I had played a certain part in this tragic affair. I had written a sharply-worded article about the Surrealists. One night we were sitting in a café and I went out to buy some tobacco. As I was crossing the street two Surrealists came up to me and one of them struck me across the face. Instead of replying in kind I stupidly asked: 'What's wrong?' The act was quite in character with the Surrealists, but the silly incident was the last drop for René Crevel. Of course a drop is not the whole cup, but it grieves me to recall it.

Aragon read Crevel's speech to the Congress. Everyone stood up. Crevel was thirty-five when he died. And so it happened that even at the Congress there had to be a suicide.

Paul Eluard asked to be allowed to speak. The audience was agitated: now trouble would start. Someone shouted at the top of his voice. Moussinac, who was presiding, gave the floor to Eluard who at the time was an orthodox Surrealist. He read a speech written by André Breton; naturally it contained attacks on the Congress: to the Surrealists we were conservatives, academicians, bureaucrats. But half an hour later the disappointed reporters went off to the refreshment room – everything had ended peacefully: we realized that the trouble was not Breton but Hitler.

I have remembered the speech of the English novelist E. M. Forster who said: '. . . You may have guessed that I am not a Communist, though perhaps I might be one if I was a younger and a braver man, for in Communism I can see hope . . . if there is another war, writers of the individualistic and liberalizing type, like myself and Mr Aldous Huxley, will be swept away . . . We have just to go on tinkering as well as we can with our old tools until the crash comes . . .' (Both the

[1] Russian saying.

younger Huxley and the older Forster survived the Second World War. And if 'old tools' are less in demand today, experts say that this is due less to a change of outlook than to the competition of television.)

Koltsov's speech was naturally far more optimistic. Addressing himself to the Fascists he recalled the proverb: 'He laughs best that laughs last'. Koltsov did not live to see the denouement. The Fascists were indeed defeated, but on 9th May 1945 we did not laugh. I remember a woman in Red Square who was quietly showing everybody the photograph of her son killed on the Volga.

(My work on this chapter has now been interrupted for a whole month: Rome, Warsaw, London – meetings, sessions, a conference – disarmament, atom bombs, Bonn, the *revanchists*. The people I saw were not writers but men from all walks of life: an American senator, members of the Labour Party, physicists, Italian deputies, Jules Moch, priests, trade unionists. Of course I want to finish writing this book, but if it is possible to convince even a dozen people that there is no other way out except to destroy all the bombs and disband all the armies, then the book can go hang – the fate of the very young is far more important: they have before them their own men, their own years, their own life.)

The Association of Anti-Fascist Writers was formed and the secretariat elected; it included two Soviet writers – Koltsov and myself. Koltsov said to me: 'As the secretariat is to be centred in Paris it's you who'll have to do the work'. With an affectionate and slightly quizzical grunt he added: 'And it's you who'll get all the kicks too'.

That I did get some kicks I have already mentioned. There was also no lack of work. We organized meetings, lectures and discussions, in Paris and in the provinces. The times were propitious: it was the Popular Front honeymoon. I lectured in Paris, Lille and Grenoble.

At the Paris Congress there were no outstanding writers from Czechoslovakia. I visited Prague and met Čapek. He had a great deal to say about the Fascist menace and agreed to come on to the committee of the Association. At that time he was working on his novel *War With the Newts*. He said smiling: 'You've probably heard the Czech anecdote: on a sunny day Čapek is walking along the Priškop with an open umbrella, and in reply to puzzled questions says: "It's raining in London"'. It's true that there are a lot of things I like about English manners and customs; for instance, I like the fact that Londoners don't jostle, and in the Underground and on buses don't shove

308

one another. This is probably because I like the dreams of the last century. But we're living in different times, society jostles man, one nation shoves another'.

In those days the secretary of the Union of Czech Writers was the poet Josef Hora; he suggested including the Czech Union in our Association. I was present at a meeting of the Slovak writers; they too joined the Association.

From Spain we had almost entirely young writers: Lorca, Alberti, Bergamín. I met my old friend Gomez de la Cerna who avoided politics, but I succeeded in persuading him to join the Association.

In June 1936 the plenary meeting of the secretariat took place in London. We were in an elated mood and discussed all kinds of plans: the awarding of international literary prizes, the setting up of a central bureau for translating the best works into a number of different languages, etc. Particularly impassioned were the discussions about the plan to compile an encyclopedia which, according to Benda, Malraux and Bloch, should become what the encyclopedias of Diderot, Voltaire and Montesquieu had been for the second half of the eighteenth century.

Quite unexpectedly H. G. Wells came to our meeting. I had first met him in the summer of 1934 at Litvinov's *dacha*. In his conversation with Litvinov, Eisenstein and myself he had said that there were many things he liked about our country, and this seemed to rile him: he resented having to acknowledge a reality that cut across his predictions. He was capable of foretelling a great deal, he was longsighted: when in 1919 Andrey Bely wrote about the atom bomb, it was the premonition of a poet, but when in 1914 Wells described the use of atomic weapons in a future war, it could be called scientific prediction. He laid great store by logic, but regarded dialectics with suspicion. At Litvinov's *dacha*, talking to Litvinov's daughter, the lively young Tania, he suddenly became natural, even benevolent.

On entering the meeting Wells laid his hat on the table and immediately threw cold water on our enthusiasm: he made it clear to us in sober terms that we were neither Diderots nor Voltaires, that we had no money and that in general we were living in a cloud-cuckoo-land. He told us a story about the nine tailors who claimed to speak for the people of England. When he had had his say, he picked up his hat and walked out.

He was of course quite right to be sceptical: we did not compile even the first volume of the encyclopedia, we did not found any literary prizes. We did not even do anything about translations. Bergamín suggested convening the Second International Writers' Congress in Madrid in 1937; this suggestion was accepted. How could we know that three weeks later a terrible destructive war would break out in Spain? Of all our decisions we carried out only one: the Congress did in fact assemble in Madrid, and we held our meetings under the fire of Fascist guns.

13

THIS IS what I wrote in *Izvestia* about France and Paris in the early spring of 1935: 'I have been thinking for a long time about why this land is so sad. Its beauty only makes the sadness more apparent. Beautiful are the old elms and ashes in the middle of a clearing. Red apples fall from the apple-trees. On the seashore fishermen mend fine, pale-blue nets. Black cows pensively dip their faces into the grass, green like childhood. White peasants' cottages are garlanded with wistaria. Life is short – that is what a shy, clumsy lad is singing under my window. He has grown out of his suit but they have not had a new one made for him. He has come to this land too late: all the novels have been written, all the waste land has been ploughed up, all the places have been filled, from the chair that the senator warms to the dustbin for the rag-and-bone man to scavenge. He can only sing on an empty stomach "Life is short" ... They are many, they were born, like everybody else, they learnt to walk, clapped their hands, sucked lollipops and looked at life with trustful blue eyes. Then it turned out that they had grown up in vain. At night in Paris, as you breathe in the briny smell of the sea, you almost seem to hear the creak of rigging. Your head swims: black is the night of Europe. The melancholy of centuries has accumulated on this small patch of land as in a casket holding the letters of one's youth. But even this melancholy is linked to life. In the early hours of the morning thrushes and factory sirens sound over dove-coloured Paris; they seem to say: "Great deeds await you, the struggle, the future!" '

I also thought about the fate of France and Paris in the little studio cluttered with canvases, jugs and bric-à-brac from the *Marché aux Puces*, looking at Robert Falk's landscapes. There is more than one Paris: we know the shining Paris of the Impressionists washed with light rain; the airy and tender Paris of Marquet; Utrillo's lyrical and provincial Paris. The Paris of Falk is heavy, twilit, grey, dove-coloured, violet; it is the Paris of the tragedy-to-come, doomed and excited, given up for lost, and yet alive. Falk had been working in Paris only nine years, but he understood this large complex city to which he might have remained a stranger.

I first met Robert Rafailovich Falk in the early thirties but it was during the last period of his life that we saw each other most often and had long talks. Ignoring the events of 1935 for the moment, let me go back to our first meeting: it was then that I first felt the full power of his painter's diction. He dragged dozens of canvases out of the corners of his studio; he was tall and gaunt, with a melancholy, not to say gloomy face, lit up now and then by a slight diffident smile. As I admired the paintings, I saw the surrounding world in a new way: the people, the epoch, the patchy sequence of events, the indecipherable shorthand of the century.

(When I was writing the novel *The Fall of Paris* I had a Paris landscape by Falk on the wall in front of me. Often I looked up from my manuscript to gaze at it – the houses, the smoke, the sky. Had it not been for that picture some of the pages might never have been written.)

I have said in these memoirs that I lived on a dozen planes at once, dissipating my energies, always in a hurry; I put it down to the times but it may have been my own fault. After all, Falk was my contemporary (he was only some three years older than I) but he worked with concentration, doggedly, fanatically. As a sixteen-year-old boy he had sat, enraptured, painting his first landscape by a small Moscow pond. He worked till his last day, frantically, painfully, destroying canvases, re-painting them for the tenth time; he scraped off the paint that had accumulated like a crust, and painted again; for the fifth, the tenth time he would return to the same figure, to the same still-life. He worked in the days when his pictures were exhibited and also when all doors were closed to him; he worked without considering whether his paintings would be shown: he spoke not because he had a packed hall before him but because he had a great deal to say.

There are artists who work easily and swiftly – I am not referring to pot-boiling but to genuine artists; they paint because, in Falk's words, 'their eyes are well-set in their heads'. Everybody has met the man who speaks readily only because he has the gift of facile, colourful speech. The ancient Greeks admired Demosthenes' oratorical talent, yet as a child he stammered. Falk in each of his works overcame his painter's stammer. But his perseverance was quite unlike the doggedness of Bryusov who called his dream an 'ox'; Falk's dream was mettlesome, he tried to bridle it, break it in to the laws of art, to his thoughts. He loved Baratynsky's verses about the sculptor: 'Fixing his deep gaze on the stone, the artist saw a nymph in it, a flame ran through his veins and his heart flew out to her. But infinitely yearning, he is already master of himself: unhurried, deliberate, the chisel removes layer upon layer to release the goddess'.

In a way he was not unlike that predecessor of his whom he most admired – Cézanne – in his incredible capacity for work, his gravity, his mild yet unaccommodating disposition, his tendency to isolation. But Robert Falk was a man of both another epoch and another land. He said of Cézanne: 'A great painter. He had perfect vision. But as a man he had a certain hardness, a dryness, traits that are frequently to be found in the French. I think these spiritual characteristics have also coloured Cézanne's painting'.

Robert Falk knew the traditions of Russian literature and Russian music; by nature he was humane and never remained a cold observer of life – he worked himself up, he suffered, he rejoiced.

He loved Vrubel. At the Art School his teacher was Konstantin Korovin. (Falk told me that he used to meet him in Paris. Korovin was then seventy-five but he still worked and explored, and said to Falk: 'D'you know who's now the greatest living painter in France? Soutine'.) Falk began exhibiting with the Jack of Diamonds group, together with Konchalovsky, Larionov, Lentulov, Goncharova, Malevich, Mashkov, Kuprin, Rozhdestvensky, Chagall. There is a widely held opinion that this group blindly imitated the French, but in fact it was an important, entirely independent current in Russian painting which has still not found an informed and honest historian. It is natural that in those days Falk should have paid his tribute to Cubism and at times he generalized too much, but his landscapes have nothing in common with geometry; they were the expression of the young artist's emotions.

Falk observed life avidly. As I have already said, he spent only nine years in Paris and during that period changed his address fourteen times, moving from one studio or attic to another; he explained that the different districts of Paris were quite unlike each other and that he wanted not only to see but also to have lived in fourteen different towns.

He knew the obscure side-streets of Moscow, the sands and stones of Central Asia, various Russian towns – he enjoyed travelling about. A recluse in painting, in life he was sociable, was always meeting people, listening attentively to discussions, stories, confidences.

Falk liked to teach; those he taught – both in the twenties and in the forties – say that he imparted to beginners not only his experience but also his findings, his insight, and that he put his whole heart into his lessons.

In his earliest youth his dream was to become a musician, and all his life he loved music. He also loved poetry; I often talked to him about it, he could grasp at once the inner rhythm of a poem, perhaps because it was rhythm that he sought in painting.

Paul Cézanne, exceptionally clearsighted in his own craft, knew little outside paint and canvas. General events left him unmoved. Zola was much ridiculed for not having understood his schoolfellow, whom he thought devoid of talent and not even particularly intelligent. People were justified in laughing at him. But one may add that neither did Cézanne understand Zola, who had revolutionized the structure of the novel: he tried to read his books and gave up, feeling bored. But Falk knew a lot and took an interest in a great many things. In his paintings Paris ('not a city but a landscape') was as he saw and understood it. In 1935 he used to say: 'France is doomed. It's difficult to work here, there's not enough air. Time to go home'. He was living quite well at the time: his pictures were exhibited, the critics wrote about him a good deal, collectors bought him. But while indifferent to money and fame, he reacted sharply to the atmosphere of the times, to the mood of those around him. He knew that France would not hold out, knew it for a certainty, and when, after the fall of Paris, I returned to Moscow he asked me about the details – the theme itself he had known long since, and not only from newspapers.

On one occasion he said to me: 'I think about all sorts of things before I get down to work. I think about the man I'm painting, and also about the age we live in, the landscape, political events, poetry, my grandmother's fairy-tales, yesterday's newspaper. When I'm painting I use only my eyes but I see quite differently because I've been thinking about things and thinking them out'. The Impressionists said that they depicted the world as they saw it. Picasso remarked once that he depicted the world as he thought it. Falk saw in the same way as he thought. He did not try to create illusionary images and he said that he disliked the term 'pictorial art', preferring 'plastic art': to him painting was not a depiction but a reflection – the creation of reality on canvas.

In one of his letters he wrote: 'Cézanne's works are not semblances of life but life itself in beautiful, precious, visual plastic forms. The

314

Cubists regard themselves as his heirs. In my view they are usurpers of his art. Frankly speaking, I do not like abstract painting. Abstraction, even in the case of the most talented painters, leads to schematization, to arbitrariness, to fortuitousness. Basically, I am a realist. In my understanding of realism Cézanne is particularly close to me. Of the later painters I am most attracted by Rouault'.

Falk had no use for decorative painting; he spoke of a painter like Matisse with respect but without warmth. He himself tried to reveal objects, nature, human character. His portraits, especially those of his last years, are striking in their depth: by means of colour he conveys the essence of his model; colour creates not only shapes and space but also shows 'the unseen side of the moon'. A writer would need volumes to describe in detail what Falk achieves with colour: face, coat, hands, a wall appear on the canvas as a complex of passions, events, meditations – a plastic biography.

In 1946 or 1947 Falk was classed as a 'formalist'. This was absurd, but in those days nothing much surprised one. He was to be brought to his knees. I remember one of the leaders of the Artists' Union in those days saying: 'Falk doesn't understand words, we shall hit his pocket'. This really amazed me even at that time: the man did not realize with whom he was dealing. I have never in my life met a painter so indifferent to all material things – to comfort, to money. Falk cooked himself peas or potatoes; he went about for years in the same shabby coat; he wore one shirt, and his only other lay in an old suitcase. In a well-furnished room he felt ill at ease and lived completely neglectful of his surroundings, concerned only with paints and brushes.

His pictures were no longer shown. He was penniless. He might have been buried alive. But he went on working. Sometimes art lovers or young painters would visit his studio: he welcomed them all, talked about art and smiled deprecatingly.

In 1954 he wrote: 'It is only now, it seems to me, that I am mature enough to understand Cézanne properly. How sad this is and what a pity! I have lived a whole life-time and have only now realized how one ought to work. But I no longer have the necessary strength, and it will go on declining'. These words show how stern and exacting Falk was with himself to the very end.

Canvases kept accumulating in the long gloomy studio near the Moscow river. When you look at the work of some elderly painters you cannot help recalling the freshness, the purity, the brightness of their youth. But Falk amazed one by his continuous growth that ceased only with life. (He once remarked that Corot painted his best picture at the age of seventy-six. Falk was seventy when he died.) His health was bad, he looked wasted and walked with difficulty but still continued to work. One exhibition, and that a very small and carefully vetted one, was held in the old premises of the Moscow Society of Soviet Painters when he was already lying in hospital near to death. And it was to those same dismal premises, soon after the exhibition, that they brought Falk in his coffin. People stood and wept; they knew what they had lost.

Today volumes of verse appear that would not have been published ten years ago; modern houses are being built. But Falk's paintings still stand with their faces to the wall.

14

ON 14th July 1935, soon after the Congress of Writers, Paris saw an unprecedented demonstration: the military parade of the Front Populaire. I spent all day walking about the streets with brief visits to cafés – I was writing a report which was to appear the next day in *Izvestia*. The demonstration began in the morning in the Place de la Bastille and the columns marched towards the Bois de Vincennes, only a few kilometres from the square; but there was such a multitude of people (the newspapers, according to their political line, later gave varying numbers – 600,000, 700,000, 800,000 –) that those who brought up the rear reached the city gates only by nightfall. The leaders of the parties that had been hostile until recently walked side by side: Thorez and Blum, Daladier and Cachin. There were also scholars and writers: Langevin, Perrin, Rivet, Aragon, Malraux, Bloch.

On that day the Fascists staged their own demonstration in the Champs Elysées; they marched smartly, raised their arms trying to be like the Nazis in every way; they shouted: *'Vive la Roque!'* – this was the name of the colonel at the head of the Croix de Feu.

'La Roque au poteau!' the people chanted rhythmically in the Place de la Bastille. The smouldering civil war was beginning to flare up. Few took any interest in the government led by the slippery Laval; he signed agreements with Mussolini, with the Soviet Union, seeking to outwit both the Front Populaire and de la Roque, to postpone the denouement if only for a year or two.

I felt very strongly that the times of peace had been left behind. Only a year ago I had read my post first thing in the morning; now I crammed the letters into my pocket and, going out to buy a paper, read it standing in the street. A radio lived in my room now, filling it with strangers who constantly imparted disquieting news. The night hours I spent listening to this hateful box were torture; speeches by Hitler or Mussolini, accounts of clashes with Fascists in the streets of French towns were interrupted by advertisements (broadcasting was still in the hands of various private companies). For some reason I still remember a jingle which glorified the healing properties of

'Baldoflorine'; what particular ailments it cured I forget, but this word 'Bal-do-florine', sandwiched between the Duce's yells of: 'Proletarian and Fascist Italy, forward!' and the description of a beheading in Hamburg, nauseated me.

On 7th September Paris was out again on the streets: they were burying Henri Barbusse who had died in Moscow. The funeral turned into a demonstration.

Of course hundreds of thousands of people thought more about the coming battles than about the dead writer: they knew that Barbusse had been a valiant comrade, a Communist, the author of a book about Stalin; the fifty-year-olds remembered *Le Feu* which told the tragedy of the Verdun generation. Barbusse was a complex personality; one cannot think of him apart from either the poems of his youth or the melancholy of his later years. He once said to me with a slight smile: 'It's difficult enough to fight capitalism but even more difficult to fight oneself'. He was, however, well able to fight himself. In one of his speeches he spoke about the function of 'modest standard-bearers', amongst whom he counted himself. On that September day it was he who became a banner. War cripples were pushed in wheel-chairs. Women held up their babies. Red flags fluttered from the windows of workers' homes, and where there were no flags people put out red curtains or cushions. On the coffin, amidst rich southern flowers, lay autumn asters and dahlias – the flowers of the Moscow countryside.

I particularly remember a contingent carrying a banner: 'The workers of Lannes will not tolerate Fascism'. A cynic might smile: Lannes is a small town of some 20,000 inhabitants. But the slogan had its own truth: France was going through a phase of unprecedented enthusiasm and each man believed that the future depended on him personally.

In February 1936 the Camelots du Roi (an extreme right-wing organization) attacked Léon Blum, beat him up and, for some un-accountable reason, kept his hat and tie as trophies.

Indignant demonstrators made their way to the Panthéon, which enshrines the ashes of Jean Jaurès who was murdered by a precursor of Fascism. Students belonging to Fascist organizations had gathered round the Panthéon. There was a lot of angry shouting. Hundreds of thousands of manual workers, of office-workers, of intellectuals raised their red flags higher and clenched their fists.

I noticed Marcel Cachin in one of the columns and went up to greet

318

him. The workers standing on the quay shouted: 'Hullo, Cachin! They won't dare touch you. We'll stand by you'. Cachin waved his hand with a faint smile.

(I once met Cachin in a café – in 1932 or 1933 – where he was sitting with Langevin and the painter Signac, telling them about his meeting with Lenin. The thought suddenly came to me: these men have come a long way to reach our present age; they have understood the present without losing the past. Cachin was well liked; he was, as it were, a living proof that profound culture is not incompatible with the every-day struggle and that Communism means neither emotional coldness nor blindness, nor yet the behaviour of one who has ambitions as a leader.)

I often attended meetings and gatherings; people were demanding the release of Ernst Thaelmann, they protested against the repression of the Asturian miners, against Italy's attack on Abyssinia; they raised all manner of questions and yet it was always the same one: you could not live in the same world with Fascists. The speakers were experienced orators and half-grown boys; they included André Gide, Langevin, Malraux and simple housewives. At one of the meetings in the mining area of the Dauphiné, when everything had already been said over and over again, an old worker with blue marks veining his face asked to speak; he mounted the platform and began to sing in a tremulous old man's voice: 'Arise ye starvelings from your slumbers . . .' Several years later I wrote the following verse about the meetings of 1935: 'I saw hope, more slender than a rose, like soft wax obedient to the hand, it was born in the fist of the drudge, and throbbed as a blood-clot on the banner's staff'.

In stuffy halls, packed with people – all strangers to me – I, too, raised my clenched fist and in it the hope of those months fluttered like a moth. And there were many grounds for hope. I was struck by the maturity of the workers. Here is one episode. In Lille I met a doctor, one of the organizers of the Franco-Soviet Friendship Society. He took me to the village of Lannoy not far from Roubaix where there was a large flax-mill. The association of factory-owners, in view of the protracted crisis, had decided to shut down a number of factories and destroy the plant. The workers, men and women, sent a letter to Laval: 'We wish to make it clear to you that we shall not allow the plant of the Boutemy factory to be destroyed. We shall see to it that the machinery, which is common property, is safeguarded'. I saw the workers who guarded the factory from its owners. A worker with a grey moustache said to me: 'I read in *L'Humanité* that Gorky's writing a history of Russian factories. Tell him how we live under capitalism: the machinery doesn't belong to us but to scoundrels, but we aren't going to give it up whatever happens, it's the property of the people. I think a writer like Gorky might mention this fact in his book'.

Under our very eyes parties, trade unions, men were being miraculously drawn closer together. There is a copy of *L'Humanité* in front of me with the list of its literary contributors of the day: the theatrical managers Jouvet and Dullen, the painter Vlaminck, the writers Gide, Malraux, Chamson, Guéhenno, Giono, Durtain, Vildrac, Cassou. Today I find this incredible.

The workers succeeded (though not for long) in winning the support of a large part of the intelligentsia, of the peasants and of the petty bourgeoisie. I witnessed this in the mining district of La Mure, near Grenoble. There was a strike on; the mineowners wanted to starve the workers into submission. The strike committee had its headquarters in the town hall; women from the neighbouring farms used to come and fetch the miners' children to stay in their homes. It was market day, and the peasants brought gifts for the miners: potatoes, eggs, bacon, geese. The local barber announced publicly that he would shave the strikers and cut their hair free of charge. In the end the miners won their strike.

At the same time one could observe almost daily how swiftly the opposite camp was organizing. There may not have been so very many Fascists all told in France, but they made a lot of noise, resorted to violence, attacked from ambush. Some of them wore little moustaches and called themselves *nacistes*; others sported badges with a skull on their sleeves and called themselves *francistes*. A *Blue House* was opened in Paris, because was there not a *Brown House* in Berlin?

Germany moved her troops into the demilitarized zone of the Rhineland. The League of Nations discussed this action for many months and in the end reached no decision. Every evening the hateful radio emitted hoarse shouts: 'Memel is ours! Strasbourg is ours! Brunn is ours!' And then, not only young fellows with small clipped moustaches but solid family men began to say that peace was far more precious than this unknown Czechoslovakia; that the Popular Front would land the country in war; that it was high time to muzzle the left-wing gasbags. Every day Italy seized some part of Abyssinia; the

Fascists waged the war ruthlessly, bombing hospitals, using poison gas. The League of Nations applied economic sanctions to Italy; in practice this remained on paper; but the Fascists in Paris organized demonstrations every week under the slogan: 'Down with sanctions!' And again middle-class Frenchmen with moderate incomes, of whom there are many in France, said: 'Why quarrel with Italy? She is our Latin sister. Mussolini will help to pacify Hitler'. Meanwhile the radio blared: 'The Mediterranean is ours! Corsica is ours! Nice is ours!' What the French middle-class feared was the victory of the Popular Front, visualizing the loss of unearned income and the introduction of communal flats and collective farms.

When newsreels showed Italian victories in Abyssinia, the audience in the workers' districts whistled deafeningly, while in the bourgeois districts many people clapped. Sometimes fighting would break out in the darkened cinema.

Complete strangers argued with one another in cafés, in the métro, in the street. Families were divided, friendships severed.

Everybody said that there would soon be war, and everybody demanded peace. The National Front of the right-wing parties swore that they would prevent war. The Popular Front prepared for the elections under the slogan: 'Peace, Bread, Liberty'. The right-wing claimed that the Communists wanted to attack the Fascist countries. Everything was confused. The Jeunesse Patriote sang the *Marseillaise* and demanded that education should be conducted in the spirit of national traditions; at the same time they organized demonstrations with shouts of: 'Down with sanctions! Down with England! Friendship with Italy!' The British urged the application of sanctions to Italy (trying, however, to avoid treading on Hitler's toes), and the writer Henri Béraud published an article in a right-wing paper entitled: 'Should England be reduced to slavery?' The younger workers preferred the *Internationale* to the *Marseillaise*, demonstrated against the Italian Fascists and against Hitler, and denounced the 'Two Hundred Families' who were betraying France.

There were also those who would not learn. One morning on opening my paper I read a manifesto which tried to justify Italy's aggression against Abyssinia as a 'cultural mission'; the text was signed by a number of writers well-known for their right-wing views, but suddenly I caught sight of the name of a man who had always been regarded as left-wing and whom I often used to meet in the twenties.

I wrote to him at once asking how he could have signed such a declaration. He answered in a long confused letter which included the following lines: 'I do not know what Fascism is or what its aims are. This may seem incredible to you, but it is now three weeks since I have read a newspaper. I am over fifty and I no longer have any opinions, I mean convinced ones of the kind that impel a man to make sacrifices. My views change twenty times a day'. He is a good writer and an amiable man, but this brought our friendship to an end; I never met him again.

I lived in a curious state of perpetual excitement. Six months later I wrote a small book of short stories and called it *Beyond a Truce*. I felt that there was a kind of tacit truce with Fascism, and that the fate of my own close associates did not come under the conditions of that truce. In an *Izvestia* article I wrote: 'Will our grandchildren realize what it meant to live under the Nazis? Wrath, shame, passion will hardly survive on the yellowed disintegrated pages. But into the high noon of another age, full of leafy sunshine, perhaps a moment's silence will fall – that will be our voice'.

Of course, at the end of 1935 I could not know that the main trials still lay ahead. All I felt was that the outcome would be tragic, and I ended my article with the words: 'The hope for peace lies in the Red Army'.

It was an unusual autumn in France: that year thunderstorms rumbled, in the gardens cherry-trees blossomed a second time. I gazed at the carefully tended plots, at the small white houses with tiled roofs, at this charming fragile world, perhaps already doomed. I was looking out of the window of a railway carriage – my paper had given me leave: I was on my way to Moscow.

15

SOON AFTER my arrival in Moscow the editor gave me a ticket for a conference of Stakhanovites. I came an hour before the appointed time but the Great Hall in the Kremlin was already packed. People in their seats talked in low voices; no one stood about. It was quite unlike the noisy Paris meetings in halls filled with tobacco smoke. I asked my neighbours to point out Stakhanov and whether they knew Krivonos, Izotov, the Vinogradovs.

Suddenly everyone rose and began to clap furiously: entering from a side door, which I could not see, Stalin appeared followed by the members of the Politburo – I had met them at Gorky's *dacha*. The audience clapped and shouted. This went on for a long time, possibly ten or fifteen minutes. Stalin clapped in response. When the applause began to die down someone shouted: 'Hurrah for the great Stalin!' and it started up all over again. At last everyone sat down and then a woman's wild cry went up: 'Glory to Stalin!' We jumped to our feet and started clapping once more.

By the time this came to an end, my palms positively hurt. I was seeing Stalin for the first time and could not take my eyes off him. I knew him from hundreds of portraits, knew his tunic and his moustache, but I had imagined him taller. His hair was very black, his forehead low, his eyes keen and expressive. At times, leaning to the right or left, he smiled, at others he sat motionless though his eyes continued to gleam brightly. I found that I was hardly listening; I was so intent on watching Stalin. Turning round I saw that everybody else was doing the same.

On my way home I felt uneasy. Of course Stalin was a great man, but he was a Communist, a Marxist; we talked a lot about a new culture, but behaved not unlike the shaman whom I had seen in Upper Shoria. I immediately pulled myself up short: I was probably reasoning in an intellectual's way. How many times I had heard it said that we, the intellectuals, did not understand the needs of the age! '*Intelligentik*', 'muddler', 'rotten liberal' . . . And yet it was incomprehensible: 'wisest of leaders', 'people's leader of genius', 'beloved father', 'great helmsman', 'reformer of the world', 'forger of peace', 'sun'. However, I succeeded in persuading myself that I did not understand the psychology of the masses and was judging everything as a member of the intelligentsia and, what was more, one who had spent half his life in Paris.

At the conference Stalin had said: 'People must be tended carefully and lovingly, as a gardener tends a favourite fruit-tree'. These words inspired everyone: after all they were human beings, not robots, who were sitting in the Kremlin, and they rejoiced at the thought that they would be treated carefully and lovingly.

Several days passed. I met lively, interesting people. I had a long talk with the weaver Dusya Vinogradova. She turned out to be intelligent and surprisingly modest; the honours, ovations and photographers had not turned her head in the least. I decided that the acclamations in the Kremlin had just been a curious way of expressing emotion, a kind of declaration of allegiance. After all, it did not grate on me when people at Paris meetings stood with clenched fists raised, rhythmically chanting: '*Les Soviets partout!*' The struggle against Fascism was so real, it absorbed me so passionately that I laughed at myself: how stupid to worry.

I met writers, painters, theatrical managers, and involuntarily got drawn into arguments – art remained very close to my heart – and I argued heatedly and also rather clumsily: I did not understand the situation clearly enough and mistook my wishes for reality.

After visiting the Dynamo Club, the University, the Timiryazev students, the regional libraries where my novel was being discussed, I wrote: 'I have heard what is said about literature by workers, students, Red Army men. The standard of our readers is far higher than our writers imagine'. I had the impression that our readers had grown up and that too often we fobbed them off with books for children. My judgment was perhaps a little premature, but at readers' conferences I did meet people with a deep inner life and high standards.

My words may also have reflected my dissatisfaction with myself, with my novel *Without Taking Breath*, written in a rather immature style, with deliberate simplifications, as if the author were not forty-three but only half that age. I felt awkward and, reading the books of some of my contemporaries, often thought that it was high time we wrote for adults in an adult way.

I wrote an article attacking 'accessibility' – the word was then coming into vogue: 'Our readers are growing up like grass in fairy-tales, overnight. It is our job to try and raise the readers' standards, even the most backward, to the level of genuine literature, and not abolish genuine literature on the grounds that some particular writer is incomprehensible to some particular reader. The author who orientates himself to the so-called "average reader" more often than not makes a fool of himself: while he sat and wrote, his reader was growing up. The author's aim was "accessibility", an appeal to the masses, while the reader who picks up his book says: "It's dull, it's flat, a long-familiar stereotype". The secret of our wonderful country is that you cannot place your stake on "today": he who gambles on "today" finds that it has become "yesterday". One must put one's stake on tomorrow'.

Izvestia printed the article. The publishing house *Sovietsky Pisatel* (Soviet Writer) decided to reprint my old novel *Jurenito*. Certain reviewers criticized me; I hit back. It seemed to me that the discussion about literature, about art, was only just beginning.

The painters organized a discussion on portraiture. I attended and spoke about academic painting, about pictures that were little different from coloured photographs and defended the right to look for a new language in painting. I said that when the bourgeois does not understand a work of art he invariably blames the artist, whereas the worker says: 'I must come again and have another look'. (I had overheard these words one day at the Museum of Western Art.) Some of the artists disliked my ideas; one of them came out with the revelation that 'Ehrenburg talks like this because his wife is a pupil of Picasso'. (Lyuba was flattered – she had never studied under Picasso.)

At the Film Centre I said I liked *Chapayev* very much but that this film was the culmination of a brilliant epoch of Soviet film-making; I said I knew Eisenstein's and Dovzhenko's boldness and expected a great deal of these artists. The newspaper *Kino* characterized my words as 'old errors on new subjects' and angrily admonished me.

When I saw Meyerhold's new production I was entranced: he really was a man of inexhaustible imagination. Griboyedov's comedy *Woe from Wit* sounded like a modern play, not only because the actors spoke the lines in a new way, but also because a freshness of thought and feeling had been injected. There was a mimed scene that is not in the text: a lot of dressed-up dummies sat at a long table, while a dirty, and perhaps murderous, piece of scandal made the rounds. I wrote:

'We hate the Famusovs and the Molchalins. They are still bogged down in the offices; they may have changed their clothes and their vocabulary but they are still as arrogant and as sycophantic as ever. We live and work to weed them out and we cannot listen with indifference to Chatsky's soliloquies, we suffer with him, we hate with him. Such is the power of true art'. For a long time I kept hearing Chatsky's words: 'I should be glad to serve, but it sickens me to be subservient'. It was then November 1935 and the paper printed my article.

How simple-minded I was! I did not realize how much depended on the tastes, and even on the mood, of one man. But even those who were well aware of this could not foresee what would happen on the morrow.

While I was in Moscow Stalin made the statement: 'Mayakovsky was and remains the best, the most talented poet of our Soviet epoch'. Immediately everybody started to talk about the importance of innovations, of new forms, of breaking away from routine.

Some months later I read an article in *Pravda* called *Muddle Instead of Music*: Stalin had been to hear Shostakovich's opera *Katerina Izmailova* and the music had made him angry. Composers and musicians were hastily convened and they convicted Shostakovich of 'clowning' and even of 'cynicism'.

From music they passed on with ease to literature, painting, the theatre, the cinema. The critics demanded 'simplicity and popular appeal'. They still continued to praise Mayakovsky, of course, but in a different way now: he was 'simple and close to the people'. (In one of his early Futuristic poems Mayakovsky begged the hairdresser: 'Please, trim my ears'. He naturally did not know that one could get more than one's ears trimmed.) A campaign began 'against formalism, leftist deformations, distortions'; the campaign was conducted fiercely and much space was allotted to it in the press.

The first victim was Marshak's book of verse for children with drawings by V. Lebedev: the drawings were condemned as scribbles and the book was pulped. The architects also got together to denounce the 'formalists'; they attacked not only Melnikov who had built the pavilion for the 1924 Paris exhibition, not only the Constructivists Leonidov and Ginsburg, but also the 'sympathizers with formalism' – Vesnin, Rudnev. The painters fared even worse: the critics said that Lentulov was incapable of drawing so much as a matchbox, that Tischler, Fonvizin and Sterenberg were 'daubers with evil intentions'.

At the meetings of theatre workers Tairov and, more vehemently,

Meyerhold were continually abused. Meyerhold's 'repentance' was stigmatized as 'vague' and 'insincere' and there was talk of closing down his theatre. Film workers went for Dovzhenko and Eisenstein. Literary critics started off by condemning Pasternak, Zabolotsky, Aseyev, Kirsanov, Olesha, but appetite grows by what it feeds on, and soon Katayev, Fedin, Leonov, Vsevolod Ivanov, Lidin and Ehrenburg were found guilty of 'formalistic eccentricities'. Finally they got down to Tikhonov, Babel, the Kukryniksi[1]. There was even one individual of singular imagination who detected formalism in the production of *Wolves and Sheep* at the Maly theatre. In *Red Virgin Soil* an article appeared calling for a struggle against formalism and a 'fight for classical rhymes, a classical, strictly constructed and precise rhythm, a classical development of the subject'.

I thought the discussion was only beginning but actually it was ending: it was replaced by hundreds of meetings at which a compulsory admission of one's formalistic errors and promises to become 'simple and accessible' were made, with familiar cries followed by 'stormy applause rising to an ovation'.

I have often been accused of a 'supercilious attitude to readers' – not by readers, but by certain critics who took an active part in the campaign. As for the readers, in those weeks and later, in hours of doubt and unhappiness, they supported me unfailingly by their understanding and maturity. The editor of the *Literary Gazette* wrote that my contemptuous attitude to the Soviet people was shown, to take an example, in my statement that not all the workers could understand all the pictures in all the galleries. 'This attitude,' wrote the editor, 'reflects the belief that the artist is the vessel of some finer, more complex, more elevated culture than that of the mass of readers.' I have copied out that sentence and it has given me pause. In this book I have frequently referred to my errors, but in this case I stand firm: I agree today with what I said a quarter of a century ago.

I believe that a writer's, an artist's place is not in the rear but in the van. People develop unevenly and in our contemporary society there are many levels of cultural development. There is no such thing as 'the mass of readers', even if books are published in mass editions: readers have differing capacities – there are books in which some things are accessible to all and other things accessible only to some. Among

[1] Combined name of Kuprianov, Krylov and Sokolov.

those who go to the Hermitage Museum some admire Rembrandt's pictures, others ask what they are all about and pass on with indifference. There are people whom you cannot get to listen to a symphony concert. Everybody knows this, but it is passed over in silence. It so happens that new forms in art have always been slow to win recognition and have caused resentment. One could quote innumerable examples, from the uproar at the first performance of one of Victor Hugo's plays and the abuse heaped on Courbet, down to the shouts of laughter with which the audience greeted Mayakovsky's reading of his poem *Man*. If a writer or an artist does not see more than the numerical 'mass', does not try to tell people something new, as yet unknown to them, then he is hardly any use to anyone.

Attacks at meetings and in the papers affected different people in different ways. Alexey Tolstoy, who liked peace and quiet, decided to play safe by repenting and publicly admitted that he had written a formalistic play. Babel said with a smile: 'In six months' time they'll leave the formalists in peace and start some other campaign'. Meyerhold was badly shaken and read over and over again some silly little article which he underlined in places. During that time in Moscow I often met Dovzhenko and we became friends. He was a great artist; it is enough to recall his film *Earth* made in 1930. He was an excellent raconteur, with the typical humour and gentle melancholy of the Ukrainian. He was tremendously distressed by what was going on. On one occasion he told me that the day before he had been summoned by Stalin who showed him the film *Chapayev* and kept on saying: 'That's the way you should do it'.

Unjust accusations hurt me, at times they made me furious, but I was better placed: the struggle with fascism was on and I was in the battlefield.

Recalling some of my Moscow impressions, the ovations and wholesale accusations, I wrote in *Book for Adults*: 'I know that people are more complex, that I myself am more complex, that life did not begin yesterday and will not end tomorrow, but sometimes one has to be blind in order to see'. (I said the same thing later in verse: 'It is not in vain that I call blindness a discovery. To clutch sorrow like a dead fledgling in one's hand, to stride in one's accustomed gait from childish vows to the full stop – to the end'.)

Work on the book absorbed me, though time and again I had to tear myself away – to write articles for *Izvestia*, to speak at various meetings, to do work for the Anti-Fascist Writers' Association. *Book for Adults* was really the first rough draft of the book I am writing now. What I had planned was entertaining though wrong-headed: I had decided to alternate chapters in which I spoke about myself and my life with others where the characters told me their secrets, worked, struggled, loved and suffered. I have called the plan wrong-headed but perhaps that is not quite accurate: I simply did not have enough talent and skill to make the characters in the novel come to life, and as a result I turned myself into a conventional literary figure.

Many pages of the book were devoted to literature and art; it was then for the first time that I began to think about how books and pictures are created. Speaking about a writer's experience I said: 'Other people's passions stick to him like burrs. Human grief knows to whom to attach itself. Even a stray dog will not attach itself to anyone: it will sniff a man, and then either run away or follow him. Not all, not all sorrows cling to the writer, but only those that ought to cling to him. Gogol died among dead souls; Plushkins and Nozdrevs crowded round his bed. Pushkin had given him the theme, life provided him with the characters. What did he add to this but his breath, and why was he obliged to pay for other people's fates with his own eccentricity, muteness, miserable death? Are books really only rough drafts of which life forces us to make a fair copy?'

My thoughts dwelt above all on the struggle that was going on all round me, on the path that I had chosen. 'Justice – this word seems to be cast in metal, it has neither warmth nor pliability. There are times when I feel it is moulded of pig-iron and others when it seems to lose weight and become tin. You have to warm it with your own passion. I have said that formerly I could not throw off my past. I think that a man never throws off anything but grows in girth like a tree: one ring added to another. Now I see why pig-iron or tin justice used to seem cold to me. I needed not only success but falls, dislocations, years of silence'.

It was probably too early to try and tell the story of my life in 1935. I did not know enough either about myself or other people and often took what was ephemeral and fortuitous for the heart of the matter. Essentially I still agree with the author of *Book for Adults*, but the war is described in it not by a veteran but by a man of middle age and average experience who is travelling to the front in a dark, warmed goods-wagon and visualizing the battles that await him.

The book is full of presentiments and foresight rather than conclusions drawn from experience. I myself cannot understand how, in the spring of 1936, before all the things I was destined to live through in the years to come, I could have written these lines: 'In my life I have had the same experiences as the majority of men of my age: the death of near ones, illness, treachery, failures in work, loneliness, emptiness. There are struggles which take place in the streets with a rifle, in workshops, in illegality, in the air, at a typewriter. But the struggle I am thinking of now is of another kind: a struggle that takes place in silence, when you find yourself staring at a light-bulb or at the printed words on the newspaper page which you are not taking in, when you have to get the better of what life has done to you, be born anew, survive at all costs'.

Slightly lifting the curtain of the confessional I may say that *Men, Years – Life* came into existence only because I succeeded in putting into practice the words I had written long ago, in getting the better of what life had done to me and, if not born anew, at least finding enough strength to advance in step with the new generation.

Book for Adults was first published in a journal; then it was to be brought out as a book; the publication took a long time – that was in the year 1937 when the tending of trees was entrusted not to devoted arborists but to woodcutters. Whole pages with names that had fallen into disfavour were taken out of the book. In the copy which I have preserved one page is whiter and shorter than the rest – it was pasted in: they had to take out the name of the latest victim of the axe: Semyon Chlenov.

I wrote that book in Paris at the beginning of 1936, I wrote it to the sound of demonstrations; the struggle was gathering strength. Now I felt certain: no matter what happened, however painful the doubts (not in the justice of the idea but in the wisdom of the men in leading positions), one had to be silent, one had to struggle, one had to win.

At the end of March I sent the manuscript to *Znamya* (Banner). And on 7th April I was talking to the miner Silverio Castañon in the Spanish town of Oviedo; he was telling me about the fighting in 1934, about his fallen comrades, about the torturing. How infinitely distant it all seemed to me now: the struggle against formalism, the pages of the manuscript, the room in Paris with its books on the shelf and its pipes on the wall! Castañon wrote poetry and at his trial had astounded the judges by his erudition: he quoted Marx, Kant, Calderón, Victor

Hugo. The judges nodded approvingly but nevertheless condemned him to death: he was chairman of the revolutionary committee in the mining district of Turón. However, the carrying out of the sentence was postponed from one day to the next. I asked Castañon how many days he had waited for death and he said: 'Fifteen months. But I wasn't waiting for death, I was waiting for the revolution'. He then recited one of his poems and suddenly said with a wide gesture: 'A man only has one life'. I looked intently at him and saw how young he was – he had the face of a child.

On returning to the cold gloomy hotel I could not get to sleep for a long time, tossing and turning and thinking – no, there is not only one life; in the course of a lifetime one has to live not one, not two lives, but many; perhaps in that lies the whole of misfortune, but also the whole of happiness.

16

I FIND it difficult today to describe the Spain of that distant spring: I spent only a fortnight there though later, during two long years, I saw it spattered with blood and in torment; I saw nightmares of war such as Goya never dreamt of; the skies exploded into the strife on earth; the peasants still fired shotguns, but Picasso, in creating *Guernica*, already felt premonitions of the nuclear insanity.

I remember huge bullfight arenas filled with tens of thousands of people: workers in caps, peasants in broad-brimmed hats, women with head shawls, potters, cobblers, schoolboys.

Rafael Alberti was standing on the platform. He was quite unlike Mayakovsky: he looked like a frail dreamer. Until recently he had been writing lyrical poetry. Now he was reciting a modern *romancero*; the verses swept over the crowd like wind over a copse, and the people, roused, rushed out into the street. The Young Socialists wore red shirts, the Young Communists blue ones with red ties. Priests turned away, old women crossed themselves in horror, respectable middle-class people looked over their shoulders, Fascists fired from windows. The brilliant sunshine alternated with heavy purple clouds.

It was an unusual spring for Spain: almost every day there were noisy showers and the red earth of Castile was dazzlingly green. Dear God, how many joyous cries I heard, how many wonderful plans, how many vows and curses! I remember at a workers' meeting in the Asturian coalfields of Mieres an old miner with a lean face raising his miner's lamp and saying: 'Three thousand comrades have died to rid us of the Fascists. They'll be wiped out. We shall go on. That's all, Spaniards!'

In Oviedo I saw the ruins of the University. The people said, like the old miner: 'No, this must never happen again'.

In the Zama district Fernando Rodríguez took me to the People's House where in 1934 the suppressors tortured and killed the miners. There were faded bloodstains on the walls, and the names of those who had been shot scratched with fingernails. Fernando Rodríguez told me: 'They hung me up by my arms and pulled at my feet. They called this the "aeroplane". They poured boiling water over my bare belly and then ice-cold water. But I didn't tell them where we had hidden our arms'.

Some boys came to me and handed me a painstakingly written letter: 'Oviedo, 22nd April 1936. Comrades, the Red Pioneers of Oviedo send May Day greetings to our comrades in the Soviet Union. Comrades, we are preparing for the second battle, it will come soon. We shall fight staunchly and bravely. *Salud y Revolución!*'

As I stood at the window I watched the boys skylarking about as they left the hotel; what was going on was little more than a game for them. I do not know what became of them but in the autumn of 1936 I read in a Fascist newspaper: 'In Oviedo, children, corrupted by Marxist teachers, attacked our officers'.

That spring I met the daughter of an Asturian miner, Dolores Ibárruri whom the workers called La Pasionaria. She was an important political figure but remained a simple woman; she had all the traits of the Spanish character: gravity, kindness, dignity, courage and, most endearing of all, humaneness. I was told how in Asturia she had released the prisoners: she arrived with a crowd of workers, gave the soldiers the command 'Dismiss!', entered the prison and, when all the prisoners had come out, laughingly showed the crowd a large rusty key.

The directors of Ciudad Lineal, the company that owned the Madrid tramways, refused to reinstate the 'rebels' dismissed in the autumn of 1934. So the workers took over the running of the trams. They bore the letters UHP – Union of Proletarian Brothers – and under this banner the workers in 1934 fought the Fascists, the Foreign Legion, the Moroccans misled by the generals. Apart from the three magic letters the trams looked the same as before – shabby, with clusters of lively urchins hanging on to them. Number 8 said: 'To the Cuatro Caminos terminus'. Nevertheless no one knew where this tram would end up – at the depot or on a battlefield.

While I was in Madrid Fascists attacked the workers. A general strike was declared. I was living in a big hotel: bootboys, lift-boys, waiters, scullery-maids, all left. The proprietor mobilized the numerous members of his family, saying: 'We shall safeguard the interests of our clients against these lazy bastards. In the meantime we shall ask our clients to do what they can to help themselves'.

Later I witnessed a tremendous strike in Barcelona. The Spanish bourgeoisie, indolent and carefree, was dismayed. A lawyer said to me: 'I could never have believed that the workers had so much power. If Europe doesn't take a hand we shall be dependent on these semi-literate loafers'.

The government tried to pacify everyone. The peasants were told that the Institute of Agrarian Reform would very quickly change their conditions. But the Institute was in no hurry. In Spain there is a saying *mañana por la mañana* (roughly: tomorrow will do) or, as the Russians put it: 'on Thursday after the rain'. The peasants began to plough up the huge derelict estates of various absentee Counts and non-Counts. They drew up title deeds. In Castilian villages I saw many such documents. Count de Romanones, a deputy to the Cortes, owned 15,000 acres on one of his numerous estates; the peasants disarmed the Civil Guards and drew up a deed transferring the land to a co-operative. In the kitchen of the house they found a ham and some potatoes and wrote a clause into the document to the effect that these provisions were to be restored to the Count. The peasants in the village of Guadamez wrote: 'We have taken over the land, the guards can bear witness that we have harmed no one by either word or deed'. The peasants of another village, Polán, wrote: 'On the morning of 30th March representatives of the Municipal Council, together with representatives of the Federation of Land Workers, have, in the presence of the estate servants, taken over Ventilozia, *viz.* 6,920 acres of land'.

In Escalona, in Malpica, in the Toledo region, I heard peasants cry joyfully: 'Land!' Old men astride undersized donkeys raised their clenched fists, girls carried kids, young men stroked old battered rifles.

In April the Civil Guard (*gendarmerie*) rose against the government. An Assault Guard (*Asaltos*) was set up but it, too, regarded the Ministers of the Popular Front Government with suspicion. The Fascists shouted: 'Down with Azaña!' Azaña was the Prime Minister and later became President of the Republic. The workers opposed the Fascists. One might have expected the guards to disband the Fascists who were clamouring against the government, but they did not dare touch the well-dressed *caballeros* and took it out on the workers.

ABC, the monarchist newspaper, openly demanded intervention: 'Hitler has said that he will not let it happen . . . Europe will refuse to live in the grip of the Bolshevik pincers'. The paper was appealing for donations; at the time I copied out the following items: 'An admirer

334

of Hitler – 1 peseta. For God and Spain – 10. Wake up Spain! – 5. A National Syndicalist – 10. A supporter of the Falange – 5'.

The Cortes passed a bill depriving retired generals who acted against the Republic of their pensions. The military sneered contemptuously: the Popular Front would not remain in power long. The generals Sanjurjo, Franco and Mola made no secret of their plans; I was told that Sanjurjo had said: 'Only a surgical operation can save Spain'. Priests and monks exhorted men to fight for God and Order. The walls were chalked with the words: 'Wake up Spain!' The former rulers strolled unperturbed in the streets of Madrid; I once caught sight of Gil Robles drinking white coffee on a café terrace. During his term of office 200,000 Fascists had been granted the right to carry arms; no one attempted to take these arms from them.

I talked to Socialists, to Companys, the Catalan Nationalist leader who had been in prison until the victory of the Popular Front. Everyone realized the danger of the situation but said that they had to observe the Constitution: liberty must not be infringed.

Nobody was frightened of the stocky, correct *caballero* called Gil Robles, or of the articles in the Fascist papers, or even of the sermons of the fanatical monks. What was frightening was that the peasants exultantly brought out their old shotguns, the unarmed workers raised their clenched fists. Meanwhile the supporters of the Falange took occasional potshots. Machine-guns were accidentally discovered in churches. The police, the Civil Guard, the army regarded the articles of the Constitution with far less respect than did the newly appointed Minister of Internal Affairs, Casares Quiroga, the Socialist Prieto, or the fiery Companys.

I had to return to Paris: the French general election was to take place on 26th April and my newspaper wanted me to cover it. I regretted leaving; I was falling more and more deeply in love with Spain. In my articles I spoke of the Fascist danger. In an old issue of *L'Humanité* I have found a short note on the speech I made in the Paris House of Culture; I said that the Spanish Fascists were bound to rise. But in my heart I did not quite believe it – because I did not want to. (Too often not only rank-and-file participants in events, like myself, but even quite important politicians have taken and still take their own desires for a sober evaluation of the real situation; this seems to be inherent in human nature.)

From time immemorial the Pyrenees have seemed to the French a

335

wall beyond which lies a different continent. When a grandson of Louis XIV ascended the Spanish throne the French king is alleged to have exclaimed: '*Il n'y a plus de Pyrénées!*' Nevertheless the Pyrenees are still there. But now, in April 1936, I did not notice them: people raised their clenched fists in just the same way; at railway stations one could see the same chalkings: 'Death to fascism!' and in the train frightened middle-class people carried on the familiar conversations about the need to 'curb the loafers'. *Frente Popular* and *Front Populaire* sounded alike. France was finding inspiration in the example of Spain.

On Sunday night, I was standing with Savich and the editor of *Lu*, Puterman, near the offices of *Le Matin*. The wide boulevard was crowded. All eyes were fixed on the screen: the results of the elections were to be announced at any minute. 'Maurice Thorez – elected'. Clapping, shouts of joy. 'Monmousseau ... Daladier ... Cot ... Vaillant-Couturier ... Blum ...' Jubilation. '*Vive le Front Populaire!*' They were singing the *Internationale*. When the names of the elected right-wing deputies appeared – Flandin, Scapini, Dommange – there was whistling. 'Traitors to the wall!' 'Down with Fascism!' All this was taking place not near *L'Humanité* but in front of the building of the newspaper that wrote every day: 'the Popular Front means the end of France'.

The papers said that nothing had been finally decided: on Sunday next the second ballot would be held. Once again a night in the streets, and once again an excited, jubilant crowd. At midnight it became clear that the Popular Front had won an assured majority. People poured down the boulevards singing the *Internationale*, embracing one another, shouting: 'The Fascists to the wall!'

I rejoiced with the others: after Spain – France! It was clear now that Hitler would not succeed in beating Europe to her knees. Our cause was being won; the revolution was passing over to the offensive. These thoughts were not yet clouded by the loss of people close to me or by the trials on the threshold of which we stood. I think back to the spring of 1936 as to the last happy spring of my life.

A few weeks later mass strikes broke out in France; the workers stopped work but stayed on the premises; the white-collar workers remained in the banks, in the offices, in the shops. The bourgeois kept saying in terror: 'They're nothing but bandits'.

Paris was unrecognizable. Red flags fluttered over the grey houses.

Everywhere the sounds of the *Internationale* or the *Carmagnole* floated out. On the Bourse share prices were falling. The rich transferred their money abroad. Everyone said over and over again, with hope or with dismay: 'This is revolution'.

I remember very clearly the window of an expensive shop in the Boulevard des Capucines: a pretty plaster model in a smart dress held a placard in her hands: 'Office staff and workers are on strike – we refuse to live on starvation wages any longer'.

Girls went around carrying sheets spread out for the people in the streets to throw in money for the strikers.

In some factories the owners proved obdurate, and the sit-down strikes lasted a long time – two or three weeks. Police surrounded the factories fearing clashes. Every day women came to the gates bringing bread, sausages and oranges.

Denise was working with a company of left-wing actors. They were invited to perform in a steel factory by the workers who had been on strike for over a fortnight. I went to the performance. Denise spoke the lines of the heroine of *Fuente Ovejuna*. She had the eyes of a sleep-walker and a vague smile. When I came out into the street a policeman searched me in case I was carrying a weapon. I was completely be-mused and kept smiling; I wished I were one of the workers whom I had just seen instead of being an *Izvestia* correspondent.

Everywhere the strikes ended in victory. In one month the French workers won not only increased wages but a genuine change in labour legislation: collective bargaining, the legal recognition of trade unions, holidays with pay.

A hot summer succeeded the spring. The west end of Paris was depopulated: the rich left for Switzerland, Belgium, Italy; they said they wanted to get away from the 'rabble let loose'. On the beaches of Normandy and Brittany they might find themselves rubbing shoul-ders with the workers: 'those loafers' who now had holidays with pay.

On 14th July over a million Parisians marched in a demonstration. There were miners from the North with their lamps, vine-growers from the South with artificial bunches of grapes, Breton fishermen carrying blue nets. The effigies of Hitler and Mussolini were burnt. Daladier, as before, embraced Communists. The premier, Léon Blum, a typical representative of the twentieth-century intelligentsia, greeted the workers, awkwardly raising his small fist. A worker's cap was carried on a pole with the legend: 'This is the French people's crown'. Portraits of Lenin, Stalin and Gorky swayed past. People shouted to the Spaniards: 'Bravo! Death to the Fascists!' They clapped when émigré workers – Italians, Poles, Germans – marched past. (I had no inkling that I would soon see many of them on the red-brown soil of Castile.)

Naturally the demonstrators demanded the disbanding of Fascist organizations and shouted as before: 'La Roque to the wall!' but the shouting was gay and good-humoured. In February the people had come out into the streets ready to plunge into battle, whereas the 14th July demonstration was like a fantastic carnival.

As always, there was dancing in the evening – in the Place de la Bastille, in hundreds of large and small streets – with the traditional Chinese lanterns, accordions, glasses of beer or bottles of lemonade, with lovers' kisses. The older workers sat and watched the young enjoying themselves. I listened to the conversations; people talked about where they should spend the holidays, about an uncle in a Limousin village, about a small house on the Loire, about fishing, walking in the mountains, sandy beaches for the children. The word 'revolution' had given place to another – 'holidays'. The easy victory had made people calm and placid.

Paris now was quite unlike Madrid: it did not have behind it the Asturian rising, the tortures, the prisons, the firing squads. Nor did it have the fanatical priesthood and the sabre-rattling generals; the French bourgeoisie was far more enlightened and shrewd: it counted on starving out the Popular Front. And the victors laughed and gave little thought to the future.

I was finishing my book of short stories *Beyond a Truce*. Irina had arrived from Moscow. It was unbearably hot in Paris; Lyuba and Irina went to Brittany; I told them that I had to send a report on the 14th July demonstration to my paper and finish the book, after which I would join them.

I remember a stifling summer evening in the rue du Cotentin. I was writing; then I laid my manuscript aside and turned on the radio: Léon Blum is consulting with the Minister of Education. In Madrid the crowd is storming the Montana barracks. Barcelona . . . The Columbus Hotel . . . Artillery . . . Colonel Aranda . . . Fighting in the region of Oviedo . . . killed, wounded . . .

I jumped up. I had to talk to someone. It was late – midnight – I

338

would not find anyone. Yet I could not remain alone in the quiet room.

And the announcer was calmly saying that at the Rose Show in the Cours-la-Reine the first prize had been won by the rose Mme A. Meilland.

For some people life was split in two on 22nd June 1941, for some on 3rd September 1939, and for others on 18th July 1936. In what I have already written about my life there must be passages very dissimilar from the experiences of my contemporaries: there was a time when we all had different destinies, different themes. But from that evening, my life began to be very much like that of millions of other people: an individual variation on a general theme. Words familiar to all of us describe the cruel decade: announcements, *démentis*, songs, tears, war communiqués, air-raid alarms, retreat, advance, short leaves, brief meetings at wayside railway stations, talk about diplomatic Notes, tactics and strategy, silence about the most important things, evacuation hospitals, a vast all-embracing blackout and, as a memory of the past, the fleeting beam of a torchlight.

17

I SPENT several unhappy and impatient weeks in Paris, sending *Izvestia* each day information about Spain culled from the French newspapers, visiting the Spanish embassy, helping the first volunteers to make their way to Barcelona. I stayed on in Paris only because I could not get a definite decision from my paper on whether or not I was to go to Spain as a war correspondent. The replies I got were laconic and obscure: we are 'co-ordinating'. I did not yet know the special meaning of this verb and it made me angry – I decided not to wait any longer. One day, when the Moscow office telephoned my Paris flat to find out why I had stopped sending telegrams, Lyuba replied: 'Didn't you know? He's in Spain'.

Picasso painted *Guernica* in 1937. But six months before that, in August–September 1936, Spain reminded me of Delacroix's paintings: beyond the Pyrenees the romanticism of the past century smouldered and briefly flared up.

Barcelona is a large industrial city but its workers for a long time past had been under the influence of the syndicalist trade unions – CNT (*Confederación Nacional del Trabajo*) and the Anarchist FAI (*Federación Anarquista Iberica*). The small bourgeoisie, the restaurant proprietors and shopkeepers told me that they preferred even the anarchists to General Franco. Here the word 'liberty', which had long ago become devalued in various European countries, still inspired many people.

Along the Ramblas lorries dashed, roughly bullet-proofed with sheets of iron; they were respectfully called 'armoured cars'. Horsemen pranced, wearing red-and-black shirts and armed with shotguns. Taxis were decorated with such inscriptions as: 'Off to Huesca!' or 'To the capture of Saragossa!' Anarchists left for the front with boxes of hand-grenades, with guitars and girl-friends. Smart women wearing incredibly high heels lugged heavy rifles. The traces of recent battles were everywhere: barricades still standing, broken glass, cartridge cases. On the spot where the heroes who had defended the city against the Fascist rebels had died, bright southern roses blazed. The people of Barcelona brought skins of wine, hams, blankets, even ancient

340

swords to give to the volunteers leaving for the front. In the Columbus Hotel, which had been shelled in July, rifles lay scattered among the dusty pouffes, and fighters slept in sumptuous beds that looked like catafalques.

'CNT–FAI' – these initials were spoken everywhere: in the Ramblas, at hundreds of meetings, in requisitioned buildings which now housed various committees, leagues and unions, from the Supporters of World Anarchy to the Fighting Esperantists. The walls were plastered with posters: 'Long live the organization of struggle against discipline!' The *Internationale* was sung as well as the anthem of the CNT: *Sons of the People*. Red-and-black flags predominated. I asked a volunteer why the Anarchists had chosen these two colours, and he said: 'Red for the struggle and black because human thought is dark'.

There was shooting from all sides, and it was difficult to know who was shooting at whom; but everybody took it calmly; the cafés and restaurants were overcrowded. The city lived in a state of feverish gaiety.

The columns and *centurias*, which were setting off to take Huesca or Saragossa, bore such names as 'Chapayev', 'Pancho Villa', 'The Neguses', 'Ethiopians', 'The Daredevils', 'The Godless', 'Bakunin'. At meetings the re-education of mankind was discussed. One speaker suggested setting up monuments to the great thinkers of the world – Socrates, Spartacus, Cervantes, Reclus, Kropotkin, Lenin. Another demanded that all money should be destroyed, all prisons demolished and labour made compulsory. A third said it was imperative to send ten of the finest men to the cruiser *Uruguay* where the leaders of the military rebellion were kept under arrest, and persuade the Fascists to join a labour commune.

The principal city barracks were renamed after Bakunin. From the roof of a bus agitators yelled: 'Down with militarism! All to the front! Freedom for everyone! Death to the Fascists!'

No one knew where the Republicans were and where the Fascists. We were driving over the red-brown stony desert of Aragon. The heat was unbearable: it was my first experience of a Spanish summer. My companion Miravilles asked the peasants if we could drive on farther. Some said the Fascists were in the next village, others assured us that our forces had liberated Huesca. The southern night fell all of a sudden. Summer lightning flooded the sky. Guns rumbled in the distance.

341

Suddenly the car stopped: a barricade rose in front of us. Someone shouted: 'The password?' We did not know the password. Miravilles pulled his revolver out of its holster. I asked him what had happened. His only answer was to hand me another revolver. I felt afraid: we were caught in a trap. I peered into the darkness and saw men standing on a rock with rifles trained on us. I was on the point of firing when someone swore in the dark: 'They're our people'. The peasants surrounded us and told us that this was the sixth night that they had been on sentry duty: they had been informed from Bujaraloz that the Fascists were advancing. We asked: 'Where is the front?' They gestured vaguely with their hands: it was seven miles to Bujaraloz, that was certain, but who was there the devil only knew. As far as they were concerned the front was everywhere.

It was not only the peasants who were ignorant of what was going on in the next village: in Barcelona no one could say in whose hands Córdoba, Malaga, Badajoz or Toledo were. The commander of each column made fantastic plans. Someone spread the rumour that the Fascists had been driven out of Seville. The Catalans decided to make a landing on Majorca. A few days later it was noised about that the Fascists had occupied Valencia and were advancing on Barcelona.

In one of the sectors of the front line I saw the notice: 'Do not go beyond this point – beware fascists'. The fighters were quite peacefully bathing in the stream; one of them stood guard over their rifles and clothes. I asked: 'What if the Fascists were to attack?' They laughed: 'We don't fight by day, it's too hot. The bastards have got a pond, they're bathing in it now. But just wait a bit, in three hours' time there'll be such a din it'll break your eardrums'.

The commander told me that Huesca would soon be taken, say in a week's time at the latest. I looked at the town, it was very close. 'What's that large building in front?' I asked. 'The asylum. Picked men are holding it. That house has to be taken first of all.' (I was near Huesca a year later, and once again heard that the asylum had to be taken. How many men died fighting for that building!)

An acquaintance of mine was going to Madrid to negotiate an agreement extending the powers of the autonomous government of Catalonia He suggested that I should go with him. We drove for a long time, the peasants had put up barricades everywhere to block the roads in case of Fascist attacks; they examined our passes carefully (I had five or six passes from all kinds of organizations, including, of

342

course, the CNT). The barricades looked very odd: barrels, furniture taken from prosperous houses, overturned carts, wooden statues that had formerly adorned some church. I still have a photograph: three peasants armed with shotguns and towering above them a baroque angel with an enormous viol.

Everywhere I saw gutted churches. When the peasants learnt of the Fascist rising the first thing they did was to set fire to a church or a monastery. One of them explained it like this: 'D'you know who's our main enemy? The *curas* (priests) and the monks. Then come the generals and the officers. And after that, of course, the rich. We didn't touch the landowner, we only took his land – let the scoundrel live like anybody else. So he signed saying he didn't object. But the *cura* climbed up to the belfry with a gun. So we sent him off to paradise'.

My companion complained about the Anarchists: 'How can you come to any agreement with them? They're honest fellows all right but even their minds are in a state of anarchy. One of them came to me in Barcelona and said: "Get rid of all traffic regulations. Why should I have to turn left if I want to turn right? It's contrary to the principles of liberty"'.

When he caught sight of a church unharmed by fire the Catalan asked the peasants: 'Why wasn't it burnt down?' After we had left the village behind I said to him: 'I don't see why it should be burnt down. They haven't got a single decent building. They could turn it into a school or a club-house'. This angered him: 'Don't you know what we've suffered from them? No, better to have no club-house than to keep that eyesore'.

In Madrid there were few Anarchists, but Madrid was still living on romantic illusions. The Fascists had seized Talavera and were within 40–50 miles of the capital. But people sat on café terraces arguing till midnight whether to go to Saragossa and link up with the Catalans or to wrest the Andalusian ports from the Fascists.

I was taken to the estate of a Fascist who had fled. 'We've organized an experimental model children's colony here.' An enthusiastic woman spent a long time proving to me that pedagogues neglected the educational importance of music. A boy of about seven or eight told us: 'They tied papa up, laid him on the road and then a lorry ran over him'. The enthusiastic woman persevered: 'And how do such beasts come to exist? As children they were not harmoniously brought up'. I could not help smiling: I remembered Kiev in 1919 and my work for

343

the aesthetic education of 'mofective children': you think, here is something unique, and then, all at once, you find that everything repeats itself.

In Madrid the mansion of a fugitive aristocrat had been made over to the writers; it had a superb library – incunabulae, rare editions, manuscripts of Spanish classics. In this mansion the poets Rafael Alberti, Manolo Altolaguirre, José Petere, Serrano Plaja, Miguel Hernández read their poems. There I met the writer José Bergamín, a left-wing Catholic, a melancholy and serene man of pure heart. We discussed Cervantes and anti-aircraft defence, Communism and Quevedo's poetry. There, too, I met Pablo Neruda, the Chilean consul and poet; he was young and full of jokes and pranks. I remember the worried bibliophile who, on hearing the air-raid sirens, put out buckets of water in the library for fear that the excessive dryness should harm the ancient manuscripts. Someone said in a hushed voice: 'They've occupied Talavera'.

At the Ateneo a meeting was held one evening in memory of Maxim Gorky. Rafael Alberti said to me with tears in his voice: 'It's been confirmed. They've killed García Lorca in Granada'.

The night of the first air-raid came. Then another. Hearing explosions I ran out into the street. An old woman was clutching a little girl tightly to her. When it was light I went to the district the Fascists had bombed and saw what I was later destined to see all too often: a shattered house, a staircase and somewhere high up a child's cot dangling.

Pablo Neruda wrote: 'And through the streets the blood of children flowed/Simply, like the blood of children'.

I went to Malpica; I had been there in April, before the war, and the peasants recognized me. The Spaniards had difficulty in pronouncing my name, they often got it wrong, and the *alcalde*, raising his clenched fist said solemnly: 'Welcome, Hindenburg! Now we can show you the castle'. In Malpica there was an estate belonging to the Duke of Oriona which the peasants had occupied. I went over the great old house. The *alcalde* carried a brass candlestick with a small candle-end. Out of the darkness emerged boars' heads, statues of the Madonna in little gold-embroidered dresses, copper saucepans, pyjamas, gramophones. The most imposing room was the bathroom where, oddly enough, there were three armchairs. The *alcalde* said: 'These are probably very valuable things. We've decided to give the castle to the writers, let them live here and write'. On the outskirts of the village, peasants stood guard armed with shotguns. The front was quite close. All around rose the smoke of campfires lit by the refugees from Estremadura.

Two days later I was again in Malpica with Alberti and María Teresa Léon; they were taking newspapers and leaflets to the front. German planes were bombing the militiamen's positions and the road. The volunteers broke and ran. At the entrance to the village of Domingo Pérez the peasants had gathered in alarm: 'Look – they're running'. An old peasant said: 'This is all we've got', and pointed to three old shotguns. We saw four militiamen who were striding away in the direction of Madrid. María Teresa ran after them; she ran very fast on very high heels, holding a tiny revolver. The deserters gave up their rifles to her; they were ashamed. The old peasant said: 'Give them to me, the young want to live but I shan't run away'. Some two hours later thirty militiamen turned back towards the enemy and dug themselves in; they had one machine-gun, but there were only a few Fascists, who, towards morning, retreated to Talavera.

Toledo was in the hands of the Republicans but the Fascists held the ancient Alcázar, half fortress, half palace. They had been there six weeks and a curious way of life had been established in the town. In some streets there were notices: 'Danger! It is prohibited to go unarmed'. There was little milk and so that they should not have to queue up under gunfire the women put their jugs, pots, or simply a pebble outside the dairies in the evening; I never once heard any squabbles. From time to time the Fascists opened fire on the town; and, facing the Alcázar, militiamen fired as they sat in wicker armchairs or rocking-chairs, shading themselves with parasols from the blazing sun, sometimes shooting in a desultory way and sometimes violently at the tremendously thick fortress walls. Occasionally a battery fired several shells. The inhabitants of the town sauntered along the streets speculating whether the shells had hit or missed.

In one of their early sorties the Fascists had taken 'hostages' – women, children. In the militiamen's barracks I saw thirty-eight photographs: a woman with a baby, an old woman, two small boys on wooden donkeys. The Fascists knew what they were about: more than once orders had been received to mine and blow up the fort but the militiamen, thinking of the women and children, replied: 'We aren't

Fascists'. They naïvely hoped to starve out the Alcázar. When the government issued a warning that its planes would bomb the fort and that the militiamen should withdraw to a distance of a hundred yards, many of them refused to do so: 'We can't – they'll escape'. Fourteen of them were killed by bomb splinters.

In this ancient capital of Spain, a city very popular with tourists, a duel was going on between the humane instincts of the people and the inhuman laws of war. The wife of the Fascist commander of the Alcázar garrison, Colonel Moscardó, lived in the town. Koltsov was amazed: 'And you haven't arrested her?' Soviet people were held in great respect but the Spaniards did not flinch: 'A woman? We aren't Fascists'.

I walked about Toledo with my friend the artist Fernando Gerassi. He lived in Paris, painting landscapes and still-lifes, and in the evening he generally went to the Dôme. He had a wife, a Ukrainian from near Lvov, the laughter-loving Stefa, and a five-year-old son, Tito. Fernando said that the Anarchists were mad, that there ought to be a unified command with discipline and order. He ridiculed the 'war in lace ruffles' but at the same time I knew that he could not find it in himself to condemn the magnanimity of the militiamen who, though they swore dreadfully and on meeting one another said 'salud y dinamita' instead of 'hullo', indignantly repudiated the idea of blowing up the Alcázar: 'What are you thinking of? There are women and children inside'.

The Madrid government wanted to demonstrate to the world how different they were from Franco, and when the Fascists in the Alcázar asked for a priest, a truce of several hours was declared.

A group of Fascists came out of the fortress. The militiamen were standing quite close and there was an exchange of abuse. This is what I recorded of it at the time: 'Bandits! We stand for God and the people.' 'You can keep God, and as for the people, that's us'. 'Liar! We're for the people. The bastards are smoking, and we've been out of tobacco for a fortnight.' (The militiaman silently takes out a packet of cigarettes. The lieutenant lights up.) 'You've sent for a priest? Looks as if it's all up with you.' 'Our fellows will be here soon, then we'll show you what's what.' 'Wait for the Second Coming.' 'We won't have long to wait – your chaps are running away like hares'. 'A lot of lies! Then why are you letting your beard grow? Getting ready for paradise?' 'What am I to shave with? My sword?' (Another militiaman

346

pulls out a packet of razor-blades and hands them to the Fascist soldier.)

At the beginning of October Colonel Varela's troops approached Toledo. The garrison of the Alcázar (where there were over a thousand Civil Guards and cadets) came out to meet them. Few of the Republicans managed to escape. The Fascists wrote a great deal about the 'heroes of the Alcázar'. Undoubtedly Colonel Moscardó's men showed staunchness and courage. The history of any war is rich in examples of military valour. But there is also no doubt that a Civil War abounds in atrocities. However, if there is anything instructive in the story of the Alcázar, it is the duel of two worlds: a people, angry but deeply humane, and a soldiery with its faultless discipline and faultless inhumanity. It was not magnanimity that conquered.

In Guadarrama I saw prisoners: among them there were soldiers, very frightened but glad to be out of the dangerous game; there were also cutthroats of the Foreign Legion. What the militiamen dreaded most were the Moroccans, who were good soldiers and understood nothing of what was going on.

With our cameraman Karmen and with Makaseyev I went to the Aragon front and saw the 'Red Wings' air force unit commanded by Alfonso Reyes, a sombre, taciturn and resolute man. The planes were pathetic: old crates that were proudly called bombers and every day bombed the Fascist positions. While we were with the squadron a plane landed riddled by the fire of German fighters. The mechanic (nicknamed 'Red Devil') was severely wounded and could barely stop himself crying out with pain, but on seeing that Karmen was photographing him, he smiled. The next day they had to amputate his leg.

The Fascists continued their advance on Madrid. People on the whole, however, were not anxious, they still firmly believed in victory; everybody said that as the Fascists had not captured the whole of Spain in July their cause was lost – the people were against them.

Only in Navarra, that Spanish Vendée, did the peasants come out in support of the rebels; there the church and the Carlists (supporters of one of the pretenders to the Spanish throne, a descendant of Don Carlos) were strong. But there were 400,000 inhabitants in Navarra and almost 30 million in Spain. In all the provinces which I had the opportunity to see during the war years – Catalonia, New Castile, Valencia, La Mancha, Murcia, Andalusia, Aragon – the overwhelming majority of the population hated the Fascists.

347

But the workers knew how to work at their benches, the peasants knew how to till the soil, the doctors how to treat the sick, the teachers how to teach, whereas on Franco's side there were professional soldiers who knew more or less how to conduct a war. The Fascists had also strong mercenary forces – the Foreign Legion and the Moroccans.

Already towards the middle of September Franco had become the dictator of all the territory seized by the rebels, and on 1st October he was declared 'leader', 'generalissimo' and Chief of State. He demanded unconditional submission. As for the Republic, it was defended by men of the most varied opinions: Communists, Catalan autonomists, Socialists – both of the left and right – bourgeois Republicans, Anarchists, Basque Catholics, POUMists (*Partido Obrero de Unificación Marxista* – Trotskyists), united only in their hatred of Fascism. In 1936 complete liberty prevailed as though what was going on was not war but an election campaign. The Catalans and Basques denounced the 'Great-Power practices of Madrid', the POUMists demanded a 'deepening of the Revolution', the right-wing Socialists, headed by Prieto, criticized the head of the government, the left-wing Socialist Largo Caballero; the Republicans looked askance at the Communists, the Anarchists swore to destroy the State they hated.

However, it was not only in the lack of professional soldiers and in the dissensions among the various anti-Fascist parties that the danger lay. On 25th July Hitler promised military aid to Franco's representative. On 30th July – a hundred days before the first Soviet fighters appeared in the skies over Madrid – Italian planes were already bombing Spanish towns.

Léon Blum was at the head of the French government, a fellow member with Largo Caballero of the Second International, but the Spanish government asked France in vain to allow the arms that had been purchased to cross her frontier. Léon Blum proclaimed the principle of non-intervention; Britain supported him. The Non-Intervention Committee met in London. Italy and Germany continued to send military equipment and men to Spain. France established a control on her frontier. I am probably repeating well-known facts. Ivan Maisky was a member of the Non-Intervention Committee; he told me recently that he was writing about it in detail in his memoirs – he has seen a great deal. I am writing only the story of my life. But how can I keep silent about hypocrisy? What happened long ago had and has a continuation: how many times have we read splendid words

348

about non-intervention, whether in Greece, in Korea, in the Congo or in Laos! After 1936 I was no longer surprised by the noble speeches of well-known murderers, by crocodile tears or by human pusillanimity. Believe me, Léon Blum was a far more decent individual than Tshombe's patrons, but he, too, frightened to death, more accustomed to the atmosphere of parliamentary intrigue than to that of the storms which burst over the world scene, said one thing and did another.

In Valencia I met Malraux; he told me that he thought he would succeed in getting ten military planes: the Spanish government had acquired them but the French had imposed an embargo. He said he wanted to create a French squadron which would bomb the Fascists, and he introduced me to the airmen Guidès and Pons.

On land there were battles enough. But in the sky the Fascists were complete masters: Junkers, Heinkels, Savoias, Fokkers – the air forces of two powerful States, Germany and Italy.

I spoke at meetings, collected material on Fascist atrocities for the western press, wrote anonymous pamphlets and completely forgot about my duties as *Izvestia* correspondent. Besides, they would have been difficult to carry out: there was no telephone communication with Moscow yet, and the editor was evidently still 'co-ordinating' and did not send any money for telegrams.

On 5th September, after a fortnight's interval, *Izvestia* printed a short paragraph: 'Barbastro, 4th September. Today your correspondent was present when the population of Mont-Florid was machine-gunned by seven three-engined Junkers supplied to the rebels by Germany'. I sent a short telegram; I had no money for a long one. For the first time I had seen people being machine-gunned by low-flying aircraft; the peasants were threshing; afterwards an old woman wept loudly: her son had been killed. The peasants knew that I was the correspondent of a Soviet newspaper and begged me: 'Write about it! Perhaps the Russians will help us'. Of course on that day more important events were taking place: the *Izvestia* correspondent in London wrote that San Sebastian had been cut off (which was true), that the Republicans had taken Huesca (this was merely a rumour); but I was in the village of Mont-Florid and it seemed to me imperative to report with all urgency that Fascists in German planes were killing unarmed peasants. This was naïve perhaps for a war correspondent, but I was thinking about Spain, not about my newspaper.

I was having a shave at a barber's. The barber started to shout: 'They get help from Hitler, from Mussolini. And we have no arms!' His eyes flashed; he repeated, brandishing the razor: 'Planes! Arms!' I thought to myself: if he's not careful he'll cut my throat. But what he was talking about was not funny.

What the Mont-Florid peasants had said had stuck in my mind; and, besides, people everywhere kept saying: 'Tell the Russians'. I began to write short dispatches and sent them to *Izvestia* by post via Paris.

A month later, having received a bundle of newspapers, I was greatly upset: my articles had been mutilated. On 26th September I wrote to the editor: 'I do not want to argue about whether I present the events in Spain in the correct light or not, but I strongly protest against the cuts which completely distort the meaning'. Of course it had no effect on the editor: my articles were varnished and took on a rosy hue. Still, I went on writing, writing hastily, not in a study but at the front; my mind was not on literary style but on bombers and tanks, without which the Spaniards could not hold out.

Alvarez del Vayo asked me to collect documentary evidence of the Fascist atrocities – for the West. In Valencia I was told that the correspondent of the Conservative *Daily Mail*, Garratt, had got away from Majorca and was denouncing the Fascists. I went to see him at the British consulate. He wrote down his evidence and told me that the Fascists had bombed a Republican field hospital: 'When their airmen came to Majorca they shouted: "Long live Spain!" but I've lived here many years and I immediately recognized the foreign accent: they were Italians. The Caproni planes had been brought over from Sardinia'. Garratt repeated several times with indignation: 'They killed my horse'. He was an elderly, thick-set Englishman with child-like eyes, the correspondent of a paper that glorified General Franco, and he could not understand why his dispatches were not being printed.

Almost two months had passed since the beginning of the rising. Although information continued to be contradictory, I saw that the Fascists were the stronger: they had occupied Seville, Córdoba, then Estremadura, Talavera, and were now pressing on to Madrid. Yet I still firmly believed in victory. There was some heartening news: the Fascists had been driven out of Malaga, out of Albacete. The resistance was growing: new *centurias*, detachments, battalions, columns appeared. Volunteers had started trickling in from France – Frenchmen, Italians, Germans, Poles.

In Barcelona I was invited to the Karl Marx barracks; the '19th July column' was being formed there. The fighters were lined up in the large courtyard. One *centuria* or, to put it more simply, one company was named the 'Ilya Ehrenburg *centuria*'. I was told I must present the colours and make a speech. I was at a total loss and felt caught up in a ridiculous situation; I said I was no politician and that I did not know how such things were done. All the same, I had to stand up and say something and was photographed holding the colours. I remember feeling both touched and foolish. People selling lemonade, fruit and boiled sweets moved about the place, and one of them pushed a handful of sweets into my hand: 'Eat up, Russian. We'll smash them yet'.

Almost on every peasant's house in Catalonia and Aragon there was the inscription: 'We want Cabanellas' head!' (General Cabanellas was the leader of the Fascist government at the time; a month later Franco got rid of him.)

I saw old peasant women who brought their sons to the barracks; when they were told that there were plenty of men already and not enough rifles, they said: 'But he's a Spaniard, he can't stay at home'.

Gerassi's wife Stefa arrived from Paris, saying that she had sent Tito to a children's colony. When she was leaving him, she could not help crying. The boy said: 'Go, mama, I'll look the other way – like this – and you, too, don't look. All right?' Stefa smiled as she repeated: 'He's a real Spaniard'.

I have just been asking myself why, while I have been describing the years of the Spanish war, I am gripped by emotion. I keep on laying my manuscript aside and before my eyes rise the red-brown rocks of Aragon, the fire-blackened houses of Madrid, the winding mountain roads, people near and dear to me – many whose names I did not even know – and all of it seems as alive as if it were today. Yet a quarter of a century has passed since then and I have lived through a far more terrible war. There are many things I can recall without emotion, but about Spain I feel a terrible tenderness and melancholy. Pablo Neruda called the book he wrote during the first months of the civil war *Spain in my Heart*; I love those poems and have translated the best of them into Russian, but it is the title I like best of all – there are no better words.

It was difficult to breathe in the disturbed and humiliated Europe of the thirties. Fascism was advancing, and advancing unhindered. Every country, and even every man, hoped to save themselves singly, save themselves at all costs, achieve safety by silence, buy themselves off. Years of the mess of pottage . . . And then, suddenly, a people arose that accepted battle. It did not save itself, nor did it save Europe, but if for men of my generation there still remains any meaning in the words 'human dignity', it is thanks to Spain. Spain became the air that allowed people to breathe.

Whom did I not meet in the bomb-shattered Spanish cities! Some came for a short while, others stayed a long time; some fought, some were war correspondents, some organized relief for the population. The paths of many diverged later, but the past cannot be obliterated. Togliatti and Nenni, Vidali ('Comandante Carlos') and Pacciardi, Koca Popovic and Kozovsky, André Malraux and Máté Zalka ('General Lukács'), Mikhail Koltsov and Louis Fischer, Pablo Neruda and Hemingway, Laszlo Rajk and Ludwig Renn, Gustav Regler and Janek Barvinski, Luigi Longo and Branting, Andersen Nexö and Ernst Busch, André Chamson and Alexey Tolstoy, Egon Erwin Kisch and Julien Benda, Saint-Exupéry and Anna Seghers, Jean-Richard Bloch and Stephen Spender, Andrée Viollis and Nicolás Guillén, Siqueiros and Dos Passos, Ralph Fox and Toller, Bodo Uhse and Willi Bredel, Isabelle Blume and the Abyssinian Ras Imru. I have probably missed out many; I merely want to show how varied were the people whose lives were bound up with Spain in those years.

At an HQ near Gomel (during the Second World War) I met Army Commander General Batov. We were talking about the coming offensive. Suddenly someone cried: 'Fritz!' – enemy aircraft came into sight. But the general and I laughed: in Spain our military advisers bore various names: Valois, Loti, Molino, Grishin, Grigorovich, Douglas, Nicolás, Xanti, Petrovich, and Pavel Ivanovich Batov was for some reason given the name Fritz. And we began to recall the Twelfth Brigade, friends, Aragon, the death of Lukács (Batov had then been wounded in the leg).

I am attending the session of the World Peace Council; the speaker at the moment is passionately demonstrating that peace is better than war; but to me he is the endearing Italian Scotti and I recall the days of Madrid. In the Kremlin the news cameraman is photographing the deputies to the Supreme Soviet; he is Boris Makaseyev, we crawled together over the rocks near Huesca. I know that at Vilna airfield I shall see a familiar face – an interpreter who was in Spain (he later took up the study of Spanish literature, but during the years of 'the struggle against cosmopolitanism' lost his job, and, in his own words, 'made a forced landing' on the Vilna airfield where he translates the questions of the customs officials to the tourists). Not so long ago, in Florence, a press photographer came to me with an elderly Italian who by way of introduction produced his membership card of the International Brigade Association, and we immediately forgot about the press photographer, sat down in a café and plunged into reminiscences of those long past days. All of us who were in Spain have bonds with that country, and bonds with one another. It seems that a man is proud not only of victories.

18

DURING THE first months of the Spanish war I gave little time to my duties as *Izvestia* correspondent. It is true that some fifty of my articles appeared in the paper between August and December, but to be frank they were written in haste and at any odd moment. I had no taste for the role of observer, I wanted to help the Spaniards in some practical way.

When I had visited Spain before the war I met for the most part writers and journalists who understood French. Now I spent my time with workers and militiamen and picked up some Spanish; I spoke badly but managed to make myself understood.

The first Soviet ambassador, Marcel Rosenberg, arrived in Madrid. I had known him in Paris where he was a counsellor at our embassy. He was a man of short stature with an amiable but slightly ironical smile. He arrived with the counsellor L. Y. Gaikis, the military attaché Gorev and his assistants Ratner and Lvovich (Loti). Koltsov was also in Madrid, doing other work besides his newspaper job; the nature of his activities is attested by eye-witnesses – Louis Fischer, Hemingway – and also by his own book *Spanish Diary*.

I made frequent trips to Barcelona, to the Aragon front; at the time (I am speaking of August–September 1936) there was not a single Soviet citizen there. When I talked about Catalonia to Rosenberg or Koltsov, they smiled: what could you do – they were all Anarchists. I probably realized better than they did how difficult it was to reach agreement with the Anarchists, but it was clear to me that without Catalonia the war could not be won. The Basque country had been cut off, and Barcelona, with her one and a half million inhabitants, was the only remaining important industrial centre.

Meanwhile in Barcelona a struggle was going on between the workers' organizations. They all hated Fascism and all of them were eager to fight, but the Aragon front could be called a front only by courtesy: various columns, in no way co-ordinated, tried to storm Saragossa, Huesca and Teruel; they had neither experienced officers, nor arms, and until the summer of 1937 General Franco did not send a single reserve unit to Aragon.

The head of the autonomous Catalan government (*Generalitat*) was Companys, a man both gentle and fiery by nature, an intellectual wedded to Catalan culture. He was over fifty; he had known prison, the Fascist terror. His fate was tragic: after the defeat of the Republic he went to France, was discovered there in 1940 by the Gestapo, handed over to Franco and shot. I remember him as a man of the highest integrity, discouraged by political intrigues and so lacking in personal ambition that he accepted power in the same spirit in which soldiers pick up and carry rifles abandoned during a retreat.

Companys was supported by the Esquerra (Left) – a party composed of the small bourgeoisie, the intellectuals and a large majority of the peasants. He was also supported by the PSUC (*Partido Socialista Unificado de Cataluña*) in which the Communists played a leading role. The Anarchists and the closely related CNT did not recognize the authority of Madrid, demanded the overthrow of the Catalan government and its replacement by 'Soviets'.

I had met Durruti as far back as 1931. He was one of the FAI leaders; I knew several other Anarchists – García Oliver, López, Vázquez, Herrera. I established friendly relations with Companys. I had to do something but I did not know exactly what. In Madrid I asked José Díaz; in Barcelona I talked to the leaders of the PSUC – Juan Comorera and others: they all said that the Anarchists were making a nuisance of themselves, that Catalonia was not helping Madrid and that the Separatists were brewing up for trouble. But what ought to be done, no one seemed to know. It was now September 1936.

I discussed the situation in Catalonia with Marcel Rosenberg several times and, at his request, sent a long telegram to Moscow.

Marcel Rosenberg has long been dead: he became one of the victims of the abuse of power. Men were cut down, but certain documents have survived, and a short time ago I obtained copies of two of my letters to Rosenberg from the archives. The following passages show not only how I assessed the events, but also what my activities were – of my own free will which, as the saying goes, drives harder than compulsion.

From my letter of 17th September 1936: 'To follow up today's telephone conversation. Companys was in a very nervous state. I talked to him for over two hours and he kept complaining about Madrid. His arguments are: the new government has changed nothing, Catalonia is treated like a province, it has refused to hand over the schools to the Generalitat, it asks for men but does not supply arms, it has not provided a single plane. He said he had received a letter from commanders serving with units on the Talavera front asking to be recalled to Catalonia. He would very much like to have a Soviet consulate in Barcelona . . . He said that the economic adviser whom they had sent to Madrid would put forward these complaints. So far neither Largo Caballero nor Prieto has found time to receive him. He pointed out that if he did not get any cotton within three weeks they would have 100,000 unemployed . . . He considers it important for Catalonia to have some sign of recognition from the Soviet Union . . . The Minister of Education Gassol also accused Madrid of ignoring Catalonia. I talked to García Oliver. He was beside himself. Irreconcilable. Whereas the leader of the Madrid syndicalists, López, told me that they do not and will not allow any attacks on the Soviet Union in the CNT newspaper, Oliver said that they do "criticize" and that Russia is not an ally because she has signed the non-intervention agreement. Durruti has learnt a good deal at the front, but Oliver is in Barcelona and nine-tenths obsessed by insane Anarchist ideas. He is, for instance, opposed to a unified command on the Aragon front: it will be needed only when a general offensive starts. Sandino was present during this part of the conversation and came out in favour of a unified command. We touched on the question of mobilization and of transforming the militia into an army. Durruti is full of the mobilization plan (I cannot understand why – there are volunteers but no rifles). Oliver said that he agreed with Durruti because "Communists and Socialists were skulking in the rear and dislodging the FAI from the towns and villages". He was in a state of frenzy at this point and might have shot me.

'I talked to the political commissar of the PSUC, Trueba (a Communist). He complained about the FAI: they will not let our men have any ammunition. The Communists have only thirty-six rounds per man left. The Anarchists have large reserves – a million and a half. Colonel Villalba's men have also only a hundred rounds each. At the CNT they complained that one of the PSUC leaders, Franzoza, had said at a meeting at San Boy that not a single rifle should be given to the Catalans because they would be bound to fall into the hands of the Anarchists.

'During the ten days that I spent in Catalonia, relations between Madrid and the Generalitat on the one side, and the Communists

356

and Anarchists on the other, have sharply deteriorated. Companys wavers: he does not know whether to try to win the support of the Anarchists, who agree to back the national and even nationalistic demands of the Esquerra, or that of the PSUC to struggle against the FAI. His advisers disagree, each alternative has its partisans. If things get worse on the Talavera front there will have to be a move in one direction or the other. It is imperative to improve relations between the PSUC and the CNT and to have closer contact with Companys.

'Today there is a meeting of Catalan writers including Bergamín who has come to fetch me. I hope that on the cultural front it will be possible to bring together the Spaniards and the Catalans. Tomorrow there is to be a public meeting – ten thousand people – and I shall be speaking in the name of the secretariat of the International Association of Anti-Fascist Writers. As this letter contains certain important corrections to what I have sent you for Moscow, please send this on too'.

From the letter of 18th September: 'Today I had another long talk with Companys. He was in a calmer frame of mind ... He suggests forming an autonomous government in this way: half Esquerra, half CNT and UGT (*Unión General de Trabajadores* – Socialist Trade Union). He called Oliver a "fanatic". He knew that I was going on to the CNT and was interested to know how the FAI would receive me; he asked me to tell him the results. He complained that the FAI were hostile to the Russians and were carrying on anti-Soviet propaganda. He is our friend. A shipload of sugar, for instance, might go some way towards appeasing them.

'At the CNT I talked to Herrera. He is much more moderate than Oliver. He immediately agreed to put a stop to anti-Soviet propaganda. With regard to "Soviets" he stands firm: the Madrid government is a party, a Marxist government. It was necessary to create a genuine workers' government etc. Still, at the end of our talk, when I pointed out the diplomatic consequences of a break in the constitutional succession, he was inclined to agree. But at that moment all sorts of international Anarchists came in and I left. It is interesting that in his attacks on the Madrid government Herrera adduced the same facts as Companys did yesterday: the detaining of two railway wagons, the refusal to provide arms to Catalonia, etc.

'Today the *Solidaridad Obrera* has printed the CNT appeal to defend small property owners, peasants, shopkeepers. A positive move.

357

'Miravilles told me that among the FAI there is already talk of a "desperate defence of Barcelona", etc. Among other things Herrera reproached Madrid for calling off the landing in Majorca – now the Fascists would start bombing Barcelona.

'The meeting was enthusiastic. The majority was from the CNT. At the moment the Anti-Fascist Militia Committee is in session. I was promised that a conciliatory line would be adopted on the question of the reorganization of the Catalan government . . .

'PS. Further to our telephone conversation and my letter. Although Oliver was adamant I have learnt that he has told *Solidaridad Obrera* to stop attacking the USSR. And indeed today *SO* has printed two telegrams from Moscow with friendly headlines.'

Soon after this I left for Paris. It was there that Antonov-Ovseyenko ran me to earth. He immediately said: 'Your telegram was discussed, and your views have been accepted. I've been appointed Consul General in Barcelona. In Moscow they believe that a *rapprochement* between Catalonia and Madrid is in the interests of Spain. I was told that I must try to make the Anarchists see reason, persuade them to take part in the defence; after all, they've got the devil of a lot of influence. But you know more about that than I do. The extraordinary thing is that the authorities should have agreed. Now I can talk with proper backing.'

I had known Antonov-Ovseyenko since pre-revolutionary years. He roamed Paris looking for work, lived in semi-starvation, but was never downhearted and was full of fight, though a dreamer who went about in downtrodden shoes and wore a cape. I remembered him in the Rotonde where he played chess, at the printers poring over the galleys of *Nashe Slovo* (Our Word), at meetings where he appealed to the audience to support Lenin. In the days of the October Revolution he proved that it was not just so much talk. In 1926 I had visited him in Prague where he was the Soviet Representative. Later I had lost sight of him.

He had aged and had a more brooding expression; only his eyes when he took off his glasses retained their childlike trustfulness. I thought: what a good thing they've chosen him for Barcelona. A man like that can influence Durruti, for there's nothing of the diplomat or of the high official about him, he's unassuming, simple and at the same time still breathes the stormy air of October – he hasn't forgotten the pre-revolutionary underground.

I proved right: Antonov-Ovseyenko quickly learnt to speak Catalan, made friends with Companys and Durruti, was liked by all. In spite of his consular rank he was a real Soviet ambassador in Catalonia. He knew the front, often talked to officers, understood the situation. He found time to send reports to *Izvestia*, which he signed *Zet*. The Catalans approved of his democratic ways. When I visited Barcelona and we were alone together, I noticed that he was depressed. He may have had a premonition of what was awaiting him. I do not know. He stayed in Barcelona for a year, and on his return to Moscow immediately disappeared; his name, too, disappeared from all the accounts of the storming of the Winter Palace. He was a man of pure heart, brave and loyal, and he perished only because the woodcutters were fulfilling and overfulfilling some devilish programme.

I wanted to go back to Barcelona with Antonov-Ovseyenko to introduce him at the start to various people, but I was detained for a week in Paris by an important job – I was buying a van.

Before I left Madrid I had informed Moscow that I intended to equip a van and work at the front with a mobile film-projector and a printing-press; I asked them to help me and to send me the films *Chapayev* and *We from Kronstadt*. In Paris I was asked to go to the bank: the Union of Writers had transferred a sum of money for the purchase of the van (I do not know why the money was sent through that organization; taking a humorous view of it, I suppose they wanted to show that the Union did actually help writers to carry out their creative plans). With the help of some Frenchmen I bought a van solid enough to negotiate the churned-up roads at the front. I do not remember who helped me to get the film-projector but, as I have said earlier, it was Eugène Merle who presented me with the printing-press. I also discovered a delightful cartoon: Mickey Mouse fights a cat, defeats him and raises a red flag over the mousetrap. I knew full well that one could not exist in Spain without a smile.

Stefa agreed to work with me. She spoke Spanish as if she had been born in Old Castile rather than in the Lvov countryside. Her job would be to translate the dialogue and help to bring out army news-sheets. Officially we were under the Commissariat of Propaganda of the Generalitat, as was stated on the sides of the van. Everyone's attention was attracted by the words: 'Printing-press and cinema'. In Barcelona we picked out a driver, a projectionist and two compositors, one of whom knew four languages.

At the beginning of October the meeting of the secretariat of the International Association of Anti-Fascist Writers took place in Madrid. We appealed to the intellectuals of the world, protested against foreign intervention and against the comedy of 'non-intervention'. The appeal was signed by many Spanish writers: Antonio Machado, Alberti, Bergamín and others, and, of the foreign writers, by Koltsov, Malraux, Louis Fischer, Andrée Viollis and myself.

On the road I met the composer Gustavo Duran, an old acquaintance of mine. Six months earlier we had discussed Prokofiev and Shostakovich; he had said with a laugh that if *Lady Macbeth* was a 'muddle' it meant that 'muddle' was just what he liked. Now he had no time for music. He commanded a detachment of 200 men and, near Bargas, had halted the advance of a Fascist column moving on Madrid from the South.

Sirens were wailing in Madrid. I had difficulty in making my way along one of the streets of the Cuatro Caminos; the ruins of a house blocked the road. Another house had been sliced open by a bomb and the rooms looked like a stage set. An old woman picked out from a heap of rubble a large framed photograph of a bridal couple, covered it carefully with a shawl and carried it away. It was raining. It was all unbearably sad, as it always is when you come upon the trivial belongings of those who have just died.

Roman Karmen went about photographing the bombed ruins. In Paris we had decided to make a film from his pictures; I wrote the script. 'They seek . . . they find . . .' On the screen mothers found their dead children in the wreckage. Many people in the audience wept. But what Madrid needed was fighter-planes, not tears.

In Barcelona disputes were still going on, but the Anarchists had become more restrained. To anticipate a little: at the end of October an agreement was signed between the PSUC and the UGT on one side and the CNT and FAI on the other. Representatives of the CNT entered the government headed by Largo Caballero. In the course of my life I have seen many unexpected, at times paradoxical things, but after reading that García Oliver – who had tried to prove to me that the State must be destroyed as no better than a prison – had been appointed Minister of Justice, I could not help laughing. But the agreement with the Anarchists seemed to me a great victory.

The ship *Zyrianin* arrived in Barcelona with a cargo of food. Other ships began to put in bringing aircraft and tanks, but in small quantities, and our aid was incomparably less than that given to Franco by the Italians and the Germans: geography played a decisive role.

I looked affectionately at the van that had at last arrived from France and photographed it as one might a woman one loves. I have before me now one of these photographs reproduced in an album. It is quite an ordinary van, but at the time it seemed to me uncommonly handsome.

The Communists – and Antonov-Ovseyenko – said: 'You must go to the Aragon front. You know how to talk to the Anarchists. There are none of our men there – the Anarchists make life impossible for everyone else. But they do at least talk to you. You might get them to see reason'.

I very much doubted it and, besides, I knew the Spanish Anarchists. But in a war one cannot choose where to go; it is not tourism. Stefa and I got into a ramshackle car and drove slowly out of Barbastro in the wake of the van.

19

'IN RUSSIA you've got a real State, but we stand for liberty', the sentry in a red-and-black shirt said to me as he checked my pass. 'We want to establish Libertarian Communism'.

Comunismo libertario – I still seem to hear these words, so many times were they uttered as a challenge, as a declaration of faith.

In an attempt to explain the sometimes inexplicable behaviour of the Anarchists it was said that their columns were packed tight with bandits. There is no denying that common burglars, men who haunted the underworld, infiltrated the Anarchists' ranks – a strong party always attracts not only honest men but also scoundrels; in those days anyone could call himself an Anarchist. In September 1936, when I was in Valencia, some hundred members of the Anarchist Iron Column stationed near Teruel rolled up. They declared that they had lost their officer and did not know what to do. In Valencia they found a job for themselves: they burnt the criminal records and tried to get into the prison to free the convicts, among whom they probably had friends.

But it was not the criminals that really mattered. In the autumn of 1936 the CNT united three-quarters of the Catalan workers. The leaders of both the CNT and the FAI were workers and most of them honest men. The trouble was that while condemning dogmatism they themselves were complete dogmatists who tried to make life conform to their theories.

The most intelligent of them saw the discrepancy between the alluring pamphlets and reality; under bombs and shells they were obliged hastily to review what only yesterday had seemed to them beyond dispute.

I first met Durruti in 1931 and had liked him at once. No writer would dare to describe his life – it was too much like an adventure story. A metal-worker, he had devoted himself from early youth to the revolutionary struggle, fought on the barricades, thrown bombs, robbed banks, kidnapped judges; he was condemned to death three times – once in Spain, once in Chile and once in the Argentine; he had seen the inside of dozens of prisons; eight countries in turn had expelled him. When the rebels tried to seize Barcelona in July, Durruti led the workers of the CNT against them.

At the beginning of September, or it may have been as early as the end of August, I drove to Durruti's HQ with Karmen and Makaseyev. At that time he was hoping to take Saragossa. His HQ was on the banks of the Ebro. I had told my companions that I knew Durruti, and they expected a hospitable welcome. But Durruti pulled out a revolver and said that, as I had slandered the Anarchists in my article about the Asturian rising, he was going to shoot me out of hand. He was not a man to waste words. 'It's up to you,' I said, 'but I must say it's a strange way of interpreting the laws of hospitality'. Durruti was an Anarchist, but he was also a Spaniard, and this embarrassed him. 'Very well, you're my guest now, but you'll get what you deserve for your article. Not here, but in Barcelona'.

Since, owing to the laws of hospitality, he could not kill me, he started to swear, shouting that the Soviet Union was no free commune, but an unmistakable State if ever there was one, that it teemed with bureaucrats, and that it was no accident that he had been expelled from Moscow.

Karmen and Makaseyev felt that something was very wrong, the more so as the sudden appearance of the revolver hardly needed interpreting. An hour later I told them: 'It's all right. He's asked us to come and have dinner'.

The militiamen sat at small tables, some in red-and-black shirts, others in blue overalls, all with huge revolvers, eating, drinking wine and laughing; nobody paid any attention to us or to Durruti. One of the men carried round the food and jugs of wine; by Durruti's plate he put a bottle of mineral water. I said jokingly: 'You said you had complete equality here, but everybody's drinking wine while you've been given mineral water'. I could never have guessed the effect my words would produce on Durruti. He jumped up and shouted: 'Take it away! Bring me water from the well'. He went on for a long time justifying himself: 'I didn't ask them. They know I can't drink wine and they got hold of a crate of mineral water somewhere. Of course it's a disgrace, you're perfectly right'. We ate in silence, then he said suddenly: 'It's difficult to change things all at once. Principles are one thing, life's another'.

During the night we went with him to inspect the positions. There was a terrible din – a convoy of lorries was passing. 'Why don't you ask me what these lorries are for?' he said. I replied that I did not want to pry into military secrets. He laughed: 'How can it be a secret when everybody knows about it? Tomorrow morning we shall cross the Ebro, that's it'. A few minutes later he started again: 'You don't ask me why I've decided to force the river'. 'I suppose it's got to be done,' I answered. 'You know best, after all you are in command of the column.' Durruti laughed: 'It isn't a matter of strategy. Yesterday a boy, about ten years old, came over from Fascist territory and said: "Why aren't you advancing? In our village everybody's asking: 'Has Durruti got cold feet?'" You understand, a child says that – it's the whole people asking. So we must advance. Strategy will come of itself'. I looked at his cheerful face and thought: why, you yourself are a child.

Later I visited Durruti several times. His column numbered ten thousand men. Durruti held firmly to his ideas but he was no dogmatist, and not a day passed without his being obliged to make concessions to reality. He was one of the first Anarchists to realize that a war cannot be carried on without discipline; he said bitterly: 'War's a bestial thing, it destroys not only houses but the highest principles'. But he did not admit this to his men.

On one occasion several militiamen left the observation post. They were discovered in the neighbouring village peacefully drinking wine. Durruti stormed: 'D'you realize that you're dishonouring the column? Hand over your CNT cards'. The culprits pulled out their trade union cards without turning a hair; this incensed Durruti still more: 'You're no Anarchists, you're just shit. I'll kick you out of the column. I'll send you home'. This was probably what the fellows were hoping for, because instead of protesting they just said: 'All right'. 'And do you know that the clothes you're wearing are the people's property? Take off your trousers'. The militiamen calmly undressed, and Durruti gave orders to escort them to Barcelona in their underpants: 'Let everyone see what you are, not Anarchists, but shit'.

He realized that in face of the Fascists there could be no quarrelling over principles and declared himself in favour of an agreement with the Communists, with the Esquerra, and sent greetings to the Soviet workers. When the Fascists approached Madrid he decided that his place was in the most dangerous spot: 'We'll show that Anarchists know how to fight'.

I had a talk with him on the eve of his departure for Madrid. He was, as usual, cheerful and full of energy; he believed in an early victory and said: 'There you are, you and I are friends. It shows that one can unite. We must unite. But after we've won, we'll see. Every nation has its own character, its own traditions. Spaniards are not like the French or the Russians. We'll find some way. But in the meantime we must destroy the Fascists'. Towards the end of our conversation he suddenly became confidential: 'Tell me, have you ever been at odds with yourself when you think one thing and do another, not out of cowardice but necessity?' I replied that I understood what he meant. As we were parting he patted me on the back, as people generally do in Spain, and I can still see his eyes with their extraordinary mixture of iron will and childlike uncertainty.

Durruti did not stay long on the Madrid front, he was killed on 19th November 1936. His death was a severe blow to all the Republican forces.

Durruti was not alone in recognizing the need to abandon pure Anarchist doctrines for the sake of victory; many other leaders of the CNT and FAI were compelled to set aside their principles. Even the fanatical García Oliver, who said that the State ought to be destroyed outright, initiated reforms as a Minister which were entirely acceptable to his liberal colleagues: he introduced measures against speculators, extended the legal rights of women, organized labour colonies for the Fascists. The Anarchist López Sanchez was Minister of Commerce, Peiró, Minister of Labour, and naturally they had to shelve their cherished projects for the organization of independent communes. The Minister of Health, the Anarchist Federica Montseny, emphasized at a meeting that while the government could not do without the Anarchists, the Anarchists could not do without the government. However, the leaders of the CNT-FAI had none of the energy, the authority and the rare spiritual integrity of Durruti. I do not know whether all of them sincerely wanted to make their followers see reason, but they seldom succeeded in doing so. Tens of thousands of courageous workers, experienced in street fighting, had been brought up on Anarchist ideas and were eager to put them into practice.

We drove our van not in order to visit Ministers but to go to the Aragon front line where things were ordered by Anarchists who had remained true to their old principles. More than once I recalled the expression coined in Russia during the Civil War: 'the authority on the spot'. I came to know this kind of authority well.

Let me briefly describe the military situation: this is what I wrote to Antonov-Ovseyenko on 17th December 1936 (this letter has also been preserved in the archives): 'The military units on the Aragon front have pulled themselves together a bit. There is better discipline. The failure of the recent attack on Huesca has had little effect on the morale of the militiamen. There are trenches here and there, rather primitive ones. The unified command still exists only on paper. Communications have improved these last few days: almost everywhere there are telephones linking the forward positions with HQ. Insofar as Durruti is now in Madrid, his column has lost half its fighting capacity. In the other Anarchist columns things are much worse; especially in the columns "Red-Black" and "Ortiz". The "Karl Marx" division remains a model compared with the other units ... As far as equipment is concerned things are in a bad way. The battalion stationed to the south-west of Huesca, in Pompenillo, has only two machine-guns, both of them jam after two belts have been used and they have to be taken to the rear, thirty miles behind the forward positions. There are few shells. The hand-grenades are no good. Despite all this the general mood is pretty cheerful'.

A month previously the picture had been much more gloomy One day I happened to be present at a meeting of the commanders of the Anarchist column. I was told that they would be discussing the vital question of how to take Huesca. A large map was spread out on the table but no one looked at it. For a solid hour everyone discussed an important piece of news: in Barcelona the red-and-black flag had been removed from the law-court building. 'It's a challenge!' shouted one of the commanders. 'We must send a hundred men to Barcelona at once. We're at the front, and the bourgeoisie's taking advantage of the fact with the help of the Marxists.' My attention was drawn to a tall elderly man with a soldierly bearing. While the discussion about the expedition to Barcelona was going on he kept silent and spoke only when one of the commanders suddenly said: 'Very well, but what are we going to do about Huesca?' The taciturn soldier, whose name was Jiménez, began to explain the plan of operations. He traced the map with his finger; the others did not look. Someone raised an objection: 'What about a frontal attack?' He was sat on: 'Jiménez knows better than you'.

When the council was over, Jiménez came up to me and introduced himself: 'Colonel Glinoyedsky'. I recalled the name: when I was in

366

Paris I had been asked to inform the Spanish embassy that Colonel Glinoyedsky – a Russian émigré, a member of the French Communist Party and a good artillery officer – wished to fight on the side of the Republicans.

There had been some talk that in the years of the Civil War in Russia Colonel Glinoyedsky had fought against Chapayev near Ufa. I do not know if there was any truth in this – he never spoke to me about his past – all I know is that he had been in the White Army and in Paris had become a worker. He was one of the first to go to Barcelona, before there were any International Brigades. He was accepted into the 'Chapayev' battalion and impressed the few Spanish officers who had remained loyal to the government with his military knowledge: he was transferred to column HQ.

He had an exceptionally attractive personality, brave, exacting but also gentle. His life had not been an easy one and this gave him a certain patient tolerance of other people's errors. He insisted on that minimum of discipline without which it would have been impossible to hold the positions that had been occupied. Twice the Anarchists wanted to shoot him for 'restoring the order of the past', but did not – they had become attached to him and felt that he was dependable. And Glinoyedsky said to me: 'It's such a muddle. I hardly know how to describe it. But what can you do with them? They're children. When they've tasted trouble they'll come to their senses'.

The Anarchists were convinced that Jiménez had come from Moscow and was concealing the fact for reasons of diplomacy. Had they realized that he had once been a White they would have shot him out of hand. In November military men arrived in Catalonia who were indeed from Moscow, and they all told the Spaniards that Jiménez was a Soviet officer. His authority grew, he became adviser on the Aragon front. The Spaniards who love conspiracy called the Soviet military men 'Mexicanos' or 'Gallegos' (inhabitants of Galicia); I remember with what pride the Anarchists used to say: 'Our Gallego is a Marxist, but he's a stout fellow'.

One day Colonel Jiménez sat down with me and began asking me about Russia, recalling his childhood. I said to him: 'Well now, after the war you can go back'. He shook his head: 'No, I'm too old. You know, there's nothing worse than to be a stranger in your own home'. He was silent for a moment and then began to talk about the situation at the front.

At our last meeting I thought he looked very tired. I have noticed more than once during war how fatigue makes men incautious; it seems as if death attracts them. Colonel Jiménez, though a member of the military council and the artillery commander of the whole front, went with a dozen men on a reconnaissance. He was fatally wounded. The hospital nurse told me that in the field hospital he had said something in Russian but nobody could understand what it was.

The whole of Barcelona attended Colonel Jiménez' funeral. Companys, Antonov-Ovseyenko, representatives of the government and of all the political parties walked behind the coffin. The Anarchists carried a wreath with a red-and-black ribbon: 'To our dear Comrade Jiménez'.

Glinoyedsky was right: I found that talking to the Anarchists, whether to their leaders – Durruti, Vázquez, García Oliver – or to militiamen near Huesca, was both touching and infuriating: they were children, there was no other word for it, though some were grey-headed and all, of course, were armed.

I got to know the Anarchists really well on the Aragon front when we were showing films in the villages, printing occasional news-sheets, eating in communal canteens, sleeping at the command posts, in ransacked presbyteries where the local committees were housed, or in peasants' huts.

I drove over and over again along the same road from Barcelona to the front, past the Catalan towns of Igualada, Tárrega, Lérida. In Tárrega there was a café called 'Kropotkin's Bar'; there the *habitués* discussed Companys' policy, the organizing of amateur theatricals, family scandal. Catalonia was emerald-green with her vineyards, gardens and kitchen-gardens: every scrap of land was lovingly cultivated. The villages had an urban look: there were cafés and clubs everywhere; smart girls strolled about the streets. Then abruptly the scene changed: the stony red desert of Aragon stretched before one's eyes. Small groups of dusty olive trees dotted the landscape. In summer the heat was intolerable; in winter icy winds blew. Occasionally a peasant would come riding along the empty twisting road on a diminutive donkey. Hungry goats nuzzled among the stones in search of a blade of grass sheltered from the blazing sun. The villages clung to the bare mountain-slopes; the houses were of the same colour as the hills and their blind walls turned towards the road made them look as though they had been abandoned.

In Catalonia the Anarchists were somewhat restrained – not by the laws of the Generalitat nor by the resistance of the Esquerra or the PSUC but by the standard of living of the population: the Catalans lived well, and the Anarchists did not always dare to attack a firmly established mode of life. Poverty-stricken, backward Aragon opened unlimited prospects to the moving spirits of the CNT-FAI. They had come here to liberate Saragossa, Huesca, Teruel from the Fascists. But the war was dragging on, the front was practically at a stalemate despite the frequent efforts to press forward. There were hotheads who decided to turn the immediate rear – the towns and villages of Aragon – into a paradise of 'Libertarian Communism'.

The peasants of Aragon led a poor kind of life, they had nothing to lose, and at first they accepted without much fuss the organization of village 'communes'. The Anarchists communized everything, down to the chickens. In many villages they took away the peasants' money and sometimes burnt it. The peasants were given ration-cards. I came across village committees which, without looking too far into the future, exchanged several wagonloads of wheat for coffee, sugar and shoes. In one village I asked a committee member what they would do in January when the reserves of grain ran out. He laughed: 'Why, we'll have smashed the Fascists before that'.

In some villages the Anarchists issued sugar, walnuts and almonds to the doctor and the teacher: they had read in the paper that these foodstuffs were necessary for brain-work. But there were also villages where the professional workers, regarded as parasites, received no rations at all. In the village of Cieza they took away the doctor's donkey so that he could no longer visit the sick in the neighbouring hamlets; there were no medical supplies at the chemist's; the committee said that 'nature was a better healer than the doctor'.

I visited the small town of Fraga; it had a population of ten thousand. The Anarchists took away everybody's money and issued books of tickets equivalent to so many pesetas a week. The cafés were open but there was nothing on sale, you could simply sit down for a while and then go away. The doctor told me that he had wanted to get a medical book from Barcelona; the chairman of the committee said: 'If you can prove that the book's necessary, we'll print it ourselves, we've got our own printing press. But we have no trade relations with Barcelona'. In the town of Pina money was also abolished and an extremely complicated system introduced; there were cards which entitled you to a hair-cut or a shave. Many committee members were sincere enthusiasts, but they had a very shaky notion of economics. In the large village of Membrilla (La Mancha) the Anarchists, after abolishing money, announced that, as the average family numbered four point five persons, they would simplify proceedings by issuing each family with provisions for four and a half people.

In one small Aragon town the committee decided to dismantle the railway line, saying that the inhabitants seldom used it and that the smoke polluted the air. The Anarchists at the front were alarmed when they got wind of the decision – food and munitions had to be sent up to them from the rear; the railway line stayed.

We organized film shows in public squares using any white wall as a screen, or in some miraculously preserved church, and also in canteens. The Anarchists adored *Chapayev*. After the first showing we cut the end of the film: the young militiamen could not reconcile themselves to Chapayev's death. They said: 'What's the point of fighting if the best men get killed?' Stefa interpreted the dialogue; sometimes she would be interrupted by cries of: 'Long live Chapayev!' Once, I remember, an Anarchist shouted: 'Down with the Commissar!' and everyone clapped. I realized, once again, that art appeals first of all to the emotions; in the film Chapayev is the hero, Furmanov the reasoner.

Still, the film occasionally produced practical results: in one unit after the performance they decided to be more cautious in future and to post night sentries.

The peasants saw *Chapayev* with different eyes. Often after the showing they would come up to me and thank the Russian commissar for prohibiting the confiscation of pigs and ask me to write and tell him what was wrong in their village: to them the film was a chronicle and they were convinced that both Chapayev and Furmanov were still living in Moscow.

The film *We from Kronstadt* elicited some peculiar reactions from the militiamen. When the sailor with a stone hung round his neck throws his guitar into the sea, there was laughter – the audience could not believe that the sailors would also be thrown into the sea. When the sole survivor emerges from the water, they laughed with delight: they had been sure beforehand that he would be saved and waited for the others to reappear. This was a reflection of the lightheartedness which still buoyed up the Catalans in the autumn of 1936. (I mentioned this in one of my articles and was rapped over the knuckles by Stavsky who was then the leader of the Writers' Union: 'If a petty bourgeois laughs, there's no harm in saying so. But no proletarian would laugh at this film'.)

In the papers that we printed for the Anarchist columns we tried – without engaging in polemics against the principles of the CNT-FAI – to explain with living examples how important it was to co-ordinate the action of one column with other units, to carry out the orders given by commanders and not to evacuate positions on the strength of the enemy's inactivity, and so on.

The Anarchists did not recognize prisons, saying that a man could not be deprived of liberty: he must be persuaded; but they were neither Tolstoyans nor pacifists and occasionally, when they found that a man would not yield to persuasion, they shot him. In one village they shot a peasant who was exchanging a hair-cut voucher for coffee or sugar. I was revolted but one of the Anarchists said to me quite seriously: 'What do you expect? We tried to persuade him for three months, but it was no use. He wasn't a man but a shark'.

I was told that in the town of Barbastro the Anarchists had closed down the brothel and made several speeches saying that the women were free from now on and must take up useful work making shirts for the militia. An elderly prostitute clawed at an Anarchist: 'I've been working here fifteen years and now you're turning me out into the street'. The Anarchists discussed at great length whether she could be persuaded; at last one of them undertook the task. This story may have been invented but it sounded quite plausible.

After describing to Antonov-Ovseyenko the way in which the Anarchists were introducing 'Libertarian Communism' in Aragon, I added: 'In all this there is more ignorance than ill-will. The Anarchists you actually talk to can be made to see reason. Unfortunately there are few men in the PSUC who understand how to talk to them; the responsible workers of the PSUC often say: "better the Fascists than the Anarchists" '.

I had apparently caught the infection from the Anarchists and believed that people could be easily persuaded. But in fact this is not at all easy: it is life that persuades. Words, even the most reasonable ones, too often remain mere words. Durruti learnt quickly; the others would not or could not part with their illusions, or their traditions; time was needed and there was none: day by day Franco was getting men and arms from his foreign supporters.

In wartime you make friends quickly, and I got on well with the Anarchists. Although they should have been abusing the Soviet Union, they realized that if anyone was helping them it was our country. I frequently got into arguments; but only once in a front-line village did a frantic youth threaten me with his revolver: 'As you can't be persuaded . . .' He was restrained in time.

Many of the Anarchists changed under my eyes; there were also those who would not budge; but even they could be prevented by a friendly word or a smile from doing many undesirable things. They shouted, they threatened, then quickly calmed down. Many of their mistaken actions should be put down to ignorance. I hardly ever met any professional soldiers, economists, agronomists or engineers among them, they were Barcelona workers; they regarded the intelligentsia with mistrust, even though they revered philosophy, science and art. They were quite capable of giving way to panic, of turning tail as a result of a single bomb, but also of attacking under heavy machine-gun fire: it all depended on their mood and on similar fortuitous factors. During the Fascist terror thousands of those whom I had met in Aragon went courageously to their death and did not recant. As in all parties, there were kind men and cruel, intelligent ones and fools among the Anarchists; but what I found attractive about them was their spontaneity and a naïvety rare in our age.

I have never felt the lure of Anarchism; obviously I lacked naïvety, but after *Julio Jurenito* several critics labelled me an 'Anarchist'. That is perhaps why – or perhaps because in my articles about Spain I insisted on the need for a unified front – one of our authors who had come to the Madrid congress said: 'Scratch Ehrenburg and you'll find an Anarchist'. This was in a house in the suburbs to which the Soviet delegation had been invited by the Communists. Dolores Ibárruri laughed: 'You also get the other sort – scratch them and you find a Fascist'.

It may be asked why I have devoted such a long chapter to the Spanish Anarchists. After all, work among them with the propaganda van took up only three or four months of my time. And, in any case, it was not only to the Anarchists that we went: we also showed the films to units commanded by Communists, we visited the international battalions, we printed news-sheets in Spanish, Catalan, German and French. In December I went to Madrid. If I have dwelt on the autumn of 1936 in Aragon it is only because in the long history of human error it is a terribly pathetic page.

Comunismo libertario – 'Free Communism' – all the Anarchists talked about it and almost all of them believed in it, arguing – and arguing well – that without liberty there cannot be genuine Communism. But the communes which they organized in Aragon reminded me of the compounds of cowed Indians in Paraguay directed by Jesuits, with uniform clothing, uniform food and uniform prayers. (It is true that the Jesuits had been dominating them for over a hundred years and had achieved perfection: Father Muratori tells us that when an erring Paraguayan was whipped he kissed the hand of his tormentor and thanked him for the blows.)

In an old notebook of mine I have found a quotation I copied out from a French author (I do not exactly remember which): 'The trouble with despotism is not that it does not love people, but that it loves them too much and trusts them too little'.

20

PEOPLE GET accustomed to anything: to plague, to terror, to war; and the population of Madrid soon became used to the bombings, the hunger and the cold, to the fact that the Fascists were at Casa del Campo, that is, within a mile or two of the densely populated quarters, and that all this was going to last a long time.

In those days *Izvestia* appeared at irregular hours of the day: sometimes at 7 a.m., sometimes, if information was received from TASS in the middle of the night — a list of people who had been decorated or found guilty — at 10 a.m., or even at noon. The Madrid newspapers continued to come out at 6 a.m., as they had done in the days when it was necessary to catch the morning trains. There had not been any trains for a long time but the habit remained.

Of the seven highroads which connected the capital with other parts of the country, six had been seized by the Fascists. Fighting flared up and died down sporadically over the control of the seventh road linking Madrid to Valencia. Several miles of this road were under Fascist fire. On one occasion I had to jump out of the car and lie in a field for half an hour. Several shells burst near me. The good thing in a war is that you are seldom alone. I could not let the Spanish driver crouching at my side see that I was not feeling particularly comfortable, for I was a 'Mexicano', while the driver, being a Spaniard, tried to show me that he felt quite at ease.

The Fascists had dug themselves in thirteen miles from Madrid near Morata de Tajuña. I was there several times; passing along the deep trenches one could hear the Fascists bickering or singing somewhere close by. For many months there was fighting for the possession of a ruined house, recalling the 'ferryman's house' which, in the years of the First World War, figured for several months in the Allied and German communiqués.

In Madrid life went on, fantastic and at the same time humdrum. No one swept the pavements, they were strewn with rubble, tattered posters, bomb splinters, broken crockery. In the morning bonfires were lit at which women and militiamen warmed themselves. The

Madrid winter is cold and the Andalusians and Catalans felt it badly. Many shops were open; what goods remained were of the kind that few people needed in those days: crystal chandeliers, scents, old novels, ties. Once in a furniture shop I saw a young militiaman and a girl asking the price of a mirror-wardrobe and exchanging tender glances; they were probably just married. On another occasion I ran into a house decorator carrying a paint-pot and ladder – he was going to whitewash walls.

In the streets they sold home-made lighters and pocket torches. In once fashionable restaurants militiamen sat happily eating chick-peas – they were to Spain what millet is to Russia. Long queues lined up outside bakeries, and it often happened that people waiting for half a pound of bread died from a bomb or a shell splinter. The trams ran almost as far as the trenches. One early morning I went to the Calle Rafael Salilla. Firemen were carrying out dead bodies. I shall never forget the sight of a small girl like a broken doll and of a sewing-machine with some blue material hanging from a rafter.

The government moved to Valencia. Endless discussions went on in the Madrid committees of the political parties. The Anarchists and the Trotskyists insisted on a 'deepening of the revolution'. Prieto wanted order to be introduced and accused his party comrade Largo Caballero of demagogy. Life went on.

It went on everywhere. The poets published a volume of verse devoted to the war and met to discuss the resurrection of the old *romancero* form. I met an elderly music teacher who told me that she had two pupils who came to her and played scales.

The theatres were open but the performances started at 6 p.m. instead of at 10 p.m., as formerly; the same plays were on: *You're a Gypsy*, *I'm a Gypsy* and *Night in the Alhambra*. The cinemas showed Chaplin's films; in *Avec le Sourire* Chevalier sang his familiar ditties. Girls wept over the seduction of an American girl, while militiamen frantically applauded Lolita Granatos. Spaniards and volunteers in the International Brigades used to come from the front to my chilly hotel room; sometimes I would have herrings sent to me from Odessa or a chicken brought from Valencia. We ate in silence after which we would talk about things that had little bearing on the situation at the front. One militiaman who had been a student argued passionately that, although *Don Quixote* was read all over the world, no one but a Spaniard understood or could understand the book. A Serb brought

375

me a thick manuscript: he had recorded his observations of the behaviour of different kinds of animals during air-raids. According to these, cats behaved perfidiously but reasonably: on hearing the hum of aircraft they immediately jumped out of a window and ran into the fields as far away as possible from human habitation. Dogs, on the contrary, blindly believing in man's omnipotence, begged to be let into the house and crept under a table or a bed. The Serb wrote his notes in the trenches while the bombing went on – a fact that came out quite casually; he was interested in zoopsychology and asked me about Durov's experiments. A Frenchman from the 'Commune de Paris' battalion read me his poems: 'The sky is bright with coloured advertisements – a bargain sale of broken bodies and Eternity'.

GHQ was housed in the centre of Madrid, in the deep cellars of the Ministry of Finance. The cellars had been divided into tiny cubicles; there people worked, ate and slept. Typewriters rattled, militiamen came and went. In one of the cubicles a sick old man, overburdened by the events, sat hunched up – General Miaja. All the newspapers of the world were writing about him at the time, but he looked at me forlornly and said: 'Yes . . . yes . . .'

Brigade Commander Gorev came in with his interpreter Emma Wolff. He had brought a map with him and spoke for a long time about the situation in the University City. Miaja listened attentively, with his sad lacklustre eyes on the map, and repeated: 'Yes . . . yes . . .'

Vladimir Yefimovich Gorev seldom looked in at the cellars of the Ministry; he spent most of his time at the front. He was under forty but had great military experience. Intelligent, reserved, and at the same time passionate – I could even call him poetical – he won everybody's esteem. To say that people had faith in him would be an understatement: they believed in his lucky star. Six months later the Spaniards had learnt how to wage war, they had talented commanders – Modesto, Lister and others less well known. But in the autumn of 1936, with the possible exception of the Chief of Staff Rojo, there were few men of vigour and military knowledge among the commanders of the Republican army. In the November days Gorev played a tremendous role, helping the Spaniards to halt the Fascists in the suburbs of Madrid.

When Franco began operations in the North, Gorev went with his interpreter to Barcelona. Franco had strong troop concentrations in the North; the German air force was dealing massive blows. The

Republicans defended themselves for four months, cut off from the main body and encircled. The end came. In Gijón, which was due to fall any day, there were twenty-six Russian officers headed by Gorev, among them sick and wounded, and also Emma Wolff.

During the first months of the war a charming gay Frenchman, the first-class pilot Abel Guidès had fought in the air force squadron organized by Malraux. In the summer of 1937 he went back to Paris. When he learnt that his Soviet comrades were unable to break out of the encirclement he managed to get hold of a tiny charter plane and flew to Gijón. Gorev wanted to be the last to leave. Guidès made three flights saving, among others, Emma Wolff, but when he flew out for the fourth time he was shot down by German fighter planes. Dear, brave Guidès perished. And he had only just got married. Gorev and the few comrades remaining with him took to the mountains with the guerrillas. They were rescued by Soviet planes. This was little short of a miracle. We rejoiced – Gorev had been saved. But six months later the hero of Madrid was calumniated and there were no miracles about. He perished.

Not only Gorev, but also Ratner and Lvovich, whom in Spain they called Loti, lived in the cellars. Ratner was a wise and modest strategist. I was told later that he had taught at one of the military academies. Loti stayed in Spain for a long time and became friendly with the Spaniards; he was an easygoing fellow with a touch of melancholy, and he loved poetry. Once, on a hot Madrid evening, we were sitting on a stone outside a bombed house, bathed in sweat; he began reciting lines from Lermontov, Blok, Mayakovsky, then he suddenly got up and said, in rhyme: 'There's a parish in Spain, Madrid by name, beautiful word, glory and fame – this means I've got to go to HQ. And do you know what you ought to be doing? Not hanging about under fire but writing. Every man has his trade. You're a writer but you don't write'. I met Loti again in General Lukács' 12th Brigade and at Gaylord's Hotel, and later in Valencia. He was exceptionally brave but tried to restrain others, saying: 'The Spaniards don't know the meaning of the word prudence. That may be all right in love but it's no good in war'. In America in 1946 I met the painter Fernando Gerassi, who had been the commander of the 12th Brigade, and his wife Stefa. Their first question was: 'What about Loti?' I turned away and said with an effort: 'Gone'.

My one thought was victory in Spain. But at the same time I met and talked to some of my countrymen, and although we did not yet know the significance of 1937, my heart was often troubled.

Marc Guelfand, the TASS correspondent, a very sick man, sent off long telegrams and made witty remarks. He wrote a funny play which he read to a chosen few; the *dramatis personae* were Koltsov, Karmen, Makaseyev, Ehrenburg and himself. Whenever we went to see him there was always laughter. One day I found him poring rather unhappily over *Pravda*. There was no one else in the room. He said to me abruptly: 'You know, we've been lucky. There's a writers' meeting, they're busy denouncing enemies ... Let's go to Carabanchel – they're going to blow up a house there. And forget about what I've just said'. I coaxed him into giving me issues of some comparatively recent newspapers. The house in Carabanchel was not blown up, the people there told us the sappers had let them down. To make up for it we were caught in a first-class bombing attack. That night I read the papers and thought: well, I really am lucky – it's much simpler to be bombed: at least you know who's your enemy and who's your friend'.

I often met Mikhail Koltsov. The Spaniards regarded him not only as a famous journalist but also as a political adviser. It would be difficult to visualize the first year of the Spanish war without Koltsov. Small, active, courageous, so acute that his intelligence positively became a burden to him, he sized up a situation at a glance, saw all the weaknesses and never pampered himself with illusions. Yet this man could hearten even those enthusiasts who easily fell into despair. The history of Soviet journalism knows no greater name, and his fame was well deserved. But having raised journalism to a high standard, having demonstrated to his readers that a report or an article could be a work of art, he did not believe it himself. More than once he said to me with wry irony: 'Other people write novels. But what will remain of me after I've gone? Newspaper articles are ephemeral stuff. Even an historian won't find them very useful, because we don't show in our articles what's going on in Spain, only what ought to be happening.' He envied Hemingway and even Regler: 'I expect he'll write a novel of 544 pages too'.

He loved the Odessa story about the old cabby who slyly asks a man new to the job what he would do if he lost a wheel in the steppe and had neither a nail nor a rope with him. 'Well, what would *you* do?' asks the nonplussed beginner. And the old man replies: 'Grin and bear it'. Koltsov often grunted: 'Grin and bear it'. But an hour later he would be putting fresh heart into some Spanish politician by persuading him that victory was certain and so everything was all right. He had a certain mistrust of people. This would sound like a criticism if I did not add that he also mistrusted himself: his feelings, his talent, his future. Nevertheless he was not dispirited but, on the contrary, rather buoyant, and after talking to him you came away with a mixed feeling: things were bitter but interesting, and life was worth living.

One day he told me: 'A bunch of people has received decorations. It won't be in the papers, but let me congratulate you on being awarded the battle Order of the Red Star'. I congratulated him too, and also Karmen and Makaseyev. Koltsov, I remember, added: 'I believe you'll be getting ten roubles a month. It won't save you from either hunger or abuse'.

For the first time in my life I had received a decoration, and what was more, one that would not be mentioned in the papers. I shall not conceal the fact that I was very pleased.

Several times I left Madrid and went back, witnessing the first victory of the Republicans at Guadalajara. The Fascists hoped to break through to Madrid with tanks. In the Siguenza region they concentrated several Italian divisions, tanks and aircraft. The battle ended unexpectedly for the Fascists: after an advance of several dozen miles they were thrown back to their initial positions with heavy casualties and the loss of a great deal of equipment. The Italians did not fight well, and calculations had been rash: the Fascists had counted on the tank formations quickly fanning out on to the plain where they would be able to encircle the enemy, but after the Republicans' counter-attack the Italian tanks found themselves caught in a narrow valley where our airmen bombed them mercilessly.

I made many trips to the Guadalajara front – with Koltsov, with Hemingway, with Savich; I visited the Palacio Ibarra – the ruins of an old manor from which the Garibaldi Battalion had driven out Italian Fascists – and bomb-shattered Brihuega. There was a special joy in treading territory freed from the Fascists, in seeing Italian inscriptions on the walls, abandoned guns, cases of hand-grenades, religious amulets, letters. I talked to the victors; soldiers of units commanded by Enrique Lister, El Campesino, fighters of the 12th Brigade, with General Lukács, with Fernando, with the Bulgarians Petrov and Belov. I also talked to captured Italians. This was during the short

379

Castilian spring. The men basked in the sun. Metallic clouds would suddenly cover the sky, rain came pattering down, and an hour later the deep southern blue presaged the approaching summer.

For those of us who had known only defeat in the past six months, Guadalajara came as a breath of joy. I felt that we had left behind not only the winter but also the chill of retreat.

Among the Italian prisoners were many wretched men who were only too ready to lay down their arms. I saw familiar Italian peasant types, kind and peaceable; they cursed their officers, the Duce, the war. A cobbler from Palermo told me that he remembered the year 1920 – at that time he was a small boy, there had been shooting in the streets, and a portrait of Lenin hung in his father's room. He was illiterate but understood pretty quickly who his friends were and, taking advantage of the general confusion, rushed off to join the Garibaldi Battalion.

There were also dyed-in-the-wool Fascists, not as brutal as their German counterparts, but arrogant and firmly convinced by Mussolini's loud demagogy. I was handed the diary of an Italian officer. A short while before Guadalajara he had written: 'All Spaniards are alike. I would dose them with castor oil, even these Falangist buffoons; all they understand is eating and drinking to the health of Spain. We are the only ones who fight seriously'.

There was a sort of musical comedy atmosphere about the Italian army. I remember the colours of the 'Black Feathers' Battalion' with the motto: 'We do not shine, but we burn'. The names of the other battalions were in the same style: 'Lions', 'Wolves', 'Eagles', 'The Untameables', 'The Arrow', 'The Storm', 'The Hurricane'. However, these battalions formed brigades and divisions. From the Italian port of Gaeta military transports set sail uninterruptedly for Cadiz, bringing men, artillery, tanks. The Republicans found documents belonging to the General Staff, including a telegram from Mussolini to General Mancini saying: 'On board the *Pola* on my way to Libya I received a report on the great battle of Guadalajara. I follow the course of the fighting with the utmost confidence, deeply convinced that the courage and fighting spirit of the legionaries will crush the enemy's resistance'. Although I was in a happy mood I did not share the optimism of those who already saw the Republicans at the walls of Saragossa. What worried me was not the fictitious bravery of the legionaries but the pusillanimity of the British and the French in the Non-Intervention Committee. In my article on the battle of Guadalajara I wrote: 'One must not under-estimate the danger – Italy is only just entering the war'.

The advance of the Republicans did not last long. On a cold night I was drinking tea with the Brigade Commander, M. P. Petrov, who was in charge of a tank unit. He was a stocky, good tempered tank-officer. He said ruefully: 'There's not enough technical equipment. They couldn't even find lorries to bring up the infantry. So now we're stuck. Well, never mind, we'll beat them yet'. (I met General Petrov in August 1941 near Bryansk. He shouted happily: 'Remember Brihuega?' Yet it was a far from happy time. He was killed in action soon after that and so did not live to see the wiping out of the Fascists.)

At the beginning of April the Republicans decided to attack the Fascists who had dug themselves in at Casa del Campo. At 5 a.m. I went to the observation post in the palace. The windows looked out to the west. We watched the men run out of the trenches and fall, and the tanks go into action. The preliminary artillery bombardment was strong but the machine-guns never stopped firing and the Republicans hardly succeeded anywhere in driving the Fascists out of their trenches.

In the evening I had to send my paper a report on the outcome of the operation. I did not know what to say and decided to give an hour-by-hour account of what I had seen, without mentioning the attack, and called the article 'A day in Casa del Campo'. In the room where we were there was a canary in a cage. The Fascists fired several shells at the palace. When the guns fell silent for a moment, the canary burst into song: evidently the din excited it. So I put in the canary too, although I realized that things of that sort were more suitable in a novel than in a correspondent's despatch. The editor cut out the bit about the canary and was even rather annoyed by it. Lyuba was in Moscow at the time and went to the newspaper office to talk to me on the telephone. 'What's this business about a canary?' she asked. But I could not tell her that the canary had burst into song in my article solely because the attack had failed.

One day I was listening to a broadcast from Seville. The Fascists were saying: 'Strong Soviet forces of up to eighty thousand men are concentrated round Madrid'. I smiled bitterly as I listened. There were not many Soviet army men; I do not know the exact number, but I had been both at Alcalá, where our tankmen were stationed, and at the two airfields – there were few of them, very few. There were also several dozen military advisers attached to various units. Few as the men were, they fought well and in the critical days heartened the Spaniards. When, in November, the inhabitants of Madrid saw Soviet fighter-planes above them (they were known as *chatos* – snub-nosed), regardless of the air-raid siren they stood in the streets and cheered – they felt that now they would be safely protected from bombs.

Amongst the commanders I met Divisional Commander G. M. Stern (in Spain he was called Grigorovich), Jan Berzin (Grishin), Corps Commander of the Air Force Y. V. Smushkevich (Douglas), tank commander Pavlov, H. D. Mamsurov (Hajji), G. L. Tumanian and others. They were all very different types but all of them genuinely loved Spain. Many of them fell victims to the abuse of power in later years but those who survive recall their Spanish comrades with affection to this day. I never noticed in any of the men I have named either arrogance or even the impatience that might so easily have been aroused in professional soldiers who found themselves up against helpless muddle, Anarchists, naïve commanders who thought that German planes could be driven off by rifle fire.

As I say, I met Soviet airmen and tankmen; with some of them I made friends and I acquired a better understanding both of the war and of our people. If, four years later, I was able to write for *Red Star* and find the right words it was because I was helped, in this as in much else, by my years in Spain.

In April the Duchess of Atholl, a Conservative MP, came to Madrid. She was given a room in the same hotel where Karmen, Savich and I were staying. While she was out looking at the town her room was demolished by a Fascist bomb splinter. The journalists asked her whether she intended the raise the question of 'non-intervention' in Parliament. She replied that she had promised not to make any political pronouncements but that she was full of admiration for the courage of Madrid and mourned for the innocent victims. She was not alone in this: many admired and mourned. Meanwhile Hitler and Mussolini got on with the job.

My faith in victory was sustained by the Spanish character. During one of the bombings Petrov and I tried to induce an old woman to go into an air-raid shelter; she did not want to come and kept saying: 'Let the scoundrels see that we aren't afraid of them'.

21

THIS WAS in March 1937 in Madrid. I was staying in the former Palace Hotel which had been turned into a hospital. The wounded groaned, there was a smell of carbolic. The building was unheated. Food was scarce and, as in Moscow in 1920, I often thought with longing of a piece of steak before I fell asleep.

One day, towards evening, I decided to go to Gaylord's Hotel where our advisers and Koltsov were staying: you could get warm there and have a good meal.

In Koltsov's room there were, as usual, both familiar people and strangers: Gaylord's tempted others besides myself. I immediately noticed a large ham and some bottles on the table. Koltsov grunted: 'Hemingway's here'. This flustered me to such an extent that I forgot all about the ham.

Every man has his favourite author, but to explain why you like some particular writer and not another is as difficult as to explain why you are in love with some particular woman. Of all my contemporaries I liked Hemingway best.

In 1931, in Spain, Toller had given me a book by an unknown author: *The Sun Also Rises*. 'I think it's about Spain, perhaps it'll help you to understand.' I read it and got hold of *A Farewell to Arms*. Hemingway helped me to understand – not bullfights, but life.

That was why I was flustered on seeing the tall, moody man who was sitting at the table drinking whisky. I started to express my feelings to him and undoubtedly did it so clumsily that Hemingway's frown deepened. A second bottle of whisky was opened; it appeared that it was he who had brought the bottles, and he drank more than the others.

I asked him what he was doing in Madrid; he said he had come as the correspondent of a newspaper agency. He spoke to me in Spanish and I to him in French. 'Do you have to telegraph only articles or news as well?' I asked. Hemingway jumped up, seized a bottle and swung it: 'I knew right off that you were trying to guy me'. News in French is *nouvelles*, but in Spanish *novelas* means novels. Someone caught hold of the bottle, the misunderstanding was cleared up and we both had a good laugh. Hemingway explained what had made him angry: the critics complained of the 'telegraphese style' of his novels. I laughed: 'And of my "chopped sentences" too'. He went on: 'It's a pity you don't like whisky. Wine's for pleasure, but whisky's fuel'.

Many people wondered at the time what Hemingway was really up to in Spain. Of course he liked the country, of course he hated Fascism. Even before the Spanish war, when the Italians attacked Abyssinia, he had come out publicly against the aggression. But why did he stay in Madrid? At first he worked with Joris Ivens on a film; from time to time he sent articles to America. He lived in the Hotel Florida, not far from the telephone exchange which was constantly under fire from Fascist artillery. The place had been badly damaged by a direct hit from a high-explosive bomb. Nobody went on living there except Hemingway. He made coffee on a spirit-lamp, ate oranges, drank whisky and was busily writing a play about love. He had a house in Florida itself, where he could have been doing what he most enjoyed: fishing, eating steaks and writing his play. In Madrid he was always hungry but this did not worry him. There were several attempts to recall him to the States but he angrily laid the cables aside: 'I'm quite happy where I am'. The writer in him was attracted by danger, by death, by heroic feats. And he said quite flatly: 'The Fascists have got to be beaten'. He was among people who refused to surrender and this refreshed and rejuvenated him.

At Gaylord's Hemingway met our army men. He liked Hajji, a man of reckless courage, who used to penetrate behind the enemy lines (he was a native of the Caucasus and could easily pass himself off as a Spaniard). Much of what Hemingway says about the activity of the guerrillas in his book *For Whom the Bell Tolls* he heard from Hajji. (What a good thing that at least Hajji has survived. I met him once later and was overjoyed.)

I was with Hemingway in Guadalajara. He understood military matters and quickly grasped the situation. I remember him watching the men bring the Italian army hand-grenades, red as large strawberries, out of the dugouts; he grinned: 'They've left the lot behind. It's just like them'.

In the First World War Hemingway had fought as a volunteer on the Italian-Austrian front; he was severely wounded by a shell. Having seen war he came to hate it. He was glad that Italian soldiers were so ready to throw down their rifles. Frederic Henry said farewell to arms: 'I was going to forget the war. I have made a separate peace'.

But at Guadalajara, at Jarama, in the University City Hemingway examined the International Brigade's machine-guns. The ancient Romans used to say: *'Tempora mutantur, nos et mutamur in illis'*. During one of our meetings Hemingway said to me: 'I don't understand much about politics and I don't like them. But I know what Fascism is. The people here are fighting for a good cause'.

He often went to the HQ of the 12th Brigade which was commanded by General Lukács – the Hungarian writer Máté Zalka. In the years of the First World War the two had faced each other from the trenches of two hostile armies. Near Madrid they conversed as friends. 'War's a dirty business,' Máté Zalka would say with a sigh. 'And how!' Hemingway would reply, adding a moment later: 'And now, Comrade General, show me where the Fascist artillery is'. They would sit for hours over the map heavily scored with coloured pencillings.

I happen to have kept a small snapshot taken at the Palacio Ibarra: Hemingway, Ivens, Regler and myself. Hemingway is still young and slim, and is faintly smiling.

On one occasion he said to me: 'Forms change, I know, but themes . . . Now what is it that all the writers on earth have written and still write about? You can count it up on the fingers of one hand – love, death, work, struggle. Everything else is included in these. War, of course. Even the sea'.

Once, too, we were sitting in a café in the Puerta del Sol talking about literature. This café had miraculously remained standing between two bombed houses. All they served was orange juice and ice-water. It was rather a cold day and Hemingway pulled a flask out of his hip-pocket and poured out some whisky. 'I believe that a writer can never describe everything,' he said. 'So there are two ways out: you describe briefly all the days, all the thoughts, all the emotions, or you try to convey the general in the particular – in one meeting, one short bit of dialogue. I write only about details, but they try to speak of the details in detail.' I told him that what struck me most in his books was the dialogue – I could not fathom how it was done. He smiled: 'One American critic claims quite seriously that I use brief dialogue because I translate the sentences from Spanish into English'.

Hemingway's dialogue still remains a puzzle to me. Of course when I am reading a novel or a story that absorbs me I do not think about how it is done. I am simply the reader; but later the writer in me starts to ponder on things that concern my craft. When I understand the technique I can say whether the book is written badly, indifferently, well or very well; I may like it even if it does not deeply affect me. But the dialogue in Hemingway's books baffles me. In art the greatest thing, perhaps, is when you do not quite understand the source of its power. Why have I been repeating to myself for half a century Blok's lines: 'I called to you, but you did not look back, I shed tears but you did not relent'? There is no new thought here on which to meditate, no uncommon words. The same thing goes for Hemingway's dialogue: it is simple and mysterious.

One day when Lily Brik was entertaining some guests, she secretly switched on the tape-recorder; later we heard our conversation and it made us feel uneasy: we spoke in long 'literary' phrases. Hemingway's characters talk differently: laconically, almost casually, and yet every word discloses the spiritual state of the speaker. When we read his novels or stories we feel that this is exactly how people do talk. But in fact these are not phrases overheard, they have not been taken down in shorthand – they are the essence of a dialogue created by an artist. One can understand the American critic who came to the conclusion that Spaniards speak in the Hemingway manner. But Hemingway did not translate dialogue from one language into another: he translated it from the language of reality into that of art.

If you had come across Hemingway by chance you might have taken him for a romantic bohemian or a typical dilettante: he drank, had various eccentricities, roamed the world, went in for deep-sea fishing, big-game hunting in Africa and appreciated all the finer points of bullfighting – nobody knew when he did his writing. But he was a hard worker; the ruins of the Florida were anything but a suitable place for a writer to work in, but he sat there writing every day; he told me that one must write doggedly, never give in – if a page turns out colourless, one must stop, re-write it, five times, ten times.

I learnt a great deal from Hemingway. I feel that before his time writers described people, sometimes brilliantly, whereas Hemingway never describes his characters – he shows them. This is perhaps the clue to the influence he exercised on writers in so many countries; not that all of them liked him, but almost all of them learnt something from him.

He was eight years younger than I, and I was surprised when he told me about the way he had lived in Paris in the early twenties – exactly as I had done eight years before; he sat over a cup of coffee at the Select – next to the Rotonde – and, like me, wished he could afford another *croissant*. I was surprised because in 1922 I had had the impression that the great days of Montparnasse were over, that the Select was crowded with rich American tourists. But Hemingway had sat there feeling hungry, writing poetry and thinking out his first novel.

As we evoked the past we discovered common friends: the poet Blaise Cendrars, the painter Pascin. Both these men shared something with Hemingway: a stormy life and a preoccupation with love, physical danger, death.

Hemingway was a stout-hearted man, strongly attached to life; he could talk for hours about some large and rare fish which passes close to the shores of Florida, about a bullfight, about his many hobby-horses. On one occasion he suddenly interrupted a fishing story: 'All the same, you know, life has a meaning. There's such a thing as human dignity. The day before yesterday an American was killed near University City. He had been to see me twice. A student. We talked about heaven knows what – poetry and hot-dogs. I wanted you to meet him. He said something rather good: "There's nothing as shittish as war. Yet it's here that I realized why I was born – they've got to be driven away from Madrid, that's as plain as two and two make four".' After a pause Hemingway added: 'You see how things have turned out – I wanted to say farewell to arms, but it didn't work out'.

At the time, he wrote that there were fifty years of undeclared wars ahead and that he had signed on for the duration. He did not know when, but he had signed on. It is one of his characters who says this, but the author himself repeated it more than once.

I remember another conversation. Hemingway said that critics were either fools, or pretended to be fools: 'I've read that all my characters are neurotics. But the fact that life on this earth is beastly is never taken into account. They just call it a "neurosis" when a man's unhappy. A bull in the ring is also a neurotic, in a meadow he's a sound fellow, that's how it is'.

At the end of 1937 I went back to Barcelona from Teruel. By the sea the orange trees were in blossom but near Teruel, which is at a high altitude, we froze and sneezed. I arrived in Barcelona shivering with cold, worn out, and fell into a heavy sleep. I woke up when someone shook me: Hemingway was standing over me. 'Well, is Teruel going to be taken?' he asked. 'I'm off there with Capa'. In the doorway stood my friend, the cameraman Robert Capa (he was killed during the war in Indo-China). I said: 'I don't know. It's started well. But they say the Fascists are bringing up reserves'. I was completely awake now and gazed with horror at Hemingway – he was wearing summer clothes. 'You're crazy – it's deadly cold out there'. He laughed: 'I've got my own central heating', and began to pull whisky flasks out of various pockets. He was cheerful and smiling: 'It's not going to be easy of course – but they'll beat them in the end'. I gave him the names of the Spanish commanders and told him to find Grigorovich: 'He'll help you'. We said good-bye in the Spanish manner – slapping each other's backs. Hemingway kept a photograph showing me in bed and him standing over me; the photograph figures in a book about his life published in America.

When I returned in June 1938 to Spain, Hemingway was no longer there. I saw him always young and slim in my mind's eye; I did not recognize him when, ten years later, I saw photographs of a stout grandfather with a great white beard.

I met him again at the end of July 1941. Almost every night in Moscow there were air-raid alarms; we were herded into the shelter. I wanted to get a good sleep, so Boris Lapin and I decided to spend the night in Peredelkino in Vishnevsky's empty *dacha*. Someone lent me the manuscript of the Russian translation of Hemingway's novel *For Whom the Bell Tolls*. We did not get our sleep: Lapin and I read through the night, passing each other the pages as we finished reading them. (The next day Lapin was due to leave for Kiev, from where he never returned.) Anti-aircraft guns roared but we went on reading. The novel was about Spain, about war; and when we finished we smiled without speaking.

It is a very tragic story but it expresses faith in man, it is about doomed and noble love, the heroism of a guerrilla detachment in enemy territory to which Robert Jordan, an American volunteer, belongs. The last pages of the book are an affirmation of life, courage, sacrifice. Robert Jordan lies on the road with a shattered leg; he has sent his comrades away. He is alone. He has an automatic rifle. He could shoot himself but, dying, he wants to kill as many Fascists as possible. Hemingway used interior monologue in this passage; here is a short fragment:

'We were going awfully good when that thing hit us, he thought. But it was only luck it didn't come while I was under the bridge . . . But later on we will have these things much better organized. We ought to have portable short-wave transmitters. *Yes, there's a lot of things we ought to have.* I ought to carry a spare leg, too . . .

'Listen, I may have to do that because if I pass out or anything like that I am no good at all and if they bring me to they will ask me a lot of questions and do things and all and that is no good . . .

'You're not so good at this, Jordan, he said. Not so good at this. And who is so good at this? I don't know and I don't really care right now. But you are not. That's right. You're not at all. Oh not at all, at all. I think it would be all right to do it now? Don't you?

'*No, it isn't.* Because there is something you can do yet. As long as you know what it is you have to do it. As long as you remember what it is you have to wait for that. *Come on, Let them come!*

'Think about them being away, he said. Think about them going through the wood. Think about them crossing a creek. Think about them riding through the heather. Think about them going up the slope. Think about them O.K. tonight . . .

'I can't wait any longer now, he said. If I wait any longer I'll pass out . . .

'*And if you wait and hold them up even for a little while or just get the officer that may make all the difference. One thing well done can make—*

'All right, he said. And he lay very quietly and tried to hold on to himself that he felt slipping away from himself as you feel snow starting to slip sometimes on a mountain slope, and he said, now quietly, then let me last until they come.

'Robert Jordan's luck held very good because he saw, just then, the cavalry ride out of the timber and cross the road.'

Hemingway took the title of his novel from the *Devotions* of the seventeenth-century poet John Donne, and used these lines for an epigraph:

'No man is an *Iland*, intire of it selfe; every man is a peece of the *Continent*, a part of the *maine*; if a *Clod* bee washed away by the *Sea*, *Europe* is the lesse, as well as if a *Promontorie* were, as well as if a *Mannor* of thy *friends* or of *thine owne* were; any mans death diminishes *me*, because I am involved in *Mankinde*; And therefore never send to know for whom the *bell* tolls; It tolls for *thee*.'

These lines could stand as an epigraph to everything Hemingway

389

ever wrote. The times changed, and so did he, but his feeling that the fate of one man is bound up with that of all others, which we bookishly call humanism, remained unchanged.

After Hemingway's death I came across an article in an American paper in which the writer said that the Civil War in Spain had meant no more to Hemingway than a chance episode sandwiched between a bullfight and a rhinoceros hunt. This is absolutely untrue. It was no chance thing that Hemingway stayed in besieged Madrid, no chance thing that, during the Second World War, when he was a war correspondent, Hemingway joined the French partisans instead of hanging about HQs, no chance thing that he welcomed Fidel Castro's victory. He charted his own course.

In August 1942, when things were very bad, I wrote: 'I would like to meet Hemingway after a great, all-European Guadalajara defeat of Fascism. We must defend life – this is the mission of our unlucky generation. And if I, and many of us, do not have the chance to see the triumph of life with our own eyes, we shall still remember at our last hour the American with a shattered leg on the Castilian road, the small machine-gun and the great heart'.

For Whom the Bell Tolls was much decried. *The Old Man and the Sea* was one thing; youth and a war for human dignity another. The novel was criticized by various people in various ways: some were repelled by Hemingway's justification of war, some did not like the description of particular episodes in the war, others objected to the passages about André Marty. (It is enough for a writer to say something fifty years, or even a single day, before it becomes common knowledge for everybody to come down on him like a ton of bricks. But if authors stuck to describing the self-evident they would be nothing better than parasites.)

When I was in the USA in the spring of 1946 I received a long letter from Hemingway; he asked me to visit him in Cuba. He recalled Spain in heartfelt terms. I was unable to go to Cuba. Shortly before his death he sent me greetings and expressed his hope that we should meet again soon. I shared his hope.

And then a brief announcement in the press. How often had Hemingway's death been announced: in 1944 and again ten years later when the plane in which he was travelling crashed over Uganda. Each time a denial had followed, but this time there was none. I do not know how it happened. Hemingway never told me that his father, a doctor, had committed suicide; I heard it from common friends. The hero of *For Whom the Bell Tolls* thinks at the last moment: 'I don't want to do that business that my father did. I will do it all right but I'd much prefer not to have to. I'm against that. Don't think about that'. Did Hemingway solve the question differently from Robert Jordan, or was it one of those stupid things that happen which he so often described? Either way, death suddenly erupted into his life and it is no more than the truth to say that he died as he had lived.

And I, looking back over the course of my life, see that of all the writers I was lucky enough to meet, two helped me not only to free myself from sentimentality, from lengthy ratiocinations and short perspectives, but also to breathe, to work, to hold out – and these two were Babel and Hemingway. At my age a man can admit it.

22

THE DUTIES of a war correspondent and perhaps my own restlessness kept me constantly on the move. One of the drivers, the young Augusto, to keep himself from falling asleep at the steering-wheel as we drove at night, used to ask: 'I say, what are the roads like in China?' I would tell him that I had never been to China, at which he would give a sceptical grin: 'I don't believe it. Why, you can't spend two nights together in the same room'.

I have looked through an old file of *Izvestia* for April 1937. On the 7th I was near Morata de Tajuña where they were fighting for the 'seventh road'; on the 9th I described the attack at Casa del Campo; on the 11th I wrote about the bombing of Sagunto; on the 17th I sent off the news about the latest offensive from near Teruel; on the 26th I was wandering about the town of Pozoblanco on the Southern front.

I also had other things to do besides newspaper work. I was told by the Propaganda Secretariat that Franco had mobilized young peasants; that it ought to be made clear to them why the Republicans were fighting the Fascists, but that the soldiers were afraid of picking up our leaflets.

The Spaniards do not smoke ready-made cigarettes, they prefer to roll their own. In Republican Spain there was no tobacco. The Fascists had tobacco but no cigarette papers which were made in the Levante; it was sold in the form of small booklets. I suggested printing all that we wanted to say on every tenth leaf and throwing the booklets, with the usual respectable firm's trademark, into the enemy trenches. It proved a rather complicated affair: I had to go to the factory myself and persuade the people to carry out the order.

Later I met men who had come over with a 'pass' – a leaflet on cigarette-paper. Everybody wanted to smoke and, though the Fascists officers gave out that the paper was poisoned, the 'booklets' were picked up gladly enough.

One day in Valencia, in the Hotel Victoria where I usually stayed, I was accosted by a Swiss, a representative of the Red Cross. He said that there were captured Soviet airmen in the Fascist prisons. The

Falangists agreed to exchange them for captured German officers. He handed me a list. I saw at once that none of the airmen had given his real name – the surnames were invented for Spain (for some reason they chose patronymics: Ivanovich, Mikhailovich, Petrovich, etc., which made them sound Serbian). I turned over the list to Stern.

A year later I was standing with a member of the Soviet embassy on the bridge which joins the French frontier-town of Hendaye to Spanish Irún. The airmen were in a terrible state – worn out, starved, in rags. The first thing we did was to feed them. This was in the evening; the shops had long been shut, but the airmen had to be fitted out. Comrades took me to the owner of a ready-made tailor's shop who had the reputation of being a 'sympathizer' and explained the position to him; an hour later the airmen could have been taken for foreign tourists returning from a holiday. They spoke with great restraint about their experiences; it was only when they got into the wagon-lit and saw the bunks with their gleaming sheets that one of them broke down; there were tears in his eyes. General Zakharov, whom I used to meet in Spain and, later, on the Byelorussian front (he commanded the air force unit which included the French 'Normandie-Niemen' squadron), told me recently that some of those airmen were still living and he knew their whereabouts. It gave me extreme pleasure to think that by chance I had had a hand in their destiny.

I am not keeping to a chronological sequence: in my memory there is a jumble of towns and dates; besides, I am not trying to write the history of the Spanish war; I am speaking only of my personal experiences and how I saw Spain in the spring of 1937.

Different towns lived in different ways. Madrid was the front line. Valencia had unexpectedly become the capital, artificial and unreal, while Barcelona remained Barcelona: a large city with its bourgeoisie, with its anarchists, its tradition of barricades and treachery, its hundreds of bars on the crowded Paralelo, lighthearted and at the same time tragic. Ration-cards and queues appeared, but the spirit did not change.

In February I made a trip to Paris and returned to Barcelona with O. G. Savich. (He wanted to write some articles for *Komsomolskaya Pravda* but soon began to work for TASS and accompanied me to Madrid – Guelfand had fallen ill and had been recalled to Moscow.) On the very first evening as we were sitting in a Barcelona restaurant peacefully discussing Spanish poetry there was a terrific crash. The lights went out. It did not sound like an air-raid and we did not realize at first what had happened. It appeared that a Fascist cruiser was shelling the city. On the Paralelo an Anarchist was firing his revolver in the direction of the sea – he thought he could sink the enemy ship.

This should have put the Barcelona people on their guard, changed their ways. But they buried the dead, cleaned up the streets, and life went on as before. A War Week was organized: the theatres were told to put on war plays, the radio broadcast anti-Fascist speeches, the streets were plastered with posters: 'Everyone to the front!' This was perhaps the most convincing sign of Barcelona's frivolity: this, the thirty-fifth week of fierce fighting and bombing, was declared a War Week. The Week ended and the theatres went back to light comedy, while in the shop-windows, pamphlets published by the Propaganda Secretariat were replaced by the usual novels, theoretical Anarchist handbooks and *erotica*.

Far more dangerous than frivolity, however, were the internal dissensions. I was a long way from Catalonia, on the Southern front, when street fighting broke out in Barcelona between the Anarchists and the Assault Guard. To pretend that what happened was merely a provocation would be just as foolish as to attribute the pre-revolutionary Socialist-Revolutionaries' passion for terrorism to Azef's directives. To the Anarchists the State was an unmitigated evil, and although Largo Caballero's government included members of the CNT, the militiamen of Barcelona and Aragon continued to 'deepen the revolution'. When I saw Barcelona again at the beginning of June I realized that there was neither genuine unity nor mutual trust. Franco was far away, and the various parties eyed one another with suspicion and even hostility. The Catalan bourgeoisie, which had begun by supporting Companys, was frightened by the Anarchists and by the strengthening of the central government's power. The workers who were under the influence of the CNT-FAI thought that the Communists, by rallying to Prieto, 'had betrayed the revolution'.

True, here and there on the Aragon front the former columns, having become divisions, had pulled themselves together. In Barcelona there were workers who realized that the first task was to defeat Franco. I remember a meeting at the General Motors factory: the men decided to work ten hours a day to provide the army with more lorries; one old syndicalist shouted: 'Ten's not enough, it ought to be sixteen'. But what one heard more frequently was fierce argument. People were

394

ambushed and killed. Barcelona, outwardly lighthearted and gay, was burning with fever.

The government established itself in Valencia, and the town was filled with civil servants, diplomats, journalists: refugees from Madrid and other towns captured by the Fascists. In the Parque del Castelar hung a faded poster: '100 miles from here to the front'.

It was less than three miles from Madrid to the front, but even in Madrid young people danced, the law courts were busy with divorce suits, the waiters' trade union negotiated new wage rates, and children begged International Brigaders for foreign stamps. As for Valencia, according to the Spaniards' notions, it was in the far rear. Were it not for the frequent air-raid alarms and occasional bombings, and also the waves of refugees, one could almost have forgotten how near the war was.

The boulevards were planted with orange-trees, the fruit lay scattered on the ground. There were queues for meat and milk; there were too many oranges: they rotted in the docks at which foreign ships seldom called. The cafés were crowded; the clients speculated about where the offensive would open – at Madrid, at Cordoba or on the Aragon front. There was talk about other battles too: political storms did not die down. Largo Caballero resigned and inveighed against Prieto. I remember how everybody in Valencia was spreading the latest piece of news: Largo Caballero wanted to speak in Alicante but motor-cyclists barred his way. The chairman of the Aragon committee, the uncompromising Anarchist Ascaso, refused to recognize the Negrín government. Azaña was distressed and said nothing. Companys talked but was also distressed. Every day commanders from the various fronts arrived in Valencia demanding arms.

In one of the Latin American embassies to which foreign journalists had been invited, I saw Fascists who had been brought out of Madrid. One lady kept saying: 'It's so terrible, so terrible!'

In the Hotel Victoria where I stayed, foreign journalists drank cocktails, played poker in the evening and complained of boredom.

Meetings were occasionally held in the square. Sometimes a spy would be discovered at the Victoria. The heat was unbearable, a humid heat that rose from the surrounding rice-fields.

During the winter I often met André Malraux in Valencia: his squadron was stationed close to the city. He is a man who is always in the grip of a single absorbing passion. I knew him during the period of his infatuation with the East, then with Dostoyevsky and Faulkner, then with the brotherhood of the workers and the revolution. In Valencia he thought and spoke only about the bombing of Fascist positions and when I started to say something about literature, he twitched and fell silent. The French volunteers had wretched obsolete aircraft but, until the Republicans received Russian machines, the squadron organized by Malraux was a great help. One day he told me of an incident which he later described in his novel *L'Espoir* (*Days of Hope*) and used as the central plot of a film made in Spain. A peasant comes from the Fascist zone and says he is willing to indicate where the Fascist airfield is. The Frenchmen take him up with them but he cannot recognize the topography from that height. The pilot has to fly at a low altitude. Bombs are released over the airfield but the plane comes under fire and the mechanic is gravely wounded. In Valencia this did not present itself as a literary subject for Malraux but as an incident in a campaign he was fighting.

The Soviet embassy was housed in the Hotel Métropole: some of the military lived there too. In the neighbouring houses the local inhabitants kept chickens on their balconies. Major Hajji went to bed late, and the cocks invariably woke him at dawn. He complained: 'It's disgusting. If I weren't a Soviet man I'd shoot all those cocks'.

At the end of May I was again in Paris, and while there had a telephone call from Savich who said that he had been summoned from Madrid to Valencia temporarily to replace Mirova who had suddenly gone to Moscow. 'Ask Irina to find out where Mirova is.' I telephoned to Irina about Mirova; she said that the weather in Moscow was lovely, real spring weather. 'And where is Mirova?' Irina did not reply.

When I got to Valencia I went to see Savich at the Métropole. He was sitting miserably in the midst of women's clothing that hung and lay about the room. 'What's happened to Mirova? I'm alone now, TASS says that I've got to stay in Valencia – the government's here.' I knew that Mirova, a large, good-natured woman, was the wife of a responsible party worker. Yes, I knew Mirova, but about 1937 I knew nothing. Moscow was a long way off.

I went to Albacete again. Before the war it had been a small provincial town trading in saffron and knives; it had no sights worth seeing and tourists did not stop there. International Brigades were being formed in Albacete. The town had been badly bombed by the Fascist air-force and was like the ruined suburbs of Madrid. I can still remem-

396

ber the museum in which a crucifixion had a fresh wound from a bomb splinter, and among the shattered remains of a café a scrap of an old poster – 'Dancing today at the Capitol'.

I met André Marty, who was imperious, very short-tempered and always suspecting everyone of treason. We talked for some two hours and this conversation left me with a sense of bitterness: he spoke (and occasionally acted) like a mentally sick man.

I found solace in the evening with the men of the International Brigade. Here were Spaniards, Frenchmen, Germans, Italians, Poles, Serbs, Britons, Negroes, Russian émigrés. They sang the *Jeune Garde*, as in the suburbs of Paris, the traditional *Bandiera Rossa* of the Italians, the mournful Madrid song about the French bridge and the four generals, our own *Partisan* song about the Volochayev days, and Bulgarian songs with comprehensible words but unfamiliar Eastern melodies, like a whirlpool of sounds. The men recalled distant cities, joked and kept up each other's spirits.

Many years later, at the first World Peace Congress, when the delegates sang, waving brightly coloured handkerchiefs and clapping wildly, I was reminded of Spain: I had seen their fathers and elder brothers in Albacete, many of whom had died at Madrid, at Huesca, by the Jarama.

It seems hardly believable that in the thirties of our century such a great and unique wave of brotherhood and self-sacrifice could rise from the depths of the people. Allegiances were pledged in those days not with signatures, not in words, but in blood. One could write a wonderful book about every one of those men. But the books were never written: the Second World War came and streams of blood washed away the drops of blood on the stones of Castile and Aragon.

At the end of April I went to Andalusia where they were fighting for the possession of a territory known as the 'Estremadura wedge'. There are hundreds of miles between Motril and Don Benito. One could say with equal justice that there was no front and that the front was everywhere.

Around Granada the hilltops were occupied by Republicans or by Fascists, and between them, in the valleys, the peasants, as accustomed to gunfire as to thunderstorms, grazed their sheep. At times the roads were not even guarded. I saw an Anarchist militiaman who had captured two Fascist officers – they had driven up in their car not knowing

397

where the enemy was (and this in Adamuz near Cordoba, which was on the most active sector of the Southern front).

The Fascists were trying to break through to Almadén: the mercury mines tempted them. Despite the bombing and the hunger the miners went on working. The 'Blue Arrows' division under Italian command was sent to reinforce the Fascists and they moved up close to Pozoblanco. This little town was mercilessly bombed and battered by gunfire. The forces were too unequal. But the Republicans held out at Pozoblanco. Their commander was a professional soldier, Colonel Pérez Sales, a man of old-fashioned courtesy, with bristling grey hair. It is hard to guess what people are from their appearance; looking at him I thought: if I were travelling in a train and a man like this sat facing me, would I have dreamt that he was capable of such things? Pérez Sales said to me: 'I am neither a Communist nor an Anarchist, I'm just a quite ordinary Spaniard, you know. But what could I do? To shoot myself would have been dishonour. From that trench over there we kept returning their fire. Two machine-guns . . . And they had nine batteries. Please don't think I'm boasting. I'm just saying that we had no other way out. I don't understand much about politics, but I'm a Spaniard, I love liberty.'

The unit known as the Stalin Battalion came to the rescue of the defenders of Pozoblanco; it was composed of Andalusians, mainly lead-miners from Linares. Their commander was a sturdy jovial southerner called Gabriel Godoy. He told me that he had worked in the mines since childhood; he looked like a good-natured bear and confided to me that he wrote poetry.

There was little discipline in Andalusia but still a great store of enthusiasm. In Jaén they made me tell them about Mayakovsky; a bombing raid started, but not a man moved, they all went on listening avidly.

Jaén was very badly bombed; I witnessed a scene there that has remained an agonizing memory even after the sights of the last war and everything we have seen since. A bomb splinter tore off the head of a little girl. The mother went mad – she would not give up the child's body and crawled about looking for the head and screaming: 'It's not true! She's alive!'

In a street in Jaén I stood watching an old potter who was making jugs. All around were demolished houses, but he unhurriedly kneaded his clay.

In Pozoblanco a bomb ripped off the roof of a textile factory. The looms were unharmed, and in that half-deserted bomb-torn town, without a roof, without bread, the workers resumed their work: they were making blankets for the soldiers. I stood watching them and thought: when all's said and done, they must win! It was contrary to logic, contrary to commonsense: Franco's army was gaining strength all the time, but one's mind refused to admit that such courage, such spiritual generosity could go for nothing.

I was on my way back from Pozoblanco to Valencia; it was a long journey, there was time to think. The driver, a cheerful Andalusian, sang mournful flamencos. For some reason I remembered the village of Buñol in the Levante; 7,000 people lived there. This village gave hospitality to 3,000 refugees – from Madrid, from Malaga, from Estremadura. In every house I saw children who did not belong to the family. In one house they made me stay and set a soup-tureen on the table. 'How many are you?' I asked my hostess. 'Six, and now three more from Madrid.' 'And you manage?' She smiled: 'We manage. And if there's not enough, we'll do without; our guests shan't suffer'.

That was something I also thought about: generosity. Nowhere did I notice any meanness, any desire to hang on to one's property or, still worse, to get rich at the expense of someone else's misfortune. They fed me; that was all right, I was a Russian. They fed Augusto – he was from Madrid. But they also fed Pepe, and Conchita, and Fernando, without asking where they came from, they just said: 'In these times . . .'

Colonel Pérez Sales had said he was fighting for liberty. I never succeeded in finding out from him exactly what kind of liberty he had in mind, it was probably the most important kind – freedom to live worthily and to die worthily. The Anarchist Pepe, the one who had crawled to the Fascist trenches and scattered the cigarette papers with the appeals, told me he was fighting for a new world. Everybody ought to work: 'Your countryman Bakunin argues correctly: to the devil with the angels, the Ministers, the generals, the policemen. Things will be better without them'. The driver was a Communist; he told me that José Diaz was the best of the lot; once the Fascists were beaten, the people would settle down to study; he himself wanted to learn how to write plays that would make everybody – including old Pérez Sales himself – laugh and cry.

It was the short southern spring; the grass was green in the valleys, the scarlet poppies glowed. At times the hills closed in on the road, at others a distant view opened out: a small house, a few green oaks, a stream. We were crossing La Mancha. Here probably, at this roadside inn, the Knight of the Sorrowful Countenance had spent a night.

I thought about that book which I have loved since childhood. *Don Quixote* has been translated into every language, it arouses people's emotions thousands of miles distant from La Mancha; but only a Spaniard could have written this book with its wonderful blend of pathos and satire, of nobility and humiliation, its sharp moral as of a fable and its moving poetry; and it is an idiotic fallacy to say that stout Sancho Panza is presented as a contrast to Don Quixote; no trials separate them. I thought about this because I had more than once seen Don Quixote and Sancho Panza face death side by side.

'Freedom, Sancho, is one of the most precious gifts that the heavens have bestowed on men; with it the treasures locked in the earth or hidden in the depths of the sea are not to be compared; for the sake of freedom, as for the sake of honour, one may and should risk one's life, and captivity, on the other hand, is the greatest evil that can befall a human being.' I recalled these words too. There was no need to ask the old colonel what kind of liberty he had in mind: he had said he was a Spaniard – the Don Quixote of Pozoblanco, the Don Quixote of the year 1937.

23

I often visited Sariñena in the days when I travelled with the mobile cinema. Now a group of our advisers was stationed there. At a table sat a short, thickset man, with a very morose expression; before him lay a map and a copy of *Pravda*. I said I had to inform *Izvestia* about the course of the fighting at Huesca. He poured me out some cold tea from a jug. 'I don't think there's ever been such heat.' He pointed to the village of Chimillas on the map. 'The idea is to cut the road to Jaca. Is that clear?' He was silent for a moment and then said, speaking rapidly: 'Have you heard the news? Tukhachevsky, Yakir, Uborevich are to be shot. Enemies of the people . . .' He threw his half-smoked cigarette on the floor, immediately lit another and, bending low over the map, began to whistle a lively tune. His face grew yet more sombre. He pored over the map for a long time and seemed to have forgotten I was there. Half an hour later, he glanced at me and said moodily: 'For *Izvestia*, you say? And where's Koltsov? . . . The road to Jaca, here's the Dombrowski Brigade with Gerassi in command, here's the Garibaldi – Pacciardi . . . Lukács will tell you all about it. I think he's still in Caspe. Drink some more – it'll be worse in the car'.

It was indeed a scorching day. The stone outcrops everywhere were ablaze with heat: not a tree, not a blade of grass – brown-red stony desert. I foolishly stuck my bare hand out of the window; the car was going fast and I felt that at least my hand would catch a little breeze. Lukács was not to be found in Caspe; I was told he was far away, in Igries. My hand had swollen up and I felt feverish. Igries with its small clay houses on the bare hillside reminded me of a red-hot Caucasian mountain village. There for the last time I saw General Lukács, or to give him his right name, Máté Zalka. I am sorry that I have no clear memory of this meeting: I was not quite myself, perhaps owing to the burn, perhaps to the conversation in Sariñena. Zalka was tired, he said he had migraine; he scolded me: 'You should take care of your hand; after all, you're a writer'. Only when we were parting he suddenly smiled: 'I say, wouldn't you like to be in the country at home? Just for a day'.

The next day I drove from Barbastro to Igries; there they told me that Lukács's HQ was in the village of Apies. We were driving along a winding road, I asked several times whether we were going in the right direction; suddenly a soldier, completely distraught, shouted: 'On the lower road . . . A shell . . . the general . . .' We turned back and drove for a long time. A stone house: this was the hospital. At first they would not let me in; then a doctor came. 'Lukács's condition is hopeless. Regler has had a blood transfusion, his life's not in danger but the wound is serious. The driver's got a head wound, he was sitting beside the general. Your countryman's got off lightly – a wound in the leg; they've just picked him up.'

I informed *Izvestia* that Zalka had been killed, Regler wounded. The next day, when I telephoned to the editor's office I asked whether the information about Regler had been published: I knew that his wife was in Moscow and feared she might hear of the report published in Madrid saying that Regler was dead. I was told that *Pravda* had printed this news. 'We can't contradict *Pravda*.' I immediately telephoned to Koltsov who was in Valencia. He grunted: 'The idiots! All right, I'll get on to them right away. Give Regler my best wishes. It's terrible about Máté'.

The next day the offensive opened. I telephoned twice a day: Chimillas, San Ramon, Heinkels, Fiats, air battles, attacks, counterattacks.

The offensive was unsuccessful. The troops deployed round Huesca were doing nothing. The fighting was confined to the Jaca road. The tanks arrived late. The International Brigade sustained heavy losses. Five or six days later it was over.

At this moment I am thinking less of Huesca than of General Lukács. When I recall the people I knew, I generally begin by talking of the day when we first met or of the moment when a casual acquaintance turned into a friend, of when, in short, they became part of my life; but what I have to say about Zalka has begun with his death: it affected me deeply.

I only got to know him shortly before he died; all my memories of him belong to the period March-April 1937. Brihuega, various HQs, then two villages where the 12th Brigade was resting (under bombing) – Fuentes and Meco – again the HQ at Morata de Tajuña, Madrid and the burnt-out village of Igries.

In the Soviet Union I had seen Máté Zalka two or three times; but

402

we only nodded to one another, we had no friends in common. I did not know Máté Zalka – I met and grew fond of General Lukács, the Hungarian who was defending the Spanish people, the writer who had exchanged his desk for the battlefield.

Of course when I talked to Lukács I saw Máté Zalka. Although he had seen a good deal of fighting in his life he had not become a soldier; his attitude to people was dictated by the fellow-feeling, the understanding of a writer who is far more familiar with the web of the emotions than with the squares of a map.

I have re-read his *Doberdo*; Zalka's genuine talent is evident, but his life was so shaped that to the end he felt himself an unsure tyro in literature. He was not yet eighteen when he published a little volume of short stories. But his father planned a different career for him: he sent him into the army before he was due to be called up. The young Máté went first to a military academy and then to the front. In 1916 he was a prisoner of war and was sent to a distant camp in Khabarovsk. After the October Revolution he formed a detachment of ex-prisoners of war and fought for the Soviet government in the Far East, then in the Ural, then in the Ukraine. He took part in the liberation of Kiev in 1920 and in the storming of Perekop. The war ended but Zalka continued to live a stormy life; he served in Food Detachments, wrote propaganda stories, became Furmanov's friend; he attended meetings of the RAPP group. Only in the thirties did he begin to think seriously about his writing and completed the novel *Doberdo*, a few weeks before leaving for Spain. Zalka was a born writer. Wars were imposed by the epoch, and his place amongst fighters was dictated by his conscience.

After the Guadalajara victory and before the operation at Morata de Tajuña (it was called a 'fighting reconnaissance' and cost many lives) Máté Zalka said to me in the village of Fuentes: 'If I don't get killed, I'll write about it in some five years' time. *Doberdo* was still only trying to find proofs. But now there's no need to try – every stone is a proof. It's enough to show how man reacts to war. And not force one's voice. I hate shouting'.

When Zalka died he was forty-one. A short time before his death, on his birthday, he wrote: 'I have been thinking about destiny, about the vicissitudes of life, about past years and I am dissatisfied with myself. I have done too little. Too few successes. Too little achieved'. Tolerant towards others, he was exigent with himself. And as a writer he found that the vicissitudes of life often intruded.

Valencia accorded a solemn burial to the famous General Lukács; only a few comrades-in-arms knew that they were saying farewell to Máté Zalka, the writer who had not written the great book he dreamt of.

Good-humoured and sociable, he loved quiet; yet almost all his life he heard gunfire and slept, as he said, 'with his ear to the ground', but he could hear the beating of the human heart; he lived loudly, but he spoke softly.

His insight as a writer may have helped him to understand soldiers. He was loved by all, although the men he commanded not only had no common tongue but sometimes no ideas in common. In the units under his command there were Polish miners, Italian émigrés – Communists, Socialists, Republicans, workers from the red suburbs of Paris and French anti-Fascists of all shades of opinion, Vilna Jews, Spaniards, veterans of the First World War and callow youths.

I visited the 12th Brigade with Hemingway, with Savich, and alone. For some reason we all enjoyed being with Lukács and his comrades-in-arms. The military adviser to the brigade was the intelligent and genial Fritz (whom I have already mentioned). Lukács's immediate aides were two Bulgarians: the tempestuous, irrepressible Petrov (Kozovsky) and his chief of staff, the quiet, modest Belov (Lukanov). I remember how in Fuentes they got hold of a kid and Petrov roasted it on dry vine-shoots; it was a real feast. The Spanish painter, my old friend Gerassi, was at first attached to Zalka's HQ and then commanded a battalion. I visited Meco with Stefa who used to go there to see her husband. Zalka's ADC, Alyosha Eisner, I also knew from Paris days. He had left Russia when still a small boy; in Paris he wrote poetry and made passionate Communist speeches at all the street-corners. In Spain he rode a horse, idolized General Lukács, engaged in literary conversations and gazed admiringly at Hemingway. He came to Moscow at a difficult time and had personal experience of what the 'cult of personality' meant. Cut off from the world, he survived spiritually better than most and when, in 1955, I met him again, he was the same lively enthusiast I had always known. Regler was the Brigade Commissar; he also enjoyed talking about literature and was always making notes in an exercise book. Zalka used to say jocularly: 'There's no doubt that he's going to write a novel, and a long one, too'. Among the commanders of the battalion I remember Janek, the French Socialist Bernard, the brave and charming Pacciardi. The Hun-

rian Nieburg limped slightly and always used a walking-stick. He
ent like that into the attack on the day following Lukács's death, and
as killed.

Regler, on regaining consciousness after being wounded, said: 'Go
o Lukács, you must save Lukács'. (They did not tell him that the
eneral had been killed.) And two days later I met one of the soldiers,
 diminutive Jew, the son of a Galician Chassid, who jumbled all the
anguages of Europe and had been wounded four times at Madrid,
who sobbed: 'That was a man!'

In Morata de Tajuña Lukács was pessimistic; he said: 'This is the
panish Doberdo'. The object was to try to draw the enemy, occupy
trongly fortified positions and evacuate them on the following day.
Lukács was nervous before the Huesca offensive opened: he realized
hat the International Brigade would bear the brunt of the battle. He
lid all he could to spare his men but never himself, and he died because
n his haste to reach HQ he had taken a road that was under fire and
which he had forbidden others to use.

As we were driving back from Fuentes to Madrid, Hemingway said
to me: 'I don't know what kind of writer he is but when I listen to
nim and look at him, it makes me feel good. A fine guy'.

Lukács had a happy disposition and could make everybody laugh –
fighters, peasants, journalists. He had a special trick of his own:
clicking out arias on his teeth; he sang and knew an extraordinary
number of songs. Once when I was present he started dancing with
some Spanish peasant women; he danced with dashing abandon and
on rejoining us said: 'You see, I can still dance. Don't forget I'm a
Hungarian hussar'.

He loved Hungary. He once said to me: 'A pity that you've never
seen the Pusta. I often think of it here. Hungary is very, very green'.

People called him Matvey Mikhailovich; he had spent many years
in the Soviet Union where he had left his wife and daughter whom he
called 'my home-base'; he loved our country, and would talk about
the wonderful summers in Poltava; he admired the Russian character
and yet remained a Hungarian through and through – it showed in his
slightly singsong pronunciation of Russian words, in his poetical
outlook, in the passionate nature which he carefully tried to conceal.

'War's a hateful thing,' he said to me more than once. There was
no affectation about him, no martial pose. On my return to Moscow I
read a letter he had written to his wife and daughter. He wrote candidly

as if making a confession: 'It is night now, dark and damp. My heart feels a certain chill. But there are such chilly moments in a war' . . . 'I got your and Talya's letter today. I go about feeling festive and happy. Everybody asks: "What's the matter with you all of a sudden? You seem a bit lit up". "Nothing's the matter," I say. I do not want to share my happiness with anyone. This is the kind of egoist I have become' . . . 'Today everything was extraordinarily quiet here. In the intervals when the men's voices fell silent, the singing of the birds in the spring bushes was almost unbearable'. It seems to me that these simple admissions reflect honesty and wisdom in equal measure.

I have said that the Spanish epic was the last wave; a certain epoch ended with it. I see Loti's room at Gaylord's. I had looked in on business. Loti kept me for dinner, there were lots of people; our military men – Grishin (Y. Berzin, one of those Latvians who during the first months of the Revolution had been Lenin's bodyguard), Grigorovich, Stern, the commander of the tank formation, the tall, powerfully built Pavlov, Máté Zalka, the attractive and intelligent Yugoslav Čopić, Janek. We were gay, we laughed, though I cannot remember the reason why. (Of all these men I was the only one to survive. Zalka was killed by an enemy shell. As for the others, they were destroyed for no reason at all by their own people.)

In Meco, while Fernando talked to Stefa, Zalka and I sat on the ground. The weather was already warm, everything around us was green. Zalka said: 'Fernando here has a small son, Tito, and my daughter who is called Talya is just about finishing school. It may sound silly, like something in the Art Theatre, but it's true – the sky will be studded with diamonds. Unless one believed this, it would be hard to live through a single day'. At the time there was a lot that Máté Zalka – like the rest of us – did not know. And today I think with sorrow, he was right: the 'diamonds' were no longer silly fancy, they *will* stud the sky, but it all takes much longer and is much more difficult than we imagined.

According to biblical tradition, Sodom and Gomorrah might have been saved had ten just men been found. This is true of all cities and all epochs. One such just man was Máté Zalka, General Lukács, dear Matvey Mikhailovich.

24

I KNEW that the planned offensive in the region of Brunete was a military secret, and did not mention it to anyone. A week before the battle began the driver Augusto said to me: 'Why are you going to Barcelona? You'll miss the show. My brother-in-law told me yesterday that we were going to strike at Brunete. But mind – it's a military secret'. It was always like that in Spain: journalists, telephone girls, quartermasters, drivers told their friends 'as a secret' that an operation was being planned. Suddenly someone would be court-martialled for spying. But the loose talk still went on.

I ought to have been glad: the Association of Anti-Fascist Writers, for whose organization I had laboured, was convening a congress in Madrid in accordance with the decision made before the war had broken out. This would give heart to the Spaniards. And it would impress everyone: for the first time writers would gather to agree on the defence of culture and this within a couple of miles of the Fascist trenches. But I must confess that I was annoyed: the forthcoming military operations interested me far more than the congress.

In spite of the unsuccessful battles at Huesca I was once again indulging in daydreams. The Aragon front with its many unreliable troops was far away. However you looked at it, the Anarchist columns, even if now they were called divisions, were not much use in modern warfare. So the military said, and I believed them. (As late as 1955 an author writing his memoirs claimed that the Huesca offensive failed because of General Lukács's death allegedly caused by the Anarchists and POUM men. I knew that Máté Zalka's death was not in any way the fault of the Anarchists and ascribed the failure of the offensive in part to the inefficiency in action of many army units.) In Madrid it was quite different: here there was discipline, there were Lister's 11th Division, the International Brigades, our tanks.

(When I look back now, I realize that the first six months of 1937 were decisive. After the March victory at Guadalajara not only we in Spain, but even military experts writing in English and French newspapers, thought that Franco's army was in peril. Our frontal attack in

Casa del Campo was unsuccessful. Italy and Germany went on supplying men and equipment. Internecine war broke out in Catalonia. Largo Caballero nursed plans for an offensive on the Southern front. The fighting for Peñarroya had given rise to great hopes, but the Fascists quickly reversed the situation. The military said that it was useless to rely on the Southern front: the army there was under strength and communications were poor. The government changed, the plan for an attack on Huesca was adopted. A month later the high command decided to pierce the enemy front in the region of Brunete. Each time the Republicans were successful in the first few days, but Franco swiftly moved up reserves; the German air force, far more numerous than ours, bombed the roads, and the offensive petered out.)

I was going to Barcelona to meet the delegation of Soviet writers, and was thinking about the coming battle for Brunete. Koltsov had said to me: 'You've got to concentrate on the Congress now, you're on the secretariat; in fact, you really started the whole thing. Personally, I shall have my hands full with the Soviet delegation'. I had agreed but, nevertheless, gave little thought to the congress.

I was not destined to reach Barcelona. Not far from Valencia, in a seaside resort, I caught sight of a number of delegates in a restaurant; they were eating fish-soup. V. P. Stavsky was wiping his face with his table-napkin and complaining: 'What heat! It's enough to kill you. And the fish-soup's nothing like ours, I can tell you'.

Judging from the papers of the time, the congress was a success. There were, of course, fewer big names than at the 1935 congress – not everyone was attracted by bombs and shells. Many writers answering the invitation had said that to discuss literary problems under such conditions was childishness, futile romanticism. The police of various countries also created obstacles: Franz Hellens, for instance, wanted to come but the Belgians would not give him a passport. Still, some well-known writers were present in Spain: Andersen Nexö, Alexey Tolstoy, Julien Benda, Antonio Machado, André Malraux, Ludwig Renn, André Chamson, Anna Seghers, Stephen Spender, Nicolás Guillén, Fadeyev, Bergamín and others.

Someone jocularly called the Congress 'a travelling circus'. We began in Valencia on 4th July, made speeches in Madrid, then again in Valencia, then in Barcelona, and a fortnight later ended up in Paris. The composition of the delegates changed: in Valencia Alvarez del Vayo took part (he had also attended the Paris congress in 1935 as an émigré), but being a Minister he could not accompany us elsewhere. Ludwig Renn was present only in Madrid: he was in command of a military unit and stayed at the front. In Paris we heard speeches by Heinrich Mann, Louis Aragon, Langston Hughes, Pablo Neruda. There was, I believe, an agenda, but no one gave it a thought. The character of the speeches changed according to circumstances.

In Madrid, under bombardment, the Congress was more like a political meeting, and the various delegates as they walked about the city, putting a good face on it but unaccustomed to being under fire, seemed like VIPs – a delegation of English MPs or American Quakers.

In Valencia, which was the seat of government, everything was formal: we were welcomed by the writer Manuel Azaña, who was also the President of the Spanish Republic; there was a banquet with toasts; there were moments when it seemed as if there was no war, and that we were at a PEN club function.

In Barcelona Companys sat on the platform, and Mikitenko spoke about the blossoming of national culture in a Socialist society.

In Paris we took the Théâtre de la Porte St Martin; a lot of people attended, there were shouts of 'Down with Non-Intervention!' But there was no longer any of the feeling that had inspired the 1935 congress. The Popular Front was going to pieces. Many left-wing intellectuals, although they shouted with the others 'Down with Non-Intervention!' as they listened to speeches about Madrid, about Guernica, privately thought: what a good thing, after all, that there's peace here. Munich was already in the offing.

There were many speeches. I remember one by José Bergamín, a very thin, big-nosed man with dark brooding eyes. I have the newspaper in which I quoted extracts from his speech: 'The word is fragile, the Spanish people call the dandelion, the flower whose life depends on a sigh, "the human word". The fragility of human words is beyond question. The word is not only the raw material with which we work, it is our link with the world. It is the affirmation of our solitude, and at the same time the denial of our isolation. Lopé de Vega has said: "Blood shouts the truth in soundless books". Blood shouts in our immortal *Don Quixote*. It is an eternal assertion of life against death. That is why the Spanish people, true to humanitarian principles, accepted this battle'. Now I understand why Bergamín's words moved me so deeply: he had given expression to what I had been vaguely thinking when I was crossing La Mancha.

There were also other good speeches; if I no longer remember them it is through no fault of the speakers. In my lifetime I have often protested against the saying of the ancient Romans: 'Amid arms the Muses are silent'. I did not and do not like the moral of this maxim as it is usually interpreted, namely, that while a storm is raging the poet should remain silent and wait till it has blown over. But now I ask myself whether the Romans did not give a different meaning to these words. They were rich in experience, they often waged wars; perhaps they had simply noticed that a poet's voice does not drown the din of battle, even though in those days there were no atom bombs and not even muskets. In the summer of 1937, in Madrid, the writers' speeches did not resound. What excited our admiration was something else. Fighters came bringing trophies: the colours of a Fascist regiment that had just been captured during the battles at Brunete. Regler came from hospital, limping with the aid of a stick; he could not speak standing up and asked permission to remain seated; the audience rose out of respect for the soldier's wound. Regler said: 'There are no problems of composition other than the problem of the struggle against the Fascists'. At that moment everyone felt this: the writers and the soldiers who had come to bring their greetings. A warm welcome was given to the writers who had taken part in the fighting: Ludwig Renn, Malraux, the young Spanish poet Aparición and others.

The speeches of many Soviet writers surprised and disturbed the Spaniards who said to me: 'We thought that twenty years after the Revolution your generals were with the people. But it appears that it's the same with you as it is with us'. I tried to reassure them, even though I myself was quite at sea. I think Agnes Barto, who spoke about Soviet children, was the only one who did not mention Tukhachevsky and Yakir; the others, raising their voices, kept on saying that some 'enemies of the people' had been liquidated, and that others would suffer the same fate. I tried to ask our delegates why they brought this up at a writers' congress, and above all in Madrid; I got no answer. Koltsov grunted: 'Serves you right. You shouldn't ask'.

The Fascists ridiculed the Congress in their broadcasts. During the night, however, they evinced some interest in it: they began shelling the centre of Madrid with all their guns. Most of the delegates took it calmly, but some who had come from quiet countries were frightened. Later on amusing stories circulated about them, but there is no denying that the bombardment was heavy, and at times one does get frightened in a war, especially when one is new to it.

The din was terrific, it was impossible to sleep. I had a long conversation with Julien Benda. He was then seventy but was very active; he spent the day walking about the city, visiting the forward positions and, when the bombardment started during the night, told me that he never slept much and he paid no attention to the explosions. About the Congress he said that he thought we had done right in convening it in Madrid: 'Just now the main thing is to show that the men who value culture are in the firing-line'. He criticized some of the speeches with a slight smile: 'Your friends attach too much importance to André Gide. He has never concealed his contempt for rationalism, he is consistently inconsistent. You believed in his value as a social entity, turned him into an apostle, and now you anathematize him. It's funny, especially here in Madrid. André Gide is a little bird that has built its nest on no-man's-land; one must fire, as the Fascists fire, at the enemy's batteries'.

The attack on Brunete began on 6th July. In the evening Vsevolod Vishnevsky took me aside: 'Let's go to Brunete. We'll take Stavsky along, he's asking to come. We're old soldiers. This is just what I came here for'.

Vishnevsky was an extremely passionate man; in a way he reminded one of a good Spanish Anarchist. When he began to speak he never knew where it would take him nor how it would end. He was a first-rate orator, and spoke better than he wrote; many Leningraders told me that during the blockade years his broadcasts were very heartening. At times he horrified our audiences of those years: people feared not only to say but even to listen to anything that was not authorized, but Vishnevsky, once he was warmed up, forgot the directives. On one occasion, at Tairov's, he got angry with me and drew his revolver, exactly like Durruti. He reviled the West, said that he was an ordinary seaman, a man of the people, but at the same time he admired Joyce and Picasso. He vehemently hated the Fascists and helped me at the time of the Soviet-German pact to publish in *Znamya* (The Banner) the first half of *The Fall of Paris*.

I went to see the Spaniards; they told me that the first day had gone well: Brunete had been occupied and at the moment fighting was going on for Villanueva de la Cañada. But the situation was fluid, Brunete was almost in a cul-de-sac, the Fascists might cut the road; in any case it would not be a good thing to take the Congress delegates there, they had better go to Jarama or have a look at Carabanchel.

On my return I told Vishnevsky: 'Nothing doing – they advise us against it'. He exploded: 'And I took you for a man with guts'. This made me angry; I said that I myself was going to Brunete, I had to inform my newspaper about what was happening there; I had a car; the Spaniards had asked me not to take any writers who had come to the Congress, but if he insisted he could please himself: we would set out next day at 5 a.m.

The heat was intolerable. I recall the nights in a blacked-out room with horror. I would be shut up for an hour, sometimes two, in an airless telephone booth dictating to the paper – 'I can't hear you, spell it out' – which delegates had spoken during the session and what villages had been occupied by the Republicans.

In the sun, the bodies of the dead tanned quickly, taking on a dark colour, and Stavsky thought that all the corpses were enemies – on this sector the Falangists had Moroccan battalions.

On our way to Brunete we met officers from the Edgar André Battalion whom I knew; they said the road was under heavy fire and that we had better not go any farther. I replied that we absolutely had to get to Brunete. 'Then don't dawdle,' they said, 'the Fascists are preparing to counter-attack.'

The Fascists had been driven out of Brunete at one blow and in the houses we saw laid tables, unfinished meals. In the Falange building leaflets, posters and Goebbels' speeches, translated into Spanish, lay scattered about. Vishnevsky picked up 'trophies' – Fascist badges, flags, documents with seals; he asked me to translate the inscriptions on the walls; in fact we dawdled. On our way to Villanueva Stavsky found a Fascist helmet, put it on his head and insisted on my photographing him with Vishnevsky.

We were on our way back. Near Villanueva the road was under heavy fire. Stavsky shouted: 'Down! Take it from me, as an old soldier'.

Vishnevsky crawled, crying ecstatically: 'Phew! That was pretty close! The devils are on the target'.

When we got back to Madrid they began describing to Fadeyev what a wonderful trip we had had. And I went off to dictate my report to the paper.

I was severely taken to task for this expedition. One of our officers

(I believe it was Maximov) shouted: 'Who gave you the right to endanger the lives of our writers? It's a disgrace!' I remarked with some embarrassment that I, too, was a writer. This did not appease him. 'That's a different matter. You and Koltsov go in the way of duty. But we have orders to keep the writers safe'. His tone changed abruptly: 'Well, what do you think of it? A wonderful job. They've occupied the cemetery of Quijorna. I was there till six o'clock; I'll sleep for three hours or so now and go back. I've got to talk to Grigorovich here . . . The bastards, I've just had a telephone call – they're bombing.'

The day before, I had written a speech for the Congress; I now decided not to speak and gave my paper to the editor of *Mundo Obrero*. There was nothing in my speech about André Gide, nor about our exterminating the 'enemies of the people'. A short time ago I was sent a copy of *Mundo Obrero* of 8th July 1937 containing my article called 'An Undelivered Speech'. Above it is printed the communiqué: 'The village of Quijorna is surrounded by our troops. The morale of our men is excellent. Some men who have come over to us say that the enemy is bringing up new units to contain our advance'.

There is one passage in my speech that seems to me to have been quite true: 'We have entered an epoch of action. Who knows whether the books we have been planning will ever be written? For years, if not for decades, culture's place will be on the battlefield. It can take cover in shelters where death will sooner or later overtake it. Or it can pass over to the counter-offensive'.

'Years' is not enough, 'decades' is exaggerated: we were destined, from the day on which I wrote these lines, to spend another eight years on the battlefield.

It is difficult for a writer to renounce 'fragile words', as Bergamín put it: literature sucks him in. Malraux had ceased to fight already in spring: there were no more planes. He started to write his novel about the Spanish war, *L'Espoir*. There was a lull on the fronts in Spain. Ludwig Renn was sent to the USA, Canada, Cuba to make public speeches about the Spanish war. Regler was doing the same thing in South America. Malraux was raising money in the States for the Spaniards. Koltsov returned to Moscow in the autumn and started on his book *Spanish Diary*.

When the Congress ended I went to a small village in the South of France. It was quiet there, at times too quiet. The tobacco fields were

413

green, the river Lot flowed lazily. I wrote a short novel about the Spanish war; it would be more correct to call it note on events and people.

One of the characters in the novel, the German émigré Walter, goes to Spain to fight the Fascists. From the train window he sees the sea. 'How pleasant it is here,' he thinks, 'stones, fishermen's nets, vineyards, quiet. What more does a man need? . . . Nonsense! He needs more, far more. Another tunnel . . . And here's the war.' I called the novel *What a Man Needs*. The thoughts are those of the hero and of the author in the interval between a life at peace and the war that has begun and will go on for a long time.

I was able to tear myself away from the life of a war correspondent for several months. But I could no longer get away from the war; there are field-glasses, field-posts, field-hospitals; my generation received the gift of long field-years.

25

THE BOMB fell close; shattered glass shivered from the windows and I heard a woman's desperate screams. The bomb had landed on a large café full of people. I was later told that there had been fifty-eight victims. The woman went on screaming. I do not know whether she was shell-shocked or whether someone belonging to her had been killed – she was incapable of speech. A quarter of an hour later firemen arrived, then ambulances. The wounded were taken away. The firemen spent a long time digging out dead bodies. I went into the hotel; I had wanted to send the news to my paper, but changed my mind: the editor had warned me that practically all the space would be taken up with the coming elections to the Supreme Soviet, and, besides, this was not pleasant news. Three days later I sent an article 'Barcelona Before the Fighting', and merely touched on the bombings; I wrote that the city was preparing to repel the Fascist attack. The article appeared on the day following the elections.

Of my old friends and acquaintances few remained in Spain. Many advisers had gone home. Antonov-Ovseyenko had also left. In a small house on the Tibidabo hill Savich pored over stacks of Spanish newspapers; Spanish journalists and those of our advisers who were left turned up there; when he had coffee, his secretary Gabrielle, small and fragile as though carved out of ivory, did the honours. Almost facing the house where Savich lived was our embassy. L. Y. Gaikis had long since been recalled to Moscow. The chargé d'affaires S. G. Marchenko replaced him.

I stayed as usual at the Majestic; some of our advisers were living there, as well as the German journalist Egon Erwin Kisch, Marthe Huysmans and Isabelle Blume. Sometimes in the middle of the night the porter would knock at our doors: 'Air-raid alarm! Go to the shelter'. I knew he would not leave us alone, so I dressed, went down into the lobby and stood about there, or else went out into the street. We did all that people do in such circumstances: shivered with cold, yawned, tried to kill time with conversation. Marthe liked to tease, to start arguments about anything: painting, strategy or the PSUC. Kisch asked me in a whisper whether it was true that Pilnyak had turned out to be a Japanese spy and complained that Tretyakov did not reply to letters; Isabelle offered chocolate, and I munched it gladly – there was very little to eat.

I was invited to a plenary meeting of writers devoted to Rustaveli, to be held in Tbilisi. It was tempting: I would see old friends like Tizian Tabidze and Paolo Yashvili; there would be a *tamada* (toastmaster), toasts, *shashlyks*. Besides, it was a long time since I had been to Moscow – two years. I had to know what was going on there. The bourgeois newspapers alleged that there had been many arrests, but that had been said before; they were probably exaggerating as usual. *Mundo Obrero* gave descriptions of the celebrations to mark the new constitution known as the 'Stalin Constitution'. I would see Irina, Lapin, Babel, Meyerhold, all my friends. I wanted a breathing-space, a change, and I rang up Lyuba in Paris saying I would come and pick her up on the 20th; we would go to Moscow for a fortnight.

It was then that Marchenko told me: 'A big attack is being mounted at Teruel'. (This time few people knew about the proposed offensive, and the Fascists were caught off their guard.)

What was I to do? I decided to remain near Teruel till the 18th – I would see the first days of the fighting. I went to Valencia. It was unusually quiet there: the government had moved to Barcelona a month before and the town pursued a peaceful provincial life, though a rather hungry one. I met some of my Spanish friends. It was warm; roses bloomed in the gardens. Along the coast the orange-trees bent under the golden load of their fruit.

The road led uphill. The gardens disappeared. A fierce wind blew from the mountains. We reached a height of 3,000 feet. It was foggy, snow driven by the wind lashed our faces.

Near Teruel it was cold, unbearably cold for the Spaniards; I believe the temperature dropped to twelve degrees of frost with a strong wind. The rocks were covered with sheets of ice, the men fell and crawled on all fours.

Exactly a year before – in December 1936 – I had been near Teruel; it had been cold then too; attempts had been made to take the town which formed a wedge thrusting into territory occupied by the Republicans, but it had come to nothing. There had been another attack in April, but at that time I had been in Madrid.

I noticed immediately that there was far more discipline now. The

416

divisions seemed better organized; even in the CNT division, under the command of the Anarchist Vivancos, there was none of the picturesque muddle of the now forgotten *centurias*.

On the eve of the attack forty Republican bombers raided the railway station, the Fascist positions, the road to Saragossa. This put heart into everyone and the offensive opened promisingly: on the very first day the Republicans advanced five and six miles at some points.

I was at the HQ of a Spanish Brigade. I shall never forget that day. Even in Spain, with its tragic quality and rich vein of fantasy, I had never witnessed such a scene. Around rose the red-brown mountains, and Teruel with its towers looked like a medieval castle; overhead hung leaden and violet clouds, torn by the wind. The fog had lifted, the light was very bright, the shadows deep. Another wave of bombers dived. It was like a combination of prehistoric nature and modern weapons. The soldiers crawled over the rocks and fell, mowed down by machine-gun fire, others crawled on. The wind kept gaining strength; in Brunete everybody had longed for shade, but here one longed, if only for a minute, to take shelter inside a house and find warmth. The village of San Blas was taken. The highway was reached; the enemy found himself surrounded: our forces swept the road with machine-gun fire.

I telephoned a description of the battle for Teruel and mentioned the success but, remembering Brihuega and Brunete, made the cautious reservation: 'In certain circumstances we could now begin to speculate about the fate of Teruel . . . But as things are it is not a matter of taking this or some other politically important centre, but of strategic aims. If the battles that have begun today have disrupted the enemy's plans for an offensive, it would be justifiable to call it a major victory'. I wanted to believe that Teruel would be taken, but I was afraid of misleading my readers.

On the second day I sought out Grigorovich. He had just returned from an observation post and was chilled to the bone. We ate hot soup out of earthenware bowls. Grigorovich said that on the next day they would occupy the town cemetery. And tomorrow I had to be on my way. It was disappointing: I would not see the outcome of the operation.

'Grigorovich, what do you think – will Teruel be taken?' He said that the southern units were lagging behind, but things were going well nevertheless; the town should fall within the next few days. Air reconnaissance had established, however, that Franco was transferring to Aragon the divisions that had become available after the liquidation of the Asturian resistance. 'It looks as though we'll take Teruel. But whether we'll be able to hold it, I can't say. We bring up a handful, and the Germans and Italians an armful . . . But what wonderful men!' Grigorovich's face broke into an affectionate smile. 'I'm a soldier, and for a soldier it's difficult here; I've had plenty of trouble, but the people are remarkable. I'll soon be leaving in all probability. But I'll never forget Spain. Koltsov told me they were honest, but though it's true, it's not important that there are very few crooks amongst them. Honour, I suppose, is an outdated notion, I mean as a word, isn't it? But here you go into a hut – you find a man who can't even read but "honour" means everything to him, like some knight of old. It hurts one to think about the Spaniards, it hurts damnably. But you will write about it all, not now, perhaps, but in another ten years or so. And when the time comes, write about our own men too; you know we did our best. All our people have come to love Spain, it explains a lot.'

He went to answer the telephone and swore; then he turned to me: 'That's what I don't like. Communications were properly established. Yet the gunners didn't know that the infantry had advanced beyond Concud and began to shell our own people. Fortunately their aim was lousy, but the impression it makes is pretty bad'.

I said I was leaving for Moscow the next day and would be back in a fortnight's time; I hoped to see him in the town. 'It's a good thing you're going. You'll see how things are at home. Till we meet again, then – soon, I hope.'

That night in Barcelona I said goodbye to Hemingway. 'But we'll be seeing each other again soon,' I said. 'You'll be here in January, won't you?' I never saw him again.

A copy of *Pravda* lay on Marchenko's table; I learnt that Grigorovich had been elected to the Supreme Soviet: 'Checheno-Ingush Autonomous Soviet Socialist Republic – Stern, Grigory Mikhailovich'. Marchenko said: 'I envy you, you'll see the New Year in at home. Well, come back soon, otherwise Savich'll be the only one left'. I gaily said: '*Au revoir!*' Even later we used to say those words, though the years were coming when not one of us knew on parting what awaited him. It would have been more honest to have said 'good-bye'.

I never saw Grigorovich or many of the other 'Mexicanos' and 'Gallegos' again.

We travelled through Austria, by-passing Germany. In Vienna we had to drive from one railway station to another. The city seemed to me quietly unconcerned. I could not know that within three months Nazi divisions would be marching through its streets.

At the station I bought a newspaper. 'The Republican army has occupied Teruel.' I sat in the dark compartment and before me rose red-brown Aragon, Augusto with his usual comment: 'So you're off somewhere again', young militiamen with raised fists, blood on the pavements of Barcelona, Grigorovich's uncertain smile – disconnected visions of a world left behind.

Here was the arch of Negoreloye. A handsome young frontier guard entered the compartment. I smiled at him. I had been friendly with a chap just like him in Alcalá de Henares. And I could not help saying: 'They've taken Teruel after all'. He returned my smile: 'It was in yesterday's paper . . . You can go on now to the customs shed'.

26

WE ARRIVED in Moscow on 24th December. Irina met us at the station. We were happy, we laughed; a taxi took us to Lavrushensky lane. In the lift my eyes fell on a hand-written notice: 'It is prohibited to put books down the lavatory. Anyone contravening this order will be traced and punished'. 'What does that mean?' I asked Irina. She replied with a sidelong glance at the lift-girl: 'I'm so glad you've come.'

Inside the flat Irina came up close to me and said in a low voice: 'Don't you know anything?'

Throughout half the night she and Lapin told us about all that had happened: an avalanche of names, and after each the single neologism: 'taken'.

'Mikitenko? But he's only just got back from Spain, he spoke at the Congress.' 'What of it?' Irina replied. 'There are people who made speeches, or had an article in *Pravda* only the day before.'

I was very agitated and at every name asked: 'But why him?' Lapin tried to think of explanations: Pilnyak had been to Japan, Tretyakov often met foreign writers, Pavel Vasilyev drank and talked too much, Bruno Jasenski was a Pole – all the Polish Communists had been arrested – Artyom Vesyoly had at one time been a member of the *Pereval* (The Pass) literary group, the wife of the painter Shukhayev was acquainted with Gogoberidze's nephew, Charents was too popular in Armenia, Natasha Stolyarova had just come from France. Irina answered my questions each time: 'How can I know? Nobody knows'. Lapin advised me with a rueful smile: 'Don't ask anyone. And if someone starts talking about it, just shut up'.

Irina was rather angry: 'Why did you ask me over the telephone about Mirova? Didn't you understand? They took her husband, then she got back here, and they arrested her too'. Lapin added: 'They often arrest the wives and put the children in homes'.

(I soon learnt that Mirova was not the only 'Spaniard' to have suffered. I found out about the fate of Antonov-Ovseyenko, his wife, Rosenberg, Gorev, Grishin, and many others.)

420

When I said that in Tbilisi we should be seeing Paolo and Tizian, Lapin was amazed: 'Don't you know that either? Tabidze has been arrested and Yashvili killed himself with a shotgun'.

The next day I went to *Izvestia*. I was well received but I could not see a single familiar face. I particularly missed Pavel Lapinsky to whom I had become greatly attached in the days of my youth – in Paris at the hotel Nice. Rayevsky was not there either. Contrary to Lapin's advice I asked the whereabouts of this or that person. Some said: 'Came a cropper', others just made a gesture of dismissal; there were also some who hastily moved away.

I dropped in on Koltsov at *Pravda* and found him sitting in a sumptuous office. On seeing me he grunted: 'Why are you here?' I said I wanted a rest and had come with Lyuba for the writers' meeting. Koltsov almost shouted: 'So Lyuba tagged along too?' I told him about Teruel, and said that before I left I had seen his wife Lisa and Maria Osten. He took me into the large bathroom adjoining the office and there let himself go: 'Here's the latest anecdote for you. Two Muscovites meet. One says: "Have you heard the news? They've taken Teruel". The other asks: "Oh, and what about his wife?" ' Koltsov smiled: 'Funny, isn't it?' 'No', I said. I was totally bewildered; I felt lost, no, that is not the word – crushed.

That same evening we left for Tbilisi. I took with me newspapers for the month of December. Matter-of-fact articles about labour, about successes achieved, were occasionally interspersed with praises of Yezhov, the 'Stalin People's Commissar'. There was his photograph: an ordinary face, rather likeable. I could not sleep and kept thinking, thinking, trying to understand what, according to Irina, no one could understand.

At the plenary meeting people spoke about Rustaveli's poetry. One speech was made by the Spanish writer Pla-y-Beltran whom I had known in Valencia; he got a warm welcome.

At the inaugural session Beria sat in the presidium. Some of the speakers praised him highly, and then everyone stood up and clapped. Beria clapped too and smiled complacently. I was prepared for the applause at every mention of Stalin's name and knew that if it came at the end of a speech everyone rose to their feet. But now I was taken by surprise – who was this Beria? I asked my neighbour in a low voice, and he replied shortly: 'A big man'.

That night Lyuba told me that Nina – Tabidze's wife – had sent a message asking us not to look her up; she did not want to compromise us.

I met many writers whom I knew well – Fedin, Tikhonov, Antokolsky, Leonidze, Vishnevsky. I also saw Isaakian; I tried to talk to him but never got a chance, and it was only once, after the war when he came to Moscow, that I had a heart-to-heart talk with him. There was the Icelandic writer Haldór Laxness. I had not read his books at the time and did not know how much I was to enjoy them. There were, as I had expected, banquets and toasts, but there is little need to say what mood I was in: I was still unable to get my bearings. We saw the New Year in at Leonidze's. We did our best to amuse our pleasant hospitable hosts, and they tried to entertain us, or rather to distract our thoughts. But it did not come off: we clinked glasses and drank in silence. I went back to Moscow with some of the writers. Jambul invited us into his compartment. He was travelling with a pupil of his who was also his interpreter. Jambul told us how forty years ago at a bey's wedding he had outdone all the other bards. Boiling water was brought in and tea was made. Jambul picked up his *dombra* and began to sing in a monotonous tone. His pupil (Jambul called him 'young', but he was close on sixty) explained that Jambul was composing verses. I asked him to translate and it appeared that the bard was simply expressing his pleasure in the tea-drinking. Then he went to the window and started to sing again; this time the interpreter recited lines that moved me: 'Here are the rails, they fly straight into a strange land, and so, too, flies my song'. His skin was like parchment but his eyes were alive, alternately sly and sad. He was then ninety-two.

Presently Fadeyev came in bringing several poems by Mandelstam which he said might be published in *Novy Mir* (New World); he talked about Madrid and his eyes, usually so cold, warmed in a smile.

When we reached Moscow I was told at the newspaper office that they intended to raise the question of my return to Spain but that nowadays everything took time – the high-ups were very busy and I would have to wait a month or two.

I spent six months in Moscow, and am grateful for it to the Fates. It was a piece of luck that I had felt the need to go to Moscow for a change and a rest just then: there are days in the history of one's people which cannot be understood from what one is told, they have to be lived through.

First of all let me describe what I did in those months. I gave various

422

talks on Spain in institutions of higher education, in factories, in military academies. Someone sent me a report taken down at the time of one such evening at the social club of a car factory, and I seem to have said that I had spoken about Spain in fifty different places.

I was glad that my audiences took the tragedy of the Spanish people to heart. I was talking to brave and honest people, devoted to Communism; they reminded me of our airmen whom I had met at Alcalá de Henares.

I could do no writing; during the whole of that time I wrote only two articles on Spain for *Izvestia*: one in March after the Fascist victories, the other for the May Day issue. The paper often asked me to write articles about the trials, about the 'Stalin People's Commissar', to compare the 'fifth column' in Spain with those who were labelled 'enemies of the people'. I said that I could not – I could write only about things I knew well – and I did not send in a line.

Even now I can write only about what I have seen for myself: my life in Moscow, the lives of fifty, or perhaps a hundred friends and acquaintances with whom I was in touch at the time; I cannot analyse the epoch nor present a large historical canvas; all I can do is to describe our day-to-day existence, as well as my own state of mind and that of my fellows, mainly writers and artists.

The life we led in those days was quite exceptional; whole books could be written about it, and it is impossible to convey it adequately in a few pages. There were so many conflicting elements: hope and despair, frivolity and courage, fear and dignity, fatalism and loyalty to the idea. There was no one in the circle of my acquaintances who could be sure about the morrow; many of them kept a small suitcase with two changes of warm underwear permanently in readiness. Some of the tenants of the house in Lavrushensky lane asked for the noisy lift to be put out of action at night. It kept them awake, listening and wondering where it would stop. Babel dropped in one day and with that humour which never forsook him, described how certain people newly appointed to various posts behaved: 'They perch on the very edge of their chairs'. In the office of *Izvestia* boards used to hang on the glass doors with the names of heads of departments, but now there was nothing; the messenger girl explained to me that it was not worth having them made: 'Here today and gone tomorrow'.

On the surface life seemed to go on as usual. It was decided to organize a Writers' Club and to have club days. In this matter, too,

S. I. Kirsanov showed himself an innovator: he arranged an exhibition in the club of pictures by Konchalovsky, Tyshler, Deineka, he even revolutionized the kitchens. I remember a lunch in honour of Zoshchenko who had come from Leningrad. There was a soup made from tinned crab which Kirsanov called 'lobster *bisque*'. An open fire was lit in the drawing-room, and bottles of *kvareli* (Georgian wine) were put near it to warm. Someone proposed a toast to me in honour of the Red Star which I had received the day before at the chancery of the Supreme Soviet.

When we all got up from table, a writer, whom I did not much care for, took me aside and whispered: 'Have you heard the latest? Stetsky has been arrested. What terrible times! You're at a loss to know whom to butter up and whom to run down'. There were people like that . . .

I once met Sergey Prokofiev at the club – he played some of his compositions. He was unhappy, even grim, and said to me: 'Today one must work. Work's the only thing, the only salvation'.

Many authors went on writing: Tynyanov completed the first part of his *Pushkin*; a new volume of Zabolotsky's verse appeared. Others admitted that they did not feel in the right mood.

Vladimir Lidin entertained us as usual with amusing stories. Once, when we were having dinner at his place, an enthusiastic young man turned up and gave a puppet show – Carmen as a scraggy old harridan, two balls exchanging vows of love – it was Sergey Obraztsov. On another occasion at Lidin's we met one of the four members of the Polar expedition, E. T. Krenkel, a modest young man; he described life on the ice-floe with a great deal of humour, and the *laika* (Eskimo dog) who had helped to frighten off the bears raiding their stores. These interludes were happy and restful.

We also used to visit the Tairovs, Yevgeny Petrov and Leonov. Babel came to see us, as did Tikhonov, Falk (who had recently returned form Paris), Vishnevsky, Lugovskoy, Tyshler, Fedin, Kirsanov; Lapin would be entertaining his friends Khatsrevin and Slavin, and we all dined together. Occasionally we indulged in literary discussions, talked about some new theatrical production, or just gossiped – after all, people still went on falling in love, having affairs and divorces; sometimes I talked about Spain: it seemed to me infinitely remote and dear; but at times the conversation would imperceptibly veer towards what we did not even want to think about.

Irina had a fat and affectionate poodle bitch Chuka who, as Durov would have said, had excellent conditioned reflexes. Lapin had taught her many tricks: she could fetch cigarettes and matches and close the dining-room door. It sometimes happened that a guest would start talking at dinner about someone who had been arrested, and black shaggy Chuka, her mind on a slice of sausage, would hastily shut the dining-room door. This made us all laugh. Even in those days we enjoyed a laugh.

Some of the people I knew tried to shut themselves off, seeing only their closest relatives; suspicion, apprehension undermined friendly intercourse. Babel said: 'Today a man talks frankly only with his wife – at night, with the blanket pulled over his head'. I, on the contrary, was drawn to human society. Almost every day we either had guests or went to see someone.

We often visited the Meyerholds. In January his theatre was shut down as 'alien'. Meyerhold's wife had a nervous breakdown. He himself bore it manfully, spoke about painting and poetry, recalled Paris. He went on working, planning the production of *Hamlet*, even though he did not believe that he would be allowed to produce the play. At the Meyerholds' I met Pyotr Konchalovsky; he was then painting portraits of Meyerhold, of the pianist Lev Oborin and of various young enthusiasts for whom Meyerhold remained a teacher.

At a writers' meeting which I once happened to attend various writers accused V. P. Stavsky of lack of vigilance: everywhere – in the journals, in the *Zhurgaz* (The Periodicals Publishing House), in the editorial offices – there were 'enemies of the people'. Stavsky sweated and kept wiping his forehead. Thinking back to the time when he had put on an enemy helmet near Brunete I thought: 'It's a good bit hotter here'.

I. K. Luppol invited us to lunch. He lived, as we did, in Lavrushensky. His wife said that they had moved in quite recently, had bought furniture and only needed a lamp; she added: 'Somehow one doesn't feel in the mood to buy things'. (Luppol held on for another eighteen months, then he was overtaken by the same fate as so many others.)

Vishnevsky roared that all writers, even the old men, should learn the art of war. He spoke about leap-frogging assault groups, strategic roads, probing the enemy.

I met people very alien to me and got on well with them: we had a feeling of being shoulder to shoulder, like soldiers in wartime. There was no war yet, but we knew that it was inevitable. We were, so to say, in a trench while the artillery, as had happened at Teruel, was shelling its own men.

Grigorovich had said that the Republican gunners which opened fire on the village occupied by their own infantry had fortunately not hit the target. Yezhov shelled town squares and did not spare the ammunition. I say Yezhov because at the time I thought that it was he who was responsible for the whole thing.

In the last part of my memoirs I shall try to sum up, to express my thoughts about Stalin, about the reasons for our errors, about all the things that weigh so heavily on the hearts of every individual of my generation. For the present I shall confine myself to describing the way I understood (or, rather, misunderstood) the happenings of that time. I realized that people were being accused of crimes which they had not and could not have committed, and I asked myself and others: why, what for? No one could give me an answer. We were completely at sea.

I was present at the opening session of the Supreme Soviet – the newspaper gave me a press card. The oldest deputy, the eighty-year-old academician A. N. Bach, who had been a member of the *Narodnaya Volya* (The People's Will) in the remote past, read his speech from a paper and, naturally, ended it with the name of Stalin. A thunder of applause greeted it. I had the impression that the old scholar reeled as from the blast of an explosion. I was sitting up above, there were ordinary Muscovites – factory and office workers – all round me, and they were in a frenzy.

But why speak of the Muscovites? In far away Andalusia I had seen militiamen go to their death with shouts of 'Estalin!' (which is how the Spaniards pronounced Stalin's name). We talk a lot about the cult of personality. At the beginning of 1938 the term 'cult' in its original, religious sense would have described it more accurately. In the minds of millions of people Stalin had become a sort of mythical demi-god; everyone uttered his name with awe and believed that he alone could save the Soviet State from invasion and disruption.

We thought (perhaps we wanted to think) that Stalin knew nothing about the senseless violence committed against the Communists, against the Soviet intelligentsia.

Meyerhold said: 'They conceal it from Stalin'.

One night, when I was taking Chuka for a run, I met Boris Pasternak

426

in Lavrushensky lane; he waved his arms about as he stood between the snowdrifts: 'If only someone would tell Stalin about it'.

Yes, not only I, but many other people, thought that the evil came from the small man whom they called the 'Stalin People's Commissar'. People who had never belonged to any opposition, who were loyal followers of Stalin or honest non-party specialists were arrested. Those years came to be known as '*Yezhovshchina*' (The Yezhov time).

In my opinion Babel was more intelligent than I, and cleverer than most. He had known Yezhov's wife before her marriage. He sometimes went to see her, aware that this was unwise, but wanting, as he told me, 'to find a key to the puzzle'. One day he said, shaking his head: 'It's not a matter of Yezhov. Of course Yezhov plays his part, but he's not at the bottom of it'. Yezhov shared the fate of Yagoda. His place was taken by Beria in whose time Babel, Meyerhold, Koltsov and many other innocent people perished.

I remember a terrible day at Meyerhold's. We were sitting peacefully looking through an illustrated monograph on Renoir, when a friend of Meyerhold, the Corps Commander I. P. Belov, arrived. He was very worked up and, without paying any attention to our presence, began to describe the trial of Tukhachevsky and other high ranking officers. Belov was a member of the Military Collegium of the Supreme Court. 'They were sitting like that – facing us. Uborevich looked me in the eyes . . .' I remember another phrase of Belov's: 'And tomorrow I'll be put in the same place'. Then he suddenly turned to me: 'Do you know Uspensky? Not Gleb, Nikolay. There's a man who wrote the truth'. And he gave us rather incoherently the gist of a story by Uspensky, I do not recall which, but a very cruel one. Belov left soon after. I glanced at Meyerhold; he sat with his eyes shut looking like a wounded bird. (Belov was arrested soon after.)

Another day I shall never forget is the one when it was announced on the radio that Gorky's murderers were being put on trial, and that doctors had been involved in the murder. Babel, who often used to visit Gorky, came rushing in, sat on the bed and tapped his forehead: they were insane. I shall have more to say about those days at the end of my memoirs.

In 1942 I wrote an article in which I said: 'Long before it attacked our country, Fascism interfered with our life and crippled the destiny of many people'. But even in the days of which I am speaking, I could not dissociate our own misfortunes from the evil news in the West.

At the end of February the Fascists reoccupied Teruel. Italy and Germany stepped up their aid to Franco. Eden raised his voice against Italy's open intervention in the Spanish war; he was forced to resign, and then came Chamberlain, an advocate of a *rapprochement* with Hitler and Mussolini. The mass bombing of Barcelona began; in a few days in March 4,000 inhabitants were killed. After concentrating their forces the Fascists broke through the Republican front in Aragon. The one and only article I wrote in the space of several months contains the following lines: 'In my room at night I listen to the broadcasts from Barcelona. Outside the window on the eighth floor I see the lights of the city. A rather muffled voice comes through: "We have beaten back the attack in the Fraga region". Perhaps at this moment they are bombing Barcelona? Perhaps the blackshirts are again attacking "in the Fraga region"?' Fraga was no abstract name to me but a town where I had often been. I saw before my eyes the streets of Barcelona and realized that the war between us and Fascism had begun. For the moment the war was not at the writers' meeting, where they were discussing who had been friendly with Bruno Jasenski, but out there – in Spain.

I thought for a long time about what I ought to do and decided to write to Stalin. Koltsov did not try to dissuade me, he only said: 'Is it worth while attracting attention to yourself?' I wrote that I had spent over a year in Spain, that my place was there, where I could join in the struggle.

A week passed, then another – there was no reply. The most unpleasant part of a situation of that sort is the waiting, but there was nothing else to do. At last I was summoned by the editor of *Izvestia*, Y. G. Selikh; he said rather pompously: 'You have written to Comrade Stalin. I've been instructed to speak to you. Comrade Stalin thinks that in view of the present international situation it is better that you should remain in the Soviet Union. You've probably got belongings and books in Paris. We can arrange for your wife to go there and collect them'.

I returned home filled with gloom, lay down and pondered. The advice transmitted to me by Selikh (if it could be called advice) seemed to me wrong. What could I do here? Tynyanov was writing about Pushkin, Tolstoy about Peter the Great. Karmen was photographing heroic expeditions and planning to go to China. Koltsov was involved in high politics. But for me there was nothing to do here.

Over there I could be useful: I hated Fascism, I knew the West. My place was not in Lavrushensky.

After lying about the whole day I got up and said: 'I'm going to write to Stalin again'. At this even Irina protested: 'You're mad! Do you mean to complain to Stalin about Stalin?' I replied grimly: 'Yes'. I realized, of course, that I was acting foolishly, that in all probability such a letter would lead to my arrest, nevertheless I sent it off.

Waiting this time was even harder than before. I did not really expect a favourable reply and knew that there was nothing more that I could do; I listened to the radio, re-read Cervantes and, in my nervous state, was hardly able to eat. At the very end of April the newspaper office rang me up: 'You can go and get your papers, foreign passports will be issued'. Why did that happen? I shall never know.

A young writer, who in 1938 was five years old, said to me recently: 'May I ask you something? How was it that you survived?' What could I say? Only what I have just written: 'I shall never know'. If I were religious, I should probably have said that the ways of God are inscrutable. I said at the very beginning of these memoirs that I lived in times when the fate of a man was not like a game of chess but like a lottery.

On May Day I was in the broadcasting studio overlooking the Red Square; poets read their verses and commented on the demonstration; I spoke about Spain. I knew that the war was going to spread and encompass the entire world.

Then came the day of departure. Many friends were at the station to see us off; we found it hard to part with them. In Leningrad, where we stayed for a few days, there were more long talks about what was going on, more warm handshakes and a hesitant *au revoir*.

In Helsinki we had to change. Lyuba and I sat in silence on a bench in a public garden: we could not even talk to one another.

I was forty-seven, an age of spiritual maturity. I knew that a misfortune had befallen us and knew also that neither I, nor my friends, nor yet the whole of our people would ever renounce October, that the crimes of individuals, or any of the things that had crippled our lives were incapable of diverting us from our hard and noble course. There were times when I no longer wanted to live, but even at those times I knew that I had chosen the right path.

After the Twentieth Party Congress, some of the people I met abroad asked me, as they also asked themselves, whether a mortal blow

429

had not been dealt to the very idea of Communism. There is something here which they do not fully appreciate but which I, an old non-party writer, know: the idea proved so strong that it was Communists who were able to tell our people and the whole world about the past crimes, about the distortions both of the philosophy of Communism and of its principles of justice, solidarity and humanity. Our people, despite everything, continued through that time to build its house; and a few years later it beat back the Fascist invasion and finished building its house in which young men and girls, who have not known the cruel errors of the past, now live, study and argue lustily.

But Lyuba and I sat silent on the bench in the scruffy little park. The thought came to me that I should have to remain silent for a very long time; in Spain people were fighting, and I should have no one with whom to share my experiences.

No, the blow was not dealt to the *idea*. It was dealt to the people of my generation. Some perished. Others will remember those years to their dying day. Their life, in truth, has not been an easy one.

27

IN FRANCE the Popular Front still existed officially but now it was no more than a peeling signboard. Daladier, the head of the new government, had entrusted the Ministry of Foreign Affairs to Bonnet who loudly proclaimed his desire for peace, adding *sotto voce* that it was necessary to come to terms with Berlin and Rome.

The tragedy of France had begun long before: as early as 1936 when Léon Blum, in fear of the right-wing, had refused to sell arms to the Spanish Government. This was contrary both to existing agreements and to the interests of France, to say nothing of Blum's political outlook. The Socialist premier admired Stendhal: in novels he liked characters with strong passions; he himself had no will power. He cried: 'It breaks my heart', and then talked about 'non-intervention'. What broke was not his heart but France.

In June 1938 many French politicians realized that Mussolini would not be content with the seizure of Addis Ababa and Malaga, that for Hitler Austria was no more than an *hors-d'œuvre* and that Spain was a dress rehearsal. But the country was divided. The opponents of the Popular Front were happy that they were neither in Barcelona nor in Vienna, that nobody bombed them, that nobody ordered them to raise their arms in the Fascist salute, that they could drink green, golden and red *apéritifs* on the terraces of large cafés and at the counters of little *bistros*. France was already launched on the slope to the coming surrender.

I bought a number of newspapers at the station and a book by Léon de Poncins – an author I did not know – with the fascinating title *The Secret History of the Spanish War*. The Fascist weekly *Gringoire* had started a competition for readers to forecast the correct date on which Barcelona would fall to Franco. The winner would get 50,000 francs. From Poncins' book I learnt that the Communists, the Socialists and the Freemasons had formed a conspiracy to hand Spain over to the Jews; for that purpose the Comintern had sent Béla Kun, Vronsky, Antonov-Ovseyenko, Ehrenburg, Koltsov, Miravilles, Gorev, Tupolev, Primakov and other 'criminals of Jewish extraction' to Barcelona.

I told myself that there were lunatics everywhere and dozed off.

I arrived in the Spanish frontier town of Port-Bou early in the morning and was at once caught in an air-raid. Spain met me with blood: on the pavement lay the corpse of a child.

I had left Spain in the days of the battles for Teruel when everyone believed in victory. On returning six months later I found a different state of affairs. Of course I had known in Moscow that the Fascists had won decisive battles, but it is one thing to read about a disaster in the papers and quite another to witness it. It is terrible, after having been parted from someone you love, whose life is bubbling over with work, anger, dreams, jealousy, to find him wasted by a cruel and possibly mortal disease. When I came away the Republicans' position was difficult but even neutral observers were uncertain about the outcome of the war. Now I tried hard to make myself believe that all was not lost and that a miracle might yet save the Republic.

On the Ebro a fifty-year-old Spaniard who had lived for a long time in Paris (his name was Angel Zapicá) and volunteered in 1938, when there was no longer any room for illusions, said to me: 'Death is a phenomenon, something that happens to you. To be born, to die, are not in our control. The main thing is to live worthily, without despising yourself'. Perhaps in saying this he had another thought: that a man wants to die worthily, to do all he can to prevent death being 'something that happens to you'.

I arrived in Barcelona. Savich was still telegraphing dispatches and saying that he was worked to death and could not even manage to get to the front. He was an old and intimate friend of mine: we had first met in 1922 and for years used to see each other daily. He is a bookish man of exceptionally mild temperament. He took air-raids without turning a hair, yet I could remember how at one time the very sight of a policeman used to frighten him. He inquired after his wife, after Mirova and some of the advisers. I told him Alya was well and trying to keep her head, that things were bad with Mirova and with many others: 'It's hard to understand why completely innocent people are arrested'. Savich looked at me with astonishment: 'What's come over you – have you become a Trotskyist?' I laughed and realized that I could not explain although this was my closest friend.

Savich lived on a hill. I went down into the town. In the Plaza de Cataluña a little old woman still collected ten centimos from people sitting in the gardens and gave them tickets. Ten centimos had become a microscopic sum; besides there were few people in the gardens – all round stood the blackened ruins of houses. But life went on. Old men scattered crumbs for the pigeons in the square. This was surprising in a way: the bread ration was six ounces, and sometimes only a quarter of a pound, scarcely enough to share with the pigeons. They, too, might have been expected to fly away – there was hardly a night without air-raids. But I was not surprised: long before this I had realized that life could be churned up, crippled, trampled down and that lovers would still kiss and exchange vows, old women would still tidy up–a room, a prison cell, a hospital bed, even perhaps their own coffin.

In the Ramblas they were still selling flowers. The theatre was giving the opening performance of *The Taming of the Shrew*. In the grounds of imposing mansions small allotments had been planted with potatoes and lettuces. Beans were served at restaurants without butter, but the tablecloths were clean, though there was no soap to be had.

The bootblacks did a roaring trade for there was plenty of boot polish, and the citizens of Barcelona, true to their habits, enjoyed the sight of well-polished shoes.

The latest issue of *The Barcelona Philatelist* came out. I counted the advertisements in it: twelve theatres and fifty-four cinemas were open. The paper gave the information that the day before had marked the hundredth bombing of Barcelona and therefore a jubilee.

The harbour quarter, the lively Barceloneta, had been destroyed by bombs. Every day the papers contained black-bordered obituary notices: so-and-so had been killed in a raid. Once a bomb fell on a cemetery and ploughed up the graves; another hit a maternity hospital and there were many victims; other bombs fell on the thirteenth-century cathedral and on the market place. *Izvestia* asked for photographs; I went about taking pictures of ruins, of soldiers dragging maimed bodies from under heaps of rubble. One can get used to anything, and I concentrated on the proper setting of the aperture. I was probably like the old woman who collected money for the chairs.

Republican Spain was already cut in two: the Fascists had succeeded in breaking through to the coast. The Germans had sent top experts: they regarded the war in Spain as first-rate manoeuvres for the forthcoming conquest of Europe. In addition to Franco's Falangists four Italian divisions were taking part in the fighting to force a passage to the Levante coast.

I started off for the front which the newspapers out of habit called

433

the Aragon front, although the Fascists had already seized all the towns and villages of Aragon – Barbastro, Fraga, Sariñena, Pina, Caspe – places where I had argued, made friends and quarrelled with the 'uncontrollable' Anarchists. I reached the suburbs of Lérida. The town was in the hands of the Fascists but the Republicans were still holding out in the district on the opposite bank of the little river Segre. Oh Lord, how often I had come to Lérida from the Aragon front! Then the town had seemed in the far rear. I used to go to the Palace Hotel, have a bath, walk about the town; the streets had arcades and at night the ancient lamps looked theatrical. You drank vermouth in the cafés. At the neighbouring tables people would be arguing about who was right – the FAI or the PSUC. And girls walked past the cafés laughing, followed by the admiring glances of both Anarchists and Socialists. Now where there had once been a café there were sandbags, the chatter of machine-guns. Before me stretched narrow, humpbacked streets and the wrecked houses of the quay. Something brought to my mind the old one-eyed barber who used to give me a shave and a hair-cut when I got back from the front. He joked, he ridiculed the generals, the Anarchists, the Ministers and proudly announced to everyone: 'I'm a moderate Anarchist and a thoroughgoing anti-Fascist'. Had he managed to leave in time or had he been killed?

An inhabitant of Lérida, who had swum across the river, said that only 400 people remained in the town (there had been 40,000): 'They've all gone. You remember the large house in the Plaza Paeria, next to the Palace Hotel? They've painted on the walls in red: "We do not want to live with murderers". It wasn't the soldiers who did it, it was one of the tenants before he left'.

It seemed almost impossible that the Fascists had been halted on the right bank of the narrow, shallow stream. In the autumn of 1936 they had been stopped on the outskirts of Madrid. The military explained at the time that the city was easy to defend. But here the Fascists had occupied the town and had then suddenly met with furious resistance.

This happened more than once in Spain, and the explanation probably lies not so much in the peculiarities of the terrain as in the peculiarities of character: the men yielded one hundred, two hundred miles practically without a fight, and then, all of a sudden, fury, rage, determination were aroused and the enemy was unable to advance another hundred yards.

I was sitting with some soldiers when a shell splinter killed hand-some, olive-skinned Currito, an Andalusian from the Sierra Morena.

434

Another man, a Barcelona tailor who was forever cracking jokes, stood for a long time over his dead comrade, his lips working, visibly holding back his tears, and at last said: 'And I'd promised to mend his shirt'.

A splinter broke the branch of a peach-tree. We ate the fragrant fruit in silence – in Lérida peaches ripen early. The Barcelona tailor said: 'Currito loved peaches'.

There were many volunteers in the battalion who had joined only recently – elderly men, young boys. The politicians said that the war was coming to an end, but these men had come to fight. They could hardly have been counting on victory, but they would not or could not stand on the side-lines. I knew Spain well, yet every day it produced some new wonder.

On my way back to Barcelona the bombers came over. We lay in the grass for half an hour. When the raid was over I saw a wheatfield completely laid waste. Strangely enough, it was an unbearably painful sight though I had seen far more terrible things. Perhaps it was because in my childhood, if I dropped a piece of bread, my nurse, Vera Platonovna, would say crossly as I picked it up: 'Kiss it', and I kissed the bread.

In Barcelona I talked to a captured German pilot, Kurt Kettner, the son of a Brandenburg architect. He had come to Spain early in the war, in October 1936; he told me at once that he was a lieutenant in the Reichswehr and flew a Heinkel 111. When I asked him why he had bombed small Spanish towns he laughed loudly: 'Are you going on again about *mujeres y niños?*' (He spoke in German but these last words he said in Spanish.) 'Rubbish! The other day I saw a cloud of smoke after the raid. Was it *mujeres y niños* smoking?'

You could not have said that he was ignorant; he had read quite a few books, he talked about the philosophy of history, but to me he seemed like a savage, bold and vicious. Such meetings helped me to get an insight into the uncomplicated but peculiar spiritual world of the officers and soldiers whom two years later I saw marching down the streets of Paris and, in 1941, in our Byelorussia.

The tragic farce of 'non-intervention' continued. In Cerbera I saw several hundreds of shovels sent to the Catalonian peasants being impounded. I went to Hendaye to find out what was going on at the frontier between France and Fascist Spain.

I had friends in Hendaye, as I mentioned when describing the exchange of airmen. These friends put me in touch with a responsible customs official who hated Fascism. He showed me papers about con-signments destined for Fascist Spain. Of course Italy and Germany sent their planes, tanks, artillery and munitions by sea to the Portu-guese ports, to Bilbao and Cadiz; but more innocuous goods they sent through France, by which route came lorries, motor-cycles, rubber, engines and chemicals for war industry. There was no control on the Franco-Spanish frontier, whatever the French government might say.

Izvestia published my article, and the French police were furious; it appeared that I was violating the principles of Non-Intervention. (All the same, it was rather naïve of me: I wanted to shame someone, to open someone's eyes, thinking that events were leading to Verdun, whereas what they were leading to was Munich.)

I must now recount a rather foolish episode. I was seized with the desire to penetrate into Fascist Spain, if only for a few hours, to see what was going on there. False documents were out of the question: in Irún there was a Gestapo official. I was told in Hendaye that smugglers often carried things over to the Spanish frontier villages. I got in touch with one of these men, a French Basque. He said to me: 'All right. But mind, I'm not having any truck with politics. I know the Fascists are bastards, but I've got a family to feed. I won't give you away, but if, God forbid, we run into frontier guards, I'll say at once that you're a stranger who picked up with me on the way'.

We crossed a stream and began to climb. I must admit that I was very excited and also rather frightened at moments. I do not even remember what my guide — I called him Jacques — was carrying. At last we found ourselves in an ordinary Spanish village, Vera, and went into a dark house that smelt of olive oil and garlic. Jacques fetched a certain Antonio who took me to another house. Immediately on our return to Hendaye I wrote down this simple record: 'The mistress of the house was old and deaf. Antonio said to me: "The *Requetés* killed her son. At the same time as Aguirre. There, where you came past with Jacques. He was lying there and swearing. She knew nothing about it. By the time she got there he was dead. They left her here because she's very old". The old woman looked in turn at me and at Antonio. Antonio shouted in her ear: "They left you here because you're very old". She nodded happily: "Yes, yes, very old". Then she clutched her black head-shawl with her sharp fingers and cried out: "But he was not old, he was young", and broke into loud sobs. Antonio put a finger to his lips: the guard. I peered through a crack between the

436

shutters. There was no one. Antonio explained: "Everybody here's afraid of him. I was at the market in Elisando. Everyone keeps his mouth shut there too. They're afraid. One man told me straight out 'I talk to nobody but my wife. And even then, I'm afraid'. I'm from Vilmediano myself, a small village, only a hundred and sixty people, but we voted for the Socialists: the *Requetés* shot twenty-nine."

'Antonio fetched four other men and said: "You can talk to him, he's a Frenchman, one of ours". The peasants cautiously told me about requisitions and fines. At that point Jacques came to say it was time to go.'

We got back towards morning, went into the railway station bar and drank brandy.

I had not really seen anything and I could have written about the old woman without taking unnecessary risks. It was an escapade more suited to a twenty-year-old; I realized this and felt less pride than shame. Added to which I was a little afraid of being recalled: it might be said that an *Izvestia* correspondent should not indulge in such antics. But nothing happened, and I went back to Barcelona.

I was not alone in my naïvety; many politicians still believed that there would be a change in the attitude of England and France. If one recalls the events of the summer of 1938, a great deal becomes clear. Hardly a day passed without Hitler threatening Czechoslovakia. Henlein, the Führer of the Sudeten Germans, went to London, but came away empty-handed. Although Chamberlain was prepared to make concessions, he had to take into account the opposition of both the Labour Party and many influential Conservatives. In France there was such confusion that it was not easy to understand how things stood: in almost every party there were both those in favour of resistance and those in favour of capitulation. The right-wing journalist de Kérillis, who only a short time before had been cursing the Spanish Republicans, now wrote that Hitler had his eye on France. The left-wing *Oeuvre*, which had until recently been hostile to Franco, now became the mouthpiece of certain circles which called themselves 'friends of peace' and were for making every concession to Hitler. There was a general atmosphere of nervousness. Hotel proprietors on the coast and in the Alps complained that people were forgetting that summer holidays had begun.

Alvarez del Vayo had always been (and remained) hopeful. I remember him assuring me that summer that war between Germany on the one hand and France with her allies on the other was inevitable: 'In Spain the French will find not only enemies ready to attack them from the rear but also allies'. He thought that the end of the summer would see many changes in the world, and kept saying: 'Our job is to hold out'.

Much has been and is still written today about the 'Miracle of Madrid', about the autumn of 1936 when the Spanish people, with the help of the International Brigades and Soviet equipment, halted the Fascist army. Much less is said about the last period: defeat has never been an inviting subject. But I must say that I see the resistance during the second half of 1938 as a still greater miracle than the defence of Madrid in the first autumn of the war.

On 15th April 1938, when Franco's armies reached the coast and cut Republican Spain in two, the outcome of the war was a foregone conclusion. There had been mistakes, confusion, many other factors, and I am writing a book of reminiscences, not the history of the war. But when I think that Catalonia held out for another ten months, and Madrid still longer, I cannot restrain my emotion. Nations are like individuals: you understand them best in times of disaster.

In June I was received by the President of the Republic, Azaña. Some people call him a 'deserter' because he and the rest of the government left for France in February 1939. Of course, the President of the Republic should have gone to Madrid; but his critics are too harsh, they seem unwilling to recognize that Azaña had become President of fighting Spain by *force majeure*. When the Republic accepted Franco's challenge and went into battle, the government was changed. It was changed many times. But the President could not be changed, he was the symbol of continuity, an emblem recognized by the democracies of the West, a standard.

Manuel Azaña became a politician by mistake; he wrote novels and essays; in common with all progressive intellectuals he detested the monarchy and the dictatorship of Primo de Rivera. He was basically a dilettante, both in literature and in politics; where he felt at ease was not in the presidential residence, not at his premier's post, not even in parliament, but in the Ateneo literary club where he engaged in erudite conversation and where interminable all-night discussions went on, which the Spaniard call *tertulias*. He could converse brilliantly with Edouard Herriot about Baroque, Madame Récamier and the all-embracing humanism of Calderón.

He had great personal courage. I was in Madrid when, on 14th April 1936, the people were celebrating the first anniversary of the Republic.

438

Azaña was then premier. A Fascist fired at him. A general panic broke out. Azaña was quite unperturbed.

But all that followed was too testing for him: he was a liberal intellectual, and when Largo Caballero brought him a list of the new government including the names of four Anarchists, he dug in his toes and argued that men who denied the State could not become Ministers of State. He argued, but others did not bother to argue back – he remained the symbol.

He received me as the correspondent of a Soviet newspaper and made a statement; it contained lines like these: 'The armed attack on the Republic, organized and supported by three European States, compels us to carry on the war for independence not only in the political sense of the word, but also in the highest, the most essential sense, more enduring than the structure and the regime of the State: the struggle going on is for the freedom of development of the Spanish spirit. It is not a question of whether there will be one more Republic in Europe or one less, or whether this or that political party will be able to carry out its programme. The question is whether a great nation, renowned in many fields, can play an independent part in the creation of modern culture or whether it will be stifled. It is that which gives world importance to the Spanish tragedy, and provides the reason and the strength for Spain's self-defence'.

After handing me his statement Azaña suddenly said with a grave smile: 'And now we can talk as two writers'. I expected him to speak about literature but he said: 'I have used the word "tragedy" in my statement; it may be unsuitable for a Head of State but I could find no better one. Negrín seems to believe that a world war would save Spain. There will certainly be a war. But they won't start it before they have throttled Spain. You know our literature. We have always striven for universal human ideals. A Spaniard created Don Quixote, whom everyone admired and who became for everyone an object of derision. People pity us and, as they pity, they smile. Spain will be put behind bars for a long, long time'.

I met Barcelona Anarchists. They reviled the government, the Communists, saying that Prieto was a sharp political dabbler, that everything that was going on proved day by day how right the Anarchists were, but at the same time they mentioned with pride that the Soviet newspapers wrote admiringly of Commander Cipriano Mera, who was an Anarchist. They insisted that the CNT-FAI would fight to the end, and deplored the fact that the government was doing so little to organize guerilla warfare: 'Every Spaniard is a natural guerrilla fighter'. One of them accompanied me to my hotel. On the way there was an air-raid alarm, the sirens wailed and we got stuck in the gateway of some warehouse. The Anarchist said: 'It's like this. I became politically conscious in 1928, when I was twenty-three. I've been at the front, I was wounded in the chest. Today I asked to be sent to the Ebro. In the first place, I'm an Anarchist, and that compels you'. He fell silent, and I asked: 'And in the second place?' He did not answer at once, and when he did his voice sounded embarrassed: 'In the second place? What can I say? I was a Spaniard before I became an Anarchist. Perhaps you think I'm not a Spaniard? I'm from Seville, like your José, only he was a baker and I was a barber. I'm more of a Spaniard than that bastard Franco. Well, what d'you think, can a real Anarchist live without Spain? I don't think so.'

Things were not easy for the Spanish Communists; the whole time they had to be explaining something to someone: to the Anarchists – the meaning of discipline without which one could not defeat the Fascists; to the Republicans – the meaning of the revolution; to the Socialists – the meaning of unity; and to the Soviet comrades – the meaning of Spain.

I met José Díaz, Dolores Ibárruri, Uribe and other Party leaders. They helped me to understand the situation. But at this point I should like to recall a conversation that has little bearing on the events.

I have never liked bullfighting and had more than one argument about it with Hemingway. I was revolted by the gored bellies of the old horses, by the banderillas goading the bemused animal, the blood on the sand, but above all by the swindle: the bull does not know the rules of the game – he runs straight at the enemy, and the *torero* moves slightly out of his path: the whole art consists in evading the rush at the right moment: not too soon, otherwise the public will whistle its contempt, but not too late, otherwise the beast might gore not an old horse, but one of Spain's idols. As a real Andalusian José Díaz loved bullfights, and he said to me in a moment of leisure: 'You think we're always on the side of the *torero*? Not at all, we're often for the bull. You don't understand anything'.

I cannot say what made me recall this conversation, probably the poet in me shouldered aside the author of this long and discursive book.

Let me return to the events of 1938. At the end of July an offensive began on the Ebro – the Republicans' last attempt to retrieve the situation. The Ebro is a broad river with a swift current. The attackers succeeded in establishing a foothold, they built pontoon-bridges, seized the small town of Mora de Ebro and a number of villages, and threatened the Fascists' left flank. A long and bloody battle began.

I went across to the right bank of the Ebro twice and observed several actions. The Fascist air force bombed the pontoons practically without interruption and the engineers rebuilt them each time; they had a special song: 'They live in a cave, they're as black as Negroes and as fierce as wild beasts, the pontooners of the Ebro'. They did in fact live among the bomb-shattered rocks. When I was photographing a bridge for *Izvestia*, one of the engineers said to me: 'Make it a quick exposure or else a bomb'll fall and spoil your picture'.

Here the war was very different from what it had been at Guadalajara or even at Teruel. Franco had eleven divisions in action. The Fascists had concentrated 170 guns on a two-mile sector. For a long time fighting went on for certain heights of the Sierra de Pandols, and I could see how the contours of a hill were changed by prolonged artillery pounding.

I met the commander Miguel Tagüeña. He was twenty-five, they called him a Young Communist. He had graduated from the University before the war, was studying optics and preparing his thesis but had had to exchange it for a rifle. He became corps commander. He still had a youthful chubby face, but professional soldiers spoke of him with respect. He said: 'We shall reach Gandesa'. And despite everything, I began to believe in the possibility of victory. In a way I felt easier at the front than in Barcelona. I did not think about what was happening in Europe, nor even about the fate of Valencia -- all my thoughts were concentrated on Hill 544, as if the outcome of the whole war depended on who would hold this bald, shell-pitted summit.

The army was commanded by Juan Modesto. We recalled the beginning of the war when he had organized a battalion named after Thaelmann, and I had originally met him on the day when they had captured their first Fascist. Modesto had been as pleased as a child: 'Do you realize, we've captured a prisoner! Of course it would have been better if we'd got two – then we could have said prisoners and material were taken'. On the Ebro he said that he remembered that day as the happiest one in his life. He told me about himself: he was an Andalusian, he had worked in a sawmill, had been a football fan and taken no interest in politics. One day the doctor gave him a tiny news-sheet *The Voice of the Proletarian*. Modesto read it and it made him think. Soon afterwards he joined the Communist Party. On the Ebro his tent was crammed with books: he was studying military science. A gay fellow, he infected everybody with his gaiety. I was told that in March, when the men had felt despondent, he had sung, cracked jokes, told Andalusian stories until, almost against their will, everyone was laughing. We discussed the prospects. Modesto was not discouraged: 'Look at the army we've got!' Then he sighed: 'But there are too few planes. You don't have to explain why, I know all about it. But there are too few'.

(Not so long ago I met Modesto in Rome after many years. I was overjoyed; it was as if I had set foot again on Spanish soil. He was still the same and said in the same tones as on the Ebro: 'Look at the young people we've got in Spain now!')

I did not lose hope even though I realized that there was nothing to hope for. One's heart often contradicts one's reason: it is like a married couple who can neither live together happily nor separate. It was always the little trivial gestures that fed my hopes. For example, there was no tobacco, but a lonely soldier at his post said: 'I've got two cigarettes, give one to any comrade you come across'. In Barcelona, in the Plaza de Cataluña, I once offered two small girls a bar of chocolate I had brought from France. The little girls called their friends and carefully broke the bar into ten tiny pieces. In the front-line village of Puigcerdá I looked in at a peasant's house and saw there were some town children. The old peasant said to me: 'There's so little land in Spain now. You see, they're from Fraga. They had land, but it was taken away from them'.

These are not just sentimental stories; they genuinely reflect the way Spain lived on the eve of defeat.

During the summer, and more particularly in the autumn, I frequently went to France: events were developing on which the fate of Europe would depend for many years to come. I suggested that Savich should write for *Izvestia* during my absence from Barcelona. He agreed, and the newspaper acquired a new correspondent with the handsome Spanish name of José García. Every time I left, I looked back anxiously at the Spanish frontier-guard; I had become superstitious. Yet at the same time I not only wrote, but actually believed that there was still hope. Despite everything.

28

In this fourth part of my memoirs almost all the chapters are about the political events in Europe between 1934–8. This is only natural: those events were of supreme importance and I did not feel myself a mere spectator. It would be impossible to dissociate my autobiography from the tremors which shook hundreds of millions of people in that epoch. To tell the story of my life in any other way would be untruthful.

When I was twenty my thoughts were about Katya, about Memling's paintings, about Blok's poems. The days had the fragrance of the tuberoses which I used to buy instead of dinner. I did not even know who was the head of the French government, although I lived in Paris; I took no interest in what was happening in Agadir, although the Agadir crisis held the threat of a world war; I did not study Stolypin's agrarian reform, although I continued to regard myself as a revolutionary.

A quarter of a century later I not only wrote for the press, but also felt my dependence on what it reported. The sense of smell evokes many significant memories, and my recollection of those days is associated less with the fragrance of flowers than with the smell of printers' ink.

I say this without regret: I could not have lived in any other way. The young man of twenty believed that he was freely choosing a life after his own heart. Towards the end of the thirties I had long since parted with a good many illusions and knew that even if a man is given the opportunity of choosing his path, the windings of that path are outside his control.

We say: 'You've called yourself a mushroom, so get into the basket'[1]. Quite true. But when all is said and done, the mushrooms in the basket differ from one another. I have been writing about the struggle in Spain, the pusillanimity of Blum and Daladier, about the peasants of Catalonia and the German pilots. Now I should like to talk about myself a little.

---

[1] Russian saying equivalent to: As you make your bed you must lie on it.

I have said that I frequently went back to Paris where great events were brewing; my paper asked me to do this, and I myself wanted to find out whether or not there would be war.

Lyuba had taken a small house in Banyuls, near the Spanish frontier. I used to go there to have a rest from the bombings; Savich sometimes came, as well as other friends from Barcelona. And there, too, came my old friend, pink-cheeked, laughter-loving Dusya from Paris. Malraux also visited us at Banyuls: he was putting the final touches to a film about the Spanish war.

There was a feeling of anxiety in Paris, and after the Spanish epic it was not easy to reconcile oneself to the cowardice, the mean-spiritedness, the clinging to endless material pleasures. Few of my old friends frequented Montparnasse. The painters now spoke less about technique than about the Sudeten Germans and Chamberlain. Irina seldom wrote, her letters were concerned with trivialities, but I did not expect anything else. The new ambassador in Paris, Yakov Suritz, was a warmhearted man, but I really made friends with him only much later, in the post-war years. It is difficult for anyone in a responsible position to talk: his task is to persuade or to dissuade.

The greatest event in my life at that time was that in 1938, quite suddenly, after an interval of fifteen years, I began to write verse. I think this came about first of all owing to grief and loneliness. In hours of happiness man is sociable, he shares his happiness with the crowd in the street or within four walls with the being he loves. And in moments of the greatest, the fullest joy he is silent, as if fearing that a word will hasten time, disrupt the inner harmony. But unhappiness calls for words, it has a tongue, though only very rarely does it find an attentive ear. Who can know how lonely we were in those years? There were speeches galore, here and there guns were already firing, the radio was never silent, but the live human voice seemed to be muted. There was much that we could not confide even to those closest to us; all we could do was to press the hands of our friends with particular warmth now and then, for we were all involved in the great conspiracy of silence.

I am devoted to my essential work – to prose; I know its pleasures and its difficulties. It is a zigzag uphill path, with landslides, loss of breath, sometimes even heart attacks. It means words addressed to people, about people; invisibly, a prose-writer's room is always crowded with the characters – agreeable or tiresome, friendly or

444

hostile, welcome or uninvited – that life has thrust upon him. The prose-writer seeks solitude for his work, he needs a desk and quiet, though in point of fact he lives and writes at a noisy, busy crossroad. A poet can compose verse in the street, in a bus, at a dull meeting, yet at such moments he is alone. No prose-writer, even in ancient times when people loved mythology, would ever dream of conversing with a Muse. But poets, including those who were never taught at school that Erato represents lyric poetry and holds a lyre, will suddenly remember the Muse. Lyric poetry is like a diary, and people often begin to compose rhymes out of loneliness. Tyutchev wrote: 'How can the heart express itself? How can another understand you? Will he understand by what you live? A thought expressed is but a lie'. In Tyutchev's poem the secret thought was no lie. Poetry has great power: born of solitude it destroys all barriers between people. The poet converses with the imaginary Muse, he pours out his heart to her, often without thinking about the fate of the lines that echo in his mind; and his words become a source of life for a multitude of people. Tyutchev's poems were published by his friends, and Ivan Aksakov later wrote: 'Tuytchev himself apparently took no part in this publication; others decided, judged and arranged things for him. We are convinced that he never even opened this slender volume'. But Leo Tolstoy with his dying breath mumbled those lines of Tyutchev which I have just quoted.

How lonely, how unhappy Lermontov was! Verlaine wrote his best poems in prison. Blok's diary impresses one deeply with its pangs of loneliness. One could fill dozens of pages with similar examples. I have not the slightest intention of glorifying solitude, but say with Bergamín: solitude does not mean isolation, it is not a programme, not an ivory tower – that outworn conception. No ivory is proof against trouble. And the world is full of trouble.

There was yet another reason why I turned to poetry once again. I wrote the short novel *What a Man Needs* in the summer of 1937, between Brunete and Teruel; I started on the novel *The Fall of Paris* in the autumn of 1940. For three years I wrote articles, essays, short accounts of military operations and political events. I wrote and dictated what I had written into a telephone, or typed Russian words in Latin characters on telegraph forms. Imperceptibly I ceased to think about words; my language became impoverished, standardized, conventional.

445

I must confess my passion. I believe no one could suspect me of nationalism; I have lived abroad a great deal and have learnt to appreciate the genius of other nations. I am no polyglot but I understand several languages and yet, from my early youth, I have been in love with the Russian language. It seems to me created for poetry. Every man loves the language which he has spoken since infancy, but I not only love the Russian language, I worship it. It has a freedom that does not exist in any other language I know; a change in the order of words in a phrase alters the meaning. There are languages with a musical stress on certain syllables, but I venture to say that the Russian language has a lyrical stress on even a particular word. This freedom, this absence of compulsory precision imposed on western European languages by the rigidity of syntax, the absence of the article – all this offers infinite possibilities to the writer: he stands not on the exhausted soil of bygone centuries but on permanently virgin soil.

Poetry became for me a laborious rarefied atmosphere, a purification. By sensing the importance of the single word I perceived both the link with the past and the reality of the future, I felt the details of life, and this helped me to overcome despair.

I composed verses in a car, in a train, in hours of rest or at noisy meetings, in the street, in front-line dugouts. I wrote them down later; the poems were short and I knew them by heart.

Fifteen-year-old Anne Frank, hiding from the Fascists, kept a diary in which she addressed herself to an imaginary friend, Kitty. I do not know to whom I opened my heart; perhaps to that same Muse, restless, spattered with the mud of front-line roads, deaf from explosions, undiscovered at writers' meetings and truly 'without passport'.

I wrote poems about events that I had previously described in my articles and which I have mentioned in this book; naturally I wrote in quite a different way. At Morata de Tajuña Lukács's brigade made a fighting reconnaissance; this was a difficult operation that cost many lives. I ended the poem *Fighting Reconnaissance* with these lines: 'An hour later the dawn gilded the inky edges of the alien hill. Let me look back – there are my graves, fighting reconnaissance, my youth!' In my report on the offensive at Casa del Campo I had mentioned a canary, which annoyed the editor, and rightly so. In a poem I returned to the little bird: 'What are the cupboard and bench doing here, these shrouded armchairs and the chest-of-drawers? There is even a cage, and in it a canary sings loudly, curse it . . . But I must confess the creature's excitement reached me for a moment, and then I remembered with fear my nightmarish craft. This spasm which seizes you by the throat will not let go till morning – how many emotions the futile game of words and sounds has killed and obliterated'. I wrote about the funeral of a Soviet airman in a Spanish village: 'Having dug a grave under the olive trees, they laid a stone on it. In what land did our comrade grow up, under what clouds did he weep? And the fighters huddled sorrowfully, and turned away swallowing their tears. Perhaps dearer to him than the olive tree would have been the simple-hearted sadness of a birch'.

I also wrote about things which I could not and did not want to tell anyone. In quoting from a poem of 1938, I naturally do not attach any importance to the poem itself, but it is easier to express some things in verse than in prose: 'Let me not think too long, silence that voice, I beseech, that memory should scatter, that grief should break asunder, that men should laugh, that there should be more noise and laughter, that, remembering, I spring up to stop thinking, and not think any more, to live unwaking like a drunkard, in one gulp and then fall to the ground, into nothingness, that the clock should tick at night, that this tap should go on dripping, that drop by drop, that figures and rhymes, that something, some semblance of precise and urgent work, that I should do battle with the foe, that I should advance with bayonet in hand against bombs and bullets, that I should out face death, looking it in the eye. Let me not see it to the end, grant me this boon, I beseech, not to see, not to remember what has happened to us in our lives'.

I wrote about the times I lived in, about the turbulent mountain torrent which later became a broad and calmly flowing river; I tried to comfort myself: 'Our age, too, will end among azure lands, where the gardener tends the seed and the mother rocks the cradle, where the day is deep and long, where the heart is full of silence, and where the weary dove pecks the corn out of one's hand'.

I dare say these are feeble verses, but I cherish them as avowals, and I could not deny them a little space in the book about my life. Perhaps this chapter will give the reader a better understanding of the author. There is a French saying that a door must be either open or shut. No, the curtain of the confessional may be simultaneously lowered and raised.

447

29

THE NEWS from Paris and London affected everybody; even in Spain the newspapers devoted whole columns to Czechoslovakia. Fighting on the Ebro front died down. Everyone was waiting for the denouement of the tragedy that was being enacted not in the theatre of military operations but in ministerial offices hidden from the eyes of the public.

I arrived in Paris on 23rd September. It was close and a storm was threatening. I went to the Czechoslovak embassy to see the Counsellor Šafranek, whom I knew and occasionally met. He was utterly dispirited and said: 'If you ask me, there's no hope at all'. He was a tall, solidly built man of great self-possession, but on that occasion he was unable to master his feelings; his voice broke, and he kept saying: 'It's very hot today, isn't it?' He poured out some water and his hand shook. Crowds gathered under the windows: there was a succession of delegations – workers, scholars, writers; they were all in a state of furious indignation at the treachery which they felt was in the air and came to express their sympathy for Czechoslovakia.

I missed my paper's telephone call because I was walking about the streets in the working-class districts. On all sides I heard the same words: 'Chamberlain', 'capitulation', 'Daladier', 'Fascism'. The people I spoke to were excited. One worker said: 'The bastards! Don't they realize that if the Czechs are handed over to the Germans, in a month's time they'll be attacking us? Traitors, that's what they are'.

In the better-off districts I watched a scene that reminded me of 1914: servants packing elegant suitcases into a car. Everything was quiet here except for some lady who was shouting at her elderly companion, evidently hard of hearing: 'Can't you understand? This Popular Front mob wants Paris to be destroyed like Madrid'.

I called at the office of *Ordre* to see Emile Buré, obese, intelligent, and something of a cynic. He was a brilliant journalist, typical of an older generation of Frenchmen; he was conservative in outlook and thought the Popular Front a dangerous thing but, as a patriot, condemned the appeasers. 'You know what they're afraid of? Victory.

448

Because then they'd have to fight the Germans in alliance with you. A deputy said to me the other day: "The army's taken leave of its senses – they're pressing for resistance; they don't seem to realize that it would encourage the Communists". What are we to do? We've degenerated. We need a Clemenceau, and what we've got is Daladier – a Tartarin without the imagination. Two years ago he raised his clenched fist and embraced Thorez. You'll see – tomorrow he'll raise his arm in the Nazi salute and embrace Hitler'.

I read an article by Giono in *Oeuvre* in which he said that 'a live coward is better than a dead hero'.

I wanted to get back to Barcelona as soon as possible. But on going out the next morning I saw people reading posters proclaiming partial mobilization. Daladier announced that France would fulfil her obligations and defend Czechoslovakia.

(When Franco started the rebellion, Blum had also promised that France would help the Spanish Republic. Talleyrand used to say that one should never follow one's first impulse – it is usually generous and therefore stupid. I do not wish, of course, to compare Talleyrand, a cynical but outstanding politician, with men like Daladier, confused and shortsighted provincials who accidentally find themselves at the helm of State.)

Men called up were on their way to the railway stations; some raised their clenched fists and sang the *Internationale*. At street corners passers-by stopped and arguments broke out. One man shouted: 'What have the Czechs got to do with us? Let the Bolsheviks defend Beneš'. Another man called him 'Fascist'. Policemen intervened monotonously: 'Move on there, move on'. They seemed rather at a loss – they did not know whom to hit.

In Paris the building trade workers were on strike. On 25th September they went back to work on the grounds that they did not want to hinder the defence of France. Sand was distributed from carts – against incendiary bombs. The roads to the south were jammed with cars: the bourgeoisie was leaving. On all sides I heard the word 'War'. Buses were requisitioned. Women took up emergency first-aid courses. Some shops closed down. At night Paris was plunged in darkness, and for a moment I felt that I was back in the streets of Barcelona.

On 30th September the Munich agreement was announced. The street-lamps shone again and ordinary Frenchmen went wild: they felt as if they had gained a victory. On a foggy evening the crowd rejoiced on the Grands Boulevards; it was disgusting to watch. People congratulated one another on the victory. The City Council decided to name one of the Paris streets 'rue du 30 Septembre'.

That evening we dined with Puterman at the Coupole in Montparnasse. I have already said that my friend Puterman edited the weekly paper *Lu*; he was a native of Bessarabia, who idolized Pushkin and collected rare editions, but his heart was not that of a bibliophile – it was warm and passionate. We sat there feeling crushed by what had happened while at neighbouring tables Frenchmen were drinking champagne and gorging. One of them suddenly noticed our distaste for the toasts, the roars of laughter, the carnival jollity, and asked: 'Are we disturbing you?' Puterman replied: 'Yes, sir, I am a Czech'. They were quiet for a moment, but then resumed their triumphant din.

I watched Daladier drive along the Champs Elysées. People threw roses into his car. He was smiling. In the Chamber of Deputies the Socialists, who the day before had condemned the Munich agreement, voted for the government. Blum wrote: 'My heart is torn between shame and a feeling of relief'. In the boulevard des Capucines I saw four flags hanging outside a cinema, including the German swastika flag. The papers invited subscriptions for a gift to the 'peacemaker Chamberlain'. In the Alsatian town of Colmar four streets were renamed, one after Adolf Hitler.

Suritz said that Daladier was a weakling, that Bonnet represented those in favour of appeasement and that Mandel had resigned in protest, but at the last moment had thought better of it.

I ended my latest dispatch with the words: 'In the Champs Elysées the capitalists cheered Monsieur Daladier. It may be that in the not too distant future they will watch Hitler's divisions marching to the Arc de Triomphe'. The editor left this sentence out; I was told that one had to wait – the intoxication might pass off; but I was asked to send frequent and detailed information about what was going on.

On 11th October *Izvestia* took on a new correspondent: Paul Jocelyn. I had chosen the pseudonym at random, without thinking, of course, of Lamartine's hero. Ehrenburg continued to send long articles while Paul Jocelyn sent brief daily dispatches.

In October I went to Alsace. The Alsatian Fascists, taking heart from Munich, had begun to talk about union with the Reich. No sooner had I arrived in Strasbourg than an agent from the Préfecture came to fetch me. The Prefect asked me whether I intended to advocate the separation of Alsace from France as the *Daily Express* correspondent had done. I laughed and explained that the attitude of the Soviet Union was in no way similar to that of Lord Beaverbrook. This pleased him, and he told me that a high ranking police official would help me to collect information on the activities of the 'autonomists' (as the pro-Hitler party called itself).

The police official proved a godsend; in the first place he disliked the Germans and secondly the autonomists had insulted him personally by calling him a cuckold in their press. He showed me some interesting documents found during a search, a list of members of a secret organization, even armbands by which, when the time came, the conspirators would be able to recognize one another. He told me that all this was known to the government but that the Minister Chautemps had decided to keep the whole thing dark for fear of offending Hitler. I met various politicians in Strasbourg and in industrial Mulhouse.

My articles did not pass unnoticed; they were quoted by newspapers who were against appeasement; the government also took an interest in them. As I learnt later, Chautemps had thought of expelling me but Mandel opposed it, and I was allowed to remain.

Among my papers I have found a telephone message I sent to the foreign department of *Izvestia*: 'Please call 25th October noon Moscow time for checking. Cabling separately short interviews various Alsatian politicians. Leaving for Marseilles evening 25th'.

In Marseilles the Congress of the Radical Party, to which Daladier and the majority of Ministers belonged, was being held. I remembered the Radical Party of the past when it had represented the small bourgeoisie, the peasants of the southern provinces, the free-thinking intelligentsia, and when it insisted on the purity of its Jacobin traditions. In Marseilles the Jacobins were not mentioned, but there was much heated talk about the 'Communist menace', although the Popular Front was still officially in existence. The speakers put all the blame on the workers, calling them lazy louts, and extolled Daladier as the man of peace. True, there were other Radicals – such as Pierre Cot and Bossoutroux – who disapproved of Daladier's policy, but I knew that they would soon be expelled from the party if they did not leave it of their own accord.

I had a talk with Edouard Herriot. He was depressed but could not make up his mind to break with Daladier; in his speech he said that the Soviet Union had been ready to fulfil its obligations, that France had lost her allies, that the menace of war had increased, and complained to me: 'The French have lost their heads. We forget we are a great power. I can't see how all this is going to end'.

During the Congress a great fire broke out; the hotel where the delegates were staying also caught fire. It turned out that the fire-brigade had not got enough ladders. Herriot was furious and shouted: 'Must I send for firemen from Lyons?' The incident seemed almost purposely arranged as a kind of foretaste of the looming catastrophe.

Soon after, another Congress assembled in Nantes – that of the C.G.T.; there, too, went the inseparables – Ilya Ehrenburg and Paul Jocelyn. The Communists called for a struggle, but in Nantes, too, there were those in favour of appeasement; one of them said: 'France's salvation lies in accepting the role of a second-rate power'.

Everything was in confusion. A thick fog hung over the towns and in the minds of men. *Oeuvre* announced that it had always stood for peace from the time when it had published Barbusse's *Le Feu* (*Under Fire*), and that it had not altered its standpoint: it was necessary to make concessions to Hitler and Mussolini in order to avoid war. There were even 'leftists' who, while protesting against the dissolution of POUM in Spain, demanded the outlawing of the Communist Party in France. The writer Céline suggested joining Hitler in a crusade against 'the Jews and the Kalmuks' (by Kalmuks he meant the Russians).

I was told to call at the Sûreté. A high-up functionary asked me whether I had noticed that I was being followed. I said that I supposed I was shadowed by police spies but I was used to it and did not mind. The functionary said that I was being followed by terrorists of the extreme right; he produced some fifty photographs and asked me to point out the men who were tailing me. I smiled: I could recognize none of them, but had no fear for myself. 'You're wrong there. We know that the organization responsible for the murder of the Rosselli brothers has decided to liquidate you'. I thanked him for his interest and left. I never found out whether this was true or only a try-on. Somehow I do not think anyone intended to shoot me, but that the Sûreté had hoped I would take fright and leave France. My newspaper work, talks with politicians, pamphlets, as well as the spate of information poured out by Paul Jocelyn could not have been much to the taste of the rulers of France at that time.

Everything went like clockwork. The government published

special decrees aimed at the workers. A general strike had been called for 30th November. The government decided to bring in troops to replace the strikers. The bus drivers who refused to work were jailed. The strike was broken. Daladier could toast yet another victory – this time over the workers. The words 'Popular Front' disappeared altogether.

In Germany large-scale Jewish pogroms were going on. Wretched people tried to cross the frontier and seek refuge in France. The frontier guards rounded them up and, on orders from Paris, handed them back to the Germans.

In the middle of December the French members of the International Brigade returned; they were welcomed by the workers at a meeting that was moving and infinitely sad: while the men of the International Brigade had been fighting at Guadalajara and Jarama, Fascism had stealthily entered their house by the backdoor.

The Civil War had begun in France as far back as 1934; it was a secret war, without guns, but with attacks and counter-attacks, with casualties and mutual hatred. Munich was neither a fortuitous event nor a miscalculation: the bourgeoisie was ready to make any sacrifice to get the better of the workers. And the workers, angered by the treachery, remained grimly silent.

I have a very clear memory of the autumn of 1938. On the surface life seemed much as usual: people worked, drank *apéritifs*, played cards, danced; but underneath it all there was bitterness, anxiety and confusion. I could not look at it with the eyes of a stranger – I knew France, I loved her and saw that, like a sleep-walker with open but unseeing eyes, she was heading for disaster, to the accompaniment of sentimental songs, chrysanthemums, rich pastry and gossip. I called an article I wrote at the end of November 'The Melancholy of France' and said: 'I am not speaking of poverty or grief but of the immense melancholy that has settled over this land: Munich has broken France'.

Meanwhile Paul Jocelyn regularly reported such items as that Jules Romains, after lunching with Ribbentrop, had come to believe in the future of a Franco-German alliance, and that armaments manufacturers were subsidizing the pacifist propaganda of the Teachers' Union.

On 5th December I wrote to Moscow: 'I should temporarily like to get rid of Jocelyn who is shouldering Ehrenburg out of existence.

I am tired, I never have a moment's leisure. I hope the editorial office will understand'.

Winter had begun; there was a smell of roasted chestnuts in the streets; lovers feeling the cold pressed closer together.

A few days later I managed to make my way back to Barcelona. Before I had time to look round I was shouting into the telephone: 'An enemy offensive has started all along the front from Tremp to the Ebro'. Men were still fighting there.

30

SOON AFTER my arrival in Barcelona – I think it was on New Year's Eve – I went to see the poet Antonio Machado: I had brought him some coffee and cigarettes from France. He lived with his old mother in a small house on the outskirts of the town. I had visited him there quite often in the summer. Machado did not look well and his shoulders drooped; he seldom shaved and this made him look still older; he was not more than sixty-three, yet he walked with difficulty; only his eyes were still bright and alive. I have kept my notes on this last meeting: 'Machado read passages from the elegies of Jorge Manrique: "Our life is rivers, and death is a sea, it takes in so many rivers, there go forever our happiness and our sorrow, all by which man lived". Then he said about death: "The whole matter is one of 'how'. A man must laugh well, write poetry well, live well and die well". With a sudden childlike smile he added: "If an actor has entered wholeheartedly into his part, it's easy for him to leave the stage" '.

Antonio Machado's death was dramatic, and unexpected in this most self-effacing of all the poets I have met in my life. When the Fascists approached Barcelona, he took his mother with him and they plodded along the terrible roads of the frontier strip. Machado lived in exile only three weeks; he died in the small town of Collioure from which one could see the mountains of Spain. His mother survived him by two days. Machado could not go on living. Today he is generally recognized as the greatest Spanish poet of our century. He is honoured by the academicians of Franco Spain, and young Spanish poets dedicate poems to his memory. He is now beyond all disputes and beyond all events; the reason why I speak of him here is because for me his figure cannot be divorced from those tragic days when Spain was forsaking Spain.

I met him for the first time in Madrid in April 1936. I remember with what admiration Rafael Alberti, Neruda and a dozen young writers listened to his poetry. I have said that he was extremely self-effacing, but that is an understatement. Chekhov was embarrassed when Bunin called him a poet and protested that he wrote crudely about crude life. As a man Machado had something of Chekhov about him. He once said to me: 'Perhaps I'm no poet. Quevedo was a poet, so were Ronsard, Verlaine, Darío. It's true that I love poetry'. This was no affectation, no pose; at sixty, he was embarrassed by rapturous admiration. And he was kindly, like Chekhov, and tolerant of the weaknesses of others; he tried to find excuses for critics soured by life, and unfortunate scribble-addicts. He found some grain of goodness or beauty in everything. His poetry is, above all, humane.

He read to me verses by Jorge Manrique. It is difficult to find a Spanish poet who has not written about death. In Barcelona, in the summer of 1938, we talked about the situation at the front, about Franco's conduct, and Machado said: 'They're mistaken abroad in thinking that Spaniards are fatalists who meet death with resignation. No, Spaniards understand how to struggle against death'.

I saw how in the last years he struggled against death. He was undismayed by the bombings, by life in temporary quarters. He did not want to leave Madrid; he was removed to Valencia in the same way as the pictures from the Prado. He wrote in Madrid, in Valencia, in Barcelona, he wrote amazing sonnets and, practically every day, articles for the front-line press.

Yet he always returned to thoughts of death; in this, as in much else, he was a true Spaniard. He wrote sonnets, elegies, blank and rhymed verse, he liked gnomic poetry which the Spaniards had borrowed from the Arabs and the Jews – short philosophical quatrains; for the most part he left them unrhymed; according to the *romancero* tradition the last words of the second and fourth line have the same stressed vowel; this has an even more subtle, more intangible effect than that of our remote Russian assonances.

'You say nothing is lost. What if you break a glass – no one will drink from it, no one, ever again . . .' 'You say that everything remains. Perhaps you are right. Yet we lose everything, and everything loses us' . . . 'Everything passes and everything stays; but we have to go on, go on making our way, our way beyond the sea'.

There are other quatrains of his that I often recall. 'Examining my skull some latter-day Hamlet will say: "The beautiful petrification of a carnival mask" ' . . . 'A man at sea has no need at all of four things – oars, rudder, anchor and the fear of sailing' . . . 'Man fights two battles, and each is defiant – he fights God in his sleep, and on awaking fights the sea' . . . 'Our hours are minutes when we thirst to know, and

centuries when we know what is knowable' . . . 'It is good to know
that glasses are for us to drink from; the bad thing is that we do not
know the reason for our thirst'.

Darío wrote of Machado: 'He shepherds a thousand lions and a
thousand kids'. In Machado's poetry there is an unusual combination
of the wormwood of the steppe with the sweetness of summer, of
wisdom with simplicity. It evokes the poverty-stricken hamlets near
Soria, the stones of Castile, human misfortune, courage, hope, and his
road is always 'step by step', a road that winds uphill and down, the
difficult road of Spain, of man.

He strode through life making his way, with others and in solitude;
he was never on the stage – although in collaboration with his brother
he wrote several plays – but lived, as it were, in the gallery. He had
started out as a teacher of French and then of Spanish literature in the
provincial towns of Soria, Baeza, Segovia, in the backwaters of Spanish
provincial life. In the spring of 1937, when I got back from a visit to the
Southern front, I decided to go and see how he was faring; he was
then living near Valencia. He questioned me about the Fascists who
were entrenched at Virgen de la Cabeza, then asked me how I had
liked La Mancha. I took down some of his remarks: 'The French
landscape is light, God painted it in His mature years, perhaps in His
old age. Everything has been well thought out, there is a sense of
proportion everywhere; a little more, a little less, and all would fall
apart. But Spain God painted in His youth. He did not think about
His brush-strokes, did not even know how many rocks He was piling
up one on top of the other. I love Chekhov's *The Steppe*. Somehow I
feel that the Russians can understand the Spanish landscape . . . La
Mancha – all know this name – Don Quixote. But why is it that so
many people don't understand that Aldonza is Dulcinea? Every
Spaniard sees his dream in the healthy, sturdy, housewifely girl, and
every Spaniard knows that the Dulcineas can keep house, gossip,
sew shirts. When Turgenev was writing about Hamlet and Don
Quixote he did not realize that Aldonza and Dulcinea were one and
the same. Perhaps it's because all his heroines are either pure heavenly
creatures or predatory ones. We have no discontinuity, but unity is
far more difficult to achieve than any contrast. And that is La Mancha,
that is the whole of Spain'.

I have quoted the poetical maxims of Don Quixote-Sancho Panza
in a literal translation. I dare not translate those sweet and mocking

457

lines which Antonio Machado composed for Aldonza-Dulcinea: they are so close to music that the slightest change in the sound of a word is enough to destroy the charm. In this there is an affinity between Machado and the Blok of *The Hours of the Night*. And, indeed, Machado was for Spain what Blok was for Russia.

'Go on making our way . . .' His behaviour during the war years was pre-determined by his whole life, there was no miracle, no sudden enlightenment, no change of direction, only loyalty: to himself, to Spain, to his times. Many people, even among those who have studied foreign languages, do not understand the language of art. The entry in the *Literary Encyclopedia* says: 'Machado is a typical representative of that section of the small bourgeois intelligentsia which, faced by the advance of capitalism, tries to withdraw into the world of self-analysis and seeks the solution of the contradictions of the present in petty bourgeois humanism'. This was written in 1934. But the *Great Soviet Encyclopedia* of 1954 says: 'The collection of poems *The Fields of Castile* (1912) is permeated with love for the poet's homeland and with bitter reflections on the fate of the Spanish people . . . In the volume *New Songs* (1924) the poet condemns reactionary bourgeois art'. Was it Machado who had changed? No, both encyclopedists were writing about books of his that had appeared in 1912 and 1924. Perhaps methods of criticism had changed? Not at all. It was simply that the war years had helped those people who understand information conveyed by newspapers but do not understand poetry to discover which label suited Machado best.

It is sad that air-raids and concentration camps should have been needed for poets to be given the right to live.

I have lost a lot of things in the course of my life but I have saved Machado's books with their dedications to me: I brought them out of Spain and, later, out of occupied Paris. I sometimes look at the handwriting, at the photograph (which I took in Barcelona) and the man seems to blend with lines of verse: 'On my life's path, art thou water or thirst? Tell me, my wild love'.

He fought together with the people. I remember on the Ebro the Divisional Commander Tagüeña reading out Machado's greeting to the men, his voice trembling with emotion: 'Spain of the Cid, Spain of 1808, has recognized her children in you'. When we were parting he said: 'Maybe, after all, we never learnt how to fight. And, besides, we didn't have enough equipment. But one shouldn't judge the Spaniards too harshly. This is the end – any day now Barcelona will fall. For the strategists, the politicians, the historians everything will be clear: we shall have lost the war. But humanly speaking I'm not so sure. Perhaps we have won it'. He went with me as far as the garden gate. I looked back and saw him, sad, round-shouldered, as old as Spain, a wise man, a tender poet, and I saw his eyes, very deep, not answering but questioning. God knows whom. I saw him for the last time. Sirens began to wail. The next air-raid had started.

31

28TH JANUARY–5TH FEBRUARY, the last week in Catalonia, the denouement. How is one to describe it? We have seen so much since then, lived through so much. Yet those days still live in my memory; the wound has not healed.

On 28th January I arrived in Gerona. This had once been a little town of narrow picturesque streets, arcades, gardens and the ancient stones of its fortress-walls; and now the town was screaming – not one man, not a hundred men but the whole town. There had once been 30,000 inhabitants in Gerona, now there were 400,000. People with sacks and baskets sat, lay, slept in the squares, in the streets, and almost without stop the Fascist planes bombed and machine-gunned the people. There were no longer any Republican fighter-planes or anti-aircraft batteries. There seemed to be nothing on that day but screams and blood – and spades in the cemetery where men were digging communal graves.

On 30th January the Divisional Commander, a tall, bony Spaniard, said: 'We haven't got any spades. We must dig in but there are no spades'. An avalanche of refugees jammed the roads; the citizens were moving out: someone was lugging an armchair; a respectable bearded man, looking like a professor, was carting huge folios tied together with rope; peasants herded sheep and goats; little girls carried dolls. A people was moving out. No one wrote on the walls now that they did not want to live with the Fascists – there was no time for words, and I do not even know whether those who were going gave a thought to life – they went forward without slogans, without hope, possibly without thoughts.

Some units continued to fight rearguard actions. The small town of Figueras, twenty miles from the French frontier, became the capital of the Spanish Republic for a short time. I saw a journalist I knew in the old smithy: this was the combined editorial office and printing press of a Barcelona newspaper. The next issue was being got out. A man with his head bandaged dictated in the semi-darkness: ' . . . we are successfully repelling the numerically superior enemy . . .'

460

I looked for Savich but could not find him. While I was in the main square another raid began. Afterwards low-flying Italian planes machine-gunned the refugees. The Chief of Staff said to me: 'I must issue a communiqué but we haven't even got a typewriter'. Sinister rumours were spreading: the Italians had landed in Port Bou and had cut Figueras off from France, the French would not allow anyone across the frontier, not even women. In a café the wounded were receiving first aid.

'I think the Russians are there,' an officer told me pointing to the school building. But the people I found there were Negrín, Alvarez del Vayo and other Ministers. They were sitting on stools at a long table; maps and folders with documents lay scattered about. Negrín said: 'We must gain time to cover the evacuation of the people to France. Once that's done we can fly to Madrid'. One of the Ministers argued that the first consideration was to evacuate the army and the equipment: from Marseilles they could go by sea to Valencia and there, jointly with the forces of the Central front, launch an offensive. Not all illusions had yet been lost.

I was told that the Soviet comrades were in a village five miles outside the town. It took me three hours to reach it. The night was cold, and the refugees were warming themselves at campfires, burning the rubbish they had been dragging with them along the roads, heaven knows what for.

I went into a peasant's house and was overwhelmed with joy: there, in front of a big open hearth with a blazing fire, were Savich and Kotov. Savich explained that for some reason the embassy library had first been evacuated by lorry, and now they had to burn it – Russian books could not be left for the Fascists. The man who was known as Kotov in Spain inspired me with a certain mistrust; he was neither a diplomat nor a soldier. He was throwing the books into the fire with evident relish, accompanying his action with a running commentary: 'Who's this? Kaverin? Here you go! Olga Forsh? I'm not sure. Still, it's warmer in there'. I was astounded by Savich – he loved books but he seemed to have caught the infection and was recklessly throwing volumes into the flames. Kotov said: 'Hmm ... *The Second Day*. I'd better cede the cremation rites to the author'. I threw the book on the fire.

Some embassy officials came in and told me that in the haste of evacuation they had forgotten to take down the escutcheon and the

461

flag from the embassy building; when they realized this someone had asked Savich: 'Will you try and get them?' Savich had gone back to Barcelona, where there was shooting in the streets, and he and his driver, the gallant Pepe, had climbed to the roof and taken down the escutcheon and the flag. (Savich was a strange man: he had gone back to Barcelona without turning a hair at the very moment when the Fascists were entering the town, he wrote reports for TASS during air-raids, he helped to burn books and made jokes, yet in Paris a week later he was almost dying of fright: he had no police permit and spent the night in hiding at Dusya's, and even she, with all her gaiety, could not get a smile out of him. He showed me a telegram sent from a little frontier town: 'Car and I at your disposal. Pepe', and gave a bitter laugh. But perhaps this is nothing to be surprised at – all men are the same.)

We were told that the Cortes would assemble in Figueras on 1st February. Savich and I spent quite a long time looking for the entrance to the cellars of the ancient castle. The Italians kept up a continuous bombing of the town. A sentry in white gloves stood at the entrance. An old man had found a small, threadbare carpet and had spread it over the steps leading to the cellar: 'After all, it is the Cortes'. Benches were reserved for the diplomatic corps and journalists. At the usher's request I took my seat on the diplomatic bench so that it should not be quite empty; later I was joined by someone from our embassy. Negrín was unshaven and his eyes were inflamed from lack of sleep. He said that Britain and France had betrayed the Republic, they were blockading Barcelona. The French were not allowing the severely wounded to cross the frontier. He also said: 'France will have cause to regret what she is doing'. It was voted that there should be an appeal to the people: the struggle would go on; the vote was taken by roll-call, the deputies rising in turn and saying: '*Si*'. One of them had an improvised bandage on his hand; blood was seeping through.

That night I drove to the French town of Perpignan to send my account of the session of the Cortes to *Izvestia* and returned in the morning.

The roads could not hold the refugees; they spread like a river in spring flood, crowding on to the rocky ledges. Near Puigcerda the snow was so deep that children sank in it. By the Ares pass I saw old women crawling over the ice-covered rocks. The peasants killed sheep, roasted them on the spot and fed the soldiers. One woman was lying in labour in the field; we shouted for a doctor. An old man came up, he was an ear, nose and throat specialist. He delivered the woman and later, warming himself at a campfire, suddenly said: 'The boy was lucky, he was just in time to be born on Spanish soil'. The doctor who spoke those rather moving words looked anything but a hero as, dressed in a woman's green jacket, he held out his swollen rheumatic fingers to the fire.

In a shepherd's hut I saw Alvarez del Vayo with a bowl of weak coffee that someone had brought him. His eyes were so grief-stricken that I turned away; but he, with great self-control, spoke about a lorry-load of bread arriving for the soldiers, about the artillery barrage and the evacuation of the wounded. (He is a man of strong faith; every two or three years I meet him in Paris, Moscow or Geneva, and each time I recall that day in February, the Minister of Foreign Affairs in the hut, with tragic eyes and a calm, steady voice.)

Three days later, somewhere on the frontier, I was standing with Savich on a rock. Endless crowds of refugees were streaming past. Small donkeys brayed. Children cried. A detachment of soldiers went by, one of them incongruously sounding a bugle. Bombs were falling. A peasant scooped up a handful of earth and tied it into a large red handkerchief.

Later I wrote a poem; it referred to many of the details mentioned in this chapter, but it was also on another, second plane, the plane of emotions that can be expressed only in verse: 'In the damp night the winds were scouring the rocks. Spain, dragging her weapons, trudged to the north. The bugle of the demented bugler shrieked till morning. Fighters were bringing their guns out of the battle. Peasants herded their bewildered animals. Children carried their toys and the doll's mouth was twisted. Women gave birth in the field, swaddled their babies in torment and went on to die standing. Campfires were still burning before the parting, the brass of the bugle still sounded. What can be more sorrowful and more wonderful than a hand still clutching a handful of earth? That night songs freed themselves from words and villages moved on like ships'.

At the frontier posts the French had stationed not only gendarmes but also troops – at first Senegalese, then French battalions. The Spanish soldiers laid down their arms and were searched; many of the refugees were also searched. At Perthus I saw women separated from their children by accident; they screamed and refused to go on, but were pushed aside.

I had a police pass, a press card issued by the Paris Préfecture. In Paris it produced little effect but here it proved an Open Sesame: I was free to go into Spain and back. I had to save many comrades from being interned in camps – a journalist, the women cleaners from our embassy, my driver, a promising young poet and men of the International Brigades. For several days I did nothing else and on some days this left me no time to send telegrams to my paper; I preferred to ring up Paris where Paul Jocelyn was supposed to be.

I came across wonderful people. A teacher from the small frontier town of Prats-de-Mollo stood practically day and night near a mountain pass distributing hot soup and bread to the refugees. Hundreds of people brought him provisions. A mechanic from Arles-sur-Tech, the owner of a small garage, drove ceaselessly in an old ramshackle car to the Ares pass picking up exhausted, frozen people and bringing them back to the town. At the pass the gendarmes were easy-going, and the mechanic helped me to get many comrades across the frontier; I am very sorry that I have failed to remember his name.

On 6th February I trod on Spanish soil for the last time: in the mountain village of Camprodón. Fighting was still going on in the neighbourhood.

The French government was issuing inhuman orders. But here, on the spot, people acted in a different spirit. Every day I witnessed gestures of solidarity, kindness, sympathy, as well as baseness. In the small town of Boulu I was looking for a peasant woman and her children for whom I had a letter and some money from her husband. The fleshy mayor, with his dull, unresponsive face, said: 'There are too many of them'. And a policeman shouted: 'It's none of your business! Get out and be quick about it'. I reminded him of human feelings, to which he replied that feelings did not concern him. In the small towns of St Laurent-de-Cerdans, Prats-de-Mollo, Arles-sur-Tech the local people fed the refugees and hid them from the police. Some groups were sent to Lyons, and the mayor of that city, Edouard Herriot, came to the railway station to supervise the feeding of the Spaniards and to house them in barracks and schools. There were, however, many French papers daily insisting that France must be protected from the Spanish 'Anarchists, Communists, murderers and criminals'.

Already in the summer I had made friends with the proprietor of a shabby old hotel in Perpignan; I used to stay there, and it was here that

464

I now brought my comrades; all the rooms were full, people had to sleep in the dining-room, in the reception office, wherever they could, but the proprietor did not inform the police of the new arrivals and no one was arrested. But in the town the hunt was up. Spanish women who had never worn anything on their heads but a shawl bought smart little hats and made up their faces to hide the traces of grief and to look as much as possible like Frenchwomen. In Banyuls the fishermen beat up a right-wing newspaper reporter who was jeering at the defeated Spaniards. Yes, there were various kinds of Frenchmen, and one cannot either condemn or justify them wholesale.

The French interned the Spaniards in concentration camps in Argelès and St Cyprien. They provided a loaf of bread to every six men and tainted drinking water, treating them with utter contempt. But in Paris Ribbentrop was being lavishly entertained. However, when one speaks of those times it is better not to think of justice – or of Ribbentrop for that matter: where was he not made welcome?

A note reached me from Herrera Petere who had been put into a concentration camp. He said that many of my friends were behind barbed wire. I went to Paris. Aragon, Bloch, Cassou and many other members of our Association took up the case of the interned writers; within two or three weeks we managed to obtain their release.

Negrín and the other Ministers left by air for Madrid. The territory still occupied by Republican troops was now encircled. England and France recognized General Franco as the legal ruler of Spain. The Republic was blockaded. Ships loaded with cargoes of bread and potatoes for Valencia were detained in Marseilles. In Madrid, on 6th March, Colonel Casado, with the blessing of that figurehead, General Miaja, staged a *coup* and replaced Negrín by a group of men who had made up their minds to surrender. However, the denouement of the Spanish tragedy was not in the death throes of doomed Madrid but had already taken place in those winter days when the army of the Ebro, in full order and under arms, crossed the French frontier in the hope of being taken across to Valencia. (The weapons the soldiers had managed to hold on to were handed over to Franco by the French.)

Hitler, encouraged by success, marched into Prague. Marina Tsvetayeva, at her last meeting with her friend – the desk – wrote: 'O eyes full of tears! Weeping of wrath and love! O Czechia in tears, Spain in blood! O black mountain that has plunged the whole world into darkness! It's time – it's time – it's time to return one's cards to the Creator'.

I find it hard to say farewell to Spain in this book. I remember on the Ares pass a Spanish soldier carrying an automatic rifle who was saying good-bye to his wife and two-year-old son; he asked me to take them to a safe place and said: 'I'm not leaving – I don't believe the French will ever take us to Valencia, they've come to an understanding with Franco. At least here I can still do in a dozen or so Fascists'. I looked back; he was lying down, his rifle to his shoulder with his eyes not on us but turned to the south from where the Fascists might appear.

By the roadside from Port Bou to Cerbère lay a heap of rifles, sub-machine-guns, tin hats, revolvers, even knives. I suddenly caught sight of a lance and an antique helmet: they were probably exhibits taken from the small Catalan museum, and the Senegalese must have thought that they were useful weapons. Yes, Don Quixote's helmet and lance had been weapons; with them Spain had defended herself for a thousand days against two Fascist powers – Italy and Germany.

Seven months later the Second World War broke out, and this chapter could well have been a prologue to the fifth part of my book; but I would rather make it an epilogue to the epoch that preceded it, when in almost every town a struggle was going on between liberty and slavery, between humanity and bestiality, between self-seeking and self-sacrifice. In the years to follow there was a great deal of heroism, as a result of which Fascism was defeated; but in this new epoch there was no place any longer for the lance and the obsolete helmet with which the Knight of the Sorrowful Countenance had gone forth to champion human dignity.

32

IN THE spring of 1939 Savich left for Moscow. We went to Le Havre to see him off. Many Spaniards were going to the Soviet Union on the same ship. We stood on the quay; a strong breeze was blowing; the Spain I had lost seemed to rise before my eyes again. I asked Savich to write to me from Moscow, but for a long time I did not know how he was getting on: in those days people were chary of sending letters abroad.

I sent daily reports to my paper signed by Paul Jocelyn – a patchy and at the same time monotonous chronicle of events: Fascist terror in Spain, Czechoslovakia's agony, the seizure of Albania by the Italians, Bonnet's and Laval's sly moves, Blum's cowardly bleating, Daladier's stupid parochial policy.

In the middle of April my reports stopped appearing. I thought at first that perhaps my stuff had deteriorated and tried to clear up the matter with the editor. At last I was informed through the embassy that for the time being *Izvestia* would not be able to print either Ehrenburg or Paul Jocelyn; I would remain their permanent correspondent, however, and would receive my salary as usual.

Completely puzzled I went to see Suritz. He reproached me: 'They aren't asking you for anything, what's there to be nervous about?' Then he grew thoughtful. 'We're informed that Litvinov's been removed from his post. Molotov's been appointed in his place. But this has got nothing to do with you as far as I can see. Why are you upset? Take a rest. Write a novel. There are lots of interesting exhibitions on just now'. (Suritz took a passionate interest in painting.)

But the fact was that my enforced leisure was owing to what the newspapers call the international situation. Paul Jocelyn continued to denounce the Fascists, but the time of complicated diplomatic negotiations was drawing near. The outlook was not clear, and my paper decided to keep me in cold storage. 'You'll be useful yet,' Suritz said. (Unfortunately he proved right: on 22nd June 1941 I had a telephone call from the editor: 'We could use your stuff now; after all, you're an old *Izvestia* hand'.)

England and France announced that they intended to halt the aggressors and come to an agreement with the Soviet Union; but after Munich it was difficult to put any faith in the good intentions of Daladier or Chamberlain. I recall those days with deep disgust. People sat by their radios – even those who did not know German – listening to Hitler's speeches and trying to guess from his intonation what the morrow would bring. France was like a sleek, well-fed rabbit hypnotized by a boa-constrictor.

In May the International Anti-Fascist Conference was held in Paris. I attended and met many old acquaintances – Langevin, Cachin, Bloch, Malraux, Aragon, César Falcón – and on that occasion I met Fierlinger for the first time. Everybody was in a black mood and the speeches seemed empty repetitions of things heard long ago – the virtue had gone out of them.

At one point Fernando Gerassi introduced me to a shy young writer who was a friend of his. His name was Jean-Paul Sartre. He squinted, which gave him a rather furtive look, but he spoke with surprising frankness about his feelings of despair. He gave me his book *Le Mur*; the stories were also about despair. When many years later I met Sartre again and got to know him, I realized that my first impression had been correct: his mind is an unusual combination of logical thinking, of sharp, even caustic intelligence and of childlike naïvety, trustfulness and sensibility.

It is difficult for me to write connectedly about that year: oppressive memories like mountain clouds descend and blot out the scene. In May Joseph Roth died. Toller hanged himself. Yakobson arrived from Prague and said that when they parted Nezval had cried like a child. Many German writers went to America. Hopeful Spaniards frequented Picasso. For the first time since I had known him Picasso said to me: '*Mon vieux*, I find it difficult to work – we're drowning in filth'. Outwardly nothing seemed to have changed. Summer holidays began: the papers announced that 'all Paris' was at Deauville, and described parties and beachwear. But it felt like a simulacrum of things as they had been in the past.

While I was in Spain I had been absorbed by the struggle and it had distracted me from many other thoughts. Now I was alone with my reflections. I often felt that it would be easier if I were in Moscow: there, at least, everybody understood you. In Paris solitude depressed me.

468

Already in Barcelona, just before the end, I had learnt Koltsov's fate. In Paris first Lisa came to me, then Maria Osten (Gresshoener). They were both leaving for Moscow. Lisa cried and said that Koltsov had been unwell even before he left Spain: 'Perhaps I'll be able to get medicines to him'.

News reached me about the fate of Meyerhold and Babel. I was losing my closest friends.

When I visited the embassy I saw new faces. All those whom I used to know – the counsellor Hirschfeld, the military attaché Ventsov, the air attaché Vasilchenko, Semyonov and many others – had disappeared. No one dared to so much as mention their names.

One day Suritz said to me: 'Raskolnikov has been to see me. He's been summoned to Moscow, but he's taken fright and lost his head. He asked me what he ought to do. I told him he must go back at once. He made a very painful impression on me'. Two days later Raskolnikov (who was then Soviet Representative in Bulgaria) came to me too and asked what he should do. I had met him in the twenties in Moscow when he had been editor of *Red Virgin Soil* and a very lively, impulsive character. He had written a preface to one of my books and criticized me for wavering and sitting on the fence. I remembered the part he had played in the October days. But here he was in my flat in the rue du Cotentin, looking like a frightened child for all his height and solidity; he said he had been recalled to Moscow and had set out with his wife and baby; on the journey his wife had wept, and suddenly at Prague he had changed his mind and, instead of going on to Moscow, had come to Paris. He kept on saying: 'I'm not afraid for myself, it's my wife. She says "I won't go on living without you" '. I had known some 'deserters' – Besedovsky, Dmitrievsky – but they had been renegades, men with an uneasy conscience. Raskolnikov was not in the least like them; I felt that he was mentally unbalanced. He did not take Suritz's advice but stayed in France; six months later he had a nervous breakdown and died.

Negotiations for a military agreement between the Soviet Union, Britain and France were going on. The Western powers were procrastinating. In the House of Commons the Labour Party attacked Chamberlain. Our Russian newspapers barely mentioned the negotiations. Everywhere preparations for war were afoot.

I did not start writing a novel as Suritz had suggested: in order to write prose one must grasp a reality and give it a meaning. And at the time I could not make out what was happening. The goal had been clear to me for a very long time, but the paths had become so convoluted that at times it was hard to know which led where. Feelings can be expressed in lyrical verse, so I wrote poetry. In 1940 a small volume called *Vernost* (Loyalty) came out in Moscow; it contained many poems I had written in the summer of 1939, among them the one that gave the book its title: 'Loyalty: together we faced the bullets, together we buried true friends. Sorrow and courage, more than I can say. Loyalty to one's bread and loyalty to the knife, loyalty to death and loyalty to affront. The wild thoughts of the heart I shall not recall and not betray. Aim at the heart! Men will march on over you. Loyalty to the heart and loyalty to fate'.

I no longer possessed that 'semblance of precise and urgent work' which frees man from unbearably difficult thoughts. Somewhere, at a small wayside halt in life, between two wars, ignorant of what awaited us, I pondered over my destiny: 'On the quiet flagstones of the fortress square the unknown guard is changing. Shall I speak of my age? I dream no longer, and the addresses in my pocket-book are of those no longer living. The sentries stand motionless. The ranks of my friends thin out, and misfortune is silent. Only the simplest words remain: care and air, wood and water'. I felt drawn to trees, to the river, to enduring things, and as I sat in the park of a Paris suburb I could not help exclaiming: 'I know, O age, I cannot escape you, your stern and noble destiny, but for a moment let me turn my gaze from you to wallflowers and see the frail, rank grass not in delirium but reality'.

Now the reaction set in and I felt terrible fatigue: Moscow, Spain – in short, all the things about which I have been writing. In August I went for a fortnight to Juliénas, a vine-growing village in the Beaujolais. I would go off in the morning, following the straight roads, climbing the low hills. On every side there were vineyards with here and there an old tree – an elm, a maple or an ash. I sought answers from the trees to the thousand questions that plagued me. Critics sometimes call such behaviour 'escapism'. But even Gramsci in prison eagerly watched the pale bean shoots; even Zalka, shortly before his death, was comforted and tormented by the song of a wild bird. After all, a man is not a machine, and life does not follow a railway timetable.

In Juliénas I lived in a small hotel. The proprietor was an Anarchist;

470

he cooked *coq au vin* admirably, broiled steaks on dried vine shoots, got drunk every morning, threw pieces of meat to my dog Bouzou and said: 'Everything's so sad that it's positively funny'. He told his customers, the vine-growing peasants, about me. Two of them came to see me – an elderly man and a young one. It appeared that there were six Communists among the vine-growers of Juliénas. They took me round the *caves*, offered me wine and, of course, asked me questions about the Soviet Union. The elderly one asked: 'Tell me, surely in the Moscow region the wine's better than ours?' (Juliénas was famous for its wines.) I hesitatingly explained that there were no vineyards near Moscow, but wine was produced in our country in the Crimea and the Caucasus. This staggered him: he thought the highest of Moscow and loved his vineyards. After some reflection he said: 'Well, never mind, one or two Five Year Plans and they'll be making better wine than ours near Moscow too'. He sent Stalin a crate of wine. (In 1946 I revisited Juliénas. The young vine-grower recognized me. He was now the mayor. 'Is the old man alive?' I asked. He took me to the fire-blackened ruins of a house: 'The old man said to everybody: "Never mind, in a year or so the Red Army'll be here". The Germans shot him and burnt his house down. I myself was in the *maquis* and you see – I survived'.)

It was not only the trees that put heart into me but also the people: such men as these two. One might say, to use a critic's expression, that my poems were not wholly devoid of optimism: '. . . I know it all: the breaks in the years, the breachings, the endless windings of steep roads. No, man cannot easily be consoled. And yet I will tell of rain and of boughs. We shall conquer. On our side is all the freshness of the world, all the veins, all the young shoots, all youth, all this blue sky, allowing for growth, like a boy's jolly sailor suit'.

In the train I read about a Frenchman of forty-two who had turned on the gas-tap in his kitchen and left a note: 'The papers will go on appearing, but people cannot go on living any more'.

Soon after my return to Paris I heard over the radio that an agreement had been signed in Moscow between the Soviet Union and Germany. Of course I did not know the details of the negotiations between the representatives of the Western powers and Molotov, but I realized that the British and the French were playing poker and not playing it very honestly either. My reason made me accept what had happened as inevitable, but my heart rejected it. Suritz showed me the latest copy of *Pravda*. I saw a photograph: Stalin, Molotov, Ribbentrop and a certain Gauss; all wearing satisfied smiles. (I saw Ribbentrop six years later at Nuremberg; there he did not smile: he knew by then that he was going to be hanged.)

Yes, I accepted everything but this did not make things easier for me. As bearded old Charles Rappoport, who had been a friend of Lenin, Plekhanov, Jaurès, Guesde, and Liebknecht, used to say: 'Capitalism may have deserved this, but we haven't'.

On that day I fell ill with a sickness that the doctors could not diagnose: for eight months I could not eat, and lost over three stone. My clothes hung on me as though on a coat-hanger, I looked like a scarecrow. The woman doctor who attended the embassy staff said angrily: 'You've no right to let yourself go like that', and wanted me to have an X-ray. It was not worth having one for I knew that the whole thing had happened suddenly: I had read the newspapers, had sat down to lunch and all of a sudden I felt that I could not swallow a morsel of bread. (The sickness left me as abruptly as it had begun – from shock: on learning that the Germans had invaded Belgium I started to eat. The doctor solemnly pronounced: 'Spasmatic phenomena'.)

Events followed each other in swift succession. The Soviet-German Non-Aggression Pact was made public on 24th August. On 1st September Molotov declared that the pact served the interests of world peace. Nevertheless, two days later Hitler launched the Second World War.

33

TIME AND again we have seen how the bloodiest battles have been started without any declaration of war. In 1939 France's declaration of war was unaccompanied by any military action. Everyone expected air-raids, advances and retreats, but nothing happened at the front. The French were astonished: '*Drôle de guerre*'.

I remember well the first weeks of this 'phoney war'. At the time I was still able to walk about the streets. Prostitutes carrying gas-masks lay in wait for customers. Window-panes were criss-crossed with strips of paper which some housewives stuck on in elaborate patterns. I had to go to the police-station to register as an alien. A wine merchant fumed: 'Why should I give up my cellar? People can shelter in the *métro*, there's room for everybody there. But I've got a stock of old Burgundy; that's none of your gassy politics, it's capital'. Some woman demanded the arrest of one of her neighbours: 'Everybody knows he was in Spain, he fought against General Franco. I tell you, he's no Frenchman, he's a proper traitor, a Communist, a spy'. Almost every night we had mock air-raid alarms. Women came out in smart dressing-gowns, with their faces made up, while the unfortunate *concierge* poured water on the floor of the air-raid shelter for some reason known only to the local air-raid warden.

Soon everyone got tired of this farce and life settled back into its rut. People earned good money and spent it freely: the thought that the war might stop being 'phoney' made even the tight-fisted extravagant. The papers said that the soldiers at the front were dying of boredom. People sent them all kinds of games, detective novels, strong drink, silk handkerchiefs with the words: 'Somewhere in France'. The 'phoney war' made a parody of military secrets: 'Where's your friend?' 'I don't know. I'm very anxious about him. He's somewhere in France'.

Maurice Chevalier sang '*Paris reste Paris*', and this became a slogan, a programme, an incantation. Newspaper columnists wrote about military prospects in the same terms as of dividends expected from some vast monopoly: they calculated the reserves of oil, iron ore, aluminium; they tried to prove that the Allies were richer, more sound than Germany and Italy. 'We shall win because we are stronger' – this could be seen on every wall side by side with advertisements for electrical gadgets and *apéritifs*. The radio broadcast each day how many tons of enemy shipping had been sunk by the Allies. No one remembered the destruction of Poland, although war had been declared because of Hitler's threat to the Poles.

A German pilot crashed on French soil and was buried with military honours. The papers gave a touching description of the ceremony. Many listened to the broadcasts in French from Stuttgart. The Stuttgart announcer claimed that Germany would be victorious because she was stronger. '*Drôle de guerre*,' said the French with a smile. They did not think about the sunk ships or about the reserves of copper, or about victory; they took life as it came.

Still, there was a war on, therefore an enemy was needed. It was discovered in the French Communists. *L'Humanité* and *Ce Soir* were closed down. Not only was the Communist Party proscribed, but also hundreds of societies, unions, leagues suspected of Communist sympathies. Mass arrests began. The Chamber allowed the State to prosecute Communist deputies: they were accused of refusing to anathematize the Soviet Union. This was a pretext; in reality the bourgeoisie was taking its revenge on the workers for the fear they had inspired in 1936.

Only a short time before the word 'Fascism' had been in every mouth. Now it disappeared as if by magic from all the speeches, from all the newspapers. One might have thought that Fascism itself had disappeared. Yet everybody knew that the Fascists were preparing a decisive onslaught.

Clémence used to come in the morning for two hours to do the housework. Her brother was a Communist, and he had said: 'I don't know what the Russians are thinking. *L'Humanité*'s been banned. Responsible comrades have been arrested. But I can see that Laval, Flandin and all the Fascist bastards go on attacking the Communists. That shows you the Communists are right'. Clémence added: 'My brother says that if he could get hold of *L'Huma*' he'd understand everything'.

I read the Moscow papers assiduously but I cannot say that I understood everything. I remembered that Bonnet and Chamberlain had hoped Hitler would attack the Ukraine; the Soviet-German pact had been dictated by necessity. The 'phoney war' and the persecution of the Communists showed that Daladier had no intention of fighting Hitler. Still, Molotov's words about 'shortsighted anti-Fascists' jarred on me. That winter, it is true, I had had to get myself some spectacles but I refused to regard myself as 'shortsighted': the scenes of the Spanish war were still fresh in my mind; Fascism remained for me the principal enemy. I was staggered by Stalin's telegram to Ribbentrop which contained the expression 'friendship cemented with blood'. I re-read it a dozen times, and although I believed in Stalin's statesman-like genius, it made my own blood boil. This was blasphemy. How could one compare the blood of Red Army men with that of the Nazis? And how forget the rivers of blood shed by the Fascists in Spain, Czechoslovakia, Poland, not to mention Germany itself?

I could not master my feelings and when Suritz called to see how I was getting on, I referred to Stalin's unfortunate telegram. At first he replied in a formal way that this was a matter of diplomacy, that one should not attach any importance to congratulatory messages. Then all of a sudden he broke out: 'The whole trouble is that you and I are men of an older generation. We were differently brought up. Now you've been upset by a telegram. There are worse things than that, let me tell you. Some day we'll be able to talk about it all. But for the moment you must think about getting well. This is no time to be ill'. And, indeed, ten years later, shortly before his death, Suritz told me many things, as I shall recount in the last part of these memoirs.

In March 1940 Suritz suddenly left Paris. He had just recovered from pneumonia. At a meeting of the embassy staff it was agreed to send a telegram of greeting to Stalin which contained, as usual, a condemnation of the Anglo-French imperialists who had declared war on Germany. It was taken to Suritz for signature. Afterwards a young and rather inexperienced member of the staff, instead of taking it to the coding clerk, took it to the post-office. The next day it was published in the French press. It was a godsend for the politicians who thought that France should be fighting the Soviet Union rather than Fascist Germany. The French government declared Suritz *persona non grata*. When I went to the embassy I was told that he had already left – 'there's been, as you might say, a little *faux pas*'.

I had grown very weak, was easily tired, could not work. That winter we had few visitors: some of our former friends thought I had betrayed France, others feared the police – I was under constant surveillance. I can count on my fingers the people who came to see me or invited me to see them: André Malraux, Jean-Richard Bloch, the airman Pons who had fought in Spain, the Hilsums, Vogel, Rafael Alberti, Gerassi, André Simon, and my friend Puterman who lived next door to us.

It was difficult to carry on a conversation with Puterman: everything infuriated him – Daladier, the Soviet-German pact, the British, Finland; his blood pressure rose alarmingly. On one of our last evenings together he suddenly began to recite by heart Pushkin's verses: 'Weep, my dear friends, over my fate in silence, fear to arouse suspicion by your tears; in our age, you know, tears are also a crime'. He died three days later. The police made a search of the place where he lay dead. They took out the volumes of Pushkin and shook them. Vogel attended the funeral. I remembered him as an animated, genial snob, a representative of *tout Paris*. At the cemetery he stood looking aged and full of grief.

The winter was exceptionally severe; the papers said that snow had fallen even in Seville. The Soviet-Finnish war was on, and the papers forgot the very existence of Germany. Many politicians advocated the sending of an expeditionary force to Finland. Marcel Déat, who until recently had been defending Hitler and had launched the catchphrase about it not being worth while 'to die for Danzig', now regarded it as necessary to die for Helsinki. In the Madeleine prayers were offered for Mannerheim's victory. Ladies knitted vests for the Finnish soldiers. Daladier wanted to show that even if he could not fight on the Rhine he could at least fight at Vyborg. Preparations were in full swing when suddenly the news broke that peace negotiations between Helsinki and Moscow had started. The Ministers gave vent to their indignation, then returned to their former concerns.

The government decided that there were too many soldiers and the front was too short; young peasants should be allowed to go home: long live agriculture!

There was enough food, but the Ministers wanted to display their foresight and introduced some innocuous restrictions – there were cakeless days, meatless days, days without *charcuterie*.

It is hard to say what the French generals expected. They had implicit faith in the two lines, the Maginot and the Siegfried line. Even I, a profoundly civilian individual, knew that in Spain the outcome of battles had been determined by air strength and large tank formations,

476

but the French generals disliked innovations; in their eyes General de Gaulle was a Futurist.

I was waiting for an exit visa. The right-wing paper *Candide* printed a nasty paragraph about me. *Je Suis Partout* asked: 'Why is Ehrenburg still in Paris?' I myself put this question to the Préfecture, but they gave no answer, they only interrogated me. I lay in weary expectation, re-reading Montaigne, Chekhov, the Bible.

In April Hitler occupied Norway and Denmark. The new premier took the decision to send a few soldiers to Norway. The names of remote fjords began to appear in the communiqués.

I still have by me a notebook with brief entries for the year 1940. Here are a few of them; they show both what was going on in France and how I reacted to it at the time. '9th April. War in Scandinavia. Oslo. Seventeen Communists arrested'. '11th April. Rue Royale. Shop-windows, brooches in the shape of tanks and planes'. '16th April. Fifty-four Communists arrested'. '17th April. A certain Peyrol, deaf and dumb, arrested for anti-national agitation'. '23rd April. Fernand told me that Regler was beaten up in the concentration camp'. '28th April. A soldier on leave, drunk, shouted in the rue de l'Armorique: "This isn't war, it's a swindle!" ' '29th April. Elsa says that Moussinac has been arrested'. '30th April. *Oeuvre* says a worker has been arrested for reading Lenin's biography'. '1st May. *Canard Enchaîné* writes: "This is the first quiet May Day since 1918".'

A 'phoney war' . . . Men were dying – in Poland, in Finland, in Norway. Ships sank, men perished in the raging seas. Sirens wailed in the night. But all this was neither like war nor like peace. The tragic farce went on.

France was rehearsing capitulation. Millions of people of different countries were rehearsing bombings, leap-frogging assaults, machine-gun firing, agony. But the rehearsals were dull, listless; no one knew his part, the actors floundered falling into an alien speech. Strategists pored like geographers over maps of the two hemispheres without the courage to undertake even the slightest reconnaissance. Did I see it all like this merely because I was condemned to complete inaction both by my illness and by circumstance? I do not know. When a man is happy he can be idle. But in misfortune action, however futile, is a necessity.

34

WE HAD stayed late at Jean-Richard Bloch's. He had been telling us about the arrest of Moussinac, a sick man at the time, who had been put in the Santé prison with ordinary criminals. Bloch also described the deportation of arrested Communists. The train was held up at a station; suddenly voices singing the *Marseillaise* issued from the closed wagons. Soldiers on their way to the front were amazed: they had been told that these people were traitors and spies. Bloch's wife, Marguerite, smiled sadly. Afterwards we walked along the blacked-out streets. I stumbled and swore: the devil take them – there was no fighting going on, but it was easy enough to break your leg.

When we reached home the sirens went; the air-raid lasted a long time. We did not go down to the shelter: we were fed up with it. Besides, there was no war. But a cat prevented us from sleeping. Goodness knows where it had come from; it mewed piteously demanding to be let into the house. Early in the morning we heard devastating news: the Germans had invaded Holland and Belgium. This was on 10th May. Fat Pons turned up and said: 'This is the start'. In *Paris-Soir* I saw photographs that reminded me of Spain – murdered children.

In my little notebook I see the entry: '11th May. Saturday. Marquet'. I remember that some time before the dramatic events of those days Luce Hilsum had told us that Marquet was expecting us; he had heard that I intended to give him an old icon and wanted to give me one of his pictures in exchange.

I must now interrupt my tale of the sinking of transports, parachutists' landings and the French disaster, to devote a chapter to the painter Albert Marquet. It is difficult to describe how that day affected everyone. Paris was like a disturbed beehive; people who only yesterday had been quite unconcerned suddenly realized that the game was over and that the day of reckoning had come. To have met any other painter or writer at this time would have been natural enough. But Marquet, with his light, translucent landscapes lived in a world of his own. Even on canvas he had never raised his voice and enjoyed above all painting water; he himself was, to use the old Russian expression, 'quieter than water'. He painted the Seine, in Paris and in Normandy, with barges and without; he painted the sea as it lost itself among the rocks of Stockholm, the canals of Venice and those of Holland, the great Nile and the small Marne, and again the Seine – at dawn, at noon, at evening, with green or leafless trees, under rain, under snow. There is nearly always water in his pictures, water, water.

In the sixteenth century the French poet Joachim du Bellay saw the ruins of ancient Rome. In the following centuries they were plundered and demolished, but in those days, according to travellers' descriptions, their grandeur was imposing. Du Bellay wrote this about Rome: '... It conquered alien cities but did not conquer itself – soldier's fortune. And only the yellow waters of the great Tiber continued to flow. What seemed eternal has fallen and crumbled. The hurrying river alone remains'.

The windows of Marquet's studio overlooked the Seine: a bridge, the quay with the booksellers' lidded stalls. We naturally began to discuss the events with his wife Marcelle: what country the Germans would next invade, whether the Belgians would resist; we condemned, we speculated. Marquet stood at the window looking at the Seine. Then he turned towards us. He had intelligent eyes, slightly mocking but not unkind. He said: 'This isn't the end yet'. What was he referring to? The outcome of the war? The destiny of mankind? On that day I realized once again the power of art. Everybody was talking about Reynaud, King Leopold, Weygand, Keitel – I have difficulty now in recalling those names. Twenty-two years have passed since then and everything seems to have changed. But the water is still there; the Seine that traverses Paris, and that in Marquet's paintings.

I have said that the most modest of all the poets I ever knew was Antonio Machado. I have never known a more modest painter than Albert Marquet. He abhorred fame. When they wanted to make him an academician it almost made him ill, he protested and implored them to leave him out. Nor did he ever try to denigrate others or write pamphlets and manifestos. In his youth he was a member of Les Fauves for some years, not because their aesthetic theories attracted him but to avoid hurting the feelings of his friend Matisse. He disliked argument, he avoided journalists. At our first meeting he said with an apologetic smile: 'I'm sorry, I can only talk with my brushes'.

He did not care what happened to his pictures and was indifferent to the material things of life. In his youth he had known poverty and had often gone hungry. When Matisse described to me how they had

479

worked together at the 1900 Exhibition, he had said with a laugh: 'Really more like house decorators'. Matisse also said: 'I don't know a more disinterested man than Marquet. His draughtsmanship is firm, sometimes as sharp as that of the ancient Japanese. But his heart's like a girl's in an old-fashioned romantic novel: it's not enough for him that he should never hurt anyone, he's positively upset if he leaves without having been hurt himself'.

In 1934 Marquet went to the Soviet Union with a group of tourists. (He travelled a great deal.) On his return to Paris he was asked whether it was true that it was like Hell there. He replied that he did not understand much about politics and had never voted in his life: 'But I enjoyed Russia. Just imagine – a great State where money doesn't determine a man's life. Isn't it extraordinary? And then, I don't think they have an Academy of Arts there, at least no one mentioned it to me'. (The Academy of Arts had been revived shortly before Marquet visited Leningrad; but he saw the Neva, workers, schoolchildren, and had no time to notice the academicians.)

Among the Communist workers in Paris there were members of art clubs who admired Marquet's painting and were devoted to the Soviet Union. They made a whip-round and when Marquet got back from Russia, they came to him with the money and said: 'This is to pay for your journey and your keep if you'll go to Leningrad for a few months and paint the Neva'.

I met Marquet again in 1946. He invited us to come and watch the fireworks over the Seine on 14th July. The war had aged him, but he was gay and treated us to some excellent claret (he was a native of Bordeaux and understood wines). The stars of the rockets fell into the black river. Marquet said: 'You're always saying water, but there are other things I like too. For instance, trees and stars'. He liked people as well, but being extremely reticent about his feelings never mentioned this. He recalled our meeting at the beginning of the French disaster: 'I've learnt a great deal during the war years. The Communists are right. It's terrible that so many people have learnt nothing and want to put the clock back'. He fell silent, and then repeated the words I had committed to memory at our meeting in 1940: 'This isn't the end yet'.

He was short, slight, very informal in manner, and neither his appearance nor choice of words betrayed the essence of the man. He spoke through his pictures. His painter's language is restrained, simple and convincing. After abandoning the riot of colour, the disjointed-

480

ness typical of many Impressionists, he never looked for geometry in life: he generalized in a human way – without a protractor, without binding logic – as poetry generalizes, or love. His pictures are impressive in their sheer economy of means, they are complex in their simplicity, subtle in their artlessness. Grey, blue, green – and the world comes alive. He loved the south – Algiers, Morocco, Egypt – but his best landscapes are of the north; apparently he himself was fascinated by the colour of the south, but it was in the grey, reticent north that he found the colours that fascinate us.

In 1940 he asked me to choose whatever landscape pleased me. I chose a picture of the Seine on a dull day, a quay, a bridge. On a wall a scrap of a Left Bloc poster – the year 1924. In 1946 Marquet gave me another picture of the Seine, quite empty, almost a bare canvas.

I could not have believed that I would never see him again. His wife wrote to me about his last days. Marquet had an operation in January 1947. The operation was no use; he grew weaker from day to day and knew that he was dying, but he went on working. He painted eight more pictures – of the Seine. In June he died.

I am writing about the years when very few people gave art a thought: men died without having time to look round them. But, after all, they died so that others should see the river, the trees, the stars, so that art should return to the blinded, deafened world. 'This isn't the end yet'.

Marquet was fond of poetry; he loved Baudelaire, Laforgue, and also, I think, Apollinaire. When I look at his pictures I sometimes repeat to myself:

> *Vienne la nuit sonne l'heure*
> *Les jours s'en vont je demeure*
> *Passent les jours et passent les semaines*
> *Ni temps passé*
> *Ni les amours reviennent*
> *Sous le pont Mirabeau coule la Seine*
> *Vienne la nuit sonne l'heure*
> *Les jours s'en vont, je demeure.*

And suddenly, in a phrase overheard in the street, I seem to hear the old poem about the Pont Mirabeau. I seem to glimpse in the eyes of a passer-by the grey Seine under Albert Marquet's studio window. Who knows, perhaps something remains of every one of us? Perhaps that is what art is.

35

ON 12th May, the next day after my visit to Marquet, the police came early in the morning and took me to the Préfecture. At first they locked me up in a cell where there were already some thirty people: Paris workers suspected of Communist sympathies, German émigrés, a Pole, a student from Barcelona. A German Jew said to me: 'Do you know why they've arrested me? My brother fought in Spain. I couldn't fight – the SS men had broken my arm. Now they've found a letter from my brother at my place, he was in the Thaelmann Battalion. The police shouted: "You're a Communist, a spy!" They aren't fighting Hitler, are they?' An elderly Frenchwoman sobbed: 'How do I know who Alfred's been meeting? It's not my business. I don't ask my husband whom he meets. I'm not a *concierge*'.

Later I was taken to the top floor, into a room where they dealt with the business of deporting foreigners. There were a lot of people about, the officials were in a hurry. 'Ehrenburg, Ilya? In three days' time.' I tried to explain that I had been waiting a long time for an exit visa, but he cut me short: 'It's not our business. Go to the second floor'.

An unpleasant thing had happened which baffled me: in the spring of 1939 certain royalties for Spanish writers had been sent to me from Moscow. These writers were on the point of leaving, some for Mexico, others for Chile. There were nine or ten of them, so it was quite a sizeable sum. When I declared my income for the past year I naturally did not include the money I had handed over to the Spaniards. At the beginning of 1940 the police raided the Banque des Pays du Nord; they checked the money-orders, the bank ledgers. It was found that I had concealed the Spanish writers' royalties from the tax inspector as well as the money for the van for Spain, acquired as long ago as 1936. I received a demand note for a sum the like of which I had never seen in my life, and was told that until it was paid I should not be allowed to leave France. On the second floor of the Préfecture I tried to explain that I was being expelled from France. An official replied in surly tones: 'That's none of my business. Go to the third floor. But until you can show us a receipt for the tax payment and the fine you won't get an exit visa'. I went back to the man in charge of deportations and stood for three hours in the queue: 'They won't let me leave'. 'I've told you that's none of my business. You must leave France before 14th May'.

As I have already said, my illness had left me very weak; my legs seemed to be made of cotton-wool. I had barely enough strength to reach home. Anti-aircraft guns were firing.

On the next day the Germans broke through the French defences near Sedan and invaded France. Terrified Belgian refugees with tear-swollen faces and loaded with hampers and bundles appeared in Paris.

Events moved swiftly. Holland capitulated. The Germans occupied Brussels. Buses disappeared from the streets; it was rumoured that they had been requisitioned for moving troops from the Maginot line to the north. Trenches were dug in the Bois de Vincennes. The wealthy districts of the city emptied as they had done in 1914. The traffic-police were issued with rifles. I saw Belgian cars pitted with bullet-holes.

Suddenly a general sigh of relief went up: the rumour spread that the Germans had turned towards the coast intending to attack England. Reynaud went to Notre-Dame where a Mass was celebrated with supplications for an Allied victory. Shares on the Bourse went up unexpectedly and the brokers yelled in happy excitement. Life went on: restaurants and cafés were full. The papers described a new style in women's millinery based on the forage cap. The radio reported fighting in the region of Narvik – beyond the Arctic Circle.

On 21st May I was again summoned to the Préfecture and asked why I had not left France. Once more I trudged in vain from one floor to the other. The sirens went. Policemen herded us into the shelter under the Conciergerie. The Préfecture officials also came hurrying down. My neighbour turned out to be the man who had been busy expelling me. He kept on saying monotonously: '*Merde . . . merde . . . merde . . .*' I could not make out what he was referring to: the anti-aircraft guns, the Germans or myself.

The premier made a speech in the Chamber saying that there had been treason, that the guilty would be punished, that France and England would halt the enemy.

Suddenly we learnt that the government had decided to send Pierre Cot to Moscow in order to 'improve relations' with the Soviet Union.

Our chargé d'affaires, N. N. Ivanov, was pleased. He told me in a whisper that Hitler was bound to attack the Soviet Union so that it might be a good thing to come to an agreement with the Allies, just to be on the safe side. But I did not believe that Reynaud could, or even wanted to restrain the pro-Fascists. A struggle was going on within the government itself. The vice-premier Pétain regarded Reynaud as a tool of the British. The Minister of Foreign Affairs, Baudouin, was in favour of a *rapprochement* with Mussolini. The Minister of the Interior, Mandel, a friend and assistant of Clemenceau in the past, wanted to fight the Germans in earnest but his hands were tied; when he ordered the arrest of five journalists who were openly advocating peace with Hitler, a storm broke out in the press and the men were released. On the other hand, Communists went on being arrested daily.

I lay in a darkened room in the rue du Cotentin. My books were packed in huge crates like coffins. Old Spanish newspapers, Popular Front leaflets and Hitler pamphlets – material for reports of long ago – were stacked in the corners.

On 24th May, de Monzie, the Minister of Public Works, whom I had known in the past, rang me up. He had been among the first Frenchmen to visit the Soviet Union; he had written a book about his trip and had more than once insisted on the need to encourage cultural and economic relations with the Soviet Union. On one occasion he had presided at a meeting where I was to speak on Soviet literature. When he set eyes on me he was furious: 'Who told you to get your hair cut?' It appeared that in his introductory speech he had intended to quote Lenin's words about 'shaggy Ilya', and I had spoilt the effect. Politically de Monzie was a dark horse: he switched from right to left-wing 'blocs', more out of caprice than calculation. He said to me over the telephone: 'Ilya, you shouldn't forget old friends. I'm told you're leaving for Russia. Why haven't you come to say good-bye?' Our relations were not close enough to allow me to put a purely personal interpretation on these words, and I realized that it was a matter of politics. De Monzie added that he wanted to see me urgently – could I come to his office in the boulevard St Germain at once?

When I arrived he was smoking a pipe as usual and, as usual, he started out in a jocular vein, but then quickly came down to brass tacks: 'Pétain, Baudouin and some of the others want to capitulate. Reynaud's against it, not to mention Mandel. It's a pretty grim picture – the General Staff have been preparing for a long war of position.

484

But the Maginot line was just a talisman, nothing more. We've got very few tanks and, above all, very few aircraft. The situation's critical'. I asked why the government continued to make war on the Communists, why did it antagonize the workers? There were almost more police agents than workers in the munitions factories. De Monzie did not try to hide the facts; he said that 30,000 Communists had been arrested and that the Minister of Justice, Sérol, a Socialist, refused to treat them as political prisoners. He added: 'I know a chap called Semard, a Communist, but a Frenchman and a patriot. He was arrested. I talked to Sérol about him but it was no good. I don't mind telling you quite frankly that I trust Semard more than I do Sérol'.

We sat for a while in silence. De Monzie put down his pipe, got up, and, without looking at me, said: 'If the Russians would sell planes to us we'd be able to hold out. What does the Soviet Union stand to gain by the defeat of France? Hitler's going to attack you. There's only one thing we want of you: sell us planes. We've decided to send Pierre Cot to Moscow. You know him – he's a friend of yours. Don't think this was easy, there were plenty who were against it. But I'm not speaking in my own name now. Transmit this to Moscow. If they don't sell us planes, the Germans will occupy the whole of France in a month or two'.

(I involuntarily recalled the summer of 1936 when the representatives of the Spanish government said over and over again in Paris: 'If France does not sell us planes we shall perish'.)

On leaving de Monzie I immediately went to our embassy and recounted this conversation to Ivanov. He made me sit down at his desk: 'It's your duty to report this. Let Moscow decide. But you must write at once'.

Before passing on let me say something about Nikolay Nikolayevich Ivanov. He was working as an economist when he was suddenly sent to Paris, first as secretary and then as counsellor at the embassy. He was a decent, honest man; his faith in people proved his salvation. He came to Paris when he was young and inexperienced; after Suritz's departure he became chargé d'affaires, which was tantamount to being ambassador. He quickly learnt French and read a great deal; he was always asking me about French writers, the theatre, what wines to order with fish or meat dishes; in short, he picked up a lot of things, important and unimportant.

Later he followed the French government to Tours, to Bordeaux, to Clermont-Ferrand. I met him at the beginning of July in the small resort of La Bourboule, near Vichy. In December 1940 he went back to Moscow; he came to see me there and told me about the start of the Resistance and the fate of various French writers. Shortly after I learnt of his arrest. When, in 1954, Ivanov was rehabilitated he was shown the sentence of the Special Conference: in September 1941 he had been given a five years' sentence for 'anti-German views'. It is difficult to credit: the Nazis were forging their way to Moscow, newspapers wrote about 'Teutonic curs'[1], yet some State Security clerk calmly rounded off the case opened during the Soviet-Nazi pact by numbering and docketing it so that it should be preserved for future generations.

Ivanov was sustained by his faith in the triumph of justice. Whilst in the camp he learnt that the State Security staff had looted his books and his pictures and, as his sentence did not include the confiscation of property, he lodged a complaint with the Procurator; to the amazement of the camp authorities he won his case. On being released he was paid an indemnity for the property he had lost. Although he was debarred from living in large cities, he immediately went to Moscow, to the Lubyanka, and began to inquire into the reasons for his five years' detention. He happened to approach a goodhearted official who said: 'Leave Moscow. By rights I ought to detain you, but I'll forget that you've been to see me'. Ivanov has kept his optimism and his faith to this day; he is married, he works, and he tells me that he is happy.

After this digression let me go back to May 1940 in Paris. Three days after my interview with de Monzie, early in the morning, the bell rang. Several policemen were on the doorstep; one of them showed me a warrant for my arrest issued by vice-premier Pétain's office.

There was a search that lasted several hours. The men opened the crates full of books, pawed the discarded heaps of old papers, even slit open a pillow. Among the policemen was a Russian whom the others called Nicolas. He was evidently a book collector, because on seeing the *Arabian Nights* in the 'Academy' edition he was overjoyed: 'Now there's one I haven't got'. The police inspector was particularly interested in the Spanish newspapers and the books with Nazi songs that were lying on the floor. He said with satisfaction: 'The evidence is clear'.

[1] Literally 'Dog-knights' – term used for the invading Teutonic knights in Alexander Nevsky's time.

Nicolas and one of the Frenchmen stayed in the flat to keep an eye on Lyuba. I was taken along the street to a police car. Our neighbours looked on with curiosity; someone asked whether I was really a spy. The police inspector replied: 'Conspiracy of Germans and Communists'. He walked behind me with a revolver, saying: 'At the first move I shoot – attempting to escape'. At the Préfecture, where the piles of 'evidence' had been taken, the interrogation started.

'You telephoned the information that everything was ready. You intended to act on Friday 31st May.'

'I was telling our chargé d'affaires that I had everything ready to leave and that I was waiting for him to ring me up. He told me he hoped to get me my exit visa on 31st May.'

'You're just being stubborn. We know that you were the head of a group of Communists who had decided to let the Germans into Paris. The documents found in your flat prove that you were in close contact with German agents.'

This sounded so funny to me that I said: 'This is silly enough for the *Canard Enchaîné*'. The police inspector produced a revolver: 'We're not standing on ceremony with the agents of Moscow and Berlin any longer. You'll find it's a mistake to laugh – in fifteen minutes' time you won't find it so funny'.

This talk about what I should be doing in fifteen minutes' time took place in the evening. The telephone rang. The police inspector jumped up: 'Yes, at your service, *Monsieur le Ministre* . . .' At the same time with one neat push he threw me out of the room and shut the door.

This is what I later learnt from Ivanov: two police agents, as I have said, had stayed behind in my flat. They would not allow Lyuba near the telephone. Clémence arrived; she, too, was detained. She protested loudly: 'You ought to arrest the Belgian king, not Monsieur Ehrenburg. Perhaps you haven't listened to the radio. The Belgian king has sold out to the Fascists and has given up. But Monsieur Ehrenburg was in Spain, he hates the Fascists'. Then she passed on to more lowly matters: 'I've got to take the dogs out. Who'll wipe the floor if they make a mess – you or me?' A few hours later there was a ring at the door; the embassy driver came in. It appeared that Ivanov had come to fetch me for a drive in the Bois de Boulogne.

Ivanov realized that the matter was serious. According to the rules he should have contacted the Ministry of Foreign Affairs, but he knew that he would not find any sympathy there. After some thought he decided to disregard diplomatic procedure and went to see the Minister of the Interior, Mandel, who, as I have said, hated the Germans and favoured a *rapprochement* with the Soviet Union.

Mandel rang up the police inspector at the precise moment when the questioning had passed from general subjects to play with a revolver.

'You can go, you're free,' the inspector said viciously. I replied that I had no intention of walking: the streets were dark, there was no public transport, it was a long way to the rue du Cotentin, and, besides, they had to return the books and papers which they had taken. The inspector was furious: 'Are you expecting us to give you a joy-ride?' But he quickly mastered himself: after all, Mandel was his supreme chief.

An hour later the residents of the rue du Cotentin saw the 'conspirator' drive up to his house and the police agents unload his books. If they were not surprised it was only because in those days no one was any longer surprised at anything.

The next morning, while I had gone out to the baker's with the dogs, our bell rang. On opening the door Lyuba saw a plain-clothes police officer who showed her his badge. Lyuba lost her temper: 'What, every day? Look at the mess you made here yesterday'. Our flat was like a bookshop after a pogrom. The police officer tried to get a word in but Lyuba would not let him. At last, taking advantage of a moment's silence he blurted out: 'But I've come on behalf of *Monsieur le Préfet* to offer his apologies'. Mandel was undoubtedly feared. (The Germans knew that they could neither frighten nor buy him, so they killed him.)

I learnt later that my arrest was connected with de Monzie's request to me. Pétain dreaded any improvement in relations with the Soviet Union. Mandel was able to get me released because the police were under him. But he could not change French foreign policy; on the same day that the police officer brought me the Prefect's apologies, the government announced that Pierre Cot's journey to Moscow had been 'postponed'.

Ivanov had saved my life: my second arrest had occurred a short time before the collapse. In those days no one could rely on legality, and it happened more than once that police reports contained the phrase 'killed while attempting to escape'.

On 26th May I saw Emile Buré. He said that Paris could quite easily

488

have been taken on the 16th. The Germans were now pushing on to Amiens: they wanted to encircle the French army. I met various people: Vogel, Bloch, Elsa Triolet, the Belgian painter Masereel; they were all very depressed.

The American ambassador William Bullitt prayed at Notre-Dame, fell on his knees and, in the name of the President, offered a rose to the statue of Joan of Arc. Buré said: 'What we need is aircraft, not flowers'. The Catholic paper *Aube* wrote about 'the motorized Joan of Arc who will save France'.

On 3rd June the Germans bombed Paris heavily. There were many victims and I witnessed scenes familiar to me from Madrid and Barcelona. But there did not seem to be any anger, only despair. Someone in the crowd said: 'We lost the war when the first shot was fired'.

The exodus of Parisians began. Long queues of cars, with mattresses on the roof, drove towards the Porte d'Italie and the Porte d'Orléans. At night anti-aircraft guns pounded away. The communiqués were vague. The radio continued to report the sinking of German vessels. Everybody said that the Germans were approaching. The Hilsums, Fotinsky, my Spanish friends left. I could not go anywhere: all my papers had been taken from me at the Préfecture. The city was deserted. Lyuba and I were the only people in the house, all the other tenants had gone. I felt confused and unhappy. Finally Ivanov left telling me that some of the embassy staff were staying on and had been told to look after me.

(It was then that a rumour was started in Moscow that I was allegedly a 'deserter'. Irina had some very unpleasant experiences; Paris was cut off, and on all sides people asked her: 'Is it true that your father is a "deserter?"')

On 9th June many shops, restaurants and cafés displayed the notice: 'Temporarily closed'. The President of the Republic received Laval. Someone we knew dropped in and said hurriedly: 'We bought a car but now there's no petrol. If only we could get a horse'. The Germans announced on the radio that they had taken Rouen and that the fate of Paris would be decided within the next few days. I tried listening in to Moscow: the broadcast went on for a long time about the *Frankfurter Zeitung*'s high opinion of the agricultural exhibition in Moscow. Clémence came to say good-bye and wept: 'What a humiliation!' Huge crowds besieged the railway stations. People left on bicycles.

489

The newspapers reported the opening of the trial of thirty-three Communists.

On 10th June Fascist Italy declared war on France. I was walking in the garden of our embassy when suddenly I heard joyful shouts and singing: the Italian embassy was next door. The Fascist diplomats had decided not to leave for home – the Germans were close at hand; they could spend a few days in 'sanctuary'. They sang *Giovinezza* without the least embarrassment.

On 11th June the rumour spread that the Soviet Union had declared war on Germany. Everybody was immensely cheered. Workers gathered at the gate of our embassy with cries of 'Long live the Soviet Union!' A few hours later a denial was issued. The people of Paris began to leave the city on foot. An old man laboriously pushed a handcart loaded with pillows on which huddled a small girl and a little old dog that howled piteously. An endless stream of refugees moved along the boulevard Raspail. Opposite the Rotonde stands Rodin's statue of Balzac who seems to be impetuously stepping off his pedestal. I stood for a long time at the crossroads, for here my youth had been spent, and I suddenly had the impression that Balzac was going off with the rest.

A shopkeeper at the corner of our street abandoned his shop without bothering so much as to shut the door; bananas and tins of food lay scattered about. People were not driving now, not walking, but running away. On 11th June I tried for a long time to find a newspaper. At last *Paris-Soir* appeared. The front page carried the photograph of an old woman bathing a dog in the Seine with the caption in large lettering: 'Paris remains Paris'. But Paris was like a house from which the inhabitants have fled in haste. Tens of thousands of people still crowded round the Gare de Lyons, although it had been announced that no trains were running – the Germans had cut the railway. Religious services and contradictory instructions were broadcast: first it was said that the evacuation had been organized, then the Parisians were asked to stay where they were and remain calm.

On 13th June I walked down the rue d'Assas. There was not a soul in sight – it was not Paris. It was Pompeii. Black rain fell (oil stocks were being burnt). At the corner of the rue de Rennes a young woman was embracing a lame soldier. Black tears streamed down her face. I realized that I was bidding farewell to a great many things.

Later I wrote a poem about it: 'To die – even that seemed easier.

Here every stone was beloved and dear. Guns were being taken away. Stores of oil were being burnt. Black rain fell on the black city. A woman said to an infantryman (black tears streaming from her eyes): "Wait, my beloved, we shall say good-bye", and his eyes stared stonily. I saw this forlorn look. It was black and empty in the city. Together with the soldier, art, as dark as the man, departed'.

In the night our bell rang. I was surprised: the authorities had left and the Germans had not yet arrived. It turned out that an embassy car had come to fetch us: they wanted us to move into the embassy in the rue de Grenelle for safety.

We were given a small room generally used by diplomatic couriers when they stayed the night. In the morning aircraft with swastikas flew over very low. We went out into the street. A French soldier rushed up to me asking the way to the Porte d'Orléans. There was nobody in the streets. Dustbins stank. Abandoned dogs howled. We walked as far as the avenue du Maine, and I suddenly saw a column of German soldiers. They were chewing as they marched.

I turned away and stood silently by the wall. This, too, had to be lived through.

36

TIME EFFACES many names, people are forgotten, years that seemed vivid fade but certain pictures remain in one's memory however much one would like to forget them. I see Paris in June 1940; it was a dead city and its beauty drove me to despair; not a car, no busy shopping, no passers-by to hide the buildings – a body whose clothing had been removed or, if you like, a skeleton with the articulation of streets. Built over many centuries, unified less by architectural planning, or the tastes of a single epoch, than by continuity, by the character of its citizens, Paris reminded me of a forest of masonry forsaken by its furred and feathered inhabitants.

The few people one met were deformed or hunchbacked, lacking an arm or a leg, cripples. In the working-class districts old, old women sat on the benches knitting; their sharp fingers seemed one with their long knitting-needles.

The Germans were taken aback; this was not how they had imagined the 'New Babylon'. They ate stolidly in the few restaurants still open and photographed one another against the background of Notre-Dame or the Eiffel tower.

Soon the fugitives began to trickle back: when, with great difficulty, they had got as far as the Loire, they found German troops on the opposite bank. Paris came to life again, but it was a ghostly, implausible life. The Germans bought souvenirs, smutty postcards, pocket dictionaries in the little shops. Notices appeared in restaurants: '*Içi on parle allemand*'. Prostitutes lisped: '*Mein Süsser*'. Petty traitors crept out of their holes. Newspapers began to appear again. *Le Matin* reported that the notorious police prefect Chiappe and his friends had remained in Paris and also that the Germans 'appreciated the delights of French cooking'. Gustav Hervé, a one-time Anarchist, later a chauvinist, resumed the publication of *Victoire*. Newspaper sellers shouted '*Victoire!*' startling the few passers-by. *Paris-Soir* took on the writer Pierre Hamp and suggested that advertisements should be drafted in German 'to stimulate trade'. There were very few advertisements: 'Aryan seeks employment, any offer accepted'; 'University graduate seeks post as waiter or shop-assistant, fluent German'; 'Genealogical trees compiled, ancestry researches made'. I went into a baker's shop in the boulevard St Germain. A respectable looking lady was saying: 'The Germans will teach our workers to work and not to organize stupid strikes'. Queues began to form outside shops. The new paper *La France au Travail* enlightened its readers: 'In every one of us there is a particle of the Jewish spirit which makes it necessary to undertake an internal spiritual pogrom'. The clocks were put forward by one hour, but even before the sun had set loud-speakers issued the warning: 'Go home!' A few restaurants and cafés sported notices saying: 'Aryan firm. No Jews admitted'. In the districts where Jews from Eastern Europe lived, in the rue de la Rosière, bearded old men scuttled about in terror; the Germans amused themselves by frightening them. The *Kommandatur* protected German troops from contact with 'suspect elements'. At the entrance to the Café Dôme in the boulevard Montparnasse, frequented by artists, there was an order: 'This café is out of bounds to German servicemen'. On the other hand, I saw this notice on the doors of a brothel: 'Local and foreign clients welcome'. A large music-hall staged the review *Immer Paris* – the German version of the French saying '*Paris reste Paris*'.

But Paris was no longer Paris: what had happened was not merely one of those military episodes which occurred in the last century, but a cataclysm.

After the experience of the Second World War it is preposterous to insist that you could not 'live in the same world with Fascists'. But at the time I had to keep a strong hold on myself. I found an outlet in poetry: 'It was not for this that Balzac wrote. The leaden tread of foreign soldiers. Night presses down, heavy and hot. Petrol and horse's piss. Not for this – I pray to the stones – that Delescluze fell on the stones. Not for this did the city grow, not for this were those years of thunderstorms, the essence of flowers and sounds, not for this, not for this'. I ended the poem with these words: 'Close your eyes and be silent – alien buglers, alien brass, alien arrogance go past. It is not for this that I grew up here'.

It was a cry from the heart, but I not only cried out, I tried also to understand the meaning of what had happened: 'The clocks did not strike. The stars came nearer. Empty, wild, to the mind unfathomable, in Paris, abandoned and forgotten by all, boundless Rome, stiffened in *rigor mortis*'.

493

After my return to Moscow Anna Akhmatova asked me about Paris. She had been there a long time ago, before the First World War, and did not know the details of its fall. Certain writers see Anna Akhmatova as a 'poetess of personal feelings in a tiny little world'. She read me a poem she had written on hearing of the fall of Paris: 'At the obsequies of an epoch no psalm is sung over the grave. Nettle and thistle will be its adornment, and only the gravediggers work with a will. Their job cannot wait. And all is silent, dear God, so silent that you can hear time pass. And then the epoch floats to the surface like a corpse on the spring flood, but son knows not mother, and grandson turns away heavy-hearted. And heads are bent lower, and moons come and go like a pendulum. And that is the silence that now reigns over dead Paris'. What strikes me in this poem is not only the accurate perception of a scene Akhmatova had not witnessed, but also its foresight. I often see the past epoch now as 'a corpse on the spring flood'. I know it beyond error, but for the grandsons it is something like a ghost, a broken mooring or a capsized boat.

We bought sausage or tinned stuff to eat at home and at other times ate in a restaurant after making sure that there were no Germans there. Once I went into a shop to buy a bottle of wine; the shopkeeper said to me: 'Have some old Burgundy. I'll sell it to you as *vin ordinaire* from the barrel – better that you should drink it than the Germans'. After our departure I am sure I must have been taken for a heavy drinker: in the diplomatic courier's room we left behind at least fifty empty bottles of renowned vintages.

One of the embassy staff told me that he had to go to the 'free zone', to Brive, and offered to take me along – he did not speak French very well. Our itinerary was Gien, Nevers, Moulins, Clermont-Ferrand, Royat, La Bourboule, Brive, Limoges, Orléans. I saw a great deal: the ruins of Gien, bomb-shattered Orléans, the confectioner's in Royat where '*tout Paris*' devoured cakes, sighing and moaning and blessing the Marshal. On the banks of the Loire wrecked cars, soldiers' tin hats and toys lay scattered about. Prisoners of war buried the bodies of the refugees who had been killed. People slept in Paris buses 'Bastille – Madeleine'.

It was on the day the government arrived in Clermont-Ferrand from Bordeaux. I had to find the whereabouts of our embassy. I was told that the Ministers were housed in the Collège building. I inquired from the porter, a little old man who looked like Voltaire. He shouted:

'No, thank God, they aren't here. I think they're at the Préfecture'. Bewildered high officials were rushing about the corridors, it was impossible to get an answer from anyone. I poked my head into one room and someone yelled at me: 'What the devil are you doing here?' It appeared that this was Laval's office.

A refugee who was sleeping rough told me that he had tried to reach Spain from Bordeaux with some other people but that the Spanish frontier guards would not allow them through. History has nothing in common with the classical novel; it either writes verse in an obscure language that none can decipher, or else it adopts the most time-honoured form of the universally understood parable.

I have frequently experienced the emotion that inspired Mayakovsky when he wrote the poem about his Soviet passport: pride when showing my passport to truculent police agents, pride, too, when I was arrested and deported, when visas were refused. I was proud of being a Soviet citizen in 1936 in Aragon, and ten years later in the racialist states of Mississippi and Alabama. But during that (fortunately short) time of which I am now speaking, things went hard with me. Once two women, working class to judge by their clothes, stopped in front of our embassy and saluted our escutcheon with raised fists. The police chased them off; a car bearing a swastika had drawn up – Hitler's officers had come to call on one of the embassy officials. I saw it all from the window and felt sick. I think the reader will understand my feelings.

I had brought my radio to the embassy and every evening listened to London. On 18th June – four days after the Germans had entered Paris – de Gaulle spoke for the first time, saying that the war was still being waged and calling on the French not to submit to the traitors. I listened and felt glad. My window was open and the two policemen on duty outside the embassy also listened; one stood to attention. I do not know what he did afterwards – perhaps he zealously served the Germans – but at that moment de Gaulle was his leader; the other policeman was smiling sceptically.

On 13th July Anna Seghers came to the embassy. She was under police surveillance and was in mortal danger. She asked for help to get to the 'free zone'.

The Vishnyaks got stuck in Paris. We often went to see them. We tried to laugh, talked of the past – of Andrey Bely, Marina, Pasternak. After the war I learnt that the Germans had murdered the Vishnyaks at Auschwitz. Dusya had also remained in Paris with her sick mother. She no longer laughed and often said: 'It's so quiet, it's frightening'. I read Ronsard's poems about noon and happiness to her. The summer was exceptionally cold and it rained a lot.

I talked to German officers in cafés – they wanted somebody to speak to and took me for a Frenchman. Some of them thought that the English ought to be smashed first, but the majority said: 'We'll soon clean up Russia'. They spoke about the Soviet Union and the Communists very frankly and with understandable spite. I remember one of them saying: 'First we'll pump oil out of Russia, then blood'.

A military band played in the Place de l'Opéra. The victors sat on the terrace of the Café de la Paix, basking in the sunshine, drinking brandy, discussing further campaigns. Paris was a marvellous rest-home for them, free of charge.

The day of our departure came at last. We boarded the train at night. We took with us the embassy driver, the chef and a clerk; I believe there were some seven or eight Soviet citizens in the train which was packed with German officers and men. A writer, asked what he had felt on being shown round a corrective labour camp, said: 'Like a live fox in a fur-shop'. That was how I felt in that train.

It was a long journey – it took a whole week. I saw the ruins of Douai, the deserted towns of northern France, German notices. We were obliged to stay some time in Brussels. We spent the night at our embassy. I tried to see Franz Hellens but was told that he had managed to get out. The Brussels population was glumly silent.

We crossed the frontier during the night. Twice there were air-raids. The train stopped. I found myself wishing: if only the English would drop a bomb! But half an hour later the train started off again. At München-Gladbach German women came to the station bringing coffee and flowers for the conquerors. Then we reached Berlin. We had to spend two nights in an hotel. There was a notice at the entrance saying: 'Jews not admitted', but I was travelling as one of the embassy staff, not as Ehrenburg, and my name did not appear in the documents. As the Germans needed Soviet oil and a great deal else, they were not prepared to make trouble over trifles.

We had a store of tea, sugar, rusks and cheese. At the sight of the cheese, the chambermaid who brought us hot water asked Lyuba where we had got this delicacy. Lyuba replied: 'We brought it from France'. At this the German woman exclaimed: 'Ah, the lucky French!'

496

It gave me pleasure to hear this: the victors, who had just seized Denmark, Holland, Belgium and France, envied the French.

I had known them as far back as 1932 in Berlin, on the eve of their first victory; I had been watching all their moves; I remembered Spain. I had seen them again in Paris. I had learnt a lot.

By nature as well as upbringing I was a man of the nineteenth century, more given to discussion than to arms. Hatred did not come to me easily. Hatred is not a particularly creditable emotion and is nothing to be proud of. But we were living in an epoch when ordinary young men, often with agreeable faces, with sentimental feelings and photographs of the girls they loved, had, in the belief that they were the elect, begun to destroy the non-elect, and only genuine and profound hatred could put an end to the triumph of Fascism. I repeat, this was not easy. I often felt pity, and perhaps I hate Fascism most bitterly because it taught me to hate not only the vile inhuman idea but also its adherents.

37

I WENT back to Moscow on 29th July 1940. I was convinced that the Germans would soon attack us; the terrible scenes of the exodus from Barcelona and from Paris were still before my eyes. But in Moscow the general mood seemed calm. The press said that friendly relations between the Soviet Union and Germany had grown stronger.

I wrote to Molotov saying that I should like to tell him about the French situation and what German officers and soldiers were saying. I was received by his deputy, S. A. Lozovsky. I had known Lozovsky since before the Revolution and had met him in Paris when he had spoken at Bolshevik meetings. He listened to me absent-mindedly, without looking at me and with a melancholy expression. I could not help saying: 'Doesn't any of this interest you at all?' Lozovsky smiled wryly: 'Personally I find it very interesting. But you know that we have a different policy'. (I was still distinctly naïve; I thought that correct information helped to determine policy: it turned out to be exactly the contrary – what was needed was information that would confirm a predetermined policy.)

(I worked with Lozovsky during the war years when he was the head of the Soviet Information Bureau. He has remained in my memory as a mild man of great personal integrity; he knew the working class in the West very well; but he had no power – at every step he had to refer to Molotov or Shcherbakov. His duties were to direct various committees set up at the beginning of the war, among them the Jewish Anti-Fascist Committee. Lozovsky was arrested with the other members of the committee at the end of 1948 and shot at the age of seventy-four; he was posthumously rehabilitated.)

Naturally I tried to see people who knew something about the Fascists and who went on hating them; N. G. Bogatyrev, who had fled from Czechoslovakia, came to see me and told me what had happened to various Czech friends; at E. F. Usevich's I met Wanda Wassilewska who told me about the fate of the poet Broniewski; former members of the International Brigades – Belov, Petrov, Baler

498

and the Spaniards La Casa, Alberto Sanchez Arcas – also came to see me. Looking through my notebook I see the names of those who visited us in the winter of 1940–1: Konchalovsky, Falk, Sterenberg, Suritz, Alexey Tolstoy, Ignatyev, Lidin, Efros, Olesha, Slavin, Akhmatova, Pasternak, Vishnevsky, Martynov, Lugovskoy. I found it easy to talk to them.

There were also some writers and journalists who said that I did not think like a Soviet citizen, I had lived too long in France, had grown attached to that country and was 'laying it on too thick' when I described the Nazis. 'People of a certain nationality dislike our foreign policy. That's quite understandable. But they'd do best to keep their feelings for the family circle'. This staggered me. I did not know yet what was in store for us.

I remember a conversation with the academician Lena Stern. We were talking about the Nazi atrocities, about Spain, France, the Non-Aggression Pact. She said: 'A responsible comrade explained to me that it was a marriage of convenience, to which I replied that even such a marriage can produce offspring'. (Eight years later Lena Stern personally experienced the correctness of her diagnosis: she was arrested with the other active members of the Jewish Anti-Fascist Committee; fortunately she survived.)

One day, at the theatre, I met Douglas – this was the name under which Y. V. Smushkevich was known in Spain where he was in charge of our air-force personnel. He was limping and used a stick. I immediately noticed two Hero of the Soviet Union stars on his chest. We talked about Spain. I was overjoyed: so not all of them had died. Savich told me that he had seen Hajji and Nikolas. I had read about Grigorovich in the press. And here was Douglas, a commander of the air force. I thought his experience in Spain would be valuable in the approaching war. (Smushkevich was arrested and shot two weeks before the Nazis attacked the Soviet Union.)

I had to work – to write and find an editor who would dare to print me. I wanted to describe all I had seen in France, to show that the swift defeat of the French army and the capitulation of Pétain were to be explained by moral weakness, by ruling class fear of the ordinary people, and not in any way by the invincible might of the Reichswehr. What mattered now, after all, was not Pétain but the fact that we would soon be at grips with the German army. I went to *Izvestia*; I had worked seven years for this paper. I was received by the foreign editor who asked me whether they owed me any money and then said straight out that they would not print me.

At the *Goslitizdat* (State Publishing House) I was told that my book on Spain would not be published: it had been held up at the printers, and then the Pact had been signed and the set-up type had been distributed. I was given a rough pull as a memento.

I cannot remember where I met L. Sheinis who worked on the paper *Trud* (Labour). He made it clear to me that I must not write anything about the Germans but was free to condemn the French traitors. The editorial office would do their best to get my articles printed. And in fact, after lengthy negotiations, amendments and cuts, they did appear in *Trud*. This cheered me up a bit.

(Later I received a pamphlet printed in Geneva – a reprint of my articles in *Trud*: the Communists were distributing it clandestinely in France.)

I was invited to a conference of Moscow writers; it was a dramatic occasion: it appeared that Stalin had summoned a group of writers, called Avdeyenko an 'enemy' and criticized Leonov's play *Metel* (Snowstorm) and Katayev's *Domik* (The Small House). We were to vote for Avdeyenko's expulsion from the Union. Various authors vied with one another in attacking Leonov and Katayev. I sat and wondered; with war looming, could Stalin be so sure of our strength that he could spare time for literary criticism? I found it utterly incomprehensible and felt miserably unhappy; also there was no 'wise Rabbi' Babel to whom I could go for enlightenment.

I wrote poetry: about Paris, about loyalty, about death. 'Daylight will come and it shall arise out of bones, as seeds germinate, from the codfishers' nets of the north to the empty sands of the Sahara, there will be a harvest of hands and bayonets, dead regiments will march again, feet without boots, boots without feet, cities of grief will march off. Drowned ships will float up, and the shade of a comrade and of clouds will take the watch without bells'.

Vishnevsky was the editor of the journal *Znanye* (Knowledge). He accepted my poems, picked out those where there was no mention of the future, and planned to publish them in the next issue. Shortly afterwards he told me that the poems were held up by the NKID (People's Commissariat for Foreign Affairs) and that the best thing would be for me to go and discuss the matter with them.

I had known N. G. Palgunov, the head of the Press Department of the NKID, in Paris when he had been TASS correspondent there. He received me cordially and said that the poems on the fall of Paris could be published. What disturbed him were the lyrical poems. He read them over and over again: '. . . The battle is over. Above grief and glory blue shows the *yavor* (sycamore) in the blazing noon'. He asked: 'Tell me frankly, whom do you mean by *yavor?*' I swore that *yavor* was a species of maple, that Pushkin uses the word. I saw that Palgunov did not quite believe me. He said: 'You realize what a responsibility I have?' In the end he agreed to pass my lyrical poems too.

Emboldened, I sent the manuscript of my collection of poems called *Loyalty* to the publishers.

At night I listened to broadcasts from London in French; how well I remember the signal, like a short rapping on the door. The news was disquieting: there were heavy German bombing raids on London. One night I wrote a poem in which I said that the fate of London closely affected me: 'It is not by its fogs which the Parcae wove, not by the couples in the green park, not by its length, longer than the spleen, not by the trident of the mistress of the seas: that city is made dear to me by a new grief. By night I see the black city, where grief is measured in tons, where sirens wail in the tender twilight damp, where houses thud to ground and grievous day rises amid strange and monstrous ruins'. I showed the poems to Vishnevsky. He said: 'Don't read that thing about London to anybody', and immediately added: 'Stalin knows better than we do'.

A poet came to see me, read me his poems and filled me with admiration: he was the Siberian Leonid Martynov. He asked me questions about the war, about Paris, said 'm-yes' and then hastily added something about the weather: 'It was a severe winter'. His poems seemed to spring from nature itself – like a noisy summer shower or the mating cry of a bird. We talked half through the night about syllabic verse. Martynov's lips moved: he was searching for a new music.

On 16th September I started on the novel *The Fall of Paris*. Of all the books I have written this is perhaps the closest to the traditional novel, though here, too, I still introduced a multiplicity of characters and swift changes of scene. I wrote it with passionate absorption. I have now re-read it; I believe that I did succeed in depicting the pre-war years in France, years which I have somewhere referred to as the latent civil war. Some of the characters seem to me alive, three-dimensional, others flat and artificial. Where did I fail? Precisely where both before and after *The Fall of Paris* many of my contemporaries failed: in showing people entirely absorbed by the political struggle, whether the Communists Michaud and Denise, or the Fascist Breteuil; I did not use enough variety of colour but only black and white brush-strokes. Apparently, though I loathed 'poster literature' and ridiculed over-zealous critics, I had nevertheless succumbed to oversimplification. By contrast, other characters in the story seem real: the actress Jeannette, the nice, intelligent, sometimes reckless capitalist Desser, the naïve engineer Pierre, the corrupt politician Tessa, the painter André and, finally, one of the precursors of many heroes of post-war French literature, the sentimental cynic Lucien.

On 21st June 1941 I was finishing the thirty-ninth chapter of the last part: seven short chapters remained to be written. The war began: I had neither thought nor time for novel writing. During the evacuation of Moscow the manuscript of the third part disappeared. I could not go back to the novel and accepted the fact that it would be unfinished. However, in December I was told that a man at the *Znamya* printing press had picked up the scattered pages. At the end of January, when there was a lull at the front, I wrote the last chapters, and the novel was published in 1942. An English translation appeared almost at once and, according to an article I have kept by chance, men and women were often found reading my novel in the London underground shelters during air-raids.

Whenever we met, Vishnevsky invariably talked about the approaching threat of war. Extracts from his diary have now been published. In December 1940 he wrote: 'Hatred for Prussian militarism, for Fascism, for the "New Order" is in our blood . . . We write in conditions of military restrictions, visible and invisible. I should like to speak out about the enemy, arouse fury at what is going on in crucified Europe. At the moment one has to keep silent'. Vishnevsky borrowed the manuscript of the first part of *The Fall of Paris* and said he would try to 'shove it through'. Two months later, on the very day when I reached the age of fifty, he came with good news: the first part had been approved though there would have to be cuts. Although it was only concerned with Paris in 1935–7 and there were no Germans in it, the word 'Fascism' had to be taken out. The text included a description of Paris demonstrations and I was asked to substitute for the slogan 'Down with Fascism!' 'Down with the reactionaries!'

I had no money and I began to give readings of extracts from my novel. There were good audiences but here, too, I ran into difficulties.

One day I was reading some chapters from the novel in the Film Club. During the interval I was told that the counsellor of the German embassy had come to hear me. I protested: 'I won't go on reading while he's here'. People tried to persuade me. A young girl attached to VOKS (All Union Society for Cultural Relations) was quite startled by my attitude: 'How can you? Naturally the subject interests him. The fact is he's a very cultured man, he likes literature. And, besides, what will they say there?' And she pointed to the ceiling. I replied that it was not an open meeting and that if a Fascist were to come into the hall I should leave. The German diplomat was told that the evening was over and when he had left I finished my reading.

These readings began to be talked about. The evenings were cancelled. I tried to see the secretary of the Writers' Union, A. A. Fadeyev, but it was hopeless. I wrote articles and earned a little money; I wrote for *Tridsat Dney* (Thirty Days), *Vokrug Sveta* (Round the World), *Globus* (The Globe), *Leningradskaya Pravda, Moskovsky Komsomolets*; most of my articles were turned down, in almost every line the editors discovered slanting references to the Fascists whom wits called our 'deadly friends'.

I have said that in that winter I reached the age of fifty. Every cloud has a silver lining: my dubious standing saved me from hypocritical congratulations and addresses in leatherette folders. Friends came to our place. Lapin, smiling shyly, filled glasses with Lvov liqueurs which were very popular in Moscow. Pasternak sent me a letter: '. . . When we first met our ages numbered as many years as have since passed. Let us husband what remains of our spent energy'. I was often ill that winter, but what I wanted rather than to husband my energy was to spend it as quickly as possible: the breathing-space was too hard to bear.

The news became increasingly alarming. Since early March London had been saying that Hitler was preparing to seize the Balkans. Our press remained unperturbed. I attended a lecture on the international situation; the lecturer gave a circumstantial account of the predatory nature of British imperialism; I waited to hear what he had to say about Germany, but he did not even mention it.

One day I went to the Café Métropole. There were Germans sitting at the next table. They were drinking and talking noisily. I got up quickly and left.

Sometimes I went to the theatre and sighed over poor Emma Bovary fluttering desperately amidst the carnival hubbub; Alice Koonen was a deeply moving actress. I went to S. N. Lebedeva's exhibition and liked the picture of an athlete and the head of a Kalmuk girl. At another exhibition I delighted in Osmerkin's use of colour.

April was unquiet. On the 6th the radio announced Germany's attack on Yugoslavia and Greece. On the 9th the Germans took Salonica, on the 13th Belgrade.

On 14th April I met Vishnevsky; he said sombrely: 'There are conflicting opinions about your novel. We aren't giving it up. But I can't say anything about the second part'. The second part dealt with the events of 1937-8 and still the Germans did not come into it. 'Who objects to it and why?' I asked. Vishnevsky did not answer.

I knew that Jean-Richard Bloch was due to arrive in Moscow: he was to come out of France with a number of Soviet clerical workers. I asked the foreign committee of the Writers' Union to let me know beforehand as I wanted to go and meet him. But the committee decided that it would be wiser for a man in my situation not to meet foreigners. However, I heard by chance that the Blochs would be arriving on 18th April. Lyuba and I went to the railway station. Jean-Richard and Marguerite looked ill, they had aged, but they smiled with confidence in their friends, in freedom, in Moscow. For the best part of the day they described to me life in France: few writers were collaborating with the Germans; *La Nouvelle Revue Française* was a poor imitation of its former self; people did not believe what the papers said; in small towns the streets were emptied of people during the French broadcasts from London; Langevin was behaving wonderfully; Aragon had written some good poems.

On 20th April I learnt that the second part of *The Fall of Paris* had not been passed. This annoyed me but I decided to carry on.

On 24th April, as I was busy writing the fourteenth chapter, a telephone call came from Stalin's secretariat. I was told to dial a certain number: 'Comrade Stalin wishes to speak to you'.

Irina hastily chased out our poodles who had chosen the wrong time to play and bark.

Stalin said that he had read the beginning of my novel and found it interesting; he wanted to send me a manuscript – a translation of André Simon's book – which might be useful to me. I thanked him and said that I had already read Simon's book in the original. (It came out later in a Russian translation and in English under the title *J'Accuse: The Men Who Betrayed France*; as for the author – Simon-Katz – he was executed in Prague shortly before Stalin's death.)

Stalin asked me whether I intended to denounce the German Fascists. I said that the last part of the novel, on which I was now working, dealt with the war, the invasion of France by the Nazis, the first weeks of occupation. I added that I was afraid the third part would not be passed, for I was not allowed to use the word 'Fascists' even where the French were concerned, even in dialogue. Stalin said jocularly: 'Just go on writing, you and I will try to push the third part through'.

Lyuba and Irina were waiting impatiently: 'What did he say?' I was looking very gloomy: 'There'll be war soon'. Of course I added that all was well with the novel. But I had immediately realized that it was not a matter of literature: Stalin knew that his telephone call would be discussed everywhere. He wanted to give warning.

(Apparently by the end of April Stalin was alarmed. And, indeed, after the seizure of Yugoslavia it would have been too much to expect Hitler to allow the Pact to stand in his way. However, two more months passed and yet the attack caught us unprepared. The blame was laid on certain military men, among them the tank officer whom I had often met in Alcalá and at Guadalajara, Army General D. G. Pavlov; he was shot.)

I went to *Znamya* and told them about the telephone call. Vishnevsky beamed and told me that he had come in for a good deal of abuse in the Central Committee. While I was there the comrade who had abused Vishnevsky rang him up and said that it had all been 'a misunderstanding'.

Various editors telephoned asking for extracts from my novel.

I met Fadeyev. He had a very powerful and complex personality; I got to know him better in post-war years and shall write about him in the last part of my memoirs. But in 1941 he represented the man in authority who spoke to me not as one writer to another but as the secretary of the Writers' Union; he explained that he had not been sure how the international situation might change (I took down at the time the phrase he used: 'On my part it was political self-insurance in the best sense of the term').

Soon after this conversation there was an evening at the Writers' Club devoted to Armenian poetry. The chairman, as his eye fell upon me, said: 'We invite Ehrenburg to join the presidium'.

I met that remarkable poet, Avetik Isaakian. Fadeyev said of him that evening that 'sunny Armenia has given him happiness' and that 'he has re-tuned his lyre'. Isaakian asked me about the tragedy of France (he had lived there for some time and we talked to each other in French). He asked me whether I had read the translation of his poem *Abul al-Maarri*[1]; I said I had read a passage from it in French. He thought for a while: 'One must know how to leave home – that's the most important thing. You've just told me how Paris left home. But that's not enough. Recently I've been thinking a great deal about Tolstoy – he, too, left home'. We were interrupted. I looked at his face and could not tear my eyes away; it was anything but 'sunny': old, not with old age but with centuries of history, of grief, of stones, of blood. Besides, one cannot re-tune a lyre.

It had been a brief interlude for me, like a breath of fresh air.

In May I travelled to Kharkov, Kiev and Leningrad. I saw many old friends: Lisa Polonskaya, Tynyanov, Kaverin, Ushakov, Olga Forsh. It was in Kharkov that I first met a young student who wrote poetry – Boris Slutsky. In Kiev there was dancing at the Hotel Continental. A young Pole who was sitting at our table began to tell us about the Germans in Warsaw. Sofia Dolmatovskaya burst into tears. In Leningrad, in the Hotel Europa, tipsy Germans shouted: '*Hoch!*' I gave a talk in the House of Culture in Vyborg; I was bombarded with questions: was it true that the Germans were preparing to violate the Non-Aggression Pact or was the rumour just a British provocation?

The Germans occupied Greece. Stalin became Chairman of the Council of People's Commissars. Hess landed by plane in England to offer peace. Churchill declared that the greatest ordeals lay ahead.

Here are my entries for those days: '1st May. Telephone call from the Political section of the War Department: "Write something for the armed forces about the Germans, but make it sound like part of your novel". Sheinis rang up: the *Trud* article is held up. Everybody talking about war. Fighting in Crete. Instructor of a Regional Committee: "No need to panic. The Germans are thinking things over". 2nd June. The English have left Crete. 3rd June. *Thirty Days* has rejected my article. London says that the Greek embassy has been forced to leave Moscow. 5th June. Anna Andreyevna came in the evening: "I shouldn't be surprised at anything". 6th June. Jean-Richard

[1] Abul Ala al-Maarri (979–1058), famous blind Syrian Arab poet.

Bloch: "I have been commissioned to write articles but they don't print them". 7th June. With Kachalov and Moskvin[1]: "What is going on in France? We don't hear anything". 9th June. Tolstoy said that he had had a letter from Bunin. "The Germans are capable of anything". 10th June. Suritz: "The most dangerous thing is moral demobilization" 11th June. Evening at the NKID: "Why don't you expose British imperialism in your novel?" 12th June. Broadcast by the American journalist Walter Duranty: the Germans are concentrating hundreds of divisions in the East. 13th June. Démenti by TASS. In the evening gave reading at General Staff HQ. 14th June. London radio repeats: the Germans have concentrated huge forces on the Soviet frontier. Gave reading to the Frontier Guards. "We've been singing *If War Breaks out Tomorrow* ... but what have we been doing? Altogether too much din". 17th June. Karmen showed a film on China. Lectured to political instructors; they asked if it was true that Stalin had telephoned to me. "One has to draw certain conclusions". 18th June. At Palgunov's, long negotiations. Pact between Germany and Turkey. 19th June. London says that the Germans are speeding up their war preparations in Finland. Lectured to civil aviation pilots. One sent up a note: "People often have uncomplicated yet original minds". 20th June. Very hot. 'Phone call from *Trud*: "Too sharp". 21st June. Lectured at a factory. The chairman said: "We are not an island, we are a huge continent of peace". A note sent up: "It makes me feel like spewing to hear things like that".'

On 21st June there was heavy rain. Lyuba planned to go into the country on the next day, Sunday, to find a *dacha* for the summer.

On 22nd June early in the morning we were awakened by a telephone call from V. A. Milman: the Germans had declared war and had bombed Soviet towns. We sat by the radio waiting to hear Stalin. Molotov spoke in his stead; he sounded overwrought. I was surprised when he said this was a treacherous attack. Treachery implies the breaking of pledges of honour, or at least of good faith. One could hardly attribute any ideas of honour or decency to Hitler. What could anyone have expected of Fascists?

We sat for a long time by the radio. Hitler made a speech. Churchill's speech was relayed. But Moscow was broadcasting gay lighthearted songs which in no way corresponded to the mood of the people.

[1] Two of the most famous actors of the Moscow Art Theatre.

No speeches, no articles had been prepared: they were playing songs.

Later I was fetched and taken to *Trud*, to *Red Star*, to the radio station. I wrote the first war article. There was a telephone call from PUR (the Political Department of the Armed Forces), asking me to come on Monday at 8 a.m. and inquiring: 'Have you any military rank?' I said that I held no rank but had a calling: I would go wherever they wanted to send me and do whatever they ordered me to do.

Late at night I saw a couple in the Ordynka. The girl was crying. The man said: 'Don't worry. Listen, Lyolya, listen to me, don't worry'.

This was the longest day of the year, and it lasted a very long time – almost four years: a day of great trials, of great courage, of great misfortune, when the Soviet people demonstrated its spiritual strength.

BIOGRAPHICAL SKETCHES

BIOGRAPHICAL SKETCHES

AFINOGENOV, ALEXANDER NIKOLAEVICH (1904–41). Soviet Russian playwright. Father a writer; mother a village schoolteacher. Graduate of Moscow School of Journalism. First play, 1926, *The Other Side of the Slit Trench*, based on a Jack London story. Put on by Moscow Workers' Proletcult Theater of which he was director 1926–29. His 1930 play *Fear* put on by Moscow Art Theater. Other plays: *Distant Point, Salute to Spain, Mashenka, On the Eve*. On Dec. 29, 1941, killed by a Nazi bomb while on air-raid duty.

AKHMATOVA, ANNA ANDREEVNA (pseudonym of ANNA A. GORENKO) (b. 1888). Soviet Russian poet with wide prerevolutionary reputation. Criticized by Soviet critics for "art for art's sake" approach and for religious mysticism in her poetry. Attacked personally in the famous 1946 resolution on literature of Central Committee of Communist Party for the Soviet Union. Supported Soviet war effort in forties and peace movement since in her poems. But considered aristocratic aesthete in SU. By many, however, considered one of great Russian poets. War poem *Courage* (*Pravda*, March 8, 1942) considered by some critics best war poem. Among well-known collections of her poems: *Evening* (1912), *Rosary Beads* (1913), *White Flock* (1917), *Plantain* (1921), *Anno Domini MCMXXI* (1921). Long silent, then in print again on eve of and during World War II but attacked as decadent. In 1950 published propeace poems from cycle *Glory and Peace*.

ANTONOV-OVSEYENKO, VLADIMIR ALEKSANDROVICH (1884–1938). One of most important of Bolshevik revolutionary leaders. Participated as revolutionary military leader in both 1905 and 1917 revolutions. Graduate of military engineering institute. In revolutionary movement from 1901; Bolshevik from 1902. Emigré in France 1910–1917. Winter Palace taken by Bolsheviks in October 1917 Revolution under his command. In Soviet military and political posts up to 1925 when appointed ambassador to Czechoslovakia; 1928 to Lithuania; 1930 to Poland; Consul General to Loyalist Spain during Civil War period. Involved in Trotskyite opposition 1923–27 but broke with them in 1928. Arrested in purge of thirties and disappeared. Rehabilitated posthumously in 1956.

BABEL, ISAAK EMMANUELOVICH (1894–1941). One of most noted of Russian writers of Soviet times. Master of the short story. Of Jewish origin. Graduate of Commercial School in Odessa where born. Then lived in Kiev and in 1915 moved to St. Petersburg. First stories published by Gorky in his magazine *Letopis* (*Annals*) in 1916. Served in Czarist army. Participated in Civil War on side of Bolsheviks. Among works—short stories: *Cavalry* (a cycle), *The King, Odessa Stories, The Awakening, Karl-Yankel, Dante Street, Oil;* plays: *Sunset, Maria;* scenario: *Wandering Stars.* Criticized for subjectivism in stories of Civil War in describing events and heroes as developing spontaneously. Showed path of the petty bourgeoisie to the revolution in his stories. Caught up in purge of late thirties. Rehabilitated posthumously.

BELY, ANDREY (pseudonym of BORIS NIKOLAEVICH BUGAEV) (1880–1934). Russian writer. Of symbolist school. Graduate of Moscow University in natural sciences. Writing career began in 1904 when he joined staff of magazine *Vesy* (*Scales*). Wrote poetry, prose, literary criticism—poetry: *Gold in Azure* (1904), *Ashes* (1907), *The Urn* (1909); prose: *Silver Pigeon* (1910), *St. Petersburg* (1916), *Kotik Letaev* (1918); theory and history of literature: *Symbolism* (1910), *Arabesques* (1911), *Dostoevsky and Tolstoy* (1911), *Poetry of the Word* (1922); memoirs: *On the Border of Two Centuries* (1930). Attacked by Soviet critics as mystical, pessimistic, obscurantist, reactionary. Especially criticized for depicting revolution as destructively violent. Philosophical sources in Kant and Schopenhauer. In early years very influential role in literature.

BEZYMENSKY, ALEKSANDR ILYICH (b. 1898). Graduate of Kiev Commercial Institute. Became Communist youth leader during Russian revolution. First in print in 1918. First book (of prose and poetry) published in Kazan in 1920 —*The Young Proletarian.* Called the Komsomol (young Communist) poet. Writes prose, poetry, plays, satire. Poetry: *Party Card 224332, Young Guard, To the Poets of the Forges* (all three written in the early twenties), *The Young Communist League* (1924), *Felix* (1927); satire: *The Shot* (a play) (1930), *A Day in Our Life* (1930). Wrote poems mobilizing youth to work in early plan years (thirties), such as *Tragedian's Night* (1931), *Night of the Chief of the Political Department* (1934). During World War II served in front-line press. Has been writing satirical antiwar poems such as *Stronger Than the Atom Bomb* (1949). Criticized occasionally for rhetorical, schematic approach in work but generally highly praised. Holds Order of Red Banner of Labor.

DEINEKA, ALEKSANDR ALEKSANDROVICH (b. 1899). Artist and sculptor.

Member of Academy of Art of USSR (since 1947). Merited Artist of RSFSR. Studied at famous Vkhulemas (higher state art studios—est. 1918) 1921–24. From early period took themes of industry and sports. Began as formalist then turned to realism. In late twenties did many political cartoons and posters. In thirties turned to genre painting—everyday life of Soviet people, and again in forties—sports and labor. In forties also used many patriotic themes related to the war against Fascism. Sculpture uses sports themes. Mosaic plafonds for subway stations (Mayakovsky Square (1938) and Novokuznetskaya (1943). Since 1928 has also been teaching art.

DOGALEVSKY, VALERIAN SAVELYEVICH (1885–1934). Soviet diplomat. Began participating actively in Russian revolutionary movement in 1904. Joined Bolshevik party in 1908. Emigré from 1908 (when arrested and exiled) to time of Revolution when returned to Russia and took part in Civil War in south, in Siberia, and outside Petrograd. From 1920 to 1923 held various government posts. In 1924 named Soviet ambassador to Sweden; 1925 to Japan; 1927 to death, ambassador to France. 1929 signatory for Soviet Union to Anglo-Soviet agreement to re-establish diplomatic relations (broken in 1927). 1932 signed nonaggression pact with France. 1933 to death, participated in Geneva disarmament talks as Soviet representative.

DOVZHENKO, ALEKSANDR PETROVICH (1894–1956). Soviet moving-picture director. People's Artist of RSFSR. Merited Artist of Ukrainian SSR. Graduate of Glukhov Teachers Institute. Painted for several years. In 1926 began his film work. First film of note: *Zvenigora* (1928). *Arsenal* (1929), *Earth* (1931)—considered his best films. But criticized as too complicated in form. *Ivan* (1932), *Aerograd* (1935)—considered less successful. *Shchors* (1939), on the man known as the Ukrainian Chapaev (said to have been inspired by talk with Stalin), popular as depiction of Revolution in Ukraine. 1940–46 did documentaries on Ukraine. During war was at front. Wrote war stories. Wrote a play on the life of the agricultural scientist Michurin and later made it into a film himself. Did all his own scenarios except those for his earliest films. Held Order of Lenin and Red Banner of Labor.

EISENSTEIN (EISENSHTEIN), SERGEI MIKHAILOVICH (1898–1948). Outstanding Soviet film director. Merited Artist of RSFSR. Doctor of Arts. 1916–18 studied at Petrograd Civil Engineering Institute. 1917 joined People's Militia as volunteer. And in 1918, the Red Army. 1921–24 was director and set designer at first workers' theater in Moscow—Proletcult. Began working

513

on films in 1924. First film *The Strike* (1925) on Russian working-class struggle. His great *Potemkin* also done in 1925. Followed by *October* (1927), *The Old and the New* (1929). 1929–31 lived in USA where he studied film-making. Did *Viva Mexico!* there (never completed). From 1932 held chair of film directing at Cinema Institute (from 1937 professor). *Bezhin Lug* (1937) criticized as formalistic, never shown. *Alexander Nevsky* (1938), *Ivan the Terrible* (1945) were great successes. Held Order of Lenin and Badge of Honor.

FADEYEV, ALEKSANDR ALEKSANDROVICH (1901–56). One of leading Soviet Russian writers and public figures. Communist Party member from 1918. Member of Central Committee of Communist Party of SU. Deputy to Supreme Soviet of USSR and RSFSR. Participated as partisan in Civil War in Far East (1919–21) where he had been brought up by revolutionary parents. Then in Red Army in 1921. 1921–22 studied at Mining Institute in Moscow. 1923–26 in political and newspaper work. From 1926 leading organizer in field of literature. On Board of Soviet Writers Union until death. Secretary-General of Writers Union through forties. Began appearing in print in 1923. *Flood* (1923), *Against the Current* (1923), *Rout* (or *The Nineteen*) (1927), *Last of the Udegs* (1929–36), *Leningrad in the Days of the Blockade* (1944), *Young Guard* (1946, revised ed. 1951). In 1954 published chapters from new book about the working class, *Ferrous Metallurgy*. Held two orders of Lenin. Committed suicide in 1956.

FEDIN, KONSTANTIN ALEKSANDROVICH (b. 1892). One of leading Soviet Russian writers. Deputy to Supreme Soviet of RSFSR. Graduate of Commercial School. 1911–14 studied at Moscow Commercial Institute, Economics Division. Went to Germany in 1914. Caught up in war. Kept as civilian prisoner four years. Returned home 1918. Served in Commissariat of People's Education for a while then went into journalism. Entered Red Army and began working in military press. Had begun writing in 1910—first published in 1913. First novel: *Wasteland* (1923). Literary philosophy during this period—art transcends classes, remove oneself from contemporaneity. *Cities and Years* (1924) one of first Soviet novels about Revolution and Civil War, however. *Morning in Vyazhny* (1926), *Muzhiks* (1926), *Transvaal* (1926), *Brothers* (1927–28) *With (Romain) Rolland* (1932). Play: *Ordeal by Feelings* (1942). 1941–45 wrote numerous essays and memoirs. *Extraordinary Summer* (1947–48). Leading positions in Union of Writers of USSR. Holds two orders of Red Banner of Labor.

FORSH, OLGA DMITRIEVNA (b. 1873). Writer. Called Dean (or Doyenne) of Russian writers because of age and length of time in print. Born a noblewoman. Born and brought up in Caucasus where father commanded a division. Up to 1917 taught drawing in school. Began literary career in 1908. Early work characterized by struggle between ideal man and the ugliness of reality. For a period under influence of the symbolists. In Soviet times, works: *Dressed in Stone* (1925), *Hot Shop* (1927), *The Mad Ship* (1931), *The Crow* (1934), *Jacobean Ferment* (1934), *Fatal Book* (1939), *Mikhailov Castle* (1946), *Forerunners of Freedom* (about the Decembrists) (1953). Two scenarios: *Palace and Fortress* (1924), *Pugachev* (1937). Holds Order of Lenin and Red Banner of Labor.

FURMANOV, DMITRI ANDREYEVICH (1891–1926). Foremost Soviet writer of early period. One of founders of Soviet literature. Communist Party member from 1918 on. Studied at Moscow University, Philosophy Department. During World War I served at front 1914–18 as volunteer in medical corps. On return home completed his higher education at Moscow University in the Social Science Department. Became a revolutionary at the front. First poems printed 1912–16 in local magazines and newspapers. First book of short stories *Red Landing* (1922), followed by novel *Chapayev* (1923) on which the film well known here was based. *Mutiny* (1925). Considered the great hope of rising proletarian literature by Soviet critics in his day.

GRABAR, IGOR EMMANUILOVICH (1871–1960). Painter and art historian. People's Artist of RSFSR and of USSR (1956). Member of Academy of Sciences of USSR (from 1943) and of Academy of Art (from 1947). Born in Budapest. In Russia from 1881. 1889–93 studied law at University of St. Petersburg. During this same period worked as writer and artist in St. Petersburg satirical journals. 1893–94 did illustrations for Gogol's collected works. 1894 entered St. Petersburg Academy of Art. 1896–1901 studied art in Munich. Came under influence of impressionists. Returned to Russia 1901. Worked on paintings depicting Russian nature. Began writing art criticism in late 1890s. 1909–14 worked as architect. 1913–25 headed Tretyakov Art Gallery in Moscow. 1909–16 wrote and published his monumental *History of Russian Art*. After October Revolution assigned task of preserving art treasures of ancient Russia. From thirties on worked on his own art. Paintings hang in many Soviet museums. Very much in realist school. 1944 became director of Inst. of Hist. of Art of Acad. of Sciences. Held two orders of Lenin and Order of Red Banner of Labor.

ILF, ILYA (pseudonym of ILYA ARNOLDOVICH FAINZILBERG) (1897–1937). One of most famous of Soviet satirists (wrote together with Evgenii Petrov). First appeared in print in 1918. Worked on satirical magazines. Wrote on everyday life and social problems and did literary criticism too. Most famous of works (together with E. Petrov) satirical novels: *12 Chairs* (1928), *Golden Calf* (1931). Their trip to New York gave Ilf and Petrov material for their *One-Storeyed America* (1936). Ilf's *Notebooks* published posthumously in 1939.

IVANOV, VSEVOLOD VYACHESLAVOVICH (b. 1895). Writer. In early life served as a sailor, then worked as an actor with a band of strolling players and in a circus too. Also worked as a printer. Participated in Civil War (in Siberia). First book: *Rogulki* (*Crooked Trees*), a collection of short stories set up and published by himself in 1919. But short stories had already appeared in magazines in 1917. Best known of his novels, plays, and short-story collections: *Partisans* (1921), *Armored Train* (1922) (did stage treatment for this novel in 1927), *Colored Winds* (1922), *Blue Sands* (1923), *Mystery of Mysteries* (1927), *Naibkhan Compromise* (a play) (1930), *Adventures of a Fakir* (autobiographic) (1935), *Parkhomenko* (on Civil War) (1939), *Uncle Kostya* (play about Belorussian partisans) (1944), *Meetings with Gorky* (who exerted strong influence on his writing and on him personally) (1947).

JAMBUL (or DZHAMBUL DZHABAEV) (1846–1945). Great Kazakh folk bard (*akyn* in Kazakh). One of most important representatives of oral folk poetry. Was deputy to Supreme Soviet of Kazakh SSR (from 1938 to death). Greatly attracted to music and song from earliest childhood. At twelve an accomplished dombra (national Kazakh instrument) player. Began his career as wandering troubador at age of fourteen traveling from Kazakh *aul* (mountain village) to *aul*. Composed poems (*aitys*) to chant his people's tales and legends and history. Master of the *aitys*. Composed cycles of poems on Soviet times, the Revolution, the Civil War, World War II. Held Order of Lenin. Translated into all languages in the Soviet Union.

KAPITSA, PETER LEONIDOVICH (b. 1894). Outstanding Soviet physicist. Member of Academy of Sciences of USSR (since 1939). Was graduated from the Petrograd Polytechnical Institute in 1918. First studies devoted to research on radioactivity. Worked in England from 1921–35 doing physical research in Lord Rutherford's Laboratory at Cambridge. Returned to USSR in 1935. 1935–46 and from 1956 on, Director of Institute of Physical Problems of Academy of Sciences of USSR. Worked on problem of liquification of air and the characteristics of liquid helium. Member of Commission on Interplanetary Communications of Academy of Sciences of USSR.

KATAYEV, VALENTIN PETROVICH (b. 1897). Writer. Wrote poetry in early youth—published in Odessa and St. Petersburg journals. 1915 went into Czarist army; wrote front-line correspondence. 1918–20 served in Red Army. Participated in Civil War in Ukraine. 1922 came to Moscow and began his literary career. Early stories were humorous and light—*Sir Henry and the Devil* (1923), *Edward the Loafer* (1925), *Bearded Baby* (1926). Then turned to Gogol-like social satire: *Embezzlers* (1927) (exposé of NEP period). Later satires lighter in treatment: *Squaring the Circle* (1928) and *The Path of Flowers* (1930)—both comedies. Play: *Time Forward!* (1932) a serious treatment of the first five-year plan. Next book a children's novel, *Lonely White Sail* (1936) (about the 1905 Revolution). Later novels: *I Am a Son of the Working People* (1937) and *Son of the Regiment* (1945) on Civil War and World War II. For *Power of the Soviets* (1949) criticized; revised edition (1951). Holds Order of Lenin.

KAVERIN, VENIAMIN ALEKSANDROVICH (b. 1902). Writer. Graduated from Leningrad University in Department of Oriental Languages in 1924. Made his literary debut while still a student in 1922 with a short story, *The Eleventh Axiom*. "Discovered" by Gorky. Was a member of the literary group called the Serapion Brothers, who were concerned with form and formal inventiveness more than with ideological content. Early work full of romantic fantasy. Moved toward realism with novel *Nine-Tenths Fate* (1926). *Scandalist* (1928). *Fulfillment of Desire* (1935–36). *Two Captains* (1940–45). *Open Book* (1952). Criticized for "contrivedness" and "inventiveness" of plots and characters in works.

KIRSANOV, SEMYON ISAAKOVICH (b. 1906). Poet. Early influenced by both Mayakovsky and the Left Front (LEF) Movement, which was searching for revolutionary original forms in style and linguistic direction. Involved in experimentation with form. *Sights* (1926) and *Experiences* (1927) were agitational in character, influenced by Mayakovsky. Of a more formalistic nature from the Soviet point of view in style but highly political in content were *Comrade Marx* (1933), *Poem about the Robot* (1934), *Cinderella* (1935), and his anti-Fascist *War—A Plague* (1937). During the war wrote agitational songs like *Foma Smyslov*. In the postwar period *Alexander Matrosov* (1946), *Sky above our Homeland* (1947), *Makar Magai* (1950), *This World* (1958).

Has translated Hikmet, Pablo Neruda in late years, and has published new collections of poems.

KOLTSOV, MIKHAIL EFIMOVICH (1898–1942). Writer and journalist. Joined Communist Party 1918. Studied at Petrograd Psychoneurological Institute. Began his literary career on student magazines. During Civil War worked on army newspaper. In 1922 became regular Pravda correspondent and columnist. Wrote sharply on both everyday problems and international affairs. Discussed problems of cultural revolution; made satirical attacks on bureaucracy, careerism, callousness, banality. Book on Spanish Civil War: *Spanish Diary* (1938). Essays on Gorky, Lunacharsky, Barbusse (1923–38). Founded and edited popular Soviet magazine *Ogonyok* (*Light*). Edited satirical magazine *Krokodil* (1934–38). Elected Deputy to Supreme Soviet of RSFSR 1938. Same year elected to corresponding membership in Academy of Sciences of USSR. Disappeared during 1938 purges. Posthumously rehabilitated 1956–57. Pungent early works being republished.

KONCHALOVSKY, PYOTR PETROVICH (1876–1956). Russian painter of prerevolutionary and Soviet fame. Was People's artist of RSFSR. Member of Academy of Arts of USSR. Studied in Paris (1897–98) and then at Petrograd Academy of Arts from which he was graduated in 1907. In early years close to famous Russian artists Surikov and Serov. Then under influence of formalists (one of organizers of the Jack of Diamonds Society around which "formalists" gathered). After October Revolution turned to realism—still lifes, landscapes, portraits, thematic compositions. Figures of people criticized as lacking in depth and psychological expressiveness. Also did stage sets (1918–21) and art teaching (1928–29). Awarded Order of Red Banner of Labor, medals, and various prizes. In 1956 posthumous show held for which he had made selections before death.

KORNEICHUK, ALEKSANDR EVDOKIMOVICH (b. 1905). Leading Soviet Ukrainian playwright and public figure. Member of CPSU since 1940 and Central Committee of CPSU since 1953. On Supreme Soviets of both Ukrainian SSR and USSR. Member of Academies of Sciences of USSR and the Ukrainian SSR. At fourteen began working on railroad. 1929 graduated from Kiev Institute of Education. 1938–41 and 1946–53 Chairman of Ukrainian Union of Soviet Writers. 1943–44 assistant People's Commissar of Foreign Affairs of USSR. 1944 People's Commissar of Foreign Affairs of Ukraine. 1944–45 Chairman of Committee on Art Affairs of Ukraine. First literary works published in 1925: *Story about Lenin*. Earliest plays: *On the Brink* (1929); *Storm* (1931) combatted Ukrainian nationalism. *Destruction of the Squadron* (1933) brought him wide fame. Followed by *Platon Krechet* (1934), *Truth* (1937), *Bogdan Khmelnitsky* (1939), *On the Steppes of the Ukraine* (1941), *Partisans on the Steppes of the Ukraine* (1942), *Front* (1942), *Come to Zvenigora* (1946), *Makar Dubrava* (1948), *Kalinovaya Grove* (1952). *Bogdan Khmelnitsky* libretto (1951), *Wings* (1954). Now active in peace work both at home and abroad. Holds Order of Lenin.

LEONOV, LEONID MAKSIMOVICH (b. 1899). Writer. Son of self-taught poet. Graduated from middle school in 1918 and joined the Red Army. Then attended Moscow University. Wrote poetry in youth. First work published, a short story, *Buryga* (1922). Early tales concerned with stylizing, abstracting character. *The Petushikhin Breakthrough* (1923). *Badgers* (1924) on class struggle in the villages considered by Soviet critics his first really mature work. Followed by *The Thief* (1927), *Untilovsk* (a play) (1928). Novels: *Sot* (1930), *Skutarevsky* (1932), *Road to the Ocean* (1936). During World War II (1941–45) wrote patriotic articles and play *Invasion* (1942). Made into film in 1944. *Lenushka* (1943). *Russian Forest* (1953). *Theater* (1960) a two-volume compilation of Lenov plays, articles 1928–57. Member of various Writers' Union executive and administrative sectors. Holds Order of Lenin and Red Banner of Labor and Patriotic War. American critics have characterized his work as long-winded and overwritten and often obscure, but have praised his keen sense of the dramatic and his psychological insight.

LOZOVSKY, SOLOMON ABRAMOVICH (1878–1952) (pseudonym taken in pre-1917 Russian revolutionary underground—real name, S. A. DRIDZO). Important figure in Soviet and international trade union movement, journalist and diplomat in Soviet foreign service. Began working at age of eleven. Entered revolutionary movement in 1900 and became Bolshevik in 1901, working for his party even in exile in Kazan in 1904. Active in 1905 Revolution. 1909–17 lived abroad (in France). 1917 returned to Russia. Immediately elected Secretary of Trade Union Council. 1921–37 General Secretary of Profintern (Left-wing international of trade unions). 1937–39 Director of State Publishing House. 1939–46 Deputy Commissar (First Deputy Minister in charge of terminology) of Foreign Affairs. 1940–49 head of History of International Relations Department at Higher Party School and concurrently (1941–48) deputy chief, then chief of Soviet Information Bureau. Doctor of Historical Sciences, member for some time of Central Committee of CPSU. Held Order of Lenin and Patriotic War. Arrested in 1949 for allegedly plotting against Stalin and executed in 1952. Rehabilitated posthumously in 1956.

MARKISH, PERETZ DAVIDOVICH (1895–1952). Soviet Jewish writer (wrote in Yiddish). First book of poems *Thresholds* (1919). Attacked idealization of small-town Jewish life. Considered anarchistic in approach by Soviet critics. Further developed in *Pranks* (1919) and *Roadlessness* (1920). 1921–25 lived abroad working on progressive Yiddish newspapers. During this period wrote his important *Heritage* (unpublished). Returned to Soviet Union in 1926. Published new book of poems there in 1927—*Everyday Affairs*. *Brothers* (1930)— on role of Jewish workers in the Russian Revolution and the Civil War. *Don't Lose Heart* (1931). *Death of a Kulak* (1933). *Dawn on the Dnieper* (1937). *War* (1948). Plays: *The Ovadis Family* (1938), *The Chronicler Arye* (1940), *Ghetto Uprising* (1946). Novels: *From Century to Century* (1929–41), *The Generations Step Forth* (written 1948—unpublished). Arrested in late forties and executed in 1952 for alleged anti-Soviet crimes. Posthumously rehabilitated in 1956—six poems published along with laudatory article on the man and his work.

MARSHAK, SAMUIL YAKOVLEVICH (b. 1887). Outstanding Soviet Russian poet, translator, children's writer. Studied in St. Petersburg and London. First published in 1907 (poems and translations of classical poetry). Association with Gorky began early. Gorky helped him become a professional writer. Considered one of founders of Soviet children's literature. His books for children most popular: *Fire* (1923), *Tale of the Little Blue Mouse* (1923), *Baggage* (1926), *The Mail* (1927), *So Absent-Minded* (1930), *Battle Against the Dnieper* (1931). Wrote many stories in verse to tell Soviet children about their country: *Military Post-Office* (1944), *Year 'Round* (1945); poems: *Fast and Fancy* (1947), *Forest Book* (1950), *How Your Book Was Printed* (1951), *Jolly Trip from A to Z* (1952); plays: *12 Months* (1945), *House of the Cat* (1945). Also wrote lyrical poems, children's satire. Also noted for his masterly translations of Shakespeare, Burns, Byron, Heine. Holds several orders including Order of Lenin.

MAYAKOVSKY, VLADIMIR VLADIMIROVICH (1893–1930). Considered probably the greatest of the Russian poets of Soviet times. As a middle school student active participant in 1905 Revolution. 1908 left school to devote self completely to underground revolutionary work. Joined the Bolsheviks at age of fifteen. Worked as a party agitator. Attended classes at Industrial Arts Institute. In and out of jails for revolutionary activity. 1911 entered Moscow

520

Art School and devoted himself to drawing. Began appearing in print 1912. Joined the futurists—signed their declaration calling for a new literature. *Night* and *Morning* published 1912 in anthology compiled by David Burliuk the painter (now living in the U.S.). Among his early poetry were poems of social protest, lyrical verse, satire (1915–17): *War and Peace, Man.* Friendship with Gorky from 1915 on. Gorky considered him a great poet and minimized his futurism. First of his political satires appeared in 1915 while he was in Czarist army—*Hymn to a Scientist, Hymn to a Judge* and others. 1917–18 became the poet of the Revolution—called on intellectuals to join the Revolution. Painted posters and wrote verse rallying people to the Civil War. Called for making the arts popular. Wrote poems in new and old forms in this period—*Mystery—Bouffe, 150,000,000* (1920–21). Among best-known poems are: *Concerning This* (1923), *Vladimir Ilyich Lenin* (1924), *All Right* (1928), *At the Top of My Voice* (1930). His satirical plays have recently enjoyed a popular revival on the Soviet stage: *The Bedbug* (1928) and *The Bathhouse* (1930). Exerted great influence on young Soviet poets. Still an important influence and still a bestseller in SU. Committed suicide at age of thirty-seven hounded by torments of an unhappy love and inner dissatisfaction.

MEYERHOLD, VSEVOLOD EMILYEVICH (1874–1942). Leading Soviet theater figure, director. Early—People's Artist of the Republic (1923). Member of the Communist Party from 1918. Was a student in Moscow University Law School 1895–96. In 1896 entered the Musical-Dramatic School of the Moscow Philharmonic Society (class in drama). On graduation worked as actor in Moscow Art Theater 1898–1902. 1902–05 worked outside Moscow. Began experimenting in theater production in Moscow and Leningrad. 1905 worked in theater studios and theaters of fame at the time such as the Komissarzhevsky Theater in St. Petersburg. After the Revolution instrumental in spreading the slogan of "Theatrical October." From 1920 on was in charge of the RSFSR Theater (later called the Meyerhold) and produced and directed Theater of the Revolution plays concurrently. Controversial figure. Criticized for formalism—but his content was always contemporary and revolutionary. Had a profound influence on the development of the directorial art in the Soviet theater. Reported arrested and deported to a labor camp where he died in 1942—for alleged counterrevolutionary activity. But is being posthumously honored.

MIKHOELS, SOLOMON MIKHAILOVICH (real name S. M. VOVSI (1890–1948). Soviet Jewish actor and director. (Performed in Yiddish). People's Artist of the USSR. Studied at Petrograd University Law School. 1919 joined

Petrograd Jewish Theater Studio on basis of which the Moscow State Jewish Theater was set up in 1921. He worked in this theater from the moment it was set up, first as an actor and then in 1929 as its director. Applied principles of Russian realistic theater movement. Among his most famous productions—*Freilakhs* (1946). His best role—that of Lear in *King Lear* (1938). Lenin Order holder. Reported killed in automobile accident. Accused posthumously (1953) of having been involved in famous alleged Jewish doctors' plot against Stalin and the SU but exonerated some months after accusation.

PASTERNAK, BORIS LEONIDOVICH (1890–1960). Poet and translator. Father a famous painter; mother a musician. Studied music, philosophy, law at Moscow University and in Germany. Began writing in 1913. First book of poems *Twin in the Storm Clouds* (1914); *Above the Barriers* (1917) and *Life, My Sister* (1922) grouped with his symbolist, escapist books by Soviet critics. Gained his fame after the Revolution. Early postrevolutionary poems lyrical—*Themes and Variations* (1923). Attempted also to present historical and revolutionary themes—*Lieutenant Schmidt* (1926), *1905* (1927). In 1932 he again began publishing his lyrical poetry. *Second Birth*—a collection of poems. During the Second World War (1941–45) patriotic themes were reflected in his work: *In Early Trains* (1943). His poetry though highly praised in the SU is criticized for subjectivism in perception of the world. Considered a translator of unequaled ability from many languages: *Georgian Poets* (1946), Goethe's *Faust* (1953), *Selected Works of Shakespeare* (1953). His first novel, *Dr. Zhivago* (1956), for which he was awarded a Nobel Prize (1958) was never published in SU and brought both political and literary attacks on him at home.

PAUSTOVSKY, KONSTANTIN GEORGIEVICH (b. 1892). Writer. Studied in Kiev in youth. Was a worker, a sailor, a reporter in turn and went through many other professions. Participated in the Civil War. First story published in 1911. Professional literary career began with 1925. Early books of a romantic, exotic nature. His heroes were far from the reality of life. His first novel concerned with Soviet life was *Kara-Bugaz* (1932) on how Soviet people change the face of nature. This became his favorite theme: *Kolkhida* (1934), *Black Sea* (1936), *Polar Novel* (1939), *Novel about the Forests* (1948), *Birth of the Sea* (1952) (the last on the Volga-Don Canal). Also wrote many historical and biographical novels: *Isaak Levitan* (1937), *Taras Shevchenko* (1939); plays: *Lieutenant Lermontov* (1941), *Our Contemporary* (Pushkin) (1949).

PILNYAK (VOGAU) BORIS ANDREEVICH (1849–1938?). Writer. Graduated from Moscow Commercial Institute in 1920. Took no part in Revolution. Traveled much after Revolution in Europe, America, and Japan. Began writing at age nineteen. First in print in 1909—in literary press. 1915 began contributing to magazines and anthologies regularly. First book of stories *The Forgotten* (1919). Developed his first novel—*The Naked Year* (1920)—from this collection and this brought him his first fame. In early works attracted to "return to nature" ideas. Inspired by symbolists in style and Slavophiles in content. Works of early thirties show more directness and simplicity of style and in his 1925–28 writing he concentrated on the problem of the triumph of intelligence over instinct and emotion. *Tale of Unextinguished Moon* (1926) caused furor, suggesting Stalin had forced Frunze (then Military Commissar) to commit suicide. *Matter of Death* and *Ivan-Moscow* belong to this latter period. In 1929 he published a lampoon on Soviet life in the emigré press— *Mahogany*. Severely attacked for this in press. With novel *Volga Flows into the Caspian* (Dec. 1929) took up theme of revolutionary Soviet life. *OK* (1932) was a critical work on the U.S. (but severely criticized in SU too). Last known novel is *Ripening of the Fruit* (1935), which was run in a journal but never published in book form. Reported arrested in 1937 and executed in 1938, accused as spy for Japanese and Trotskyites. Rehabilitated to extent in 1957.

PRISHVIN, MIKHAIL MIKHAILOVICH (1873–1954). Writer. Active in Marxist groups as youth. Arrested and imprisoned (1897–99). Then went abroad. Got university training in agronomy at Leipzig University. Returned to Russia and worked as agronomist. Hiked all over north Russia. His first book, *In the Country of Unfrightened Birds* (1905), brought him membership in the Russian Geographical Society (the book was a record of his ethnographic observations of life in the little-known north). In all of his early books Prishvin looked for the inner man through his perception of untouched nature in the far north, in Kazakhstan, in the Crimea: *The Little Round Loaf* (1906), *The Black Arab* (1911), *Glorious the Tambourines* (1914). It was after the October Revolution in 1917 that he gained a wide public popularity and he turned to a more realistic style. His autobiographic *Chain of Kashchey* (1923–36) describes the developing consciousness of an artist in the Russia of the nineties. His books continued, however, to reflect his love of nature and man with great understanding and humor: *Hunter's Tales* (1920–26), *Calendar of Nature* (1925), *Springs of Berendey* (1926), *Root of Life* (1932), *Tree Drippings* (1940–43), *Storehouse of the Sun* (1945) (a children's fairy tale), *Honey from beyond the Pale* (1957), *Ships' Thicket* (1954). Holds Order of Red Banner of Labor.

RADEK, KARL BERNGARDOVICH (1885– 1945?). Was in his day one of most famous of Soviet Communist political figures and political writers. Associated with working-class movement from age of fourteen (in Galicia). From 1901 active leader of Galician Bolsheviks. 1904–08 active in Polish revolutionary Socialist movement and 1908 in left wing of German social democratic movement. After Bolshevik Revolution came to Petrograd. Was Left Communist. After conclusion of Brest Peace worked in People's Commissariat of Foreign Affairs in charge of Central European Affairs. Went to Germany illegally after German revolution broke out in 1918, arrested in 1919. On liberation from prison returned to Russia. Active leader in Communist International. 1919–24 member of Central Committee of CPSU. 1924 joined the Trotskyite opposition and in 1927 was expelled from the Party. In 1930 reinstated. Books: *5 Years of Comintern, German Revolution*. Wrote for *Pravada* and *Izvestia*. Arrested in 1936 and tried and sentenced in 1937 on charge of treason in concert with the "Anti-Soviet Trotskyite Center". Judged responsible for "criminal activities" of this Center but not directly participating in organization and execution of it and so sentenced to ten years' imprisonment rather than death as were many of the others in the "Center". Reported to have died in later years of World War II in a prison camp in Yakutia, the victim of a fellow prisoner who killed him in a quarrel.

SLUTSKY, BORIS ABRAMOVICH (b. early twenties?). Spent early childhood and school years in Kharkov—in thirties. Came to the attention of the reading public after World II but first poem published in 1941. Also translates foreign and non-Russian Soviet poets into Russian. In his poems uses commonplace incident to bring to his reader topical, philosophical, or ethical problems. Style involved. Has had a few collections published but appears mainly in literary journals. Very popular among young poets. In 1962 *Literary Gazette* published his *Poems of Various Years* critical of Stalin (written before the "Thaw") and about contemporary living, calling on the Soviet people to work to bring their dreams of the future to pass. Among recent collections of poems: *Memory* (1957).

TAIROV, ALEKSANDR YAKOVLEVICH (pseudonym—real name, KORNBLITT) (1885–1950). Famous Soviet theater figure. Director. People's Artist of RSFSR (from 1935). Graduate of St. Petersburg University Law School in 1913. While still student in 1905 joined the St. Petersburg Komissarzhevsky Theater. 1905–09 worked as both actor and director with Gaideburov and Skarskaya Mobile Dramatic Theater and 1910–11 as director in theaters in Riga, St. Petersburg, and Moscow. In 1914 organized and ran the Moscow

Kamerny (Chamber) Theater with which he was connected until 1949 (the theater itself was in operation until 1950). He was responsible for mounting over sixty productions in this theater. Early productions called formalistic; stylized, illustrating the illusoriness of life. In the twenties became interested in monumental tragedies and in social problem plays. In 1933 he produced Vishnevsky's *Optimistic Tragedy* considered an important play in the history of the Soviet theater. In forties concentrated on Russian and foreign classics (Flaubert, Chekhov, Gorky) as well as Soviet dramas (Vishnevsky, Grin, Yakobson). Held Order of Lenin and Red Banner of Labor.

TIKHONOV, NIKOLAI SEMYONOVICH (b. 1896). Writer and public figure. Chairman of Soviet Peace Committee (since 1950). Deputy to Supreme Soviets of RSFSR and USSR. 1915 soldier in First World War. 1918 entered Red Army as volunteer. Began appearing in print 1918. After demobilization from Army (1922) devoted himself completely to literature. In early searchings for literary form came under influence of formalism for a short period. His first collection of poems *The Horse* (1922), and *Home Brew* (1922), reflected the revolutionary romanticism of the Civil War. His romantic *Ballad of the Blue Package* (1922) and *Ballad of the Nails* (1919–22) brought him fame and a wide audience. His wide travels through the Caucasus and Central Asia gave him material for *Yurga* (1926–30), *Nomads* (1931), *Everlasting Transit* (1934) and *Poems of Kakhetia* (1935), which depict Socialist construction and the class struggle in Turkmenistan and Georgia. Both his poetry and his prose characterized by reserve, laconic language, poetic images in this period, and these qualities deepened with the years. His involvement in the international writers' struggle against rising fascism in the middle and late thirties influenced *Shadow of a Friend* (1935–36). 1939–45 participated in wars first against Finland and then Germany. Was in Leningrad during siege of that city. Wrote much about the siege then (1941), also collection of poems *Fiery Year* (1942). *Poems about Yugoslavia* (1947). *Georgian Spring* (1948–49). Wrote about the peace movement in his *2nd World Peace Congress* (1951). Traveled much in Europe and Asia. Wrote *Stories about Pakistan* (1950). Novel—*White Miracle* (1956). Was active in Soviet Writers Union (Chairman in 1950). In recent years very busy with his work in peace organization at home and abroad but has been translating poetry—Soviet and foreign (Hungarian)—and has been publishing poems in magazines. Holds Order of Lenin.

TRETYAKOV, SERGEI MIKHAILOVICH (1892–1939?). Poet and playwright. Was a futurist and member of LEF (the Left literary front). Early writing—

poetry. First poems 1914. His 1923 *Summation* summed up all his poetry published 1914–22. His Chinese travels in later twenties gave him material for his book *Deng-Shi-Hua* and his famous play *Roar China!*—both 1926. 1929 brought out a book of poems. In late twenties, early thirties wrote for theater and films, wrote movies and literary criticism. Considered at the time petty bourgeois, a futurist but on path of literary ideological reconstruction taking up concrete problems of the period as in *The Cell* (early thirties). In late twenties had proposed the creation of literary workshops headed by "literary formulators," supervised by experts to be called Fixators going further than colleagues in the RAPP (leftist Russian Association of Proletarian Writers) movement. Disappeared in purges of thirties. Posthumously rehabilitated. To be published soon again.

TSVETAYEVA, MARINA IVANOVNA (1894–1941). Moscow-born poet. Father professor of art; grandfather famous historian Ilovaisky. Educated in Switzerland, France, Germany. First book of poems published in 1910—*Evening Album*. It was her book of poems *Versts* (1922) that first brought her fame. In 1922 she emigrated abroad, a firm opponent of Communism (she called herself the Poet of the White Dreams). Her life abroad in Prague, Berlin, and Paris was hounded by great hardship. She went through a change of attitude abroad and drew closer to the Communists, becoming associated with left-wing groups and in 1938 she returned to Russia with her husband, who had joined the Communists. He was rumored arrested and executed later; and when the Germans moved closer to Moscow during World War II, she was evacuated to a village in the Volga and there committed suicide in 1941. She wrote lyrics, love poems, epic poems, drama in rhyme, historical and biographical poems. She was among the great experimenters in Russian poetry. Interested in language and problems of tone. Compared to Gertrude Stein. Little published until very recent years in SU but widely known and respected as force among Soviet writers and poets. Best-known books (published outside the SU in main): *The Czar-Maiden* (1922), *Parting* (1922), *Poems to Blok* (1922), *A Bold Fellow* (1924), *Craft* (1923), *After Russia* (1928). In 1961 *Selections* was published in the SU. She also translated work of other Slavic poets. Many poems published only in various emigré magazines. Some of unpublished manuscripts saved by friends. Others lost. In recent Soviet evaluation of Tsvetayeva she has been called a great poet who has made a significant contribution to the Russian culture of the 20th century. Her own evaluation of herself was of a "lonely soul."

TYUTCHEV, FEDOR IVANOVICH (1803–1873). Outstanding Russian poet.

Born in nobleman's family. Got preparatory schooling at home; tutored by the Decembrist poet-translator Raich. Graduate of Moscow University Philological School. 1822–39 served in Russian diplomatic corps in Germany and Italy. In Germany became friend of Heine. Returned to Russia in 1844. Continued in foreign service in various offices until death (from 1858 on in charge of censorship of foreign materials). Began writing poetry early in youth. First appeared in print in 1819 but from then on infrequently and with wide intervals of time. Highly praised by Pushkin who published a sizable cycle of Tyutchev's poems in *Sovremennik* (*The Contemporary*) in 1836. Also given high praise by Nekrasov and Turgenev. Poetry highly complex and full of contradictions. Books of essays—*Russia and Germany* (1844), *Russia and Revolution* (1849). His political lyrical poems in book *Sea and Cliff* (1848) agitated for pan-Slavism. The Crimean War (1853–56) made him conscious, however, of the rottenness of serfdom in Russia. He turned in his poetry to love lyrics; lyrics to nature in his literary work of 1857 and 1865. Although writers of the period of the most varied schools of thinking were great admirers of Tyutchev, he was better known abroad. At present he is being studied and read again in the SU. The estate outside Moscow where he was born has been turned into a Tyutchev museum. His works have been republished in a number of editions.

VAKHTANGOV, EVGENII BAGRATIONOVICH (1883–1922). Among greatest of Russian actors, directors, and theater figures. Of Russian-Armenian origin. Studied at A. L. Adashev's actor's school of the Moscow Art Theater 1909–11. On graduation joined the Moscow Art Theater. Played minor roles and in mass scenes. One of Stanislavsky's first students; highly praised by him. Taught the Stanislavsky method in many of Moscow's schools and studios. Moscow Art Theater First Studio set up 1912 and V. became actor and director there—playing top roles. Dissatisfied there. Criticized bourgeois sentimentality. Just before October Revolution swayed by dream of a "theater of mysteries." Criticized for "decadence" in this period. Excited by the Revolution. Dreamed of theater that could portray the rebellious spirit of the people. Organized the People's Art Theater which lasted only one season. Continued to look for way to a theater of criticism of the morality of the bourgeois world and at same time expressive of revolutionary contemporaneity through his Studio which became the Moscow Art Theater's Second Studio in 1920, and in 1926 the Vakhtangov Theater, which has trained such well-known Soviet actors and directors as Shchukin, Zavadsky, Mansurov.

VISHNEVSKY, VSEVOLOD VITALYEVICH (1900–51). Writer-playwright.

Member of CPSU from 1937. Active participant in October Revolution and Civil War both on land and sea. First appeared in print in 1920 in Crimean newspaper (notes on battles). First play written and produced in Novorosiisk in 1921—*The Count*. With his *First Cavalry* (1929) he began a whole cycle of revolutionary romantic plays using the Civil War as the theme: *Final and Decisive* (1931), *Optimistic Tragedy* (1932) (enjoying a successful popular revival on stage and screen these last few years), *Battle in the West* (1932), *We Are from Kronstadt* (1933) (a scenario). *We, the Russian People* (1937) (a film-play). During war *Pravda* military correspondent. Wrote on Nuremberg trials. *Walls of Leningrad* (1943)—a play on the siege of that city during the war. *Unforgettable 1919* (1949)—a play returning to his Civil War theme. Held fifteen orders and medals including two orders of Lenin and three Order of the Red Banner. Was on administration board of Union of Soviet Writers.

YAGODA, GENRIKH GRIGORYEVICH (1891–1938). Discredited Party and government leader. In his autobiography claimed to have worked in an underground printing press as a compositor at age of fourteen (1904–05) and to have joined the Bolsheviks in 1907, to have been arrested for revolutionary activity in 1911 and sent into exile. This was brought into question by his enemies during his 1938 trial and later by proof offered he had not joined until 1917. However in 1917 he was in Petrograd (Leningrad), an active member of the military organization of the October Revolution. 1918–19 in Higher Organ of Military Inspection on Southern and Eastern Fronts (during Civil War). 1919 on governing board of People's Commissariat of Foreign Trade. 1920 on presidium of Cheka (Soviet secret service). In 1924 became deputy chairman of the GPU (at the same time alternate member of Central Committee of CPSU) and finally head of the NKVD (until 1936) which succeeded the GPU as the Soviet secret-service organ. In 1937 himself arrested, tried, and executed (in 1938) as a foreign spy working in a conspiratorial group called the "Bloc of Rights and Trotskyites."

YESENIN (Called ESSENIN in books published here), SERGEI ALEKSANDRO-VICH (1895–1925). Poet. Of peasant origin. Brought up by well-to-do grand-father, an Old Believer. Began writing poetry at age of fourteen. His first collection of poems, *Radunitsa*, came out in 1916. Belonged to imagist group of poets. Early poems gave idyllic picture of the Russian village. Some of his postrevolutionary poems showed a love for the cause of the revolution, gave a picture of the victorious people, hatred of the White Guard enemy: *Heavly Drummer* (1918), *Ballad on the 26* (1924), *Captain of the Land* (1925), *Anna Snegina* (1925). Criticized for his imagism and symbolism and Bohemianism.

His so-called "Bohemian" poems very popular among sections of the Soviet Youth during the NEP period. Met and married Isadora Duncan in early twenties and lived with her in Berlin, Paris, and New York. Very turbulent life. Drank a great deal. Wrote in this period *Moscow of Taverns* (1924), *Confession of a Hooligan* (1924). 1924 returned to native village looking for his roots. Disillusioned in it. Everything about Revolution now strange to him as he wrote in *Soviet Russia* (1924). Depressed and guilt-ridden about himself, committed suicide. *Black Man* (1925) most revealing of his poems. Long shunned in SU after death then reprinted in 1948 and immediately sold out. Now newly popular.

YEZHOV, NIKOLAI IVANOVICH (1895–1939?). Discredited Party and government leader. Began working at age of fourteen—in St. Petersburg factories. Joined CPSU in 1917. Active participant in October Revolution and Civil War. In Red Army to 1921 as military commissar. 1922–37 in various top government and Party posts and (as of 1935) in governing body of Communist International. 1937–39 succeeded Yagoda, preceded Beria as head of NKVD (People's Commissariat of Internal Affairs). In 1936 appointed to NKVD and put in charge of preparing second Moscow "purge" trial of "Anti-Soviet Bloc of Rights and Trotskyites." Responsible for the mass arrests that followed and the source of the coining of the hate-filled word "Yezhovshchina" describing this period of witch hunt and purge and spy trials. Subsequently himself declared an "Enemy of the People," arrested and disappeared. Rumored in Moscow that he went insane after his arrest.

ZASLAVSKY, DAVID (b. 1880). Journalist now in retirement. Was for many years on editorial staff of *Pravda*. Wrote on international affairs. Active in International Organization of Journalists, a left-wing grouping (on Executive Committee). Long considered spokesman for Soviet policies in *Pravda*. Holds Order of Lenin and Red Banner.

ZOSHCHENKO, MIKHAIL MIKHAILOVICH (1895–1958). Humorist. Studied at St. Petersburg University Law School but was not graduated. Volunteered for front in 1915. Served as officer. After October Revolution wandered about Russia working as carpenter, hunter, shoemaker, telephone operator, militiaman, office worker, actor, card player, Red Army volunteer. Joined the Serapion Brothers, a neorealist literary grouping concerned with expressing the grotesque and the fantastic. First appeared in print in 1921 and immediately became immensely popular. Brought fame by his *Tales of Nagar*

Ilyich Sinebriukhov (1922) in which comedy close to the grotesque (Sinebriukhov means Blue Belly). Wrote in what received label of "Zoshchenko language," a kind of obscure, semiliterate speech mixed with malaprop bookish words. His favorite genre short humorous novelettes full of absurdities of Soviet life. 1930 Zoshchenko's satire questioned as not so innocent vis-à-vis Soveit ideology. Resulted in his broadening his range of satire: *Restored Youth* (1933); *Pale-Blue Book* (1934), a parody of history. Autobiographical *Before the Sunrise* (1943). Analyzed reasons for his melancholy and unhappiness. Attacked as individualistic, bourgeois, unfriendly to Soviet thinking. Called "brainless, pornographic scribbler." Afterwards became very popular again. But his *Adventures of an Ape* (1946), which shows Soviet people as gossipy half-wits, was attacked as calumny. Expelled from Writers Union. Didn't appear in press again until 1947 and 1950—with pieces (in magazine *New World* and others) on the German invasion and the heroism of the partisans. Even did a critical analysis of Soviet literature in the humorous magazine *Krokodil* in 1954. Nevertheless denounced again that year by Soviet literary critics as "preacher of apologetics." Collection of hitherto unpublished short stories, satirical articles, and comedies published posthumously in 1962. Well received in Soviet press.

INDEX

537